How to Use the Maps in *The Essential World History,* *Third Edition*

Here are some basic map concepts that will help you to get the most out of the maps in this textbook.

- Always look at the scale, which allows you to determine the distance in miles or kilometers between locations on the map.

- Examine the legend carefully. It explains the colors and symbols used on the map.

- Note the locations of mountains, rivers, oceans, and other geographic features, and consider how these would affect such human activities as agriculture, commerce, travel, and warfare.

- Read the map caption thoroughly. It provides important information, sometimes not covered in the text itself, and poses a thought question to encourage you to think beyond the mere appearance of the map and make connections across chapters, regions, and concepts.

- Several "spot maps" appear in each chapter, to allow you to view in detail smaller areas that may not be apparent in larger maps. For example, a spot map in Chapter 12 lets you zoom in on Charlemagne's Empire.

- Many of the text's maps also carry a globe icon, which indicates that they or similar maps appear in interactive form at http://worldrc.wadsworth.com/

VOLUME II: SINCE 1500

ENHANCED THIRD EDITION

THE ESSENTIAL WORLD HISTORY

WILLIAM J. DUIKER

The Pennsylvania State University

JACKSON J. SPIELVOGEL

The Pennsylvania State University

THOMSON
WADSWORTH

Australia • Brazil • Canada • Mexico • Singapore • Spain
United Kingdom • United States

THOMSON

★

WADSWORTH

The Essential World History Enhanced Third Edition, Volume II: Since 1500
William J. Duiker
Jackson J. Spielvogel

Publisher: *Clark Baxter*
Senior Acquisitions Editor: *Ashley Dodge*
Senior Development Editor: *Sue Gleason*
Assistant Editor: *Ashley Spicer*
Editorial Assistant: *Heidi Kador*
Associate Development Project Manager: *Lee McCracken*
Executive Marketing Manager: *Diane Wenckebach*
Marketing Assistant: *Aimee Lewis*
Lead Marketing Communications Manager: *Tami Strang*
Senior Production Manager: *Michael Burggren*
Senior Content Project Manager: *Lauren Wheelock*
Senior Art Director: *Cate Rickard Barr*

Manufacturing Manager: *Marcia Locke*
Permissions Editor: *Bob Kauser*
Production Service: *International Typesetting and Composition*
Text Designer: *Kathleen Cunningham and Dutton & Sherman Design*
Photo Researcher: *Sarah Evertson*
Cover Designer: *Dutton & Sherman Design*
Cover Image: *British and other foreign vessels off Yokohama. Four rowing boats carry passengers to a sailship. Complete view. Color print. 1860. Coll. C.D. Wertheim. Werner Forman/Art Resource, NY.*
Cover/Text Printer: *Transcontinental-Beauceville*
Compositor: *International Typesetting and Composition*

Printed in Canada
1 2 3 4 5 6 7 11 10 09 08

Thomson Higher Education
10 Davis Drive
Belmont, CA 94002-3098
USA

For more information about our products, contact us at:
Thomson Learning Academic Resource Center
1-800-423-0563
For permission to use material from this text or product,
submit a request online at
http://www.thomsonrights.com.
Any additional questions about permissions
can be submitted by e-mail to
thomsonrights@thomson.com.

Library of Congress Control Number: 2007937376

Student Edition:
ISBN-13: 978-0-495-56628-1
ISBN-10: 0-495-56628-4

Brief Contents

DETAILED CONTENTS

PART III
THE EMERGENCE OF NEW WORLD PATTERNS (1500–1800)   286

13 NEW ENCOUNTERS: THE CREATION OF A WORLD MARKET   288

14 EUROPE TRANSFORMED: REFORM AND STATE BUILDING   311

15 THE MUSLIM EMPIRES   333

CHRONOLOGIES

MAPS

PREFACE

*F*OR SEVERAL MILLION YEARS after primates first appeared on the surface of the earth, human beings lived in small communities, seeking to survive by hunting, fishing, and foraging in a frequently hostile environment. Then suddenly, in the space of a few thousand years, there was an abrupt change of direction as human beings in a few widely scattered areas of the globe began to master the art of cultivating food crops. As food production increased, the population in those areas rose correspondingly, and people began to congregate in larger communities. Governments were formed to provide protection and other needed services to the local population. Cities appeared and became the focal point of cultural and religious development. Historians refer to this process as the beginnings of civilization.

For generations, historians in Europe and the United States pointed to the rise of such civilizations as marking the origins of the modern world. Courses on Western civilization conventionally began with a chapter or two on the emergence of advanced societies in Egypt and Mesopotamia and then proceeded to ancient Greece and the Roman Empire. From Greece and Rome, the road led directly to the rise of modern civilization in the West.

There is nothing inherently wrong with this approach. Important aspects of our world today can indeed be traced back to these early civilizations, and all human beings the world over owe a considerable debt to their achievements. But all too often this interpretation has been used to imply that the course of civilization has been linear in nature, leading directly from the emergence of agricultural societies in ancient Mesopotamia to the rise of advanced industrial societies in Europe and North America. Until recently, most courses on world history taught in the United States routinely focused almost exclusively on the rise of the West, with only a passing glance at other parts of the world, such as Africa, India, and East Asia. The contributions made by those societies to the culture and technology of our own time were often passed over in silence.

Two major reasons have been advanced to justify this approach. Some have argued that it is more important that young minds understand the roots of their own heritage than that of peoples elsewhere in the world. In many cases, however, the motivation for this Eurocentric approach has been the belief that since the time of Socrates and Aristotle Western civilization has been the sole driving force in the evolution of human society.

Such an interpretation, however, represents a serious distortion of the process. During most of the course of human history, the most advanced civilizations have been not in the West, but in East Asia or the Middle East. A relatively brief period of European dominance culminated with the era of imperialism in the late nineteenth century, when the political, military, and economic power of the advanced nations of the West spanned the globe. During recent generations, however, that dominance has gradually eroded, partly as the result of changes taking place within Western societies and partly because new centers of development are emerging elsewhere on the globe—notably in East Asia, where the growing economic strength of China and Japan and many of their neighbors has led to the now familiar prediction that the twenty-first century will be known as the Pacific Century.

World history, then, has been a complex process in which many branches of the human community have taken an active part, and the dominance of any one area of the world has been a temporary rather than a permanent phenomenon. It will be our purpose in this book to present a balanced picture of this story, with all respect for the richness and diversity of the tapestry of the human experience. Due attention must be paid to the rise of the West, of course, since that has been the most dominant aspect of world history in recent centuries. But the contributions made by other peoples must be given adequate consideration as well, not only in the period prior to 1500 when the major centers of civilization were located in Asia, but also in our own day, where a multipolar picture of development is clearly beginning to emerge.

Anyone who wishes to teach or write about world history must decide whether to present the topic as an integrated whole or as a collection of different cultures. The world that we live in today, of course, is in many respects an interdependent one in terms of economics as well as culture and communications, a reality that is often expressed by the phrase "global village." The convergence of peoples across the surface of the earth into an integrated world system began in early times and intensified after the rise of capitalism in the early modern era. In growing recognition of this trend, historians trained in global history, as well as instructors in the growing number of world history courses, have now begun to speak and write of a "global approach" that turns attention away from the study of individual civilizations and focuses instead on the "big picture" or, as the world historian Fernand Braudel termed it, interpreting world history as a river with no banks.

On the whole, this development is to be welcomed as a means of bringing the common elements of the evolution of human society to our attention. But there is a problem involved in this approach. For the vast majority of their time on earth, human beings have lived in partial or virtually total isolation from each other. Differences in climate, location, and geographical features have created human societies very different from each other in culture and historical experience. Only in relatively recent times—(the commonly accepted date has long been the beginning of the age of European exploration at the end of the fifteenth century, but some would now push it back to the era of the Mongol empire or even further)— have cultural interchanges begun to create a common "world system," in which events taking place in one part of the world are rapidly transmitted throughout the globe, often with momentous consequences. In recent generations, of course, the process of global interdependence has been proceeding even more rapidly. Nevertheless, even now the process is by no means complete, as ethnic and regional differences continue to exist and to shape the course of world history. The tenacity of these differences and sensitivities is reflected not only in the rise of internecine conflicts in such divergent areas as Africa, India, and Eastern Europe, but also in the emergence in recent years of such regional organizations as the Organization of African Unity, the Association for the Southeast Asian Nations, and the European Union.

The second problem is a practical one. College students today are all too often not well informed about the distinctive character of civilizations such as China and India and, without sufficient exposure to the historical evolution of such societies, will assume all too readily that the peoples in these countries have had historical experiences similar to ours and will respond to various stimuli in a similar fashion to those living in Western Europe or the United States. If it is a mistake to ignore those forces that link us together, it is equally a mistake to underestimate those factors that continue to divide us and to differentiate us into a world of diverse peoples.

Our response to this challenge has been to adopt a global approach to world history while at the same time attempting to do justice to the distinctive character and development of individual civilizations and regions of the world. The presentation of individual cultures will be especially important in Parts I and II, which cover a time when it is generally agreed that the process of global integration was not yet far advanced. Later chapters will begin to adopt a more comparative and thematic approach, in deference to the greater number of connections that have been established among the world's peoples since the fifteenth and sixteenth centuries. Part V will consist of a series of chapters that will center on individual regions of the world while at the same time focusing on common problems related to the Cold War and the rise of global problems such as overproduction and environmental pollution.

We have sought balance in another way as well. Many textbooks tend to simplify the content of history courses by emphasizing an intellectual or political perspective or, most recently, a social perspective, often at the expense of sufficient details in a chronological framework. This approach is confusing to students whose high school social studies programs have often neglected a systematic study of world history. We have attempted to write a well-balanced work in which political, economic, social, religious, intellectual, cultural, and military history have been integrated into a chronologically ordered synthesis.

To enliven the past and let readers see for themselves the materials that historians use to create their pictures of the past, we have included primary sources (boxed documents) in each chapter that are keyed to the discussion in the text. The documents include examples of the religious, artistic, intellectual, social, economic, and political aspects of life in different societies and reveal in a vivid fashion what civilization meant to the individual men and women who shaped it by their actions. We have added questions to help guide students in analyzing the documents, as well as references to related documents that are available online.

Each chapter has a lengthy introduction and conclusion to help maintain the continuity of the narrative and to provide a synthesis of important themes. Anecdotes in the chapter introductions convey more dramatically the major theme or themes of each chapter. Timelines, at the end of each chapter enable students to see the major developments of an era at a glance and within cross-cultural categories, while the more detailed chronologies reinforce the events discussed in the text. An annotated bibliography at the end of each chapter reviews the most recent literature on each period and also gives references to some of the older, "classic" works in each field.

Updated maps and extensive illustrations serve to deepen the reader's understanding of the text. Map captions are designed to enrich students' awareness of the importance of geography to history, and numerous spot maps enable students to see at a glance the region or subject being discussed in the text. In addition, special globe icons indicate maps for which an interactive version appears on the Web site. The maps have also been revised where needed. To facilitate understanding of cultural movements, illustrations of artistic works discussed in the text are placed near the discussions. Chapter outlines and focus and critical thinking questions have been combined in a new format at the beginning of each chapter to help students with an overview and guide them to the main subjects of each chapter. A glossary of important terms (now boldfaced in the text when they are introduced and defined) and a pronunciation guide are provided at the back of the book to maximize reader comprehension.

After reexamining the entire book and analyzing the comments and reviews of many colleagues who have found the book to be a useful instrument for introducing their students to world history, we have also made a number of other changes for the third edition. In the first place, we have reorganized the material by ending Part II at 1500, reversing the order of Chapters 13 and 14, and redoing Chapter 12, "The Making of Europe." The Renaissance is now covered in Chapter 12, and Chapter 14, "Europe Transformed: Reform and State Building," begins with the Reformation. Chapter 5, now titled "The First World Civilization: Rome, China, and the Emergence of the Silk Road," includes a discussion of both the Roman and Han Chinese empires.

Second, we have sought to strengthen the global framework of the book, but not at the expense of reducing the attention assigned to individual regions of the world. New comparative essays have been added to each chapter. Keyed to the seven major themes of world history (see p. xxiii), these essays enable us to more concretely draw comparisons and contrasts across geographical, cultural, and chronological lines. Moreover, additional comparative material has been added to each chapter to help students be aware of similar developments globally. Among other things, this material includes new comparative sections as well as comparative illustrations in each chapter that are keyed to the seven major themes of world history. We hope that these techniques will assist instructors who wish to encourage their students to adopt a comparative approach to their understanding of the human experience.

Third, this new edition contains additional information on the role of women in world history. In conformity with our own convictions, as well as what we believe to be recent practice in the field, we have tried where possible to introduce such material at the appropriate point in the text, rather than to set aside separate sections devoted exclusively to women's issues.

Finally, a number of new illustrations, boxed documents, and maps have been added, and the bibliographies have been revised to take account of newly published material. The chronologies and maps have been fine-tuned as well, to help the reader locate in time and space the multitude of individuals and place names that appear in the book. To keep up with the ever-growing body of historical scholarship, new or revised material has been added throughout the book on many topics.

Chapter 1 The Code of Hammurabi; urbanization in the first civilizations; gender issues in Mesopotamia; and new section, "The Spread of Egyptian Influence: Nubia." New comparative illustration on early writing. New comparative essay, "From Hunter-Gatherers and Herders to Farmers."

Chapter 2 New material on Hinduism and Buddhism, and ancient Indian achievements in mathematics. New comparative essay, "Writing and Civilization."

Chapter 3 New material on early Chinese religion compared with that in Mesopotamia and Greece; the evolution of autocratic rule in ancient China; and bronze-casting factories. New comparative illustration on early agricultural technology. New comparative essay, "The Use of Metals."

Chapter 4 New material on Hellenistic urbanization; trade and cultural diffusion; Alexander's connections to the East; Greek science in the classical and Hellenistic periods; Minoan Crete; the effects of colonization; and the development of Athenian democracy, especially under Pericles. New comparative essay, "Demos and Despots."

Chapter 5 New material on trade between Rome and China; slaves; the crises of the third century and the end of the Western Empire; and new section, "The Glorious Han Empire (202 B.C.E. – 221 C.E.)." New comparative essay, "Rulers and Gods."

Chapter 6 New material on the Maya; Caral and Chavín de Huantar; environmental problems in ancient South America; and the Anasazi. New comparative essay, "History and the Environment."

Chapter 7 New material on early Islam; early Muslim brotherhoods; and iconoclasm in Islam. New comparative essay, "Trade and Civilization."

Chapter 8 New material on the Husuni Kubwa; comparison of building techniques of the Inka and Great Zimbabwe; the Khoi and the San; and African wood carving. New comparative essay, "The Migration of Peoples." New spot map of the Swahili coast.

Chapter 9 New comparative illustration of rock architecture. New comparative essay, "Caste, Class, and Family."

Chapter 10 New material on the Silk Road and the School of Mind compared with Greek philosophy. New comparative essay, "The Spread of Technology."

Chapter 11 New comparative essay, "Feudal Orders Around the World."

Chapter 12 New material on decentralization versus centralization of state power in the Middle Ages and Renaissance and long-distance trade with the East. New comparative essay, "The Role of Disease."

Chapter 13 New material on the Middle Passage and an overall assessment of the Age of Exploration. New comparative illustration of Christianity in Asia. New comparative essay, "Marriage in the Early Modern World."

Chapter 14 New material on Jesuit missionary activities in Asia. New comparative essay, "Marriage in the Early Modern World."

Chapter 15 New material on Safavid Iran. New comparative illustration of war commemorations. New comparative essay, "The Changing Face of War."

Chapter 16 New comparative essay, "Population Explosion."

Chapter 17 New comparative essay, "The Scientific Revolution."

Chapter 18 New material on nationalism and a changed interpretation of the Battle of Königgrätz. New comparative essay, "The Industrial Revolution."

Chapter 19 New material on trade unions and Canada. New comparative essay, "The Rise of Nationalism."

Chapter 20 New comparative illustration on cultural influences. New comparative essay, "Imperialism: The Balance Sheet."

Chapter 21 New comparative illustration of female rulers. New comparative essay, "Imperialism and the Global Environment."

Chapter 22 New material on the Russian Revolution; casualties of World War I; genocide of Armenians by Turks at end of World War I; and Dadaism. New comparative essay, "A Revolution in the Arts."

Chapter 23 New material on women's rights in India and early twentieth-century nation building in Iraq. New comparative essay, "Out of the Doll's House."

Chapter 24 New material on Japanese motives for expansion; the Japanese path to war; and Japan in the war. New comparative essay, "Paths to Modernization."

Chapter 25 New comparative illustration, "The Iron Curtain Falls." New comparative essay, "One World, One Environment." New map of the Chinese civil war; new spot map of South Vietnam at war.

Chapter 26 New comparative essay, "Family and Society in an Era of Change."

Chapter 27 New section on the European Union. New material on Yugoslavia; immigration laws in Europe; and postmodernism. All nations updated to the present. New comparative essay, "From the Industrial to the Technological Revolution." New spot map of Central America.

Chapter 28 New material on Muslim fundamentalism and the growth of Islam in the West, and society and culture in the Middle East. All nations updated to the present. New comparative illustration on traditional patterns in the countryside. New comparative essay, "Religion and Society." New spot map of present-day Iraq.

Chapter 29 All nations updated to the present. New comparative illustration on the new technology. New comparative essay, "Global Village or Clash of Civilizations?"

Because courses in world history at American and Canadian colleges and universities follow different chronological divisions, a one-volume comprehensive edition, a two-volume edition of this text, and a volume covering events to 1500 are being made available to fit the needs of instructors. Teaching and learning ancillaries include:

Multimedia Manager for World History with Instructor's Resources: A Microsoft® Powerpoint® Tool Includes the Instructor's Manual, Resource Integration Guide (grids that link each chapter of the text to instructional ideas and corresponding supplemental resources), ExamView® computerized testing, and Microsoft® PowerPoint® slides with lecture outlines and images that can be used as offered, or customized by importing personal lecture slides or other material. ExamView allows you to create, deliver, and customize tests and study guides (both print and online) in minutes with its easy-to-use assessment and tutorial system. It offers both a Quick Test Wizard and an Online Test Wizard that guide you step by step through the process of creating tests, while its "what you see is what you get" capability allows you to see the test you are creating on the screen exactly as it will print or display online. You can build tests of up to 250 questions using up to 12 question types. Using ExamView's complete word-processing capabilities, you can enter an unlimited number of new questions or edit existing questions.

Instructor's Manual with Test Bank Prepared by Eugene Larson, Los Angeles Pierce College. Includes chapter outlines reflecting the main headings; class lecture/discussion topics; thought/discussion questions for the boxed documents; possible student projects; and examination questions (essay, identification, and 50 multiple-choice questions, the latter with correct answers and text page references indicated). Available on the Book Companion Site and the Multimedia Manager.

Transparency Acetates for World History Each package contains more than 100 four-color map images from the text and other sources. Packages are three-hole punched and shrinkwrapped. Map commentary is provided by James Harrison, Siena College.

Sights and Sounds of History Prepared by David Redles, Cuyahoga Community College. Short, focused VHS video clips, photos, artwork, animations, music, and dramatic readings are used to bring life to historical topics and events which are most difficult for students to appreciate from a textbook alone. For example, students will experience the grandeur of Versailles and the defeat felt by a German soldier at Stalingrad. The video segments average 4 minutes in length and make excellent lecture launchers.

JoinIn™ on TurningPoint®—World History JoinIn™ on TurningPoint® is the easiest way to turn your lecture hall into a personal, fully interactive experience for your students. JoinIn turns your ordinary PowerPoint® application into powerful audience response software, allowing you to take attendance, poll students on key issues to spark discussion, check student comprehension of difficult concepts, collect student demographics to better assess student needs, and even administer quizzes without collecting papers or grading. In addition, we provide interactive slide sets for many of our leading products that you can modify and merge with any existing PowerPoint lecture slides for a seamless classroom presentation.

Music CDs Available to instructors upon request, these CDs include musical selctions from Henry Purcell through Ravi Shankar to enrich lectures. A correlation guide is available in the Resource Integration Guide in the Multimedia Manager and the Multimedia Manager.

HistoryNow Available via access card, this web-based intelligent study system saves time for students and instructors by providing a complete package of diagnostic quizzes, a personalized study plan, integrated multimedia, over 450 primary source readings, and an instructor gradebook.

HistoryUnbound: Online Explorations in World History HistoryUnbound's online modules bring the past to life through seamless integration of interactive maps and timelines, images, and primary-source readings. Available as a bundle item or as a standalone product, the *HistoryUnbound* access code is packaged with a text-specific Correlation Guide.

Wadsworth History Resource Center Wadworth History Resource Centers (http://worldrc.wadsworth.com/) for American History, World History, and Western Civilization have significantly expanded! Now chronologically organized with a user-friendly timeline navigation bar, these centers act as a primary source e-reader with over 300 primary source documents and feature numerous resources, such as timelines, photos, interactive maps, exercises, and more. Your students obtain access to the appropriate resource center when you package an access code with any Thomson Wadsworth history textbook. Access codes are available free when packaged with most new books and at a nominal price when packaged with our Thomson Advantage Books. If need be, you can also order it by itself. All access codes last for one complete year. Demo the resource centers at http://history.wadsworth.com, by clicking on your area (American, Western Civilization,

World Civilization) on the left-hand navigation bar, and then contact your local representative for ordering details.

Book Companion Web Site

http://www.thomsonedu.com/history/duiker

Both instructors and students will enjoy the chapter-by-chapter resources for Duiker and Spielvogel's *World History*, with access to the Wadsworth World History Resource Center. Text-specific content for students includes interactive maps, interactive timelines, tutorial quizzes, glossary, hyperlinks, InfoTrac College Edition exercises, Internet activities, and an annotated bibliography. Instructors also have access to the Instructor's Manual and PowerPoint slides (access code required). From the History homepage, instructors and students can access many selections, such as primary source documents, interactive simulations, an Internet Guide for History, a career center, lessons on surfing the web, the World History Image Bank, and links to great history-related web sites.

The Journey of Civilization Prepared by David Redles, Cuyahoga Community College. This CD-ROM takes the student on 18 interactive journeys through history. Enhanced with QuickTime movies, animations, sound clips, maps, and more, the journeys allow students to engage in history as active participants rather than as readers of past events. Contact your local sales representative for bundle pricing.

Migrations in Modern World History 1500–2000 CD-ROM with User Guide (Student Version) An interactive multimedia curriculum on CD-ROM developed by Patrick Manning and the World History Center at Northeastern University. *Migration* goes beyond the mere chronicling of migratory paths. Over 400 primary source documents in *Migration* provide a springboard to explore a wide range of global issues in social, cultural, economic, and political history during the period 1500–2000.

InfoTrac® College Edition with InfoMarks® Now available, free four-month access to InfoTrac® College Edition's online database of more than 18 million reliable, full-length articles from 5,000 academic journals and periodicals (including *the New York Times, Science, Forbes,* and *USA Today*) includes access to InfoMarks—stable URLs that can be linked to articles, journals, and searches. InfoMarks allow you to use a simple "copy and paste" technique to create instant and continually updated online readers, content services, bibliographies, electronic "reserve" readings, and current topic sites. And incorporating InfoTrac College Edition into your course is easy—references to this virtual library are built into many of our texts in margins, exercises, and so forth. In addition, ask about other InfoTrac College Edition resources available, including InfoMarks print and online readers with readings, activities, and exercises hand selected to work with the text. And to help students use the research they gather, their free four-month subscription to InfoTrac College Edition includes access to InfoWrite, a complete set of online critical thinking and paper writing tools. To take a quick tour of InfoTrac

College Edition, visit http://www.infotrac-college.com/ and select the "User Demo." (Journals subject to change. Certain restrictions may apply. For additional information, please consult your local Thomson representative.)

A Civilization Primer, 5th Edition This proven supplement for the introductory Western civilization course, by Edward M. Anson, University of Arkansas, Little Rock, is designed to help history students develop their knowledge of core social science concepts and terminology. This brief text defines and clarifies the basics of history, culture, religion, government, economics, and geography.

Document Exercise Workbook for World History, 3rd Edition Prepared by Donna Van Raaphorst, Cuyahoga Community College, this two-volume workbook provides a collection of exercises based around primary source documents in history. Contact your local sales representative for bundle pricing.

Magellan World History Atlas Available to bundle with any history text. Contains 44 four-color historical maps, including The Conflict in Afghanistan, 2001, and States of the World, 2001. Contact your local sales representative for bundle pricing.

Map Exercise Workbook, 3rd Edition Prepared by Cynthia Kosso, Northern Arizona University, this two-volume workbook features approximately 30 map exercises. Designed to help students feel comfortable with maps by having them work with different kinds of maps to identify places and improve their geographic understanding of world history. Contact your local sales representative for bundle pricing.

Scientific American—Ancient Civilizations Bring your students into current activity in the field with *Scientific American* magazine. As an exclusive offer from Thomson, this magazine is available as a bundle item for your course. This issue includes coverage by region, including such topics as the Iceman, Death Cults of Prehistoric Malta, Keys to the Lost Indus Cities, Women and Men at Catalhuyuk, Rock Art in Southern Africa, Life and Death in Nabada, Tapestry of Power in a Mesopotamian City, Daily Life in Ancient Egypt, Great Zimbabwe, Precious Metal Objects of the Middle Sican, Life in the Provinces of the Aztec Empire, Reading the Bones of La Florida, and more.

Sources of World History This two-volume reader, edited by Mark Kishlansky, Harvard University, is a collection of primary source documents designed to supplement any world history text. Provides a balance of constitutional documents, political theory, philosophy, imaginative literature, and social description. Contact your local sales representative for bundle pricing.

Primary Source Reader for World History Edited by Elsa A. Nystrom, Kennesaw State University. A thoughtful collection of important primary source documents essential to world history, this two-volume reader is an affordable supplement for students and a valuable complement to any world history or world civilization class. More than 50 percent of the primary source documents are non-Western, giving students a broad perspective on the history of the world. The readings are divided by eras and organized according to principal themes, such as religion, law and government, and everyday life. Each group of readings has a section describing the signficance of subsequent readings and how those readings interrelate. Individual readings include a headnote and various study questions intended to guide student reading and understanding.

A Custom Reader for Western Civilization Written by leading educators and historians, this fully customizable reader of primary and secondary sources, appropriate for the text's European coverage, is enhanced with an online collection of visual sources, including maps, animations and interactive exercises. Each reading also comes with an introduction and a series of review questions. To learn more visit www.ThomsonCustom.com or call Thomson Custom Publishing at 1-800-355-9983.

ABOUT THE AUTHORS

WILLIAM J. DUIKER is liberal arts professor emeritus of East Asian studies at The Pennsylvania State University. A former U.S. diplomat with service in Taiwan, South Vietnam, and Washington, D.C., he received his doctorate in Far Eastern history from Georgetown University in 1968, where his dissertation dealt with the Chinese educator and reformer Cai Yuanpei. At Penn State, he has written widely on the history of Vietnam and modern China, including the widely acclaimed *The Communist Road to Power in Vietnam* (revised edition, Westview Press, 1996), which was selected for a Choice Outstanding Academic Book Award in 1982–1983 and 1996–1997. Other recent books are *China and Vietnam: The Roots of Conflict* (Berkeley, 1987), *Sacred War: Nationalism and Revolution in a Divided Vietnam* (McGraw-Hill, 1995), and *Ho Chi Minh: A Life* (Hyperion, 2000). While his research specialization is in the field of nationalism and Asian revolutions, his intellectual interests are considerably more diverse. He has traveled widely and has taught courses on the History of Communism and non-Western civilizations at Penn State, where he was awarded a Faculty Scholar Medal for Outstanding Achievement in the spring of 1996.

To Yvonne,
for adding sparkle to this book, and to my life
W.J.D.

JACKSON J. SPIELVOGEL is associate professor emeritus of history at The Pennsylvania State University. He received his Ph.D. from The Ohio State University, where he specialized in Reformation history under Harold J. Grimm. His articles and reviews have appeared in such journals as *Moreana, Journal of General Education, Catholic Historical Review, Archiv für Reformationsgeschichte,* and *American Historical Review.* He has also contributed chapters or articles to *The Social History of the Reformation, The Holy Roman Empire: A Dictionary Handbook, Simon Wiesenthal Center Annual of Holocaust Studies,* and *Utopian Studies.* His work has been supported by fellowships from the Fulbright Foundation and the Foundation for Reformation Research. At Penn State, he helped inaugurate the Western civilization course as well as a popular course on Nazi Germany. His book *Hitler and Nazi Germany* was published in 1987 (fifth edition, 2005). He is the author of *Western Civilization* published in 1991 (sixth edition, 2006). Professor Spielvogel has won five major university-wide teaching awards. During the year 1988–1989, he held the Penn State Teaching Fellowship, the university's most prestigious teaching award. In 1996, he won the Dean Arthur Ray Warnock Award for Outstanding Faculty Member and in 2000 received the Schreyer Honors College Excellence in Teaching Award.

To Diane,
whose love and support made it all possible
J.J.S.

ACKNOWLEDGMENTS

$\mathcal{B}$OTH AUTHORS GRATEFULLY acknowledge that without the generosity of many others, this project could not have been completed.

William Duiker would like to thank Kumkum Chatterjee and On-cho Ng for their helpful comments about issues related to the history of India and premodern China. His longtime colleague Cyril Griffith, now deceased, was a cherished friend and a constant source of information about modern Africa. Art Goldschmidt has been of invaluable assistance in reading several chapters of the manuscript, as well as in unraveling many of the mysteries of Middle Eastern civilization. Finally, he remains profoundly grateful to his wife, Yvonne V. Duiker, Ph.D. She has not only given her usual measure of love and support when this appeared to be an insuperable task, but she has also contributed her own time and expertise to enrich the sections on art and literature, thereby adding life and sparkle to this, as well as the earlier editions of the book. To her, and to his daughters Laura and Claire, he will be forever thankful for bringing joy to his life.

Jackson Spielvogel would like to thank Art Goldschmidt, David Redles, and Christine Colin for their time and ideas. Daniel Haxall and Kathryn Spielvogel of The Pennsylvania State University provided valuable assistance with materials on postwar art, popular culture, and Postmodern art and thought. Above all, he thanks his family for their support. The gifts of love, laughter, and patience from his daughters, Jennifer and Kathryn, his sons, Eric and Christian, and daughters-in-law, Liz and Laurie, and his son-in-law, Daniel, were invaluable. Diane, his wife and best friend, provided him with editorial assistance, wise counsel, and the loving support that made a project of this magnitude possible.

Thanks to Wadsworth's comprehensive review process, many historians were asked to evaluate our manuscript. We are grateful to the following for the innumerable suggestions that have greatly improved our work. This edition's map reviewers (asterisked) deserve our particular thanks.

Henry Abramson
  Florida Atlantic University
Eric H. Ash
  Wayne State University
William Bakken
  Rochester Community College
Suzanne Balch-Lindsay
  Eastern New Mexco University
Michael E. Birdwell
  Tennessee Technological University
*Connie Brand
  Meridien Community College
Eileen Brown
  Norwalk Community College
Thomas Cardoza
  University of California, San Diego
Alistair Chapman
  Westmont College
Nupur Chaudhuri
  Texas Southern University
Richard Crane
  Greensboro College
Wade Dudley
  East Carolina University
E.J. Fabyan
  Vincennes University
Kenneth Faunce
  Washington State University
Jaime Crozier Garcia
  Hawaii Pacific University
Steven Gosch
  University of Wisconsin—Eau Claire

Donald Harreld
  Brigham Young University
Janine C. Hartman
  University of Connecticut
Greg Havrilcsak
  University of Michigan—Flint
Thomas Hegerty
  University of Tampa
Sanders Huguenin
  University of Science and Arts of Oklahoma
Ahmed Ibrahim
  Southwest Missouri State University
C. Barden Keeler
  Gulf Coast High School
Marilynn Fox Kokoszka
  Orchard Ridge Campus, Oakland Community College
James Krippner-Martinez
  Haverford College
Oscar Lansen
  University of North Carolina—Charlotte
David Leinweber
  Oxford College, Emory University
Susie Ling
  Pasadena City College
*Moira Maguire
  University of Arkansas—Little Rock
Andrew McGreevy
  Ohio University
Daniel Miller
  Calvin College

Michael Murdock
  Brigham Young University
Elsa A. Nystrom
  Kennesaw State University
S. Mike Pavelec
  Hawaii Pacific University
Randall L. Pouwels
  University of Central Arkansas
Margaret Power
  Illinois Institute of Technology
Pamela Sayre
  Henry Ford Community College
Philip Curtis Skaggs
  Grand Valley State University
Laura Smoller
  University of Arkansas at Little Rock
Beatrice Spade
  University of Southern Colorado
Jeremy Stahl
  Middle Tennessee State University
Kate Transchel
  California State University, Chico
Justin Vance
  Hawaii Pacific University
Lorna VanMeter
  Ball State University
Michelle White
  University of Tennessee at Chattanooga
Edna Yahil
  Washington State University—Swiss Center

A Note to Students About Languages and the Dating of Time

*O*NE OF THE MOST difficult challenges in studying world history is coming to grips with the multitude of names, words, and phrases in unfamiliar languages. Unfortunately, this problem has no easy solution. We have tried to alleviate the difficulty, where possible, by providing an English-language translation of foreign words or phrases, a glossary, and a pronunciation guide. The issue is especially complicated in the case of Chinese, since two separate systems are commonly used to transliterate the spoken Chinese language into the Roman alphabet. The Wade-Giles system, invented in the nineteenth century, was the most frequently used until recent years, when the pinyin system was adopted by the People's Republic of China as its own official form of transliteration. We have opted to use the latter, since it appears to be gaining acceptance in the United States, but the initial use of a Chinese word is accompanied by its Wade-Giles equivalent in parentheses for the benefit of those who may encounter the term in their outside reading.

In our examination of world history, we need also to be aware of the dating of time. In recording the past, historians try to determine the exact time when events occurred. World War II in Europe, for example, began on September 1, 1939, when Adolf Hitler sent German troops into Poland, and ended on May 7, 1945, when Germany surrendered. By using dates, historians can place events in order and try to determine the development of patterns over periods of time.

If someone asked you when you were born, you would reply with a number, such as 1988. In the United States, we would all accept that number without question, because it is part of the dating system followed in the Western world (Europe and the Western Hemisphere). In this system, events are dated by counting backward or forward from the birth of Christ (assumed to be the year 1). An event that took place 400 years before the birth of Christ would most commonly be dated 400 B.C. (before Christ). Dates after the birth of Christ are labeled as A.D. These letters stand for the Latin words *anno domini*, which mean "in the year of the Lord" (or the year of the birth of Christ). Thus an event that

took place 250 years after the birth of Christ is written A.D. 250, or in the year of the Lord 250. It can also be written as 250, just as you would not give your birth year as A.D. 1988, but simply 1988.

Some historians now prefer to use the abbreviations B.C.E. ("before the common era") and C.E. ("common era") instead of B.C. and A.D. This is especially true of world historians who prefer to use symbols that are not so Western or Christian oriented. The dates, of course, remain the same. Thus, 1950 B.C.E. and 1950 B.C. would be the same year, as would A.D. 40 and 40 C.E. In keeping with the current usage by many world historians, this book will use the terms B.C.E. and C.E.

Historians also make use of other terms to refer to time. A decade is 10 years; a century is 100 years; and a millennium is 1,000 years. The phrase fourth century B.C.E. refers to the fourth period of 100 years counting backward from 1, the assumed date of the birth of Christ. Since the first century B.C.E would be the years 100 B.C.E. to 1 B.C.E., the fourth century B.C.E would be the years 400 B.C.E. to 301 B.C.E. We could say, then, that an event in 350 B.C.E. took place in the fourth century B.C.E.

The phrase fourth century C.E. refers to the fourth period of 100 years after the birth of Christ. Since the first period of 100 years would be the years 1 to 100, the fourth period or fourth century would be the years 301 to 400. We could say, then, for example, that an event in 350 took place in the fourth century. Likewise, the first millennium B.C.E refers to the years 1000 B.C.E to 1 B.C.E; the second millennium C.E refers to the years 1001 to 2000.

The dating of events can also vary from people to people. Most people in the Western world use the Western calendar, also known as the Gregorian calendar after Pope Gregory XIII who refined it in 1582. The Hebrew calendar, on the other hand, uses a different system in which the year 1 is the equivalent of the Western year 3760 B.C.E, considered by Jews to be the date of the creation of the world. Thus, the Western year 2007 will be the year 5767 on the Jewish calendar. The Islamic calendar begins year 1 on the day Muhammad fled Mecca, which is the year 622 on the Western calendar.

THEMES FOR UNDERSTANDING WORLD HISTORY

As they pursue their craft, historians often organize their material on the basis of themes that enable them to ask and try to answer basic questions about the past. Such is our intention here. In preparing the third edition of this book, we have selected several major themes that we believe are especially important in understanding the course of world history. These themes transcend the boundaries of time and space and have relevance to all cultures since the beginning of the human experience.

In the chapters that follow, we will refer to these themes frequently as we advance from the prehistoric era to the present. Where appropriate, we shall make comparisons across cultural boundaries, or across different time periods. To facilitate this process, we have included a comparative essay in each chapter that focuses on a particular theme within the specific time period dealt with in that section of the book. For example, the comparative essays in Chapters 1 and 6 deal with the human impact on the natural environment during the premodern era, while those in Chapters 21 and 25 discuss the issue during the age of imperialism and in the contemporary world. Each comparative essay is identified with a particular theme, although it will be noted that many essays deal with several themes at the same time.

We have sought to illustrate these themes through the use of comparative illustrations in each chapter. These illustrations are comparative in nature and seek to encourage the reader to think about thematic issues in cross-cultural terms, while not losing sight of the unique characteristics of individual societies. Our seven themes, each divided into two subtopics, are listed below.

1. *Politics and Government*   The study of politics seeks to answer certain basic questions that historians have about the structure of a society: How were people governed? What was the relationship between the ruler and the ruled? What people or groups of people (the political elites) held political power? What actions did people take to guarantee their security or change their form of government?

2. *Arts and Ideas*   We cannot understand a society without looking at its culture, or the common ideas, beliefs, and patterns of behavior that are passed on from one generation to the next. Culture includes both high culture and popular culture. High culture consists of the writings of a society's thinkers and the works of its artists. A society's popular culture is the world of ideas and experiences of ordinary people. Today the media have embraced the term popular culture to describe the current trends and fashionable styles.

3. *Religion and Philosophy*   Throughout history, people have sought to find a deeper meaning to human life. How have the world's great religions, such as Hinduism, Buddhism, Judaism, Christianity, and Islam, influenced people's lives? How have they spread to create new patterns of culture in other parts of the world?

4. *Family and Society*   The most basic social unit in human society has always been the family. From a study of family and social patterns, we learn about the different social classes that make up a society and their relationships with one another. We also learn about the role of gender in individual societies. What different roles did men and women play in their societies? How and why were those roles different?

5. *Science and Technology*   For thousands of years, people around the world have made scientific discoveries and technological innovations that have changed our world. From the creation of stone tools that made farming easier to advanced computers that guide our airplanes, science and technology have altered how humans have related to their world.

6. *Earth and the Environment*   Throughout history, peoples and societies have been affected by the physical world in which they live. Climatic changes alone have been an important factor in human history. Through their economic activities, peoples and societies, in turn, have also made an impact on their world. Human activities have affected the physical environment and even endangered the very existence of entire societies and species.

7. *Interaction and Exchange*   Many world historians believe that the exchange of ideas and innovations is the driving force behind the evolution of human societies. The introduction of agriculture, writing and printing, metal working, and navigational techniques, for example, spread gradually from one part of the world to other regions and eventually changed the face of the entire globe. The process of cultural and technological exchange took place in various ways, including trade, conquest, and the migration of peoples.

STUDYING FROM PRIMARY SOURCE MATERIALS

ASTRONOMERS investigate the universe through telescopes. Biologists study the natural world by collecting plants and animals in the field and then examining them with microscopes. Sociologists and psychologists study human behavior through observation and controlled laboratory experiments.

Historians study the past by examining historical "evidence" or "source" materials—church or town records, letters, treaties, advertisements, paintings, menus, literature, buildings, clothing—anything and everything written or created by our ancestors that give clues about their lives and the times in which they lived.

Historians refer to written material as "documents." Excerpts of more than 100 documents—some in shaded boxes, and others in the text narrative itself—appear in every chapter of this textbook. Each chapter also includes several photographs of buildings, paintings, and other kinds of historical evidence.

As you read each chapter, the more you examine all this "evidence" better, the more you will understand the main ideas of the course. This introduction to studying historical evidence, and the visual summaries at the end of each chapter, will help you learn how to look at evidence the way your instructor does. The better you become at reading evidence, the better the grade you will earn in your course.

Source material comes in two main types: primary and secondary

"Primary" evidence is material that comes to us exactly as it left the pen of the person who wrote or created it. Letters between King Louis XIV of France and the king of Tonkin (now Vietnam) are primary evidence (p. 306). So is the court transcript of a witchcraft trial in France (p. 321), a poem by Shakespeare, or a diagram of the solar system drawn by Copernicus (p. 379).

"Secondary" evidence is an account by someone about the life or activity of someone else. A story about Abraham Lincoln written by his Secretary of War would give us primary source information about Lincoln by someone who knew him. Reflections about Lincoln's presidency written by a historian might give us insights into how, for example, Lincoln governed during wartime. But because the historian did not know Lincoln firsthand, we would consider this information a secondary source of information about Lincoln. Secondary sources such as historical essays (and textbooks!) can therefore be very helpful in

understanding the past. But it is important to remember that a secondary source can reveal as much about its author as it does about its subject.

Reading Documents

We will turn to a specific document in a moment and analyze it in some detail. For now, however, the following are a few basic things to be aware of—and to ask yourself—as you read any written document.

1. Who wrote it? The authors of the textbook answer this question for you at the beginning of each document in the book. But your instructors may give you other documents to read, and the authorship of each document is the first question you need to answer.
2. What do we know about the author of the document? The more you know about the author, the better and more reliable information you can extract from the document.
3. Is it a primary or a secondary document?
4. When was the document written?
5. What is the purpose of the document? Closely tied to the question of document type is the document's purpose. A work of fiction might have been written to entertain, whereas an official document was written to convey a particular law or decree to subjects, citizens, or believers.
6. Who was the intended audience? An excerpt from a play is meant to be performed, whereas a copy of Martin Luther's Ninety-Five Theses was posted publicly.
7. Can you detect a bias in this document? As the two documents on the Siege of Jerusalem (p. 275) suggest, first-hand accounts of the Crusades written by Christian and Muslims tend to differ. Each may be "accurate" as far as the writer is concerned, but your job as a historian is to decide whether this written evidence gives a reliable account of what happened. You cannot always believe everything you read, but the more you read, the more you can decide what is, in fact, accurate.

"Reading" and Studying Photographs and Artwork

This book pays particular attention to primary source material and written documents, but historians also view works of art as primary sources. Consider this painting of the medieval French writer Christine de Pizan holding

British Library, London, folio 290, Harley ms. 4431

Christine de Pizan

an early book. Christine was a poet and author of *Book of the City of Ladies,* in which she describes women whose lives counter the antifeminist prejudices shared by some of her male contemporaries. The women facing her represent Reason, Righteousness, and Justice, three virtues Christine claimed helped her write the book. The women appear before her in a dream.

A historian might ask questions about the painting like those that follow to try to learn more about Christine and about life in medieval France. The more you study and learn about medieval and cultural history, the history of women, and other related topics, of course, the more information this painting will reveal. To help you look at and interpret art like a historian, ask yourself the following:

1. After taking a good look at what Christine is wearing and holding and where she is standing, what do you judge to be her social and economic status? Does she seem wealthy, poor, or somewhere in between?
2. Christine died before the publication of the first book printed with movable type. How were the books in the picture prepared? Do you think that books were as available and as common in households as they are now?
3. How many women in medieval Europe do you think were able to read and write?
4. What kind of room are these three women standing in? Why is it so plain? Why is there a table and

not a chair? For what was the room most often used?
5. Keep in mind that many pieces of art, particularly in the Middle Ages and Renaissance, were commissioned by wealthy rulers and aristocrats. Who do you think might have commissioned this piece of art and why? Why is this information useful to know?
6. Symbols are a common feature of much medieval European artwork (as well as of artwork throughout Western history). The women facing Christine wear crowns and represent the virtues of Reason, Righteousness, and Justice. Each woman is holding an object that symbolizes her virtue. Can you make a connection between the object and the virtue it represents? What do their crowns symbolize?
7. What "symbols" in advertisements, television shows, or movies help reveal the character of the people you see in them? How, for example, might a typical ad make it obvious at first glance that a person was smart or rich?

Reading and Studying Maps

Historical events do not just "happen." They happen in a specific place. It is important to learn all you can about that place, and a good map can help you do this.

Your textbook includes several kinds of maps. The pull-out map of the world bound into the inside front cover of the textbook is a good place to start. Map basics include taking care to read and understand every label on whatever map you study. The textbook's pullout map has labels for six kinds of information. Each of the following is important:

1. Names of countries
2. Names of major cities
3. Names of oceans and large bodies of water
4. Names of rivers
5. Longitude and latitude. Lines of longitude extend from the North Pole to the South Pole; one such line intersects Iceland in the top left (or northwest) corner of the map. Lines of latitude circle the globe east to west and intersect lines of longitude. These imaginary lines place countries and oceans in their approximate setting on the face of the earth. Not every map includes latitude and longitude.
6. Mileage scale. A mileage scale shows how far apart, in miles and kilometers, each location is from other locations.

Most maps include three basic types of information:

1. The boundaries of countries, cities, empires, and other kinds of "political" information. A good map shows each political division in a different color to make them all easy to find. The color of each region

or country is the decision of the mapmaker (also known as a cartographer).

2. Mountains, oceans, rivers, and other "physical" or "topographic" information. The mountains on this map appear as wavy lines: Ethiopia and the western United States are mountainous; Sudan and Kazakhstan are flat.

3. Latitude, longitude, a mileage scale, and other information: These elements help the reader place the information in some kind of context. Some maps include an N with an arrow that points north. Most maps show northern areas (Alaska, Norway, etc.) at the top. A map that does not do this is not misleading or wrong. But if an N arrow appears on the map, be sure you know where north is.

"Political" information tends to change a great deal. Maps usually change after the winners of a major war take more territory. "Physical" information changes slowly. Latitude, north, distances, and the like do not change.

In addition, many maps include information about the spread of disease, the location of cathedrals and universities, trade routes, and any number of other things. There is no real limit to the kinds of information a map can show, and the more information a map can display clearly, the more useful it is. Any good map will include a boxed "legend" stating the information that makes that map useful. The more detailed the map, the more information the mapmaker should provide in the legend.

Again, note that only the names of oceans, large bodies of water, and rivers, the "physical" features in this map, really exist in nature. They are relatively changeless. All other features on this map are made up and change fairly often. The maps you see here and on the next page all show the same familiar "boot," which we call Italy. But all or part of this landmass has also been called Latium, Campania, the Duchy of Benevento, the Kingdom of Lothair, the Papal States, the Kingdom of Sicily, Tuscany, Lombardy, Piedmont, Savoy, and finally, in 1870, Italy. People and places change; mountains and oceans do not, at least not much. Whenever you have trouble finding a region or a place on a map, look for a permanent feature to help you get your bearings.

In addition to kingdoms, cities, and mountains, maps can show the physical proximity of any two or more ideas, movements, or developments. Map 13.2 (p. 294) shows the movement of several voyages of the sixteenth and seventeenth centuries. Note that the boxed legend associates the color of a route (shown as a line) with its nation of origin. This map makes it possible to see a number of useful things at a glance that could take several maps to describe, including:

1. Where each voyage began (Note the places that launch the most voyages and those that launch none.)
2. How long each voyage was (Note the mileage key.)
3. Which route each explorer took (Note the letters labeling each line.)

Ancient Italy

The Byzantine Empire in the Time of Justinian

Europe in the High Middle Ages

Europe in 1763

The New Europe

The Unification of Italy

4. The trading cities that were established (Which nation established the most?)
5. The location of the trade winds (What effect did they have on the voyages, such as Vasco da Gama's?)

Another kind of movement appears in Map 9.3 (p. 198). This map shows the spread of religions in southern and eastern Asia between 600 and 1900 C.E. Using the legend, trace the movement of each major religion.

Putting It Together: Reading and Studying Documents, Supported by Maps and Images

Learning to read a document is no different from learning to read a restaurant menu. The more you practice, the quicker your eyes will find the lobster and pastries.

Let's explore a pair of primary sources.

As the introduction to the reading on the next page makes clear, King Louis XIV of France is writing the king of Tonkin to ask permission to send Christian missionaries to Southeast Asia. But this exchange of letters tells a great deal more than that.

Before you read this document, take a careful look at the portrait of Louis XIV next to it. As this image makes clear, Louis lived during an age of flourishes and excess. Among many other questions, including some that appear later, you may ask yourself how Louis's manner of speaking reflects the public presentation you see in his portrait.

Your textbook does not show a corresponding portrait of the king of Tonkin, but you might try to create a picture of him in your mind as you read his response to the letter he receives from his fellow king.

Next, look at the two maps, on pages xxviii and xxix. Find Vietnam (of which Tonkin was a province) and France. Look at the arrows that correspond to France on the map of trade routes. See what you can learn about the economic and other interests of each of these countries at the time of this exchange of letters.

The following questions about this document are the kinds of questions your instructor would ask about the document.

1. Why does Louis refer to the king of Tonkin, whom he never met, as his "very dear and good friend" (line 2)? Do you think that this French king would begin a conversation with, say, a French shopkeeper in quite the same way? If not, why does he identify more with a fellow king than with a fellow Frenchman?
2. How often do you imagine that the king of France had to persuade people to do what he wanted rather than order them to do so? Who might these people have been?
3. Note that Louis uses what is referred to as the "Royal 'We'" and refers to himself in the third person singular. When does the king of Tonkin refer to himself in the first person ("I"), and when does he refer to himself in the third person ("we")?

Louis XIV

A LETTER TO THE KING OF TONKIN

1. Most high, most excellent, most mighty and most mag-
2. nanimous Prince, our very dear and good friend, may it
3. please God to increase your greatness with a happy end!
4. We hear from our subjects who were in your Realm
5. what protection you accorded them. We appreciate this all
6. the more since we have for you all the esteem that one can
7. have for a prince as illustrious through his military valor as
8. he is commendable for the justice which he exercises in his
9. Realm.... Since the war which we have had for several
10. years, in which all of Europe had banded together against
11. us, prevented our vessels from going to the Indies, at the
12. present time, when we are at peace after having gained
13. many victories and expanded our Realm through the con-
14. quest of several important places, we have immediately
15. given orders to the Royal Company to establish itself in
16. your kingdom as soon as possible.... We have given orders
17. to have brought to you some presents which we believe
18. might be agreeable to you. But the one thing in the world
19. which we desire most, both for you and for your Realm,
20. would be to obtain for your subjects who have already
21. embraced the law of the only true God of heaven and earth,
22. the freedom to profess it, since this law is the highest, the
23. noblest, the most sacred and especially the most suitable to
24. have kings reign absolutely over the people.
25.   We are even quite convinced that, if you knew the
26. truths and the maxims which it teaches, you would give
27. first of all to your subjects the glorious example of
28. embracing it. We wish you this incomparable blessing
29. together with a long and happy reign, and we pray God
30. that it may please Him to augment your greatness with
31. the happiest of endings.
32.   Your very dear and good friend,
33.   Louis
34.   Written at Sainte-Germain-en-Laye
35.   the 10th day of January, 1681

The Qing Empire in the Eighteenth Century

4. Why does Louis say that he is writing when he does, instead of earlier (lines 9–16)? Consider the map on the
   next page: Does France dominate overseas trade as thoroughly as it dominated its European neighbors? What
   does this map suggest about Louis's request of Tonkin?
5. How does Louis say that Christian missionaries will
   be good for Tonkin and its people (lines 25–28)? What
   reason in Louis's own letter makes you wonder if

ANSWERS FROM THE KING OF TONKIN TO LOUIS XIV

36. The King of Tonkin sends to the King of France a letter to
37. express to him his best sentiments.... Your communica-
38. tion, which comes from a country which is a thousand
39. leagues away, and which proceeds from the heart as a
40. testimony of your sincerity, merits repeated consideration
41. and infinite praise. Politeness toward strangers is nothing
42. unusual in our country. There is not a stranger who is not
43. well received by us. How then could we refuse a man from
44. France, which is the most celebrated among the kingdoms
45. of the world and which for love of us wishes to frequent us
46. and bring us merchandise? These feelings of fidelity and
47. justice are truly worthy to be applauded. As regards your
48. wish that we should cooperate in propagating your reli-
49. gion, we do not dare to permit it, for there is an ancient
50. custom, introduced by edicts, which formally forbids it.
51. Now, edicts are promulgated only to be carried out faith-
52. fully; without fidelity nothing is stable. How could we
53. disdain a well-established custom to satisfy a private
54. friendship?... This then is my letter. We send you here-
55. with a modest gift which we offer you with a glad heart.
56.   This letter was written at the beginning of winter
57. and on a beautiful day.

converting the people of Tonkin to Christianity is "the one thing in the world which we desire most"?

6. Does the king of Tonkin seem pleased to hear from Louis and by his request (lines 36–41)? How does he refer to the gift Louis offers him?

7. Louis mentions his gratitude for the good treatment of some French subjects when they were "in your realm." What do you imagine these Frenchmen were actually doing there? Do you imagine they were invited, or did they arrive on their own? How does the king of Tonkin respond when Louis mentions his appreciation for the "protection" they were accorded (lines 41–43)? And protection from what?

8. What reason does the king of Tonkin give for refusing Louis's offer of Christian missionaries (lines 47–54)? He takes care to explain to Louis that "edicts are promulgated . . . nothing is stable." What does this suggest about the king of Tonkin's attitude toward

Louis and the "incomparable blessing" of faith in the Christian god? How many French people (or Europeans, for that matter) is the king of Tonkin likely to have met? What French person or persons might have already given the king ideas about Louis and his offer?

9. Compare the final line of each letter. What significance do you draw from the fact that Louis names the day, month, year, and location in which he writes? Apart from later historians, who in particular is most likely to have been most interested in having this information? What is the significance of the king of Tonkin's closing line?

If you can propose thoughtful answers to these questions, you will have gotten to know the material very well and will be ready for whatever examinations and papers await you in your course.

Global Trade Patterns of the European States in the Eighteenth Century

ISTORIANS OFTEN REFER to the period from the sixteenth through eighteenth centuries as the early modern era. During these years, several factors were at work that created the conditions of our own time.

From a global perspective, perhaps the most noteworthy event of the period was the extension of the maritime trade network throughout the entire populated world. The Chinese had inaugurated the process with their groundbreaking voyages to East Africa in the early fifteenth century. Muslim traders had contributed their part by extending their mercantile network as far as China and the Spice Islands in Southeast Asia. The final instrument of that expansion was a resurgent Europe, which exploded onto the world scene with the initial explorations of the Portuguese and the Spanish at the end of the fifteenth century and then gradually came to dominate shipping on international trade routes during the next three centuries.

Some contemporary historians argue that it was this sudden burst of energy from Europe that created the first truly global economic network. According to Immanuel Wallerstein, one of the leading proponents of this theory, the Age of Exploration led to the creation of a new "world system" characterized by the emergence of global trade networks dominated by the rising force of European capitalism, which now began to scour the periphery of the system for access to markets and cheap raw materials.

Other historians, however, qualify Wallerstein's view and point to the Mongol expansion beginning in the thirteenth century or even to the rise of the Arab Empire in the Middle East a few centuries earlier as signs of the creation of a global communications network enabling goods and ideas to travel from one end of the Eurasian supercontinent to the other.

Whatever the truth of this debate, there are still many reasons for considering the end of the fifteenth century as a crucial date in world history. In the most basic sense, it marked the end of the long isolation of the Western Hemisphere from the rest of the inhabited world. In so doing, it led to the creation of the first truly global network of ideas and commodities, which would introduce plants, ideas, and (unfortunately) many new diseases to all humanity (see the comparative essay in Chapter 13). Second, the period gave birth to a stunning increase in trade and manufacturing that stimulated major economic changes not only in Europe but in other parts of the world as well.

The period from 1500 to 1800, then, was an incubation period for the modern world and the launching pad for an era of European domination that would reach fruition in the nineteenth century. To understand why the West emerged as the leading force in the world at that time, it is necessary to grasp what factors were at work in Europe and why they were absent in other major civilizations around the globe.

Historians have identified improvements in navigation, shipbuilding, and weaponry that took place in Europe in the early modern era as essential elements in the Age of Exploration. As we have seen, many of these technological advances were based on earlier discoveries that had taken place elsewhere—in China, India, and the Middle East—and had then been brought to Europe on Muslim ships or along

The Art Archive

the trade routes through Central Asia. But it was the capacity and the desire of the Europeans to enhance their wealth and power by making practical use of the discoveries of others that was the significant factor in the equation and enabled them to dominate international sea-lanes and create vast colonial empires in the New World.

European expansion was not fueled solely by economic considerations, however. As had been the case with the rise of Islam, religion played a major role in motivating the European Age of Exploration in the early modern era. Although Christianity was by no means a new religion in the sixteenth century (as Islam had been at the moment of Arab expansion), the world of Christendom was in the midst of a major period of conflict with the forces of Islam, a rivalry that had been exacerbated by the conquest of the Byzantine Empire by the Ottoman Turks in 1453.

Although the claims of Portuguese and Spanish adventurers that their activities were motivated primarily by a desire to bring the word of God to non-Christian peoples undoubtedly included a considerable measure of hypocrisy, there is no doubt that religious motives played a major part in the European Age of Exploration. Religious motives were less evident in the activities of the non-Catholic powers that entered the competition in the seventeenth century. English and Dutch merchants and officials were more inclined to be motivated purely by the pursuit of economic profit.

Conditions in many areas of Asia were less conducive to these economic and political developments. In China, a centralized monarchy continued to rely on a prosperous agricultural sector as the economic foundation of the empire. In Japan, power was centralized under the powerful Tokugawa shogunate, and the era of peace and stability that ensued saw an increase in manufacturing and commercial activity. But Japanese elites, after initially expressing interest in the outside world, abruptly shut the door on European trade and ideas in an effort to protect the "land of the gods" from external contamination.

In India and the Middle East, commerce and manufacturing had played a vital role in the life of societies since the emergence of the Indian Ocean trade network in the first centuries C.E. But beginning in the eleventh century, the area had suffered through an extended period of political instability, marked by invasions by nomadic peoples from Central Asia. The violence of the period and the local rulers' lack of experience in promoting maritime commerce had a severe depressing effect on urban manufacturing and commerce.

In the early modern era, then, Europe was best placed to take advantage of the technological innovations that had become increasingly available throughout the Old World. It possessed the political stability, the capital, and the "modernizing elite" that spurred efforts to wrest the greatest benefit from the new conditions. Whereas other regions were beset by internal obstacles or had deliberately turned inward to seek their destiny, Europe now turned outward to seek a new and dominant position in the world. Nevertheless, significant changes were taking place in other parts of the world as well, and many of these changes had relatively little to do with the situation in the West. As we shall see, the impact of European expansion on the rest of the world was still limited at the end of the eighteenth century. While European political authority was firmly established in a few key areas, such as the Spice Islands and Latin America, traditional societies remained relatively intact in most regions of Africa and Asia. And processes at work in these societies were often operating independently of events in Europe and would later give birth to forces that acted to restrict or shape the Western impact. One of these forces was the progressive emergence of centralized states, some of them built on the concept of ethnic unity. ◈

13

NEW ENCOUNTERS:
THE CREATION OF A WORLD MARKET

CHAPTER OUTLINE
AND FOCUS QUESTIONS

An Age of Exploration and Expansion

◻ How did Muslim merchants expand the world trade network at the end of the fifteenth century?

The Portuguese Maritime Empire

◻ Why were the Portuguese so successful in taking over the spice trade?

Spanish Conquests in the "New World"

◻ How did Portugal and Spain acquire their overseas empires, and how did their methods differ?

The Impact of European Expansion

◻ What were some of the consequences of the arrival of the European traders and missionaries for the peoples of Asia and the Americas?

Africa in Transition

◻ What were the main features of the African slave trade, and what effects did European participation have on traditional practices?

Southeast Asia in the Era of the Spice Trade

◻ What were the main characteristics of Southeast Asian societies, and how were they affected by the coming of Islam and the Europeans?

CRITICAL THINKING

◻ Christopher Columbus has recently become a controversial figure in world history. Why do you think this is so, and how would you evaluate his contribution to the modern world?

CALECHVT CELEBERRI:
MVM INDIÆ EMPORIVM,

Courtesy of tthe Beinecke Rare Book and Manuscript Library, Yale University

The port of Calicut in the mid-1500s

*W*HEN, IN THE SPRING OF **1498,** the Portuguese fleet arrived at the town of Calicut (now known as Kozhikode), on the western coast of India, fleet commander Vasco da Gama ordered a landing party to go ashore to contact the local authorities. The first to greet them, a Muslim merchant from Tunisia, said, "May the Devil take thee! What brought thee hither?" "Christians and spices," replied the visitors. "A lucky venture, a lucky venture," replied the Muslim. "Plenty of rubies, plenty of emeralds! You owe great thanks to God, for having brought you to a country holding such riches!"[1]

Such words undoubtedly delighted the Portuguese, who sent a landing party ashore and concluded that the local population appeared to be Christians. Although it later turned out that they were mistaken—the local faith was a form of Hinduism—their spirits were probably not seriously dampened, for God was undoubtedly less important than gold and glory to sailors like themselves who had gone through considerable hardship to become the first Europeans since the ancient Greeks to sail across the Indian Ocean. They left two months later with a cargo of spices and the determination to return soon with a second and larger fleet.

Vasco da Gama's maiden voyage to India inaugurated an extended period of European expansion into Asia, led by merchant adventurers and missionaries, that lasted several hundred years and had effects that are still felt today. Eventually, it resulted in a Western takeover of existing trade routes in the Indian Ocean and the establishment of colonies throughout Asia, Africa, and Latin America. In later years, Western historians would react to these events by describing the era as an "Age of Discovery" that significantly broadened the maritime trade network and set the stage for the emergence of the modern world.

In fact, however, the voyages of Vasco da Gama and his European successors were only the latest stage in a process that had begun generations earlier, at a time when European explorations were still restricted to the stormy waters of the North Atlantic Ocean. As we have seen in Chapter 10, Chinese fleets had roamed the Indian Ocean for several years during the early fifteenth century, linking the Middle Kingdom with societies as distant as the Middle East and the coast of East Africa. Although the voyages of Zhenghe were short in duration and had few lasting effects, the world of Islam was also on the march, as Muslim traders blazed new trails into Southeast Asia and across the Sahara to the civilizations that flourished along the banks of the Niger River. In this chapter, we turn our attention to the stunning expansion in the scope and volume of commercial and cultural contacts that took place in the generations preceding and following da Gama's historic voyage to India, as well as to the factors that brought about this expansion. ◆

An Age of Exploration and Expansion

The voyage of Vasco da Gama has customarily been seen as a crucial step in the opening of trade routes to the East. In the sense that the voyage was a harbinger of future European participation in the spice trade, this view undoubtedly has merit. In fact, however, as has been pointed out in earlier chapters, the Indian Ocean had been a busy thoroughfare for centuries. The spice trade had been carried on by sea in the region since the days of the legendary Queen of Sheba, and Chinese junks had sailed to the area in search of cloves and nutmeg since the Tang dynasty (see Chapter 10).

Islam and the Spice Trade

By the fourteenth century, a growing percentage of the spice trade was being transported in Muslim ships sailing from ports in India or the Middle East. Muslims, either Arabs or Indian converts, had taken part in the Indian Ocean trade for centuries, and by the thirteenth century, Islam had established a presence in seaports on the islands of Sumatra and Java and was gradually moving inland. In 1292, the Venetian traveler Marco Polo observed that Muslims were engaging in missionary activity in northern Sumatra: "This kingdom is so much frequented by the Saracen merchants that they have converted the natives to the Law of Mahomet—I mean the townspeople only, for the hill people live for all the world like beasts, and eat human flesh, as well as other kinds of flesh, clean or unclean."[2]

But the major impetus for the spread of Islam in Southeast Asia came in the early fifteenth century, with the foundation of a new sultanate at Malacca, on the strait that today bears the same name. The founder was Paramesvara, a vassal of the Hindu state of Majapahit on Java, whose original base of operations had been at Palembang, on the island of Sumatra. In 1390, he had moved his base to Tumasik (modern Singapore), at the tip of the Malayan peninsula, hoping to enhance his ability to play a role in the commerce passing

The Strait of Malacca

through the region. Under pressure from the expanding power of the Thai state of Ayuthaya (see "Southeast Asia in the Era of the Spice Trade" later in this chapter), in the early fifteenth century Paramesvara moved once again to Malacca. The latter's potential strategic importance was confirmed in the sixteenth century by a visitor from Portugal, who noted that Malacca "is a city that was made for commerce; . . . the trade and commerce between the different nations for a thousand leagues on every hand must come to Malacca."[3]

Shortly after its founding, Malacca was visited by a Chinese fleet under the command of Admiral Zhenghe (see Chapter 10). In order to protect his patrimony from local rivals, Paramesvara accepted Chinese vassalage and cemented the new relationship by making an official visit to the Ming emperor in Beijing (see the box on p. 290). More importantly, perhaps, he also converted to Islam. The move was undoubtedly undertaken with a view to enhancing Malacca's ability to participate in the trade that passed through the strait, much of which was dominated by Muslim merchants. Within a few years, Malacca had become the leading economic power in the region and helped to promote the spread of Islam to trading ports throughout the islands of Southeast Asia, including Java, Borneo, Sulawesi, and the Philippines. Adoption of the Muslim faith was eased by the popularity of Sufism, which expressed a marked tolerance for mysticism and local religious beliefs.

The Spread of Islam in West Africa

In the meantime, Muslim trade and religious influence continued to expand south of the Sahara into the Niger

A CHINESE DESCRIPTION OF MALACCA

INTERACTION & EXCHANGE

Malacca, located on the west coast of the Malayan peninsula, first emerged as a major trading port in the early fifteenth century, when its sultan, Paramesvara, avoided Thai rule with the aid of the emperor of China. This description of the area was written by a naval officer who served in one of the famous Chinese fleets that visited the city in the early fifteenth century.

Why was Malacca such an importance center of world trade?

Ma Huan, *Description of a Starry Raft*

This place did not formerly rank as a kingdom. It can be reached from Palembang on the monsoon in eight days. The coast is rocky and desolate, the population sparse. The country (used to) pay an annual tax of 40 taels of gold to Siam. The soil is infertile and yields low. In the interior there is a mountain from (the slopes of) which a river takes its rise. The (local) folk pan the sands (of this river) to obtain tin, which they melt into ingots called *tou*. These weigh 1 kati 4 taels standard weight. (The inhabitants) also weave banana fiber into mats. Apart from tin, no other product enters into (foreign) trade. The climate is hot during the day but cool at night. (Both) sexes coil their hair into a knot. Their skin resembles black lacquer, but there are (some) white-complexioned folk among them who are of Chinese descent. The people esteem sincerity and honesty.

They make a living by panning tin and catching fish. Their houses are raised above the ground. (When constructing them) they refrain from joining planks and restrict the building to the length of a (single) piece of timber. When they wish to retire, they spread their bedding side by side. They squat on their haunches when taking their meals. The kitchen and all its appurtenances is (also) raised (on the stilts). The goods (used in trading at Malacca) are blue and white porcelain, colored beads, colored taffetas, gold and silver. In the seventh year of Yung-lo (1409), the imperial envoy, the eunuch Cheng-Ho, and his lieutenants conferred (on the ruler), by Imperial command, a pair of silver seals, and a headdress, girdle and robe. They also set up a tablet (stating that) Malacca had been raised to the rank of a kingdom, but at first Siam refused to recognize it. In the thirteenth year (of Yung-lo) (1415), the ruler (of Malacca, desirous of) showing his gratitude for the Imperial bounty, crossed the ocean and, accompanied by his consort and son, came to court with tribute. The Emperor rewarded him (appropriately), whereupon (the ruler of Malacca) returned to his (own) country.

ThomsonNOW™ To read more about Ma Huan's voyages, enter the *ThomsonNOW* documents area using the access card that is available for *The Essential World History*.

River valley in West Africa. The area had been penetrated by traders from across the Sahara since ancient times, and contacts undoubtedly increased after the establishment of Muslim control over the Mediterranean coastal regions. Muslim traders crossed the desert carrying Islamic values, political culture, and legal traditions along with their goods. The early stage of state formation had culminated with the kingdom of Mali, symbolized by the renowned Mansa Musa, whose pilgrimage to Mecca in the fourteenth century had left an indelible impression on observers (see Chapter 8).

With the decline of Mali in the late fifteenth century, a new power eventually appeared with the creation of the kingdom of Songhai. The founder of Songhai was Sonni Ali, a local chieftain who seized Timbuktu from its Berber overlords in 1468 and then sought to restore the formidable empire of his predecessors. Rumored to possess magical powers, Sonni Ali was criticized by Muslim scholars for supporting traditional religious practices, but under his rule, Songhai emerged as a major trading state in the region (see Map 13.1). When he died in 1492, his son ascended to the throne, but was deposed shortly thereafter by one of his military commanders, who seized power as king under the name Askia Mohammed (r. 1493–1528).

Under the new ruler, a fervent Muslim, Songhai increasingly relied on Islamic institutions and ideology to strengthen national unity and centralize authority. Askia Mohammed himself embarked on a pilgrimage to Mecca and was recognized by the caliph of Cairo as the Muslim ruler of the Niger River valley. On his return from Mecca, he tried to revive Timbuktu as a major center of Islamic learning, but had less success in converting his subjects, many of whom—especially in rural regions—continued to resist conversion to Islam. He did preside over a significant increase in trans-Saharan trade (notably in salt and gold), which provided a steady source of income to Songhai and other kingdoms in the region (see the box on p. 291). Despite the efforts of Askia Mohammed and his successors, however, centrifugal forces within Songhai eventually led to its breakup after his death.

A New Player: Europe

For almost a millennium, Catholic Europe had been confined to one area. Its one major attempt to expand beyond those frontiers, the Crusades, had largely failed. Of course, Europe had never completely lost contact with the outside world: the goods of Asia and Africa made their

THE GREAT CITY OF TIMBUKTU

 INTERACTION & EXCHANGE

After its founding in the twelfth century, Timbuktu became a great center of Islamic learning and a fabled city of mysteries and riches to Europeans. In the sixteenth century, Timbuktu was still a major commercial center on the trade route through the Sahara. This description of the city was written in 1526 by Leo Africanus, a Muslim from the Islamic state of Granada and one of the great travelers of his time.

What role did the city of Timbuktu play in regional commerce, according to the author of this document? What were the chief means of payment?

Leo Africanus, *History and Description of Africa*

Here are many shops of artificers and merchants, and especially of such as weave linen and cotton cloth. And hither do the Barbary merchants bring cloth of Europe. All the women of this region, except the maid-servants, go with their faces covered, and sell all necessary victuals. The inhabitants, and especially strangers there residing are exceeding rich, insomuch that the king that now is, married both his daughters to rich merchants. Here are many wells containing sweet water; and so often as the river Niger overfloweth, they convey the water thereof by certain sluices into the town. Corn, cattle, milk, and butter this region yieldeth in great abundance: but salt is very scarce here; for it is brought hither by land from Taghaza which is 500 miles distant. When I myself was here, I saw one camel's load of salt sold for 80 ducats. The rich king of Timbuktu hath many plates and scepters of gold, some whereof weigh 1,300 pounds: and he keeps a magnificent and well-furnished court. When

he travelleth any whither he rideth upon a camel which is led by some of his noblemen; and so he doth likewise when he goeth forth to warfare, and all his soldiers ride upon horses. Whoever will speak unto this king must first fall down before his feet, and then taking up earth must first sprinkle it upon his own head and shoulders: which custom is ordinarily observed by . . . ambassadors from other princes. He hath always 3,000 horsemen, and a number of footmen that shoot poisoned arrows, attending upon him. They have often skirmishes with those that refuse to pay tribute, and so many as they take, they sell unto the merchants of Timbuktu. Here are very few horses bred, and the merchants and courtiers keep certain little nags which they use to travel upon: but their best horses are brought out of Barbary. . . . Here are great store of doctors, judges, priests, and other learned men, that are bountifully maintained at the king's cost and charges, and hither are brought divers manuscripts or written books out of Barbary, which are sold for more money than any other merchandise. The coin of Timbuktu is of gold without any stamp or superscription but in matters of small value they use certain shells brought hither out of the kingdom of Persia, 400 of which are worth a ducat: and $6^2/_3$ pieces of their gold coin weigh an ounce. The inhabitants are people of gentle and cheerful disposition, and spend a great part of the night singing and dancing through all the streets of the city.

ThomsonNOW To read an annotated version of Leo Africanus's account, enter the *ThomsonNOW* documents area using the access card that is available for *The Essential World History*.

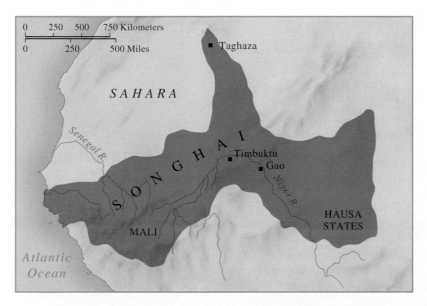

MAP 13.1 **The Songhai Empire.** Songhai was the last of the great states to dominate the region of the Niger River valley prior to the European takeover in the nineteenth century ❓ What were the predecessors of the Songhai Empire in the region? What explains the importance of the area in African history?

way into medieval castles, the works of Muslim philosophers were read in medieval universities, and the Vikings in the ninth and tenth centuries had even explored the eastern fringes of North America. Nevertheless, Europe's contacts with non-European civilizations remained limited until the fifteenth century, when Europeans began to embark on a remarkable series of overseas journeys. What caused European seafarers to undertake such dangerous voyages to the ends of the earth?

Europeans had long been attracted to the East. In the Middle Ages, myths and legends of an exotic land of great riches and magic were widespread. The most famous medieval travelers to the East were the Polos of Venice. In 1271, Nicolò and Maffeo, merchants from Venice, accompanied by Nicolò's son Marco, undertook the lengthy journey to the court of the great Mongol ruler Khubilai Khan (see Chapter 10). As one of the Great Khan's ambassadors, Marco traveled to Japan as well and did not return to Italy until 1295. An account of his experiences, the *Travels,* proved to be the most informative of all the descriptions of Asia by medieval European travelers. Others, like the Franciscan friar John Plano Carpini, had preceded the Polos, but in the fourteenth century, the conquests of the Ottoman Turks and then the breakup of the Mongol Empire reduced Western traffic to the East. With the closing of the overland routes, a number of people in Europe became interested in the possibility of reaching Asia by sea.

The Motives An economic motive thus looms large in Renaissance European expansion (see Chapter 12). The rise of capitalism in Europe was undoubtedly a powerful spur to the process. Merchants, adventurers, and government officials had high hopes of finding precious metals and expanding the areas of trade, especially for the spices of the East. Spices continued to be transported to Europe via Arab intermediaries but were outrageously expensive. Adventurous Europeans did not hesitate to express their desire to share in the wealth. As one Spanish conquistador explained, he and his kind went to the Americas to "serve God and His Majesty, to give light to those who were in darkness, and to grow rich, as all men desire to do."[4]

This statement expresses another major reason for the overseas voyages—religious zeal. A crusading mentality was particularly strong in Portugal and Spain, where the Muslims had largely been driven out in the Middle Ages. Contemporaries of Prince Henry the Navigator of Portugal said that he was motivated by "his great desire to make increase in the faith of our Lord Jesus Christ and to bring him all the souls that should be saved." Although most scholars believe that the religious motive was secondary to economic considerations, it would be foolish to overlook the genuine desire on the part of both explorers and conquistadors, let alone missionaries, to convert the heathen to Christianity. Hernán Cortés, the conqueror of Mexico, asked his Spanish rulers if it was not their duty to ensure that the native Mexicans were "introduced into and instructed in the holy Catholic faith."[5]

The Means If "God, glory, and gold" were the primary motives, what made the voyages possible? First of all, the expansion of Europe was a state enterprise, tied to the growth of centralized monarchies during the Renaissance. By the second half of the fifteenth century, European monarchies had increased both their authority and their resources and were in a position to turn their energies beyond their borders. That meant the invasion of Italy for France, but for Portugal, a state not strong enough to

A Sixteenth-Century Map of Africa. Advances in mapmaking also contributed to the European Age of Exploration. Here a section of a world map by the early-sixteenth-century Spanish cartographer Juan de la Cosa shows the continent of Africa. Note the drawing of the legendary Prester John, mentioned in Chapter 8, at the right, and the Portuguese caravels with their lateen sails in the South Atlantic Ocean. In the minds of Europeans at the time, the legend of Prester John had been identified with the Christian king of Ethiopia.

pursue power in Europe, it meant going abroad. The Spanish scene was more complex, since the Spanish monarchy was strong enough by the sixteenth century to pursue power both on the Continent and beyond.

At the same time, by the end of the fifteenth century, European states had a level of knowledge and technology that enabled them to achieve a regular series of voyages beyond Europe. Although the highly schematic and symbolic medieval maps were of little help to sailors, the **portolani,** or detailed charts made by medieval navigators and mathematicians in the thirteenth and fourteenth centuries, were more useful. With details on coastal contours, distances between ports, and compass readings, they proved of great value for voyages in European waters. But because the *portolani* were drawn on a flat surface and took no account of the curvature of the earth, they were of little use for longer overseas voyages. Only when seafarers began to venture beyond the coasts of Europe did they begin to accumulate information about the actual shape of the earth. By the end of the fifteenth century, cartography had developed to the point that Europeans possessed fairly accurate maps of the known world.

In addition, Europeans had developed remarkably seaworthy ships as well as new navigational techniques. European shipbuilders had mastered the use of the sternpost rudder (an import from China) and had learned how to combine the use of lateen sails with a square rig. With these innovations, they could construct ships mobile enough to sail against the wind and engage in naval warfare and also large enough to mount heavy cannons and carry a substantial amount of goods over long distances. Previously, sailors had used a quadrant and their knowledge of the position of the polestar to ascertain their latitude. Below the equator, however, this technique was useless. Only with the assistance of new navigational aids such as the compass (a Chinese invention) and the astrolabe (an astronomical instrument, reportedly devised by Arab sailors, that was used to measure the altitude of the sun and the stars above the horizon) were they able to explore the high seas with confidence.

The Portuguese Maritime Empire

Portugal took the lead in exploration when it began exploring the coast of Africa under the sponsorship of Prince Henry the Navigator (1394–1460). Prince Henry's motives were a blend of seeking a Christian kingdom as an ally against the Muslims and acquiring new trade opportunities for Portugal. In 1419, he founded a school for navigators on the southwestern coast of Portugal. Shortly thereafter, Portuguese fleets began probing southward along the western coast of Africa in search of gold. In 1441, Portuguese ships reached the Senegal River, just north of Cape Verde, and brought home a cargo of black Africans, most of whom were sold as slaves to wealthy buyers elsewhere in Europe. Within a few years, an estimated thousand slaves were shipped annually from the area back to Lisbon.

Continuing southward, in 1471 the Portuguese discovered a new source of gold along the southern coast of the hump of West Africa (an area that would henceforth be known to Europeans as the Gold Coast). To facilitate trade in gold, ivory, and slaves (some slaves were brought back to Lisbon and others were bartered to local merchants for gold), the Portuguese leased land from local rulers and built stone forts along the coast.

The Portuguese in India

Hearing reports of a route to India around the southern tip of Africa, Portuguese sea captains continued their probing (see Map 13.2 on p. 294). In 1487, Bartolomeu Dias took advantage of westerly winds in the South Atlantic to round the Cape of Good Hope, but he feared a mutiny from his crew and returned home without continuing onward. Ten years later, a fleet under the command of Vasco da Gama rounded the cape and stopped at several ports controlled by Muslim merchants along the coast of East Africa, including Sofala, Kilwa, and Mombasa. Then da Gama's fleet crossed the Arabian Sea and arrived off the port of Calicut on the southwestern coast of India, on May 18, 1498. The Portuguese crown had sponsored da Gama's voyage with the clear objective of destroying the Muslim monopoly over the spice trade, a monopoly that had been intensified by the Ottoman conquest of Constantinople in 1453 (see Chapter 15). Calicut was a major entrepôt on the long route from the Spice Islands to the Mediterranean Sea, but the ill-informed Europeans believed it was the source of the spices themselves. Although he lost two ships en route, da Gama's remaining vessels returned to Europe with their holds filled with ginger and cinnamon, a cargo that earned the investors a profit of several thousand percent.

The Search for Spices

During the next years, the Portuguese set out to gain control of the spice trade. In 1510, Admiral Afonso de Albuquerque established his headquarters at Goa, on the western coast of India south of present-day Bombay. From there, the Portuguese raided Arab shippers, provoking the following comment from an Arab source: "[The Portuguese] took about seven vessels, killing those on board and making some prisoner. This was their first action, may God curse them."[6] In 1511, Albuquerque attacked Malacca itself.

For Albuquerque, control of Malacca would serve two purposes. It could help to destroy the Arab

The Spice Islands

Principal Voyages of Exploration

A Portuguese expeditions, 1430s–1480s
B Dias, 1487–1488
C da Gama, 1497–1499
D Portuguese voyages to the Orient, 1509–1514
E Columbus's first voyage, 1492

F Columbus's three successive voyages, 1493–1504
G Voyages attended by Vespucci, 1499–1502
H Magellan–del Cano, 1519–1522
I Cabot, 1497

Trade winds	
Areas under Spanish control	Spanish trading cities
Areas under Portuguese control	Portuguese trading cities
	Independent trading cities

Spanish routes
Portuguese routes
Other routes

MAP 13.2 **European Voyages and Possessions in the Sixteenth and Seventeenth Centuries.**
This map indicates the most important voyages launched by Europeans during their momentous
Age of Exploration in the sixteenth and seventeenth centuries. ❓ Why did Vasco da Gama sail so
far into the South Atlantic on his voyage to Asia? 🌐 **View an animated version of this map or related**
maps at http://worldrc.wadsworth.com/

spice trade network by blocking passage through the
Strait of Malacca, and it could also provide the
Portuguese with a way station en route to the Spice
Islands and other points east. After a short but bloody
battle, the Portuguese seized the city and put the local
Muslim population to the sword. They then proceeded to
erect a fort, a factory (a common term at the time for a
warehouse), and a church.

From Malacca, the Portuguese launched expeditions
farther east, to China and the Moluccas, then known as
the Spice Islands. There they signed a treaty with a local
sultan for the purchase and export of cloves to the
European market. Within a few years, they had managed
to seize control of the spice trade from Muslim traders
and had garnered substantial profits for the Portuguese
monarchy.

Why were the Portuguese so successful? Basically,
their success was a matter of guns and seamanship. The
first Portuguese fleet to arrive in Indian waters was relatively modest in size. It consisted of three ships and
twenty guns, a force sufficient for self-defense and intimidation but not for serious military operations. Sixteenth-
century Portuguese fleets were more heavily armed and
were capable of inflicting severe defeats if necessary on
local naval and land forces. The Portuguese by no means
possessed a monopoly on the use of firearms and explosives, but they used the maneuverability of their light
ships to maintain their distance while bombarding the
enemy with their powerful cannons. Such tactics gave
them a military superiority over lightly armed rivals that
they were able to exploit until the arrival of other
European forces several decades later.

Columbus Lands in the Americas. In the log that he wrote during his first voyage to the Americas, Christopher Columbus noted that the peoples of the New World were intelligent and friendly, and relations between them and the Spanish were amicable at first. Later, however, the conquistadors began to mistreat the local people. Here is a somewhat imaginative painting of the first encounter from a European perspective. Note the upturned eyes of Columbus and several of his companions, implying that their motives were spiritual rather than material.

Spanish Conquest in the "New World"

While the Portuguese were seeking access to the spice trade of the Indies by sailing eastward through the Indian Ocean, the Spanish attempted to reach the same destination by sailing westward across the Atlantic. Although the Spanish came to overseas discovery and exploration later than the Portuguese, their greater resources enabled them to establish a far grander overseas empire.

The Voyages

An important figure in the history of Spanish exploration was an Italian from Genoa, Christopher Columbus (1451–1506). Knowledgeable Europeans were aware that the world was round but had little understanding of its circumference or the extent of the continent of Asia. Convinced that the circumference of the earth was smaller than contemporaries believed and that Asia was larger, Columbus felt that Asia could be reached by sailing due west instead of eastward around Africa. After being rejected by the Portuguese, he persuaded Queen Isabella of Spain to finance his exploratory expedition, which reached the Americas in October 1492 and explored the coastline of Cuba and the northern shores of the neighboring island of Hispaniola. Columbus believed that he had reached Asia and in three subsequent voyages (1493, 1498, and 1502) sought in vain to find a route through the outer islands to the Asian mainland. In his four voyages, Columbus reached all the major islands of the Caribbean, which he called the Indies, as well as Honduras in Central America.

Although Columbus clung to his belief until his death, other explorers soon realized that he had discovered a new frontier altogether. State-sponsored explorers joined the race to what Europeans began to call the "New World." A Venetian seafarer, John Cabot, explored the New England coastline of the Americas under a license from King Henry VII of England. The continent of South America was discovered accidentally by the Portuguese sea captain Pedro Cabral in 1500. Amerigo Vespucci, a Florentine, accompanied several voyages and wrote a series of letters describing the geography of the New World. The publication of these letters led to the use of the name "America" (after Amerigo) for the new lands.

The Conquests

The newly discovered territories were referred to as the New World, even though they possessed flourishing civilizations populated by millions of people when the Europeans arrived. But the Americas were new to the Europeans, who quickly saw opportunities for conquest and exploitation. The Spanish, in particular, were interested because in 1494 the Treaty of Tordesillas had divided the newly discovered world into separate Portuguese and Spanish spheres of influence. Thereafter the route east around the Cape of Good Hope was to be reserved for the Portuguese, while the route across the Atlantic (except for the eastern hump of South America) was assigned to Spain. The Spanish conquistadors were a hardy lot of mostly upper-class individuals motivated by a typical sixteenth-century blend of glory, greed, and religious crusading zeal. Although sanctioned by the Castilian crown, these groups were financed and outfitted privately, not by the government.

Christopher Columbus's first voyage to the Americas	1492
Last voyages of Columbus	1502–1504
Spanish conquest of Mexico	1519–1522
Francisco Pizarro's conquest of the Inkas	1531–1536

Their superior weapons, organizational skills, and determination brought the conquistadors incredible success. Beginning in 1519 with a small band of men, Hernán Cortés took three years to overthrow the mighty Aztec Empire in central Mexico, led by the chieftain Moctezuma (see Chapter 6). By 1550, the Spanish had gained control of northern Mexico. Between 1531 and 1536, another expedition led by a hardened and somewhat corrupt soldier, Francisco Pizarro (1470–1541), took control of the Inka Empire high in the Peruvian Andes. The Spanish conquests were undoubtedly facilitated by the previous arrival of European diseases, which had decimated the local population. Although it took another three decades before the western part of Latin America was brought under Spanish control (the Portuguese took over Brazil), already by 1535, the Spanish had created a system of colonial administration that made the New World an extension of the old—at least in European eyes.

Governing the Empire

Spanish policy toward the inhabitants of the Americas, whom the Europeans called Indians, was a combination of confusion, misguided paternalism, and cruel exploitation. Confusion arose over the nature of the Indians. Queen Isabella declared the Indians to be subjects of Castile and instituted the *encomienda* system, which permitted the conquering Spaniards to collect tribute from the natives and use them as laborers. In return, the holders of an *encomienda* were supposed to protect the Indians and supervise their spiritual and material needs. In practice, this meant that the settlers were free to implement the system as they pleased. Three thousand miles from Spain, Spanish settlers largely ignored their government and brutally used the Indians to pursue their own economic interests. Indians were put to work on sugar plantations and in the lucrative gold and silver mines. Forced labor, starvation, and especially disease took a fearful toll on Indian lives. With little or no natural resistance to European diseases, the Indians of America were ravaged by smallpox, measles, and typhus brought by the explorers and the conquistadors. Although scholarly estimates of native populations vary drastically, a reasonable guess is that at least half of the natives died of European diseases. On Hispaniola alone, out of an initial population of 100,000 natives when Columbus arrived in 1493, only 300 Indians survived by 1570. In 1542, largely in response to the publications of Bartolomé de Las Casas, a Dominican monk who championed the Indians, the government abolished the *encomienda* system and provided more protection for the natives.

The chief organ of colonial administration was the Council of the Indies. The council nominated colonial viceroys, oversaw their activities, and kept an eye on ecclesiastical affairs in the colonies. Spanish possessions in the Americas were initially divided between New Spain (Mexico, Central America, and the Caribbean islands), with its center in Mexico City, and Peru (western South America), with its capital at Lima. Each area was governed by a viceroy who served as the king's chief civil and military officer.

By papal agreement, the Catholic monarchs of Spain were given extensive rights over ecclesiastical affairs in the Americas. They could nominate church officials, build churches, collect fees, and supervise the various religious orders that conducted missionary activities. Catholic monks had remarkable success converting and baptizing hundreds of thousands of Indians in the early years of the conquest. Soon after the missionaries came the establishment of dioceses, parishes, schools, and hospitals—all the trappings of a European society.

The Impact of European Expansion

The arrival of the Europeans had an enormous impact on both the conquerors and the conquered. The native American civilizations, which (as we discussed in Chapter 6) had their own unique qualities and a degree of sophistication rarely appreciated by the conquerors, were virtually destroyed, while the native populations were ravaged by diseases introduced by the Europeans. Ancient social and political structures were ripped up and replaced by European institutions, religion, language, and culture.

How does one evaluate the psychological impact of colonization on the colonizers? The relatively easy European success in dominating native peoples undoubtedly reinforced the Europeans' belief in the inherent superiority of their civilization. The Scientific Revolution of the seventeenth century, to be followed by the era of imperialism a century later, then served to strengthen the Eurocentric perspective that has long pervaded Western civilization in its relationship with the rest of the world.

European expansion also affected the conquerors in the economic arena. Wherever they went in the Americas, Europeans sought gold and silver. One Aztec observer commented that the Spanish conquerors "longed and lusted for gold. Their bodies swelled with greed, and their hunger was ravenous; they hungered like pigs for that gold."[7] Rich silver deposits were found and exploited in Mexico and southern Peru (modern Bolivia). When the mines at Potosí in Peru were opened in 1545, the value of precious metals imported into Europe quadrupled. It has been estimated that between 1503 and 1650, some 16 million kilograms of silver and 185,000 kilograms of gold entered the port of Seville, fueling a price revolution that affected the Spanish economy.

COMPARATIVE ESSAY

THE COLUMBIAN EXCHANGE

INTERACTION & EXCHANGE

In the Western world, the discovery of the Americas has traditionally been viewed essentially in a positive sense, as the first step in a process that expanded the global trade network and eventually led to economic well-being and the spread of civilization throughout the world. In recent years, however, that view has come under sharp attack from some observers, who claim that for the peoples of the Americas, the primary legacy of the European conquest was not improved living standards but harsh colonial exploitation and the spread of pestilential diseases that decimated the local population. The brunt of such criticism has been directed at Christopher Columbus, one of the chief initiators of the discovery and conquest of the Americas. Taking issue with the prevailing image of Columbus as a heroic figure in world history, critics view him as a symbol of Spanish colonial repression and a prime mover in the virtual extinction of the peoples and cultures of the Americas.

There is no doubt that the record of the European conquistadors in the Western Hemisphere leaves much to be desired, and certainly the voyages of Columbus were not of universal benefit to his contemporaries or to the generations later to come. They not only resulted in the destruction of vibrant civilizations that were evolving in the Americas but also led ultimately to the enslavement of millions of Africans, who were separated from their families and shipped to a new world in conditions of inhuman bestiality.

But to focus solely on the evils that were committed in the name of civilization misses a larger point and distorts the historical realities of the era. The age of European expansion that began with Prince Henry the Navigator and Christopher Columbus was only the latest in a series of population movements that included the spread of nomadic peoples across Central Asia and the expansion of Islam from the Middle East after the death of the prophet Muhammad. In fact, the migration of peoples in search of survival and a better livelihood has been a central theme in the evolution of the human race since the dawn of prehistory. Virtually all of them involved acts of unimaginable cruelty and the forcible displacement of peoples and societies.

Even more important, it seems clear that the consequences of such population movements are too complex to be summed up in moral or ideological simplifications. The European expansion into the Americas, for example, not only brought the destruction of cultures and dangerous new diseases but also initiated the exchange of plant and animal species that have ultimately been of widespread benefit to peoples throughout the globe. The introduction of the horse, cow, and various grain crops vastly increased food productivity in the Western Hemisphere. The cultivation of corn, manioc, and the potato, all of them products of the Americas, have had the same effect in Asia, Africa, and Europe.

Christopher Columbus was a man of his time, with many of the character traits and prejudices common to his era. Whether he was hero or a villain is a matter of debate. That he and his contemporaries played a key role in the emergence of the modern world is a matter of which there can be no doubt.

Library of Congress, Prints and Photographs Division

Massacre of the Indians. This sixteenth-century engraving is an imaginative treatment of what was probably an all-too-common occurrence as the Spanish attempted to enslave the American peoples and convert them to Christianity.

But gold and silver were only two of the products sent to Europe from the Western Hemisphere. Into Seville flowed sugar, dyes, cotton, vanilla, and hides from livestock raised on the South American pampas. New agricultural products native to the Americas, such as potatoes, cacao, corn, manioc, and tobacco, were also imported (see the comparative essay "The Columbian Exchange" above). Because of its trading posts in Asia, Portugal soon challenged the Italian states as the chief entry point of the eastern trade in spices, jewels, silk, carpets, ivory, leather, and perfumes. Economic historians believe that the increase in the volume and area of European trade and the rise in fluid capital due to this expansion were crucial factors in producing a new era of commercial capitalism that represented the first step toward the world economy that has characterized the modern era.

New Rivals

Portugal's efforts to dominate the trade of the Indian Ocean were never totally successful. The Portuguese lacked both the numbers and the wealth to overcome

Cape Horn and the Strait of Magellan

local resistance and colonize the Asian regions. Moreover, their massive investments in ships and laborers for their empire (hundreds of ships and hundreds of thousands of workers in shipyards and overseas bases) proved very costly. Disease, shipwreck, and battles took a heavy toll of life. The empire was simply too large and Portugal too small to maintain it, and by the end of the century, the Portuguese were being severely challenged by rivals.

Europeans in Asia   The Spanish had established themselves in Asia in the early 1520s, when Ferdinand Magellan, seeking a western route to the Spice Islands across the Pacific Ocean, had sailed around the southern tip of South America, crossed the Pacific, and landed on the island of Cebu in the Philippine Islands. Although Magellan and some forty of his crew were killed in a skirmish with the local population, one of the two remaining ships sailed on to Tidor, in the Moluccas, and thence around the world via the Cape of Good Hope. In the words of a contemporary historian, they arrived in Cádiz "with precious cargo and fifteen men surviving out of a fleet of five sail."[8]

As it turned out, the Spanish could not follow up on Magellan's accomplishment, and in 1529, they sold their rights in Tidor to the Portuguese. But Magellan's voyage was not a total loss. In the absence of concerted resistance from the local population, the Spanish managed to consolidate their control over the Philippines, which eventually became a major Spanish base in the carrying trade across the Pacific.

The primary threat to the Portuguese toehold in Southeast Asia, however, came from the English and the Dutch. In 1591, the first English expedition to the Indies through the Indian Ocean arrived in London with a cargo of pepper. Nine years later, a private joint-stock company, the East India Company, was founded to provide a stable source of capital for future voyages. In 1608, an English fleet landed at Surat, on the northwestern coast of India. Trade with Southeast Asia soon followed.

The Dutch were quick to follow suit, and the first Dutch fleet arrived in India in 1595. In 1602, the Dutch East India Company was established under government sponsorship and was soon actively competing with the English and the Portuguese in the region.

Europeans in the Americas   The Dutch, the French, and the English also began to make inroads on Spanish and Portuguese possessions in the Americas. War and steady pressure from their Dutch and English rivals eroded Portuguese trade in both the West and the East, although Portugal continued to profit from its large colonial empire in Brazil. A formal administration system had been instituted in Brazil in 1549, and Portuguese migrants had established massive plantations there to produce sugar for export to the Old World. The Spanish also maintained an enormous South American empire, but Spain's importance as a commercial power declined rapidly in the seventeenth century because of a drop in the output of the silver mines and the poverty of the Spanish monarchy.

The Dutch formed their own Dutch West India Company in 1621 to compete with Spanish and Portuguese interests in the Americas. But although it made some inroads in Portuguese Brazil and the Caribbean (see Map 13.3), the company's profits were never large enough to compensate for the expenditures. Dutch settlements were also established on the North American continent. The mainland colony of New Netherland stretched from the mouth of the Hudson River as far north as Albany, New York. In the meantime, French colonies appeared in the Lesser Antilles, and in Louisiana, at the mouth of the Mississippi River.

In the second half of the seventeenth century, however, rivalry and years of warfare with the English and the French (who had also become active in North America) brought the decline of the Dutch commercial empire in the Americas. In 1664, the English seized the colony of New Netherland and renamed it New York, and the Dutch West India Company soon went bankrupt. In 1663, Canada became the property of the French crown and was administered like a French province. But

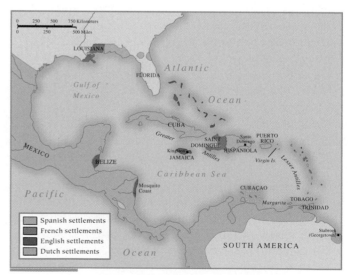

MAP 13.3   European Possessions in the West Indies.   After the first voyage of Christopher Columbus, other European adventurers followed on his trail, seeking their share of the alleged riches of the Americas. ❓ Where else did the French, Dutch, and English settle that proved more profitable for them?

the French failed to provide adequate men or money, allowing their continental wars to take precedence over the conquest of the North American continent. By the early eighteenth century, the French began to cede some of their American possessions to their English rival.

The English, meanwhile, had proceeded to create a colonial empire along the Atlantic seaboard of North America. The desire to escape from religious oppression combined with economic interests did make successful colonization possible, as the Massachusetts Bay Company demonstrated. The Massachusetts colony had only four thousand settlers in its early years, but by 1660, their number had swelled to forty thousand.

Africa in Transition

Although the primary objective of the Portuguese in rounding the Cape of Good Hope was to find a sea route to the Spice Islands, they soon discovered that profits were to be made en route, along the eastern coast of Africa.

Europeans in Africa

In the early sixteenth century, a Portuguese fleet seized a number of East African port cities, including Kilwa, Sofala, and Mombasa, and built forts along the coast in an effort to control the trade in the area (see Map 13.2 on p. 294). Above all, the Portuguese wanted to monopolize the trade in gold, which was mined by Bantu workers in the hills along the upper Zambezi River and then shipped to Sofala on the coast (see Chapter 8). For centuries, the gold trade had been monopolized by local Shona peoples at Zimbabwe. In the fifteenth century, it had come under the control of a Shona dynasty known as the Mwene Metapa. The Portuguese opened treaty relations with the Mwene Metapa, and Jesuit priests were eventually posted to the court in 1561. At first, the Mwene Metapa found the Europeans useful as an ally against local rivals, but by the end of the sixteenth century, the Portuguese had established a protectorate and forced the local ruler to grant title to large tracts of land to European officials and private individuals living in the area. The Portuguese, however, lacked the personnel, the capital, and the expertise to dominate local trade, and in the late seventeenth century, a vassal of the Mwene Metapa succeeded in driving them from the plateau; his descendants maintained control of the area for the next two hundred years.

The first Europeans to settle in southern Africa were the Dutch. After an unsuccessful attempt to seize the Portuguese settlement on the island of Mozambique off the East African coast, in 1652 the Dutch set up a way station at the Cape of Good Hope to serve as a base for their fleets en route to the East Indies. At first, the new settlement was meant simply to provide food and other supplies to Dutch ships, but eventually it developed into a permanent colony. Dutch farmers, known as Boers and speaking a Dutch dialect that evolved into Afrikaans, began to settle in the sparsely occupied areas outside the city of Cape Town. The temperate climate and the absence of tropical diseases made the territory near the cape practically the only land south of the Sahara that the Europeans had found suitable for habitation.

The Slave Trade

The European exploration of the African coastline had little apparent significance for most peoples living in the interior of the continent, except for a few who engaged in direct or indirect trade with the foreigners. But for peoples living on or near the coast, the impact was often great indeed. As the trade in slaves increased during the sixteenth through the eighteenth centuries, thousands, and then millions, were removed from their homes and forcibly exported to plantations in the Western Hemisphere.

Origins of Slavery in Africa Traffic in slaves had existed for centuries before the arrival of Portuguese fleets along African shores. The primary market for African slaves was the Middle East, where most were used as domestic servants. Slavery also existed in many European countries, where a few slaves from Africa or war captives from the regions north of the Black Sea were used for domestic purposes or as agricultural workers in the lands adjacent to the Mediterranean.

At first, the Portuguese simply replaced European slaves with African ones. During the second half of the fifteenth century, about a thousand slaves were taken to Portugal each year; the vast majority were apparently destined to serve as domestic servants for affluent families throughout Europe. But the discovery of the New World in the 1490s and the subsequent planting of sugarcane in South America and the islands of the Caribbean changed the situation. Cane sugar was native to Indonesia and had first been introduced to Europeans from the Middle East during the Crusades. By the fifteenth century, it was grown (often by slaves from Africa or the region of the Black Sea) in modest amounts on Cyprus, Sicily, and southern regions of the Iberian peninsula. But when the Ottoman Empire seized much of the eastern Mediterranean (see Chapter 15), the Europeans needed to seek out new areas suitable for cultivation. Demand increased as sugar gradually replaced honey as a sweetener, especially in northern Europe.

The primary impetus to the sugar industry came from the colonization of the Americas. During the sixteenth century, plantations were established along the eastern coast of Brazil and on several islands in the Caribbean. Because the cultivation of cane sugar is an arduous process demanding both skill and large quantities of labor, the new plantations required more workers than could be provided by the Indian population in the New World, many of whom had died of diseases imported from the Old World. Since the climate and soil of much of West Africa were not especially conducive to the cultivation of sugar, African slaves began to be shipped to Brazil and the Caribbean to work on the plantations. The first were sent from Portugal, but in 1518, a Spanish ship carried the first boatload of African slaves directly from Africa to the Americas.

Growth of the Slave Trade   During the next two centuries, the trade in slaves increased by massive proportions (see Map 13.4). An estimated 275,000 enslaved Africans were exported to other countries during the sixteenth century, with 2,000 going annually to the Americas alone. During the next century, the total climbed to over a million and jumped to six million in the eighteenth century, when the trade spread from West and Central Africa to East Africa. It has been estimated that altogether as many as ten million African slaves were transported to the Americas between the early sixteenth and the late nineteenth centuries. As many as two million were exported to other areas during the same period.

The Middle Passage   One reason for these astonishing numbers, of course, was the tragically high death rate. In what is often called the **Middle Passage,** the arduous voyage from Africa to the Americas, losses were frequently appalling. Although figures on the number of slaves who died on the journey are almost entirely speculative, during the first shipments, up to one-third of the human cargo may have died of disease or malnourishment. Even

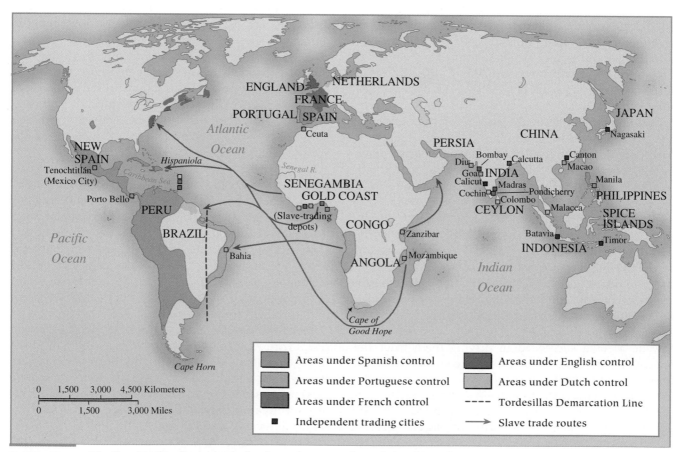

MAP 13.4   The Slave Trade.   Beginning in the sixteenth century, the trade in African slaves to the Americas became a major source of profit to European merchants. This map traces the routes taken by slave-trading ships, as well as the territories and ports of call of European powers in the seventeenth century. **?** What were the major destinations for the slave trade? **◉ View an animated version of this map or related maps at** http://worldrc.wadsworth.com/

among crew members, mortality rates were sometimes as high as one in four. Later merchants became more efficient and reduced losses to about 10 percent. Still, the future slaves were treated in an inhumane manner, chained together in the holds of ships reeking with the stench of human waste and diseases carried by vermin.

Ironically, African slaves who survived the brutal voyage fared somewhat better than whites after their arrival. Mortality rates for Europeans in the West Indies, in fact, were ten to twenty times higher than in Europe, and death rates for those newly arrived in the islands averaged more than 125 per 1,000 annually. But the figure for Africans, many of whom had developed at least a partial immunity to yellow fever, was only about 30 per 1,000.

The reason for these staggering death rates was clearly more than maltreatment, although that was certainly a factor. As we have seen, the transmission of diseases from one continent to another brought high death rates among those lacking immunity. African slaves were somewhat less susceptible to European diseases than the American Indian populations. Indeed, they seem to have possessed a degree of immunity, perhaps because their ancestors had developed antibodies to "white people's diseases" owing to the trans-Saharan trade. The Africans would not have had immunity to native American diseases, however.

Sources of Slaves   Slaves were obtained by traditional means. Before the coming of the Europeans in the fifteenth century, most slaves in Africa were prisoners or war captives or had inherited their status. Many served as domestic servants or as wageless workers for the local ruler. When Europeans first began to take part in the slave trade, they would normally purchase slaves from local African merchants at the infamous slave markets in exchange for gold, guns, or other European manufactured goods such as textiles or copper or iron utensils (see the box on p. 302). At first, local slave traders obtained their supply from immediately surrounding regions, but as demand increased, they had to move farther inland to locate their victims. In a few cases, local rulers became concerned about the impact of the slave trade on the political and social well-being of their societies. In a letter to the king of Portugal in 1526, King Affonso of Congo (Bakongo) complained that "so great, Sire, is the corruption and licentiousness that our country is being completely depopulated."[9] As a general rule, however, local monarchs viewed the slave trade as a source of income, and many launched forays against defenseless villages in search of unsuspecting victims.

The Effects of the Slave Trade   The effects of the slave trade varied from area to area. It might be assumed that apart from the tragic effects on the lives of individual

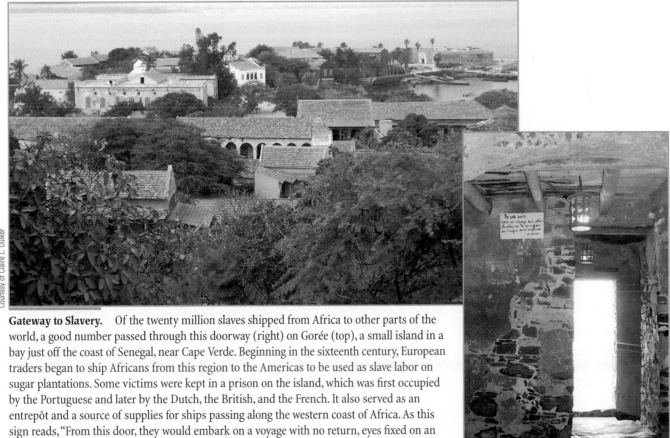

Gateway to Slavery.   Of the twenty million slaves shipped from Africa to other parts of the world, a good number passed through this doorway (right) on Gorée (top), a small island in a bay just off the coast of Senegal, near Cape Verde. Beginning in the sixteenth century, European traders began to ship Africans from this region to the Americas to be used as slave labor on sugar plantations. Some victims were kept in a prison on the island, which was first occupied by the Portuguese and later by the Dutch, the British, and the French. It also served as an entrepôt and a source of supplies for ships passing along the western coast of Africa. As this sign reads, "From this door, they would embark on a voyage with no return, eyes fixed on an infinity of suffering."

Courtesy of Claire L. Duiker

Courtesy of Claire L. Duiker

A Slave Market in Africa

FAMILY & SOCIETY

Traffic in slaves had been carried on in Africa since the kingdom of the pharaohs in ancient Egypt. But the slave trade increased dramatically after the arrival of European ships off the coast of West Africa. The following passage by a Dutch observer describes a slave market in Africa and the conditions on the ships that carried the slaves to the Americas. Note the difference in tone between this account and the far more critical views expressed in Chapter 20.

What is the author's overall point of view with respect to the institution of slavery? Does he justify the practice? How does he compare Dutch behavior with that of other European countries involved?

Slavery in Africa: A Firsthand Report

Not a few in our country fondly imagine that parents here sell their children, men their wives, and one brother the other. But those who think so deceive themselves, for this never happens on any other account but that of necessity, or some great crime; most of the slaves that are offered to us are prisoners of war, who are sold by the victors as their booty.

When these slaves come to Fida, they are put in prison all together; and when we treat concerning buying them, they are brought out into a large plain. There, by our surgeons, whose province it is, they are thoroughly examined, even to the smallest member, and that naked too, both men and women, without the least distinction or modesty. Those that are approved as good are set on one side; and the lame or faulty are set by as invalids. . . .

The invalids and the maimed being thrown out, . . . the remainder are numbered, and it is entered who delivered them. In the meanwhile, a burning iron, with the arms or name of the companies, lies in the fire, with which ours are marked on the breast. This is done that we may distinguish them from the slaves of the English, French, or others (which are also marked with their mark), and to prevent the Negroes exchanging them for worse, at which they have a good hand.

I doubt not but this trade seems very barbarous to you, but since it is followed by mere necessity, it must go on; but we take all possible care that they are not burned too hard, especially the women, who are more tender than the men.

When we have agreed with the owners of the slaves, they are returned to their prison. There from that time forward they are kept at our charge, costing us two pence a day a slave; which serves to subsist them, like our criminals, on bread and water. To save charges, we send them on board our ships at the very first opportunity, before which their masters strip them of all they have on their backs so that they come aboard stark naked, women as well as men. In this condition they are obliged to continue, if the master of the ship is not so charitable (which he commonly is) as to bestow something on them to cover their nakedness.

You would really wonder to see how these slaves live on board, for though their number sometimes amounts to six or seven hundred, yet by the careful management of our masters of ships, they are so regulated that it seems incredible. And in this particular our nation exceeds all other Europeans, for the French, Portuguese and English slave ships are always foul and stinking; on the contrary, ours are for the most part clean and neat.

The slaves are fed three times a day with indifferent good victuals, and much better than they eat in their own country. Their lodging place is divided into two parts, one of which is appointed for the men, the other for the women, each sex being kept apart. Here they lie as close together as it is possible for them to be crowded.

We are sometimes sufficiently plagued with a parcel of slaves which come from a far inland country who very innocently persuade one another that we buy them only to fatten and afterward eat them as a delicacy. When we are so unhappy as to be pestered with many of this sort, they resolve and agree together (and bring over the rest to their party) to run away from the ship, kill the Europeans, and set the vessel ashore, by which means they design to free themselves from being our food.

I have twice met with this misfortune; and the first time proved very unlucky to me, I not in the least suspecting it, but the uproar was quashed by the master of the ship and myself by causing the abettor to be shot through the head, after which all was quiet.

ThomsonNOW To read excerpts from a slave's autobiography, enter the *ThomsonNOW* documents area using the access card that is available for *The Essential World History*.

---

victims and their families, the practice would have led to the depopulation of vast areas of the continent. This did occur in some areas, notably in modern Angola, south of the Congo River basin, and in thinly populated areas in East Africa, but it was less true in West Africa. There high birthrates were often able to counterbalance the loss of able-bodied adults, and the introduction of new crops from the Western Hemisphere, such as maize, peanuts, and manioc, led to an increase in food production that made it possible to support a larger population. One of the many cruel ironies of history is that while the institution of slavery was a tragedy for many, it benefited others.

Still, there is no denying the reality that from a moral point of view, the slave trade represented a tragic loss for millions of Africans, not only for the individual victims, but also for their families. One of the more poignant aspects of the trade is that as many as 20 percent of those sold to European slavers were children, a statistic that may be partly explained by the fact that many European countries had enacted regulations that permitted more children than adults to be transported aboard the ships.

How did Europeans justify cruelty of such epidemic proportions? In some cases, they rationalized that slave traders were only carrying on a tradition that had existed for centuries throughout the Mediterranean and African world. In fact, African intermediaries were active in the process and were often able to dictate the price, volume, and availability of slaves to European purchasers. In others, they eased their consciences by noting that slaves brought from Africa would now be exposed to the Christian faith and would be able to replace American Indian workers, many of whom were considered too physically fragile for the heavy human labor involved in cutting sugarcane.

Political and Social Structures in a Changing Continent

Of course, the Western economic penetration of Africa had other dislocating effects. As in other parts of the non-Western world, the importation of manufactured goods from Europe undermined the foundations of local cottage industry and impoverished countless families. The demand for slaves and the introduction of firearms intensified political instability and civil strife. At the same time, the impact of the Europeans should not be exaggerated. Only in a few isolated areas, such as South Africa and Mozambique, were permanent European settlements established. Elsewhere, at the insistence of African rulers and merchants, European influence generally did not penetrate beyond the coastal regions.

Nevertheless, inland areas were often affected by events taking place elsewhere. In the western Sahara, for example, the diversion of trade routes toward the coast led to the weakening of the old Songhai trading empire and its eventual conquest by a vigorous new Moroccan dynasty in the late sixteenth century. In 1590, Moroccan forces defeated Songhai's army at Gao, on the Niger River, and then occupied the great caravan center of Timbuktu.

European influence had a more direct impact along the coast of West Africa, especially in the vicinity of European forts such as Dakar and Sierra Leone, but no European colonies were established there before 1800. Most of the numerous African states in the area from Cape Verde to the delta of the Niger River were sufficiently strong to resist Western encroachments, and they often allied with each other to force European purchasers to respect their monopoly over trading operations. Some, like the powerful Ashanti kingdom, established in 1680 on the Gold Coast, profited substantially from the rise in seaborne commerce. Some states, particularly along the so-called Slave Coast, in what is now Dahomey and Togo, or in the densely populated Niger River delta, took an active part in the slave trade. The demands of slavery and

the temptations of economic profit, however, also contributed to the increase in conflict among the states in the area.

This was especially true in the region of the Congo River, where Portuguese activities eventually led to the splintering of the Congo Empire and two centuries of rivalry and internal strife among the successor states in the area. A similar pattern developed in East Africa, where Portuguese activities led to the decline and eventual collapse of the Mwene Metapa. Northward along the coast, in present-day Kenya and Tanzania, African rulers, assisted by Arab forces from Oman and Muscat in the Arabian peninsula, expelled the Portuguese from Mombasa in 1728. Swahili culture now regained some of the dynamism it had possessed before the arrival of Vasco da Gama and his successors. But with much shipping now diverted southward to the route around the Cape of Good Hope, the commerce of the area never completely recovered and was increasingly dependent on the export of slaves and ivory obtained through contacts with African states in the interior.

Southeast Asia in the Era of the Spice Trade

In Southeast Asia, the encounter with the West that began with the arrival of Portuguese fleets in the Indian Ocean at the end of the fifteenth century eventually resulted in the breakdown of traditional societies and the advent of colonial rule. The process was a gradual one, however.

The Arrival of the West

As we have seen, the Spanish soon followed the Portuguese into Southeast Asia. By the seventeenth century, the Dutch, English, and French had begun to join the scramble for rights to the lucrative spice trade.

Within a short time, the Dutch, through the aggressive and well-financed Dutch East India Company (Vereenigde Oost-Indische Compagnie, or VOC), had not only succeeded in elbowing their rivals out of the spice trade but had also begun to consolidate their political and military control over the area. On the island of Java, where they established a fort at Batavia (today's Jakarta) in 1619 (see the comparative illustration on p. 304), the Dutch found that it was necessary to bring the inland regions under their control to protect their position. Rather than establishing a formal colony, however, they tried to rule as much as possible through the local landed aristocracy. On Java and the neighboring island of Sumatra, the VOC established pepper plantations, which soon became the source of massive profits for Dutch merchants in Amsterdam. Elsewhere they attempted to monopolize the clove trade by limiting cultivation of the crop to one island. By the end of the eighteenth century, the Dutch had succeeded in bringing almost the entire Indonesian archipelago under their control.

CALECHVT CELEBERRI:
MVM INDIÆ EMPORIVM.

INTERACTION &
EXCHANGE

COMPARATIVE ILLUSTRATION

Europe in Asia.   As Europeans began to move into parts of Asia, they reproduced
many of the physical surroundings of their homeland in the port cities they built
there. This is evident in comparing these two scenes. The etching of the port at
Calicut, India (upper figure), reveals many architectural details brought by the Portuguese in the
1500s. The lower figure is a seventeenth-century view of Batavia, which the Dutch built as their
headquarters on the northern coast of Java in 1619. Eventually, the canals of Batavia became breeding
grounds for malaria-bearing mosquitoes, forcing the Dutch to move a few miles to the south, the site
of modern-day Jakarta.

The arrival of the Europeans had somewhat less
impact on mainland Southeast Asia, where cohesive
monarchies in Burma, Thailand, and Vietnam resisted
foreign encroachment. In addition, the coveted spices
did not thrive on the mainland, so the Europeans'
efforts there were far less determined than in the
islands. The Portuguese did establish limited trade relations with several mainland states, including the Thai

kingdom at Ayuthaya, Burma, Vietnam, and the remnants of the old Angkor kingdom in Cambodia. By the
early seventeenth century, other nations had followed
and had begun to compete actively for trade and missionary privileges. As was the case elsewhere, the
Europeans soon became involved in local factional disputes as a means of obtaining political and economic
advantages.

In Vietnam, the arrival of Western merchants and missionaries coincided with a period of internal conflict among ruling groups in the country. After their arrival in the mid-seventeenth century, the European powers characteristically began to intervene in local politics, with the Portuguese and the Dutch supporting rival factions. By the end of the century, when it became clear that economic opportunities were limited, most European states abandoned their factories (trading stations) in the area. French missionaries attempted to remain, but their efforts were hampered by the local authorities, who viewed the Catholic insistence that converts give their primary loyalty to the pope as a threat to the legal status and prestige of the Vietnamese emperor (see the box on p. 306).

State and Society in Precolonial Southeast Asia

Between 1400 and 1800, Southeast Asia experienced the last flowering of traditional culture before the advent of European rule in the nineteenth century. Although the coming of the Europeans had an immediate and direct impact in some areas, notably the Philippines and parts of the Malay world, in most areas Western influence was still relatively limited.

Nevertheless, Southeast Asian societies were changing in several subtle ways—in their trade patterns, their means of livelihood, and their religious beliefs. In some ways, these changes accentuated the differences between individual states in the region. Yet beneath these differences was an underlying commonality of life for most people. Despite the diversity of cultures and religious beliefs in the area, Southeast Asians were in most respects closer to each other than they were to peoples outside the region. For the most part, the states and peoples of Southeast Asia were still in control of their own destiny.

Religion and Kingship   During the early modern era, both Buddhism and Islam became well established in Southeast Asia, and Christianity began to attract some converts, especially in the Philippines. Buddhism was dominant in lowland areas on the mainland, from Burma to Vietnam. At first, Muslim influence was felt mainly on the Malayan peninsula and along the northern coast of Java and Sumatra, where local merchants encountered their Muslim counterparts from foreign lands on a regular basis.

Buddhism and Islam also helped shape Southeast Asian political institutions. As the political systems began to mature, they evolved into four main types: Buddhist kings, Javanese kings, Islamic sultans, and Vietnamese emperors (for the case of Vietnam, which was strongly influenced by China, see Chapter 11). In each case, institutions and concepts imported from abroad were adapted to local circumstances.

The Buddhist style of kingship took shape between the eleventh and the fifteenth centuries. It became the predominant political system in the Buddhist states of mainland Southeast Asia—Burma, Ayuthaya, Laos, and Cambodia. Perhaps the dominant feature of the Buddhist model was the godlike character of the monarch, who was considered by virtue of his karma to be innately superior to other human beings and served as a link between human society and the cosmos.

The Javanese model was a blend of Buddhist and Islamic political traditions. Like their Buddhist counterparts, Javanese monarchs possessed a sacred quality and maintained the balance between the sacred and the material world.

The Islamic model was found mainly on the Malayan peninsula and along the coast of the Indonesian archipelago. In this pattern, the head of state was a sultan, who was viewed as a mortal, although he still possessed some magical qualities.

The Economy   During the early period of European penetration, the economy of most Southeast Asian societies was based on agriculture, as it had been for thousands of years. Still, by the sixteenth century, commerce was beginning to affect daily life, especially in the cities that were beginning to proliferate along the coasts or on navigable rivers. In part, this was because agriculture itself was becoming more commercialized as cash crops like sugar and spices replaced subsistence farming in rice or other cereals in some areas.

Regional and interregional trade were already expanding before the coming of the Europeans. The central geographic location of Southeast Asia enabled it to become a focal point in a widespread trading network. Spices, of course, were the mainstay of the interregional trade, but Southeast Asia exchanged other products as well. The region exported tin (mined in Malaya since the tenth century), copper, gold, tropical fruits and other agricultural products, cloth, gems, and luxury goods in exchange for manufactured goods, ceramics, and high-quality textiles such as silk from China.

AN EXCHANGE OF ROYAL CORRESPONDENCE

INTERACTION & EXCHANGE

In 1681, King Louis XIV of France wrote a letter to the "king of Tonkin" (the Trinh family head, then acting as viceroy to the Vietnamese ruler) requesting permission for Christian missionaries to proselytize in Vietnam. The latter politely declined the request on the grounds that such activity was prohibited by ancient custom. In fact, Christian missionaries had been active in Vietnam for years, and their intervention in local politics had aroused the anger of the court in Hanoi.

Compare the response given here to Louis XIV's request to the answer given to the pope by the Mongol emperor Kuyuk Khan in 1244, presented in the box on page 228 Which do you believe was the more conciliatory?

A Letter to the King of Tonkin from Louis XIV

Most high, most excellent, most mighty, and most magnanimous Prince, our very dear and good friend, may it please God to increase your greatness with a happy end!

We hear from our subjects who were in your Realm what protection you accorded them. We appreciate this all the more since we have for you all the esteem that one can have for a prince as illustrious through his military valor as he is commendable for the justice which he exercises in his Realm. We have even been informed that you have not been satisfied to extend this general protection to our subjects but, in particular, that you gave effective proofs of it to Messrs. Deydier and de Bourges. We would have wished that they might have been able to recognize all the favors they received from you by having presents worthy of you offered you; but since the war which we have had for several years, in which all of Europe had banded together against us, prevented our vessels from going to the Indies, at the present time, when we are at peace after having gained many victories and expanded our Realm through the conquest of several important places, we have immediately given orders to the Royal Company to establish itself in your kingdom as soon as possible, and have commanded Messrs. Deydier and de Bourges to remain with you in order to maintain a good relationship between our subjects and yours, also to warn us on occasions that might present themselves when we might be able to give you proofs of our esteem and of our wish to concur with your satisfaction as well as with your best interests.

By way of initial proof, we have given orders to have brought to you some presents which we believe might be agreeable to you. But the one thing in the world which we desire most, both for you and for your Realm, would be to obtain for your subjects who have already embraced the law of the only true God of heaven and earth, the freedom to profess it, since this law is the highest, the noblest, the most sacred, and especially the most suitable to have kings reign absolutely over the people.

We are even quite convinced that, if you knew the truths and the maxims which it teaches, you would give first of all to your subjects the glorious example of embracing it. We wish you this incomparable blessing together with a long and happy reign, and we pray God that it may please Him to augment your greatness with the happiest of endings.

Written at Saint-Germain-en-Laye, the 10th day of January, 1681,

Your very dear and good friend,
Louis

Answer from the King of Tonkin to Louis XIV

The King of Tonkin sends to the King of France a letter to express to him his best sentiments, saying that he was happy to learn that fidelity is a durable good of man and that justice is the most important of things. Consequently practicing of fidelity and justice cannot but yield good results. Indeed, though France and our Kingdom differ as to mountains, rivers, and boundaries, if fidelity and justice reign among our villages, our conduct will express all of our good feelings and contain precious gifts. Your communication, which comes from a country which is a thousand leagues away, and which proceeds from the heart as a testimony of your sincerity, merits repeated consideration and infinite praise. Politeness toward strangers is nothing unusual in our country. There is not a stranger who is not well received by us. How then could we refuse a man from France, which is the most celebrated among the kingdoms of the world and which for love of us wishes to frequent us and bring us merchandise? These feelings of fidelity and justice are truly worthy to be applauded. As regards your wish that we should cooperate in propagating your religion, we do not dare to permit it, for there is an ancient custom, introduced by edicts, which formally forbids it. Now, edicts are promulgated only to be carried out faithfully; without fidelity nothing is stable. How could we disdain a well-established custom to satisfy a private friendship? . . .

We beg you to understand well that this is our communication concerning our mutual acquaintance. This then is my letter. We send you herewith a modest gift, which we offer you with a glad heart.

This letter was written at the beginning of winter and on a beautiful day.

ThomsonNOW For insights into Louis XIV, enter the *ThomsonNOW* documents area using the access card that is available for *The Essential World History*.

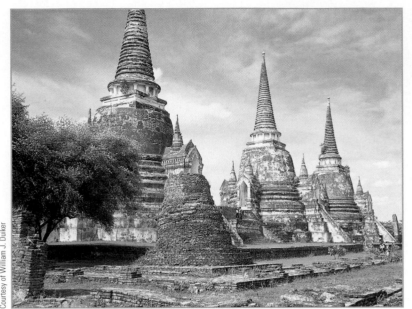

Courtesy of William J. Duiker

The Thai Capital at Ayuthaya. The Thai arrived in Southeast Asia in the thirteenth century, driven out of southern China by the Mongols. They then destroyed the Angkor empire and set up their capital at Ayuthaya, which was one of the finest cities in Asia from the fifteenth to the eighteenth century. After a Burmese invasion in 1767, most of Ayuthaya's inhabitants were killed, and all official Thai records were destroyed. Here the remains of some Buddhist stupas, erected in a ceremonial precinct in the center of the city, are a visual confirmation of the influence of Theravada Buddhism on Thai society.

Society In general, Southeast Asians probably enjoyed a somewhat higher living standard than most of their contemporaries elsewhere in Asia. Although most of the population was poor by modern Western standards, hunger was not a widespread problem. Several factors help explain this relative prosperity. In the first place, most of Southeast Asia has been blessed by a salubrious climate. The uniformly high temperatures and the abundant rainfall enable as many as two or even three crops to be grown each year. Second, although the soil in some areas is poor, the alluvial deltas on the mainland are fertile, and the volcanoes of Indonesia periodically spew forth rich volcanic ash that renews the mineral resources of the soil of Sumatra and Java. Finally, with some exceptions, most of Southeast Asia was relatively thinly populated.

Social institutions tended to be fairly homogeneous throughout Southeast Asia. Compared with China and India, there was little social stratification, and the nuclear family predominated. In general, women fared better in the region than anywhere else in Asia. Daughters often had the same inheritance rights as sons, and family property was held jointly between husband and wife. Wives were often permitted to divorce their husbands, and monogamy was the rule rather than the exception. Although women were usually restricted to specialized work, such as making ceramics, weaving, or transplanting the rice seedlings into the main paddy fields, and rarely possessed legal rights equal to those of men, they enjoyed a comparatively high degree of freedom and status in most societies in the region and were sometimes involved in commerce.

CONCLUSION

*D*URING THE FIFTEENTH CENTURY, the pace of international commerce increased dramatically. Chinese fleets visited the Indian Ocean while Muslim traders extended their activities into the Spice Islands and sub-Saharan West Africa. Then the Europeans burst onto the world scene. Beginning with the seemingly modest ventures of the Portuguese ships that sailed southward along the West African coast, the process accelerated with the epoch-making voyages of Christopher Columbus to the Americas and Vasco da Gama to the Indian Ocean in the 1490s. Soon a number of other European states had entered the scene, and by the end of the eighteenth century, they had created a global trade network dominated by Western ships and Western power that distributed foodstuffs, textile goods, spices, and precious minerals from one end of the globe to the other (see Map 13.5).

In less than three hundred years, the European Age of Exploration changed the face of the world. In some areas, such as the Americas and the Spice Islands, it led to the destruction of indigenous civilizations and the establishment of European colonies. In others, as in Africa, South Asia, and mainland Southeast Asia, it left native regimes intact but had a strong impact on local societies and regional trade patterns.

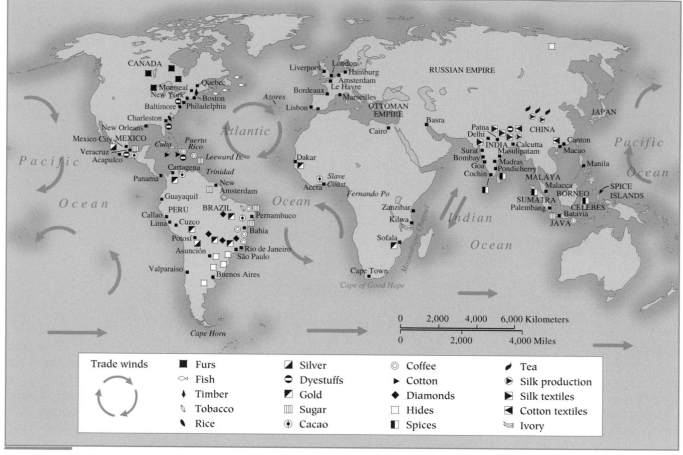

MAP 13.5 **The Pattern of World Trade from the Sixteenth to the Eighteenth Centuries.** This map shows the major products that were traded by European merchants throughout the world during the era of European exploration. Prevailing wind patterns in the oceans are shown on the map.
❓ What were the primary sources of gold and silver, so sought after by Columbus and his successors?
🌐 **View an animated version of this map or related maps at** http://worldrc.wadsworth.com/

At the time, many European observers viewed the process in a favorable light. Not only did it expand world trade and foster the exchange of new crops and discoveries between the Old and New Worlds, but it also introduced Christianity to "heathen peoples" around the globe. Many modern historians have been much more critical, concluding that European activities during the sixteenth and seventeenth centuries created a "tributary mode of production" based on European profits from unequal terms of trade that foreshadowed the exploitative relationship characteristic of the later colonial period. Other scholars have questioned that contention, however, and argue that although Western commercial operations had a significant impact on global trade patterns, they did not—at least not before the eighteenth century—freeze out non-European participants. Muslim merchants, for example, were

long able to evade European efforts to eliminate them from the spice trade, and the trans-Saharan caravan trade was relatively unaffected by European merchant shipping along the West African coast. In some cases, the European presence may even have encouraged new economic activity, as in the Indian subcontinent (see Chapter 15).

By the same token, the Age of Exploration did not, as some have claimed, usher in an era of Western dominance over the rest of the world. In the Middle East, powerful empires continued to hold sway over the lands washed by the Muslim faith. Beyond the Himalayas, Chinese emperors in their new northern capital of Beijing retained proud dominion over all the vast territory of continental East Asia. We shall deal with these regions, and how they confronted the challenges of a changing world, in Chapter 15 and 16.

TIMELINE

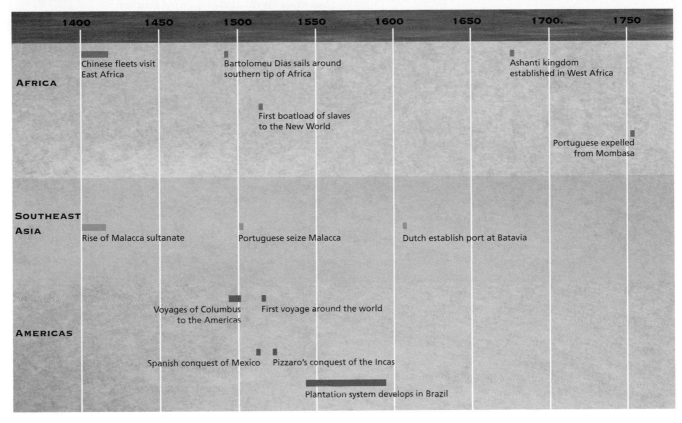

	1400	1450	1500	1550	1600	1650	1700.	1750

AFRICA

Chinese fleets visit East Africa

Bartolomeu Dias sails around southern tip of Africa

Ashanti kingdom established in West Africa

First boatload of slaves to the New World

Portuguese expelled from Mombasa

SOUTHEAST ASIA

Rise of Malacca sultanate

Portuguese seize Malacca

Dutch establish port at Batavia

Voyages of Columbus to the Americas

First voyage around the world

AMERICAS

Spanish conquest of Mexico   Pizzaro's conquest of the Incas

Plantation system develops in Brazil

CHAPTER NOTES

1. *A Journal of the First Voyage of Vasco da Gama* (London, 1898), cited in J. H. Parry, *The European Reconnaissance: Selected Documents* (New York, 1968), p. 82.
2. H. J. Benda and J. A. Larkin, eds., *The World of Southeast Asia: Selected Historical Readings* (New York, 1967), p. 13.
3. Parry, *European Reconnaissance*, quoting from A. Cortesão, *The Summa Oriental of Tomé Pires* (London, 1944), vol. 2, pp. 283, 287.
4. Quoted in J. H. Parry, *The Age of Reconnaissance: Discovery, Exploration, and Settlement, 1450 to 1650* (New York, 1963), p. 33.
5. Quoted in R. B. Reed, "The Expansion of Europe," in R. DeMolen, ed., *The Meaning of the Renaissance and Reformation* (Boston, 1974), p. 308.
6. K. N. Chaudhuri, *Trade and Civilization in the Indian Ocean: An Economic History from the Rise of Islam to 1750* (Cambridge, 1985), p. 65.
7. Quoted in M. Leon-Portilla, ed., *The Broken Spears: The Aztec Account of the Conquest of Mexico* (Boston, 1969), p. 51.
8. Quoted in Parry, *Age of Reconnaissance*, pp. 176–177.
9. Quoted in B. Davidson, *Africa in History: Themes and Outlines* (London, 1968), p. 137.

SUGGESTED READING

On the technological aspects of European expansion, see **C. M. Cipolla, *Guns, Sails, and Empires: Technological Innovation and the Early Phases of European Expansion, 1400–1700*** (New York, 1965); **F. Fernandez-Armesto**, ed., ***The Times Atlas of World Exploration***

(New York, 1991); and **R. C. Smith, *Vanguard of Empire: Ships of Exploration in the Age of Columbus*** (Oxford, 1993); also see **A. Pagden, *Lords of All the World: Ideologies of Empire in Spain, Britain, and France, c. 1500–c. 1800*** (New Haven, Conn., 1995). For an overview on the impact of European expansion in the Indian Ocean, see **K. N. Chaudhuri, *Trade and Civilization in the Indian Ocean: An Economic History from the Rise of Islam to 1750*** (Cambridge, 1985). For a series of stimulating essays reflecting modern scholarship, see **J. D. Tracy, *The Rise of Merchant Empires: Long-Distance Trade in the Early Modern World, 1350–1750*** (Cambridge, 1990).

On European expansion in the Americas, see **S. E. Morison, *The European Discovery of America: The Southern Voyages, 1492–1616*** (New York, 1974). A gripping work on the conquistadors is **H. Thomas, *Conquest: Montezuma, Cortés, and the Fall of Old Mexico*** (New York, 1993). The human effects of the interaction of New and Old World cultures are examined thoughtfully in **A. W. Crosby, *The Columbian Exchange: Biological and Cultural Consequences of 1492*** (Westport, Conn., 1972).

On Portuguese expansion, the fundamental work is **C. R. Boxer, *The Portuguese Seaborne Empire, 1415–1825*** (New York, 1969). On the Dutch, see **J. I. Israel, *Dutch Primacy in World Trade, 1585–1740*** (Oxford, 1989). British activities are chronicled in **S. Sen, *Empire of Free Trade: The East India and the Making of the Colonial Marketplace*** (Philadelphia, 1998), and **Anthony Wild's** elegant work ***The East India Company: Trade and Conquest from 1600*** (New York, 2000).

The effects of European trade in Southeast Asia are discussed in **A. Reid, *Southeast Asia in the Age of Commerce, 1450–1680*** (New Haven, Conn., 1989). On the spice trade, see **A. Dalby, *Dangerous Tastes: The Story of Spices*** (Berkeley, Calif., 2000) and **J. Turner, *Spice: The History of a Temptation*** (New York, 2004).

On the African slave trade, the standard work is **P. Curtin**, *The African Slave Trade: A Census* (Madison, Wis., 1969). For more recent treatments, see **P. Lovejoy**, *Transformations in Slavery: A History of Slavery in Africa* (1983), and **P. Manning**, *Slavery and African Life* (Cambridge, 1990); **H. Thomas**, *The Slave Trade* (New York, 1997), provides a useful overview. Also see **C. Palmer**, *Human Cargoes: The British Slave Trade to Spanish America, 1700–1739* (Urbana, Ill., 1981), and **K. F. Kiple**, *The Caribbean Slave: A Biological History* (Cambridge, 1984).

For a brief introduction to women's experiences during the Age of Exploration and global trade, see **S. Hughes** and **B. Hughes**, *Women in World History,* vol. 2 (Armonk, N.Y., 1997). For a more theoretical discussion of violence and gender in the early modern period, consult **R. Trexler**, *Sex and Conquest: Gendered Violence, Political Order, and the European Conquest of the Americas* (Ithaca, N.Y., 1995). The native American female experience with the European encounter is presented in **R. Gutierrez**, *When Jesus Came the Corn Mothers Went Away: Marriage, Sexuality and Power in New Mexico, 1500–1846* (Stanford, Calif., 1991), and **K. Anderson**, *Chain Her by One Foot: The Subjugation of Women in Seventeenth-Century New France* (London, 1991).

InfoTrac College Edition

Visit this chapter's InfoTrac College Edition/Research activities at the *Essential World History* Companion Website for activities related to early explorations.

ThomsonNOW™ for Duiker and Spielvogel's *The Essential World History, Third Edition*

Enter *ThomsonNOW* using the access card that is available with this text. *ThomsonNOW* will assist you in understanding the content in this chapter with lesson plans generated for your needs, as well as provide you with a connection to the *Wadsworth World History Resource Center* (see description below for details).

WORLD HISTORY
RESOURCE CENTER

Enter the Resource Center using either your *ThomsonNOW* access card or your standalone access card for the *Wadsworth World History Resource Center*. Organized by topic, this website includes quizzes; images; over 350 primary source documents; interactive simulations, maps, and timelines; movie explorations; and a wealth of other resources. You can read the following documents, and many more, at http://worldrc.wadsworth.com/

> Vasco da Gama, "Round Africa to India"
> Fra Soncino, "Regarding John Cabot's First Voyage"

Visit the *Essential World History* Companion Website for chapter quizzes and more.

> http://www.thomsonedu.com/history/duiker

DISCOVERY

How was European expansion into the rest of the world both a positive and a negative experience for Europeans and non-Europeans?

In thinking about this question, begin by breaking it down into the components shown below. A discussion of the significance of each component should appear in your answer.

POLITICS AND GOVERNMENT: What were the social and cultural results of empire building in Europe? Why did Louis XIV want to send missionaries, and why did the King of Tonkin oppose it? In what ways did Louis see his culture as superior to the King of Tonkin's? Compare the final sentence of each letter. How do they differ? What do these differences tell you about European and East Asian culture in the 1600s?

AN EXCHANGE OF ROYAL CORRESPONDENCE

A Letter to the King of Tonkin from Louis XIV

Most high, most excellent, most mighty, and most magnanimous Prince, our very dear and good friend, may it please God to increase your greatness with a happy end!

We hear from our subjects who were in your Realm what protection you accorded them. We appreciate this all the more since we have for you all the esteem that one can have for a prince as illustrious through his military valor as he is commendable for the justice which he exercises in his Realm. We have even been informed that you have not been satisfied to extend this general protection to our subjects but, in particular, that you gave effective proofs of it to Messrs. Deydier and de Bourges. We would have wished that they might have been able to recognize all the favors they received from you by having presents worthy of you offered you; but since the war which we have had for several years, in which all of Europe had banded together against us, prevented our vessels from going to the Indies, at the present time, when we are at peace after having gained many victories and expanded our Realm through the conquest of several important places, we have immediately given orders to the Royal Company to establish itself in your kingdom as soon as possible, and have commanded Messrs. Deydier and de Bourges to remain with you in order to maintain a good relationship between our subjects and yours, also to warn us on occasions that might present themselves when we might be able to give you proofs of our esteem and of our wish to concur with your satisfaction as well as with your best interests.

By way of initial proof, we have given orders to have brought to you some presents which we believe might be agreeable to you. But the one thing in the world which we desire most, both for you and for your Realm, would be to obtain for your subjects who have already embraced the law of the only true God of heaven and earth, the freedom to profess it, since this law is the highest, the noblest, the most sacred, and especially the most suitable to have kings reign absolutely over the people.

We are even quite convinced that, if you knew the truths and the maxims which it teaches, you would give first of all to your subjects the

glorious example of embracing it. We wish you this incomparable blessing together with a long and happy reign, and we pray God that it may please Him to augment your greatness with the happiest of endings.

Written at Saint-Germain-en-Laye, the 10th day of January, 1681,

Your very dear and good friend,
Louis

Answer from the King of Tonkin to Louis XIV

The King of Tonkin sends to the King of France a letter to express to him his best sentiments, saying that he was happy to learn that fidelity is a durable good of man and that justice is the most important of things. Consequently practicing of fidelity and justice cannot but yield good results. Indeed, though France and our Kingdom differ as to mountains, rivers, and boundaries, if fidelity and justice reign among our villages, our conduct will express all of our good feelings and contain precious gifts. Your communication, which comes from a country which is a thousand leagues away, and which proceeds from the heart as a testimony of your sincerity, merits repeated consideration and infinite praise. Politeness toward strangers is nothing unusual in our country. There is not a stranger who is not well received by us. How then could we refuse a man from France, which is the most celebrated among the kingdoms of the world and which for love of us wishes to frequent us and bring us merchandise? These feelings of fidelity and justice are truly worthy to be applauded. As regards your wish that we should cooperate in propagating your religion, we do not dare to permit it, for there is an ancient custom, introduced by edicts, which formally forbids it. Now, edicts are promulgated only to be carried out faithfully; without fidelity nothing is stable. How could we disdain a well-established custom to satisfy a private friendship? . . .

We beg you to understand well that this is our communication concerning our mutual acquaintance. This then is my letter. We send you herewith a modest gift, which we offer you with a glad heart.

This letter was written at the beginning of winter and on a beautiful day.

INTERACTION AND EXCHANGE: Based on this fanciful image of Columbus's landing and the Comparative Essay, with its telling print, what do you think was the European attitude toward native peoples? What does it reveal about European cultural attitudes at that time?

Look at the maps of European voyages and European trade. Compare the key areas of European exploration with what became key centers of trade. What major products were valued by the Europeans? Note which areas of the European trade map do not indicate trade products. What does this indicate about the flow of products in the world trade of the sixteenth to eighteenth centuries? Who controlled this trade, and who benefited?

© North Wind Picture Archives

Columbus Lands in the Americas

In the Western world, the discovery of the Americas has traditionally been viewed essentially in a positive sense, as the first step in a process that expanded the global trade network and eventually led to economic well-being and the spread of civilization throughout the world. In recent years, however, that view has come under sharp attack from some observers, who claim that for the peoples of the Americas, the primary legacy of the European conquest was not improved living standards but harsh colonial exploitation and the spread of pestilential diseases that decimated the local population. The brunt of such criticism has been directed at Christopher Columbus, one of the chief initiators of the discovery and conquest of the Americas. Taking issue with the prevailing image of Columbus as a heroic figure in world history, critics view him as a symbol of Spanish colonial repression and a prime mover in the virtual extinction of the peoples and cultures of the Americas.

There is no doubt that the record of the European conquistadors in the Western Hemisphere leaves much to be desired, and certainly the voyages of Columbus were not of universal benefit to his contemporaries or to the generations later to come. They not only resulted in the destruction of vibrant civilizations that were evolving in the Americas but also led ultimately to the enslavement of millions of Africans, who were separated from their families and shipped to a new world in conditions of inhuman bestiality.

But to focus solely on the evils that were committed in the name of civilization misses a larger point and distorts the historical realities of the era. The age of European expansion that

began with Prince Henry the Navigator and Christopher Columbus was only the latest in a series of population movements that included the spread of nomadic peoples across Central Asia and the expansion of Islam from the Middle East after the death of the prophet Muhammad. In fact, the migration of peoples in search of survival and a better livelihood has been a central theme in the evolution of the human race since the dawn of prehistory. Virtually all of them involved acts of unimaginable cruelty and the forcible displacement of peoples and societies.

Even more important, it seems clear that the consequences of such population movements are too complex to be summed up in moral or ideological simplifications. The European expansion into the Americas, for example, not only brought the destruction of cultures and dangerous new diseases but also initiated the exchange of plant and animal species that have ultimately been of widespread benefit to peoples throughout the globe. The introduction of the horse, cow, and various grain crops vastly increased food productivity in the Western Hemisphere. The cultivation of corn, manioc, and the potato, all of them products of the Americas, have had the same effect in Asia, Africa, and Europe.

Christopher Columbus was a man of his time, with many of the character traits and prejudices common to his era. Whether he was hero or a villain is a matter of debate. That he and his contemporaries played a key role in the emergence of the modern world is a matter of which there can be no doubt.

Library of Congress, Prints and Photographs Division

Massacre of the Indians

Look at the maps of European voyages and European trade. Compare the key areas of European exploration with what became key centers of trade. What were the major products valued by the Europeans? Note which areas of the European trade map do

The Pattern of World Trade from the Sixteenth to the Eighteenth Centuries

European Voyages and Possessions in the Sixteenth and Seventeenth Centuries

not indicate trade products. What does this indicate about the flow of products in the world trade of the sixteenth to eighteenth centuries? Who controlled this trade, and who benefited? Compare this with the development of modern world economies and centers of economic power.

14

EUROPE TRANSFORMED: REFORM AND STATE BUILDING

CHAPTER OUTLINE AND FOCUS QUESTIONS

The Reformation of the Sixteenth Century

◻ What were the main tenets of Lutheranism and Calvinism, and how did they differ from each other and from Catholicism?

Europe in Crisis, 1560–1650

◻ Why is the period between 1560 and 1650 in Europe called an age of crisis, and how did the turmoil contribute to the artistic developments of the period?

Response to Crisis: The Practice of Absolutism

◻ What was absolutism, and what were the main characteristics of the absolute monarchies that emerged in France, Prussia, Austria, and Russia?

England and Limited Monarchy

◻ How and why did England avoid the path of absolutism?

The Flourishing of European Culture

◻ How did the artistic and literary achievements of this era reflect the political and economic developments of the period?

CRITICAL THINKING

◻ What was the relationship between European overseas expansion (as seen in Chapter 13) and political, economic, and social developments in Europe?

A sixteenth-century engraving of Martin Luther in front of Charles V at the Diet of Worms

*O*N APRIL 18, 1520, A LOWLY MONK stood before the emperor and princes of Germany in the city of Worms. He had been called before this august gathering to answer charges of heresy, charges that could threaten his very life. The monk was confronted with a pile of his books and asked if he wished to defend them all or reject a part. Courageously, Martin Luther defended them all and asked to be shown where any part was in error on the basis of "Scripture and plain reason." The emperor was outraged by Luther's response and made his own position clear the next day: "Not only I, but you of this noble German nation, would be forever disgraced if by our negligence not only heresy but the very suspicion of heresy were to survive. After having heard yesterday the obstinate defense of Luther, I regret that I have so long delayed in proceeding against him and his false teaching. I will have no more to do with him." Luther's appearance at Worms set the stage for a serious challenge to the authority of the Catholic church. This was by no means the first crisis in the church's fifteen-hundred-year history, but its consequences were more far-reaching than anyone at Worms in 1520 could have imagined.

After the disintegrative patterns of the fourteenth century, Europe began a remarkable recovery that encompassed a revival of arts and letters in the fifteenth century, known as the Renaissance, and a religious renaissance in the sixteenth century, known as the Reformation. The religious division of Europe (Catholics versus Protestants) that was a result of the Reformation was instrumental in beginning a series of wars that dominated much of European history from 1560 to 1650 and exacerbated the economic and social crises that were besetting the region.

One of the responses to the crises of the seventeenth century was a search for order. The most general trend was an extension of monarchical power as a stablizing force. This development, which historians have called absolutism or absolute monarchy, was most evident in France during the flamboyant reign of Louis XIV, regarded by some as the perfect embodiment of an absolute monarch.

But absolutism was not the only response to the search for order in the seventeenth century. Other states, such as England, reacted very differently to domestic crisis, and another very different system emerged where monarchs were limited by the power of their representative assemblies. Absolute and limited monarchy were the two poles of seventeenth-century state building. ◇

The Reformation of the Sixteenth Century

The **Protestant Reformation** is the name given to the religious reform movement that divided the western Christian church into Catholic and Protestant groups. Although Martin Luther began the Reformation in the early sixteenth century, several earlier developments had set the stage for religious change.

Background to the Reformation

Changes in the fifteenth century—the age of the Renaissance—helped prepare the way for the dramatic upheavals in sixteenth-century Europe.

The Growth of State Power In the first half of the fifteenth century, European states had continued the disintegrative patterns of the previous century. In the second half of the fifteenth century, however, recovery had set in, and attempts had been made to reestablish the centralized power of monarchical governments. To characterize the results, some historians have used the label "Renaissance states"; others have spoken of the "**new monarchies,**" especially those of France, England, and Spain at the end of the fifteenth century (see Chapter 12).

Although appropriate, the term *new monarch* can also be misleading. What was new about these Renaissance monarchs was their concentration of royal authority, their attempts to suppress the nobility, their efforts to control the church in their lands, and their desire to obtain new sources of revenue in order to increase royal power and enhance the military forces at their disposal. Like the rulers of fifteenth-century Italian states, the Renaissance monarchs were often crafty men obsessed with the acquisition and expansion of political power. Of course, none of these characteristics was entirely new; a number of medieval monarchs, especially in the thirteenth century, had also exhibited them. Nevertheless, the Renaissance period does mark the further extension of centralized royal authority.

No one gave better expression to the Renaissance preoccupation with political power than Niccolò Machiavelli (1469–1527), an Italian who wrote *The Prince* (1513), one of the most influential works on political power in the Western world. Machiavelli's major concerns in *The Prince* were the acquisition, maintenance, and expansion of political power as the means to restore and maintain order in his time. In the Middle Ages, many political theorists stressed the ethical side of a prince's activity—how a ruler ought to behave based on Christian moral principles. Machiavelli bluntly contradicted this approach: "For the gap between how people actually behave and how they ought to behave is so great that anyone who ignores everyday reality in order to live up to an ideal will soon discover he had been taught how to destroy himself, not how to preserve himself."[1] Machiavelli considered his approach far more realistic than that of his medieval forebears. Political activity, in his view, could not be restricted by moral considerations. The prince acts on behalf of the state and for the sake of the state must be willing to let his conscience sleep. Machiavelli was among the first Western thinkers to abandon morality as the basis for the analysis of political activity. The same emphasis on the ends justifying the means, or on achieving results regardless of the methods employed, had in fact been expressed a thousand years earlier by a court official in India named Kautilya in his treatise on politics, the *Arthasastra* (see Chapter 2).

Social Changes in the Renaissance Social changes in the fifteenth century also had an impact on the Reformation of the sixteenth century. After the severe economic reversals and social upheavals of the fourteenth century, the European economy gradually recovered as manufacturing and trade increased in volume. The Italians and especially the Venetians expanded their wealthy commercial empire, rivaled only by the increasingly powerful Hanseatic League, a commercial and military alliance of north German coastal towns. Not until the sixteenth century, when overseas discoveries gave new importance to the states facing the Atlantic, did the Italian city-states begin to suffer from the competitive advantages of the more powerful national territorial states.

As noted in Chapter 12, society in the Middle Ages was divided into three estates: the clergy, or first estate, whose preeminence was grounded in the belief that people should be guided to spiritual ends; the nobility, or second estate, whose privileges rested on the principle that nobles provided security and justice for society; and the peasants and inhabitants of the towns and cities, the third estate. Although this social order continued into the Renaissance, some changes also became evident.

Throughout much of Europe, the landholding nobles faced declining real incomes during most of the fourteenth and fifteenth centuries. Many members of the old nobility survived, however, and new blood also infused its ranks. By 1500, the nobles, old and new, who constituted between 2 and 3 percent of the population in most countries, managed to dominate society, as they had done in the Middle Ages, holding important political posts and serving as advisers to the king.

Except in the heavily urban areas of northern Italy and Flanders, peasants made up the overwhelming mass of the third estate—they constituted 85 to 90 percent of the total European population. Serfdom decreased as the manorial system continued its decline. Increasingly, the labor dues owed by a peasant to his lord were converted into rents paid in money. By 1500, especially in western Europe, more and more peasants were becoming legally free. At the same time, peasants in many areas resented their social superiors and sought a greater share of the benefits coming from their labor. In the sixteenth century, the grievances of peasants, especially in Germany, led many of them to support religious reform movements.

The remainder of the third estate were inhabitants of towns and cities, originally merchants and artisans. But by the fifteenth century, the Renaissance town or city had become more complex. At the top of urban society were the patricians, whose wealth from capitalistic enterprises in trade, industry, and banking enabled them to dominate their urban communities economically, socially, and politically. Below them were the petty burghers—the shopkeepers, artisans, guildmasters, and guildsmen—who were largely concerned with providing goods and services for local consumption. Below these two groups were the propertyless workers earning pitiful wages and the unemployed, living squalid and miserable lives. These poor city-dwellers constituted 30 to 40 percent of the urban population. The pitiful conditions of the lower groups in urban society often led them to support calls for radical religious reform in the sixteenth century.

The Impact of Printing The Renaissance witnessed the development of printing, which made an immediate impact on European intellectual life and thought. Printing from hand-carved wooden blocks had been done in the West since the twelfth century and in China even before that. What was new in the fifteenth century in Europe was multiple printing with movable metal type. The development of printing from movable type was a gradual process that culminated sometime between 1445 and 1450; Johannes Gutenberg of Mainz played an important role in bringing the process to completion.

Gutenberg's Bible, completed in 1455 or 1456, was the first true book produced from movable type.

By 1500, there were more than a thousand printers in Europe, who collectively had published almost forty thousand titles (between eight and ten million copies). Probably half of these books were religious—Bibles and biblical commentaries, books of devotion, and sermons.

The printing of books encouraged the development of scholarly research and the desire to attain knowledge. Printing also stimulated the development of an ever-expanding lay reading public, a development that had an enormous impact on European society. Indeed, without the printing press, the new religious ideas of the Reformation would never have spread as rapidly as they did in the sixteenth century. Moreover, printing allowed European civilization to compete for the first time with the civilization of China.

Prelude to Reformation During the second half of the fifteenth century, the new classical learning of the Italian Renaissance spread to the European countries north of the Alps and spawned a movement called **Christian humanism** or **northern Renaissance humanism,** whose major goal was the reform of Christendom. The Christian humanists believed in the ability of human beings to reason and improve themselves and thought that through education in the sources of classical, and especially Christian, antiquity, they could instill an inner piety or an inward religious feeling that would bring about a reform of the church and society. To change society, they must first change the human beings who compose it.

The most influential of all the Christian humanists was Desiderius Erasmus (1466–1536), who formulated and popularized the reform program of Christian humanism. He called his conception of religion "the philosophy of Christ," by which he meant that Christianity should be a guiding philosophy for the direction of daily life rather than the system of dogmatic beliefs and practices that the medieval church seemed to stress. No doubt his work helped prepare the way for the Reformation; as contemporaries proclaimed, "Erasmus laid the egg that Luther hatched."

Church and Religion on the Eve of the Reformation Corruption in the Catholic church was another factor that encouraged people to want reform. Between 1450 and 1520, a series of popes—called the Renaissance popes—failed to meet the church's spiritual needs. The popes were supposed to be the spiritual leaders of the Catholic church, but as leaders of the Papal States, they were all too often involved in worldly interests. Julius II (1503–1513), the fiery "warrior-pope," personally led armies against his enemies, much to the disgust of pious Christians, who viewed the pope as a spiritual leader. As one intellectual wrote, "How, O bishop standing in the room of the Apostles, dare you teach the people the things that pertain to war?" Many high church officials were also concerned with money and used their church offices as opportunities to advance their careers and their wealth, and many ordinary parish priests seemed ignorant of their spiritual duties.

While the leaders of the church were failing to meet their responsibilities, ordinary people were clamoring for meaningful religious expression and certainty of salvation. As a result, for some the process of salvation became almost mechanical. Collections of **relics** grew as more and more people sought certainty of salvation through veneration of objects associated with the saints and martyrs or with Jesus himself. Frederick the Wise, elector of Saxony and Martin Luther's prince, had amassed over five thousand relics to which were attached **indulgences** that could reduce one's time in purgatory by 1,443 years. (An indulgence is a remission, after death, of all or part of the punishment due to sin.)

Martin Luther and the Reformation in Germany

Martin Luther was a monk and a professor at the University of Wittenberg, where he lectured on the Bible. Probably sometime between 1513 and 1516, through his study of the Bible, he arrived at an answer to a problem—the assurance of salvation—that had disturbed him since his entry into the monastery.

Catholic doctrine had emphasized that both faith and good works were required for a Christian to achieve personal salvation. In Luther's eyes, human beings, weak and powerless in the sight of an almighty God, could never do enough good works to merit salvation. Through his study of the Bible, Luther came to believe that humans are not saved through their good works but through faith in the promises of God, made possible by the sacrifice of Jesus on the cross. This doctrine of salvation, or justification by grace through faith alone, became the primary doctrine of the Protestant Reformation (**justification by faith** is the act by which a person is made deserving of salvation). Because Luther had arrived at this doctrine from his study of the Bible, the Bible became for Luther as for all other Protestants the chief guide to religious truth.

Luther did not see himself as a rebel, but he was greatly upset by the widespread selling of indulgences. Especially offensive in his eyes was the monk Johann Tetzel, who hawked indulgences with the slogan: "As soon as the coin in the coffer [money box] rings, the soul from purgatory springs." Greatly angered, in 1517 Luther issued a stunning indictment of the abuses in the sale of indulgences, known as the Ninety-Five Theses (see the box on p. 315). Thousands of copies were printed and quickly spread to all parts of Germany.

Unable to accept Luther's ideas, the church excommunicated him in January 1521. He had also been summoned in 1520 to appear before the imperial diet or Reichstag of the Holy Roman Empire, convened by the newly elected Emperor Charles V (1519–1556).

Ordered to recant the heresies he had espoused, Luther refused and made the famous reply that became the battle cry of the Reformation:

> Unless I am convicted by Scripture and plain reason—I do not accept the authority of popes and councils, for they have contradicted each other—my conscience is captive to the Word of God. I cannot and I will not recant anything, for to go against conscience is neither right nor safe. Here I stand, I cannot do otherwise. God help me. Amen.[2]

Members of the Reichstag were outraged and demanded that Luther be captured and delivered to the emperor. But Luther's ruler, Elector Frederick of Saxony, stepped in and protected him.

During the next few years, Luther's religious movement became a revolution. Luther was able to gain the support of many of the German rulers among the three hundred or so states that made up the Holy Roman Empire. These rulers quickly took control of the churches in their territories. The Lutheran churches in Germany (and later in Scandinavia) quickly became territorial or state churches in which the state supervised the affairs of the church. As part of the development of these state-dominated churches, Luther also instituted new religious services to replace the Catholic Mass. These focused on Bible reading, preaching the word of God, and song.

Politics and Religion in the German Reformation From its very beginning, the fate of Luther's movement was closely tied to political affairs. In 1519, Charles I, king of Spain and the grandson of Emperor Maximilian, was elected Holy Roman Emperor as Charles V. Charles V ruled over an immense empire, consisting of Spain and its overseas possessions, the traditional Austrian Habsburg lands, Bohemia, Hungary, the Low Countries, and the kingdom of Naples in southern Italy. Politically, Charles wanted to maintain his enormous empire; religiously, he hoped to preserve the unity of his empire in the Catholic faith.

The internal political situation in the Holy Roman Empire was not in Charles's favor, however. Although all the German states owed loyalty to the emperor, in the Middle Ages these states had become quite independent of imperial authority. By the time Charles V was able to bring military forces to Germany in 1546, Lutheranism had become well established, and the Lutheran princes were well organized. Unable to defeat them, Charles was forced to negotiate a truce. Religious warfare in Germany came to an end in 1555 with the Peace of Augsburg. The division of Christianity was formally acknowledged; Lutheran states were to have the same legal rights as Catholic states. Although the German states were now free to choose between Catholicism and Lutheranism, the peace settlement did not recognize the principle of religious toleration for individuals. The right of each German ruler to determine the religion of his subjects was accepted, but not the right of the subjects to choose their own religion.

LUTHER AND THE NINETY-FIVE THESES

RELIGION & PHILOSOPHY

To most historians, the publication of Luther's Ninety-Five Theses marks the beginning of the Reformation. To Luther, they were simply a response to what he considered blatant abuses committed by sellers of indulgences. Although written in Latin, the theses were soon translated into German and disseminated widely across Germany. They made an immense impression on Germans already dissatisfied with the ecclesiastical and financial policies of the papacy.

What are the major ideas of Luther's Ninety-Five Theses? Why did they have such a strong appeal in Germany?

Martin Luther, Selections from the Ninety-Five Theses

5. The Pope has neither the will nor the power to remit any penalties beyond those he has imposed either at his own discretion or by canon law.
20. Therefore the Pope, by his plenary remission of all penalties, does not mean "all" in the absolute sense, but only those imposed by himself.
21. Hence those preachers of Indulgences are wrong when they say that a man is absolved and saved from every penalty by the Pope's Indulgences.
27. It is mere human talk to preach that the soul flies out [of purgatory] immediately [when] the money clinks in the collection box.
28. It is certainly possible that when the money clinks in the collection box greed and avarice can increase; but the intercession of the Church depends on the will of God alone.
50. Christians should be taught that, if the Pope knew the exactions of the preachers of Indulgences, he would rather have the basilica of St. Peter reduced to ashes than built with the skin, flesh, and bones of his sheep [the indulgences that so distressed Luther were being sold to raise money for the construction of the new St. Peter's Basilica in Rome].
81. This wanton preaching of pardons makes it difficult even for learned men to redeem respect due to the Pope from the slanders or at least the shrewd questionings of the laity.
82. For example: "Why does not the Pope empty purgatory for the sake of most holy love and the supreme need of souls? This would be the most righteous of reasons, if he can redeem innumerable souls for sordid money with which to build a basilica, the most trivial of reasons."
86. Again: "Since the Pope's wealth is larger than that of the crassest Crassi of our time, why does he not build this one basilica of St. Peter with his own money, rather than with that of the faithful poor?"
90. To suppress these most conscientious questionings of the laity by authority only, instead of refuting them by reason, is to expose the Church and the Pope to the ridicule of their enemies, and to make Christian people unhappy.
94. Christians should be exhorted to seek earnestly to follow Christ, their Head, through penalties, deaths, and hells.
95. And let them thus be more confident of entering heaven through many tribulations rather than through a false assurance of peace.

ThomsonNOW To read a full version of this document, enter the *ThomsonNOW* documents area using the access card that is available for *The Essential World History*.

The Spread of the Protestant Reformation

With the Peace of Augsburg, what had at first been merely feared was now certain: the ideal of Christian unity was forever lost. The rapid spread of new Protestant groups made this a certainty.

Calvin and Calvinism   John Calvin (1509–1564) was educated in his native France but after his conversion to Protestantism was forced to flee to the safety of Switzerland. In 1536, he published the first edition of the *Institutes of the Christian Religion*, a masterful synthesis of Protestant thought that immediately secured Calvin's reputation as one of the new leaders of Protestantism.

On most important doctrines, Calvin stood very close to Luther. He adhered to the doctrine of justification by faith alone to explain how humans achieved salvation. But Calvin also placed much emphasis on the absolute sovereignty of God or the all-powerful nature of God—what Calvin called the "power, grace, and glory of God." One of the ideas derived from his emphasis on the absolute sovereignty of God—**predestination**—gave a unique cast to Calvin's teachings. This "eternal decree," as Calvin called it, meant that God had predestined some people to be saved (the elect) and others to be damned (the reprobate). According to Calvin, "He has once for all determined, both whom He would admit to salvation, and whom He would condemn to destruction."[3] Although Calvin stressed that there could be no absolute certainty of salvation, his followers did not always make this distinction. The practical psychological effect of predestination was to give later Calvinists an unshakable conviction that they were doing God's work on earth, making Calvinism a dynamic and activist faith.

In 1536, Calvin began working to reform the city of Geneva. He was able to fashion a tightly organized church

Luther Versus the Pope. In the 1520s, after Luther's return to Wittenberg, his teachings began to spread rapidly, ending ultimately in a reform movement supported by state authorities. Pamphlets containing picturesque woodcuts were important in the spread of Luther's ideas. In the woodcut shown here, the crucified Jesus attends Luther's service on the left, while on the right the pope is at a table selling indulgences.

order that employed both clergy and laymen in the service of the church. The Consistory, a special body for enforcing moral discipline, functioned as a court to oversee the moral life, daily behavior, and doctrinal orthodoxy of Genevans and to admonish and correct deviants. Citizens of Geneva were punished for such varied "crimes" as dancing, singing obscene songs, drunkenness, swearing, and playing cards.

Calvin's success in Geneva enabled the city to become a vibrant center of Protestantism. Following Calvin's lead, missionaries trained in Geneva were sent to all parts of Europe. Calvinism became established in France, the Netherlands, Scotland, and central and eastern Europe, and by the mid-sixteenth century, Calvin's Geneva stood as the fortress of the Reformation.

The English Reformation   The English Reformation was rooted in politics, not religion. King Henry VIII (1509–1547) had a strong desire to divorce his first wife, Catherine of Aragon, with whom he had a daughter, Mary, but no male heir. He wanted to marry Anne Boleyn, with whom he had fallen in love. Impatient with the pope's unwillingness to grant him an annulment of his marriage, Henry turned to England's own church courts. As archbishop of Canterbury and head of the highest church court in England, Thomas Cranmer ruled in May 1533 that the king's marriage to Catherine was "absolutely void." At the beginning of June, Anne was crowned queen, and three months later a child was born, a girl (the future queen Elizabeth I), much to the king's disappointment.

In 1534, at Henry's request, Parliament moved to finalize the break of the Church of England with Rome. The Act of Supremacy of 1534 declared that the king was "the only supreme head on earth of the Church of England," a position that gave him control of doctrine, clerical appointments, and discipline. Although Henry VIII had broken with the papacy, little change occurred in matters of doctrine, theology, and ceremony. Some of his supporters, including Archbishop Cranmer, sought a religious reformation as well as an administrative one, but Henry was unyielding. But he died in 1547 and was succeeded by his son, the underage and sickly Edward VI (1547–1553), and during Edward's reign, Cranmer and others inclined toward Protestant doctrines were able to move the Church of England (or Anglican church) in a more Protestant direction. New acts of Parliament gave the clergy the right to marry and created a new Protestant church service.

Edward VI was succeeded by Mary (1553–1558), a Catholic who attempted to return England to Catholicism. Her actions aroused much anger, however, especially when "bloody Mary" burned more than three hundred Protestant heretics. By the end of Mary's reign, England was more Protestant than it had been at the beginning.

The Social Impact of the Protestant Reformation

The Protestants were especially important in developing a new view of the family (see the comparative essay "Marriage in the Early Modern World" on p. 317). Because Protestantism had eliminated any idea of special holiness for celibacy and had abolished both monasticism and a celibate clergy, the family could be placed at the center of human life, and a new stress on "mutual love between man and wife" could be extolled.

But were doctrine and reality the same? Most often, reality reflected the traditional roles of husband as the

MARRIAGE IN THE EARLY MODERN WORLD

FAMILY & SOCIETY

Marriage is an ancient institution. In China, mythical stories about the beginnings of Chinese civilization maintain that the rites of marriage began with the primordial couple Fuxi and Nugun and that these rites actually preceded such discoveries as fire, farming, and medicine. In the early modern world, family and marriage were inseparable and at the center of all civilizations.

In the early modern period, the family was still at the heart of Europe's social organization. For the most part, people still thought of the family in traditional terms, as a patriarchal institution with the husband dominating his wife and children. The upper classes in particular were still concerned for the family as a "house," an association whose collective interests were more important than those of its individual members. Parents (especially the fathers) still generally selected marriage partners for their children, based on the interests of the family. One French noble responded to his son's inquiry about his upcoming marriage, "Mind your own business." Details were worked out well in advance, sometimes when children were only two or three years old, and reinforced by a legally binding contract. The important aspect of the contract was the size of the dowry, money presented by the wife's family to the husband upon marriage. The dowry could involve large sums and was expected of all families.

Arranged marriages were not unique to Europe but were common throughout the world. In China, marriages were normally arranged for the benefit of the family, often by a go-between, and the groom and bride were usually not consulted. Frequently, they did not meet until the marriage ceremony. Love was obviously not a reason for marriage and in fact was often viewed as a distraction because it took the married couple's attention away from their chief responsibility to the larger family unit. In Japan too, marriages were arranged, often by the heads of dominant families in rural areas, and the new wife moved in with the family of her husband. In India, not only were marriages arranged, but it was not uncommon for women to be married before the age of ten. In colonial Latin America, parents also determined the choice of a spouse and often chose a dwelling for the couple as well. The process of selection was frequently complicated by the need for the lower classes to present gifts to powerful landlords who dominated their regions in order to gain their permission to marry. These nobles often stopped unmarried women from marrying in order to keep them as servants.

Arranged marriages were the logical result of a social system in which men dominated and women's primary role was to bear children, manage the household, and work in the fields. Not until the nineteenth century did a feminist movement emerge in Europe to improve the rights of women. By the beginning of the twentieth century, that movement had spread to other parts of the world. The New Culture Movement in China, for example, advocated the free choice of spouses. Despite the progress that has been made throughout the world in allowing people to choose their spouses, in some places, especially in rural areas, families still play an active role in the choice of marriage partners.

---

ruler and wife as the obedient servant whose chief duty was to please her husband. Luther stated it clearly:

> The rule remains with the husband, and the wife is compelled to obey him by God's command. He rules the home and the state, wages war, defends his possessions, tills the soil, builds, plants, etc. The woman on the other hand is like a nail driven into the wall . . . so the wife should stay at home and look after the affairs of the household, as one who has been deprived of the ability of administering those affairs that are outside and that concern the state. She does not go beyond her most personal duties.[4]

Obedience to her husband was not a wife's only role; her other important duty was to bear children. To Calvin and Luther, this function of women was part of the divine plan, and for most Protestant women, family life was their only destiny. Overall, the Protestant Reformation did not noticeably alter women's subordinate place in society.

The Catholic Reformation

By the mid-sixteenth century, Lutheranism had become established in Germany and Scandinavia and Calvinism in Scotland, Switzerland, France, the Netherlands, and eastern Europe. In England, the split from Rome had resulted in the creation of a national church. The situation in Europe did not look particularly favorable for the Roman Catholic church. Nevertheless, the Catholic church also underwent a revitalization in the sixteenth century, giving it new strength. There were three chief pillars of the **Catholic Reformation:** the Jesuits, a reformed papacy, and the Council of Trent.

The Society of Jesus The Society of Jesus, known as the Jesuits, was founded by a Spanish nobleman, Ignatius of Loyola (1491–1556). Loyola gathered together a small group of individuals who were recognized as a religious order by the pope in 1540. The new order was grounded on the principles of absolute obedience to the papacy, a strict hierarchical order for the society, the use of education to achieve its goals, and a dedication to engage in "conflict for God." A special vow of absolute obedience to the pope made the Jesuits an important instrument for papal policy. Jesuit missionaries proved singularly successful in restoring Catholicism to parts of Germany and eastern Europe.

Ignatius of Loyola. The Jesuits became the most important new religious order of the Catholic Reformation. Shown here in a sixteenth-century painting by an unknown artist is Ignatius of Loyola, founder of the Society of Jesus. Loyola is seen kneeling before Pope Paul III, who officially recognized the Jesuits in 1540.

Another prominent Jesuit activity was the propagation of the Catholic faith among non-Christians. Francis Xavier (1506–1552), one of the original members of the Society of Jesus, carried the message of Catholic Christianity to the East. After converting tens of thousands in India, he traveled to Malacca and the Moluccas before finally reaching Japan in 1549. He spoke highly of the Japanese: "They are a people of excellent morals— good in general and not malicious."[5] Thousands of Japanese, especially in the southernmost islands, became Christians. In 1552, Xavier set out for China but died of fever before he reached the mainland.

Although conversion efforts in Japan proved short-lived, Jesuit activity in China, especially that of the Italian Matteo Ricci, was more long-lasting. Recognizing the Chinese pride in their own culture, the Jesuits attempted to draw parallels between Christian and Confucian concepts and to show the similarities between Christian morality and Confucian ethics. For their part, the missionaries were much impressed with many aspects of Chinese civilization, and reports of their experiences heightened European curiosity about this great society on the other side of the world.

A Reformed Papacy A reformed papacy was another important factor in the development of the Catholic Reformation. The involvement of Renaissance popes in dubious finances and Italian political and military affairs had created numerous sources of corruption. It took the jolt of the Protestant Reformation to bring about serious reform. Pope Paul III (1534–1549) perceived the need for change and took the audacious step of appointing a reform commission to ascertain the church's ills. The commission's report in 1537 blamed the church's problems on the corrupt policies of popes and cardinals. Paul III also formally recognized the Jesuits and summoned the Council of Trent.

The Council of Trent In March 1545, a group of high church officials met in the city of Trent on the border between Germany and Italy and initiated the Council of Trent, which met intermittently from 1545 to 1563 in three major sessions. The final decrees of the Council of Trent reaffirmed traditional Catholic teachings in opposition to Protestant beliefs. Scripture and tradition were affirmed as equal authorities in religious matters; only the church could interpret Scripture. Both faith and good works were declared necessary for salvation. Belief in purgatory and in the use of indulgences was strengthened, although the selling of indulgences was prohibited.

By the mid-sixteenth century, the Roman Catholic church had become one Christian denomination among many. Nevertheless, after the Council of Trent, the Roman Catholic church possessed a clear body of doctrine and a unified church under the acknowledged supremacy of the popes. With a new spirit of confidence, the Catholic church entered a militant phase, as well prepared as the Calvinists to do battle for the Lord. An era of religious warfare was about to unfold.

Europe in Crisis, 1560–1650

Between 1560 and 1650, Europe experienced religious wars, revolutions and constitutional crises, economic and social disintegration, and a witchcraft craze. It was truly an age of crisis.

Politics and the Wars of Religion in the Sixteenth Century

By 1560, Calvinism and Catholicism had become militant religions dedicated to spreading the word of God as they interpreted it. Although their struggle for the minds and hearts of Europeans was at the center of the religious wars of the sixteenth century, economic, social, and political forces also played an important role in these conflicts.

The French Wars of Religion (1562–1598) Religion was central to the French civil wars of the sixteenth century. The growth of Calvinism had led to persecution by the French kings, but the latter did little to stop the spread of Calvinism. Huguenots (as the French Calvinists were called) constituted only about 7 percent of the population, but 40 to 50 percent of the French nobility became Huguenots, including the house of Bourbon, which stood next to the Valois in the royal line of succession. The conversion of so many nobles made the Huguenots a potentially dangerous political threat to monarchical power. Still, the Calvinist minority was greatly outnumbered by the Catholic majority, and the Valois monarchy was staunchly Catholic.

For thirty years, battles raged in France between Catholic and Calvinist parties. Finally, in 1589, Henry of Navarre, the political leader of the Huguenots and a member of the Bourbon dynasty, succeeded to the throne as Henry IV (1589–1610). Realizing, however, that he would never be accepted by Catholic France, Henry converted to Catholicism. With his coronation in 1594, the Wars of Religion had finally come to an end. The Edict of Nantes in 1598 solved the religious problem by acknowledging Catholicism as the official religion of France while guaranteeing the Huguenots the right to worship and to enjoy all political privileges, including the holding of public offices.

Philip II and Militant Catholicism   The greatest advocate of militant Catholicism in the second half of the sixteenth century was King Philip II of Spain (1556–1598), the son and heir of Charles V. Philip's reign ushered in an age of Spanish greatness, both politically and culturally. Philip II had inherited from his father Spain, the Netherlands, and possessions in Italy and the Americas. To strengthen his control, Philip insisted on strict conformity to Catholicism and strong monarchical authority. Achieving the latter was not an easy task, because each of the lands of his empire had its own structure of government.

Philip's attempt to strengthen his control over the Spanish Netherlands, which consisted of seventeen provinces (the modern Netherlands and Belgium), soon led to a revolt. The nobles, who stood to lose the most politically, strongly opposed Philip's efforts. Religion also became a major catalyst for rebellion when Philip attempted to crush Calvinism. Violence erupted in 1566, and the revolt became organized, especially in the northern provinces, where the Dutch, under the leadership of William of Nassau, the prince of Orange, offered growing resistance. The struggle dragged on for decades until 1609, when the war ended with a twelve-year truce that virtually recognized the independence of the northern provinces. These seven northern provinces, which called themselves the United Provinces of the Netherlands, became the core of the modern Dutch state.

At the beginning of the seventeenth century, most Europeans still regarded Spain as the greatest power of the age, but the reality was quite different. The Spanish treasury was empty, the armed forces were obsolescent, and the government was inefficient. Spain continued to play the role of a great power, but real power had shifted to England.

The England of Elizabeth   When Elizabeth Tudor, the daughter of Henry VIII and Anne Boleyn, ascended the throne in 1558, England was home to fewer than four million people. Yet during her reign, the small island

Courtesy of J. K. Wingfield Digby, Sherborne Castle, England

Procession of Queen Elizabeth I.   Intelligent and learned, Elizabeth Tudor was familiar with Latin and Greek and spoke several European languages. Served by able administrators, Elizabeth ruled for nearly forty-five years and generally avoided open military action against any major power. This picture, painted near the end of her reign, shows the queen in a ceremonial procession.

kingdom became leader of the Protestant nations of Europe and laid the foundations for a world empire.

Intelligent, cautious, and self-confident, Elizabeth moved quickly to solve the difficult religious problem she inherited from her half-sister, Queen Mary. Elizabeth's religious policy was based on moderation and compromise. She repealed the Catholic laws of Mary's reign, and a new Act of Supremacy designated Elizabeth as "the only supreme governor" of both church and state. The Church of England under Elizabeth was basically Protestant, but it was of a moderate bent that kept most people satisfied.

Caution and moderation also dictated Elizabeth's foreign policy. Gradually, however, Elizabeth was drawn into conflict with Spain. Having resisted for years the idea of invading England as too impractical, Philip II of Spain was finally persuaded to do so by advisers who assured him that the people of England would rise against their queen when the Spaniards arrived. A successful invasion of England would mean the overthrow of heresy and the return of England to Catholicism. Philip ordered preparations for a fleet of warships, the *Armada,* to spearhead the invasion of England.

The Armada was a disaster. The Spanish fleet that finally set sail had neither the ships nor the manpower that Philip had planned to send. Battered by a number of encounters with the English, the Spanish fleet sailed back to Spain by a northward route around Scotland and Ireland, where it was further pounded by storms.

Economic and Social Crises

The period of European history from 1560 to 1650 witnessed severe economic and social crises as well as political upheaval. Economic contraction began to be evident in some parts of Europe by the 1620s. In the 1630s and 1640s, as imports of silver from the Americas declined, economic recession intensified, especially in the Mediterranean area. Once the industrial and financial center of Europe in the age of the Renaissance, Italy was now becoming an economic backwater.

Population Decline   Population trends of the sixteenth and seventeenth centuries also reveal Europe's worsening conditions. The population of Europe increased from 60 million in 1500 to 85 million by 1600, the first major recovery of the European population since the devastation of the Black Death in the mid-fourteenth century. By 1650, however, records also indicate a decline in the population, especially in central and southern Europe. Europe's longtime adversaries—war, famine, and plague—continued to affect population levels. Europe's problems created social tensions, some of which were manifested in an obsession with witches.

Witchcraft Mania   Hysteria over witchcraft affected the lives of many Europeans in the sixteenth and seventeenth centuries. Perhaps more than 100,000 people were prosecuted throughout Europe on charges of witchcraft.

As more and more people were brought to trial, the fear of witches, as well as the fear of being accused of witchcraft, escalated to frightening levels (see the box on p. 321).

Common people—usually those who were poor and without property—were more likely to be accused of witchcraft. Indeed, where lists are given, those mentioned most often are milkmaids, peasant women, and servant girls. In the witchcraft trials of the sixteenth and seventeenth centuries, more than 75 percent of the accused were women, most of them single or widowed and many over fifty years old.

That women should be the chief victims of witchcraft trials was hardly accidental. Nicholas Rémy, a witchcraft judge in France in the 1590s, found it "not unreasonable that this scum of humanity, i.e., witches, should be drawn chiefly from the feminine sex." To another judge, it came as no surprise that witches would confess to sexual experiences with Satan: "The Devil uses them so, because he knows that women love carnal pleasures, and he means to bind them to his allegiance by such agreeable provocations."[6]

By the mid-seventeenth century, the witchcraft hysteria had begun to subside. As governments grew stronger, fewer magistrates were willing to accept the unsettling and divisive conditions generated by the trials of witches. Moreover, by the beginning of the eighteenth century, more and more people were questioning altogether their old attitudes toward religion and found it especially contrary to reason to believe in the old view of a world haunted by evil spirits.

Economic Trends in the Seventeenth Century   In the course of the seventeenth century, new economic trends also emerged. **Mercantilism** is the name historians apply to the set of economic tendencies that came to dominate economic practices in the seventeenth century. According to the mercantilists, the prosperity of a nation depended on a plentiful supply of bullion (gold and silver). For this reason, it was desirable to achieve a favorable balance of trade in which goods exported were of greater value than those imported, promoting an influx of gold and silver payments that would increase the quantity of bullion. Furthermore, to encourage exports, governments should stimulate and protect export industries and trade by granting trade monopolies, encouraging investment in new industries through subsidies, importing foreign artisans, and improving transportation systems by building roads, bridges, and canals. By placing high tariffs on foreign goods, they could reduce imports and prevent them from competing with domestic industries. Colonies were also deemed valuable as sources of raw materials and markets for finished goods.

Mercantilist theory on the role of colonies was matched in practice by Europe's overseas expansion. With the development of colonies and trading posts in the Americas and the East, Europeans embarked on an adventure in international commerce in the seventeenth

A WITCHCRAFT TRIAL IN FRANCE

FAMILY & SOCIETY

Persecutions for witchcraft reached their high point in the sixteenth and seventeenth centuries, when tens of thousands of people were brought to trial. In this excerpt from the minutes of a trial in France in 1652, we can see why the accused witch stood little chance of exonerating herself.

Why were women, particularly older women, especially vulnerable to accusations of witchcraft? What "proofs" are offered here that Suzanne Gaudry had consorted with the devil? What does this account tell us about the spread of witchcraft persecutions in the seventeenth century?

The Trial of Suzanne Gaudry

28 May, 1652. . . . Interrogation of Suzanne Gaudry, prisoner at the court of Rieux. . . . During interrogations on May 28 and May 29, the prisoner confessed to a number of activities involving the devil.

Deliberation of the Court—June 3, 1652

The undersigned advocates of the Court have seen these interrogations and answers. They say that the aforementioned Suzanne Gaudry confesses that she is a witch, that she had given herself to the devil, that she had renounced God, Lent, and baptism, that she has been marked on the shoulder, that she has cohabited with the devil and that she has been to the dances, confessing only to have cast a spell upon and caused to die a beast of Philippe Cornié. . . .

Third Interrogation, June 27

This prisoner being led into the chamber, she was examined to know if things were not as she had said and confessed at the beginning of her imprisonment.

—Answers no, and that what she has said was done so by force.

Pressed to say the truth, that otherwise she would be subjected to torture, having pointed out to her that her aunt was burned for this same subject.

—Answers that she is not a witch. . . .

She was placed in the hands of the officer in charge of torture, throwing herself on her knees, struggling to cry, uttering several exclamations, without being able, nevertheless, to shed a tear. Saying at every moment that she is not a witch.

The Torture

On this same day, being at the place of torture.

This prisoner, before being strapped down, was admonished to maintain herself in her first confessions and to renounce her lover.

—Says that she denies everything she has said, and that she has no lover. Feeling herself being strapped down, says that she is not a witch, while struggling to cry . . . and upon being asked why she confessed to being one, said that she was forced to say it.

Told that she was not forced, that on the contrary she declared herself to be a witch without any threat.

—Says that she confessed it and that she is not a witch, and being a little stretched [on the rack] screams ceaselessly that she is not a witch.

Asked if she did not confess that she had been a witch for twenty-six years.

—Says that she said it, that she retracts it, crying that she is not a witch.

Asked if she did not make Philippe Cornié's horse die, as she confessed.

—Answers no, crying Jesus-Maria, that she is not a witch.

The mark having been probed by the officer, in the presence of Doctor Bouchain, it was adjudged by the aforesaid doctor and officer truly to be the mark of the devil.

Being more tightly stretched upon the torture rack, urged to maintain her confessions.

—Said that it was true that she is a witch and that she would maintain what she had said.

Asked how long she has been in subjugation to the devil.

—Answers that it was twenty years ago that the devil appeared to her, being in her lodgings in the form of a man dressed in a little cowhide and black breeches. . . .

Verdict

July 9, 1652. In the light of the interrogations, answers, and investigations made into the charge against Suzanne Gaudry, . . . seeing by her own confessions that she is said to have made a pact with the devil, received the mark from him, . . . and that following this, she had renounced God, Lent, and baptism and had let herself be known carnally by him, in which she received satisfaction. Also, seeing that she is said to have been a part of nocturnal carols and dances.

For expiation of which the advice of the undersigned is that the office of Rieux can legitimately condemn the aforesaid Suzanne Gaudry to death, tying her to a gallows, and strangling her to death, then burning her body and burying it here in the environs of the woods.

century. Although some historians speak of a nascent world economy, we should remember that local, regional, and intra-European trade still predominated. At the end of the seventeenth century, for example, English imports totaled 360,000 tons, but only 5,000 tons came from the East Indies. What made the transoceanic trade rewarding, however, was not the volume of its goods but their value. Dutch, English, and French merchants were bringing back products that were still consumed largely by the wealthy but were beginning to make their way into the lives of artisans and merchants. Pepper and spices from the Indies, West Indian and Brazilian sugar, and Asian coffee and tea were becoming more readily available to European consumers.

The commercial expansion of the sixteenth and seventeenth centuries was made easier by new forms of commercial organization, especially the **joint-stock company.** Individuals bought shares in a company and received dividends on their investment while a board of directors ran the company and made the important business decisions. The return on investments could be spectacular. During its first ten years, investors received 30 percent annually on their money from the Dutch East India Company, which opened the Spice Islands and Southeast Asia to Dutch activity. The joint-stock company made it easier to raise large amounts of capital for world trading ventures.

Despite the growth of commercial capitalism, most of the European economy still depended on an agricultural system that had experienced few changes since the thirteenth century. At least 80 percent of Europeans still worked on the land. Almost all of the peasants of western Europe were free of serfdom, although many still owed a variety of feudal dues to the nobility. Despite the expanding markets and rising prices, European peasants saw little or no improvement in their lot as they faced increased rents and fees and higher taxes imposed by the state.

Seventeenth-Century Crises: Revolution and War

During the first half of the seventeenth century, a series of rebellions and civil wars rocked the domestic stability of many European governments. A devastating war that affected much of Europe also added to the sense of crisis.

The Thirty Years' War (1618–1648) The Thirty Years' War began in 1618 in the Germanic lands of the Holy Roman Empire as a struggle between Catholic forces, led by the Habsburg Holy Roman Emperors, and Protestant—primarily Calvinist—nobles in Bohemia who rebelled against Habsburg authority (see Map 14.1). What began as a struggle over religious issues soon became a wider conflict perpetuated by political motivations as both minor and major European powers—Denmark, Sweden, France, and Spain—entered the war. The competition for European leadership between the Bourbon dynasty of France and the Habsburg dynasties of Spain and the Holy Roman Empire was an especially important factor. Nevertheless, most of the battles were fought on German soil (see the box on p. 324).

The war in Germany was officially ended in 1648 by the Peace of Westphalia, which proclaimed that all German states, including the Calvinist ones, were free to determine their own religion. The major contenders gained new territories, and France emerged as the dominant nation in Europe. The more than three hundred entities that made up the Holy Roman Empire were recognized as independent states, and each was given the power to conduct its own foreign policy; this brought an end to the Holy Roman Empire and ensured German disunity for another two hundred years. The Peace of Westphalia made it clear that political motives, not religious convictions, had become the guiding force in public affairs.

A Military Revolution? By the seventeenth century, war played an increasingly important role in European affairs. As military power was considered essential to a ruler's reputation and power, the pressure to build an effective military machine was intense. Some historians believe that the changes that occurred in the science of warfare between 1560 and 1650 warrant the title of military revolution.

These changes included increased use of firearms and cannons, greater flexibility and mobility in tactics, and better-disciplined and better-trained armies. These innovations necessitated standing armies, based partly on conscription, which grew ever larger and more expensive as the seventeenth century progressed. Such armies could be maintained only by levying heavier taxes, making war an economic burden and an ever more important part of the early modern European state. The creation of large bureaucracies to supervise the military resources of the state led to a growth in the power of state governments.

Response to Crisis: The Practice of Absolutism

Many people responded to the crises of the seventeenth century by searching for order. An increase in monarchical power became an obvious means for achieving stability. The result was what historians have called **absolutism** or absolute monarchy. Absolutism meant that the sovereign power or ultimate authority in the state rested in the hands of a king who claimed to rule by divine right—the idea that kings received their power from God and were responsible to no one but God. Late-sixteenth-century political theorists believed that sovereign power consisted of the authority to make laws, levy taxes, administer justice, control the state's administrative system, and determine foreign policy.

MAP 14.1 **Europe in the Seventeenth Century.** This map shows Europe at the time of the Thirty Years' War (1618–1648). Although the struggle began in Bohemia and much of the fighting took place in the Germanic lands of the Holy Roman Empire, the conflict became a Europe-wide struggle. 🔲 Which countries engaged in the war were predominantly Protestant, which were Catholic, and which were mixed? 🌐 **View an animated version of this map or related maps at** http://worldrc.wadsworth.com/

France Under Louis XIV

France during the reign of Louis XIV (1643–1715) has traditionally been regarded as the best example of the practice of absolute or **divine-right monarchy** in the seventeenth century. French culture, language, and manners reached into all levels of European society. French diplomacy and wars overwhelmed the political affairs of western and central Europe. The court of Louis XIV seemed to be imitated everywhere in Europe (see the comparative illustration on p. 325).

Political Institutions One of the keys to Louis's power was his control of the central policy-making machinery of government, which he made part of his own court and household. The royal court located at Versailles served

three purposes simultaneously: it was the personal household of the king, the location of central governmental machinery, and the place where powerful subjects came to find favors and offices for themselves and their clients. The greatest danger to Louis's personal rule came from the very high nobles and princes of the blood (the royal princes), who considered it their natural role to assert the policy-making role of royal ministers. Louis eliminated this threat by removing them from the royal council, the chief administrative body of the king, and enticing them to his court at Versailles, where he could keep them preoccupied with court life and out of politics. Instead of the high nobility and royal princes, Louis relied for his ministers on nobles who came from relatively new aristocratic families. His ministers were expected to be subservient: "I had no intention of sharing my authority with them," Louis said.

THE FACE OF WAR IN THE SEVENTEENTH CENTURY

FAMILY & SOCIETY

We have a firsthand account of the face of war in Germany from a picaresque novel called *Simplicius Simplicissimus*, written by Jakob von Grimmelshausen. The author's experiences as a soldier in the Thirty Years' War give his descriptions of the effect of the war on ordinary people a certain vividness and reality. This selection describes the fate of a peasant farm, an experience all too familiar to thousands of German peasants between 1618 and 1648.

What does this document reveal about the effect of war on ordinary Europeans?

Jakob von Grimmelshausen, *Simplicius Simplicissimus*

The first thing these horsemen did in the nice back rooms of the house was to put in their horses. Then everyone took up a special job, one having to do with death and destruction. Although some began butchering, heating water, and rendering lard, as if to prepare for a banquet, others raced through the house, ransacking upstairs and down; not even the privy chamber was safe, as if the golden fleece of Jason might be hidden there. Still others bundled up big packs of cloth, household goods, and clothes, as if they wanted to hold a rummage sale somewhere. What they did not intend to take along they broke and spoiled. Some ran their swords into the hay and straw, as if there hadn't been hogs enough to stick. Some shook the feathers out of beds and put bacon slabs, hams, and other stuff in the ticking, as if they might sleep better on these. Others knocked down the hearth and broke the windows, as if announcing an everlasting summer. They flattened out copper and pewter dishes and baled the ruined goods. They burned up bedsteads, tables, chairs, and benches, though there were yards and yards of dry firewood outside the kitchen. Jars and crocks, pots and casseroles all were broken, either because they preferred their meat broiled or because they thought they'd eat only one meal with us. In the barn, the hired girl was handled so roughly that she was unable to walk away, I am ashamed to report. They stretched the hired man out flat on the ground, stuck a wooden wedge in his mouth to keep it open, and emptied a milk bucket full of stinking manure drippings down his throat; they called it a Swedish cocktail. He didn't relish it and made a very wry face. By this means they forced him to take a raiding party to some other place where they carried off men and cattle and brought them to our farm. Among those were my father, mother, and [sister] Ursula.

Then they used thumbscrews, which they cleverly made out of their pistols, to torture the peasants, as if they wanted to burn witches. Though he had confessed to nothing as yet, they put one of the captured hayseeds in the bake-oven and lighted a fire in it. They put a rope around someone else's head and tightened it like a tourniquet until blood came out of his mouth, nose, and ears. In short, every soldier had his favorite method of making life miserable for peasants, and every peasant had his own misery. My father was, as I thought, particularly lucky because he confessed with a laugh what others were forced to say in pain and martyrdom. No doubt because he was the head of the household, he was shown special consideration; they put him close to a fire, tied him by his hands and legs, and rubbed damp salt on the bottoms of his feet. Our old nanny goat had to lick it off and this so tickled my father that he could have burst laughing. This seemed so clever and entertaining to me—I had never seen or heard my father laugh so long—that I joined him in laughter, to keep him company or perhaps to cover up my ignorance. In the midst of such glee he told them the whereabouts of hidden treasure much richer in gold, pearls, and jewelry than might have been expected on a farm.

I can't say much about the captured wives, hired girls, and daughters because the soldiers didn't let me watch their doings. But I do remember hearing pitiful screams from various dark corners and I guess that my mother and our Ursula had it no better than the rest.

ThomsonNOW To read a full version of this document, enter the *ThomsonNOW* documents area using the access card that is available for *The Essential World History*.

Louis's domination of his ministers and secretaries gave him control of the central policy-making machinery of government and thus authority over the traditional areas of monarchical power: the formulation of foreign policy, the making of war and peace, the assertion of the secular power of the crown against any religious authority, and the ability to levy taxes to fulfill these functions. Louis had considerably less success with the internal administration of the kingdom, however.

The Economy and the Military The cost of building palaces, maintaining his court, and pursuing his wars made finances a crucial issue for Louis XIV. He was most fortunate in having the services of Jean-Baptiste Colbert (1619–1683) as controller general of finances. Colbert sought to increase the wealth and power of France by general adherence to mercantilism, which focused on the role of the state and maintained that state intervention in the economy was desirable for the sake of the national good. To decrease imports and increase exports, Colbert granted subsidies to individuals who established new industries. To improve communications and the transportation of goods internally, he built roads and canals. To decrease imports directly, Colbert raised tariffs on foreign goods.

POLITICS & GOVERNMENT

COMPARATIVE ILLUSTRATION

Sun Kings, West and East.   At the end of the seventeenth century, two powerful rulers dominated their kingdoms. Both monarchs ruled states that dominated the affairs of the regions around them. And both rulers saw themselves as favored by divine authority—Louis XIV as a divine-right monarch and Kangxi as possessing the mandate of Heaven. Thus, both rulers saw themselves not as divine beings but as divinely ordained beings whose job was to govern organized societies. On the left, Louis XIV, who ruled France from 1643 to 1715, is seen in a portrait by Hyacinth Rigaud that captures the king's sense of royal dignity and grandeur. On the right, Kangxi, who ruled China from 1661 to 1722, is seen in a nineteenth-century portrait that shows the ruler seated in majesty on his imperial throne.

The increase in royal power that Louis pursued led the king to develop a professional army numbering 100,000 men in peacetime and 400,000 in time of war. To achieve the prestige and military glory befitting an absolute king as well as to ensure the domination of his Bourbon dynasty over European affairs, Louis waged four wars between 1667 and 1713. His ambitions roused much of Europe to form coalitions that were determined to prevent the certain destruction of the European balance of power by Bourbon hegemony. Although Louis added some territory to France's northeastern frontier and established a member of his own Bourbon dynasty on the throne of Spain, he also left France impoverished and surrounded by enemies.

Absolutism in Central and Eastern Europe

During the seventeenth century, a development of great importance for the modern Western world took place with the appearance in central and eastern Europe of three new powers: Prussia, Austria, and Russia.

Prussia   Frederick William the Great Elector (1640–1688) laid the foundation for the Prussian state. Realizing that the land he had inherited, known as Brandenburg-Prussia, was a small, open territory with no natural frontiers for defense, Frederick William built an army of forty thousand men, the fourth largest in Europe. To sustain the army, Frederick William established the General

Interior of Versailles: The Hall of Mirrors. Pictured here is the exquisite Hall of Mirrors in King Louis XIV's palace at Versailles. Located on the second floor, the hall overlooks the park below. Hundreds of mirrors were placed on the wall opposite the windows to create an illusion of even greater width. Careful planning went into every detail of the interior decoration. Even the doorknobs were specially designed to reflect the magnificence of Versailles.

© Giraudon/Art Resource, NY

War Commissariat to levy taxes for the army and oversee its growth. The Commissariat soon evolved into an agency for civil government as well. The new bureaucratic machine became the elector's chief instrument to govern the state. Many of its officials were members of the Prussian landed aristocracy, the Junkers, who also served as officers in the all-important army.

In 1701, Frederick William's son Frederick officially gained the title of king. Elector Frederick III became King Frederick I, and Brandenburg-Prussia simply Prussia. In the eighteenth century, Prussia emerged as a great power in Europe.

Austria The Austrian Habsburgs had long played a significant role in European politics as Holy Roman Emperors, but by the end of the Thirty Years' War, their hopes of creating an empire in Germany had been dashed. In the seventeenth century, the house of Austria created a new empire in eastern and southeastern Europe.

The nucleus of the new Austrian Empire remained the traditional Austrian hereditary possessions: Lower and Upper Austria, Carinthia, Carniola, Styria, and Tyrol. To these had been added the kingdom of Bohemia and parts of northwestern Hungary. After the defeat of the Turks in 1687 (see Chapter 15), Austria took control of all of Hungary, Transylvania, Croatia,

and Slovenia, thus establishing the Austrian Empire in southeastern Europe. By the beginning of the eighteenth century, the house of Austria had assembled an empire of considerable size.

The Austrian monarchy, however, never became a highly centralized, absolutist state, primarily because it contained so many different national groups. The Austrian Empire remained a collection of territories held together by the Habsburg emperor, who was archduke of Austria, king of Bohemia, and king of Hungary. Each of these regions, however, had its own laws and political life.

From Muscovy to Russia A new Russian state had emerged in the fifteenth century under the leadership of the principality of Muscovy and its grand dukes. In the sixteenth century, Ivan IV (1533–1584) became the first ruler to take the title of *tsar* (the Russian word for *Caesar*). Ivan expanded the territories of Russia eastward and crushed the power of the Russian nobility. He was known as Ivan the Terrible because of his ruthless deeds, among them stabbing his son to death in a heated argument. When Ivan's dynasty came to an end in 1598, it was followed by a period of anarchy that did not end until the Zemsky Sobor (national assembly) chose Michael Romanov as the new tsar, establishing a dynasty that lasted until 1917. One of its most prominent members was Peter the Great.

Peter the Great (1689–1725) was an unusual character. A towering, strong man at 6 feet 9 inches tall, Peter enjoyed a low kind of humor—belching contests and crude jokes—and vicious punishments, including floggings, impalings, and roastings. Peter got a firsthand view of the West when he made a trip there in 1697–1698 and returned to Russia with a firm determination to Westernize or Europeanize Russia. He was especially eager to borrow European technology in order to create the army and navy he needed to make Russia a great power.

As could be expected, one of his first priorities was the reorganization of the army and the creation of a navy. Employing both Russians and Europeans as officers, he conscripted peasants for twenty-five-year stints of service to build a standing army of 210,000 men. Peter has also been given credit for forming the first Russian navy.

To impose the rule of the central government more effectively throughout the land, Peter divided Russia into provinces. Although he hoped to create a "police state," by which he meant a well-ordered community governed in accordance with law, few of his bureaucrats shared his concept of duty to the state. Peter hoped for a sense of civic duty, but his own forceful personality created an atmosphere of fear that prevented it.

The object of Peter's domestic reforms was to make Russia into a great state and military power. His primary goal was to "open a window to the west," meaning an ice-free port easily accessible to Europe. This could only be achieved on the Baltic, but at that time, the Baltic coast was controlled by Sweden, the most important power in northern Europe. A long and hard-fought war with Sweden won Peter the lands he sought. In 1703, Peter began the construction of a new city, Saint Petersburg, his window to the west and a symbol that Russia was looking westward to Europe. Under Peter, Russia became a great military power and, by his death in 1725, an important European state.

England and Limited Monarchy

Not all states were absolutist in the seventeenth century. One of the most prominent examples of resistance to absolute monarchy came in England, where king and Parliament struggled to determine the roles each should play in governing England.

Conflict Between King and Parliament

With the death of Queen Elizabeth I in 1603, the Tudor dynasty became extinct, and the Stuart line of rulers was inaugurated with the accession to the throne of Elizabeth's cousin, King James VI of Scotland, who became James I (1603–1625) of England. James espoused the divine right of kings, a viewpoint that alienated

Parliament, which had grown accustomed under the Tudors to act on the premise that monarch and Parliament together ruled England as a "balanced polity." Then, too, the Puritans—Protestants within the Anglican church who, inspired by Calvinist theology, wished to eliminate every trace of Roman Catholicism from the Church of England—were alienated by the king's strong defense of the Anglican church. Much of England's gentry, mostly well-to-do landowners, had become Puritans, and this Puritan gentry formed an important and substantial part of the House of Commons, the lower house of Parliament. It was not wise to alienate these men.

The conflict that had begun during the reign of James came to a head during the reign of his son Charles I (1625–1649). Charles also believed in divine-right monarchy, and religious differences added to the hostility between Charles I and Parliament. The king's attempt to impose more ritual on the Anglican church struck the Puritans as a return to Catholic practices. When Charles tried to force the Puritans to accept his religious policies, thousands of them went off to the "howling wildernesses" of America.

Civil War and Commonwealth

Grievances mounted until England finally slipped into a civil war (1642–1648) won by the parliamentary forces, due largely to the New Model Army of Oliver Cromwell, the only real military genius of the war. The New Model Army was composed primarily of more extreme Puritans known as the Independents, who, in typical Calvinist fashion, believed they were doing battle for God. As Cromwell wrote in one of his military reports, "Sir, this is none other but the hand of God; and to Him alone belongs the glory." We might give some credit to Cromwell; his soldiers were well trained in the new military tactics of the seventeenth century.

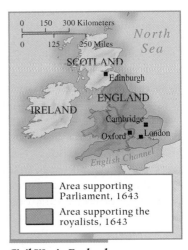

Civil War in England

After the execution of Charles I on January 30, 1649, Parliament abolished the monarchy and the House of Lords and proclaimed England a republic or commonwealth. But Cromwell and his army, unable to work effectively with Parliament, dispersed it by force and established a military dictatorship. After Cromwell's death in 1658, the army decided that military rule was no longer feasible and restored the monarchy in the person of Charles II, the son of Charles I.

France	
Louis XIV	1643–1715
Brandenburg-Prussia	
Frederick William the Great Elector	1640–1688
Elector Frederick III (King Frederick I)	1688–1713
Russia	
Ivan IV the Terrible	1533–1584
Peter the Great	1689–1725
First trip to the West	1697–1698
Construction of Saint Petersburg begins	1703
England	
Civil wars	1642–1648
Commonwealth	1649–1653
Charles II	1660–1685
Declaration of Indulgence	1672
James II	1685–1688
Glorious Revolution	1688
Bill of Rights	1689

Restoration and a Glorious Revolution

Charles II was sympathetic to Catholicism, and Parliament's suspicions were aroused in 1672 when he took the audacious step of issuing the Declaration of Indulgence, which suspended the laws that Parliament had passed against Catholics and Puritans after the restoration of the monarchy. Parliament forced the king to suspend the declaration.

The accession of James II (1685–1688) to the crown virtually guaranteed a new constitutional crisis for England. An open and devout Catholic, his attempt to further Catholic interests made religion once more a primary cause of conflict between king and Parliament. James named Catholics to high positions in the government, army, navy, and universities. Parliamentary outcries against James's policies stopped short of rebellion because the members knew that he was an old man and that his successors were his Protestant daughters Mary and Anne, born to his first wife. But on June 10, 1688, a son was born to James II's second wife, also a Catholic. Suddenly, the specter of a Catholic hereditary monarchy loomed large. A group of prominent English noblemen invited the Dutch chief executive, William of Orange, husband of James's daughter Mary, to invade England. William and Mary raised an army and invaded England while James, his wife, and their infant son fled to France. With little bloodshed, England had undergone its "Glorious Revolution."

In January 1689, Parliament offered the throne to William and Mary, who accepted it along with the provisions of the Bill of Rights (see the box on p. 329). The Bill of Rights affirmed Parliament's right to make laws and levy taxes. The rights of citizens to keep arms and have a

jury trial were also confirmed. By deposing one king and establishing another, Parliament had destroyed the divine-right theory of kingship (William was, after all, king by grace of Parliament, not God) and asserted its right to participate in the government. Parliament did not have complete control of the government, but it now had the right to participate in affairs of state. Over the next century, it would gradually prove to be the real authority in the English system of **limited (constitutional) monarchy.**

The Flourishing of European Culture

Despite religious wars and the growth of absolutism, European culture continued to flourish. The era was blessed with a number of prominent artists and writers.

Art: The Baroque

The artistic movement known as the **Baroque** dominated the Western artistic world for a century and a half. The Baroque began in Italy in the last quarter of the sixteenth century and spread to the rest of Europe and Latin America. Baroque artists sought to harmonize the classical ideals of Renaissance art with the spiritual feelings of the sixteenth-century religious revival. In large part, Baroque art and architecture reflected the search for power that was characteristic of much of the seventeenth century. Baroque churches and palaces featured richly ornamented facades, sweeping staircases, and an overall splendor meant to impress people. Kings and princes wanted other kings and princes, as well as their own subjects, to be in awe of their power.

Baroque painting was known for its use of dramatic effects to arouse the emotions, especially evident in the works of Peter Paul Rubens (1577–1640), a prolific artist and an important figure in the spread of the Baroque from Italy to other parts of Europe. In his artistic masterpieces, bodies in violent motion, heavily fleshed nudes, a dramatic use of light and shadow, and rich sensuous pigments converge to express intense emotions.

Art: Dutch Realism

The supremacy of Dutch commerce in the seventeenth century was paralleled by a brilliant flowering of Dutch painting. Wealthy patricians and burghers of Dutch urban society commissioned works of art for their guildhalls, town halls, and private dwellings. The interests of this burgher society were reflected in the subject matter of many Dutch paintings: portraits of themselves, group portraits of their military companies and guilds, landscapes, seascapes, genre scenes, still lifes, and the interiors of their residences. Neither classical nor Baroque, Dutch painters were primarily interested in the realistic portrayal of secular everyday life.

THE BILL OF RIGHTS

POLITICS & GOVERNMENT

In 1688, the English experienced a bloodless revolution in which the Stuart king James II was replaced by Mary, James's daughter, and her husband, William of Orange. After William and Mary had assumed power, Parliament passed a Bill of Rights that specified the rights of Parliament and laid the foundation for a constitutional monarchy.

How did the Bill of Rights lay the foundation for a constitutional monarchy in England?

The Bill of Rights

Whereas the said late King James II having abdicated the government, and the throne being thereby vacant, his Highness the prince of Orange (whom it hath pleased Almighty God to make the glorious instrument of delivering this kingdom from popery and arbitrary power) did (by the device of the lords spiritual and temporal, and diverse principal persons of the Commons) cause letters to be written to the lords spiritual and temporal, being Protestants, and other letters to the several counties, cities, universities, boroughs, and Cinque Ports, for the choosing of such persons to represent them, as were of right to be sent to parliament, to meet and sit at Westminster upon the two and twentieth day of January, in this year 1689, in order to such an establishment as that their religion, laws, and liberties might not again be in danger of being subverted; upon which letters elections have been accordingly made.

And thereupon the said lords spiritual and temporal and Commons, pursuant to their respective letters and elections, being now assembled in a full and free representation of this nation, taking into their most serious consideration the best means for attaining the ends aforesaid, do in the first place (as their ancestors in like case have usually done), for the vindication and assertion of their ancient rights and liberties, declare:

1. That the pretended power of suspending laws, or the execution of laws, by regal authority, without consent of parliament is illegal.

2. That the pretended power of dispensing with the laws, or the execution of law by regal authority, as it hath been assumed and exercised of late, is illegal.

3. That the commission for erecting the late court of commissioners for ecclesiastical causes, and all other commissions and courts of like nature, are illegal and pernicious.

4. That levying money for or to the use of the crown by pretense of prerogative, without grant of parliament, for longer time or in other manner than the same is or shall be granted, is illegal.

5. That it is the right of the subjects to petition the king, and all commitments and prosecutions for such petitioning are illegal.

6. That the raising or keeping a standing army within the kingdom in time of peace, unless it be with consent of parliament, is against law.

7. That the subjects which are Protestants may have arms for their defense suitable to their conditions, and as allowed by law.

8. That election of members of parliament ought to be free.

9. That the freedom of speech, and debates or proceedings in parliament, ought not to be impeached or questioned in any court or place out of parliament.

10. That excessive bail ought not to be required, nor excessive fines imposed, nor cruel and unusual punishments inflicted.

11. That jurors ought to be duly impaneled and returned, and jurors which pass upon men in trials for high treason ought to be freeholders.

12. That all grants and promises of fines and forfeitures of particular persons before conviction are illegal and void.

13. And that for redress of all grievances, and for the amending, strengthening, and preserving of the laws, parliament ought to be held frequently.

ThomsonNOW To read a full version of this document, enter the *ThomsonNOW* documents area using the access card that is available for *The Essential World History.*

A Golden Age of Literature in England

In England, writing for the stage reached new heights between 1580 and 1640. The golden age of English literature is often called the Elizabethan Era because much of the English cultural flowering occurred during Elizabeth's reign. Elizbethan literature exhibits the exuberance and pride associated with English exploits under Queen Elizabeth. Of all the forms of Elizabethan literature, none expressed the energy and intellectual versatility of the era better than drama. And no dramatist is more famous or more accomplished than William Shakespeare (1564–1614).

Shakespeare was a "complete man of the theater." Although best known for writing plays, he was also an actor and a shareholder in the chief acting company of the time, the Lord Chamberlain's Company, which played in various London theaters. Shakespeare is to this day hailed as a genius. A master of the English language, he imbued its words with power and majesty. And his technical proficiency was matched by incredible insight into human psychology. Whether writing tragedies or comedies, Shakespeare exhibited a remarkable understanding of the human condition.

Peter Paul Rubens, *The Landing of Marie de' Medici at Marseilles.* The Flemish painter Peter Paul Rubens played a key role in spreading the Baroque style from Italy to other parts of Europe. In *The Landing of Marie de' Medici at Marseilles,* Rubens made a dramatic use of light and color, bodies in motion, and luxurious nudes to heighten the emotional intensity of the scene. This was one of a cycle of twenty-one paintings dedicated to the queen mother of France.

CONCLUSION

N Chapter 13, we observed how the movement of Europeans outside of Europe began to change the shape of world history. But what had made this development possible? After all, the religious division of Europe had led to almost a hundred years of religious warfare complicated by serious political, economic, and social issues—the worst series of wars and civil wars since the collapse of the western Roman Empire—before Europeans finally admitted that they would have to tolerate different ways to worship God.

At the same time, the concept of a united Christendom, held as an ideal since the Middle Ages, had been irrevocably destroyed by the religious wars, enabling a system of nation-states to emerge in which power politics took on increasing significance. Within those states slowly emerged some of the machinery that made possible a growing centralization of power. In absolutist states,

strong monarchs with the assistance of their aristocracies took the lead in promoting greater centralization. In all the major European states, a growing concern for power led to larger armies and greater conflict, stronger economies, and more powerful governments. From a global point of view, Europeans—with their strong governments, prosperous economies, and strengthened military forces—were beginning to dominate other parts of the world, leading to a growing belief in the superiority of their civilization.

Yet despite Europeans' increasing domination of global trade markets, they had not achieved their goal of diminishing the power of Islam, first pursued during the Crusades. In fact, as we shall see in the next chapter, in the midst of European expansion and exploration, three new and powerful Muslim empires were taking shape in the Middle East and South Asia.

CHAPTER NOTES

1. N. Machiavelli, *The Prince,* trans. D. Wootton (Indianapolis, Ind., 1995), p. 48.

2. Quoted in R. Bainton, *Here I Stand: A Life of Martin Luther* (New York, 1950), p. 144.

3. J. Calvin, *Institutes of the Christian Religion,* trans. J. Allen (Philadelphia, 1936), vol. 1, p. 228; vol. 2, p. 181.

TIMELINE

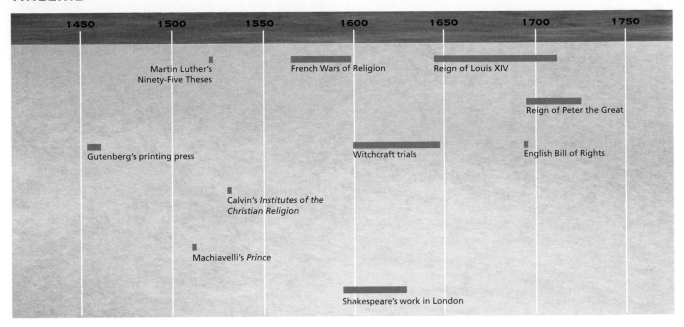

1450	1500	1550	1600	1650	1700	1750

Martin Luther's Ninety-Five Theses

French Wars of Religion

Reign of Louis XIV

Reign of Peter the Great

Gutenberg's printing press

Witchcraft trials

English Bill of Rights

Calvin's *Institutes of the Christian Religion*

Machiavelli's *Prince*

Shakespeare's work in London

---

4. Quoted in B. S. Anderson and J. P. Zinsser, *A History of Their Own: Women in Europe from Prehistory to the Present* (New York, 1988), vol. 1, p. 259.

5. Quoted in J. O'Malley, *The First Jesuits* (Cambridge, Mass., 1993), p. 76.

6. Quoted in J. Klaits, *Servants of Satan: The Age of Witch Hunts* (Bloomington, Ind., 1985), p. 68.

SUGGESTED READING

Basic surveys of the Reformation period include **H. J. Grimm, *The Reformation Era, 1500–1650,*** 2d ed. (New York, 1973); **D. L. Jensen, *Reformation Europe,*** 2d ed. (Lexington, Mass., 1990); **J. D. Tracy, *Europe's Reformations, 1450–1650*** (Oxford, 1999); **D. MacCulloch, *The Reformation*** (New York, 2003); and **C. Lindberg, *The European Reformations*** (Cambridge, Mass., 1996). Also see the interesting and useful book by **S. Ozment, *Protestants: The Birth of a Revolution*** (New York, 1992).

The classic account of Martin Luther's life is **R. Bainton, *Here I Stand: A Life of Martin Luther*** (New York, 1950). More recent works include **J. M. Kittelson, *Luther the Reformer: The Story of the Man and His Career*** (Minneapolis, Minn., 1986), and **H. A. Oberman, *Luther: Man Between God and the Devil*** (New York, 1992). See also the brief biography by **M. Marty, *Martin Luther*** (New York, 2004). On the role of Charles V, see **W. Maltby, *The Reign of Charles V*** (New York, 2002). A good survey of the English Reformation is **A. G. Dickens, *The English Reformation,*** 2d ed. (New York, 1989). On John Calvin, see **A. McGrath, *A Life of John Calvin: A Study in the Shaping of Western Culture*** (Cambridge, Mass., 1990), and **W. J. Bouwsma, *John Calvin*** (New York, 1988).

On the impact of the Reformation on the family, see **J. F. Harrington, *Reordering Marriage and Society in Reformation Germany*** (New York, 1995). A good introduction to the Catholic Reformation can be found in **R. P. Hsia, *The World of Catholic Renewal, 1540–1770*** (Cambridge, 1998).

On the French Wars of Religion, see **M. P. Holt, *The French Wars of Religion, 1562–1629*** (New York, 1995), and **R. J. Knecht, *The French Wars of Religion, 1559–1598,*** 2d ed. (New York, 1996). A good biography of Philip II is **G. Parker, *Philip II,*** 3d ed. (Chicago, 1995). Elizabeth's reign can be examined in **C. Haigh, *Elizabeth I,*** 2d ed. (New York, 1998). On the Thirty Years' War, see **R. G. Asch, *The Thirty Years' War: The Holy Roman Empire and Europe, 1618–1648*** (New York, 1997).

Witchcraft hysteria can be examined in **B. P. Levack, *The Witch-Hunt in Early Modern Europe*** (London, 1987).

For a brief account of seventeenth-century French history, see **J. B. Collins, *The State in Early Modern France*** (Cambridge, 1995). A solid and very readable biography of Louis XIV is **J. Levi, *Louis XIV*** (New York, 2004). For a brief study, see **P. R. Campbell, *Louis XIV, 1661–1715*** (London, 1993). On the creation of an Austrian state, see **P. S. Fichtner, *The Habsburg Monarchy, 1490–1848*** (New York, 2003). See **P. H. Wilson, *Absolutism in Central Europe*** (New York, 2000), on both Prussia and Austria. Works on Peter the Great include **M. S. Anderson, *Peter the Great,*** 2d ed. (New York, 1995), and **L. Hughes, *Russia in the Age of Peter the Great*** (New Haven, Conn., 1998). On England, see **M. A. Kishlansky, *A Monarchy Transformed*** (London, 1996) on the English Revolution, and **W. A. Speck, *The Revolution of 1688*** (Oxford, 1988).

For a general survey of Baroque culture, see **J. S. Held, *Seventeenth and Eighteenth Century Art: Baroque Painting, Sculpture, Architecture*** (New York, 1971). The literature on Shakespeare is enormous. For a biography, see **A. L. Rowse, *The Life of Shakespeare*** (New York, 1963).

InfoTrac College Edition

Visit this chapter's InfoTrac College Edition/Research activities at the *Essential World History* Companion Website for activities related to the transformation of Europe.

ThomsonNOW™ for Duiker and Spielvogel's *The Essential World History, Third Edition*

Enter *ThomsonNOW* using the access card that is available with this text. *ThomsonNOW* will assist you in understanding the content in this chapter with lesson plans generated for your needs, as well as provide you with a connection to the *Wadsworth World History Resource Center* (see description at the right for details).

WORLD HISTORY
RESOURCE CENTER

Enter the Resource Center using either your *ThomsonNOW* accesss card or your standalone access card for the *Wadsworth World History Resource Center*. Organized by topic, this website includes quizzes; images; over 350 primary source documents; interactive simulations, maps, and timelines; movie explorations; and a wealth of other resources. You can read the following documents, and many more, at http://worldrc.wadsworth.com/

Niccolò Machiavelli, *The Prince,* selected chapters

Erasmus and Luther, "On Free Will and Salvation"

Saint-Simon, "The Daily Ritual of the King and His Courtiers"

Visit the *Essential World History* Companion Website for chapter quizzes and more.

http://www.thomsonedu.com/history/duiker

DISCOVERY

What was the relationship between European overseas expansion (as seen in Chapter 13) and political, economic, and social developments in Europe?

In thinking about this question, begin by breaking it down into the components shown below. A discussion of the significance of each component should appear in your answer.

RELIGION AND PHILOSOPHY: Look at the map of religious divisions in Europe before the Thirty Years' War. How does this correspond to the different sides in the war? Was this war a religious or a political one? How would the cost of such wars affect overseas trade?

How did this war affect the average peasant? How might the atrocities of war for a thirty-year period influence the average person's view of government? What might they seek in future governments? Do you see any parallels in the modern world?

Catholics and Protestants in Europe, 1560

JAKOB VON GRIMMELSHAUSEN, *SIMPLICIUS SIMPLICISSIMUS*

The first thing these horsemen did in the nice back rooms of the house was to put in their horses. Then everyone took up a special job, one having to do with death and destruction. Although some began butchering, heating water, and rendering lard, as if to prepare for a banquet, others raced through the house, ransacking upstairs and down; not even the privy chamber was safe, as if the golden fleece of Jason might be hidden there. Still others bundled up big packs of cloth, household goods, and clothes, as if they wanted to hold a rummage sale somewhere. What they did not intend to take along they broke and spoiled. Some ran their swords into the hay and straw, as if there hadn't been hogs enough to stick. Some shook the feathers out of beds and put bacon slabs, hams, and other stuff in the ticking, as if they might sleep better on these. Others knocked down the hearth and broke the windows, as if announcing an ever-lasting summer. They flattened out copper and pewter dishes and baled the ruined goods. They burned up bedsteads, tables, chairs, and benches, though there were yards and yards of dry firewood outside the kitchen. Jars and crocks, pots and casseroles all were broken, either because they preferred their meat broiled or because they thought they'd eat only one meal with us. In the barn, the hired girl was handled so roughly that she was unable to walk away, I am ashamed to report. They stretched the hired man out flat on the ground, stuck a wooden wedge in his mouth to keep it open, and emptied a milk bucket full of stinking manure drippings down his throat; they called it a Swedish cocktail. He didn't relish it and made a very wry face. By this means they forced him to take a raiding party to some other place where they carried off men and cattle and brought them to our farm. Among those were my father, mother, and [sister] Ursula.

Then they used thumbscrews, which they cleverly made out of their pistols, to torture the peasants, as if they wanted to burn witches. Though he had confessed to nothing as yet, they put one of the captured hayseeds in the bake-oven and lighted a fire in it. They put a rope around someone else's head and tightened it like a tourniquet until blood came out of his mouth, nose, and ears. In short, every soldier had his favorite method of making life miserable for peasants, and every peasant had his own misery.

My father was, as I thought, particularly lucky because he confessed with a laugh what others were forced to say in pain and martyrdom. No doubt because he was the head of the household, he was shown special consideration; they put him close to a fire, tied him by his hands and legs, and rubbed damp salt on the bottoms of his feet. Our old nanny goat had to lick it off and this so tickled my father that he could have burst laughing. This seemed so clever and entertaining to me—I had never seen or heard my father laugh so long—that I joined him in laughter, to keep him company or perhaps to cover up my ignorance. In the midst of such glee he told them the whereabouts of hidden treasure much richer in gold, pearls, and jewelry than might have been expected on a farm.

I can't say much about the captured wives, hired girls, and daughters because the soldiers didn't let me watch their doings. But I do remember hearing pitiful screams from various dark corners and I guess that my mother and our Ursula had it no better than the rest.

POLITICS AND GOVERNMENT: What do the artists seem to be attempting to portray about both rulers in these paintings? What features are most prominent? What might this say about how these monarchs wanted their people to view them? How had kingship changed? What are some similarities of and differences between Elizabeth I and Louis XIV?

Procession of Queen Elizabeth I

Louis XIV

RELIGION AND PHILOSOPHY: What are the main ways in which Lutheranism and Catholicism differed in their basic views of faith? To what groups or classes within European society would Luther appeal, and why? How might kings or political leaders react to Luther's new tenets? How would the Catholic Church respond to Luther? What problems would this cause throughout Europe?

Luther Versus the Pope

MARTIN LUTHER, SELECTIONS FROM THE NINETY-FIVE THESES

5. The Pope has neither the will nor the power to remit any penalties beyond those he has imposed either at his own discretion or by canon law.
20. Therefore the Pope, by his plenary remission of all penalties, does not mean "all" in the absolute sense, but only those imposed by himself.
21. Hence those preachers of Indulgences are wrong when they say that a man is absolved and saved from every penalty by the Pope's Indulgences.
27. It is mere human talk to preach that the soul flies out [of purgatory] immediately [when] the money clinks in the collection box.
28. It is certainly possible that when the money clinks in the collection box greed and avarice can increase; but the intercession of the Church depends on the will of God alone.
50. Christians should be taught that, if the Pope knew the exactions of the preachers of Indulgences, he would rather have the basilica of St. Peter reduced to ashes than built with the skin, flesh, and bones of his sheep [the indulgences that so distressed Luther were being sold to raise money for the construction of the new St. Peter's Basilica in Rome].
81. This wanton preaching of pardons makes it difficult even for learned men to redeem respect due to the Pope from the slanders or at least the shrewd questionings of the laity.

82. For example: "Why does not the Pope empty purgatory for the sake of most holy love and the supreme need of souls? This would be the most righteous of reasons, if he can redeem innumerable souls for sordid money with which to build a basilica, the most trivial of reasons."
86. Again: "Since the Pope's wealth is larger than that of the crassest Crassi of our time, why does he not build this one basilica of St. Peter with his own money, rather than with that of the faithful poor?"
90. To suppress these most conscientious questionings of the laity by authority only, instead of refuting them by reason, is to expose the Church and the Pope to the ridicule of their enemies, and to make Christian people unhappy.
94. Christians should be exhorted to seek earnestly to follow Christ, their Head, through penalties, deaths, and hells.
95. And let them thus be more confident of entering heaven through many tribulations rather than through a false assurance of peace.

15

THE MUSLIM EMPIRES

CHAPTER OUTLINE AND FOCUS QUESTIONS

The Ottoman Empire

☐ What was the ethnic composition of the Ottoman Empire, and how did the government of the sultan administer such a diverse population? How did Ottoman policy in this regard compare with that applied in Europe and Asia?

The Safavids

☐ What role did women play in each of the Muslim empires? Compare Safavid policy toward women with that followed in other parts of the world.

The Grandeur of the Mughals

☐ Although the Ottoman, Safavid, and Mughal Empires all adopted Islam as their state religion, their approach was often different. Describe the differences, and explain why they might have occurred.

CRITICAL THINKING

☐ What were the main characteristics of each of the Muslim empires, and in what ways did they resemble each other? How were they distinct from their European counterparts?

The Battle of Mohács

℡HE OTTOMAN ARMY, led by Sultan Suleyman the Magnificent, arrived at Mohács, on the plains of Hungary, on an August morning in 1526. The Turkish force numbered about 100,000 men, and in its baggage were three hundred new long-range cannons. Facing them was a somewhat larger European force, clothed in heavy armor but armed with only one hundred older cannons.

The battle began at noon and was over in two hours. The flower of the Hungarian cavalry had been destroyed, and twenty thousand foot soldiers had drowned in a nearby swamp. The Ottomans had lost fewer than two hundred men. Two weeks later, they seized the Hungarian capital at Buda and prepared to lay siege to the nearby Austrian city of Vienna. Europe was in a panic. It was to be the high point of Turkish expansion in Europe.

In launching their Age of Exploration, European rulers had hoped that by controlling global markets, they could cripple the power of Islam and reduce its threat to the security of Europe. But the Christian nations' dream of expanding their influence around the globe at the expense of their great Muslim rival had not been achieved. On the contrary, the Muslim world, which appeared to have entered a period of decline with the collapse of the Abbasid caliphate during the era of the Mongols, managed to revive in the shadow of Europe's Age of Exploration, a period that also saw the rise of three great Muslim empires. These powerful Muslim states—those of the Ottomans, the Safavids, and the Mughals—dominated the Middle East and the South Asian subcontinent and brought stability to a region that had been in turmoil for centuries. ◇

The Ottoman Empire

The Ottoman Turks were among the various Turkic-speaking peoples who had spread westward from Central Asia in the ninth, tenth, and eleventh centuries. The first to dominate were the Seljuk Turks, who initially attempted to revive the declining Abbasid caliphate in Baghdad. Later they established themselves in the Anatolian peninsula at the expense of the Byzantine Empire. Turks served as warriors or administrators, while the peasants who tilled the farmland were mainly Greek.

The Rise of the Ottoman Turks

In the late thirteenth century, a new group of Turks under the tribal leader Osman (1280–1326) began to consolidate their power in the northwestern corner of the Anatolian peninsula. At first, the Osman Turks were relatively peaceful and engaged in pastoral pursuits, but as the Seljuk Empire began to disintegrate in the early fourteenth century, they began to expand and founded the Osmanli (later to be known as Ottoman) dynasty.

The Ottomans gained a key advantage by seizing the Bosporus and the Dardanelles, between the Mediterranean and the Black seas. The Byzantine Empire, of course, had controlled the area for centuries, serving as a buffer between the Muslim Middle East and the Latin West. The Byzantines, however, had been severely weakened by the sack of Constantinople in the Fourth Crusade (in 1204) and the Western occupation of much of the empire for the next half century. In 1345, Ottoman forces under their leader Orkhan I (1326–1360) crossed the Bosporus for the first time to support a usurper against the Byzantine emperor in Constantinople. Setting up their first European base at Gallipoli at the Mediterranean entrance to the Dardanelles, Turkish forces expanded gradually into the Balkans and allied with fractious Serbian and Bulgar forces against the Byzantines. In these unstable conditions, the Ottomans gradually established permanent settlements throughout the area, where Turkish **beys** (provincial governors in the Ottoman Empire; from the Turkish *beg*, "knight") drove out the previous landlords and collected taxes from the local Slavic peasants. The Ottoman leader now began to claim the title of **sultan** or sovereign of his domain.

In 1360, Orkhan was succeeded by his son Murad I, who consolidated Ottoman power in the Balkans and gradually reduced the Byzantine emperor to a vassal. Murad now began to build up a strong military administration based on the recruitment of Christians into an elite guard. Called **Janissaries** (from the Turkish *yeni cheri*, "new troops"), they were recruited from the local Christian population in the Balkans and then converted to Islam and trained as foot soldiers or administrators. One of the major advantages of the Janissaries was that they were directly subordinated to the sultanate and therefore owed their loyalty to the person of the sultan. Other military forces were organized by the beys and were thus loyal to their local tribal leaders.

The Janissary corps also represented a response to changes in warfare. As the knowledge of firearms spread in the late fourteenth century, the Turks began to master the new technology, including siege cannons and muskets (see the comparative essay "The Changing Face of War" on p. 335). The traditional nomadic cavalry charge was now outmoded and was superseded by infantry forces armed with muskets. Thus, the Janissaries provided a well-armed infantry who served both as an elite guard to protect the palace and as a means of extending Turkish control in the Balkans. With his new forces, Murad defeated the Serbs at the famous Battle of Kosovo in 1389 and ended Serbian hegemony in the area.

Expansion of the Empire

Under Murad's successor, Bayazid I (1389–1402), the Ottomans advanced northward, annexed Bulgaria, and slaughtered the French cavalry at a major battle on the Danube. When Mehmet II (1451–1481) succeeded to the throne, he was determined to capture Constantinople. Already in control of the Dardanelles, he ordered the construction of a major fortress on the Bosporus just north of the city, which put the Turks in a position to strangle the Byzantines.

The Fall of Constantinople The last Byzantine emperor issued a desperate call for help from the Europeans, but only the Genoese came to his defense. With eighty thousand troops ranged against only seven thousand defenders, Mehmet laid siege to Constantinople in 1453. In their attack on the city, the Turks made use of massive cannons with 26-foot barrels that could launch stone balls weighing up to 1,200 pounds each. The Byzantines stretched heavy chains across the Golden Horn, the inlet that forms the city's harbor, to prevent a naval attack from the north and prepared to make their final stand behind the 13-mile-long wall along the western edge of the city. But Mehmet's forces seized the tip of the peninsula north of the Golden Horn and then dragged their ships overland across the peninsula from the Bosporus and put them into the water behind the chains. Finally, the walls were breached; the Byzantine emperor died in the final battle.

The Advance into Western Asia and Africa With their new capital at Constantinople, renamed Istanbul, the

THE CHANGING FACE OF WAR

SCIENCE &
TECHNOLOGY

"War," as the renowned French historian Fernand Braudel once observed, "has always been a matter of arms and techniques. Improved techniques can radically alter the course of events." Braudel's remark was directed to the situation in the Mediterranean region during the sixteenth century, when the adoption of artillery changed the face of warfare and gave enormous advantages to the countries that stood at the head of the new technological revolution. But it could as easily have been applied to the present day, when potential adversaries possess weapons capable of reaching across oceans and continents.

One crucial aspect of military superiority, of course, lies in the nature of weaponry. From the invention of the bow and arrow to the advent of the atomic era, the possession of superior instruments of war has provided a distinct advantage against a poorly armed enemy. It was at least partly the possession of iron weapons, for example, that enabled the invading Hyksos to conquer Egypt during the second millennium B.C.E.

Mobility is another factor of vital importance. During the second millennium B.C.E., horse-drawn chariots revolutionized the art of war from the Mediterranean Sea to the Yellow River valley in northern China. Later, the invention of the stirrup enabled mounted warriors to shoot arrows from horseback, a technique applied with great effect by the Mongols as they devastated civilizations across the Eurasian supercontinent.

To protect themselves from marauding warriors, settled societies began to erect massive walls around their cities and fortresses. That in turn led to the invention of siege weapons like the catapult and the battering ram. The Mongols allegedly even came up with an early form of chemical warfare, hurling human bodies infected with the plague into the bastions of their enemies.

The invention of explosives launched the next great revolution in warfare. First used as a weapon of war by the Tang dynasty in China, explosives were brought to the West by the Turks, who used them with great effectiveness in the fifteenth century against the Byzantine Empire. But the Europeans quickly mastered the new technology and took it to new heights, inventing handheld firearms and mounting iron cannons on their warships. The latter represented a significant advantage to European fleets as they began to compete with rivals for control of the Indian and Pacific oceans.

The twentieth century saw revolutionary new developments in the art of warfare, from armed vehicles to airplanes and on to the nuclear age. But as weapons grow ever more fearsome, they are more risky to use, resulting in the paradox of the Vietnam War, when lightly armed Viet Cong guerrilla units were able to fight the world's mightiest army to a virtual standstill. As the Chinese military strategist Sun Tzu had long ago observed, victory in war often goes to the smartest, not the strongest.

Ottoman Turks were now a dominant force in the Balkans and the Anatolian peninsula. They now began to advance to the east against the Shi'ite kingdom of the Safavids in Persia (see "The Safavids" later in this chapter), which had been promoting rebellion among the Anatolian tribal population and disrupting Turkish trade through the Middle East. After defeating the Safavids at a major battle in 1514, Emperor Selim I (1512–1520) consolidated Turkish control over the territory that had been ancient Mesopotamia and then turned his attention to the Mamluks in Egypt, who had failed to support the Ottomans in their struggle against the Safavids. The Mamluks were defeated in Syria in 1516; Cairo fell a year later. Now controlling several of the holy cities of Islam, including Jerusalem, Mecca, and Medina, Selim declared himself to be the new caliph, or successor to Muhammad. During the next few years, Turkish armies and fleets advanced westward along the African coast, occupying Tripoli, Tunis, and Algeria and eventually penetrating almost to the Strait of Gibraltar (see Map 15.1).

The impact of Turkish rule on the peoples of North Africa was relatively light. Like their predecessors, the Turks were Muslims, and they preferred where possible to administer their conquered regions through local rulers. Central government direction was achieved through appointed pashas who collected taxes (and then paid a fixed percentage as tribute to the central government), maintained law and order, and were directly responsible to Istanbul. The Turks ruled from coastal cities like Algiers, Tunis, and Tripoli and made no attempt to control the interior beyond maintaining the trade routes through the Sahara to the trading centers along the Niger River. Meanwhile, local pirates along the Barbary Coast—the northern coast of Africa from Egypt to the Atlantic Ocean—competed with their Christian rivals in raiding the shipping that passed through the Mediterranean.

By the seventeenth century, the links between the imperial court in Istanbul and its appointed representatives in the Turkish regencies in North Africa had begun

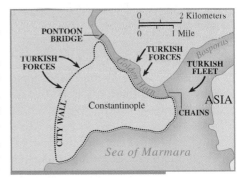

The Fall of Constantinople, 1453

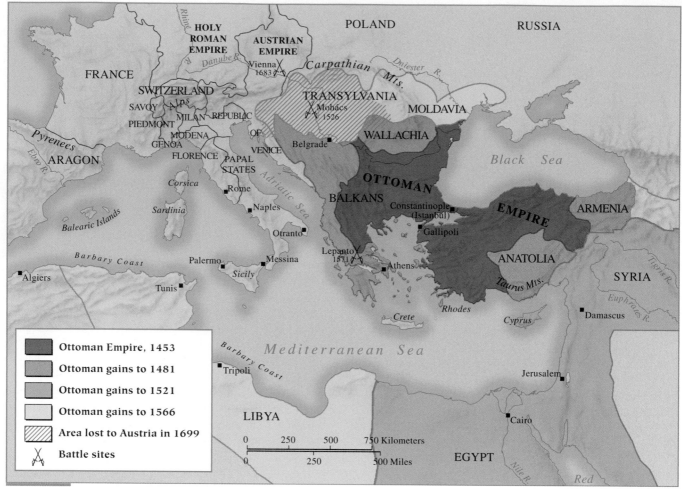

MAP 15.1 **The Ottoman Empire.** This map shows the territorial growth of the Ottoman Empire from the eve of the conquest of Constantinople in 1453 to the end of the seventeenth century, when a defeat at the hands of Austria led to the loss of a substantial portion of central Europe. ❓ Where did the Ottomans come from? 🌐 **View an animated version of this map or related maps at** http://worldrc.wadsworth.com/

to decline. Some of the pashas were dethroned by local elites, while others, such as the bey of Tunis, became hereditary rulers. Even Egypt, whose agricultural wealth and control over the route to the Red Sea made it the most important country in the area to the Turks, gradually became autonomous under a new official class of Janissaries.

Turkish Expansion in Europe   After their conquest of Constantinople in 1453, the Ottoman Turks tried to extend their territory in Europe. Under the leadership of Suleyman I the Magnificent (1520–1566), Turkish forces advanced up the Danube, seizing Belgrade in 1521 and winning a major victory over the Hungarians at the Battle of Mohács on the Danube in 1526. Subsequently, the Turks overran most of Hungary, moved into Austria, and advanced as far as Vienna, where they were finally repulsed in 1529. At the same time, they extended their power into the western Mediterranean and threatened to turn it into a Turkish lake until a large Turkish fleet

was destroyed by the Spanish at Lepanto in 1571 (see the comparative illustration on p. 337).

In the second half of the seventeenth century, the Ottoman Empire again took the offensive. By mid-1683, the Ottomans had marched through the Hungarian plain and laid siege to Vienna. Repulsed by a mixed army of Austrians, Poles, Bavarians, and Saxons, the Turks retreated and were pushed out of Hungary by a new European coalition. Although they retained the core of their empire, the Ottoman Turks would never again be a threat to Europe. The Turkish empire held together for the rest of the seventeenth and the eighteenth centuries, but it faced new challenges from the ever-growing Austrian Empire in southeastern Europe and the new Russian giant to the north.

The Nature of Turkish Rule

Like other Muslim empires in Persia and India, the Ottoman political system was the result of the evolution

COMPARATIVE ILLUSTRATION

Commemorating Victory, from Mohács to Lepanto. In 1526, the Ottoman army won an important victory over European forces at Mohács, on the plains of Hungary. Less than half a century later, the Ottoman advance was halted at Lepanto, off the coast of Greece, where a Turkish fleet met defeat at the hands of the Europeans. Both victories reflected the importance of modern technology. Not surprisingly, both battles were commemorated in important paintings by the victors. On the left, Ottoman forces advance against their adversaries at Mohács; on the right, the victorious European fleet arrives at Messina, a port city on the island of Sicily.

of tribal institutions into a sedentary empire. At the apex of the Ottoman system was the sultan, who was the supreme authority in both a political and a military sense. The origins of this system can be traced back to the bey, who was only a tribal leader, a first among equals, who could claim loyalty from his chiefs so long as he could provide booty and grazing lands for his subordinates. Disputes were settled by tribal law, while Muslim laws were secondary. Tribal leaders collected taxes—or booty—from areas under their control and sent one-fifth on to the bey. Both administrative and military power were centralized under the bey, and the capital was wherever the bey and his administration happened to be.

But the rise of empire brought about an adaptation to Byzantine traditions of rule. The status and prestige of the sultan now increased relative to the subordinate tribal leaders, and the position took on the trappings of imperial rule. Court rituals inherited from the Byzantines and Persians were adopted, as was a centralized administrative system that increasingly isolated the sultan in his palace. The position of the sultan was hereditary, with a son, although not necessarily the eldest, always succeeding the father. This practice led to chronic succession struggles upon the death of individual sultans, and the losers were often executed (strangled with a silk bowstring) or imprisoned. Heirs to the throne were assigned as provincial governors to provide them with experience.

The Harem The heart of the sultan's power was in the Topkapi Palace in the center of Istanbul. Topkapi (meaning "cannon gate") was constructed in 1459 by Mehmet II and served as an administrative center as well as the private residence of the sultan and his family. Eventually, it had a staff of twenty thousand employees. The private domain of the sultan was called the **harem** ("sacred place"). Here he resided with his concubines. Normally, a sultan did not marry but chose several concubines as his favorites; they were accorded this status after they gave birth to sons. When a son became a sultan, his mother became known as the queen mother and served as adviser to the throne. This tradition, initiated by the influential wife of Suleyman the Magnificent, often resulted in considerable authority for the queen mother in the affairs of state.

Members of the harem, like the Janissaries, were often of slave origin and formed an elite element in Ottoman society. Since the enslavement of Muslims was forbidden, slaves were taken among non-Islamic peoples. Some concubines were prisoners selected for the position, while others were purchased or offered to the sultan as a gift. They were then trained and educated like the Janissaries

CHRONOLOGY The Ottoman Empire

Reign of Osman I	1280–1326
Ottoman Turks first cross the Bosporus	1345
Murad I consolidates Turkish power in the Balkans	1360
Ottomans defeat Serbian army at Kosovo	1389
Rule of Mehmet II (the Conqueror)	1451–1481
Turkish conquest of Constantinople	1453
Turks defeat Mamluks in Syria and seize Cairo	1516–1517
Reign of Suleyman I (the Magnificent)	1520–1566
Defeat of Hungarians at Battle of Mohács	1526
Defeat of Turks at Vienna	1529
Battle of Lepanto	1571
Second siege of Vienna	1683
Treaty of Carlowitz	1699

in a system called **devshirme** ("collection"). *Devshirme* had originated in the practice of requiring local clan leaders to provide prisoners to the sultan as part of their tax obligation. Talented males were given special training for eventual placement in military or administrative positions, while their female counterparts were trained for service in the harem, with instruction in reading, the Qur'an, sewing and embroidery, and musical performance. They were ranked according to their status, and some were permitted to leave the harem to marry officials.

Unique to the Ottoman Empire from the fifteenth century onward was the exclusive use of slaves to reproduce its royal heirs. Contrary to myth, few of the women of the imperial harem were used for sexual purposes, as the majority were members of the sultan's extended family—sisters, daughters, widowed mothers, and in-laws, with their own personal slaves and entourage. Contemporary European observers compared the atmosphere in the Topkapi harem to a Christian nunnery, with its hierarchical organization, enforced chastity, and rule of silence.

Because of their proximity to the sultan, the women of the harem often wielded so much political power that the era has been called "the sultanate of women." Queen mothers administered the imperial household and engaged in diplomatic relations with other countries while controlling the marital alliances of their daughters with senior civilian and military officials or members of other royal families in the region. One princess was married seven separate times from the age of two after her previous husbands died either in battle or by execution.

Administration of the Government The sultan ruled through an imperial council that met four days a week and was chaired by the chief minister known as the

grand vezir (*wazir,* sometimes rendered in English as *vizier*). The sultan often attended behind a screen, whence he could privately indicate his desires to the grand vezir. The latter presided over the imperial bureaucracy. Like the palace guard, the bureaucrats were not an exclusive group but were chosen at least partly by merit from a palace school for training officials. Most officials were Muslims by birth, but some talented Janissaries became senior members of the bureaucracy, and almost all the later grand vezirs came from the *devshirme* system.

Local administration during the imperial period was a product of Turkish tribal tradition and was similar in some respects to fief-holding in Europe. The empire was divided into provinces and districts governed by officials who, like their tribal predecessors, combined both civil and military functions. Senior officials were assigned land in fief by the sultan and were then responsible for collecting taxes and supplying armies to the empire. These lands were then farmed out to the local cavalry elite called the **sipahis,** who exacted a tax from all peasants in their fiefdoms for their salary.

Religion and Society in the Ottoman World

Like most Turkic-speaking peoples in the Anatolian peninsula and throughout the Middle East, the Ottoman ruling elites were Sunni Muslims. Ottoman sultans had claimed the title of caliph ("defender of the faith") since the early sixteenth century and thus theoretically were responsible for guiding the flock and maintaining Islamic law, the *Shari'a.* In practice, the sultan assigned these duties to a supreme religious authority, who administered the law and maintained a system of schools for educating Muslims.

Islamic law and customs were applied to all Muslims in the empire. Like their rulers, most Turkic-speaking people were Sunni Muslims, but some communities were attracted to Sufism (see Chapter 7) or other heterodox doctrines. The government tolerated such activities so long as their practitioners remained loyal to the empire, but in the early sixteenth century, unrest among these groups—some of whom converted to the Shi'ite version of Islamic doctrine—outraged the conservative *ulama* and eventually led to war against the Safavids (see "The Safavids" later in this chapter).

The Treatment of Minorities Non-Muslims—mostly Orthodox Christians (Greeks and Slavs), Jews, and Armenian Christians—formed a significant minority within the empire, which treated them with relative tolerance. Non-Muslims were compelled to pay a head tax (because of their exemption from military service), and they were permitted to practice their religion or convert to Islam, although Muslims were prohibited from adopting another faith. Most of the population in European areas of the empire remained Christian, but in some places, such as the territory now called Bosnia, substantial numbers converted to Islam.

Recruitment of the Children. The Ottoman Empire, like its Chinese counterpart, sought to recruit its officials on the basis of merit. Through the system called *devshirme* ("collection"), youthful candidates were selected from the non-Muslim population in villages throughout the empire. In this painting, an imperial officer is counting coins to pay for the children's travel expenses to Istanbul, where they will undergo extensive academic and military training. Note the concern of two of the mothers and a priest as they question the official, who undoubtedly underwent the process himself as a child. As they leave their family and friends, the children carry their worldly possessions in bags slung over their shoulders.

Technically, women in the Ottoman Empire were subject to the same restrictions that afflicted their counterparts in other Muslim societies, but their position was ameliorated to some degree by various factors. In the first place, non-Muslims were subject to the laws and customs of their own religions; thus, Orthodox Christian, Jewish, and Armenian Christian women were spared some of the restrictions applied to their Muslim sisters. In the second place, Islamic laws as applied in the Ottoman Empire defined the legal position of women comparatively tolerantly. Women were permitted to own and inherit property, including their dowries. They could not be forced into marriage and in certain cases were permitted to seek a divorce. As we have seen, women often exercised considerable

influence in the palace and in a few instances even served as senior officials, such as governors of provinces. The relatively tolerant attitude toward women in Ottoman-held territories has been ascribed by some to Turkish tribal traditions, which took a more egalitarian view of gender roles than the sedentary societies of the region did.

The Ottomans in Decline

By the seventeenth century, signs of internal rot had begun to appear in the empire, although the first loss of imperial territory did not occur until 1699, when Transylvania and much of Hungary were ceded to Austria at the Treaty of Carlowitz. Apparently, a number of factors were involved. In the first place, the administrative system inherited from the tribal period began to break down. Although the *devshirme* system of training officials continued to function, *devshirme* graduates were now permitted to marry and inherit property and to enroll their sons in the palace corps. Thus, they were gradually transformed from a meritocratic administrative elite into a privileged and often degenerate hereditary caste. Local administrators were corrupted and taxes rose as the central bureaucracy lost its links with rural areas. The imperial treasury was depleted by constant wars, and transport and communications were neglected. Interest in science and technology, once a hallmark of the Arab Empire, was in decline. In addition, the empire was increasingly beset by economic difficulties caused by the diversion of trade routes away from the eastern Mediterranean and the price inflation brought about by the influx of cheap American silver.

Another sign of change within the empire was the increasing degree of material affluence and the impact of Western ideas and customs. Sophisticated officials and merchants began to mimic the habits and lifestyles of their European counterparts, dressing in the European fashion, purchasing Western furniture and art objects, and ignoring Muslim strictures against the consumption of alcohol and sexual activities outside marriage. During the sixteenth and early seventeenth centuries, coffee and tobacco were introduced into polite Ottoman society, and cafés for the consumption of both began to appear in the major cities (see the box on p. 340). One sultan in the early seventeenth century issued a decree prohibiting the consumption of both coffee and tobacco, arguing (correctly, no doubt) that many cafés were nests of antigovernment intrigue. He even began to wander incognito through the streets of Istanbul at night. Any of his subjects detected in immoral or illegal acts were summarily executed and their bodies left on the streets as an example to others.

There were also signs of a decline in competence within the ruling family. Whereas the first sultans reigned twenty-seven years on average, later ones averaged only thirteen years, suggesting an increase in turmoil within the ruling cliques. The throne now went to the oldest surviving male, while his rivals were kept secluded in a latticed cage and thus had no governmental experience if

A TURKISH DISCOURSE ON COFFEE

INTERACTION & EXCHANGE

Coffee was first introduced to Turkey from the Arabian peninsula in the mid-sixteenth century and allegedly came to Europe during the Turkish siege of Vienna in 1529. The following account was written by Katib Chelebi, a seventeenth-century Turkish author who, among other things, compiled an extensive encyclopedia and bibliography. Here, in The Balance of Truth, he describes how coffee entered the empire and the problems it caused for public morality. (In the Muslim world, as in Europe and later in colonial America, the drinking of coffee was associated with coffeehouses, where rebellious elements often gathered to promote antigovernment activities.) Chelebi died in Istanbul in 1657, reportedly while drinking a cup of coffee.

Why do you think coffee became identified as a dangerous substance in the Ottoman Empire? Were the authorities successful in suppressing its consumption?

Katib Chelebi, *The Balance of Truth*

[Coffee] originated in Yemen and has spread, like tobacco, over the world. Certain sheikhs, who lived with their dervishes in the mountains of Yemen, used to crush and eat the berries . . . of a certain tree. Some would roast them and drink their water. Coffee is a cold dry food, suited to the ascetic life and sedative of lust. . . .

It came to Asia Minor by sea, about 1543, and met with a hostile reception, fetwas [decrees] being delivered against it. For they said, Apart from its being roasted, the fact that it is drunk in gatherings, passed from hand to hand, is suggestive of loose living. It is related of Abul-Suud Efendi that he had holes bored in the ships that brought it, plunging their cargoes of coffee into the sea. But these strictures and prohibitions availed nothing. . . . One coffeehouse was opened after another, and men would gather together, with great eagerness and enthusiasm, to drink. Drug addicts in particular, finding it a life-giving thing, which increased their pleasure, were willing to die for a cup.

Storytellers and musicians diverted the people from their employments, and working for one's living fell into disfavor. Moreover the people, from prince to beggar, amused themselves with knifing one another. Toward the end of 1633, the late Ghazi Gultan Murad, becoming aware of the situation, promulgated an edict, out of regard and compassion for the people, to this effect: Coffeehouses throughout the Guarded Domains shall be dismantled and not opened hereafter. Since then, the coffeehouses of the capital have been as desolate as the heart of the ignorant. . . . But in cities and towns outside Istanbul, they are opened just as before. As has been said above, such things do not admit of a perpetual ban.

---

they succeeded to rule. Later sultans also became less involved in government, and more power flowed to the office of the grand vezir (called the Sublime Porte) or to eunuchs and members of the harem. Palace intrigue increased as a result.

Ottoman Art

The Ottoman sultans were enthusiastic patrons of the arts and maintained large ateliers of artisans and artists, primarily at the Topkapi Palace in Istanbul but also in other important cities of the vast empire. The period from Mehmet II in the fifteenth century to the early eighteenth century witnessed the flourishing of pottery, rugs, silk and other textiles, jewelry, arms and armor, and calligraphy. All adorned the palaces of the rulers, testifying to their opulence and exquisite taste. The artists came from all parts of the realm and beyond.

Architecture By far the greatest contribution of the Ottoman Empire to world art was its architecture, especially the magnificent mosques of the second half of the sixteenth century. Traditionally, prayer halls in mosques were subdivided by numerous pillars that supported small individual domes, creating a private, forestlike atmosphere. The Turks, however, modeled their new mosques on the open floor plan of the Byzantine church of Hagia Sophia (completed in 537), which had been turned into a mosque by Mehmet II, and began to push the pillars toward the outer wall to create a prayer hall with an uninterrupted central area under one large dome. With this plan, large numbers of believers could worship in unison in accordance with Muslim preference. By the mid-sixteenth century, the greatest of all Ottoman architects, Sinan, began erecting the first of his eighty-one mosques with an uncluttered prayer area. Each was topped by an imposing dome, and often, as at Edirne, the entire building was framed with four towering narrow minarets. By emphasizing its vertical lines, the minarets camouflaged the massive stone bulk of the structure and gave it a feeling of incredible lightness. These four graceful minarets would find new expression sixty years later in India's white marble Taj Mahal (see "Mughal Culture" later in this chapter).

Earlier, in the thirteenth-century the Seljuk Turks of Anatolia had created beautiful tile decorations with two-color mosaics. Now Ottoman artists invented a new glazed tile art with painted flowers and geometrical designs in brilliant blue, green, yellow, and their own secret "tomato red." Entire walls, both interior and exterior, were covered with the painted tiles, which adorned palaces as well as mosques.

The Suleymaniye Mosque, Istanbul. The magnificent mosques built under the patronage of Suleyman the Magnificent are a great legacy of the Ottoman Empire and a fitting supplement to Santa Sophia (Hagia Sophia) Cathedral, built by the Byzantine emperor Justinian in the sixth century C.E. Towering under a central dome, these mosques seem to defy gravity and, like European Gothic cathedrals, convey a sense of weightlessness. The Suleymaniye Mosque is one of the most impressive and most graceful in Istanbul. A far cry from the seventh-century desert mosques constructed of palm trunks, the Ottoman mosques stand among the architectural wonders of the world. Under the massive dome, the interior of the Suleymaniye Mosque offers a quiet refuge for prayer and reflection, bathed in muted sunlight and the warmth of plush carpets, as shown in the inset photo.

Textiles The sixteenth century also witnessed the flourishing of textiles and rugs. The Byzantine emperor Justinian had introduced the cultivation of silkworms to the West in the sixth century, and the silk industry resurfaced under the Ottomans. Perhaps even more famous than Turkish silks are the rugs. But whereas silks were produced under the patronage of the sultans, rugs were a peasant industry. Each village boasted its own distinctive design and color scheme for the rugs it produced.

The Safavids

After the collapse of the empire of Tamerlane in the early fifteenth century, the area extending from Persia into Central Asia lapsed into anarchy. The Uzbeks, Turkic-speaking peoples from Central Asia, were the chief political and military force in the area. From their capital at Bokhara, east of the Caspian Sea, they maintained a semblance of control over the highly fluid tribal alignments until the emergence of the Safavid dynasty in Persia at the beginning of the sixteenth century.

The Safavid dynasty was founded by Shah Ismail (1487–1524), the descendant of a sheikh called Safi al-Din (thus the name Safavid), who traced his origins to Ali, the fourth imam of the Muslim faith. In the early fourteenth century, Safi had been the leader of a community of Turkic-speaking tribespeople in Azerbaijan, near the Caspian Sea. Safi's community was only one of many Sufi mystical religious groups throughout the area. In time, the doctrine spread among nomadic groups throughout the Middle East and was transformed into the more activist Shi'ite version of Islam. Its adherents were known as "red heads" because of their distinctive red cap with twelve folds, meant to symbolize allegiance to the twelve imams of the Shi'ite faith.

In 1501, Ismail's forces seized much of Iran and Iraq, and he called himself the shah of a new Persian state. Baghdad was subdued in 1508 and the Uzbeks and their capital at Bokhara shortly thereafter. Ismail now sent Shi'ite preachers into Anatolia to proselytize and promote rebellion among Turkish tribal peoples in the Ottoman Empire. In retaliation, the Ottoman sultan, Selim I, advanced against the Safavids in Iran and won a major battle near Tabriz in 1514. But Selim could not maintain control of the area, and Ismail regained Tabriz a few years later.

The Ottomans returned to the attack in the 1580s and forced the new Safavid shah, Abbas I the Great (1587–1629), to sign a punitive peace in which much territory was lost. The capital was subsequently moved from

Tabriz in the northwest to Isfahan in the south. Still, it was under Shah Abbas that the Safavids reached the zenith of their glory. He established a system similar to the Janissaries in Turkey to train administrators to replace the traditional warrior elite. He also used the period of peace to strengthen his army, now armed with modern weapons, and in the early seventeenth century, he attempted to regain the lost territories. Although he had some initial success, war resumed in the 1620s, and a lasting peace was not achieved until 1638 (see Map 15.2).

Abbas the Great had managed to strengthen the dynasty significantly, and for a time after his death in 1629, it remained stable and vigorous. But succession conflicts plagued the dynasty. Partly as a result, the power of the more militant Shi'ites began to increase at court and in Safavid society at large. The intellectual freedom that had characterized the empire at its height was curtailed under the pressure of religious orthodoxy, and Iranian women, who had enjoyed considerable freedom and influence during the early empire, were forced to withdraw into seclusion and behind the veil. Meanwhile, attempts to suppress the religious beliefs of minorities led to increased popular unrest. In the early eighteenth century, Afghan warriors took advantage of local revolts to seize the capital of Isfahan, forcing the remnants of the Safavid ruling family to retreat to Azerbaijan, their original homeland. The Ottomans seized territories along the western border. Eventually, order was restored by the military adventurer Nadir Shah Afshar, who launched an extended series of campaigns that restored the country's borders and even occupied the Mughal capital of Delhi (see "Twilight of the Mughals" later in this chapter). After his death, the Zand dynasty ruled until the end of the eighteenth century.

Safavid Politics and Society

Like the Ottoman Empire, Iran under the Safavids was a mixed society. The Safavids had come to power with the support of nomadic Turkic-speaking tribal groups, and

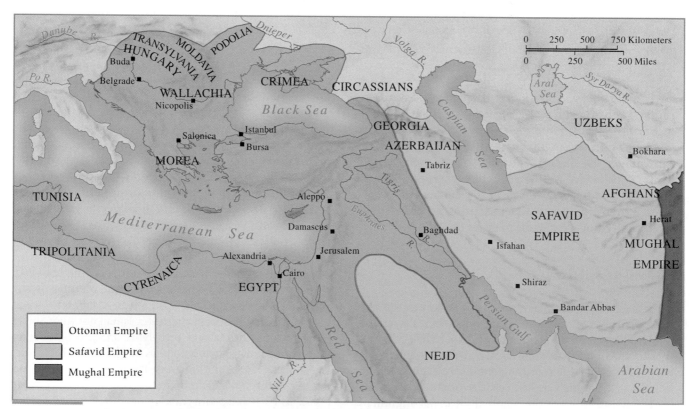

MAP 15.2 **The Ottoman and Safavid Empires, c. 1683.** During the seventeenth century, the two empires contested vigorously for hegemony in the eastern Mediterranean and the Middle East. This map shows the territories controlled by each state in the late seventeenth century. ❓ Which countries shared control over the ancient lands in the Tigris and Euphrates valleys? What modern-day countries are they?

THE RELIGIOUS ZEAL OF SHAH ABBAS THE GREAT

RELIGION &
PHILOSOPHY

Shah Abbas I, probably the greatest of the Safavid rulers, expanded the borders of his empire into areas of the southern Caucasus inhabited by Christians and other non-Muslim peoples. After Persian control was assured, he instructed that the local population be urged to convert to Islam for its own protection and the glory of God. In this passage, his biographer, the Persian historian Eskander Beg Monshi, recounts the story of that effort.

How do the efforts to convert nonbelievers to Islam compare with similar programs by Muslim rulers in India, as described in Chapter 9? What is the author's point of view on the matter?

The Conversion of a Number of Christians to Islam

This year the Shah decreed that those Armenians and other Christians who had been settled in [the southern Caucasus] and had been given agricultural land there should be invited to become Muslims. Life in this world is fraught with vicissitudes, and the Shah was concerned lest, in a period when the authority of the central government was weak, these Christians . . . might be subjected to attack by the neighboring Lor tribes (who are naturally given to causing injury and mischief), and their women and children carried off into captivity. In the areas in which these Christian groups resided, it was the Shah's purpose that the places of worship which they had built should become mosques, and the muezzin's call should be heard in them, so that these Christians might assume the guise of Muslims, and their future status accordingly be assured. . . .

Some of the Christians, guided by God's grace, embraced Islam voluntarily; others found it difficult to abandon their Christian faith and felt revulsion at the idea. They were encouraged by their monks and priests to remain steadfast in their faith. After a little pressure had been applied to the monks and priests, however, they desisted, and these Christians saw no alternative but to embrace Islam, though they did so with reluctance. The women and children embraced Islam with great enthusiasm, vying with one another in their eagerness to abandon their Christian faith and declare their belief in the unity of God. Some five thousand people embraced Islam. As each group made the Muslim declaration of faith, it received instruction in the Koran and the principles of the religious law of Islam, and all bibles and other Christian devotional material were collected and taken away from the priests.

In the same way, all the Armenian Christians who had been moved to [the area] were also forcibly converted to Islam. . . . Most people embraced Islam with sincerity, but some felt an aversion to making the Muslim profession of faith. True knowledge lies with God! May God reward the Shah for his action with long life and prosperity!

---

leading elements from those groups retained considerable influence within the empire. But the majority of the population were Iranian; most of them were farmers or townspeople, with attitudes inherited from the relatively sophisticated and urbanized culture of pre-Safavid Iran. Faced with the problem of integrating unruly Turkic-speaking tribal peoples with the sedentary Persian-speaking population of the urban areas, the Safavids used the Shi'ite faith as a unifying force (see the box above). The shah himself acquired an almost divine quality and claimed to be the spiritual leader of all Islam. Shi'ism was declared the state religion.

Although there was a landed aristocracy, aristocratic power and influence were firmly controlled by strong-minded shahs, who confiscated aristocratic estates when possible and brought them under the control of the crown. Appointment to senior positions in the bureaucracy was by merit rather than birth.

The Safavid shahs took a direct interest in the economy and actively engaged in commercial and manufacturing activities, although there was also a large and affluent urban bourgeoisie. Like the Ottoman sultan, one shah regularly traveled the city streets incognito to check on the honesty of his subjects. When he discovered that a baker and butcher were overcharging for their products, he had the baker cooked in his own oven and the butcher roasted on a spit.

At its height, Safavid Iran was a worthy successor to the great Persian empires of the past, although it was probably not as wealthy as its Mughal and Ottoman neighbors to the east and west. Hemmed in by the sea power of the Europeans to the south and by the land power of the Ottomans to the west, the early Safavids had no navy and were forced to divert overland trade with Europe through southern Russia to avoid an Ottoman blockade. In the early seventeenth century, the situation improved when Iranian forces, in cooperation with the English, seized the island of Hormuz from Portugal and established a new seaport on the southern coast at Bandar Abbas. As a consequence, commercial ties with Europe began to increase.

Safavid Art and Literature

Persia witnessed an extraordinary flowering of the arts during the reign of Shah Abbas I. His new capital of Isfahan was a grandiose planned city with wide visual perspectives and a sense of order almost unique in the region. Shah Abbas ordered his architects to position his palaces, mosques, and bazaars around the Maydan-i-Shah,

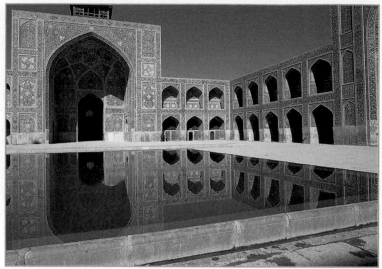

The Royal Academy of Isfahan. Along with institutions such as libraries and hospitals, theological schools were often included in the mosque compound. One of the most sumptuous was the Royal Academy of Isfahan, built by the shah of Iran in the early eighteenth century. This view shows the large courtyard surrounded by arcades of student rooms, reminiscent of the arrangement of monks' cells in European cloisters. Note the similarities with the buildings in Tamerlane's capital at Samarkand, as shown on page 201.

a massive rectangular polo ground. Much of the original city is still in good condition and remains the gem of modern Iran. The immense mosques are richly decorated with elaborate blue tiles. The palaces are delicate structures with unusual slender wooden columns. These architectural wonders of Isfahan epitomize the grandeur, delicacy, and color that defined the Safavid golden age. To adorn the splendid buildings, Safavid artisans created imaginative metalwork, tile decorations, and original and delicate glass vessels.

The greatest area of productivity, however, was in textiles. Silk weaving based on new techniques became a national industry. The silks depicted birds, animals, and flowers in a brilliant mass of color with silver and gold threads. Above all, carpet weaving flourished, stimulated by the great demand for Persian carpets in the West.

The long tradition of Persian painting continued in the Safavid era but changed from paintings to line drawings and from landscape scenes to portraits, mostly of young ladies, boys, lovers, or dervishes. Although some Persian artists studied in Rome, Safavid art was little influenced by the West. Riza-i-Abassi, the most famous artist of this period, created exquisite works on simple naturalistic subjects, such as an ox plowing, hunters, or lovers. Soft colors, delicacy, and flowing movement were the dominant characteristics of the painting of this era.

The Grandeur of the Mughals

In retrospect, the period from the sixteenth to the eighteenth centuries can be viewed as a high point of traditional culture in India. The era began with the creation of one of the subcontinent's greatest empires—that of the Mughals. For the first time since the Mauryan dynasty, the entire subcontinent was united under a single government, with a common culture that inspired admiration and envy throughout the entire region.

The Mughal Empire reached its peak in the sixteenth century under the famed Emperor Akbar and maintained its vitality under a series of strong rulers for another century (see Map 15.3). Then the dynasty began to weaken, a process that was hastened by the increasingly insistent challenge of the foreigners arriving by sea. The Portuguese, who first arrived in 1498, were little more than an irritant. Two centuries later, however, Europeans began to seize control of regional trade routes and to meddle in the internal politics of the subcontinent. By the end of the eighteenth century, nothing remained of the empire but a shell. But some historians see the seeds of decay less in the challenge from abroad than in internal weakness—in the very nature of the empire itself, which was always more a heterogeneous collection of semiautonomous political forces than a centralized empire in the style of neighboring China.

The Founding of the Empire

When the Portuguese fleet led by Vasco da Gama arrived at the port of Calicut in the spring of 1498, the Indian subcontinent was still divided into a number of Hindu and Muslim kingdoms. But it was on the verge of a new era of unity that would be brought about by a foreign dynasty called the Mughals. Like so many recent rulers of northern India, the founders of the Mughal Empire were not natives of India but came from the mountainous region north of the Ganges River. The founder of the dynasty, known to history as Babur (1483–1530), had an illustrious pedigree. His father was descended from the great Asian conqueror Tamerlane, his mother from the Mongol conqueror Genghis Khan.

Babur had inherited a fragment of Tamerlane's empire in an upland valley of the Syr Darya River (see Map 15.2 on p. 342). Driven south by the rising power of the Uzbeks and then the Safavid dynasty in Persia, Babur and his warriors seized Kabul in 1504 and, thirteen years later, crossed the Khyber Pass to India.

Following a pattern that we have seen before, Babur began his rise to power by offering to help an ailing

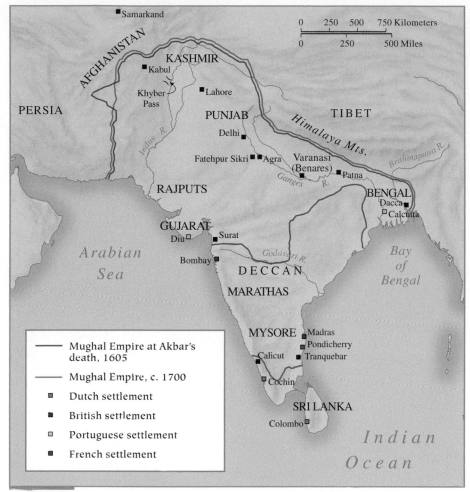

MAP 15.3   The Mughal Empire.   This map indicates the expansion of the Mughal Empire from the death of Akbar in 1605 to the rule of Aurangzeb at the end of the seventeenth century. [?] In which cities on the map were European settlements located? When did each group of Europeans arrive, and how did the settlements spread?   🌐 **View an animated version of this map or related maps at** http://worldrc.wadsworth.com/

Humayun was succeeded by his son Akbar (1556–1605). Born while his father was living in exile, Akbar was only fourteen when he mounted the throne. Illiterate but highly intelligent and industrious, Akbar set out to extend his domain, then limited to Punjab and the upper Ganges River valley. "A monarch," he remarked, "should be ever intent on conquest, otherwise his neighbors rise in arms against him. The army should be exercised in warfare, lest from want of training they become self-indulgent."[1] By the end of his life, he had brought Mughal rule to most of the subcontinent, from the Himalaya Mountains to the Godavari River in central India and from Kashmir to the mouths of the Brahmaputra and the Ganges. In so doing, Akbar had created the greatest Indian empire since the Mauryan dynasty nearly two thousand years earlier. It was an empire that appeared highly centralized from the outside but was actually a collection of semiautonomous principalities ruled by provincial elites and linked together by the overarching majesty of the Mughal emperor.

dynasty against its opponents. Although his own forces were far smaller than those of his adversaries, he possessed advanced weapons, including artillery, and used them to great effect. His use of mobile cavalry was particularly successful against the massed forces, supplemented by mounted elephants, of his enemy. In 1526, with only twelve thousand troops against an enemy force nearly ten times that size, Babur captured Delhi and established his power in the plains of northern India. Over the next several years, he continued his conquests in northern India, until his early death in 1530 at the age of forty-seven.

Babur's success was due in part to his vigor and his charismatic personality, which earned him the undying loyalty of his followers. His son and successor Humayun (1530–1556) was, in the words of one British historian, "intelligent but lazy." In 1540, he was forced to flee to Persia, where he lived in exile for sixteen years. Finally, with the aid of the Safavid shah of Persia, he returned to India and reconquered Delhi in 1555 but died the following year in a household accident, reportedly from injuries suffered in a fall after smoking a pipeful of opium.

Akbar and Indo-Muslim Civilization

Although Akbar was probably the greatest of the conquering Mughal monarchs, like his famous predecessor Asoka, he is best known for the humane character of his rule. Above all, he accepted the diversity of Indian society and took steps to reconcile his Muslim and Hindu subjects.

Religion   Though raised an orthodox Muslim, Akbar had been exposed to other beliefs during his childhood and had little patience with the pedantic views of Muslim scholars at court. As emperor, he displayed a keen interest in other religions, not only tolerating Hindu practices in his own domains but also welcoming the expression of Christian views by his Jesuit advisers. Akbar put his policy of religious tolerance into practice by taking a Hindu princess as one of his wives, and the success of this marriage may well have had an effect on his religious convictions. He patronized classical Indian arts and architecture and abolished many of the restrictions faced by Hindus in a Muslim-dominated society.

A RELIGION FIT FOR A KING

RELIGION & PHILOSOPHY

Emperor Akbar's attempt to create a new form of religion, known as the "Divine Faith," was partly a product of his inquisitive mind. But it was also influenced by Akbar's long friendship with Abu'l Fazl Allami, a courtier who introduced the young emperor to the Shi'ite tradition that each generation produced an individual (imam) who possessed a "divine light" capable of interpreting the holy scriptures. One of the sources of this Muslim theory was the Greek philosopher Plato's idea of a "philosopher king," who in his wisdom could provide humanity with an infallible guide in affairs of religion, morality, and statecraft. Akbar, of course, found the idea appealing, since it provided support for his efforts to reform religious practices in the empire. Abu'l Fazl, however, had made many enemies with his advice and was assassinated, probably at the order of Akbar's son and successor, Jahangir. The following excerpt is from Abu'l Fazl's writings on the subject.

In this account, what role does the Mughal emperor play in promoting public morality? What tactics must he apply to bring about success in his efforts?

Abu'l Fazl, *Institutes of Akbar*

Royalty is a light emanating from God, and a ray from the sun, the illuminator of the universe, the argument of the book of perfection, the receptacle of all virtues. Modern language calls this light the divine light, and the tongue of antiquity called it the sublime halo. It is communicated by God to kings without the intermediate assistance of anyone, and men, in the presence of it, bend the forehead of praise toward the ground of submission.

Again, many excellent qualities flow from the possession of this light:

1. *A paternal love toward the subjects.* Thousands find rest in the love of the king, and sectarian differences do not raise the dust of strife. In his wisdom, the king will understand the spirit of the age, and shape his plans accordingly.

2. *A large heart.* The sight of anything disagreeable does not unsettle him, nor is want of discrimination for him a source of disappointment. His courage steps in. His divine firmness gives him the power of requittal, nor does the high position of an offender interfere with it. The wishes of great and small are attended to, and their claims meet with no delay at his hands.

3. *A daily increasing trust in God.* When he performs an action, he considers God as the real doer of it [and himself as the medium] so that a conflict of motives can produce no disturbance.

4. *Prayer and devotion.* The success of his plans will not lead him to neglect, nor will adversity cause him to forget God and madly trust in man. He puts the reins of desire into the hands of reason; in the wide field of his desires he does not permit himself to be trodden down by restlessness; neither will he waste his precious time in seeking after that which is improper. He makes wrath, the tryant, pay homage to wisdom, so that blind rage may not get the upper hand, and inconsiderateness overstep the proper limits. . . . He is forever searching after those who speak the truth and is not displeased with words that seem bitter but are, in reality, sweet. He considers the nature of the words and the rank of the speaker. He is not content with not committing violence, but he must see that no injustice is done within his realm.

ThomsonNOW To read more of Abu'l Fazl's writings about Akbar, enter the *ThomsonNOW* documents area using the access card that is available for *The Essential World History*.

During his later years, Akbar became steadily more hostile to Islam. To the dismay of many Muslims at court, he sponsored a new form of worship called the Divine Faith (*Din-i-Ilahi*), which combined characteristics of several religions with a central belief in the infallibility of all decisions reached by the emperor. The new faith aroused deep hostility in Muslim circles and rapidly vanished after his death (see the box above).

Society and the Economy Akbar also extended his innovations to the empire's administration. Although the upper ranks of the government continued to be dominated by nonnative Muslims, a substantial proportion of lower-ranking officials were Hindus, and a few Hindus were appointed to positions of importance. At first, most officials were paid salaries, but later they were ordinarily assigned sections of agricultural land for their temporary use; they kept a portion of the taxes paid by the local peasants in lieu of a salary. These local officials, known as **zamindars,** were expected to forward the rest of the taxes from the lands under their control to the central government.

The same tolerance that marked Akbar's attitude toward religion and administration extended to the Mughal legal system. While Muslims were subject to the Islamic codes (the *Shari'a*), Hindu law applied to areas settled by Hindus, who after 1579 were no longer required to pay the hated *jizya*, or poll tax on non-Muslims. Punishments for crime were relatively mild, at least by the standards of the day, and justice was administered in a relatively impartial and efficient manner.

Overall, Akbar's reign was a time of peace and prosperity. Although all Indian peasants were required to pay about one-third of their annual harvest to the state through the *zamindars*, the system was applied fairly, and when drought struck in the 1590s, the taxes were reduced or even suspended altogether. Thanks to a long period of relative peace and political stability, commerce and manufacturing flourished. Foreign trade, in particular, thrived as Indian goods, notably textiles, tropical food products, spices, and precious stones, were exported in exchange for gold and silver. Tariffs on imports were low. Much of the foreign commerce was handled by Arab traders, since the Indians, like their Mughal rulers, did not care for travel by sea. Internal trade, however, was dominated by large merchant castes, who also were active in banking and handicrafts.

Twilight of the Mughals

Akbar died in 1605 and was succeeded by his son Jahangir (1605–1628). During the early years of his reign, Jahangir continued to strengthen central control over the vast empire. Eventually, however, his grip began to weaken (according to his memoirs, he "only wanted a bottle of wine and a piece of meat to make merry"), and the court fell under the influence of one of his wives, the Persian-born Nur Jahan. The empress took advantage of her position to enrich her own family and arranged for her niece Mumtaz Mahal to marry her husband's third son and ultimate successor, Shah Jahan. When Shah Jahan succeeded to the throne in 1628, he quickly demonstrated the single-minded quality of his grandfather (albeit in a much more brutal manner), ordering the assassination of all of his rivals in order to secure his position.

The Reign of Shah Jahan During a reign of three decades, Shah Jahan maintained the system established by his predecessors while expanding the boundaries of the empire by successful campaigns in the Deccan Plateau and against Samarkand, north of the Hindu Kush. But Shah Jahan's rule was marred by his failure to deal with the growing domestic problems. He had inherited a nearly empty treasury because of Empress Nur Jahan's penchant for luxury and ambitious charity projects. Though the majority of his subjects lived in grinding poverty, Shah Jahan's frequent military campaigns and expensive building projects put a heavy strain on the imperial finances and compelled him to raise taxes. At the same time, the government did little to improve rural conditions. In a country where transport was primitive (it often took three months to travel the 600 miles between Patna, in the middle of the Ganges River valley, and Delhi) and drought conditions frequent, the dynasty made few efforts to increase agricultural efficiency or to improve the roads or the irrigation network. A Dutch merchant in Gujarat described conditions during a famine in the mid-seventeenth century:

> As the famine increased, men abandoned towns and villages and wandered helplessly. It was easy to recognize their condition: eyes sunk deep in head, lips pale and covered with slime, the skin hard, with the bones showing through, the belly nothing but a pouch hanging down empty,

knuckles and kneecaps showing prominently. One would cry and howl for hunger, while another lay stretched on the ground dying in misery; wherever you went, you saw nothing but corpses.[2]

In 1648, Shah Jahan moved his capital from Agra to Delhi and built the famous Red Fort in his new capital city. But he is best known for the Taj Mahal in Agra, widely considered to be the most beautiful building in India, if not in the entire world. The story is a romantic one—that the Taj was built by the emperor in memory of his wife Mumtaz Mahal, who had died giving birth to her thirteenth child at the age of thirty-nine. But the story has a less attractive side: the expense of the building, which employed twenty thousand masons over twenty years, forced the government to raise agricultural taxes, further impoverishing many Indian peasants.

Rule of Aurangzeb Succession struggles returned to haunt the dynasty in the mid-1650s when Shah Jahan's illness led to a struggle for power between his sons Dara Shikoh and Aurangzeb. Dara Shikoh was described by his contemporaries as progressive and humane, but he apparently lacked political acumen and was outmaneuvered by Aurangzeb (1658–1707), who had Dara Shikoh put to death and then imprisoned his father in the fort at Agra.

Aurangzeb is one of the most controversial individuals in the history of India. A man of high principle, he attempted to eliminate many of what he considered to be India's social evils, prohibiting the immolation of widows on their husband's funeral pyre (*sati*), the castration of eunuchs, and the exaction of illegal taxes. With less success, he tried to forbid gambling, drinking, and prostitution. But Aurangzeb, a devout and somewhat doctrinaire Muslim, also adopted a number of measures that reversed the policies of religious tolerance established by his predecessors. The building of new Hindu temples was prohibited, and the Hindu poll tax was restored. Forced conversions to Islam were resumed, and non-Muslims were driven from the court. Aurangzeb's heavy-handed religious policies led to considerable domestic unrest and to a revival of Hindu fervor during the last years of his reign. A number of revolts also broke out against imperial authority.

Decline of the Mughals During the eighteenth century, Mughal power was threatened from both within and without. Fueled by the growing power and autonomy of the local gentry and merchants, rebellious groups in provinces throughout the empire, from the Deccan to the Punjab, began to reassert local authority and reduce the power of the Mughal emperor to that of a "tinsel sovereign." Increasingly divided, India was vulnerable to attack from abroad. In 1739, Delhi was sacked by the Persians, who left it in ashes.

A number of obvious reasons for the virtual collapse of the Mughal Empire can be identified, including the draining of the imperial treasury and the decline in

THE CAPTURE OF PORT HOOGLY

In 1632, the Mughal ruler, Shah Jahan, ordered an attack on the city of Hoogly, a fortified Portuguese trading post on the northeastern coast of India. For the Portuguese, who had profited from half a century of triangular trade between India, China, and various countries in the Middle East and Southeast Asia, the loss of Hoogly at the hands of the Mughals hastened the decline of their influence in the region. Presented here are two contemporary versions of the battle. The first, from the Padshahnama (Book of Kings), relates the course of events from the Mughal point of view. The second account is by John Cabral, a Jesuit missionary who was resident in Hoogly at the time.

How do these two accounts of the Battle of Hoogly differ? Is there any way to reconcile the two into a single account?

The *Padshahnama*

During the reign of the Bengalis, a group of Frankish [European] merchants . . . settled in a place one *kos* from Satgaon on the banks of the [?] and, on the pretext that they needed a place for trading, they received permission from the Bengalis to construct a few edifices. Over time, due to the indifference of the governors of Bengal, many Franks gathered there and built dwellings of the utmost splendor and strength, fortified with cannons, guns, and other instruments of war. It was not long before it became a large settlement and was named Hoogly. . . . The Franks' ships trafficked at this port, and commerce was established, causing the market at the port of Satgaon to slump. . . . Of the peasants of those places, they converted some to

Christianity by force and others through greed and sent them off to Europe in their ships. . . .

Since the improper actions of the Christians of Hoogly Port toward the Muslims was accurately reflected in the mirror of the mind of the Emperor before his accession to the throne, when the imperial banners cast their shadows over Bengal, and inasmuch as he was always inclined to propagate the true religion and eliminate infidelity, it was decided that when he gained control over this region he would eradicate the corruption of these abominators from the realm.

John Cabral, *Travels of Sebastian Manrique, 1629–1649*

Hugli continued at peace all the time of the great King Jahangir. For, as this Prince, by what he showed, was more attached to Christ than to Mohammad and was a Moor in name and dress only. . . . Sultan Khurram was in everything unlike his father, especially as regards the latter's leaning towards Christianity. . . . He declared himself the mortal enemy of the Christian name and the restorer of the law of Mohammad. . . . He sent a firman [order] to the Viceroy of Bengal, commanding him without reply or delay, to march upon the Bandel of Hugli and put it to fire and the sword. He added that, in doing so, he would render a signal service to God, to Mohammad, and to him. . . .

Consequently, on a Friday, September 24, 1632, . . . all the people [the Portuguese] embarked with the utmost secrecy. . . . Learning what was going on, and wishing to be able to boast that they had taken Hugli by storm, they [the imperialists] made a general attack on the Bandel by Saturday noon. They began by setting fire to a mine, but lost in it more men than we. Finally, however, they were masters of the Bandel.

---

competence of the Mughal rulers. But it should also be noted that even at its height under Akbar, the empire was a loosely knit collection of heterogeneous principalities held together by the authority of the throne, which tried to combine Persian concepts of kingship with the Indian tradition of decentralized power. Decline set in when centrifugal forces gradually began to predominate over centripetal ones.

The Impact of Western Power in India

As we have seen, the first Europeans to arrive were the Portuguese. Although they established a virtual monopoly over regional trade in the Indian Ocean, they did not aggressively seek to penetrate the interior of the subcontinent. The situation changed at the end of the sixteenth century, when the English and the Dutch entered the scene. Soon both powers were in active competition with Portugal, and with each other, for trading privileges in the region (see the box above).

Penetration of the new market was not easy. When the first English fleet arrived at Surat, a thriving port on the northwestern coast of India, in 1608, their request for trading privileges was rejected by Emperor Jahangir. Needing lightweight Indian cloth to trade for spices in the East Indies, the English persisted, and in 1616, they were finally permitted to install their own ambassador at the imperial court in Agra. Three years later, the first English factory (trading station) was established at Surat.

During the next several decades, the English presence in India steadily increased while Mughal power gradually waned. By midcentury, additional English factories had been established at Fort William (now the great city of Calcutta) on the Hoogly River near the Bay of Bengal and in 1639 at Madras on the southeastern coast. From there, English ships carried Indian-made cotton goods to the East Indies, where they were bartered for spices, which were shipped back to England.

English success in India attracted rivals, including the Dutch and the French. The Dutch abandoned their interests

Arrival of Vasco da Gama at Calicut	1498
Babur seizes Delhi	1526
Death of Babur	1530
Humayun recovers throne in Delhi	1555
Death of Humayun and accession of Akbar	1556
Death of Akbar and accession of Jahangir	1605
Arrival of English at Surat	1608
Reign of Emperor Shah Jahan	1628–1657
Mughals attack Port Hoogly	1632
Foundation of English fort at Madras	1639
Aurangzeb succeeds to the throne	1658
Death of Aurangzeb	1707
Delhi sacked by Persians	1739
Battle of Plassey	1757

British East India Company exacted from the now-decrepit Mughal court the authority to collect taxes from extensive lands in the area surrounding Calcutta. Less than ten years later, British forces seized the reigning Mughal emperor in a skirmish at Buxar, and the British began to consolidate their economic and administrative control over Indian territory through the surrogate power of the now powerless Mughal court (see Map 15.4).

To officials of the East India Company, the expansion of their authority into the interior of the subcontinent probably seemed like a simple commercial decision, a move designed to seek guaranteed revenues to pay for the increasingly expensive military operations in India. To historians, it marks a major step in the gradual transfer of all of the Indian subcontinent to the British East India Company and later, in 1858, to the British crown. The process was more haphazard than deliberate.

Economic Difficulties The company's takeover of vast landholdings, notably in the eastern Indian states of Orissa and Bengal, may have been a windfall for enterprising

to concentrate on the spice trade in the middle of the seventeenth century, but the French were more persistent and established factories of their own. For a brief period, under the ambitious empire builder Joseph François Dupleix, the French competed successfully with the British. But the military genius of Sir Robert Clive, an aggressive British administrator and empire builder who eventually became the chief representative of the East India Company in the subcontinent, and the refusal of the French government to provide financial support for Dupleix's efforts eventually left the French with only their fort at Pondicherry and a handful of small territories on the southeastern coast.

In the meantime, Clive began to consolidate British control in Bengal, where the local ruler had attacked Fort William and imprisoned the local British population in the infamous Black Hole of Calcutta (an underground prison for holding the prisoners, many of whom died in captivity). In 1757, a small British force numbering about three thousand defeated a Mughal-led army over ten times that size in the Battle of Plassey. As part of the spoils of victory, the

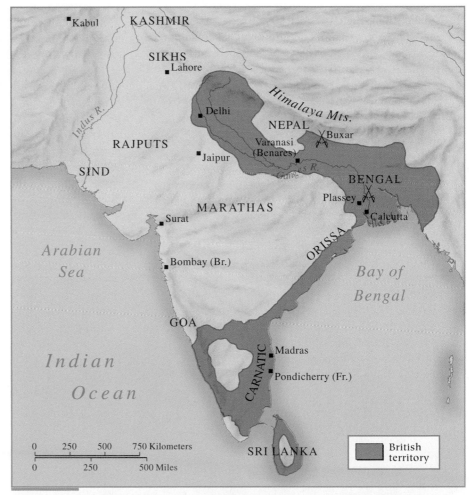

MAP 15.4 **India in 1805.** By the early nineteenth century, virtually all of the Indian subcontinent had fallen under British domination. The extent of British territory, with prominent cities and major geographic terms indicated, is shown here. ? Where was the capital of the Mughal Empire? View an animated version of this map or related maps at http://worldrc.wadsworth.com/

British officials, but it was a disaster for the Indian economy. In the first place, it resulted in the transfer of capital from the local Indian aristocracy to company officials, most of whom sent their profits back to Britain. Second, it hastened the destruction of once healthy local industries because British goods such as machine-made textiles were imported duty-free into India to compete against local products. Finally, British expansion hurt the peasants. As the British took over the administration of the land tax, they also applied British law, which allowed the lands of those unable to pay the tax to be confiscated. In the 1770s, a series of massive famines led to the death of an estimated one-third of the population in the areas under company administration. The British government attempted to resolve the problem by assigning tax lands to the local revenue collectors (*zamindars*) in the hope of transforming them into English-style rural gentry, but many collectors themselves fell into bankruptcy and sold their lands to absentee bankers while the now landless peasants remained in abject poverty. It was hardly an auspicious beginning to "civilized" British rule.

Resistance to the British As a result of such problems, Britain's rise to power in India did not go unchallenged. Astute Indian commanders avoided pitched battles with the well-armed British troops but harassed and ambushed them in the manner of guerrillas in our time. Haidar Ali, one of Britain's primary rivals for control in southern India, said:

> You will in time understand my mode of warfare. Shall I risk my cavalry which cost a thousand rupees each horse, against your cannon ball which cost two pice? No! I will march your troops until their legs swell to the size of their bodies. You shall not have a blade of grass, nor a drop of water. I will hear of you every time your drum beats, but you shall not know where I am once a month. I will give your army battle, but it must be when I please, and not when you choose.[3]

Unfortunately for India, not all its commanders were as astute as Haidar Ali. In the last years of the eighteenth century, the stage was set for the final consolidation of British rule over the subcontinent.

Society and Economy Under the Mughals

The Mughals were the last of the great traditional Indian dynasties. Like so many of their predecessors since the fall of the Guptas nearly a thousand years before, the Mughals were Muslims. But like the Ottoman Turks, the best Mughal rulers did not simply impose Islamic institutions and beliefs on a predominantly Hindu population; they combined Muslim with Hindu and even Persian concepts and cultural values in a unique social and cultural synthesis that still today seems to epitomize the greatness of Indian civilization.

The Position of Women Whether Mughal rule had much effect on the lives of ordinary Indians seems somewhat problematic. The treatment of women is a good example. Women had traditionally played an active role in Mongol tribal society—many actually fought on the battlefield alongside the men—and Babur and his successors often relied on the women in their families for political advice. Women from aristocratic families were often awarded honorific titles, received salaries, and were permitted to own land and engage in business. Women at court sometimes received an education, and aristocratic women often expressed their creative talents by writing poetry, painting, or playing music. Women of all classes were adept at spinning thread, either for their own use or

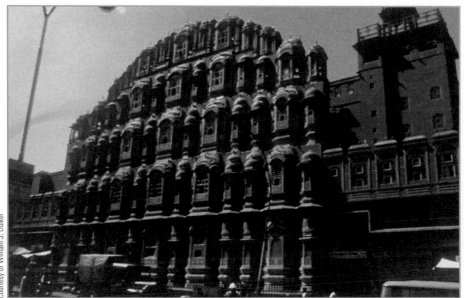

Courtesy of William J. Duiker

The Palace of the Winds at Jaipur. Built by the maharaja of Jaipur in 1799, this imposing building, part of a palace complex, is today actually only a facade. Behind the intricate pink sandstone window screens, the women of the palace were able to observe city life while at the same time remaining invisible to prying eyes. The palace, like most of the buildings in the city of Jaipur, was constructed of sandstone, a product of the nearby desert of Rajasthan.

to sell to weavers to augment the family income. They sold simple cloth to local villages and fine cottons, silks, and wool to the Mughal court. By Akbar's rule, in fact, the textile manufacturing was of such high quality and so well established that India sold cloth to much of the world: Arabia, the coast of East Africa, Egypt, Southeast Asia, and Europe.

To a certain degree, these Mughal attitudes toward women may have had an impact on Indian society. Women were allowed to inherit land, and some even possessed *zamindar* rights. Women from mercantile castes sometimes took an active role in business activities. At the same time, however, as Muslims, the Mughals subjected women to certain restrictions under Islamic law. On the whole, these Mughal practices coincided with and even accentuated existing tendencies in Indian society. The Muslim practice of isolating women and preventing them from associating with men outside the home (**purdah**) was adopted by many upper-class Hindus as a means of enhancing their status or protecting their women from unwelcome advances by Muslims in positions of authority. In other ways, Hindu practices were unaffected. The custom of *sati* continued to be practiced despite efforts by the Mughals to abolish it, and child marriage (most women were betrothed before the age of ten) remained common. Women were still instructed to obey their husbands without question and to remain chaste.

For their part, Hindus sometimes attempted to defend themselves and their religious practices against the efforts of some Mughal monarchs to impose the Islamic religion and Islamic mores on the indigenous population. In some cases, despite official prohibitions, Hindu men forcibly married Muslim women and then converted them to the native faith, while converts to Islam normally lost all of their inheritance rights within the Indian family. Government orders to destroy Hindu temples were often ignored by local officials, sometimes as the result of bribery or intimidation. Sometimes Indian practices had an influence on the Mughal elites, as many Mughal chieftains married Indian women and adopted Indian forms of dress.

The Economy   Long-term stability led to increasing commercialization and the spread of wealth to new groups within Indian society. The Mughal era saw the emergence of an affluent landed gentry and a prosperous merchant class. Members of prestigious castes from the pre-Mughal period reaped many of the benefits of the increasing wealth, but some of these changes transcended caste boundaries and led to the emergence of new groups who achieved status and wealth on the basis of economic achievement rather than traditional kinship ties. During the late eighteenth century, this economic prosperity was shaken by the decline of the Mughal Empire and the increasing European presence. But many prominent Indians reacted by establishing commercial relationships with the foreigners.

Mughal Culture

The era of the Mughals was one of synthesis in culture as well as in politics and religion. The Mughals combined Islamic themes with Persian and indigenous motifs to produce a unique style that enriched and embellished Indian art and culture. The Mughal emperors were zealous patrons of the arts and enticed painters, poets, and artisans from as far away as the Mediterranean. Apparently, the generosity of the Mughals made it difficult to refuse a trip to India. It was said that they would reward a poet with his weight in gold.

Architecture   Undoubtedly, the Mughals' most visible achievement was in architecture. Here they integrated Persian and Indian styles in a new and sometimes breathtakingly beautiful form best symbolized by the Taj Mahal, built by the emperor Shah Jahan in the mid-seventeenth century (see the comparative illustration on p. 352). Although the human and economic cost of the Taj tarnishes the romantic legend of its construction, there is no denying the beauty of the building. It had evolved from a style that originated several decades earlier with the tomb of Humayun.

Humayun's mausoleum had combined Persian and Islamic motifs in a square building finished in red sandstone and topped with a dome. The Taj brought the style to perfection. Working with a model created by his Persian architect, Shah Jahan raised the dome and replaced the red sandstone with brilliant white marble. The entire exterior and interior surface is decorated with cut-stone geometrical patterns, delicate black stone tracery, or intricate inlay of colored precious stones in floral and Qur'anic arabesques. The technique of creating dazzling floral mosaics of lapis lazuli, malachite, carnelian, turquoise, and mother of pearl may have been introduced by Italian artists at the Mughal court. Shah Jahan spent his last years imprisoned in a room in the Red Fort at Agra; from his windows, he could see the beautiful memorial to his beloved wife.

The Taj was by no means the only magnificent building erected during the Mughal era. Akbar, who, in the words of a contemporary, "[dressed] the work of his mind and heart in the garment of stone and clay," was the first of the great Mughal builders. His first palace at Agra, the Red Fort, was begun in 1565. A few years later, he ordered the construction of a new palace at Fatehpur Sikri, 26 miles west of Agra. The new palace was built in honor of a Sufi mystic who had correctly forecast the birth of a son to the emperor. In gratitude, Akbar decided to build a new capital city and palace on the site of the mystic's home in the village of Sikri. Over a period of fifteen years, from 1571 to 1586, a magnificent new city in red sandstone was constructed. Although the city was abandoned before completion and now stands almost untouched, it is a popular destination for tourists and pilgrims.

Painting   The other major artistic achievement of the Mughal period was painting. As in so many other areas of

COMPARATIVE ILLUSTRATION

The Taj Mahal: Symbol of the Exotic East.   The Taj Mahal, completed in 1653, was built by the Mughal emperor Shah Jahan as a tomb to glorify the memory of his beloved wife. Raised on a marble platform above the Jumna River, the Taj is dramatically framed by contrasting twin red sandstone mosques, magnificent gardens, and a long reflecting pool that mirrors and magnifies its beauty. The effect is one of monumental size, near blinding brilliance, and delicate lightness, a startling contrast to the heavier and more masculine Baroque style then popular in Europe. The Taj Mahal inspired many imitations, including the Royal Pavilion at Brighton, England (see inset), constructed in 1815 to commemorate the British victory over Napoleon at Waterloo. The Pavilion is a good example of the way Europeans portrayed the "exotic" East.

endeavor, painting in Mughal India resulted from the blending of two cultures. While living in exile, Emperor Humayun had learned to admire Persian miniatures. On his return to India in 1555, he invited two Persian masters to live in his palace and introduce the technique to his adopted land. His successor, Akbar, appreciated the new style and popularized it with his patronage. He established a state workshop at Fatehpur Sikri for two hundred artists, mostly Hindus, who worked under the guidance of the Persian masters to create the Mughal school of painting.

The "Akbar style" combined Persian with Indian motifs, such as the use of extended space and the portrayal of physical human action, characteristics not usually seen in Persian art. Akbar also apparently encouraged the imitation of European art forms, including the portrayal of Christian subjects, the use of perspective, lifelike portraits, and the shading of colors in the Renaissance style. The depiction of the human figure in Mughal painting outraged orthodox Muslims at court, but Akbar argued that the painter, "in sketching anything that has life . . . must come to feel that he cannot bestow individuality upon his work, and is thus forced to think of God, the Giver of Life, and will thus increase in knowledge."[4]

Literature   The development of Indian literature was held back by the absence of printing, which was not introduced until the end of the Mughal era. Literary works were inscribed by calligraphers, and one historian has estimated that the library of Agra contained more than 24,000 volumes. Poetry, in particular, flourished under the Mughals, who established poet laureates at court. Poems were written in the Persian style and in the Persian language. In fact, Persian became the official language of the court until the sack of Delhi in 1739.

Another aspect of the long Mughal reign was a Hindu revival of devotional literature, much of it dedicated to Krishna and Rama. The retelling of the Ramayana in the vernacular culminated in the sixteenth-century Hindi version by the great poet Tulsidas (1532–1623). His *Ramcaritmanas* presents the devotional story with a deified Rama and Sita. Tulsidas's genius was in combining the conflicting cults of Vishnu and Shiva into a unified and overwhelming love for the divine, which he expressed in some of the most moving of all Indian poetry. The *Ramcaritmanas* has eclipsed its two-thousand-year-old Sanskrit ancestor in popularity and even became the basis of an Indian television series in the late 1980s.

CONCLUSION

$\mathcal{T}$HE THREE EMPIRES THAT we have discussed in this chapter exhibit a number of striking similarities. First of all, they were Muslim in their religious affiliation, although the Safavids were Shi'ite rather than Sunni, a distinction that often led to mutual tensions and conflict. More important, perhaps, they were all of nomadic origin, and the political and social institutions that they adopted carried the imprint of their preimperial past. Once they achieved imperial power, however, all three ruling dynasties displayed an impressive capacity to administer a large empire and brought a degree of stability to peoples who had all too often lived in conditions of internal division and war.

Another similarity is that the mastery of the techniques of modern warfare, including the use of firearms, played a central role in all three empires' ability to overcome their rivals and rise to regional hegemony. Some scholars have therefore labeled them "gunpowder empires" in the belief that technical prowess in the art of warfare was a key element in their success. Although that is undoubtedly true, we should not forget that other factors, such as dynamic leadership, political acumen, and the possession of an ardent following motivated by religious zeal, were equally if not more important in their drive to power and ability to retain it. Weapons by themselves do not an empire make.

The rise of these powerful Muslim states coincided with the opening period of European expansion at the end of the fifteenth century and the beginning of the sixteenth. The military and political talents of these empires helped protect much of the Muslim world from the resurgent forces of Christianity. To the contrary, the Ottoman Turks carried their empire into the heart of Christian Europe and briefly reached the gates of the great city of Vienna. By the end of the eighteenth century, however, the Safavid dynasty had imploded, and the powerful Mughal Empire was in a state of virtual collapse. Only the Ottoman Empire was still functioning. Yet it too had lost much of its early expansionistic vigor and was showing signs of internal decay.

The reasons for the decline of these empires have inspired considerable debate among historians. One factor was undoubtedly the expansion of European power into the Indian Ocean and the Middle East. But internal causes were probably more important in the long run. All three empires experienced growing factionalism within the ruling elite, incompetence within the palace, and the emergence of divisive forces in the empire at large—factors that have marked the passing of traditional empires since early times. Paradoxically, one of the greatest strengths of these empires—their mastery of gunpowder—may have simultaneously been a serious weakness in that it allowed them to develop a complacent sense of security. With little incentive to turn their attention to new developments in science and technology, they were increasingly vulnerable to attack by the advanced nations of the West. The weakening of the gunpowder empires created a political vacuum into which the dynamic and competitive forces of European capitalism were quick to enter.

The gunpowder empires, however, were not the only states in the Old World that were able to resist the first outward thrust of European expansion. Farther to the east, the mature civilizations in China and Japan successfully faced a similar challenge from Western merchants and missionaries. Unlike their counterparts in South Asia and the Middle East, as the nineteenth century dawned, they continued to thrive.

CHAPTER NOTES

1. Vincent A. Smith, *The Oxford History of India* (Oxford, 1967), p. 341.
2. Quoted in Michael Edwardes, *A History of India: From the Earliest Times to the Present Day* (London, 1961), p. 188.
3. Quoted in Edwardes, *History of India*, p. 220.
4. Quoted in Roy C. Craven, *Indian Art: A Concise History* (New York, 1976), p. 205.

SUGGESTED READING

The most complete general survey of the Ottoman Empire is **S. J. Shaw, *History of the Ottoman Empire and Modern Turkey*** (Cambridge, 1976). Shaw is difficult reading but informative on administrative matters. A more readable albeit less definitive account is **Lord Kinross, *The Ottoman Centuries: The Rise and Fall of the Ottoman Empire*** (New York, 1977), which is larded with human interest stories.

For a dramatic account of the conquest of Constantinople in 1453, see **S. Runciman, *The Fall of Constantinople, 1453*** (Cambridge, 1965). The life of Mehmet II is chronicled in **F. Babinger, *Mehmed the Conqueror and His Time*,** trans. **R. Manheim** (Princeton, N.J., 1979). On Suleyman the Magnificent, see **R. Merriman, *Suleiman the Magnificent,*** 1520–1566 (Cambridge, 1944). On the Safavids, see **R. M. Savory, *Iran Under the Safavids*** (Cambridge, 1980), and **E. B. Monshi, *History of Shah Abbas the Great,*** 2 vols. (Boulder, Colo., 1978).

For an overview of the Mughal era, see **S. Wolpert, *New History of India*** (New York, 1989). Also see **J. Richards, *The Mughal Empire*** (Cambridge, 1993), part of a series entitled "The New Cambridge History of India." For a comparative look at the "gunpowder empires," see **Michael Adas,** ed., ***Islamic and European Expansion: The Forging of a Global Order*** (Philadelphia, 1993).

There are a number of specialized works on various aspects of the period. For a treatment of the Mughal era in the context of Islamic

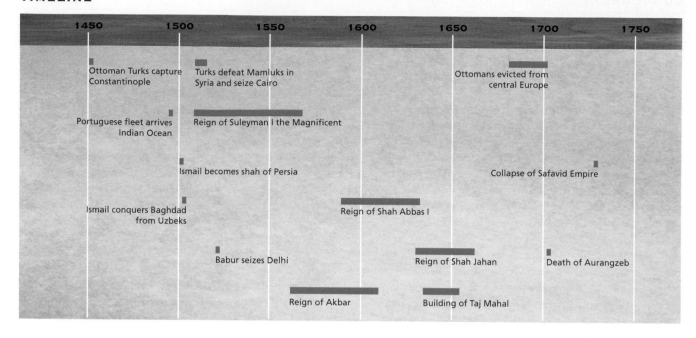

rule in India, see **S. M. Ikram**, *Muslim Civilization in India* (New York, 1964). The concept of "gunpowder empires" is persuasively analyzed in **D. E. Streusand**, *The Formation of the Mughal Empire* (Delhi, 1989). Economic issues predominate in much recent scholarship. For example, **S. Subrahmanyan**, *The Political Economy of Commerce: Southern India, 1500–1650* (Cambridge, 1990), focuses on the interaction between internal and external trade in southern India during the early stages of the period. The Mughal Empire is analyzed in a broad Central Asian context in **R. C. Foltz**, *Mughal India and Central Asia* (Karachi, 1998). Finally, **K. N. Chaudhuri**, *Trade and Civilization in the Indian Ocean: An Economic History from the Rise of Islam to 1750* (Cambridge, 1985), views Indian commerce in the perspective of the regional trade network throughout the Indian Ocean.

For treatments of all three Muslim empires in a comparative context, see **J. J. Kissling** et al., *The Last Great Muslim Empires* (Princeton, N.J., 1996), and **M. G. S. Hodgson**, *Rethinking World History: Essays on Europe, Islam, and World History* (Cambridge, 1993).

For an introduction to the women of the Ottoman Empire and those of the Mughal Empire, see **S. Hughes** and **B. Hughes**, *Women in World History,* vol. 2 (Armonk, N.Y., 1997). For a more detailed presentation of women in the imperial harem, consult **L. P. Peirce**, *The Imperial Harem: Women and Sovereignty in the Ottoman Empire* (Oxford, 1993). The fascinating story of the royal woman who played an important role behind the scenes is found in **E. B. Findly**, *Nur Jahan: Empress of Mughal India* (Oxford, 1993).

On the art of this era, see **R. C. Craven**, *Indian Art: A Concise History,* rev. ed. (New York, 1997); **J. Bloom** and **S. Blair**, *Islamic Arts* (London, 1997); **M. C. Beach**, *The Imperial Image* (Washington, D.C., 1981); **M. C. Beach** and **E. Koch**, *King of the World: The Padshahnama* (London, 1997); and **M. Hattstein** and **P. Delius**, *Islam: Art and Architecture* (Konigwinter, Germany, 2004).

InfoTrac College Edition

Visit this chapter's InfoTrac College Edition/Research activities at the *Essential World History* Companion Website for activities related to the Muslim empirer.

ThomsonNOW™ for Duiker and Spielvogel's *The Essential World History, Third Edition*

Enter *ThomsonNOW* using the access card that is available with this text. *ThomsonNOW* will assist you in understanding the content in this chapter with lesson plans generated for your needs, as well as provide you with a connection to the *Wadsworth World History Resource Center* (see description below for details).

WORLD HISTORY
RESOURCE CENTER

Enter the Resource Center using either your *ThomsonNow* access card or your standalone access card for the *Wadsworth World History Resource Center.* Organized by topic, this website includes quizzes; images; over 350 primary source documents; interactive simulations, maps, and timelines; movie explorations; and a wealth of other resources. You can read the following documents, and many more, at http://worldrc.wadsworth.com/

> Lady Mary Wortley Montagu, "Dining with the Sultana"
>
> Travels of Ibn Battuta
>
> Classical Persian Poetry

Visit the *Essential World History* Companion Website for chapter quizzes and more.

http://www.thomsonedu.com/history/duiker

DISCOVERY

What were the main characteristics of each of the Muslim empires, and in what ways did they resemble each other? How were they distinct from their European counterparts?

In thinking about this question, begin by breaking it down into the components shown below. A discussion of the significance of each component should appear in your answer.

POLITICS AND GOVERNMENT: Compare the size and scope of each of these Muslim empires over time. How did their size and population affect the types of government imposed and attitudes toward the diverse ethnic groups within each empire?

The Ottoman Empire

The Mughal Empire

The Ottoman and Safavid Empires, c. 1683

INTERACTION AND EXCHANGE: How was each of these empires eventually affected by Europeans? How does the decline of these empires correspond to the rise of European exploration?

RELIGION AND PHILOSOPHY: Both of the illustrations on the next page represent victory. How do they differ, though, in how they represent the reasons for those victories? What does this say about the societies that created them? What does this say about their faiths?

In a similar vein, what reasons does Shah Abbas give for urging the conversion of Christians to the Muslim faith? How does this compare to the treatment of Muslims in Jerusalem under the victorious Christian crusaders?

Commemorating Victory, from Mohács to Lepanto

THE CONVERSION OF A NUMBER OF CHRISTIANS TO ISLAM

This year the Shah decreed that those Armenians and other Christians who had been settled in [the southern Caucasus] and had been given agricultural land there should be invited to become Muslims. Life in this world is fraught with vicissitudes, and the Shah was concerned lest, in a period when the authority of the central government was weak, these Christians . . . might be subjected to attack by the neighboring Lor tribes (who are naturally given to causing injury and mischief), and their women and children carried off into captivity. In the areas in which these Christian groups resided, it was the Shah's purpose that the places of worship which they had built should become mosques, and the muezzin's call should be heard in them, so that these Christians might assume the guise of Muslims, and their future status accordingly be assured. . . .

Some of the Christians, guided by God's grace, embraced Islam voluntarily; others found it difficult to abandon their Christian faith and felt revulsion at the idea. They were encouraged by their monks and priests to remain steadfast in their faith. After a little pressure had been applied to the monks and priests, however, they desisted, and these Christians saw no alternative but to embrace Islam, though they did so with reluctance. The women and children embraced Islam with great enthusiasm, vying with one another in their eagerness to abandon their Christian faith and declare their belief in the unity of God. Some five thousand people embraced Islam. As each group made the Muslim declaration of faith, it received instruction in the Koran and the principles of the religious law of Islam, and all bibles and other Christian devotional material were collected and taken away from the priests.

In the same way, all the Armenian Christians who had been moved to [the area] were also forcibly converted to Islam. . . . Most people embraced Islam with sincerity, but some felt an aversion to making the Muslim profession of faith. True knowledge lies with God! May God reward the Shah for his action with long life and prosperity!

THE SIEGE OF JERUSALEM: CHRISTIAN AND MUSLIM PERSPECTIVES

Fulcher of Chartres, *Chronicle of the First Crusade*

Then the Franks entered the city magnificently at the noonday hour on Friday, the day of the week when Christ redeemed the whole world on the cross. With trumpets sounding and with everything in an uproar, exclaiming: "Help, God!" they vigorously pushed into the city, and straightaway raised the banner on the top of the wall. All the heathen, completely terrified, changed their boldness to swift flight through the narrow streets of the quarters. The more quickly they fled, the more quickly they were put to flight.

Count Raymond and his men, who were bravely assailing the city in another section, did not perceive this until they saw the Saracens [Muslims] jumping from the top of the wall. Seeing this, they joyfully ran to the city as quickly as they could, and helped the others pursue and kill the wicked enemy.

Then some, both Arabs and Ethiopians, fled into the Tower of David; others shut themselves in the Temple of the Lord and of Solomon, where in the halls a very great attack was made on them. Nowhere was there a place where the Saracens could escape swordsmen.

On the top of Solomon's Temple, to which they had climbed in fleeing, many were shot to death with arrows and cast down headlong from the roof. Within this Temple, about ten thousand were beheaded. If you had been there, your feet would have been stained up to the ankles with the blood of the slain. What more shall I tell? Not one of them was allowed to live. They did not spare the women and children.

Account of Ibn al-Athir

In fact Jerusalem was taken from the north on the morning of Friday 22 Sha'ban 492/15 July 1099. The population was put to the sword by the Franks, who pillaged the area for a week. A band of Muslims barricaded themselves into the Oratory of David and fought on for several days. They were granted their lives in return for surrendering. The Franks honored their word, and the group left by night for Ascalon. In the Masjid al-Aqsa the Franks slaughtered more than 70,000 people, among them a large number of Imams and Muslim scholars, devout and ascetic men who had left their homelands to live lives of pious seclusion in the Holy Place. The Franks stripped the Dome of the Rock of more than forty silver candelabra, each of them weighing 3,600 drams, and a great silver lamp weighing forty-four Syrian pounds, as well as a hundred and fifty smaller candelabra and more than twenty gold ones, and a great deal more booty. Refugees from Syria reached Baghdad in Ramadan, among them the qadi Abu sa'd al-Harawi. They told the Caliph's ministers a story that wrung their hearts and brought tears to their eyes. On Friday they went to the Cathedral Mosque and begged for help, weeping so that their hearers wept with them as they described the sufferings of the Muslims in the Holy City: the men killed, the women and children taken prisoner, the homes pillaged. Because of the terrible hardships they had suffered, they were allowed to break the fast.

16

THE EAST ASIAN WORLD

CHAPTER OUTLINE
AND FOCUS QUESTIONS

China at Its Apex

▢ Why were the Manchus so successful at establishing a foreign dynasty in China, and what were the main characteristics of Manchu rule?

Changing China

▢ How did the economy and society change during the Ming and Qing eras, and to what degree did these changes seem to be leading toward an industrial revolution on the European model?

Tokugawa Japan

▢ How did the society and economy of Japan change during the Tokugawa era, and how did Japanese culture reflect those changes?

Korea: The Hermit Kingdom

▢ To what degree did developments in Korea during this period reflect conditions in China and Japan? What were the most unique aspects of Korean civilization?

CRITICAL THINKING

▢ How did China and Japan respond to the coming of the Europeans, and what explains the differences? What impact did European contacts have on these two East Asian civilizations through the end of the eighteenth century?

Emperor Kangxi

© Pierre Colombel/CORBIS

*I*N DECEMBER 1717, Emperor Kangxi returned from a hunting trip north of the Great Wall and began to suffer from dizzy spells. Conscious of his approaching date with mortality—he was now nearly seventy years of age—the emperor called together his sons and leading government officials in the imperial palace and issued an edict summing up his ideas on the art of statecraft. Rulers, he declared, should be sincere in their reverence for Heaven's laws as the fundamental strategy for governing the country. Among those laws were the following: show concern for the welfare of the people, practice diligence, protect the state from its enemies, choose able advisers, and strike a careful balance between leniency and strictness, principle and expedience. That, he concluded, was all there was to it.[1]

Any potential successor to the throne would have been well advised to attend to the emperor's advice. Kangxi was not only one of the longest reigning of all Chinese rulers but also one of the wisest. His era was one of peace and prosperity, and after half a century of rule, the empire was now at the zenith of its power and influence. As his life approached its end, Heaven must indeed have been pleased at the quality of his stewardship.

As for the emperor's edict, it clearly reflected the genius of Confucian teachings at their best and has a timeless quality that applies to our age as well as to the Golden Age of the Qing dynasty.

Kangxi reigned during one of the most glorious eras in the long history of China. Under the Ming (1369–1644) and the early Qing (1644–1911) dynasties, the empire expanded its borders to a degree not seen since the Han and the Tang. Chinese culture was the envy of its neighbors and earned the admiration of many European visitors, including Jesuit priests and Enlightenment philosophes.

On the surface, China appeared to be an unchanging society patterned after the Confucian vision of a "golden age" in the remote past. This indeed was the image presented by China's rulers, who referred constantly to tradition as a model for imperial institutions and cultural values. Although few observers could have been aware of it at the time, however, China was changing—and rather rapidly.

A similar process was under way in neighboring Japan. A vigorous new shogunate called the Tokugawa rose to power in the early seventeenth century and managed to revitalize the traditional system in a somewhat more centralized form that enabled it to survive for another 250 years. But major structural changes were taking place in Japanese society, and by the nineteenth century, tensions were growing as the gap between theory and reality widened.

One of the many factors involved in the quickening pace of change in both countries was contact with the West, which began with the arrival of Portuguese ships in Chinese and Japanese ports in the first half of the sixteenth century. The Ming and the Tokugawa initially opened their doors to European trade and missionary activity. Later, however, Chinese and Japanese rulers became concerned about the corrosive effects of Western ideas and practices and attempted to protect their traditional societies from external intrusion. But neither could forever resist the importunities of Western trading nations, and when the doors to the West were finally reopened in the mid-nineteenth century, both societies were ripe for radical change. ◆

China at Its Apex

In 1514, a Portuguese fleet dropped anchor off the coast of China, just south of the Pearl River estuary and present-day Hong Kong. It was the first direct contact between the Chinese Empire and the West since the arrival of the Venetian adventurer Marco Polo two centuries earlier, and it opened an era that would eventually change the face of China and, indeed, all the world.

From the Ming to the Qing

Marco Polo had reported on the magnificence of China after visiting Beijing during the reign of Khubilai Khan, the great Mongol ruler. By the time the Portuguese fleet arrived off the coast of China, of course, the Mongol Empire had long since disappeared. It had gradually weakened after the death of Khubilai Khan and was finally overthrown in 1368 by a massive peasant rebellion under the leadership of Zhu Yuanzhang, who had declared himself the founding emperor of a new Ming (Bright) dynasty and assumed the reign title of Ming Hongwu (Ming Hung Wu, or Ming Martial Emperor).

As we have seen, the Ming inaugurated a period of territorial expansion westward into Central Asia and southward into Vietnam while consolidating control over China's vast heartland. At the same time, between 1405 and 1433 the dynasty sponsored a series of voyages under Admiral Zhenghe that spread Chinese influence far into the Indian Ocean. Then suddenly the voyages were discontinued, and the dynasty turned its attention to domestic concerns (see Chapter 10).

First Contacts with the West Despite the Ming's retreat from active participation in maritime trade, when the Portuguese arrived in 1514, China was in command of a vast empire that stretched from the steppes of Central Asia to the China Sea, from the Gobi Desert to the tropical rain forests of Southeast Asia. From the lofty perspective of the imperial throne in Beijing, the Europeans could only have seemed like an unusually exotic form of barbarian to be placed within the familiar framework of the tributary system, the hierarchical arrangement in which rulers of all other countries were regarded as "younger brothers" of the Son of Heaven. Indeed, the bellicose and uncultured behavior of the Portuguese so outraged Chinese officials that they expelled the Europeans, but after further negotiations, the Portuguese were permitted to occupy the tiny territory of Macao, a foothold they would retain until the end of the twentieth century.

Initially, the arrival of the Europeans did not have much impact on Chinese society. Direct trade between Europe and China was limited, and Portuguese ships became involved in the regional trade network, carrying silk to Japan in return for Japanese silver. Eventually, the Spanish also began to participate, using the Philippines as an anchor in the galleon trade between China and the great silver mines in the Americas.

More influential than trade, perhaps, were the ideas introduced by Christian missionaries. Among the most active and the most effective were highly educated Jesuits, who were familiar with European philosophical and scientific developments. Recognizing the Chinese pride in their own culture, the Jesuits attempted to draw parallels between Christian and Confucian concepts (for example, they identified the Western concept of God with the Chinese character for Heaven) and to show the similarities between Christian morality and Confucian ethics. European inventions such as the clock, the prism, and various astronomical and musical instruments impressed Chinese officials, hitherto deeply imbued with a sense of the superiority of Chinese civilization, and helped Western

THE ART OF PRINTING

ARTS & IDEAS

Europeans obtained much of their early information about China from the Jesuits who served at the Ming court in the sixteenth and seventeenth centuries. Clerics such as the Italian Matteo Ricci (1552–1610) found much to admire in Chinese civilization. Here Ricci expresses a keen interest in Chinese printing methods, which at that time were well in advance of the techniques used in the West. Later Christian missionaries expressed strong interest in Confucian philosophy and Chinese ideas of statecraft.

How did the Chinese method of printing differ from that developed in Europe at that time? What were its advantages?

Matteo Ricci, *The Diary of Matthew Ricci*

The art of printing was practiced in China at a date somewhat earlier than that assigned to the beginning of printing in Europe, which was about 1405. It is quite certain that the Chinese knew the art of printing at least five centuries ago, and some of them assert that printing was known to their people before the beginning of the Christian era, about 50 B.C.E. Their method of printing differs widely from that employed in Europe, and our method would be quite impracticable for them because of the exceedingly large number of Chinese characters and symbols. . . .

Their method of making printed books is quite ingenious. The text is written in ink, with a brush made of very fine hair, on a sheet of paper which is inverted and pasted on a wooden tablet. When the paper has become thoroughly dry, its surface is scraped off quickly and with great skill, until nothing but a fine tissue bearing the characters remains on the wooden tablet. Then, with a steel graver, the workman cuts away the surface following the outlines of the characters until these alone stand out in low relief. From such a block a skilled printer can make copies with incredible speed, turning out as many as fifteen hundred copies in a single day. . . . This scheme of engraving wooden blocks is well adapted for the large and complex nature of the Chinese characters, but I do not think it would lend itself very aptly to our European type, which could hardly be engraved upon wood because of its small dimensions.

Their method of printing has one decided advantage, namely, that once these tablets are made, they can be preserved and used for making changes in the text as often as one wishes. Additions and subtractions can also be made as the tablets can be readily patched. . . . We have derived great benefit from this method of Chinese printing, as we employ the domestic help in our homes to strike off copies of the books on religious and scientific subjects which we translate into Chinese from the languages in which they were written originally. In truth, the whole method is so simple that one is tempted to try it for himself after once having watched the process. The simplicity of Chinese printing is what accounts for the exceedingly large numbers of books in circulation here and the ridiculously low prices at which they are sold.

ThomsonNOW To read a memorial to Matteo Ricci, enter the *ThomsonNOW* documents area using the access card that is available for *The Essential World History*.

---

ideas win acceptance at court. An elderly Chinese scholar expressed his wonder at the miracle of eyeglasses:

> *White glass from across the Western Seas*
> *Is imported through Macao:*
> *Fashioned into lenses big as coins,*
> *They encompass the eyes in a double frame.*
> *I put them on—it suddenly becomes clear;*
> *I can see the very tips of things!*
> *And read fine print by the dim-lit window*
> *Just like in my youth.[2]*

For their part, the missionaries were much impressed with many aspects of Chinese civilization, and reports of their experiences heightened European curiosity about this great society on the other side of the world (see the box above).

The Ming Brought to Earth During the late sixteenth century, the Ming began to decline as a series of weak rulers led to an era of corruption, concentration of landownership, and ultimately peasant rebellions and tribal unrest along the northern frontier. The inflow of vast amounts of foreign silver led to an alarming increase in inflation. Then the arrival of the English and the Dutch disrupted the silver trade; silver imports plummeted, severely straining the Chinese economy by raising the value of the metal relative to that of copper. Crop yields declined due to harsh weather, and the resulting scarcity reduced the ability of the government to provide food in times of imminent starvation. High taxes, provoked in part by increased official corruption, led to peasant unrest and worker violence in urban areas.

As always, internal problems were accompanied by unrest along the northern frontier. Following long precedent, the Ming had attempted to pacify the frontier tribes by forging alliances with them and granting trade privileges. One of the alliances was with the Manchus (also known as the Jurchen), the descendants of peoples who had briefly established a kingdom in northern China during the early thirteenth century. The Manchus, a mixed agricultural and hunting people, lived northeast of the Great Wall in the area known today as Manchuria.

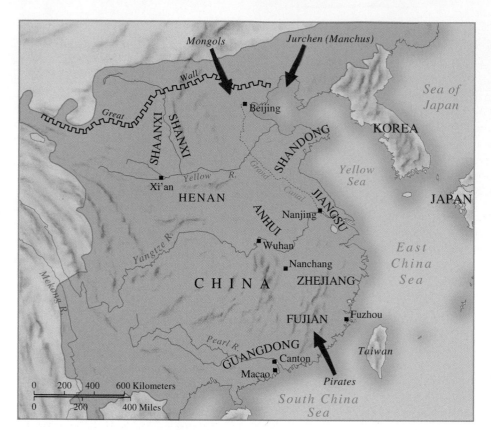

MAP 16.1 **China and Its Enemies During the Late Ming Era.** During the seventeenth century, the Ming dynasty faced challenges on two fronts, from China's traditional adversaries— nomadic groups north of the Great Wall—and from new arrivals— European merchants—who had begun to press for trading privileges along the southern coast. **?** How did these threats differ from those faced by previous dynasties in China?

At first, the Manchus were satisfied with consolidating their territory and made little effort to extend their rule south of the Great Wall. But during the first decades of the seventeenth century, a major epidemic devastated the population in many areas of the country. The suffering brought on by the epidemic helped spark a vast peasant revolt led by Li Zicheng (Li Tzu-ch'eng, 1604–1651), a postal worker in central China who had been dismissed from his job as part of a cost-saving measure by the imperial court. In the 1630s, Li managed to extend the revolt throughout the country and finally occupied the capital of Beijing in 1644. The last Ming emperor committed suicide by hanging himself from a tree in the palace gardens.

But Li was unable to hold his conquest. The overthrow of the Ming dynasty presented a great temptation to the Manchus. With the assistance of many military commanders who had deserted from the Ming, they conquered Beijing on their own (see Map 16.1). Li Zicheng's army disintegrated, and the Manchus declared the creation of a new dynasty with the reign title of the Qing (Ch'ing, or Pure). Once again, China was under foreign rule.

The Greatness of the Qing

The accession of the Manchus to power in Beijing was not universally applauded. Some Ming loyalists fled to Southeast Asia, but others continued their resistance to the new rulers from inside the country. To make it easier to identify the rebels, the government ordered all Chinese to adopt Manchu dress and hairstyles. All Chinese males were

to shave their foreheads and braid their hair into a queue; those who refused were to be executed. As a popular saying put it, "Lose your hair or lose your head."[3]

But the Manchus eventually proved to be more adept at adapting to Chinese conditions than their predecessors, the Mongols. Unlike the latter, who had tried to impose their own methods of ruling, the Manchus adopted the Chinese political system (although, as we shall see, they retained their distinct position within it) and were gradually accepted by most Chinese as the legitimate rulers of the country.

Like all of China's great dynasties, the Qing was blessed with a series of strong early rulers who pacified the country, rectified many of the most obvious social and economic inequities, and restored peace and prosperity. For the Ming dynasty, these strong emperors had been Hongwu and Yongle; under the Qing, they would be Kangxi (K'ang Hsi) and Qianlong (Ch'ien Lung). The two Qing monarchs ruled China for well over a century, from the middle of the seventeenth century to the end of the eighteenth, and were responsible for much of the greatness of Manchu China.

The Reign of Kangxi Kangxi (1661–1722) was arguably the greatest ruler in Chinese history. Ascending to the throne at the age of seven, he was blessed with diligence, political astuteness, and a strong character and began to take charge of Qing administration while still an adolescent. During the six decades of his reign, Kangxi not only stabilized imperial rule by pacifying the restive peoples along the northern and western frontiers but also managed to make the dynasty acceptable to the general population. As an ordering all missionaries and converts to conform to the official orthodoxy set forth in Europe. At first, Kangxi attempted to resolve the problem by appealing directly to the Vatican, but the pope was uncompromising. After Kangxi's death, his successor began to suppress Christian activities throughout China.

The Reign of Qianlong   Kangxi's achievements were carried on by his successors, Yongzheng (Yung Cheng, 1722–1736) and Qianlong (1736–1795). Like Kangxi, Qianlong was known for his diligence, tolerance, and intellectual curiosity, and he too combined vigorous military action against the unruly tribes along the frontier with active efforts to promote economic prosperity, administrative efficiency, and scholarship and artistic excellence. The result was continued growth for the Manchu Empire throughout much of the eighteenth century.

But it was also under Qianlong that the first signs of the internal decay of the Manchu dynasty began to appear. The clues were familiar ones. Qing military campaigns along the frontier were expensive and placed heavy demands on the imperial treasury. As the emperor aged, he became less astute in selecting his subordinates and fell under the influence of corrupt elements at court.

Corruption at the center led inevitably to unrest in rural areas, where higher taxes, bureaucratic venality, and rising pressure on the land because of the growing population had produced economic hardship. The heart of the unrest was in central China, where discontented peasants who had recently been settled on infertile land launched a revolt known as the White Lotus Rebellion (1796–1804). The revolt was eventually suppressed but at great expense.

Qing Politics   One reason for the success of the Manchus was their ability to adapt to their new environment. They retained the Ming political system with relatively few changes. They also tried to establish their legitimacy as China's rightful rulers by stressing their devotion to the principles of Confucianism. Emperor Kangxi ostentatiously studied the sacred Confucian classics and issued a "sacred edict" that proclaimed to the entire empire the importance of the moral values established by the master (see the box on p. 371).

Still, the Manchus, like the Mongols, were ethnically, linguistically, and culturally distinct from their subject population. The Qing attempted to cope with this reality by adopting a two-pronged strategy. On the one hand, the Manchus, representing less than 2 percent of the entire population, were legally defined as distinct from everyone else in China. The Manchu nobles retained their aristocratic privileges, while their economic base was protected by extensive

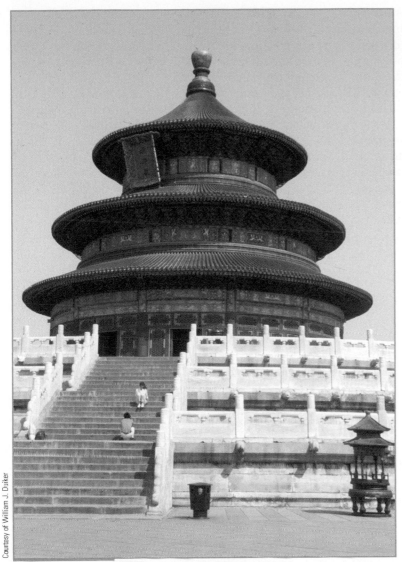

The Temple of Heaven.   This temple, located in the capital city of Beijing, is one of the most important historical structures in China. Built in 1420 at the order of the Ming emperor Yongle, it served as the location for the emperor's annual ceremony appealing to Heaven for a good harvest. As a symbol of their efforts to continue the imperial traditions, the Manchu emperors embraced the practice as well. Yongle's temple burned to the ground in 1889 but was immediately rebuilt according to the original design.

active patron of arts and letters, he cultivated the support of scholars through a number of major projects.

During Kangxi's reign, the activities of the Western missionaries, Dominicans and Franciscans as well as Jesuits, reached their height. The emperor was quite tolerant of the Christians, and several Jesuit missionaries became influential at court. Several hundred court officials converted to Christianity, as did an estimated 300,000 ordinary Chinese. But the Christian effort was ultimately undermined by squabbling among the Western religious orders over the Jesuit policy of accommodating local beliefs and practices in order to facilitate conversion. Jealous Dominicans and Franciscans complained to the pope, who issued an edict landholdings and revenues provided from the state treasury. Other Manchus were assigned farmland and organized into military units, called **banners**, which were stationed as separate units in various strategic positions throughout China. These "bannermen" were the primary fighting force of the empire. Ethnic Chinese were prohibited from settling in Manchuria and were still compelled to wear their hair in a queue as a sign of submission to the ruling dynasty.

But while the Qing attempted to protect their distinct identity within an alien society, they also recognized the need to bring ethnic Chinese into the top ranks of imperial administration. Their solution was to create a system, known as **dyarchy**, in which all important administrative positions were shared equally by Chinese and Manchus. Meanwhile, the Manchus themselves, despite official efforts to preserve their separate language and culture, were increasingly assimilated into Chinese civilization.

China on the Eve of the Western Onslaught Unfortunately for China, the decline of the Qing dynasty occurred just as China's modest relationship with the West was about to give way to a new era of military confrontation and increased pressure for trade. The first problems came in the north, where Russian traders seeking skins and furs began to penetrate the region between Siberian Russia and Manchuria. Earlier the Ming dynasty had attempted to deal with the Russians by the traditional method of placing them in a tributary relationship. But the tsar refused to play by Chinese rules. His envoys to Beijing ignored the tribute system and refused to perform the kowtow (the ritual of prostration and knocking the head on the ground performed by foreign emissaries before the emperor), the classic symbol of fealty demanded of all foreign ambassadors to the Chinese court. Formal diplomatic relations were finally established in 1689, when the Treaty of Nerchinsk settled the boundary dispute and provided for regular trade between the two countries. Through such arrangements, the Manchus were able not only to pacify the northern frontier but also to extend their rule over Xinjiang and Tibet to the west and southwest (see Map 16.2).

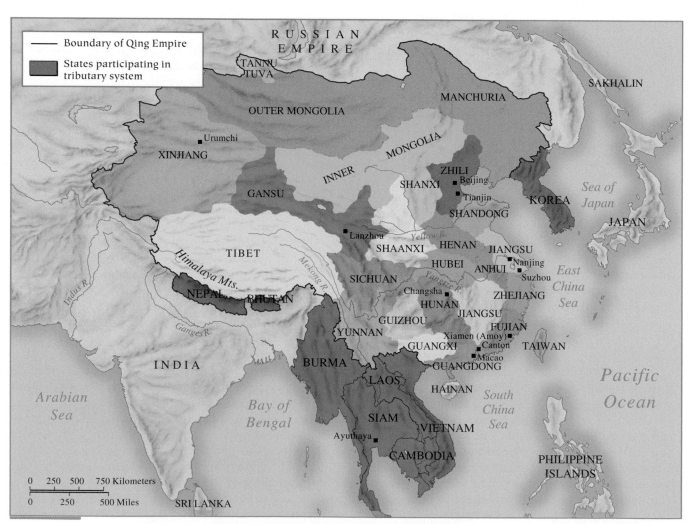

MAP 16.2 **The Qing Empire in the Eighteenth Century.** The boundaries of the Chinese Empire at the height of the Qing dynasty in the eighteenth century are shown on this map. ❓ What areas were linked in tributary status to the Chinese Empire, and how did they benefit the empire?

🐾 View an animated version of this map or related maps at http://worldrc.wadsworth.com/

The European Warehouses at Canton. Aggravated by the growing presence of foreigners in the eighteenth century, the Chinese court severely restricted the movement of European traders in China. They were permitted to live only in a compound near Canton during the seven months of the trading season and could go into the city only three times a month. In this painting, the Dutch and British flags fly over the warehouses and residences of the foreign community, while Chinese sampans and junks sit anchored in the river.

Canton in the Eighteenth Century

Dealing with the foreigners who arrived by sea was more difficult. By the end of the seventeenth century, the English had replaced the Portuguese as the dominant force in European trade. Operating through the East India Company, which served as both a trading unit and the administrator of English territories in Asia, the English established their first trading post at Canton in 1699. Over the next decades, trade with China, notably the export of tea and silk to England, increased rapidly. To limit contact between Chinese and Europeans, the Qing licensed Chinese trading firms at Canton to be the exclusive conduit for trade with the West. Eventually, the Qing confined the Europeans to a small island just outside the city wall and permitted them to reside there only from October through March.

For a while, the British tolerated this system, but by the end of the eighteenth century, the British government became restive at the uneven balance of trade between the two countries, which forced the British to ship vast amounts of silver bullion to China in exchange for its silks, porcelains, and teas. In 1793, a mission under Lord Macartney visited Beijing to press for liberalization of trade restrictions. A compromise was reached on the kowtow (Macartney was permitted to bend on one knee as was

the British custom), but Qianlong expressed no interest in British manufactured products (see the box on p. 362). An exasperated Macartney compared the Chinese Empire to "an old, crazy, first-rate man-of-war" that had once awed its neighbors "merely by her bulk and appearance" but was now destined under incompetent leadership to be "dashed to pieces on the shore."[4] With his contemptuous dismissal of the British request, the emperor had inadvertently sowed the seeds for a century of humiliation.

Changing China

During the Ming and Qing dynasties, China remained a predominantly agricultural society; nearly 85 percent of its people were farmers. But although most Chinese still lived in rural villages, the economy was undergoing a number of changes.

THE TRIBUTE SYSTEM IN ACTION

INTERACTION & EXCHANGE

In 1793, the British emissary Lord Macartney visited the Qing Empire to request the opening of formal diplomatic and trading relations between his country and China. Emperor Qianlong's reply, addressed to King George III of Britain, illustrates how the imperial court in Beijing viewed the world. King George could not have been pleased. The document provides a good example of the complacency with which the Celestial Empire viewed the world beyond its borders.

What reasons does the emperor give for refusing Macartney's request to have a permanent British ambassador in Beijing? How does the tribute system differ from the principles of international relations as practiced in the West?

A Decree of Emperor Qianlong

An Imperial Edict to the King of England: You, O King, are so inclined toward our civilization that you have sent a special envoy across the seas to bring to our Court your memorial of congratulations on the occasion of my birthday and to present your native products as an expression of your thoughtfulness. On perusing your memorial, so simply worded and sincerely conceived, I am impressed by your genuine respectfulness and friendliness and greatly pleased.

As to the request made in your memorial, O King, to send one of your nationals to stay at the Celestial Court to take care of your country's trade with China, this is not in harmony with the state system of our dynasty and will definitely not be permitted. Traditionally people of the European nations who wished to render some service under the Celestial Court have been permitted to come to the capital. But after their arrival they are obliged to wear Chinese court costumes, are placed in a certain residence, and are never allowed to return to their own countries. This is the established rule of the Celestial Dynasty with which presumably you, O King, are familiar. Now you, O King, wish to send one of your nationals to live in the capital, but he is not like the Europeans who come to Peking as Chinese employees, live there, and never return home again, nor can he be allowed to go and come and maintain any correspondence. This is indeed a useless undertaking.

Moreover the territory under the control of the Celestial Court is very large and wide. There are well-established regulations governing tributary envoys from the outer states to Peking [Beijing], giving them provisions (of food and traveling expenses) by our post-houses and limiting their going and coming. There has never been a precedent for letting them do whatever they like. Now if you, O King, wish to have a representative in Peking, his language will be unintelligible and his dress different from the regulations; there is no place to accommodate him. . . .

The Celestial Court has pacified and possessed the territory within the four seas. Its sole aim is to do its utmost to achieve good government and to manage political affairs, attaching no value to strange jewels and precious objects. The various articles presented by you, O King, this time are accepted by my special order to the office in charge of such functions in consideration of the offerings having come from a long distance with sincere good wishes. As a matter of fact, the virtue and prestige of the Celestial Dynasty having spread far and wide, the kings of the myriad nations come by land and sea with all sorts of precious things. Consequently there is nothing we lack, as your principal envoy and others have themselves observed. We have never set much store on strange or ingenious objects, nor do we need any more of your country's manufactures. . . .

ThomsonNOW To read more about Macartney's mission, enter the *ThomsonNOW* documents area using the access card that is available for *The Essential World History.*

The Population Explosion

In the first place, the center of gravity was continuing to shift steadily from the north to the south. In the early centuries of Chinese civilization, the administrative and economic center of gravity was clearly in the north. By the early Qing, the economic breadbasket of China was located along the Yangtze River and regions to the south. One concrete indication of this shift occurred during the Ming dynasty, when Emperor Yongle ordered the renovation of the Grand Canal to facilitate the shipment of rice from the Yangtze delta to the food-starved north.

Moreover, the population was beginning to increase rapidly (see the comparative essay "Population Explosion" on p. 363). For centuries, China's population had remained within a range of 50 to 100 million, rising in times of peace and prosperity and falling in periods of foreign invasion and internal anarchy. During the Ming and the early Qing, however, the population increased from an estimated 70 to 80 million in 1390 to over 300 million at the end of the eighteenth century. There were probably several reasons for this population increase: the relatively long period of peace and stability under the early Qing; the introduction of new crops from the Americas, including peanuts, sweet potatoes, and maize; and the planting of a new species of faster-growing rice from Southeast Asia.

Of course, this population increase meant much greater population pressure on the land, smaller farms, and a razor-thin margin of safety in case of climatic disaster. The imperial court attempted to deal with the problem through a variety of means, most notably by preventing the concentration of land in the hands of wealthy landowners. Nevertheless, by the eighteenth century, almost all the land

THE POPULATION EXPLOSION

EARTH & ENVIRONMENT

Between 1700 and 1800, Europe, China, and to a lesser degree India and the Ottoman Empire experienced a dramatic growth in population. In Europe, the population grew from 120 million people to almost 200 million by 1800; China, from less than 200 million to 300 million during the same period.

Four factors were important in causing this population explosion. First, better growing conditions, made possible by an improvement in climate, affected wide areas of the world and enabled people to produce more food. Summers in both China and Europe were warmer beginning in the early eighteenth century. Second, by the eighteenth century, people had begun to develop immunities to the epidemic diseases that had caused such widespread loss of life between 1500 and 1700. The spread of people by ship after 1500 had led to devastating epidemics. For example, the arrival of Europeans in Mexico led to smallpox, measles, and chicken pox among a native population that had no immunities to European diseases. In 1500, between 11 and 20 million people lived in the area of Mexico; by 1650, only 1.5 million remained. Gradually, however, people developed immunities to these diseases.

Festival of the Yam. The spread of a few major food crops made possible new sources of nutrition to feed more people. The importance of the yam to the Ashanti people of West Africa is evident in this celebration of a yam festival at harvest time in 1817.

© The Art Archive/Eileen Tweedy

A third factor in the population increase came from new food sources. As a result of the Columbian exchange (see the box on p. 297) American food crops—such as corn, potatoes, and sweet potatoes—were brought to other parts of the world, where they became important food sources. China had imported a new species of rice from Southeast Asia that had a shorter harvest cycle than that of existing varieties. These new foods provided additional sources of nutrition that enabled more people to live for a longer time. At the same time, land development and canal building in the eighteenth century also enabled government authorities to move food supplies to areas threatened with crop failure and famine.

Finally, the use of new weapons based on gunpowder allowed states to control larger territories and ensure a new degree of order. The early rulers of the Qing dynasty, for example, pacified the Chinese Empire and ensured a long period of peace and stability. Absolute monarchs achieved similar goals in a number of European states. Thus, less violence led to fewer deaths at the same time that an increase in food supplies and a decrease in deaths from diseases were occurring, thus making possible in the eighteenth century the beginning of the world population explosion that persists to this day.

that could be irrigated was already under cultivation, and the problems of rural hunger and landlessness became increasingly serious.

Seeds of Industrialization

Another change that took place during the early modern period in China was the steady growth of manufacturing and commerce. Taking advantage of the long era of peace and prosperity, merchants and manufacturers began to expand their operations beyond their immediate provinces. Commercial networks began to operate on a regional and sometimes even a national basis, as trade in silk, metal and wood products, porcelain, cotton goods, and cash crops like cotton and tobacco developed rapidly. Foreign trade also expanded as Chinese merchants set up extensive contacts with countries in Southeast Asia.

Although this rise in industrial and commercial activity resembles the changes occurring in western Europe, China and Europe differed in several key ways. In the first place, members of the bourgeoisie in China were not as independent as their European counterparts. In China, trade and manufacturing remained under the firm control of the state. In addition, political and social prejudices against commercial activity remained strong. Reflecting an ancient preference for agriculture over manufacturing and trade, the state levied heavy taxes on manufacturing and commerce while attempting to keep agricultural taxes low.

One of the consequences of these differences was a growing technological gap between China and Europe. The Chinese reaction to European clockmaking techniques provides an example. In the early seventeenth century, the Jesuit Matteo Ricci introduced advanced

Rise of Ming dynasty	1369
Voyages of Zhenghe	1405–1433
Portuguese arrive in southern China	1514
Matteo Ricci arrives in China	1601
Li Zicheng occupies Beijing	1644
Manchus seize China	1644
Reign of Kangxi	1661–1722
Treaty of Nerchinsk	1689
First English trading post at Canton	1699
Reign of Qianlong	1736–1793
Lord Macartney's mission to China	1793
White Lotus Rebellion	1796–1804

European clocks driven by weights or springs. The emperor was fascinated and found the clocks more reliable than Chinese methods of keeping time. Over the next decades, European timepieces became a popular novelty at court, but the Chinese expressed little curiosity about the technology involved, provoking one European to remark that playthings like cuckoo clocks "will be received here with much greater interest than scientific instruments or *objets d'art.*"[5]

Daily Life in Qing China

Daily life under the Ming and early Qing dynasties continued to follow traditional patterns. As in earlier periods, Chinese society was organized around the family. The ideal family unit in Qing China was the joint family, in which as many as three or even four generations lived under the same roof. When sons married, they brought their wives to live with them in the family homestead. Unmarried daughters would also remain in the house. Aging parents and grandparents remained under the same roof and were cared for by younger members of the household until they died. This ideal did not always correspond to reality, however, since many families did not possess sufficient land to support a large household.

The Family   The family continued to be important in early Qing times for much the same reasons as in earlier times. As a labor-intensive society based primarily on the cultivation of rice, China needed large families to help with the harvest and to provide security for parents too old to work in the fields. Sons were particularly prized, not only because they had strong backs but also because they would raise their own families under the parental roof. With few opportunities for employment outside the family, sons had little choice but to remain with their parents and help on the land. Within the family, the oldest male was king, and his wishes theoretically had to be obeyed by all family members. Marriages were normally

arranged for the benefit of the family, often by a go-between, and the groom and bride were usually not consulted. Frequently, they did not meet until the marriage ceremony. Under such conditions, love was clearly a secondary consideration. In fact, it was often viewed as detrimental since it inevitably distracted the attention of the husband and wife from their primary responsibility to the larger family unit.

Although this emphasis on filial piety might seem to represent a blatant disregard for individual rights, the obligations were not all on the side of the children. The father was expected to provide support for his wife and children and, like the ruler, was supposed to treat those in his care with respect and compassion. All too often, however, the male head of the family was able to exact his privileges without performing his responsibilities in return.

Beyond the joint family was the clan. Sometimes called a lineage, a clan was an extended kinship unit consisting of dozens or even hundreds of joint and nuclear families linked together by a clan council of elders and a variety of other common social and religious functions. The clan served a number of useful purposes. Some clans possessed lands that could be rented out to poorer families, or richer families within the clan might provide land for the poor. Since there was no general state-supported educational system, sons of poor families might be invited to study in a school established in the home of a more prosperous relative. If the young man succeeded in becoming an official, he would be expected to provide favors and prestige for the clan as a whole.

The Role of Women   In traditional China, the role of women had always been inferior to that of men. A sixteenth-century Spanish visitor to South China observed that Chinese women were "very secluded and virtuous, and it was a very rare thing for us to see a woman in the cities and large towns, unless it was an old crone." Women were more visible, he said, in rural areas, where they frequently could be seen working in the fields.[6]

The concept of female inferiority had deep roots in Chinese history. This view was embodied in the belief that only a male would carry on sacred family rituals and that men alone had the talent to govern others. Only males could aspire to a career in government or scholarship. Within the family system, the wife was clearly subordinated to the husband. Legally, she could not divorce her husband or inherit property. The husband, however, could divorce his wife if she did not produce male heirs, or he could take a second wife as well as a concubine for his pleasure. A widow suffered especially, because she had to either raise her children on a single income or fight off her former husband's greedy relatives, who would coerce her to remarry since, by law, they would then inherit all of her previous property and her original dowry.

Female children were less desirable because of their limited physical strength and because their parents would have to pay a dowry to the parents of their future husband. Female children normally did not receive an education, and in times of scarcity when food was in short supply, daughters might even be put to death.

Though women were clearly inferior to men in theory, this was not always the case in practice. Capable women often compensated for their legal inferiority by playing a strong role within the family. Women were often in charge of educating the children and handled the family budget. Some privileged women also received training in the Confucian classics, although their schooling was generally for a shorter time and less rigorous than that of their male counterparts. A few produced significant works of art and poetry.

Cultural Developments

During the late Ming and the early Qing dynasties, traditional culture in China reached new heights of achievement. With the rise of a wealthy urban class, the demand for art, porcelain, textiles, and literature grew significantly.

The Rise of the Chinese Novel   During the Ming dynasty, a new form of literature arose that eventually evolved into the modern Chinese novel. Although considered less respectable than poetry and nonfiction prose, these groundbreaking works (often written anonymously or under pseudonyms) were enormously popular, especially among well-to-do urban dwellers.

Written in a colloquial style, the new fiction was characterized by a realism that resulted in vivid portraits of Chinese society. Many of the stories sympathized with society's downtrodden—often helpless maidens—and dealt with such crucial issues as love, money, marriage, and power. Adding to the realism were sexually explicit passages that depicted the private side of Chinese life. Readers delighted in sensuous tales that, no matter how pornographic, always professed a moral lesson; the villains were punished and the virtuous rewarded.

The Dream of the Red Chamber is generally considered China's most distinguished popular novel. Published in 1791, it tells of the tragic love between two young people caught in the financial and moral disintegration of a powerful Chinese clan. The hero and the heroine, both sensitive and spoiled, represent the inevitable decline of the Chia family and come to an equally inevitable tragic end, she in death and he in an unhappy marriage to another.

The Art of the Ming and the Qing   During the Ming and the early Qing, China produced its last outpouring of traditional artistic brilliance. Although most of the creative work was modeled on past examples, the art of this period is impressive for its technical perfection and breathtaking quantity.

In architecture, the most outstanding example is the Imperial City in Beijing. Building on the remnants of the palace of the Yuan dynasty, the Ming emperor Yongle ordered renovations when he returned the capital to Beijing in 1421. Succeeding emperors continued to add to the palace, but the basic design has not changed since the Ming era. Surrounded by high walls, the immense compound is divided into a maze of private apartments and

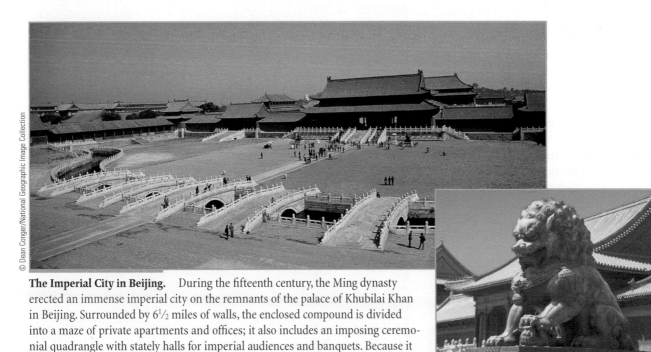

The Imperial City in Beijing.   During the fifteenth century, the Ming dynasty erected an immense imperial city on the remnants of the palace of Khubilai Khan in Beijing. Surrounded by 6½ miles of walls, the enclosed compound is divided into a maze of private apartments and offices; it also includes an imposing ceremonial quadrangle with stately halls for imperial audiences and banquets. Because it was off-limits to commoners, the compound was known as the Forbidden City. The fearsome lion shown in the inset, representing the omnipotence of the Chinese Empire, guards the entrance to the private apartments of the palace.

© Dean Conger/National Geographic Image Collection

Courtesy of William J. Duiker

Beijing Under the Ming and the Manchus, 1400–1911

offices and an imposing ceremonial quadrangle with a series of stately halls for imperial audiences and banquets. The grandiose scale, richly carved marble, spacious gardens, and graceful upturned roofs also contribute to the splendor of the "Forbidden City."

The decorative arts flourished in this period, especially the intricately carved lacquerware and the boldly shaped and colored cloisonné, a type of enamelwork in which colored areas are separated by thin metal bands. Silk production reached its zenith, and the best-quality silks were highly prized in Europe, where chinoiserie, as Chinese art of all kinds was called, was in vogue. Perhaps the most famous of all the achievements of the Ming era was its blue-and-white porcelain, still prized by collectors throughout the world.

During the Qing dynasty, artists produced great quantities of paintings, mostly for home consumption. Inside the Forbidden City in Beijing, court painters worked alongside Jesuit artists and experimented with Western techniques. Most scholarly painters and the literati, however, totally rejected foreign techniques and became obsessed with traditional Chinese styles. As a result, Qing painting became progressively more repetitive and stale.

Tokugawa Japan

At the end of the fifteenth century, the traditional Japanese system was at a point of near anarchy. With the decline in the authority of the Ashikaga shogunate at Kyoto, clan rivalries had exploded into an era of warring states. Even at the local level, power was frequently diffuse. The typical daimyo (great lord) domain had often become little more than a coalition of fief-holders held together by a loose allegiance to the manor lord. Nevertheless, Japan was on the verge of an extended era of national unification and peace under the rule of its greatest shogunate—the Tokugawa.

The Three Great Unifiers

The process began in the mid-sixteenth century with the emergence of three very powerful political figures, Oda Nobunaga (1568–1582), Toyotomi Hideyoshi (1582–1598), and Tokugawa Ieyasu (1598–1616). In 1568, Oda Nobunaga, the son of a samurai and a military commander under the Ashikaga shogunate, seized the imperial capital of Kyoto and placed the reigning shogun under his domination. During the next few years, the brutal and ambitious Nobunaga attempted to consolidate his rule throughout the central plains by defeating his rivals and suppressing the power of the Buddhist estates, but he was killed by one of his generals in 1582 before the process was complete. He was succeeded by Toyotomi Hideyoshi, a farmer's son who had worked his way up through the ranks to become a military commander. Hideyoshi located his capital at Osaka, where he built a castle to accommodate his headquarters, and gradually extended his power outward to the southern islands of Shikoku and Kyushu (see Map 16.3). By 1590, he had persuaded most of the daimyo on the Japanese islands to accept his authority and created a national currency. Then he invaded Korea in an abortive effort to export his rule to the Asian mainland.

Despite their efforts, however, neither Nobunaga nor Hideyoshi was able to eliminate the power of the local daimyo. Both were compelled to form alliances with some daimyo in order to destroy other more powerful rivals. At the conclusion of his conquests in 1590, Toyotomi Hideyoshi could claim to be the supreme proprietor of all registered lands in areas under his authority. But he then reassigned those lands as fiefs to the local daimyo, who

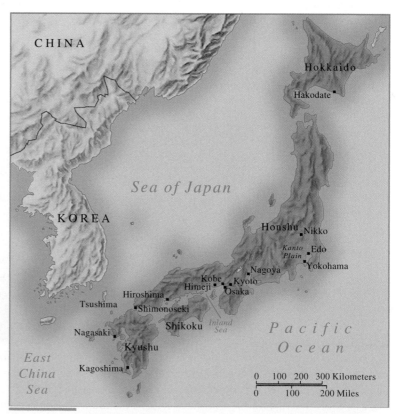

MAP 16.3 Tokugawa Japan. This map shows the Japanese islands during the long era of the Tokugawa shogunate. Key cities, including the shogun's capital of Edo, are shown. ❓ Where was the imperial court located ? 🌐 **View an animated version of this map or related maps at** http://worldrc.wadsworth.com/

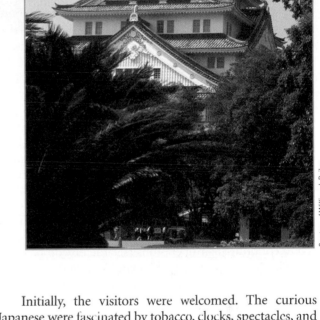

The Siege of Osaka Castle. In imitation of European castle architecture, the Japanese perfected a new type of fortress-palace in the early seventeenth century. Strategically placed high on a hilltop, constructed of heavy stone with tiny windows, and fortified by numerous watchtowers and massive walls, these strongholds were impregnable to arrows and catapults. They served as a residence for the local daimyo, while the castle compound also housed his army and contained the seat of the local government. Osaka Castle (on the right) was built by Hideyoshi essentially as a massive stage set to proclaim his power and grandeur. In 1615, the powerful warlord Tokugawa Ieyasu seized the castle, as shown in the screen painting above. The family's control over Japan lasted nearly 250 years. Note the presence of firearms, introduced by the Europeans half a century earlier.

declared their allegiance to him. The daimyo in turn began to pacify the countryside, carrying out extensive "sword hunts" to disarm the population and attracting samurai to their service. The Japanese tradition of decentralized rule had not been overcome.

After Hideyoshi's death in 1598, Tokugawa Ieyasu, the powerful daimyo of Edo (modern Tokyo), moved to fill the vacuum. Neither Hideyoshi nor Oda Nobunaga had claimed the title of shogun, but Ieyasu named himself shogun in 1603, initiating the most powerful and long-lasting of all Japanese shogunates. The Tokugawa rulers completed the restoration of central authority begun by Nobunaga and Hideyoshi and remained in power until 1868, when a war dismantled the entire system. As a contemporary phrased it, "Oda pounds the national rice cake, Hideyoshi kneads it, and in the end Ieyasu sits down and eats it."[7]

Opening to the West

The unification of Japan took place almost simultaneously with the coming of the Europeans. Portuguese traders sailing in a Chinese junk that may have been blown off course by a typhoon had landed on the islands in 1543. Within a few years, Portuguese ships were stopping at Japanese ports on a regular basis to take part in the regional trade between Japan, China, and Southeast Asia. The first Jesuit missionary, Francis Xavier, arrived in 1549.

Initially, the visitors were welcomed. The curious Japanese were fascinated by tobacco, clocks, spectacles, and other European goods, and local daimyo were interested in purchasing all types of European weapons and armaments. Oda Nobunaga and Toyotomi Hideyoshi found the new firearms helpful in defeating their enemies and unifying the islands. The effect on Japanese military architecture was particularly striking as local lords began to erect castles on the European model, many of which still exist today.

The missionaries also had some success in converting a number of local daimyo, some of whom may have been motivated in part by the desire for commercial profits. By the end of the sixteenth century, thousands of Japanese in the southernmost islands of Kyushu and Shikoku had become Christians. But papal claims to the loyalty of all Japanese Christians and the European habit of intervening in local politics soon began to arouse suspicion in official circles. Missionaries added to the problem by deliberately destroying local idols and shrines and turning some temples into Christian schools or churches.

The Christians Are Expelled Inevitably, the local authorities reacted. In 1587, Toyotomi Hideyoshi issued an edict prohibiting further Christian activities within his

The Portuguese Arrive at Nagasaki. Portuguese traders landed in Japan by accident in 1543. In a few years, they arrived regularly, taking part in a regional trade network between Japan, China, and Southeast Asia. In these panels done in black lacquer and gold leaf, we see a late-sixteenth-century Japanese interpretation of the first Portuguese landing at Nagasaki.

domains. Japan, he declared, was "the land of the Gods," and the destruction of shrines by the foreigners was "something unheard of in previous ages."[8] The Jesuits were ordered to leave the country within twenty days. Hideyoshi was careful to distinguish missionary from trading activities, however, and merchants were permitted to continue their operations (see the box on p. 370).

The Jesuits protested the expulsion, and eventually Hideyoshi relented, permitting them to continue proselytizing so long as they were discreet. But he refused to repeal the edicts, and when the aggressive activities of newly arrived Spanish Franciscans aroused his ire, he ordered the execution of nine missionaries and a number of their Japanese converts. When the missionaries continued to interfere in local politics, Tokugawa Ieyasu ordered the eviction of all missionaries in 1612.

At first, Japanese authorities hoped to maintain commercial relations with European countries even while suppressing the Western religion, but eventually they decided to prohibit foreign trade altogether and closed the two major foreign factories on the island of Hirado and at Nagasaki. The sole remaining opening to the West was at Deshima Island in Nagasaki Harbor, where a small Dutch community was permitted to engage in limited trade with Japan (the Dutch,

Nagasaki and Hirado Island

unlike the Portuguese and the Spanish, had not allowed missionary activities to interfere with their commercial interests). Dutch ships were permitted to dock at Nagasaki Harbor only once a year and, after close inspection, were allowed to remain for two or three months. Conditions on the island of Deshima itself were quite confining: the Dutch physician Engelbert Kaempfer complained that the Dutch lived in "almost perpetual imprisonment."[9] Nor were the Japanese free to engage in foreign trade. A small amount of commerce took place with China, but Japanese subjects of the shogunate were forbidden to leave the country on penalty of death.

The Tokugawa "Great Peace"

Once in power, the Tokugawa attempted to strengthen the system that had governed Japan for over three hundred years. They followed precedent in ruling through the *bakufu*, composed now of a coalition of daimyo, and a council of elders. But the system was more centralized than it had been previously. Now the shogunate government played a dual role. It set national policy on behalf of the emperor in Kyoto while simultaneously governing the shogun's own domain, which included about one-quarter of the national territory as well as the three great cities of Edo, Kyoto, and Osaka. As before, the state was divided into separate territories, called domains (**han**), which were ruled by a total of about 250 individual daimyo.

In theory, the daimyo were essentially autonomous in that they were able to support themselves from taxes on their lands (the shogunate received its own revenues from its extensive landholdings). In actuality, the shogunate was able to guarantee their loyalty by compelling the daimyo to maintain two residences, one in their own domains and the other at Edo, and to leave their families in Edo as hostages for the daimyo's good behavior. Keeping up two residences also put the Japanese nobility in a difficult economic position. Some were able to defray the high costs by concentrating on cash crops such as sugar, fish, and forestry products; but most were rice producers, and their revenues remained roughly the same throughout the period. The daimyo were also able to protect their economic interests by depriving their samurai retainers of their proprietary rights over the land and transforming them into salaried officials. The fief thus became a stipend, and the personal relationship between the daimyo and his retainers gradually gave way to a bureaucratic authority.

The Tokugawa also tinkered with the social system by limiting the size of the samurai class and reclassifying samurai who supported themselves by tilling the land as commoners. In fact, with the long period of peace brought about by Tokugawa rule, the samurai gradually ceased to be a warrior class and were required to live in the castle towns. As a gesture to their glorious past, samurai were still permitted to wear their two swords, and a rigid separation was maintained between persons of samurai status and the nonaristocratic segment of the population.

Seeds of Capitalism   The long period of peace under the Tokugawa shogunate made possible a dramatic rise in commerce and manufacturing, especially in the growing cities of Edo, Kyoto, and Osaka. By the mid-eighteenth century, Edo, with a population of more than one million, was one of the largest cities in the world. The growth of trade and industry was stimulated by a rising standard of living—driven in part by technological advances in agriculture and an expansion of arable land—and the voracious appetites of the aristocrats for new products.

Most of this commercial expansion took place in the major cities and the castle towns, where the merchants and artisans lived along with the samurai, who were clustered in neighborhoods surrounding the daimyo's castle. Banking flourished and paper money became the normal medium of exchange in commercial transactions. Merchants formed guilds not only to control market conditions but also to facilitate government control and the collection of taxes. Under the benign if somewhat contemptuous supervision of Japan's noble rulers, a Japanese merchant class gradually began to emerge from the shadows to play a significant role in the life of the Japanese nation. Some historians view the Tokugawa era as the first stage in the rise of an indigenous form of capitalism.

Eventually, the increased pace of industrial activity spread beyond the cities into rural areas. As in Great Britain, cotton was a major factor. Cotton had been introduced to China during the Song dynasty and had spread to Korea and Japan shortly thereafter. Traditionally, however, cotton cloth had been too expensive for the common people, who instead wore clothing made of hemp. Imports

CHRONOLOGY   Japan and Korea During the Early Modern Era

First phonetic alphabet in Korea	Fifteenth century
Portuguese merchants arrive in Japan	1543
Francis Xavier arrives in Japan	1549
Rule of Oda Nobunaga	1568–1582
Seizure of Kyoto	1568
Rule of Toyotomi Hideyoshi	1582–1598
Edict prohibiting Christianity in Japan	1587
Invades Korea	1592
Death of Toyotomi Hideyoshi and withdrawal of army from Korea	1598
Rule of Tokugawa Ieyasu	1598–1616
Creation of Tokugawa shogunate	1603
Dutch granted permission to trade at Nagasaki	1609
Order evicting Christian missionaries	1612
Yi dynasty of Korea declares fealty to China	1630s

increased during the sixteenth century, however, when cotton cloth began to be used for uniforms, matchlock fuses, and sails. Eventually, technological advances reduced the cost, and specialized communities for producing cotton cloth began to appear in the countryside and were gradually transformed into towns. By the eighteenth century, cotton had firmly replaced hemp as the cloth of choice for most Japanese.

Not everyone benefited from the economic changes of the seventeenth and eighteenth centuries, however; the samurai were barred by tradition and prejudice from commercial activities. Most samurai still relied on their revenues from rice lands, which were often insufficient to cover their rising expenses; consequently, they fell heavily into debt. Others were released from servitude to their lord and became "masterless samurai." Occasionally, these unemployed warriors (known as **ronin**, or "wave men") revolted or plotted against the local authorities.

Land Problems   The effects of economic developments on the rural population during the Tokugawa era are harder to estimate. Some farm families benefited by exploiting the growing demand for cash crops. But not all prospered. Most peasants continued to rely on rice cultivation and were whipsawed between declining profits and rising costs and taxes (as daimyo expenses increased, land taxes often took up to 50 percent of the annual harvest). Many were forced to become tenants or to work as wage laborers on the farms of wealthy neighbors or in village industries. When rural conditions in some areas became desperate, peasant revolts erupted. According

TOYOTOMI HIDEYOSHI EXPELS THE MISSIONARIES

RELIGION & PHILOSOPHY

When Christian missionaries in sixteenth-century Japan began to interfere in local politics and criticize traditional religious practices, Toyotomi Hideyoshi issued an edict calling for their expulsion. In this letter to the Portuguese viceroy in Asia, Hideyoshi explains his decision. Note his conviction that Buddhists, Confucianists, and followers of Shinto all believe in the same God and his criticism of Christianity for rejecting all other faiths.

What reason does Hideyoshi give for prohibiting the practice of Christianity in Japan? How do his religious beliefs, as expressed in this document, differ from those of other religions like Christianity and Islam?

Toyotomi Hideyoshi, Letter to the Viceroy of the Indies

Ours is the land of the Gods, and God is mind. Everything in nature comes into existence because of mind. Without God there can be no spirituality. Without God there can be no way. God rules in times of prosperity as in times of decline. God is positive and negative and unfathomable. Thus, God is the root and source of all existence. This God is spoken of by Buddhism in India, Confucianism in China, and Shinto in Japan. To know Shinto is to know Buddhism as well as Confucianism.

As long as man lives in this world, Humanity will be a basic principle. Were it not for Humanity and Righteousness, the sovereign would not be a sovereign, nor a minister of a state a minister. It is through the practice of Humanity and Righteousness that the foundations of our relationships between sovereign and minister, parent and child, and husband and wife are established. If you are interested in the profound philosophy of God and Buddha, request an explanation and it will be given to you. In your land one doctrine is taught to the exclusion of others, and you are not yet informed of the [Confucian] philosophy of Humanity and Righteousness. Thus there is no respect for God and Buddha and no distinction between sovereign and ministers. Through heresies you intend to destroy the righteous law. Hereafter, do not expound, in ignorance of right and wrong, unreasonable and wanton doctrines. A few years ago the so-called Fathers came to my country seeking to bewitch our men and women, both of the laity and clergy. At that time punishment was administered to them, and it will be repeated if they should return to our domain to propagate their faith. It will not matter what sect or denomination they represent—they shall be destroyed. It will then be too late to repent. If you entertain any desire of establishing amity with this land, the seas have been rid of the pirate menace, and merchants are permitted to come and go. Remember this.

---

to one estimate, nearly seven thousand disturbances took place during the Tokugawa era.

Some Japanese historians, influenced by a Marxist view of history, have interpreted such evidence as an indication that the Tokugawa economic system was highly exploitative, with feudal aristocrats oppressing powerless peasants. Recent scholars, however, have tended to adopt a more balanced view, maintaining that in addition to agriculture, manufacturing and commerce experienced extensive growth. Some point out that although the population doubled in the seventeenth century, a relatively low rate for the time period, so did the amount of cultivable land, while agricultural technology made significant advances.

The relatively low rate of population growth probably meant that Japanese peasants were spared the kind of land hunger that many of their counterparts in China faced. Recent evidence indicates that the primary reasons for the relatively low rate of population growth were late marriage, abortion, and infanticide.

Life in the Village

The changes that took place during the Tokugawa era had a major impact on the lives of ordinary Japanese. In some respects, the result was an increase in the power of the central government at the village level. The shogunate increasingly relied on Confucian maxims advocating

obedience and hierarchy to enhance its authority with the general population. Decrees from the *bakufu* instructed the peasants on all aspects of their lives, including their eating habits and their behavior (see the box on p. 371). At the same time, the increased power of the government led to more autonomy from the local daimyo for the peasants. Villages now had more control over their local affairs.

At the same time, the Tokugawa era saw the emergence of the nuclear family (*ie*) as the basic unit in Japanese society. In previous times, Japanese peasants had few legal rights. Most were too poor to keep their conjugal family unit intact or to pass property on to their children. Many lived at the manorial residence or worked as servants in the households of more affluent villagers. Now, with farm income on the rise, the nuclear family took on the same form as in China, although without the joint family concept. The Japanese system of inheritance was based on primogeniture. Family property was passed on to the eldest son, although younger sons often received land from their parents to set up their own families after marriage.

The Role of Women Another result of the changes under the Tokugawa was that women were somewhat more restricted than they had been previously. The rights of females were especially restricted in the samurai class,

SOME CONFUCIAN COMMANDMENTS

FAMILY & SOCIETY

Although the Qing dynasty was of foreign origin, its rulers found Confucian maxims convenient for maintaining the social order. In 1670, the great emperor Kangxi issued the Sacred Edict to popularize Confucian values among the common people. The edict was read publicly at periodic intervals in every village in the country and set the standard for behavior throughout the empire. Like the Qing dynasty in China, the Tokugawa shoguns attempted to keep their subjects in line with decrees that carefully prescribed all kinds of behavior. As this decree, which was circulated in all Japanese villages, shows, the bakufu sought to be the moral instructor as well as the guardian and protector of the Japanese people.

In what ways does Kangxi's set of commandments conform to the principles of State Confucianism? How do these standards compare with those applied in Japan, shown on the right?

Kangxi's Sacred Edict

1. Esteem most highly filial piety and brotherly submission, in order to give due importance to the social relations.
2. Behave with generosity toward your kindred, in order to illustrate harmony and benignity.
3. Cultivate peace and concord in your neighborhoods, in order to prevent quarrels and litigations.
4. Recognize the importance of husbandry and the culture of the mulberry tree, in order to ensure a sufficiency of clothing and food.
5. Show that you prize moderation and economy, in order to prevent the lavish waste of your means.
6. Give weight to colleges and schools, in order to make correct the practice of the scholar.
7. Extirpate strange principles, in order to exalt the correct doctrine.
8. Lecture on the laws, in order to warn the ignorant and obstinate.
9. Elucidate propriety and yielding courtesy, in order to make manners and customs good.
10. Labor diligently at your proper callings, in order to stabilize the will of the people.
11. Instruct sons and younger brothers, in order to prevent them from doing what is wrong.
12. Put a stop to false accusations, in order to preserve the honest and good.
13. Warn against sheltering deserters, in order to avoid being involved in their punishment.
14. Fully remit your taxes, in order to avoid being pressed for payment.
15. Unite in hundreds and tithing, in order to put an end to thefts and robbery.
16. Remove enmity and anger, in order to show the importance due to the person and life.

Maxims for Peasant Behavior

1. Young people are forbidden to congregate in great numbers.
2. Entertainments unsuited to peasants, such as playing the samisen or reciting ballad dramas, are forbidden.
3. Staging sumo matches is forbidden for the next five years.
4. The edict on frugality issued by the *han* at the end of last year must be observed.
5. Social relations in the village must be conducted harmoniously.
6. If a person has to leave the village for business or pleasure, that person must return by ten at night.
7. Father and son are forbidden to stay overnight at another person's house. An exception is to be made if it is to nurse a sick person.
8. Corvée [obligatory labor] assigned by the *han* must be performed faithfully.
9. Children who practice filial piety must be rewarded.
10. One must never get drunk and cause trouble for others.
11. Peasants who farm especially diligently must be rewarded.
12. Peasants who neglect farm work and cultivate their paddies and upland fields in a slovenly and careless fashion must be punished.
13. The boundary lines of paddy and upland fields must not be changed arbitrarily.
14. Recognition must be accorded to peasants who contribute greatly to village political affairs.
15. Fights and quarrels are forbidden in the village.
16. The deteriorating customs and morals of the village must be rectified.
17. Peasants who are suffering from poverty must be identified and helped.
18. This village has a proud history compared to other villages, but in recent years bad times have come upon us. Everyone must rise at six in the morning, cut grass, and work hard to revitalize the village.
19. The punishments to be meted out to violators of the village code and gifts to be awarded the deserving are to be decided during the last assembly meeting of the year.

ThomsonNOW To read more of Confucius's Analects, enter the *ThomsonNOW* documents area using the access card that is available for *The Essential World History*.

where Confucian values were highly influential. Male heads of households had broad authority over property, marriage, and divorce; wives were expected to obey their husbands on pain of death. Males often took concubines or homosexual partners, while females were expected to remain chaste. The male offspring of samurai parents studied the Confucian classics in schools established by the daimyo, while females were reared at home, where only the fortunate might receive a rudimentary training in reading and writing Chinese characters. Some women, however, became accomplished poets and painters since, in aristocratic circles, female literacy was prized for enhancing the refinement, social graces, and moral virtue of the home.

Women were similarly at a disadvantage among the common people. Marriages were arranged, and as in China, the new wife moved in with the family of her husband. A wife who did not meet the expectations of her spouse or his family was likely to be divorced. Still, gender relations were more egalitarian than among the nobility. Women were generally valued as childbearers and home-makers, and both men and women worked in the fields. Coeducational schools were established in villages and market towns, and about one-quarter of the students were female. Poor families, however, often put infant daughters to death or sold them into prostitution.

Such attitudes toward women operated within the context of the increasingly rigid stratification of Japanese society. Deeply conservative in their social policies, the Tokugawa rulers established strict legal distinctions between the four main classes in Japan (warriors, artisans, peasants, and merchants). Intermarriage between classes was forbidden in theory, although sometimes the prohibitions were ignored in practice. Below these classes were Japan's outcasts, the *eta.* Formerly, they were permitted to escape their status, at least in theory. The Tokugawa made their status hereditary and enacted severe discriminatory laws against them, regulating their place of residence, their dress, and even their hairstyles.

Tokugawa Culture

Under the Tokugawa, a vital new set of cultural values began to appear, especially in the cities. This innovative era witnessed the rise of popular literature written by and for the townspeople. With the development of woodblock printing in the early seventeenth century, literature became available to the common people, literacy levels rose, and lending libraries increased the accessibility of the printed word.

The Literature of the New Middle Class
The best examples of this new urban fiction are the works of Saikaku (1642–1693), considered one of Japan's finest novelists. Saikaku's greatest novel, *Five Women Who Loved Love*, relates the amorous exploits of five women of the merchant class. Based partly on real-life experiences, it broke from the Confucian ethic of wifely fidelity to her husband

and portrayed women who were willing to die for love— and all but one eventually did. Despite the tragic circumstances, the tone of the novel is upbeat and sometimes comic, and the author's wry comments prevent the reader from becoming emotionally involved with the heroines' misfortunes.

In the theater, the rise of *Kabuki* threatened the long dominance of the *No* play, replacing the somewhat restrained and elegant thematic and stylistic approach of the classical drama with a new emphasis on violence, music, and dramatic gestures. Significantly, the new drama emerged not from the rarefied world of the court but from the new world of entertainment and amusement (see the comparative illustration on p. 373). Its very commercial success, however, led to difficulties with the government, which periodically attempted to restrict or even suppress it. Early *Kabuki* was often performed by prostitutes, and shogunate officials, fearing that such activities could have a corrupting effect on the nation's morals, prohibited women from appearing on the stage; at the same time, they attempted to create a new professional class of male actors to impersonate female characters on stage.

In contrast to the popular literature of the Tokugawa period, poetry persevered in its more serious tradition. The most exquisite poetry was produced in the seventeenth century by the greatest of all Japanese poets, Basho (1644–1694). He was concerned with the search for the meaning of existence and the poetic expression of his experience. With his love of Daoism and Zen Buddhism, Basho found answers to his quest for the meaning of life in nature, and his poems are grounded in seasonal imagery. The following are among his most famous poems:

> The ancient pond
> A frog leaps in
> The sound of the water.
> On the withered branch
> A crow has alighted–
> The end of autumn.

His last poem, dictated to a disciple only three days prior to his death, succinctly expressed his frustration with the unfinished business of life:

> On a journey, ailing–
> my dreams roam about
> on a withered moor.

Like all great artists, Basho made his poems seem effortless and simple. He speaks directly to everyone, everywhere.

Tokugawa Art
Art also reflected the dynamism and changes in Japanese culture under the Tokugawa regime. The shogun's order that all daimyo and their families live every other year in Edo set off a burst of building as provincial rulers competed to erect the most magnificent mansion. Furthermore, the shoguns themselves constructed splendid castles adorned with sumptuous,

COMPARATIVE ILLUSTRATION
Popular Culture: East and West. By the eighteenth century, a popular culture distinct from the elite culture of the nobility was beginning to emerge in the urban worlds of both the East and the West. At the left is a scene from the "floating world," as the pleasure district in Edo, Japan, was called. Seen here are courtesans, storytellers, jesters, and various other entertainers. Below is a scene from the celebration of Carnival on the Piazza Sante Croce in Florence, Italy. Carnival was a period of festivities before Lent, mostly celebrated in Roman Catholic countries. Carnival became an occasion for indulgence in food, drink, games, and practical jokes.

almost ostentatious decor and furnishings. And the prosperity of the newly rising merchant class added fuel to the fire. Japanese paintings, architecture, textiles, and ceramics all flourished during this affluent era.

Although Japan was isolated from the Western world during much of the Tokugawa era, Japanese art was enriched by ideas from other cultures. Japanese pottery makers borrowed both techniques and designs from Korea to produce handsome ceramics. The passion for "Dutch learning" inspired Japanese to study Western medicine, astronomy, and languages and also led to experimentation with oil painting and Western ideas of perspective and the interplay of light and dark. Europeans

desired Japanese lacquerware and metalwork, inlaid with ivory and mother-of-pearl, and especially the ceramics, which were now as highly prized as those of the Chinese.

Perhaps the most famous of all Japanese art of the Tokugawa era is the woodblock print. Genre painting, or representations of daily life, began in the sixteenth century and found its new mass-produced form in the eighteenth-century woodblock print. The now literate mercantile class was eager for illustrated texts of the amusing and bawdy tales that had circulated in oral tradition. Some prints depict entire city blocks filled with people, trades, and festivals, while others show the interiors of houses; thus, they provide us with excellent visual documentation of the times. Others portray the "floating world" of the entertainment quarter, with scenes of carefree revelers enjoying the pleasures of life.

One of the most renowned of the numerous blockprint artists was Utamaro (1754–1806), who painted erotic and sardonic women in everyday poses, such as walking down the street, cooking, or drying their bodies after a bath. Hokusai (1760–1849) was famous for *Thirty-Six Views of Mount Fuji*, a new and bold interpretation of the Japanese landscape.

Korea: The Hermit Kingdom

While Japan was gradually moving away from its agrarian origins, the Yi dynasty in Korea was attempting to pattern its own society on the Chinese model. The dynasty had been founded by the military commander Yi Song Gye in the late fourteenth century and immediately set out to establish close political and cultural relations with the Ming dynasty. From their new capital at Seoul, located on the Han River in the center of the peninsula, the Yi rulers accepted a tributary relationship with their powerful neighbor and engaged in the wholesale adoption of Chinese institutions and values. As in China, the civil service examinations tested candidates on their knowledge of the Confucian classics, and success was viewed as an essential step toward upward mobility.

There were differences, however. As in Japan, the dynasty continued to restrict entry into the bureaucracy to members of the aristocratic class, known in Korea as the *yangban* (or "two groups," the civilian and military). At the same time, the peasantry remained in serflike conditions, working on government estates or on the manor holdings of the landed elite. A class of slaves (*chonmin*) labored on government plantations or served in certain occupations, such as butchers and entertainers, considered beneath the dignity of other groups in the population.

Eventually, Korean society began to show signs of independence from Chinese orthodoxy. In the fifteenth century, a phonetic alphabet for writing the Korean spoken language (*hangul*) was devised. Although it was initially held in contempt by the elites and used primarily as a teaching device, eventually it became the medium for private correspondence and the publishing of fiction for a popular audience. At the same time, changes were taking place in the economy, where rising agricultural production contributed to a population increase and the appearance of a small urban industrial and commercial sector, and in society, where the long domination of the *yangban* class began to weaken. As their numbers increased and their power and influence declined, some *yangban* became merchants or even moved into the ranks of the peasantry, further blurring the distinction between the aristocratic class and the common people.

In general, Korean rulers tried to keep the country isolated from the outside world, but they were not always successful. The Japanese invasion under Toyotomi Hideyoshi in the late sixteenth century had a disastrous impact on Korean society. A Manchu force invaded northern Korea in the 1630s and eventually compelled the Yi dynasty to declare allegiance to the new imperial government in Beijing. Korea was relatively untouched by the arrival of European merchants and missionaries, although information about Christianity was brought to the peninsula by Koreans returning from tribute missions to China, and a small Catholic community was established there in the late eighteenth century.

CONCLUSION

*W*HEN CHRISTOPHER COLUMBUS sailed from southern Spain in his three ships in August 1492, he was seeking a route to China and Japan. He did not find it, but others soon did. In 1514, Portuguese ships arrived on the coast of southern China. Thirty years later, a small contingent of Portuguese merchants became the first Europeans to set foot on the islands of Japan.

At first, the new arrivals were welcomed, if only as curiosities. Eventually, several European nations established trade relations with China and Japan, and Christian missionaries of various religious orders were active in both countries and in Korea as well. But their success was short-lived. Europeans eventually began to be perceived as detrimental to law and order, and during the seventeenth century, the majority of the foreign merchants and missionaries were evicted from all three

countries. From that time until the middle of the nineteenth century, China, Japan, and Korea were relatively little affected by events taking place beyond their borders.

That fact deluded many observers into the assumption that the societies of East Asia were essentially stagnant, characterized by agrarian institutions and values reminiscent of those of the feudal era in Europe. As we have seen, however, that picture is misleading, for all three countries were changing and by the early nineteenth century were quite different from what they had been three centuries earlier.

Ironically, these changes were especially marked in Tokugawa Japan, an allegedly "closed country," where traditional classes and institutions were under increasing strain, not only from the emergence of a new merchant

TIMELINE

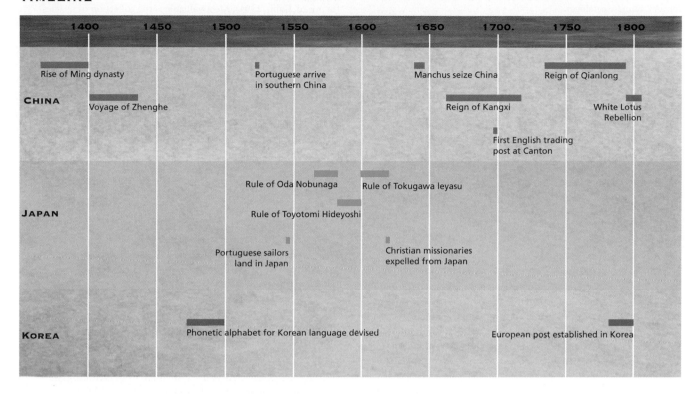

class but also from the centralizing tendencies of the powerful Tokugawa shogunate. Some historians have seen strong parallels between Tokugawa Japan and early modern Europe, which gave birth to centralized empires and a strong merchant class during the same period. The image of the monarchy is reflected in a song sung at the shrine of Toyotomi Hideyoshi in Kyoto:

Who's that
Holding over four hundred provinces
In the palm of his hand

And entertaining at a tea-party?
It's His Highness
So mighty, so impressive![10]

By the beginning of the nineteenth century, then, powerful tensions, reflecting a growing gap between ideal and reality, were at work in both Chinese and Japanese society. Under these conditions, both countries were soon forced to face a new challenge from the aggressive power of an industrializing Europe.

CHAPTER NOTES

1. From Jonathan D. Spence, *Emperor of China: Self-Portrait of K'ang Hsi* (New York, 1974), pp. 143–144.
2. Richard Strassberg, *The World of K'ang Shang-jen: A Man of Letters in Early Ch'ing China* (New York, 1983), p. 275.
3. Lynn Struve, *The Southern Ming, 1644–1662* (New Haven, Conn., 1984), p. 61.
4. J. L. Cranmer-Byng, *An Embassy to China: Lord Macartney's Journal, 1793–1794* (London, 1912), p. 340.
5. Daniel J. Boorstin, *The Discoverers: A History of Man's Search to Know His World and Himself* (New York, 1983), p. 63.
6. C. R. Boxer, ed., *South China in the Sixteenth Century* (London, 1953), p. 265.
7. Chie Nakane and Sinzaburo Oishi, eds., *Tokugawa Japan* (Tokyo, 1990), p. 14.
8. Quoted in Jurgis Elisonas, "Christianity and the Daimyo," in John Whitney Hall, ed., *The Cambridge History of Japan,* vol. 4 (Cambridge, 1991), p. 360.
9. Engelbert Kaempfer, *The History of Japan: Together with a Description of the Kingdom of Siam, 1690–1692,* vol. 2 (Glasgow, 1906), pp. 173–174.
10. Quoted in Ryusaku Tsunda et al., *Sources of Japanese Tradition* (New York, 1964), p. 313.

SUGGESTED READING

For a general overview of this period in East Asian history, see volumes 8 and 9 of **F. W. Mote** and **D. Twitchett,** eds., ***The Cambridge History of China*** (Cambridge, 1976), and **J. W. Hall,** ed., ***The Cambridge History of Japan,*** vol. 4 (Cambridge, 1991).

For information on Chinese voyages into the Indian Ocean, see **P. Snow, *The Star Raft: China's Encounter with Africa*** (Ithaca, N.Y., 1988). Also see **Ma Huan, *Ying-hai Sheng-lan: The Overall Survey of the Ocean's Shores*** (Bangkok, 1996), an ocean survey by a fifteenth-century Chinese cataloger.

On the late Ming, see **J. D. Spence, *The Search for Modern China*** (New York, 1990), and **L. Struve, *The Southern Ming, 1644–1662*** (New Haven, Conn., 1984). On the rise of the Qing, see **F. Wakeman Jr., *The Great Enterprise: The Manchu Reconstruction of Imperial Order in Seventeenth-Century China*** (Berkeley, Calif., 1985). On Kangxi, see **J. D. Spence, *Emperor of China: Self-Portrait of K'ang Hsi*** (New York, 1974). Social issues are discussed in **S. Naquin** and **E. Rawski, *Chinese Society in the Eighteenth Century*** (New Haven, Conn., 1987). Also see **J. D. Spence** and **J. Wills, eds., *From Ming to Ch'ing*** (New Haven, Conn., 1979). For a very interesting account of Jesuit missionary experiences in China, see **L. J. Gallagher**, ed. and trans., ***China in the Sixteenth Century: The Journals of Matthew Ricci, 1583–1616*** (New York, 1953). For brief biographies of Ming-Qing luminaries such as Wang Yangming, Zheng Chenggong, and Emperor Qianlong, see **J. E. Wills Jr., *Mountains of Fame: Portraits in Chinese History*** (Princeton, N.J., 1994).

The best surveys of Chinese literature are **S. Owen, *An Anthology of Chinese Literature: Beginnings to 1911*** (New York, 1996), and **V. Mair, *The Columbia Anthology of Traditional Chinese Literature*** (New York, 1994). For a comprehensive introduction to the Chinese art of this period, see **M. Sullivan, *The Arts of China*,** 4th ed. (Berkeley, Calif., 1999), and **C. Clunas, *Art in China*** (Oxford, 1997). For the best introduction to the painting of this era, see **J. Cahill, *Chinese Painting*** (New York, 1977).

On Japan before the rise of the Tokugawa, see **J. W. Hall** et al., eds., ***Japan Before Tokugawa: Political Consolidation and Economic Growth*** (Princeton, N.J., 1981), and **G. Elison** and **B. L. Smith, eds., *Warlords, Artists, and Commoners: Japan in the Sixteenth Century*** (Honolulu, 1981). See also **M. E. Berry, *Hideyoshi*** (Cambridge, Mass., 1982), the first biography of this fascinating figure in Japanese history. On early Christian activities, see **G. Elison, *Deus Destroyed: The Image of Christianity in Early Modern Japan*** (Cambridge, Mass., 1973). Buddhism is dealt with in **N. McMullin, *Buddhism and the State in Sixteenth Century Japan*** (Princeton, N.J., 1984).

On the Tokugawa era, see **H. Bolitho, *Treasures Among Men: The Fudai Daimyo in Tokugawa Japan*** (New Haven, Conn., 1974), and **R. B. Toby, *State and Diplomacy in Early Modern Japan: Asia in the Development of the Tokugawa Bakufu*** (Princeton, N.J., 1984). See also **C. I. Mulhern, ed., *Heroic with Grace: Legendary Women of Japan*** (Armonk, N.Y., 1991). Three other worthwhile studies are **S. Vlastos, *Peasant Protests and Uprisings in Tokugawa Japan*** (Berkeley, Calif., 1986); **H. Ooms, *Tokugawa Ideology: Early Constructs, 1570–1680*** (Princeton, N.J., 1985); and **C. Nakane, ed., *Tokugawa Japan: The Social and Economic Antecedents of Modern Japan*** (Tokyo, 1990).

For a brief introduction to women in the Ming and Qing dynasties as well as the Tokugawa era, see **S. Hughes** and **B. Hughes, *Women in World History*,** vol. 2 (Armonk, N.Y., 1997), and

S. Mann and **Y. Cheng,** eds, ***Under Confucian Eyes: Writings on Gender in Chinese History*** (Berkeley, Calif., 2001). On women's literacy in seventeenth-century China, see **D. Ko, *Teachers of the Inner Chambers: Women and Culture in Seventeenth Century China*** (Stanford, Calif., 1994). Most valuable is the collection of articles edited by **G. L. Bernstein, *Re-Creating Japanese Women, 1600–1945*** (Berkeley, Calif., 1991).

Of specific interest to Japanese literature of the Tokugawa era is **D. Keene, *World Within Walls: Japanese Literature of the Pre-Modern Era, 1600–1867*** (New York, 1976). For an introduction to Basho's life, poems, and criticism, consult the stimulating ***Basho and His Interpreters: Selected Hokku with Commentary*** (Stanford, Calif., 1991), by **M. Ueda.**

For the most comprehensive and accessible overview of Japanese art, see **P. Mason, *Japanese Art*** (New York, 1993). For a concise introduction to Japanese art of the Tokugawa era, see **J. Stanley-Baker, *Japanese Art*** (London, 1984).

InfoTrac College Edition

Visit this chapter's InfoTrac College Edition/Research activities at the *Essential World History* Companion Website for activities related to this era in East Asia.

ThomsonNOW™ **for Duiker and Spielvogel's *The Essential World History, Third Edition***

Enter *ThomsonNOW* using the access card that is available with this text. *ThomsonNOW* will assist you in understanding the content in this chapter with lesson plans generated for your needs, as well as provide you with a connection to the *Wadsworth World History Resource Center* (see description below for details).

WORLD HISTORY
RESOURCE CENTER

Enter the Resource Center using either your *ThomsonNOW* access card or your standalone access card for the *Wadsworth World History Resource Center*. Organized by topic, this website includes quizzes; over 350 primary source documents; interactive simulations, maps, and timelines; movie explorations; and a wealth of other resources. You can read the following documents, and many more, at http://worldrc.wadsworth.com/

 The Dream of the Red Chamber

  Honda Toshiaki, "A Secret Plan for Government, 1798"

Visit the *Essential World History* Companion Website for chapter quizzes and more.

  http://www.thomsonedu.com/history/duiker

DISCOVERY

How did China and Japan respond to the coming of the Europeans, and what explains the differences in their approach? What impact did European contacts have on these two East Asian civilizations through the end of the eighteenth century?

In thinking about this question, begin by breaking it down into the components shown below. A discussion of the significance of each component should appear in your answer.

POLITICS AND GOVERNMENT: How are the views of China and Japan each represented in these documents? What reasons do both leaders give for their actions? How were these similar to European views and actions toward non-Europeans that you have learned about previously?

How would you imagine their responses might influence the future of both nations? What do you think are the positives and negatives of having an open society as opposed to an insular one?

A DECREE OF EMPEROR QIANLONG

An Imperial Edict to the King of England: You, O King, are so inclined toward our civilization that you have sent a special envoy across the seas to bring to our Court your memorial of congratulations on the occasion of my birthday and to present your native products as an expression of your thoughtfulness. On perusing your memorial, so simply worded and sincerely conceived, I am impressed by your genuine respectfulness and friendliness and greatly pleased.

As to the request made in your memorial, O King, to send one of your nationals to stay at the Celestial Court to take care of your country's trade with China, this is not in harmony with the state system of our dynasty and will definitely not be permitted. Traditionally people of the European nations who wished to render some service under the Celestial Court have been permitted to come to the capital. But after their arrival they are obliged to wear Chinese court costumes, are placed in a certain residence, and are never allowed to return to their own countries. This is the established rule of the Celestial Dynasty with which presumably you, O King, are familiar. Now you, O King, wish to send one of your nationals to live in the capital, but he is not like the Europeans who come to Peking as Chinese employees, live there, and never return home again, nor can he be allowed to go and come and maintain any correspondence. This is indeed a useless undertaking.

Moreover the territory under the control of the Celestial Court is very large and wide. There are well-established regulations governing tributary envoys from the outer states to Peking [Beijing], giving them provisions (of food and traveling expenses) by our post-houses and limiting their going and coming. There has never been a precedent for letting them do whatever they like. Now If you, O King, wish to have a representative in Peking, his language will be unintelligible and his dress different from the regulations; there is no place to accommodate him. . . .

The Celestial Court has pacified and possessed the territory within the four seas. Its sole aim is to do its utmost to achieve good government and to manage political affairs, attaching no value to strange jewels and precious objects. The various articles presented by you, O King, this time are accepted by my special order to the office in charge of such functions in consideration of the offerings having come from a long distance with sincere good wishes. As a matter of fact, the virtue and prestige of the Celestial Dynasty having spread far and wide, the kings of the myriad nations come by land and sea with all sorts of precious things. Consequently there is nothing we lack, as your principal envoy and others have themselves observed. We have never set much store on strange or ingenious objects, nor do we need any more of your country's manufactures. . . .

TOYOTOMI HIDEYOSHI, LETTER TO THE VICEROY OF THE INDIES

Ours is the land of the Gods, and God is mind. Everything in nature comes into existence because of mind. Without God there can be no spirituality. Without God there can be no way. God rules in times of prosperity as in times of decline. God is positive and negative and unfathomable. Thus, God is the root and source of all existence. This God is spoken of by Buddhism in India, Confucianism in China, and Shinto in Japan. To know Shinto is to know Buddhism as well as Confucianism.

As long as man lives in this world, Humanity will be a basic principle. Were it not for Humanity and Righteousness, the sovereign would not be a sovereign, nor a minister of a state a minister. It is through the practice of Humanity and Righteousness that the foundations of our relationships between sovereign and minister, parent and child, and husband and wife are established. If you are interested in the profound philosophy of God and Buddha, request an

explanation and it will be given to you. In your land one doctrine is taught to the exclusion of others, and you are not yet informed of the [Confucian] philosophy of Humanity and Righteousness. Thus there is no respect for God and Buddha and no distinction between sovereign and ministers. Through heresies you intend to destroy the righteous law. Hereafter, do not expound, in ignorance of right and wrong, unreasonable and wanton doctrines. A few years ago the so-called Fathers came to my country seeking to bewitch our men and women, both of the laity and clergy. At that time punishment was administered to them, and it will be repeated if they should return to our domain to propagate their faith. It will not matter what sect or denomination they represent— they shall be destroyed. It will then be too late to repent. If you entertain any desire of establishing amity with this land, the seas have been rid of the pirate menace, and merchants are permitted to come and go. Remember this.

INTERACTION AND EXCHANGE: Both of these paintings depict economic interaction between Europeans and societies in East Asia. How do they differ? What do you see in the painting of Canton that is absent from the painting of Nagasaki? What does this tell you about how each government approached the idea of cultural and economic interaction? Which painting seems more "European," and why?

Why do you think that the Japanese and Chinese did not attempt to make inroads in Europe? Did either of them ever attempt exploration as the Europeans did? If so, why do you think they stopped? How might history have been different if they had undertaken such voyages?

The Portuguese Arrive at Nagasaki

The European Warehouses at Canton

ARTS AND IDEAS: Look at the photographs of the Imperial City and Osaka Castle. What do these structures say about the dynasties that built them? How do they differ stylistically? What role might geography have played in choosing their design? What image were the builders attempting to portray to both their subjects and to foreigners? Which photograph most mirrors what Europeans were doing at the time? Why?

The Imperial City in Beijing

Osaka Castle

17

THE WEST ON THE EVE
OF A NEW WORLD ORDER

CHAPTER OUTLINE
AND FOCUS QUESTIONS

Toward a New Heaven and a New Earth: An Intellectual Revolution in the West

▣ Who were the leading figures of the Scientific Revolution and the Enlightenment, and what were their main contributions?

Economic Changes and the Social Order

▣ What changes occurred in the European economy in the eighteenth century, and to what degree were these changes reflected in social patterns?

Colonial Empires and Revolution in the Western Hemisphere

▣ How did Spain and Portugal administer their American colonies, and what were the main characteristics of Latin American society in the eighteenth century?

Toward a New Political Order and Global Conflict

▣ What do historians mean by the term *enlightened absolutism*, and to what degree did eighteenth-century Prussia, Austria, and Russia exhibit its characteristics?

The French Revolution

▣ What were the causes, the main events, and the results of the French Revolution?

The Age of Napoleon

▣ Which aspects of the French Revolution did Napoleon preserve, and which did he destroy?

CRITICAL THINKING

▣ In what ways were the American Revolution, the French Revolution, and the seventeenth-century English revolutions alike? In what ways were they different?

The storming of the Bastille

$\mathcal{O}$N THE MORNING OF JULY 14, 1789, a Parisian mob of some eight thousand men and women in search of weapons streamed toward the Bastille, a royal armory filled with arms and ammunition. The Bastille was also a state prison, and although it held only seven prisoners at the time, in the eyes of these angry Parisians, it was a glaring symbol of the government's despotic policies. It was defended by the marquis de Launay and a small garrison of 114 men. The attack on the Bastille began in earnest in the early afternoon, and after three hours of fighting, de Launay and the garrison surrendered. Angered by the loss of ninety-eight protesters, the victors beat de Launay to death, cut off his head, and carried it aloft in triumph through the streets of Paris. When King Louis XVI was told the news of the fall of the Bastille by the duc de La Rochefoucauld-Liancourt, he exclaimed, "Why, this is a revolt." "No, Sire," replied the duke. "It is a revolution."

The French Revolution was a key factor in the emergence of a new world order. Historians have often portrayed the eighteenth century as the final phase of Europe's old order, before the violent upheaval and reordering of society associated with the French Revolution. The old order—still largely agrarian, dominated by kings and landed aristocrats, and grounded in privileges for nobles, clergy, towns, and provinces—seemed to continue a basic pattern that had prevailed in Europe since medieval times. But, just as a new intellectual order based on rationalism and secularism was emerging in Europe, demographic, economic, social, and political patterns were beginning to change in ways that proclaimed the emergence of a modern new order.

The French Revolution demolished the institutions of the old regime and established a new order based on individual rights, representative institutions, and a concept of loyalty to the nation rather than to the monarch. The revolutionary upheavals of the era, especially in France, created new liberal and national political ideals, summarized in the French revolutionary slogan, "Liberty, Equality, Fraternity," that transformed France and then spread to other European countries and the rest of the world. ◆

Toward a New Heaven and a New Earth: An Intellectual Revolution in the West

In the seventeenth century, a group of scientists set the Western world on a new path known as the **Scientific Revolution,** which brought to Europeans a new way of viewing the universe and their place in it. The Scientific Revolution affected only a small number of Europe's educated elite. But in the eighteenth century, this changed dramatically as a group of intellectuals popularized the ideas of the Scientific Revolution and used them to undertake a dramatic reexamination of all aspects of life. The widespread impact of these ideas on their society has caused historians ever since to call the eighteenth century in Europe the Age of Enlightenment.

The Scientific Revolution

The Scientific Revolution ultimately challenged conceptions and beliefs about the nature of the external world that had become dominant by the Late Middle Ages.

Toward a New Heaven: A Revolution in Astronomy   The philosophers of the Middle Ages had used the ideas of Aristotle, Ptolemy (the greatest astronomer of antiquity, who lived in the second century C.E.), and Christianity to form the Ptolemaic or **geocentric theory** of the universe. In this conception, the universe was seen as a series of concentric spheres with a fixed or motionless earth at its center. Composed of material substance, the earth was imperfect and constantly changing. The spheres that surrounded the earth were made of a crystalline, transparent substance and moved in circular orbits around the earth. The heavenly bodies, which numbered ten in 1500, were pure orbs of light, embedded in the moving, concentric spheres. Working outward from the earth, the first eight spheres contained the moon, Mercury, Venus, the sun, Mars, Jupiter, Saturn, and the fixed stars. The ninth sphere imparted to the eighth sphere of the fixed stars its daily motion, while the tenth sphere was frequently described as the prime mover that moved itself and imparted motion to the other spheres. Beyond the tenth sphere was the Empyrean Heaven—the location of God and all the saved souls. God and the saved souls were at one end of the universe, then, and humans were at the center. They had power over the earth, but their real purpose was to achieve salvation.

Nicholas Copernicus (1473–1543), a native of Poland, was a mathematician who felt that Ptolemy's geocentric system failed to accord with the observed motions of the heavenly bodies and hoped that his **heliocentric** (sun-centered) **theory** would offer a more accurate explanation. Copernicus argued that the sun was motionless at the center of the universe. The planets revolved around the sun in the order of Mercury, Venus, the earth, Mars, Jupiter, and Saturn. The moon, however, revolved around the earth. Moreover, what appeared to be the movement of the sun around the earth was really explained by the daily rotation of the earth on its axis and the journey of the earth around the sun each year. But Copernicus did not reject the idea that the heavenly spheres moved in circular orbits.

The next step in destroying the geocentric conception and supporting the Copernican system was taken by Johannes Kepler (1571–1630). A brilliant German mathematician and astronomer, Kepler arrived at laws of planetary motion that confirmed Copernicus's heliocentric theory. In his first law, however, he contradicted Copernicus by showing that the orbits of the planets around the sun were not circular but elliptical, with the sun at one focus of the ellipse rather than at the center.

Kepler's work destroyed the basic structure of the Ptolemaic system. People could now think in new terms of the actual paths of planets revolving around the sun in elliptical orbits. But important questions remained unanswered. For example, what were the planets made of? An Italian scientist achieved the next important breakthrough to a new cosmology by answering that question.

Galileo Galilei (1564–1642) taught mathematics and was the first European to make systematic observations of the heavens by means of a telescope, inaugurating a new age in astronomy. Galileo turned his telescope to the skies and made a remarkable series of discoveries: mountains on the moon, four moons revolving around Jupiter, and sunspots. Galileo's observations seemed to destroy yet another aspect of the traditional cosmology in that the universe seemed to be composed of material similar to that of earth rather than a perfect and unchanging substance.

Galileo's revelations, published in *The Starry Messenger* in 1610, made Europeans aware of a new picture of the universe. But the Catholic church condemned Copernicanism and ordered Galileo to abandon the Copernican thesis. The church attacked the Copernican system because it threatened not only Scripture but also an entire conception of the universe. The heavens were no longer a spiritual world but a world of matter.

Medieval Conception of the Universe. As this sixteenth-century illustration shows, the medieval cosmological view placed the earth at the center of the universe, surrounded by a series of concentric spheres. The earth was imperfect and constantly changing, while the heavenly bodies that surrounded it were perfect and incorruptible. Beyond the tenth and final sphere was heaven, where God and all the saved souls were located. (The circles read, from the center outward: 1. Moon, 2. Mercury, 3. Venus, 4. Sun, 5. Mars, 6. Jupiter, 7. Saturn, 8. Firmament of the Stars, 9. Crystalline Sphere, 10. Prime Mover, and at the end, Empyrean Heaven—Home of God and all the Elect, that is, saved souls.)

The Copernican System. The Copernican system was presented in *On the Revolutions of the Heavenly Spheres,* published shortly before Copernicus's death. As shown in this illustration from the first edition of the book, Copernicus maintained that the sun was the center of the universe while the planets, including the earth, revolved around it. Moreover, the earth rotated daily on its axis. (The circles read, from the outside in: 1. Immobile Sphere of the Fixed Stars, 2. Saturn, orbit of 30 years, 3. Jupiter, orbit of 12 years, 4. Mars, orbit of 2 years, 5. Earth, with the moon, orbit of one year, 6. Venus, 7. Mercury, orbit of 80 days, 8. Sun.)

By the 1630s and 1640s, most astronomers had come to accept the new heliocentric conception of the universe. Nevertheless, the problem of explaining motion in the universe and tying together the ideas of Copernicus, Galileo, and Kepler had not yet been done. This would be the work of an Englishman who has long been considered the greatest genius of the Scientific Revolution.

Isaac Newton (1642–1727) taught at Cambridge University, where he wrote his major work, *Mathematical Principles of Natural Philosophy,* known simply as the *Principia* by the first word of its Latin title. In the first book of the *Principia,* Newton defined the three laws of motion that govern the planetary bodies, as well as objects on earth. Crucial to his whole argument was the universal law of gravitation, which explained why the planetary bodies did not go off in straight lines but continued in elliptical orbits about the sun. In mathematical terms, Newton explained that every object in the universe is attracted to every other object by a force called gravity.

Newton had demonstrated that one mathematically proven universal law could explain all motion in the universe. At the same time, the Newtonian synthesis created a new cosmology in which the universe was seen as one huge, regulated machine that operated according to natural laws in absolute time, space, and motion. Newton's **world-machine** concept dominated the modern worldview until the twentieth century, when Albert Einstein's concept of relativity created a new picture of the universe.

Europe, China, and Scientific Revolutions An interesting question that arises is why the Scientific Revolution occurred in Europe and not in China. In the Middle Ages, China had been the most technologically advanced civilization in the world. After 1500, that distinction passed to the West (see the comparative essay "The Scientific Revolution" on p. 380). Historians are not sure why. Some have compared the sense of order in Chinese society to the competitive spirit existing in Europe. Others have emphasized China's ideological viewpoint that favored living in harmony with nature rather than trying to dominate it. One historian has even suggested that China's civil service system drew the "best and the brightest" into government service, to the detriment of other occupations.

Background to the Enlightenment

The impetus for political and social change in the eighteenth century stemmed in part from the **Enlightenment.**

COMPARATIVE ESSAY

THE SCIENTIFIC REVOLUTION

SCIENCE & TECHNOLOGY

When Catholic missionaries began to arrive in China during the sixteenth century, they marveled at the sophistication of Chinese civilization and its many accomplishments, including woodblock printing and the civil service examination system. In turn, their hosts were impressed with European inventions such as the spring-driven clock and eyeglasses.

It is no surprise that the visitors from the West were impressed with what they saw in China, for that country had long been at the forefront of human achievement. From now on, however, Europe would take the lead in the advance of science and technology, a phenomenon that would ultimately result in bringing about the Industrial Revolution and beginning a transformation of human society that would lay the foundations of the modern world.

Why did Europe suddenly become the engine for rapid global change in the seventeenth and eighteenth centuries? One factor was the change in the European worldview, the shift from a metaphysical to a materialist perspective and the growing inclination among European intellectuals to question first principles. Whereas in China, for example, the "investigation of things" proposed by Song dynasty thinkers had been put to the use of analyzing and confirming principles first established by Confucius and his contemporaries, empirical scientists in early modern Europe rejected received religious ideas, developed a new conception of the universe, and sought ways to improve material conditions around them.

Why were European thinkers more interested in practical applications of their discoveries than their counterparts elsewhere? No doubt the literate mercantile and propertied elites of Europe were attracted to the new science because it offered new ways to exploit resources for profit. Some of the early scientists made it easier for these groups to accept the new ideas by showing how they could be applied directly to specific industrial and technological needs. Galileo, for example, consciously sought an alliance between science and the material interests of the educated elite when he assured his listeners that the science of mechanics would be quite useful "when it becomes necessary to build bridges or other structures over water, something occurring mainly in affairs of great importance."

A final factor was the political changes that were beginning to take place in Europe during this period. Many European states enlarged their bureaucratic machinery and consolidated their governments in order to collect the revenues and amass the armies needed to compete militarily with rivals. Political leaders desperately sought ways to enhance their wealth and power and grasped eagerly at whatever tools were available to guarantee their survival and prosperity.

The Enlightenment was a movement of intellectuals who were greatly impressed with the accomplishments of the Scientific Revolution. When they used the word *reason*—one of their favorite words—they were advocating the application of the scientific method to the understanding of all life. All institutions and all systems of thought were subject to the rational, scientific way of thinking if people would only free themselves from the shackles of past, worthless traditions, especially religious ones. If Isaac Newton could discover the natural laws regulating the world of nature, they too, by using reason, could find the laws that governed human society. This belief in turn led them to hope that they could make progress toward a better society than the one they had inherited. *Reason, natural law, hope, progress*—these were the buzzwords in the heady atmosphere of eighteenth-century Europe.

Major sources of inspiration for the Enlightenment were two Englishmen, Isaac Newton and John Locke (1632–1704). As mentioned earlier, Newton contended that the world and everything in it worked like a giant machine. Enchanted by the grand design of this world-machine, the intellectuals of the Enlightenment were convinced that by following Newton's rules of reasoning, they could discover the natural laws that governed politics, economics, justice, and religion.

John Locke's theory of knowledge also made a great impact. In his *Essay Concerning Human Understanding*, written in 1690, Locke denied the existence of innate ideas and argued instead that every person was born with a *tabula rasa*, a blank mind:

> Let us then suppose the mind to be, as we say, white paper, void of all characters, without any ideas. How comes it to be furnished? Whence comes it by that vast store which the busy and boundless fancy of man has painted on it with an almost endless variety? Whence has it all the materials of reason and knowledge? To this I answer, in one word, from experience. . . . Our observation, employed either about external sensible objects or about the internal operations of our minds perceived and reflected on by ourselves, is that which supplies our understanding with all the materials of thinking.[1]

By denying innate ideas, Locke's philosophy implied that people were molded by their environment, by whatever they perceived through their senses from their surrounding world. By changing the environment and subjecting people to proper influences, they could be changed and a new society created. And how should the environment be changed? Newton had paved the way: reason enabled enlightened people to discover the natural laws to which all institutions should conform.

The Philosophes and Their Ideas

The intellectuals of the Enlightenment were known by the French term *philosophes,* although they were not all French and few were philosophers in the strict sense of the term. The **philosophes** were literary people, professors, journalists, economists, political scientists, and above all, social reformers. Although it was a truly international and cosmopolitan movement, the Enlightenment also enhanced the dominant role being played by French culture; Paris was its recognized capital. Most of the leaders of the Enlightenment were French. The French philosophes, in turn, affected intellectuals elsewhere and created a movement that touched the entire Western world, including the British and Spanish colonies in the Americas.

To the philosophes, the role of philosophy was not just to discuss the world but to change it. A spirit of rational criticism was to be applied to everything, including religion and politics. Spanning almost a century, the Enlightenment evolved with each succeeding generation, becoming more radical as new thinkers built on the contributions of their predecessors. A few individuals, however, dominated the landscape so completely that we can gain insight into the core ideas of the philosophes by focusing on the three French giants—Montesquieu, Voltaire, and Diderot.

Montesquieu Charles de Secondat, the baron de Montesquieu (1689–1755), came from the French nobility. His most famous work, *The Spirit of the Laws,* was published in 1748. In this comparative study of governments, Montesquieu attempted to apply the scientific method to the social and political arena to ascertain the "natural laws" governing the social and political relationships of human beings. Montesquieu distinguished three basic kinds of governments: republic, monarchy, and despotism.

Montesquieu used England as an example of monarchy, and it was his analysis of England's constitution that led to his most lasting contribution to political thought—the importance of checks and balances achieved by means of a **separation of powers.** He believed that England's system, with its separate executive, legislative, and judicial powers that served to limit and control each other, provided the greatest freedom and security for a state. The translation of his work into English two years after publication ensured its being read by American political leaders, who eventually incorporated its principles into the U.S. Constitution.

Voltaire The greatest figure of the Enlightenment was François-Marie Arouet, known simply as Voltaire (1694–1778). Son of a prosperous middle-class family from Paris, he studied law, although he achieved his first success as a playwright. Voltaire was a prolific author and wrote an almost endless stream of pamphlets, novels, plays, letters, philosophical essays, and histories.

Voltaire was especially well known for his criticism of traditional religion and his strong attachment to the ideal of religious toleration. As he grew older, Voltaire became ever more strident in his denunciations. "Crush

the infamous thing," he thundered repeatedly—the infamous thing being religious fanaticism, intolerance, and superstition.

Throughout his life, Voltaire championed not only religious tolerance but also **deism,** a religious outlook shared by most other philosophes. Deism was built on the Newtonian world-machine, which implied the existence of a mechanic (God) who had created the universe. To Voltaire and most other philosophes, the universe was like a clock, and God was the clockmaker who had created it, set it in motion, and allowed it to run according to its own natural laws.

Diderot Denis Diderot (1713–1784) was the son of a skilled craftsman from eastern France who became a writer so that he could be free to study and read in many subjects and languages. One of Diderot's favorite topics was Christianity, which he condemned as fanatical and unreasonable. Of all religions, Christianity, he averred, was the worst, "the most absurd and the most atrocious in its dogma."

Diderot's most famous contribution to the Enlightenment was the *Encyclopedia, or Classified Dictionary of the Sciences, Arts, and Trades,* a twenty-eight-volume compendium of knowledge that he edited and referred to as the "great work of his life." Its purpose, according to Diderot, was to "change the general way of thinking." It did precisely that in becoming a major weapon of the philosophes' crusade against the old French society. The contributors included many philosophes who attacked religious intolerance and advocated a program for social, legal, and political improvements that would lead to a society that was more cosmopolitan, more tolerant, more humane, and more reasonable. The *Encyclopedia* was sold to doctors, clergymen, teachers, lawyers, and even military officers, thus spreading the ideas of the Enlightenment.

Toward a New "Science of Man" The Enlightenment belief that Newton's scientific methods could be used to discover the natural laws underlying all areas of human life led to the emergence in the eighteenth century of what the philosophes called a "science of man," or what we would call the social sciences. In a number of areas, such as economics, politics, and education, the philosophes arrived at natural laws that they believed governed human actions.

Adam Smith (1723–1790) has been viewed as one of the founders of the modern discipline of economics. Smith believed that individuals should be free to pursue their own economic self-interest. Through the actions of these individuals, all society would ultimately benefit. Consequently, the state should in no way interrupt the free play of natural economic forces by imposing government regulations on the economy but should leave it alone, a doctrine that subsequently became known as *laissez-faire* (French for "leave it alone").

Smith gave to government only three basic functions: it should protect society from invasion (army), defend its citizens from injustice (police), and keep up certain public works, such as roads and canals, that private individuals could not afford.

The Later Enlightenment   By the late 1760s, a new generation of philosophes who had grown up with the worldview of the Enlightenment began to move beyond their predecessors' beliefs. Most famous was Jean-Jacques Rousseau (1712–1778), whose political beliefs were presented in two major works. In his *Discourse on the Origins of the Inequality of Mankind,* Rousseau argued that people had adopted laws and governors in order to preserve their private property. In the process, they had become enslaved by government. What, then, should people do to regain their freedom? In his celebrated treatise *The Social Contract,* published in 1762, Rousseau found an answer in the concept of the social contract whereby an entire society agreed to be governed by its general will. Each individual might have a particular will contrary to the general will, but if the individual put his particular will (self-interest) above the general will, he should be forced to abide by the general will. "This means nothing less than that he will be forced to be free," said Rousseau, because the general will was not only political but also ethical; it represented what the entire community ought to do.

Another influential treatise by Rousseau was his novel *Émile,* one of the Enlightenment's most important works on education. Rousseau's fundamental concern was that education should foster, rather than restrict, children's natural instincts. Rousseau's own experiences had shown him the importance of the emotions. What he sought was a balance between heart and mind, between emotion and reason.

But Rousseau did not necessarily practice what he preached. His own children were sent to orphanages, where many children died at a young age. Rousseau also viewed women as "naturally" different from men. In Rousseau's *Émile,* Sophie, Émile's intended wife, was educated for her role as wife and mother by learning obedience and the nurturing skills that would enable her to provide loving care for her husband and children. Not everyone in the eighteenth century, however, agreed with Rousseau.

The "Woman Question" in the Enlightenment   For centuries, many male intellectuals had argued that the nature of women made them inferior to men and made male domination of women necessary and right. In the Scientific Revolution, however, some women had made notable contributions. Maria Winkelmann in Germany, for example, was an outstanding practicing astronomer. Nevertheless, when she applied for a position as assistant astronomer at the Berlin Academy, for which she was highly qualified, she was denied the post by the academy's members, who feared that hiring her would establish a precedent ("mouths would gape").

Female thinkers in the eighteenth century disagreed with this attitude and provided suggestions for improving the conditions of women. The strongest statement for the rights of women was advanced by the English writer Mary Wollstonecraft (1759–1797), viewed by many as the founder of modern European **feminism.**

In her *Vindication of the Rights of Woman,* written in 1792, Wollstonecraft pointed out two contradictions in the views of women held by such Enlightenment thinkers as Rousseau. To argue that women must obey men, she said, was contrary to the beliefs of the same individuals that a system based on the arbitrary power of monarchs over their subjects or slave owners over their slaves was wrong. The subjection of women to men was equally wrong. In addition, she argued that the Enlightenment was based on an ideal of reason innate in all human beings. If women have reason, then they too are entitled to the same rights that men have in education and in economic and political life (see the box on p. 383).

Culture in an Enlightened Age

Although the Baroque style that had dominated the seventeenth century continued to be popular, by the 1730s, a new style affecting decoration and architecture known as **Rococo** had spread throughout Europe. Unlike the Baroque, which stressed power, grandeur, and movement, Rococo emphasized grace, charm, and gentle action. Rococo rejected strict geometrical patterns and had a fondness for curves; it liked to follow the wandering lines of natural objects, such as seashells and flowers. It made much use of interlaced designs colored in gold with delicate contours and graceful arcs. Highly secular, its lightness and charm spoke of the pursuit of pleasure, happiness, and love.

Some of Rococo's appeal is evident already in the work of Antoine Watteau (1684–1721), whose lyrical views of aristocratic life, refined, sensual, and civilized, with gentlemen and ladies in elegant dress, revealed a world of upper-class pleasure and joy. Underneath that exterior, however, was an element of sadness as the artist revealed the fragility and transitory nature of pleasure, love, and life.

High Culture   Historians have grown accustomed to distinguishing between a civilization's high culture and its popular culture. **High culture** is the literary and artistic culture of the educated and wealthy ruling classes; **popular culture** is the written and unwritten culture of the masses, most of which has traditionally been passed down orally.

By the eighteenth century, the two forms were beginning to blend, owing to the expansion of both the reading public and publishing. Whereas French publishers issued three hundred titles in 1750, about sixteen hundred were being published yearly in the 1780s. Although many of these titles were still geared for small groups of the educated elite, many were also directed to the new reading public of the middle classes, which included women and even urban artisans.

THE RIGHTS OF WOMEN

FAMILY & SOCIETY

Mary Wollstonecraft responded to an unhappy childhood in a large family by seeking to lead an independent life. Few occupations were available for middle-class women in her day, but she survived by working as a teacher, chaperone, and governess to aristocratic children. All the while, she wrote and developed her ideas on the rights of women. This excerpt is taken from her *Vindication of the Rights of Woman,* written in 1792. This work led to her reputation as the foremost British feminist thinker of the eighteenth century.

What picture does the author paint of the women of her day? Why are they in such a deplorable state? How does Wollstonecraft suggest that both women and men are at fault for the "slavish" situation of females?

Mary Wollstonecraft, *Vindication of the Rights of Woman*

It is a melancholy truth—yet such is the blessed effect of civilization—the most respectable women are the most oppressed; and, unless they have understandings far superior to the common run of understandings, taking in both sexes, they must, from being treated like contemptible beings, become contemptible. How many women thus waste life away the prey of discontent, who might have practiced as physicians, regulated a farm, managed a shop, and stood erect, supported by their own industry, instead of hanging their heads surcharged with the dew of sensibility, that consumes the beauty to which it at first gave luster. . . .

Proud of their weakness, however, [women] must always be protected, guarded from care, and all the rough toils that dignify the mind. If this be the fiat of fate, if they will make themselves insignificant and contemptible, sweetly to waste "life away," let them not expect to be valued when their beauty fades, for it is the fate of the fairest flowers to be admired and pulled to pieces by the careless hand that plucked them. In how many ways do I wish, from the purest benevolence, to impress this truth on my sex; yet I fear that they will not listen to a truth that dear-bought experience has brought home to many an agitated bosom, nor willingly resign the privileges of rank and sex for the privileges of humanity, to which those have no claim who do not discharge its duties. . . .

Would men but generously snap our chains, and be content with rational fellowship instead of slavish obedience, they would find us more observant daughters, more affectionate sisters, more faithful wives, and more reasonable mothers—in a word, better citizens. We should then love them with true affection, because we should learn to respect ourselves; and the peace of mind of a worthy man would not be interrupted by the idle vanity of his wife.

ThomsonNOW To read a full version of this document, enter the *ThomsonNOW* documents area using the access card that is available for *The Essential World History.*

An important aspect of the growth of publishing and reading in the eighteenth century was the development of magazines for the general public. Great Britain saw 25 different periodicals published in 1700, 103 in 1760, 158 in 1780. Along with magazines came daily newspapers. The first was printed in London in 1702, but by 1780, thirty-seven other English towns had their own newspapers.

Popular Culture   The distinguishing characteristic of popular culture is its collective nature. Group activity was especially common in the *festival*, a broad name used to cover a variety of celebrations: community festivals in Catholic Europe that celebrated the feast day of the local patron saint; annual festivals, such as Christmas and Easter, that go back to medieval Christianity; and the ultimate festival, Carnival, which was celebrated in the Mediterranean world of Spain, Italy, and France as well as in Germany and Austria.

Carnival began after Christmas and lasted until the start of Lent, the forty-day period of fasting and purification leading up to Easter. Because during Lent people were expected to abstain from meat, sex, and most recreations, Carnival was a time of great indulgence when heavy consumption of food and drink were the norm. It was a time of intense sexual activity as well. Songs with double meanings that would ordinarily be considered offensive could be sung publicly at this time of year. A float of Florentine "keymakers," for example, sang this ditty to the ladies: "Our tools are fine, new and useful. We always carry them with us. They are good for anything. If you want to touch them, you can."[2]

Economic Changes and the Social Order

The eighteenth century in Europe witnessed the beginning of economic changes that ultimately had a strong impact on the rest of the world.

New Economic Patterns

Europe's population began to grow around 1750 and continued to increase steadily. The total European population was probably around 120 million in 1700, 140 million in 1750, and 190 million in 1790. A falling death rate was perhaps the most important reason for this population growth. Of great significance in lowering death rates was the

Equality and Slavery: Revolution in Haiti Early in the French Revolution, the desire for equality led to a discussion of what to do about slavery. A club called Friends of the Blacks advocated the abolition of slavery, which was achieved in France in September 1791. However, French planters in the West Indies, who profited greatly from the use of slaves on their sugar plantations, opposed the abolition of slavery in the French colonies. When the National Convention came to power, the issue was revisited, and on February 4, 1794, guided by ideals of equality, the government abolished slavery in the colonies.

In one French colony, slaves had already rebelled for their freedom. In 1791, black slaves in the French sugar colony of Saint Domingue (the western third of the island of Hispaniola), inspired by the ideals of the revolution occurring in France, revolted against French plantation owners. Led by Toussaint L'Ouverture (1746–1803), a son of African slaves, over 100,000 black slaves rose in revolt and seized control of all of Hispaniola. Later, an army sent by Napoleon captured L'Ouverture, who died in captivity in France. But the French soldiers, weakened by disease, soon succumbed to the slave forces. On January 1, 1804, the western part of Hispaniola, now called Haiti, announced its freedom and became the first independent state in Latin America. One of the French revolutionary ideals had triumphed abroad.

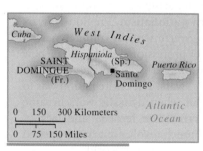

Revolt in Saint Domingue

Reaction and the Directory

By the summer of 1794, the French had been successful on the battlefield against their foreign foes, making the Terror less necessary. But the Terror continued because Robespierre, who had become a figure of power and authority, became obsessed with purifying the body politic of all the corrupt. Many deputies in the National Convention were fearful, however, that they were not safe while Robespierre was free to act and gathered enough votes to condemn him. Robespierre was guillotined on July 28, 1794.

After the death of Robespierre, a reaction set in as more moderate middle-class leaders took control. The Reign of Terror came to a halt, and the National Convention reduced the power of the Committee of Public Safety. In addition, a new constitution was drafted in August 1795 that reflected the desire for a stability that did not sacrifice the ideals of 1789. Five directors—the Directory—acted as the executive authority.

The period of the Revolution under the government of the Directory (1795–1799) was an era of stagnation and corruption. At the same time, the Directory faced political enemies from both the left and the right of the political spectrum. On the right, royalists who wanted to restore the monarchy continued their agitation. On the left, radical hopes of power were revived by continuing economic problems. Battered from both sides, unable to solve the country's economic problems, and still carrying on the wars inherited from the Committee of Public Safety, the Directory increasingly relied on the military to maintain its power. This led to a coup d'état in 1799 in which the popular military general Napoleon Bonaparte seized power.

The Age of Napoleon

Napoleon dominated both French and European history from 1799 to 1815. He was born in 1769 in Corsica shortly after France had annexed the island. The young Napoleon Bonaparte was sent to France to study in one of the new military schools and was a lieutenant when the Revolution broke out in 1789. The Revolution and the European war that followed gave him new opportunities, and Napoleon rose quickly through the ranks. In 1794, at the age of only twenty-five, he was made a brigadier general by the Committee of Public Safety. Two years later, he commanded the French armies in Italy, where he won a series of victories and returned to France as a conquering hero (see the box on p. 395). After a disastrous expedition to Egypt, Napoleon returned to Paris, where he participated in the coup that gave him control of France. He was only thirty years old.

After the coup of 1799, a new form of the Republic—called the Consulate—was proclaimed in which Napoleon, as first consul, controlled the entire executive authority of government. He had overwhelming influence over the legislature, appointed members of the administrative bureaucracy, commanded the army, and conducted foreign affairs. In 1802, Napoleon was made consul for life, and in 1804, he returned France to monarchy when he had himself crowned as Emperor Napoleon I.

CHRONOLOGY	The French Revolution
Meeting of Estates-General	May 5, 1789
Formation of National Assembly	June 17, 1789
Fall of the Bastille	July 14, 1789
Declaration of the Rights of Man and the Citizen	August 26, 1789
Civil Constitution of the Clergy	July 12, 1790
Flight of the king	June 20–21, 1791
Attack on the royal palace	August 10, 1792
Abolition of the monarchy	September 21, 1792
Execution of the king	January 21, 1793
Levy-in-mass	August 23, 1793
Execution of Robespierre	July 28, 1794
Adoption of Constitution of 1795 and the Directory	August 22, 1795

NAPOLEON AND PSYCHOLOGICAL WARFARE

POLITICS & GOVERNMENT

In 1796, at the age of twenty-seven, Napoleon Bonaparte was given command of the French army in Italy, where he won a series of stunning victories. His use of speed, deception, and surprise to overwhelm his opponents is well known. In this selection from a proclamation to his troops in Italy, Napoleon also appears as a master of psychological warfare.

What themes did Napoleon use to play on the emotions of his troops and inspire them to greater efforts? Do you think Napoleon believed these words? Why or why not?

Napoleon Bonaparte, Proclamation to French Troops in Italy (April 26, 1796)

Soldiers:

In a fortnight you have won six victories, taken twenty-one standards [flags of military units], fifty-five pieces of artillery, several strong positions, and conquered the richest part of Piedmont [in northern Italy]; you have captured 15,000 prisoners and killed or wounded more than 10,000 men. . . . You have won battles without cannon, crossed rivers without bridges, made forced marches without shoes, camped without brandy and often without bread. Soldiers of liberty, only republican troops could have endured what you have endured. Soldiers, you have our thanks! The grateful *Patrie* [nation] will owe its prosperity to you. . . .

The two armies which but recently attacked you with audacity are fleeing before you in terror; the wicked men who laughed at your misery and rejoiced at the thought of the triumphs of your enemies are confounded and trembling.

But, soldiers, as yet you have done nothing compared with what remains to be done. . . . Undoubtedly the greatest obstacles have been overcome; but you still have battles to fight, cities to capture, rivers to cross. Is there one among you whose courage is abating? No. . . . All of you are consumed with a desire to extend the glory of the French people; all of you long to humiliate those arrogant kings who dare to contemplate placing us in fetters; all of you desire to dictate a glorious peace, one which will indemnify the *Patrie* for the immense sacrifices it has made; all of you wish to be able to say with pride as you return to your villages, "I was with the victorious army of Italy!"

ThomsonNOW To read a related document, enter the *ThomsonNOW* documents area using the access card that is available for *The Essential World History.*

Domestic Policies

One of Napoleon's first domestic policies was to establish peace with the oldest and most implacable enemy of the Revolution, the Catholic church. In 1801, Napoleon arranged a concordat with the pope that recognized Catholicism as the religion of a majority of the French people. In return, the pope agreed not to raise the question of the church lands confiscated in the Revolution. As a result of the concordat, the Catholic church was no longer an enemy of the French government.

Napoleon's most enduring domestic achievement was his codification of the laws. Before the Revolution, France had some three hundred local legal systems. During the Revolution, efforts were made to prepare a single code of laws for the entire nation, but it remained for Napoleon to bring the work to completion in the famous Civil Code. This preserved most of the revolutionary gains by recognizing the principle of the equality of all citizens before the law, the abolition of serfdom and feudalism, and religious toleration. Property rights were also protected.

At the same time, the Civil Code strictly curtailed the rights of some people. During the radical phase of the French Revolution, new laws had made divorce an easy process for both husbands and wives and allowed sons and daughters to inherit property equally. Napoleon's Civil Code undid these laws. Divorce was still allowed but was made more difficult for women to obtain. Women were now "less equal than men" in other ways as well. When they married, their property came under the control of their husbands.

Napoleon also developed a powerful, centralized administrative machine and worked hard to develop a bureaucracy of capable officials. Early on, the regime showed that it cared little whether the expertise of officials had been acquired in royal or revolutionary bureaucracies. Promotion, whether in civil or military offices, was to be based not on rank or birth but on ability only. This principle of a government career open to talent was, of course, what many bourgeois had wanted before the Revolution.

In his domestic policies, then, Napoleon both destroyed and preserved aspects of the Revolution. Liberty had been replaced by an initially benevolent despotism that grew increasingly arbitrary as the demands of war overwhelmed Napoleon and the French. The Civil Code, however, preserved the equality of all citizens before the law. The concept of careers open to talent was also a gain of the Revolution that Napoleon preserved.

Napoleon's Empire

When Napoleon became consul in 1799, France was at war with a second European coalition of Russia, Great Britain, and Austria. Napoleon realized the need for a pause and made a peace treaty in 1802. But war was renewed in 1803 with Britain, which was soon joined by Austria, Russia, and Prussia in the Third Coalition. In a series of battles from 1805 to 1807, Napoleon's Grand Army defeated the

The Coronation of Napoleon. In 1804, Napoleon restored monarchy to France when he had himself crowned as emperor. In the coronation scene painted by Jacques-Louis David, Napoleon is shown crowning his wife, the empress Josephine, while the pope looks on. The painting shows Napoleon's mother seated in the box in the background, even though she was not at the ceremony.

Austrian, Prussian, and Russian armies, giving Napoleon the opportunity to create a new European order.

The Grand Empire From 1807 to 1812, Napoleon was the master of Europe. His Grand Empire was composed of three major parts: the French Empire, dependent states, and allied states (see Map 17.3). Dependent states were kingdoms under the rule of Napoleon's relatives; these came to include Spain, the Netherlands, the kingdom of Italy, the Swiss Republic, the Grand Duchy of Warsaw, and the Confederation of the Rhine (a union of all German states except Austria and Prussia). Allied states were those defeated by Napoleon and forced to join his struggle against Britain; these included Prussia, Austria, Russia, and Sweden.

Within his empire, Napoleon sought acceptance of certain revolutionary principles, including legal equality, religious toleration, and economic freedom. In the inner core and dependent states of his Grand Empire, Napoleon tried to destroy the old order. Nobility and clergy everywhere in these states lost their special privileges. He decreed equality of opportunity with offices open to talent, equality before the law, and religious toleration. This spread of French revolutionary principles was an important factor in the development of liberal traditions in these countries.

Napoleon hoped that his Grand Empire would last for centuries; it collapsed almost as rapidly as it had been

formed. As long as Britain ruled the waves, it was not subject to military attack. Napoleon hoped to invade Britain, but he could not overcome the British navy's decisive defeat of a combined French-Spanish fleet at Trafalgar in 1805. To defeat Britain, Napoleon turned to his **Continental System.** An alliance put into effect between 1806 and 1808, it attempted to prevent British goods from reaching the European continent in order to weaken Britain economically and destroy its capacity to wage war. But the Continental System failed. Allied states resented it; some began to cheat and others to resist.

Napoleon also encountered new sources of opposition. His conquests made the French hated oppressors and aroused the patriotism of the conquered people. A Spanish uprising against Napoleon's rule, aided by British support, kept a French force of 200,000 pinned down for years.

The Fall of Napoleon The beginning of Napoleon's downfall came in 1812 with his invasion of Russia. The refusal of the Russians to remain in the Continental System left Napoleon with little choice. Although aware of the risks in invading such a huge country, he also knew that if the Russians were allowed to challenge the Continental System unopposed, others would soon follow suit. In June 1812, he led his Grand Army of more than 600,000 men into Russia. Napoleon's hopes for victory

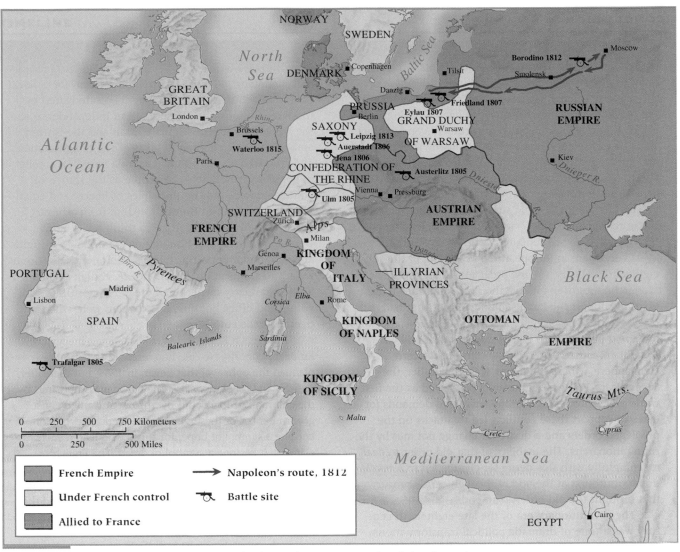

MAP 17.3 **Napoleon's Grand Empire.** Napoleon's Grand Army won a series of victories against Britain, Austria, Prussia, and Russia that gave the French emperor full or partial control over much of Europe by 1807. ❓ On the Continent, what is the overall relationship between distance from France and degree of French control, and how can you account for this?

depended on quickly defeating the Russian armies, but the Russian forces retreated and refused to give battle, torching their own villages and countryside to keep Napoleon's army from finding food. When the Russians did stop to fight at Borodino, Napoleon's forces won an indecisive and costly victory. When the remaining troops of the Grand Army arrived in Moscow, they found the city ablaze. Lacking food and supplies, Napoleon abandoned Moscow late in October and made a retreat across Russia in terrible winter conditions. Only 40,000 of the original 600,000 men managed to arrive back in Poland in January 1813.

This military disaster led other European states to rise up and attack the crippled French army. Paris was captured in March 1814, and Napoleon was sent into exile on the island of Elba, off the coast of Italy. Meanwhile, the Bourbon monarchy was restored in the person of Louis XVIII, the count of Provence, brother of the executed king. (Louis XVII, son of Louis XVI, had died in prison at

age ten.) Napoleon, bored on Elba, slipped back into France. When troops were sent to capture him, Napoleon opened his coat and addressed them: "Soldiers of the 5th regiment, I am your Emperor. . . . If there is a man among you would kill his Emperor, here I am!" No one fired a shot. Shouting *"Vive l'Empereur! Vive l'Empereur!"* the troops went over to his side, and Napoleon entered Paris in triumph on March 20, 1815.

The powers that had defeated him pledged once more to fight him. Having decided to strike first at his enemies, Napoleon raised yet another army and moved to attack the allied forces stationed in what is now Belgium. At Waterloo on June 18, Napoleon met a combined British and Prussian army under the duke of Wellington and suffered a bloody defeat. This time, the victorious allies exiled him to Saint Helena, a small, forsaken island in the South Atlantic, off the coast of Africa. Only Napoleon's memory continued to haunt French political life.

LOOKING BACK, LOOKING AHEAD

*W*ITHIN THE CENTRALIZED STATES at the end of the eighteenth century, the steady growth of a commercial and manufacturing sector was beginning to create the conditions for a future industrial revolution. A number of Asian societies had made technological advances during this period and witnessed the emergence of a more visible and articulate urban bourgeoisie. For the moment, however, such forces were mere portents for the future, not

TIMELINE

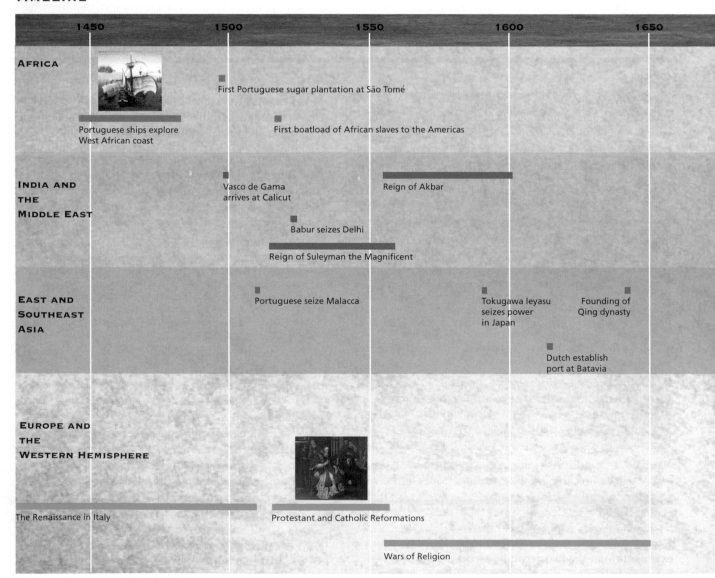

	1450	1500	1550	1600	1650
AFRICA		First Portuguese sugar plantation at São Tomé			
	Portuguese ships explore West African coast	First boatload of African slaves to the Americas			
INDIA AND THE MIDDLE EAST		Vasco de Gama arrives at Calicut	Reign of Akbar		
		Babur seizes Delhi			
		Reign of Suleyman the Magnificent			
EAST AND SOUTHEAST ASIA		Portuguese seize Malacca		Tokugawa Ieyasu seizes power in Japan	Founding of Qing dynasty
				Dutch establish port at Batavia	
EUROPE AND THE WESTERN HEMISPHERE	The Renaissance in Italy	Protestant and Catholic Reformations			
			Wars of Religion		

signs of an imminent industrial revolution. At the beginning of the nineteenth century, the primary fact of life for most Asian and African societies was the expansionist power of an industrializing and ever more aggressive Europe. The power and ambition of the West provided an immediate challenge to the independence and destiny of societies throughout the rest of the world. The nature of that challenge will be the subject of our next section.

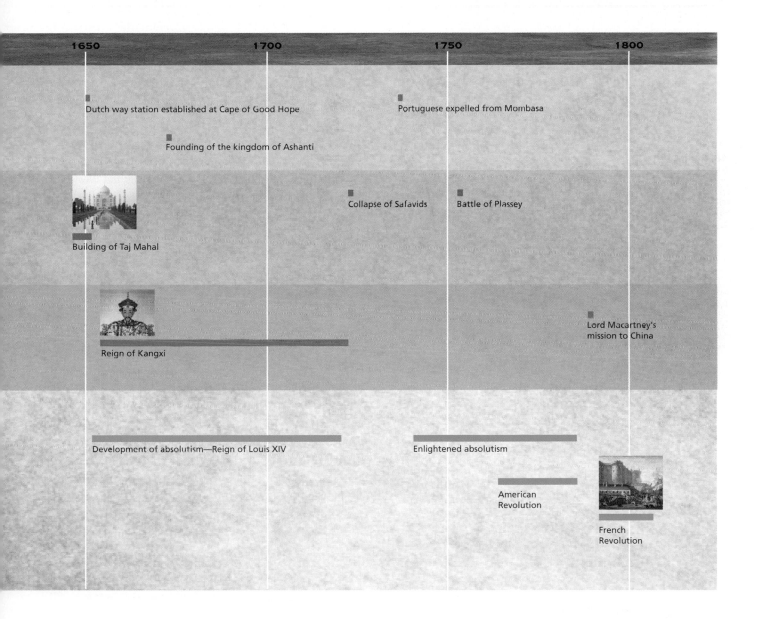

1650 — 1700 — 1750 — 1800

Dutch way station established at Cape of Good Hope

Portuguese expelled from Mombasa

Founding of the kingdom of Ashanti

Collapse of Safavids

Battle of Plassey

Building of Taj Mahal

Reign of Kangxi

Lord Macartney's mission to China

Development of absolutism—Reign of Louis XIV

Enlightened absolutism

American Revolution

French Revolution

MODERN PATTERNS OF WORLD HISTORY (1800–1945)

THE PERIOD OF WORLD HISTORY from 1800 to 1945 was characterized, above all, by two major developments: the growth of industrialization and Western domination of the world. The two developments were, of course, interconnected. The Industrial Revolution became one of the major forces of change in the nineteenth century as it led Western civilization into the industrial era that has characterized the modern world. Beginning in Britain, it spread to the Continent and the Western Hemisphere in the course of the nineteenth century. At the same time, the Industrial Revolution created the technological means, including new weapons, by which the West achieved domination of much of the rest of the world by the end of the nineteenth century.

Europeans had begun to explore the world in the fifteenth century, but even as late as 1870, they had not yet completely penetrated North America, South America, Australia, or most of Africa. In Asia and Africa, with few exceptions, the Western presence was limited to trading posts. Between 1870 and 1914, Western civilization expanded into the rest of the Americas and Australia, while the bulk of Africa and Asia was divided into European colonies or spheres of influence. Two major events explain this remarkable expansion: the migration of many Europeans to other parts of the world due to population growth and the revival of imperialism, which was made possible by the

The Art Archive

West's technological advances. Beginning in the 1880s, European states began an intense scramble for overseas territory. During this revival of imperialism—the "new imperialism," some have called it—Europeans carved up Asia and Africa.

What was the overall economic effect of imperialism on the subject peoples? For most of the population in colonial areas, Western domination was rarely beneficial and often destructive. Although a limited number of merchants, large landowners, and traditional hereditary elites undoubtedly prospered under the umbrella of the expanding imperialistic economic order, the majority of colonial peoples, urban and rural alike, probably suffered considerable hardship as a result of the policies adopted by their foreign rulers.

Some historians point out, however, that for all the inequities of the colonial system, there was a positive side to the experience as well. The expansion of markets and the beginnings of a modern transportation and communications network, while bringing few immediate benefits to the colonial peoples, offered considerable promise for future economic growth. At the same time, the introduction of new ways of looking at human freedom and the relationship between the individual and society set the stage for a reevaluation of such ideas after the restoration of independence following World War II.

Perhaps the Western concept that had the most immediate impact on the era was the rise of nationalism. Like the Industrial Revolution, the idea of nationalism originated in eighteenth-century Europe, where it was a product of the secularization of the age and the experiences of the French revolutionary and Napoleonic eras. Although the concept provided the basis for a new sense of community and the rise of the modern nation-state, it also gave birth to ethnic tensions and hatred that resulted in bitter disputes and civil strife and contributed to the competition that eventually erupted into world war. Nevertheless, colonial peoples soon learned the power of nationalism, and in the twentieth century, nationalism would become a powerful force in the rest of the world as nationalist revolutions moved through Asia, Africa, and the Middle East. Moreover, the exhaustive struggles of two world wars sapped the power of the European states, and the colonial powers no longer had the energy or the wealth to maintain their colonial empires after World War II. ◆

18

THE BEGINNINGS OF MODERNIZATION: INDUSTRIALIZATION AND NATIONALISM, 1800–1870

CHAPTER OUTLINE AND FOCUS QUESTIONS

The Industrial Revolution and Its Impact

☐ What were the basic features of the new industrial system created by the Industrial Revolution, and what effects did the new system have on urban life, social classes, family life, and standards of living?

Reaction and Revolution: The Growth of Nationalism

☐ What were the major ideas associated with conservatism, liberalism, and nationalism, and what role did each ideology play in Europe and Latin America between 1800 and 1870?

☐ What were the causes of the revolutions of 1848, and why did these revolutions fail?

National Unification and the National State, 1848–1871

☐ What actions did Cavour and Bismarck take to bring about unification in Italy and Germany, respectively, and what role did war play in their efforts?

Cultural Life: Romanticism and Realism in the Western World

☐ What were the main characteristics of Romanticism and Realism?

CRITICAL THINKING

☐ In what ways were the intellectual and artistic developments of the age related to the development of industrialization and the growth of nationalism?

A meeting of the Congress of Vienna

© Scala/Art Resource, NY

$\mathscr{I}$N SEPTEMBER 1814, hundreds of foreigners began to converge on Vienna, the capital city of the Austrian Empire. Many were members of European royalty–kings, archdukes, princes, and their wives–accompanied by their diplomatic advisers and scores of servants. Their congenial host was the Austrian emperor, Francis I, who never tired of regaling Vienna's guests with concerts, glittering balls, sumptuous feasts, and innumerable hunting parties. One participant remembered, "Eating, fireworks, public illuminations. For eight or ten days, I haven't been able to work at all. What a life!" Of course, not every waking hour was spent in pleasure during this gathering of notables, known to history as the Congress of Vienna. These people were also representatives of all the states that had fought Napoleon, and their real business was to arrange a final peace settlement after almost a decade of war. On June 8, 1815, they finally completed their task.

The forces of upheaval unleashed during the French revolutionary and Napoleonic wars were temporarily quieted in 1815 as rulers sought to restore stability by reestablishing much of the old order to a Europe ravaged by war. But the Western world had been changed, and it would not readily go back to the old system. New ideologies of change, especially liberalism and nationalism, products of the upheaval initiated in France, had become too powerful to be contained. The forces of change called forth revolts that periodically shook the West and culminated in a spate of revolutions in 1848. Some of the revolutions and revolutionaries were successful; most were not. And yet by 1870, many of the goals sought by the liberals and nationalists during the first half of the nineteenth century seemed to have been achieved. National unity became a reality in Italy and Germany, and many Western states developed parliamentary features.

During the late eighteenth and early nineteenth centuries, another revolution—an industrial one—transformed the economic and social structure of Europe and spawned the industrial era that has characterized modern world history. ◇

The Industrial Revolution and Its Impact

The enormous leap in industrial production triggered by the Industrial Revolution relied largely on coal and steam, which replaced wind and water as new sources of energy and power to drive laborsaving machines. In turn, these machines called for new ways of organizing human labor to maximize the benefits and profits from the new machines; factories replaced shop and home workrooms. During the Industrial Revolution, Europe shifted from an economy based on agriculture and handicrafts to an economy based on manufacturing by machines and automated factories. Large numbers of people moved from the countryside to cities to work in the new factories. The creation of a wealthy industrial middle class and a huge industrial working class (or proletariat) substantially transformed traditional social relationships.

The Industrial Revolution in Great Britain

The Industrial Revolution began in Britain in the 1780s. Improvements in agricultural practices in the eighteenth century led to a significant increase in food production. British agriculture could now feed more people at lower prices with less labor; even ordinary British families did not have to use most of their income to buy food, giving them the wherewithal to purchase manufactured goods. At the same time, rapid population growth in the second half of the eighteenth century provided a pool of surplus labor for the new factories of the emerging British industry.

A crucial factor in Britain's successful industrialization was the ability to produce cheaply the articles in greatest demand. The traditional methods of cottage industry could not keep up with the growing demand for cotton clothes throughout Britain and its vast colonial empire. Faced with this problem, British cloth manufacturers sought and accepted the new methods of manufacturing that a series of inventions provided. In so doing, these individuals ignited the Industrial Revolution.

Changes in Textile Production The invention of the flying shuttle made weaving on a loom faster and enabled weavers to double their output. This created shortages of yarn until James Hargreaves's spinning jenny, perfected by 1768, allowed spinners to produce yarn in greater quantities. Edmund Cartwright's loom, powered by water and invented in 1787, allowed the weaving of cloth to catch up with the spinning of yarn. It was now more efficient to bring workers to the machines and organize their labor collectively in factories located next to rivers and streams, the sources of power for these early machines.

The invention of the steam engine pushed the cotton industry to even greater heights of productivity. In the 1760s, a Scottish engineer, James Watt (1736–1819), built an engine powered by steam that could pump water from mines three times as quickly as previous engines. In 1782, Watt developed a rotary engine that could turn a shaft and thus drive machinery. Steam power could now be applied to spinning and weaving cotton, and before long, cotton mills using steam engines were multiplying across Britain. Fired by coal, these steam engines could be located anywhere.

The boost given to cotton textile production by these technological changes was readily apparent. In 1760, Britain had imported 2.5 million pounds of raw cotton, which was farmed out to cottage industries. In 1787, the British imported 22 million pounds of cotton; most of it was spun on machines, some powered by water in large mills. By 1840, some 366 million pounds of cotton—now Britain's most important product in value—were being imported. By this time, British cotton goods were sold everywhere in the world.

Other Technological Changes The British iron industry also was radically transformed during the Industrial Revolution. A better quality of iron came into being in the 1780s when Henry Cort developed a system called puddling, in which coke, derived from coal, was used to burn away impurities in pig iron (crude iron) and produce an iron of high quality. A boom then ensued in the British iron industry. In 1740, Britain produced 17,000 tons of iron; by the 1840s, over 2 million tons; and by 1852, almost 3 million tons, more than the rest of the world combined.

The new high-quality wrought iron was in turn used to build new machines and ultimately new industries. In 1804, Richard Trevithick pioneered the first steam-powered locomotive on an industrial rail line in southern Wales. It pulled 10 tons of ore and seventy people at 5 miles per hour. Better locomotives soon followed. Engines built by George Stephenson and his son proved superior, and it was Stephenson's *Rocket* that was used on the first public railway line, which opened in 1830, extending 32 miles from Liverpool to Manchester. *Rocket* sped along at 16 miles per hour.

Within twenty years, locomotives were traveling at 50 miles per hour. By 1840, Britain had almost 6,000 miles of railroads.

The railroad was an important contributor to the success and maturing of the Industrial Revolution. Railway construction created new job opportunities, especially for farm laborers and peasants who had long been accustomed to finding work outside their local villages. Perhaps most important, the proliferation of a cheaper and faster means of transportation had a ripple effect on the growth of the industrial economy. As the prices of goods fell, markets grew larger; increased sales meant more factories and more machinery, thereby reinforcing the self-sustaining aspect of the Industrial Revolution, a fundamental break with the traditional European economy. Continuous, self-sustaining economic growth came to be accepted as a fundamental characteristic of the new economy.

The Industrial Factory Another visible symbol of the Industrial Revolution was the factory (see the comparative illustration at the right). From its beginning, the factory created a new labor system. Factory owners wanted to use their new machines constantly. Workers were therefore obliged to work regular hours and in shifts to keep the machines producing at a steady rate. Early factory workers, however, came from rural areas, where they were used to a different pace of life. Peasant farmers worked hard, especially at harvest time, but they were also used to periods of inactivity.

Early factory owners therefore had to institute a system of work discipline in which employees became accustomed to working regular hours and doing the same work over and over. Of course, such work was boring, and factory owners resorted to tough methods to accomplish their goals. They issued minute and detailed factory regulations. Adult workers were fined for a wide variety of minor infractions, such as being a few minutes late for work, and dismissed for more serious misdoings, especially drunkenness, which set a bad example for younger workers and also courted disaster in the midst of dangerous machinery. Employers found that dismissals and fines worked well for adult employees; in a time when great population growth had produced large masses of unskilled labor, dismissal meant disaster. Children were less likely to understand the implications of dismissal, so they were sometimes disciplined more directly—often by beating. As the nineteenth century progressed, the second and third generations of workers came to view a regular workweek as a natural way of life.

By the mid-nineteenth century, Great Britain had become the world's first and richest industrial nation. Britain was the "workshop, banker, and trader of the world." It produced one-half of the world's coal and manufactured goods; in 1850, its cotton industry alone was equal in size to the industries of all other European countries combined.

The Spread of Industrialization

From Great Britain, industrialization spread to the continental countries of Europe and the United States at

COMPARATIVE ILLUSTRATION
Textile Factories, West and East. The development of the factory changed the relationship between workers and employers as workers were encouraged to adjust to a new system of discipline that forced them to work regular hours under close supervision. At the top is an 1851 illustration that shows women working in a British cotton factory. The factory system came later to the rest of the world than it did in Britain. Shown at the bottom is one of the earliest industrial factories in Japan, the Tomioka silk factory, built in the 1870s. Note that although women are doing the work in both factories, the managers are men.

MAP 18.1 **The Industrialization of Europe by 1850.** Great Britain was Europe's first industrialized country; by the middle of the nineteenth century, however, several regions on the Continent, especially in Belgium, France, and the German states, had made significant advances in industrialization. ❓ What reasons could explain why coal mining and iron industries are densely clustered in manufacturing and industrial areas? In what areas was there a population boom?

different times and speeds during the nineteenth century. First to be industrialized on the Continent were Belgium, France, and the German states (see Map 18.1). Their governments were especially active in encouraging the development of industrialization by, among other things, setting up technical schools to train engineers and mechanics and providing funds to build roads, canals, and railroads. By 1850, a network of iron rails had spread across Europe.

The Industrial Revolution also transformed the new nation in North America, the United States. In 1800, six out of every seven American workers were farmers, and there were no cities with more than 100,000 people. By 1860, however, the population had sextupled to 30 million people (larger than Great Britain), nine U.S. cities had

populations over 100,000, and only 50 percent of American workers were farmers.

In sharp contrast to Britain, the United States was a large country. Thousands of miles of roads and canals were built linking east and west. The steamboat facilitated transportation on the Great Lakes, Atlantic coastal waters, and rivers. Most important in the development of an American transportation system was the railroad. Beginning with 100 miles in 1830, by 1860 there were over 27,000 miles of railroad track covering the United States. This transportation revolution turned the United States into a single massive market for the manufactured goods of the Northeast, the early center of American industrialization.

COMPARATIVE ESSAY

THE INDUSTRIAL REVOLUTION

 SCIENCE & TECHNOLOGY

Why some societies were able to embark on the road to industrialization during the nineteenth century and others were not has long been debated. Some historians have found an answer in the cultural characteristics of individual societies, such as the Protestant work ethic in parts of Europe or the tradition of social discipline and class hierarchy in Japan. Others have placed more emphasis on practical reasons. To the historian Peter Stearns, for example, the availability of capital, natural resources, a network of trade relations, and navigable rivers all helped stimulate industrial growth in nineteenth-century Britain. By contrast, the lack of an urban market for agricultural goods (which reduced the landowners' incentives to introduce mechanized farming) is sometimes cited as a reason for China's failure to set out on its own path toward industrialization.

To some observers, the ability of western European countries to exploit the wealth and resources of their colonies in Asia, Africa, and Latin America was crucial to their success in achieving industrial prowess. In their view, the Age of Exploration led to the creation of a new "world system" characterized by the emergence of global trade networks, propelled by the rising force of European capitalism in pursuit of precious metals, markets, and cheap raw materials.

These views are not mutually exclusive. In his recent book titled *The Great Divergence: China, Europe, and the Making of the Modern World Economy,* Kenneth Pomeranz argued that coal resources and access to the cheap raw materials of the Americas were both assets for Great Britain as it became the first to enter the industrial age.

Clearly, there is no single answer to this controversy. Whatever the case, the advent of the industrial age had a number of lasting consequences for the world at large. On the one hand, the material wealth of the nations that successfully passed through the process increased significantly. In many cases, the creation of advanced industrial societies strengthened democratic institutions and led to a higher standard of living for the majority of the population. It also helped reduce class barriers and bring about the emancipation of women from many of the legal and social restrictions that had characterized the previous era.

On the other hand, not all the consequences of the Industrial Revolution were beneficial. In the industrializing societies themselves, rapid economic change often led to widening disparities in the distribution of wealth and a sense of rootlessness and alienation among much of the population. Although some societies were able to manage these problems with a degree of success, others experienced a breakdown of social values and widespread political instability. In the meantime, the transformation of Europe into a giant factory sucking up raw materials and spewing manufactured goods out to the entire world had a wrenching impact on traditional societies whose own economic, social, and cultural foundations were forever changed by absorption into the new world order.

Limiting the Spread of Industrialization to the Rest of the World

Before 1870, the industrialization that was transforming western and central Europe and the United States did not extend in any significant way to the rest of the world (see the comparative essay "The Industrial Revolution" above). Even in eastern Europe, industrialization lagged far behind. Russia, for example, was still largely rural and agricultural, ruled by an autocratic regime that preferred to keep the peasants in serfdom.

In other parts of the world where they had established control (see Chapter 20), newly industrialized European states pursued a deliberate policy of preventing the growth of mechanized industry. A good example is India. In the eighteenth century, India had become one of the world's greatest exporters of cotton cloth produced by hand labor. In the first half of the nineteenth century, much of India fell under the control of the British East India Company. With British control came inexpensive British factory-produced textiles, and soon thousands of Indian spinners and handloom weavers were

unemployed. British policy encouraged Indians to export their raw materials while buying British-made goods.

The Social Impact of the Industrial Revolution

Eventually, the Industrial Revolution revolutionized the social life of Europe and the world. This change was already evident in the first half of the nineteenth century in the growth of cities and the emergence of new social classes.

Population Growth and Urbanization Population increases had already begun in the eighteenth century, but they became dramatic in the nineteenth century. In 1750, the total European population stood at an estimated 140 million; by 1850, it had almost doubled to 266 million. The key to the expansion of population was the decline in death rates throughout Europe. Wars and major epidemic diseases, such as plague and smallpox, became less frequent, which led to a drop in the number of deaths. Thanks to the increase in the food supply, more people were better fed and more resistant to disease.

Throughout Europe, cities and towns grew dramatically in the first half of the nineteenth century, a phenomenon related to industrialization. By 1850, especially in Great Britain and Belgium, cities were rapidly becoming home to many industries. With the steam engine, factory owners could locate their manufacturing plants in urban centers where they had ready access to transportation facilities and large numbers of new arrivals from the country looking for work.

In 1800, Great Britain had one major city, London, with a population of 1 million, and six cities with populations between 50,000 and 100,000. Fifty years later, London's population had swelled to 2,363,000, and there were nine cities with populations over 100,000 and eighteen cities with populations between 50,000 and 100,000. Over 50 percent of the British population lived in towns and cities by 1850. Urban populations also grew on the Continent, but less dramatically.

The dramatic growth of cities in the first half of the nineteenth century produced miserable living conditions for many of the inhabitants. Located in the center of most industrial towns were the row houses of the industrial workers. Rooms were not large and were frequently overcrowded, as a government report of 1838 in Britain revealed: "I entered several of the tenements. In one of them, on the ground floor, I found six persons occupying a very small room, two in bed, ill with fever. In the room above this were two more persons in one bed, ill with fever." Another report said: "There were 63 families where there were at least five persons to one bed; and there were some in which even six were packed in one bed, lying at the top and bottom—children and adults."[1]

Sanitary conditions in these towns were appalling; sewers and open drains were common on city streets: "In the centre of this street is a gutter, into which the refuse of animal and vegetable matters of all kinds, the dirty water from the washing of clothes and of the houses, are all poured, and there they stagnate and putrefy."[2] Unable to deal with human excrement, cities in the early industrial era smelled horrible and were extraordinarily unhealthy.

New Social Classes: The Industrial Middle Class   The rise of industrial capitalism produced a new middle-class group. The bourgeoisie or middle class was not new; it had existed since the emergence of cities in the Middle Ages. Originally, the bourgeois was a burgher or town dweller, active as a merchant, official, artisan, lawyer, or man of letters. As wealthy townspeople bought land, the original meaning of the word *bourgeois* became lost, and the term came to include people involved in commerce, industry, and banking as well as professionals such as teachers, physicians, and government officials.

The new industrial middle class was made up of the people who constructed the factories, purchased the machines, and figured out where the markets were (see the box on p. 410). Their qualities included resourcefulness, single-mindedness, resolution, initiative, vision,

ambition, and often, of course, greed. As Jedediah Strutt, a cotton manufacturer said, "Getting of money . . . is the main business of the life of men."

Members of the industrial middle class sought to reduce the barriers between themselves and the landed elite, but it is clear that they tried at the same time to separate themselves from the laboring classes below them. The working class was actually a mixture of different groups in the first half of the nineteenth century, but in the course of the nineteenth century, factory workers would form an industrial **proletariat** that constituted a majority of the working class.

New Social Classes: The Industrial Working Class   Early industrial workers faced wretched working conditions. Work shifts ranged from twelve to sixteen hours a day, six days a week, with a half hour for lunch and dinner. There was no security of employment and no minimum wage. The worst conditions were in the cotton mills, where temperatures were especially debilitating. One report noted that "in the cotton-spinning work, these creatures are kept, fourteen hours in each day, locked up, summer and winter, in a heat of from eighty to eighty-four degrees." Mills were dirty, dusty, and unhealthy.

Conditions in the coal mines were also harsh. Although steam-powered engines were used to lift coal from the mines to the top, inside the mines, men still bore the burden of digging the coal out while horses, mules, women, and children hauled coal carts on rails to the lift. Dangerous conditions, including cave-ins, explosions, and gas fumes, were a way of life. The cramped conditions in mines—tunnels were often only 3 or 4 feet high—and their constant dampness led to deformed bodies and ruined lungs.

Both children and women worked in large numbers in early factories and mines. Children had been an important part of the family economy in preindustrial times, working in the fields or carding and spinning wool at home. In the Industrial Revolution, however, child labor was exploited more than ever. The owners of cotton factories found child labor very helpful. Children had a particular delicate touch as spinners of cotton. Their smaller size made it easier for them to move under machines to gather loose cotton. Moreover, children were more easily trained to do factory work. Above all, children represented a cheap supply of labor. In 1821, about half of the British population was under twenty years of age. Hence children made up an abundant supply of labor, and they were paid only about one-sixth to one-third of what a man was paid. In the cotton factories in 1838, children under eighteen made up 29 percent of the total workforce; children as young as seven worked twelve to fifteen hours per day, six days a week, in cotton mills.

By 1830, women and children made up two-thirds of the cotton industry's labor. After the Factory Act of 1833, however, the number of children employed declined, and their places were taken by women, who came to dominate the labor forces of the early factories. Women made up 50 percent of the labor force in textile (cotton and woolen)

In the nineteenth century, a new industrial middle class in Great Britain took the lead in creating the Industrial Revolution. Japan did not begin to industrialize until after 1870 (see Chapter 21). There, too, an industrial middle class emerged, although there were also important differences in the attitudes of business leaders in Britain and Japan. Some of these differences can be seen in these documents. The first is an excerpt from *Self-Help,* a book first published in 1859, by Samuel Smiles, who espoused the belief that people succeed through "individual industry, energy, and uprightness." The two additional selections are by Shibuzawa Eiichi, a Japanese industrialist who supervised textile factories. Although he began his business career in 1873, he did not write his autobiography, the source of his first excerpt, until 1927.

What do you think are the major similarities and differences between the business attitudes of Samuel Smiles and Shibuzawa Eiichi? How do you explain the differences?

Samuel Smiles, *Self-Help*

"Heaven helps those who help themselves" is a well-worn maxim, embodying in a small compass the results of vast human experience. The spirit of self-help is the root of all genuine growth in the individual; and, exhibited in the lives of many, it constitutes the true source of national vigor and strength. Help from without is often enfeebling in its effects, but help from within invariably invigorates. Whatever is done for men or classes, to a certain extent takes away the stimulus and necessity of doing for themselves; and where men are subjected to overguidance and overgovernment, the inevitable tendency is to render them comparatively helpless. . . .

National progress is the sum of individual industry, energy, and uprightness, as national decay is of individual idleness, selfishness, and vice. . . . If this view be correct, then it follows that the highest patriotism and philanthrophy consist, not so much in altering laws and modifying institutions as in helping and stimulating men to elevate and improve themselves by their own free and independent action as individuals. . . .

Many popular books have been written for the purpose of communicating to the public the grand secret of making money. But there is no secret whatever about it, as the proverbs of every nation abundantly testify. . . . "A penny saved is a penny gained."—"Diligence is the mother of good-luck."—"No pains no gains."—"No sweat no sweet."—"Sloth, the key of poverty."—"Work, and thou shalt have."—"He who will not work, neither shall he eat."—"The world is his, who has patience and industry."

Shibuzawa Eiichi, *Autobiography*

I . . . felt that it was necessary to raise the social standing of those who engaged in commerce and industry. By way of setting an example, I began studying and practicing the teachings of the *Analects of Confucius.* It contains teachings first enunciated more than twenty-four hundred years ago. Yet it supplies the ultimate in practical ethics for all of us to follow in our daily living. It has many golden rules for businessmen. For example, there is a saying: "Wealth and respect are what men desire, but unless a right way is followed, they cannot be obtained; poverty and lowly position are what men despise, but unless a right way is found, one cannot leave that status once reaching it." It shows very clearly how a businessman must act in this world.

Shibuzawa Eiichi on Progress

One must beware of the tendency of some to argue that it is through individualism or egoism that the State and society can progress most rapidly. They claim that under individualism, each individual competes with the others, and progress results from this competition. But this is to see merely the advantages and ignore the disadvantages, and I cannot support such a theory. Society exists, and a State has been founded. Although people desire to rise to positions of wealth and honor, the social order and the tranquility of the State will be disrupted if this is done egoistically. Men should not do battle in competition with their fellow men. Therefore, I believe that in order to get along together in society and serve the State, we must by all means abandon this idea of independence and self-reliance and reject egoism completely.

ThomsonNOW™   To read more of *Self-Help,* enter the *ThomsonNOW* documents area using the access card that is available for *The Essential World History.*

---

factories before 1870. They were mostly unskilled laborers and were paid half or less of what men received.

Reaction and Revolution: The Growth of Nationalism

After the defeat of Napoleon, European rulers moved to restore much of the old order. This was the goal of the great powers—Great Britain, Austria, Prussia, and Russia—when they met at the Congress of Vienna in September 1814 to arrange a final peace settlement after the Napoleonic wars. The leader of the congress was the Austrian foreign minister, Prince Klemens von Metternich (1773–1859), who claimed that he was guided at Vienna by the **principle of legitimacy.** To reestablish peace and stability in Europe, he considered it necessary to restore the legitimate monarchs who would preserve traditional institutions (see Map 18.2). This had already been done in France with the restoration of the Bourbon monarchy.

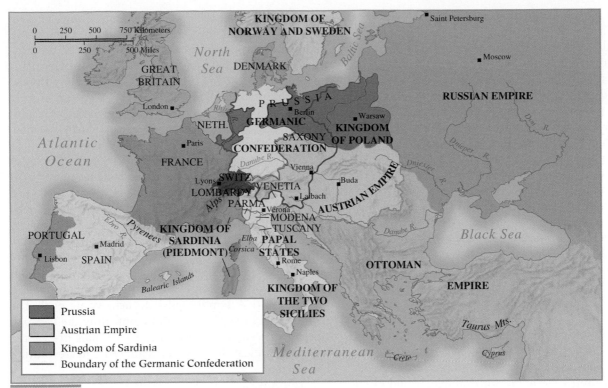

MAP 18.2 **Europe After the Congress of Vienna, 1815.** The Congress of Vienna imposed order on Europe based on the principles of monarchical government and a balance of power. Monarchs were restored in France, Spain, and other states recently under Napoleon's control, and much territory changed hands, often at the expense of small and weak states. ❓ How did Europe's major powers manipulate territory to decrease the probability that France could again threaten the Continent's stability? ✎ **View an animated version of this map or related maps at** http://worldrc.wadsworth.com/

The peace arrangements of 1815 were but the beginning of a conservative reaction determined to contain the liberal and nationalist forces unleashed by the French Revolution. Metternich and his kind were representatives of the ideology known as **conservatism.** Most conservatives favored obedience to political authority, believed that organized religion was crucial to social order, hated revolutionary upheavals, and were unwilling to accept either the liberal demands for civil liberties and representative governments or the nationalistic aspirations generated by the French revolutionary era. After 1815, the political philosophy of conservatism was supported by hereditary monarchs, government bureaucracies, landowning aristocracies, and revived churches, both Protestant and Catholic. The conservative forces were dominant after 1815.

One method used by the great powers to maintain the new status quo they had constructed was the Concert of Europe, according to which Great Britain, Russia, Prussia, and Austria (and later France) agreed to meet periodically in conferences to take steps that would maintain the peace in Europe. Eventually, the great powers adopted a **principle of intervention** that was based on their right to send armies into countries where there were revolutions to restore legitimate monarchs to their thrones.

Forces for Change

Between 1815 and 1830, conservative governments throughout Europe worked to maintain the old order. But, powerful forces for change—liberalism and nationalism—were also at work. **Liberalism** owed much to the Enlightenment of the eighteenth century and the American and French Revolutions at the end of that century; it was based on the idea that people should be as free from restraint as possible.

Liberals came to hold a common set of political beliefs. Chief among them was the protection of civil liberties, or the basic rights of all people, which included equality before the law; freedom of assembly, speech, and the press; and freedom from arbitrary arrest. All of these freedoms should be guaranteed by a written document, such as the American Bill of Rights. In addition to religious toleration for all, most liberals advocated separation of church and state. Liberals also demanded the right of peaceful opposition to the government in and out of parliament and the making of laws by a representative assembly (legislature) elected by qualified voters. Many liberals believed, then, in a constitutional monarchy or constitutional state with limits on the powers of government in order to prevent despotism and in written constitutions that would guarantee these rights. Liberals were not democrats, however. They thought that the right to vote and hold office should be open only to men of property. As a political philosophy, liberalism was adopted by middle-class men, especially industrial middle-class men, who favored voting rights for themselves so that they could share power with the landowning classes.

Nationalism was an even more powerful ideology for change in the nineteenth century. Nationalism arose out of an awareness of being part of a community that has common institutions, traditions, language, and customs. This community is called a nation, and the primary political loyalty of individuals would be to the nation. Nationalism did not become a popular force for change until the French Revolution. From then on, nationalists came to believe that each nationality should have its own government. Thus, the Germans, who were not united, wanted national unity in a German nation-state with one central government. Subject peoples, such as the Hungarians, wanted the right to establish their own autonomy rather than be subject to a German minority in the multinational Austrian Empire.

Nationalism, then, was a threat to the existing political order. A united Germany, for example, would upset the balance of power established at Vienna in 1815. Conservatives feared such change and tried hard to repress nationalism. The conservative order dominated much of Europe after 1815, but the forces of liberalism and nationalism, first generated by the French Revolution, continued to grow as that second great revolution, the Industrial Revolution, expanded and brought in new groups of people who wanted change. In 1848, these forces for change erupted.

The Revolutions of 1848

Revolution in France was the spark for revolution in other countries. Beginning in 1846, a severe industrial and agricultural depression in France brought untold hardship to the lower middle class, workers, and peasants, while the government's persistent refusal to lower the property qualification for voting angered the disenfranchised members of the middle class. When the government of King Louis-Philippe (1830–1848) refused to make changes, opposition grew and finally overthrew the monarchy on February 24, 1848. A group of moderate and radical republicans established a provisional government and called for the election by universal male suffrage of a "constituent assembly" that would draw up a new constitution.

The new constitution, ratified on November 4, 1848, established a republic (the Second Republic) with a single legislature elected to three-year terms by universal male suffrage and a president elected to a four-year term, also by universal male suffrage. In the elections for the presidency held in December 1848, Charles Louis Napoleon Bonaparte, the nephew of the famous French ruler, won a resounding victory.

News of the 1848 revolution in France led to upheaval in central Europe as well (see the box on p. 413). The Vienna settlement in 1815 had recognized the existence of thirty-eight sovereign states (called the Germanic Confederation) in what had once been the Holy Roman Empire. Austria and Prussia were the two great powers in terms of size and might; the other states varied considerably. In 1848, cries for change caused many German rulers to promise constitutions, a free press, jury trials, and other liberal reforms. In Prussia, King Frederick William IV (1840–1861) agreed to establish a new constitution and work for a united Germany.

The promise of unity reverberated throughout all the German states as governments allowed elections by universal male suffrage for deputies to an all-German parliament called the Frankfurt Assembly. Its purpose was to fulfill a liberal and nationalist dream—the preparation of a constitution for a new united Germany. But the Frankfurt Assembly failed to achieve its goal. The members had no real means of compelling the German rulers to accept the constitution they had drawn up. German unification was not achieved; the revolution had failed.

The Austrian Empire needed only the news of the revolution in Paris to erupt in flames in March 1848. The Austrian Empire was a multinational state, a collection of at least eleven ethnically distinct peoples, including Germans, Czechs, Magyars (Hungarians), Slovaks, Romanians, Serbians, and Italians, who had pledged their loyalty to the Habsburg emperor. The Germans, though only a quarter of the population, were economically dominant and played a leading role in governing Austria. In March, demonstrations in Buda, Prague, and Vienna led to the dismissal of Metternich, the Austrian foreign minister and the archsymbol of the conservative order, who fled abroad. In Vienna, revolutionary forces took control of the capital and demanded a liberal constitution. Hungary was given its own legislature and a separate national army.

Austrian officials had made concessions to appease the revolutionaries, but they were determined to reestablish firm control. As in the German states, they were increasingly encouraged by the divisions between radical and moderate revolutionaries. By the end of October 1848, Austrian military forces had crushed the radical rebels in Vienna, but it was only with the assistance of a Russian army of 140,000 men that the Hungarian revolution was finally put down in 1849. The revolutions in the Austrian Empire had failed.

So did revolutions in Italy. The Congress of Vienna had established nine states in Italy, including the Kingdom of Sardinia in the north, ruled by the house of Savoy; the Kingdom of the Two Sicilies (Naples and Sicily); the Papal States; a handful of small duchies; and the important northern provinces of Lombardy and Venetia, which were now part of the Austrian Empire. Italy was largely under Austrian domination, but a new movement for Italian unity known as Young Italy led to

REVOLUTIONARY EXCITEMENT: CARL SCHURZ AND THE REVOLUTION OF 1848 IN GERMANY

POLITICS & GOVERNMENT

The excitement with which German liberals and nationalists received the news of the 1848 revolution in France and their own expectations for Germany are well captured in this selection from the *Reminiscences of Carl Schurz*. Schurz (1829–1906) made his way to the United States after the failure of the German revolution and eventually became a U.S. senator.

How did the fervent desire expressed by Schurz for "German unity" and the founding of a great national German Empire express itself in nineteenth-century German history?

Carl Schurz, *Reminiscences*

One morning, toward the end of February, 1848, I sat quietly in my attic-chamber, working hard at my tragedy of "Ulrich von Hutten" [a sixteenth-century German humanist and knight], when suddenly a friend rushed breathlessly into the room, exclaiming: "What, you sitting here! Do you not know what has happened?"

"No; what?"

"The French have driven away Louis Philippe and proclaimed the republic."

I threw down my pen—and that was the end of "Ulrich von Hutten" I never touched the manuscript again. We tore down the stairs, into the street, to the market-square, the accustomed meeting-place for all the student societies after their midday dinner. Although it was still forenoon, the market was already crowded with young men talking excitedly. There was no shouting, no noise, only agitated conversation. What did we want there? This probably no one knew. But since the French had driven away Louis Philippe and proclaimed the republic, something of course must happen here, too. . . . We were dominated by a vague feeling as if a great outbreak of elemental forces had begun, as if an earthquake was impending of which we had felt the first shock, and we instinctively crowded together. . . .

The next morning there were the usual lectures to be attended. But how profitless! The voice of the professor sounded like a monotonous drone coming from far away. What he had to say did not seem to concern us. The pen that should have taken notes remained idle. At last we closed with a sigh the notebook and went away, impelled by a feeling that now we had something more important to do—to devote ourselves to the affairs of the fatherland. And this we did by seeking as quickly as possible again the company of our friends, in order to discuss what had happened and what was to come. In these conversations, excited as they were, certain ideas and catchwords worked themselves to the surface, which expressed more or less the feelings of the people. Now had arrived in Germany the day for the establishment of "German Unity," and the founding of a great, powerful national German Empire. In the first line the convocation of a national parliament. Then the demands for civil rights and liberties, free speech, free press, the right of free assembly, equality before the law, a freely elected representation of the people with legislative power, responsibility of ministers, self-government of the communes, the right of the people to carry arms, the formation of a civic guard with elective officers, and so on—in short, that which was called a "constitutional form of government on a broad democratic basis." Republican ideas were at first only sparingly expressed. But the word democracy was soon on all tongues, and many, too, thought it a matter of course that if the princes should try to withhold from the people the rights and liberties demanded, force would take the place of mere petition. Of course the regeneration of the fatherland must, if possible, be accomplished by peaceable means. . . . Like many of my friends, I was dominated by the feeling that at last the great opportunity had arrived for giving to the German people the liberty which was their birthright and to the German fatherland its unity and greatness, and that it was now the first duty of every German to do and to sacrifice everything for this sacred object.

ThomsonNOW To read more of this document, enter the *ThomsonNOW* documents area using the access card that is available for *The Essential World History*.

---

initially successful revolts in 1848. By 1849, however, the Austrians had reestablished complete control over Lombardy and Venetia, and the old order also prevailed in the rest of Italy.

Throughout Europe in 1848–1849, moderate, middle-class liberals and radical workers soon divided over their aims, and the failure of the revolutionaries to stay united soon led to the reestablishment of authoritarian regimes. In other parts of the Western world, revolutions took somewhat different directions.

Independence and the Development of the National State in Latin America

By the end of the eighteenth century, the ideas of the Enlightenment and the new political ideals stemming from the successful revolution in North America were beginning to influence the creole elites (descendants of Europeans who became permanent inhabitants of Latin America). The principles of the equality of all people in the eyes of the law, free trade, and a free press proved very attractive. Sons of creoles, such as Simón Bolívar and José de San Martín, who became leaders of the independence movement, even attended European universities, where they imbibed the ideas of the Enlightenment.

Nationalistic Revolts   The creole elites soon began to use their new ideas to denounce the rule of the Iberian monarchs and the peninsulars (Spanish and Portuguese officials who resided in Latin America for political and economic gain). When Napoleon Bonaparte toppled the monarchies of Spain and Portugal, the authority of the Spaniards and Portuguese in their colonial empires was weakened, and between 1807 and 1825, a series of revolts enabled most of Latin America to become independent.

Beginning in 1810, Mexico too experienced a revolt, fueled initially by the desire of the creole elites to overthrow the rule of the peninsulars. But when Indians and *mestizos* joined the revolt, both creoles and peninsulars, fearful of the masses, cooperated in defeating the popular revolutionary forces. Nevertheless, independence still came to Mexico, but it was now the elites—both creoles and peninsulars—who decided to overthrow Spanish rule as a way of preserving their own power. They selected a creole military leader, Augustín de Iturbide (1783–1824), as the first emperor of Mexico in 1821.

Independence movements elsewhere in Latin America were the work of elites—primarily creoles—who overthrew Spanish rule and set up new governments that they could dominate. Two of the most prominent leaders were both members of the creole elite—José de San Martín (1778–1850) of Argentina and Simón Bolívar (1783–1830) of Venezuela.

By 1810, the forces of San Martín had freed Argentina from Spanish authority, while in Venezuela, Bolívar, hailed as the Liberator, led the bitter struggle for independence. San Martín, who believed that the Spaniards must be removed from all of South America if any nation was to be free, led his forces into Chile in 1817 and then in 1821 moved on to Lima, Peru, the center of Spanish authority. He was soon joined by Bolívar, who in 1824 assumed the task of crushing the last significant Spanish army. Soon, Peru, Uruguay, Paraguay, Colombia, Venezuela, Argentina, Bolivia, and Chile had all become free states (see Map 18.3). The Central American states became independent in 1823 and subsequently divided into five republics in 1838–1839: Guatemala, El Salvador, Honduras, Costa Rica, and Nicaragua. Earlier, in 1822, the prince regent of Brazil had declared Brazil's independence from Portugal.

The Difficulties of Nation Building   The new Latin American nations faced a number of serious problems. The wars for independence had themselves resulted in a staggering loss of population, property, and livestock; at the same time, disputes arose between nations over their precise boundaries.

The new nations of Latin America began with republican governments, but they had no experience in ruling themselves. Soon after independence, strong leaders

José de San Martín.   José de San Martín of Argentina was one of the famous leaders of the Latin American independence movement. His forces liberated Argentina, Chile, and Peru from Spanish authority. In this painting by Theodore Géricault, San Martín is shown leading his troops at the Battle of Chacabuco in Chile in 1817.

known as *caudillos* came into power. They ruled chiefly by military force and were usually supported by the landed elites. Many kept the new national states together.

Although political independence brought economic independence, old patterns were hard to extinguish. Instead of Spain and Portugal, Great Britain now dominated the Latin American economy. Old trade patterns soon reemerged. Because Latin America served as a source of raw materials and foodstuffs for the industrializing nations of Europe and North America, exports, especially of wheat, tobacco, wools, sugar, coffee, and hides, to the North Atlantic countries increased noticeably. At the same time, the importation of finished consumer goods, especially textiles, also grew and caused a decline in industrial production in Latin America.

A fundamental underlying problem for all of the new nations was the persistent domination of Latin America's economic and social life by the landed elites. Large estates remained the basis of wealth, social prestige, and political power throughout the nineteenth century. Landed elites ran governments, controlled courts, and maintained a system of inexpensive labor. These landowners made enormous profits growing single, specialized crops (such as coffee) for export, while the masses, unable to have land to grow basic food crops, experienced dire poverty.

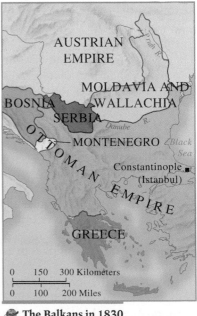

MAP 18.3 **Latin America in the First Half of the Nineteenth Century.** Latin American colonies took advantage of Spain's weakness during the Napoleonic wars to fight for independence, beginning with Argentina in 1810 and spreading throughout the region over the next decade with the help of leaders like Simón Bolívar and José de San Martín. **?** Where did the last battles for independence take place? Why?

Nationalism in the Balkans: The Ottoman Empire and the Eastern Question

The Ottoman Empire had long been in control of much of the Balkans in southeastern Europe. By the beginning of the nineteenth century, however, the Ottoman Empire was in decline, and authority over its outlying territories in the Balkans waned. As a result, European governments, especially those of Russia and Austria, began to take an active interest in the disintegration of the empire, which they called the "sick man of Europe."

When the Russians invaded the Ottoman provinces of Moldavia and Wallachia, the Ottoman Turks declared war on Russia on October 4, 1853. In the following year,

on March 28, Great Britain and France, fearful of Russian gains, declared war on Russia. The Crimean War, as the conflict came to be called, was poorly planned and poorly fought. Heavy losses caused the Russians to sue for peace. By the Treaty of Paris, signed in March 1856, Russia agreed to allow Moldavia and

🐌 **The Balkans in 1830**

Wallachia to be placed under the protection of all the great powers.

The Crimean War destroyed the Concert of Europe. Austria and Russia, the two chief powers maintaining the status quo in the first half of the nineteenth century, were now enemies because of Austria's unwillingness to support Russia in the war. Russia, defeated and humiliated by the obvious failure of its armies, withdrew from European affairs for the next two decades. Great Britain, disillusioned by its role in the war, also pulled back from continental affairs. Austria, paying the price for its neutrality, was now without friends among the great powers. This new international situation opened the door for the unification of Italy and Germany.

National Unification and the National State, 1848–1871

The revolutions of 1848 had failed, but within twenty-five years, many of the goals sought by liberals and nationalists during the first half of the nineteenth century were achieved. Italy and Germany became nations, and many European states were led by constitutional monarchs.

The Unification of Italy

The Italians were the first people to benefit from the breakdown of the Concert of Europe. In 1850, Austria was still the dominant power on the Italian peninsula. After the failure of the revolution of 1848–1849, more and more Italians looked to the northern Italian state of Piedmont, ruled by the royal house of Savoy, as their best hope to achieve the unification of Italy. It was, however, doubtful that the little state could provide the leadership needed to unify Italy until King Victor Emmanuel II (1849–1878; 1861–1878 as king of Italy) named Count Camillo di Cavour (1810–1861) prime minister in 1852.

As prime minister, Cavour pursued a policy of economic expansion that increased government revenues and enabled Piedmont to equip a large army. Cavour, allied with the French emperor, Louis Napoleon, defeated the Austrians and gained control of Lombardy. Cavour's success caused nationalists in some northern Italian states (Parma, Modena, and Tuscany) to overthrow their governments and join Piedmont.

Meanwhile, in southern Italy, Giuseppe Garibaldi (1807–1882), a dedicated Italian patriot, raised an army of a thousand volunteers called Red Shirts because of the color of their uniforms. Garibaldi's forces swept through Sicily and then crossed over to the mainland and began a victorious march up the Italian peninsula. Naples, and with it the Kingdom of the Two Sicilies, fell in early September in 1860. Ever the patriot, Garibaldi chose to turn over his conquests to Cavour's Piedmontese

forces. On March 17, 1861, the new kingdom of Italy was proclaimed under a centralized government subordinated to the control of Piedmont and King Victor Emmanuel II of the house of Savoy. The task of unification was not yet complete, however. Venetia in the north was taken from Austria in 1866. The Italian army annexed the city of Rome on September 20, 1870, and it became the new capital of the united Italian state.

The Unification of Germany

After the failure of the Frankfurt Assembly to achieve German unification in 1848–1849, more and more Germans looked to Prussia for leadership in the cause of German unification. Prussia had become a strong, prosperous, and authoritarian state, with the Prussian

The Unification of Italy

king in firm control of both the government and the army. In 1862, King William I (1861–1888) appointed a new prime minister, Count Otto von Bismarck (1815–1898). Bismarck has often been portrayed as the ultimate realist, the foremost nineteenth-century practitioner of *Realpolitik*—the "politics of reality." He said, "Not by speeches and majorities will the great questions of the day be decided—that was the mistake of 1848–1849 —but by iron and blood."[3] Opposition to his domestic policy determined Bismarck on an active foreign policy, which led to war and German unification.

After defeating Denmark with Austrian help in 1864 and gaining control over the duchies of Schleswig and Holstein, Bismarck created friction with the Austrians and goaded them into a war on June 14, 1866. Though the Austrians were barely defeated at Königgrätz on July 3, Prussia proceeded to organize the German states north of the Main River into the North German Confederation. The southern German states, largely Catholic, remained independent but signed military alliances with Prussia due to their fear of France, their western neighbor.

Prussia now dominated all of northern Germany, but problems with France soon arose. Bismarck realized that France would never be content with a strong German state to its east because of the potential threat to French security. Bismarck goaded the French into declaring war on Prussia on July 15, 1870. The Prussian armies advanced into France, and at Sedan, on September 2, 1870, they captured an entire French army and the French emperor Napoleon III himself. Paris capitulated on January 28, 1871. France had to give up the provinces of Alsace and Lorraine to the new German state, a loss that left the French burning for revenge.

Even before the war had ended, the southern German states had agreed to enter the North German Confederation. On January 18, 1871, in the Hall of Mirrors in Louis XIV's palace at Versailles, William I was proclaimed kaiser (emperor) of the Second German Empire (the first was the medieval Holy Roman Empire). German unity had been achieved by the Prussian monarchy and the Prussian army. The Prussian leadership of German unification meant the triumph of authoritarian, militaristic values over liberal, constitutional sentiments in the development of the new German state. With its

industrial resources and military might, the new state had become the strongest power on the Continent. A new European balance of power was at hand.

Nationalism and Reform: The European National State at Mid-Century

Unlike nations on the Continent, Great Britain managed to avoid the revolutionary upheavals of the first half of the nineteenth century. In the early part of the century, Great Britain was governed by the aristocratic landowning classes that dominated both houses of Parliament. But in 1832, to avoid the turmoil on the Continent,

CHRONOLOGY   The Unification of Germany

King William I of Prussia	1861–1888
Danish War	1864
Austro-Prussian War	1866
Franco-Prussian War	1870–1871
German Empire is proclaimed	January 18, 1871

© Bildarchiv Preussischer Kulturbesitz, Berlin/Art Resource, NY

The Unification of Germany.   Under Prussian leadership, a new German empire was proclaimed on January 18, 1871, in the Hall of Mirrors in the palace of Versailles. King William of Prussia became Emperor William I of the Second German Empire. Otto von Bismarck, the man who had been so instrumental in creating the new German state, is shown here, resplendently attired in his white uniform, standing at the foot of the throne.

🌀 **The Unification of Germany**

Map legend:
- Prussia, 1862
- United in 1866–1867 with Prussia as North German Confederation
- South German Confederation
- Annexed in 1871 after Franco-Prussian War

Parliament passed a reform bill that increased the number of male voters, chiefly by adding members of the industrial middle class. By allowing the industrial middle class to join the landed interests in ruling Britain, Britain avoided revolution in 1848.

In the 1850s and 1860s, the liberal parliamentary system of Britain made both social and political reforms that enabled the country to remain stable. One of the other reasons for Britain's stability was its continuing economic growth. After 1850, middle-class prosperity was at last coupled with some improvements for the working classes as real wages for laborers increased more than 25 percent between 1850 and 1870. The British sense of national pride was well reflected in Queen Victoria (1837–1901), whose sense of duty and moral respectability reflected the attitudes of her age, which has ever since been known as the Victorian Age.

Events in France after the revolution of 1848 moved toward the restoration of monarchy. Four years after his election as president, Louis Napoleon restored an authoritarian empire. On December 2, 1852, Louis Napoleon assumed the title of Napoleon III (the first Napoleon had abdicated in favor of his son, Napoleon II, on April 6, 1814). The Second Empire had begun.

The first five years of Napoleon III's reign were a spectacular success. He took many steps to expand industrial growth. Government subsidies helped foster the rapid construction of railroads as well as harbors, roads, and canals. The major French railway lines were completed during Napoleon III's reign, and iron production tripled. In the midst of this economic expansion, Napoleon III also undertook a vast reconstruction of the city of Paris. The medieval Paris of narrow streets and old city walls was destroyed and replaced by a modern Paris of broad boulevards, spacious buildings, an underground sewage system, a new public water supply, and gaslights.

In the 1860s, as opposition to his rule began to mount, Napoleon III began to liberalize his regime. He gave the Legislative Corps more say in affairs of state, including debate over the budget. Liberalization policies worked initially; in a plebiscite in May 1870 on whether to accept a new constitution that might have inaugurated a parliamentary regime, the French people gave Napoleon III a resounding victory. This triumph was short-lived, however. War with Prussia in 1870 brought Napoleon III's ouster, and a republic was proclaimed.

Although nationalism was a major force in nineteenth-century Europe, one of the region's most powerful states, the Austrian Empire, managed to frustrate the desire of its numerous ethnic groups for self-determination. After the Habsburgs had crushed the revolutions of 1848–1849, they restored centralized, autocratic government to the empire. But Austria's defeat at the hands of the Prussians in 1866 forced the Austrians to deal with the fiercely nationalistic Hungarians.

The result was the negotiated *Ausgleich,* or Compromise, of 1867, which created the dual monarchy of Austria-Hungary. Each part of the empire now had its own constitution, its own legislature, its own governmental bureaucracy, and its own capital (Vienna for Austria and Budapest for Hungary). Holding the two states together were a single monarch—Francis Joseph (1848–1916) was emperor of Austria and king of Hungary—and a common army, foreign policy, and system of finances.

At the beginning of the nineteenth century, Russia was overwhelmingly rural, agricultural, and autocratic. The Russian imperial autocracy, based on soldiers, secret police, and repression, had withstood the revolutionary fervor of the first half of the nineteenth century. Defeat in the Crimean War in 1856, however, led even staunch conservatives to realize that Russia was falling hopelessly behind the western European powers. Tsar Alexander II (1855–1881) decided to make serious reforms.

Serfdom was the most burdensome problem in tsarist Russia. On March 3, 1861, Alexander issued his emancipation edict (see the box on p. 419). Peasants were now free to own property and marry as they chose. But the system of land redistribution instituted after emancipation was not that favorable to them. The government provided land for the peasants by purchasing it from the landlords, but the landowners often chose to keep the best lands. The Russian peasants soon found that they had inadequate amounts of good arable land to support themselves.

Nor were the peasants completely free. The state compensated the landowners for the land given to the peasants, but the peasants were expected to repay the state in long-term installments. To ensure that the payments were made, peasants were subjected to the authority of their *mir* or village commune, which was collectively responsible for the land payments to the government. And since the village communes were responsible for the payments, they were reluctant to allow peasants to leave their land. Emancipation, then, led not to a free, landowning peasantry along the Western model but to an unhappy, land-starved peasantry that largely followed the old ways of agricultural production.

The Growth of the United States

The U.S. Constitution, ratified in 1789, committed the United States to two of the major forces of the first half of the nineteenth century, liberalism and nationalism. The election of Andrew Jackson (1767–1845) as president in 1828 opened a new era in American politics. Jacksonian democracy introduced a mass democratic politics as property qualifications for voting were dropped. By the 1830s, suffrage had been extended to almost all adult white males.

By the mid-nineteenth century, the issue of slavery had become a threat to American national unity. Like the North, the South had grown dramatically in population during the first half of the nineteenth century. But the South's economy was based on growing cotton on plantations, chiefly by slave labor. Although new slave imports had been barred in 1808, there were 4 million African

EMANCIPATION: SERFS AND SLAVES

FAMILY & SOCIETY

Although overall their histories have been quite different, Russia and the United States shared a common feature in the 1860s. They were the only states in the Western world that still had large enslaved populations (the Russian serfs were virtually slaves). The leaders of both countries issued emancipation proclamations within two years of each other. The first excerpt is taken from the imperial decree of March 3, 1861, which freed the Russian serfs. The second excerpt is from Abraham Lincoln's Emancipation Proclamation, issued on January 1, 1863.

What changes did Tsar Alexander II's emancipation of the serfs initiate in Russia? What effect did Lincoln's Emancipation Proclamation have on the southern "armed rebellion"? What reasons does each leader give for his action?

Alexander II's Imperial Decree, March 3, 1861

By the grace of God, we, Alexander II, Emperor and Autocrat of all the Russias, King of Poland, Grand Duke of Finland, etc., to all our faithful subjects, make known:

Called by Divine Providence and by the sacred right of inheritance to the throne of our ancestors, we took a vow in our innermost heart to respond to the mission which is intrusted to us as to surround with our affection and our Imperial solicitude all our faithful subjects of every rank and of every condition, from the warrior, who nobly bears arms for the defense of the country, to the humble artisan devoted to the works of industry; from the official in the career of the high offices of the State to the laborer whose plough furrows the soil. . . .

We thus came to the conviction that the work of a serious improvement of the condition of the peasants was a sacred inheritance bequeathed to us by our ancestors, a mission which, in the course of events, Divine Providence called upon us to fulfill. . . .

In virtue of the new dispositions above mentioned, the peasants attached to the soil will be invested within a term fixed by the law with all the rights of free cultivators. . . .

At the same time, they are granted the right of purchasing their close, and, with the consent of the proprietors, they may acquire in full property the arable lands and other appurtenances which are allotted to them as a permanent holding. By the acquisition in full property of the quantity of land fixed, the peasants are free from their obligations toward the proprietors for land thus purchased, and they enter definitely into the condition of free peasant-landholders.

Lincoln's Emancipation Proclamation, January 1, 1863

Now therefore, I, Abraham Lincoln, President of the United States, by virtue of the power in me vested as Commander-in-Chief of the Army and Navy of the United States in time of actual armed rebellion against the authority and government of the United States, and as a fit and necessary war measure for suppressing such rebellion, do, on this 1st day of January, A.D. 1863, and in accordance with my purpose to do so, . . . order and designate as the States and parts of States wherein the people thereof, respectively, are this day in rebellion against the United States the following, to wit:

Arkansas, Texas, Louisiana, . . . Mississippi, Alabama, Florida, Georgia, South Carolina, North Carolina, and Virginia . . .

And by virtue of the power for the purpose aforesaid, I do order and declare that all persons held as slaves within said designated States and parts of States are, and henceforward shall be free; and that the Executive Government of the United States, including the military and naval authorities thereof, will recognize and maintain the freedom of said persons.

ThomsonNOW To read all of Alexander's decree, enter the *ThomsonNOW* documents area using the access card that is available for *The Essential World History*.

American slaves in the South by 1860—four times the number sixty years earlier. The cotton economy and plantation-based slavery were related, and the South was determined to maintain them. In the North, many people feared the spread of slavery into western territories.

As polarization over the issue of slavery intensified, compromise became less feasible. When Abraham Lincoln, who had said in a speech in Illinois in 1858 that "this government cannot endure permanently half slave and half free," was elected president in November 1860, the die was cast. Lincoln carried only 2 of the 1,109 counties in the South. In February 1861, seven southern states formed a rival nation, the Confederate States of America, and in April, fighting erupted between North and South.

The American Civil War (1861–1865) was an extraordinarily bloody struggle. Over 600,000 soldiers died, either in battle or from deadly infectious diseases spawned by filthy camp conditions. Over a period of four years, the Union (Northern) states mobilized their superior assets and gradually wore down the South. Moreover, what had begun as a war to save the Union became a war against slavery. On January 1, 1863, Lincoln's Emancipation Proclamation made most of the nation's slaves "forever free" (see the box above). The surrender of Confederate forces on April 9, 1865, confirmed that the United States would be "one nation, indivisible." National unity had prevailed in the United States.

The Emergence of a Canadian Nation

By the Treaty of Paris in 1763, Canada—or New France, as it was called—passed into the hands of the British. By 1800, most Canadians favored more autonomy, although differences existed among the colonists on the form this autonomy should take. Upper Canada (now Ontario) was predominantly English-speaking, while Lower Canada (now Quebec) was dominated by French Canadians. After two short rebellions against the government broke out in Upper and Lower Canada in 1837 and 1838, the British moved toward change. In 1840, the British Parliament formally joined Upper and Lower Canada into the United Provinces of Canada, without granting self-government.

The head of Upper Canada's Conservative Party, John Macdonald, became an avid apostle for self-government. Fearful of American designs on Canada, the British government finally capitulated to Macdonald's campaign, and in 1867, Parliament passed the British North American Act, which established a Canadian nation—the Dominion of Canada—with its own constitution. John Macdonald became the first prime minister of the Dominion.

Cultural Life: Romanticism and Realism

At the end of the eighteenth century, a new intellectual movement known as **Romanticism** emerged to challenge the ideas of the Enlightenment. The Enlightenment stressed reason as the chief means for discovering truth. Although the Romantics by no means disparaged reason, they tried to balance its use by stressing the importance of feeling, emotion, and imagination as sources of knowing.

The Characteristics of Romanticism

Romantic writers emphasized emotion and sentiment and believed that these inner feelings were understandable only to the person experiencing them. In their novels, Romantic writers created figures who were often misunderstood and rejected by society but who continued to believe in their own worth through their inner feelings.

Many Romantics also possessed a passionate interest in the past. They revived medieval Gothic architecture and left European countrysides adorned with pseudo-medieval castles and cities bedecked with grandiose neo-Gothic cathedrals, city halls, and parliamentary buildings. Literature, too, reflected this historical consciousness. The novels of Walter Scott (1771–1832) became European best-sellers in the first half of the nineteenth century. *Ivanhoe*, in which Scott tried to evoke the clash between Saxon and Norman knights in medieval England, became one of his most popular.

Many Romantics had a deep attraction to the exotic and unfamiliar. In an exaggerated form, this preoccupation gave rise to so-called **Gothic literature**, chillingly evident in Mary Shelley's *Frankenstein* and Edgar Allan Poe's short stories of horror (see the box on p. 421). Some Romantics even brought the unusual into their own lives by experimenting with cocaine, opium, and hashish in an attempt to find extraordinary states of experience in drug-induced altered states of consciousness.

To the Romantics, poetry was the direct expression of the soul and therefore ranked above all other literary forms. Romantic poetry gave full expression to one of the most important characteristics of Romanticism: love of nature, especially evident in the poetry of William Wordsworth (1770–1850). His experience of nature was almost mystical as he claimed to receive "authentic tidings of invisible things":

> One impulse from a vernal wood
> May teach you more of man,
> Of Moral Evil and of good,
> Than all the sages can.[4]

Romantics believed that nature served as a mirror into which humans could look to learn about themselves.

Like the literary arts, the visual arts were also deeply affected by Romanticism. To Romantic artists, all artistic expression was a reflection of the artist's inner feelings; a painting should mirror the artist's vision of the world and be the instrument of his own imagination.

Eugène Delacroix (1798–1863) was one of the most famous French exponents of the Romantic school of painting. Delacroix visited North Africa in 1832 and was strongly impressed by its vibrant colors and the brilliant dress of the people. His paintings came to exhibit two primary characteristics, a fascination with the exotic and a passion for color. Both are apparent in his *Women of Algiers*. Significant for its use of light and its patches of interrelated color, this portrayal of the world of harem concubines in exotic Algeria was actually somewhat scandalous to the early nineteenth century. In Delacroix, theatricality and movement combined with a daring use of color. Many of his works reflect his own belief that "a painting should be a feast to the eye."

A New Age of Science

With the Industrial Revolution came a renewed interest in basic scientific research. By the 1830s, new scientific discoveries led to many practical benefits that caused science to have an ever-greater impact on European life.

In biology, the Frenchman Louis Pasteur (1822–1895) discovered the germ theory of disease, which had enormous practical applications in the development of modern scientific medical practices. In chemistry, the Russian Dmitri Mendeleev (1834–1907) in the 1860s classified all the material elements then known on the basis of their atomic weights and provided the systematic foundation for the periodic law.

GOTHIC LITERATURE: EDGAR ALLAN POE

American writers and poets made significant contributions to the movement of Romanticism. Although Edgar Allan Poe (1809–1849) was influenced by the German Romantic school of mystery and horror, many literary historians give him the credit for pioneering the modern short story. This selection from the conclusion of "The Fall of the House of Usher" gives a feeling for the nature of so-called Gothic literature.

What were the aesthetic aims of Gothic literature? How did it come to be called "Gothic"? How did its values relate to those of the Romantic movement as a whole?

Edgar Allan Poe, "The Fall of the House of Usher"

No sooner had these syllables passed my lips, than—as if a shield of brass had indeed, at the moment, fallen heavily upon a floor of silver—I became aware of a distinct, hollow, metallic, and clangorous, yet apparently muffled, reverberation. Completely unnerved, I leaped to my feet; but the measured rocking movement of Usher was undisturbed. I rushed to the chair in which he sat. His eyes were bent fixedly before him, and throughout his whole countenance there reigned a stony rigidity. But, as I placed my hand upon his shoulder, there came a strong shudder over his whole person; a sickly smile quivered about his lips; and I saw that he spoke in a low, hurried, and gibbering murmur, as if unconscious of my presence. Bending closely over him, I at length drank in the hideous import of his words.

"Not hear it?—yes, I hear it, and *have* heard it. Long-long-long-many minutes, many hours, many days, have I heard it—yet I dared not—oh, pity me, miserable wretch that I am!—I dared not—I *dared* not speak! We *have put her living*

in the tomb! Said I not that my senses were acute? I *now* tell you that I heard her first feeble movements in the hollow coffin. I heard them—many, many days ago—yet I dared not—*I dared not speak!* And now—to-night— . . . the rending of her coffin, and the grating of the iron hinges of her prison, and her struggles within the coppered archway of the vault! Oh whither shall I fly? Will she not be here anon? Is she not hurrying to upbraid me for my haste? Have I not heard her footstep on the stair? Do I not distinguish that heavy and horrible beating of her heart? MADMAN!"—here he sprang furiously to his feet, and shrieked out his syllables, as if in the effort he were giving up his soul—"MADMAN! I TELL YOU THAT SHE NOW STANDS WITHOUT THE DOOR!"

As if in the superhuman energy of his utterance there had been found the potency of a spell, the huge antique panels to which the speaker pointed threw slowly back, upon the instant, their ponderous and ebony jaws. It was the work of the rushing gust—but then without those doors there DID stand the lofty and enshrouded figure of the lady Madeline of Usher. There was blood upon her white robes, and the evidence of some bitter struggle upon every portion of her emaciated frame. For a moment she remained trembling and reeling to and fro upon the threshold, then, with a low moaning cry, fell heavily inward upon the person of her brother, and in her violent and now final death-agonies, bore him to the floor a corpse, and a victim to the terrors he had anticipated.

ThomsonNOW™ To explore all of Poe's work, enter the *ThomsonNOW* documents area using the access card that is available for *The Essential World History.*

The popularity of scientific and technological achievement produced a widespread acceptance of the **scientific method** as the only path to objective truth and objective reality. This in turn undermined the faith of many people in religious revelation. It is no accident that the nineteenth century was an age of increasing **secularization,** evident in the belief that truth was to be found in the concrete material existence of human beings. No one did more to create a picture of humans as material beings that were simply part of the natural world than Charles Darwin.

In 1859, Charles Darwin (1809–1882) published *On the Origin of Species by Means of Natural Selection.* The basic idea of this book was that all plants and animals had each evolved over a long period of time from earlier and simpler forms of life, a principle known as **organic evolution.** In every species, he argued, "many more individuals of each species are born than can possibly survive." This results in a "struggle for existence." Darwin

believed that some organisms were more adaptable to the environment than others, a process that Darwin called **natural selection.** Those that were naturally selected for survival ("survival of the fit") reproduced and thrived. The unfit did not and became extinct. The fit who survived passed on small variations that enhanced their survival until, from Darwin's point of view, a new and separate species emerged. In *The Descent of Man,* published in 1871, he argued for the animal origins of human beings. Humans were not an exception to the rule governing other species.

Realism in Literature and Art

The name **Realism** was first employed in 1850 to describe a new style of painting and soon spread to literature. The literary Realists of the mid-nineteenth century rejected Romanticism. They wanted to deal with ordinary characters from actual life rather than Romantic heroes in exotic settings.

Eugène Delacroix, *Women of Algiers*. A characteristic of Romanticism was its love of the exotic and unfamiliar. In his *Women of Algiers*, Delacroix reflected this fascination with the exotic in this portrayal of harem concubines from North Africa in which the clothes and jewelry of the women combine with their calm facial expressions to create an atmosphere of peaceful sensuality. At the same time, Delacroix's painting reflects his preoccupation with light and color.

The leading novelist of the 1850s and 1860s, the Frenchman Gustave Flaubert (1821–1880), perfected the Realist novel. His *Madame Bovary* (1857) was a straightforward description of barren and sordid provincial life in France. Emma Bovary is trapped in a marriage to a drab provincial doctor. Impelled by the images of romantic love she has read about in novels, she seeks the same thing for herself in adulterous love affairs but is ultimately driven to suicide.

In art, too, Realism became dominant after 1850. Gustave Courbet (1819–1877), the most famous artist of the Realist school, reveled in realistic portrayals of everyday life. His subjects were factory workers, peasants, and the wives of saloonkeepers. "I have never seen either angels or goddesses, so I am not interested in painting them," he exclaimed. One of his famous works, *The Stonebreakers*, painted in 1849, shows two road workers engaged in the deadening work of breaking stones to build a road.

Gustave Courbet, *The Stonebreakers*. Realism, largely developed by French painters, aimed at a lifelike portrayal of the daily activities of ordinary people. Gustave Courbet was the most famous of the Realist artists. As is evident in *The Stonebreakers*, he sought to portray things as they really appear. He shows an old road builder and his young assistant in their tattered clothes, engrossed in their dreary work of breaking stones to construct a road.

CONCLUSION

HE FORCES UNLEASHED between 1800 and 1870 by two revolutions—the French Revolution and the Industrial Revolution—led to Western global dominance by the end of the nineteenth century. The Industrial Revolution seemed to prove to Europeans the underlying assumption of the Scientific Revolution of the seventeenth century—that human beings were capable of dominating nature. By rationally manipulating the material environment for human benefit, people could achieve new levels of material prosperity and produce machines not dreamed of in their wildest imaginings. Some of these new machines included weapons of war that enabled the Western world to devastate and dominate non-Western civilizations.

In 1815, a conservative order had been reestablished throughout Europe, but the revolutionary waves in Latin America and Europe in the first half of the nineteenth century made it clear that the ideologies of liberalism and nationalism, unleashed by the French Revolution and now reinforced by the spread of industrialization, were still alive and active in the Western world. Between 1850 and 1871, the national state became the focus of people's loyalty. Wars, both foreign and civil, were fought to create unified nation-states, and both wars and changing political alignments served as catalysts for domestic reforms that made the nation-state the center of attention. Liberal nationalists had believed that unified nation-states would preserve individual rights and lead to a greater community of peoples. But the new nationalism of the late nineteenth century, loud and chauvinistic, did not unify peoples but divided them instead as the new national states became embroiled in bitter competition after 1870.

Many people, however, were hardly aware of nationalism's dangers in 1870. The spread of industrialization and the growing popularity of science and technology were sources of optimism, not pessimism. After the revolutionary and military upheavals of the mid-century decades, many Westerners believed that they stood on the verge of a new age of progress.

CHAPTER NOTES

1. Quoted in E. Royston Pike, *Human Documents of the Industrial Revolution in Britain* (London, 1966), pp. 314, 343.
2. Ibid., p. 315.
3. Quoted in Louis L. Snyder, ed., *Documents of German History* (New Brunswick, N.J., 1958), p. 202.
4. William Wordsworth, "The Tables Turned," *Poems of Wordsworth*, ed. Matthew Arnold (London, 1963), p. 138.

SUGGESTED READING

For a good survey of the entire nineteenth century, see **R. Gildea, Barricades and Borders: Europe, 1800–1914,** 2d ed. (Oxford, 1996). The well-written work by **D. Landes, The Unbound Prometheus: Technological Change and Industrial Development in Western Europe from 1750 to the Present** (Cambridge, 1969), is still a good introduction to the Industrial Revolution. Also of value is **D. Fisher, The Industrial Revolution** (New York, 1992). For a broader perspective, see **P. Stearns, The Industrial Revolution in World History** (Boulder, Colo., 1993).

On the social impact of the Industrial Revolution, see **P. Pilbeam, The Middle Classes in Europe, 1789–1914** (Basingstoke, England, 1990); **T. Koditschek, Class Formation and Urban Industrial Society** (New York, 1990); and **F. Crouzet, The First Industrialists: The Problems of Origins** (Cambridge, 1985), on British entrepreneurs. A classic work on female labor patterns is **L. A. Tilly** and **J. W. Scott, Women, Work, and Family** (New York, 1978). See also **J. Lown, Women and Industrialization: Gender at Work in Nineteenth-Century England** (Minneapolis, Minn., 1990). For a global approach to the modern economy, see **K. Pomeranz, The Great Deliverance: China, Europe, and the Making of the Modern World Economy** (Princeton, N.J., 2002).

For a survey of the period 1814–1848, see **M. Broers, Europe After Napoleon: Revolution, Reaction, and Romanticism, 1814–1848** (New York, 1996). There are some useful books on individual countries that cover more than this chapter. These include **R. Magraw, France, 1815–1914: The Bourgeois Century** (London, 1983); **D. Saunders, Russia in the Age of Reaction and Reform, 1801–1881** (London, 1992); **J. J. Sheehan, German History, 1770–1866** (New York, 1989); **N. McCord, British History, 1815–1906** (New York, 1991); and **A. Sked, The Decline and Fall of the Habsburg Empire, 1815–1918** (London, 1989). The best introduction to the revolutions of 1848 is **J. Sperber, The European Revolutions, 1848–1851** (New York, 1994).

For a comprehensive survey of Latin American history, see **E. Williamson, The Penguin History of Latin America** (London, 1992). A good survey of nineteenth-century developments can be found in **D. Bushnell** and **N. Macaulay, The Emergence of Latin America in the Nineteenth Century** (Oxford, 1988).

The unification of Italy can be examined in **H. Hearder, Cavour** (New York, 1994). The unification of Germany can be pursued first in two good biographies of Bismarck, **E. Crankshaw, Bismarck** (New York, 1981), and **E. Feuchtwanger, Bismarck** (London, 2002). Louis Napoleon's role can be examined in **J. F. McMillan, Napoleon III** (New York, 1991). On the emancipation of the Russian serfs, see **D. Field, The End of Serfdom: Nobility and Bureaucracy in Russia, 1855–1861** (Cambridge, 1976). A good one-volume survey of the Civil War can be found in **P. J. Parish, The American Civil War** (New York, 1975). For a general history of Canada, see **C. Brown,** ed., **The Illustrated History of Canada** (Toronto, 1991).

For an introduction to the intellectual changes of the nineteenth century, see **O. Chadwick, The Secularization of the European Mind in the Nineteenth Century** (Cambridge, 1975). On the ideas of the Romantics, see **M. Cranston, The Romantic Movement** (Oxford, 1994). A detailed biography of Darwin can be found in **J. Bowlby, Charles Darwin: A Biography** (London, 1990). On Realism, **J. Malpas, Realism** (Cambridge, 1997), is a good introduction.

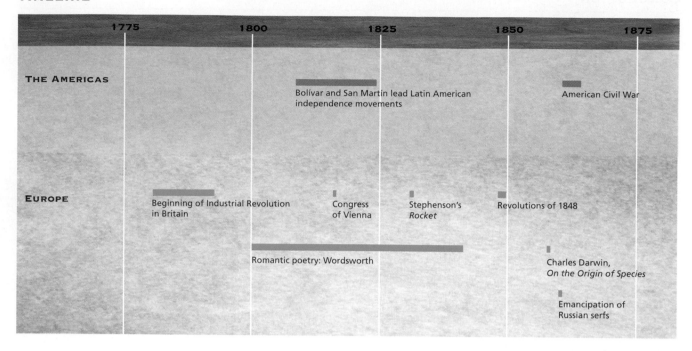

	1775	1800	1825	1850	1875

THE AMERICAS

Bolívar and San Martín lead Latin American independence movements

American Civil War

EUROPE

Beginning of Industrial Revolution in Britain

Congress of Vienna

Stephenson's *Rocket*

Revolutions of 1848

Romantic poetry: Wordsworth

Charles Darwin, *On the Origin of Species*

Emancipation of Russian serfs

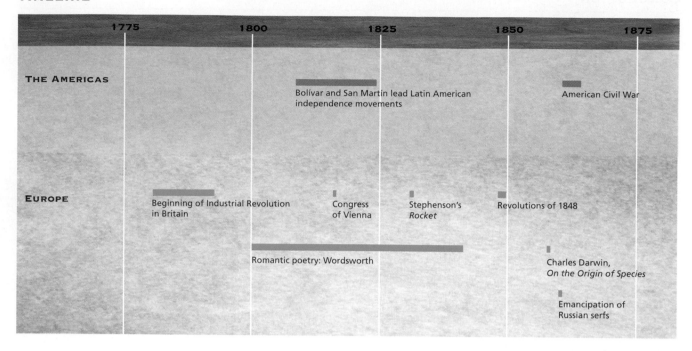

InfoTrac College Edition

Visit this chapter's InfoTrac College Edition/Research activities at the *Essential World History* Companion Website for activities related to industrialization and nationalism.

ThomsonNOW™ for Duiker and Spielvogel's *The Essential World History, Third Edition*

Enter *ThomsonNOW* using the access card that is available with this text. *ThomsonNOW* will assist you in understanding the content in this chapter with lesson plans generated for your needs, as well as provide you with a connection to the *Wadsworth World History Resource Center* (see description at the right for details).

WORLD HISTORY
RESOURCE CENTER

Enter the Resource Center using either your *ThomsonNOW* access card or your standalone access card for the *Wadsworth World History Resource Center.* Organized by topic, this website includes quizzes; images; over 350 primary source documents; interactive simulations, maps, and timelines; movie explorations; and a wealth of other resources. You can read the following documents, and many more, at http://worldrc.wadsworth.com/

> Thomas Malthus, *An Essay on the Principle of Population*
>
> The Chartist Petition

Visit the *Essential World History* Companion Website for chapter quizzes and more:

http://www.thomsonedu.com/history/duiker

DISCOVERY

In what ways were the intellectual and artistic developments of the age related to the development of industrialization and the growth of nationalism?

In thinking about this question, begin by breaking it down into the components shown below. A discussion of the significance of each component should appear in your answer.

ARTS AND IDEAS: How do the two portraits reflect a sense of independence in both nations? What symbols are used to illustrate the power of these new nations? How can art help create a sense of national identity? Does the art of nationalism need to be accurate in its historical depiction? Do you think that these are historically accurate? Do you think that they give a realistic portrayal of their leaders? Do you see any modern comparisons?

José de San Martín

The Unification of Germany

SCIENCE AND TECHNOLOGY: How do both the pictures and the documents reflect the differing views of the importance of industrialization in Eastern and Western societies? What does the focus of industrialization in the East seem to be, compared with its focus in the West? Does it serve the same purpose? Why did industrialization come much later to Eastern societies? How would this affect the growth of nationalism?

Textile Factories, West and East

INDUSTRIAL ATTITUDES IN BRITAIN AND JAPAN

Samuel Smiles, *Self-Help*

"Heaven helps those who help themselves" is a well-worn maxim, embodying in a small compass the results of vast human experience. The spirit of self-help is the root of all genuine growth in the individual; and, exhibited in the lives of many, it constitutes the true source of national vigor and strength. Help from without is often enfeebling in its effects, but help from within invariably invigorates. Whatever is done for men or classes, to a certain extent takes away the stimulus and necessity of doing for themselves; and where men are subjected to overguidance and overgovernment, the inevitable tendency is to render them comparatively helpless. . . .

National progress is the sum of individual industry, energy, and uprightness, as national decay is of individual idleness, selfishness, and vice. . . . If this view be correct, then it follows that the highest patriotism and philanthrophy consist, not so much in altering laws and modifying institutions as in helping and stimulating men to elevate and improve themselves by their own free and independent action as individuals. . . .

Many popular books have been written for the purpose of communicating to the public the grand secret of making money. But there is no secret whatever about it, as the proverbs of every nation abundantly testify. . . . "A penny saved is a penny gained."—"Diligence is the mother of good-luck."—"No pains no gains."—"No sweat no sweet."—"Sloth, the key of poverty."—"Work, and thou shalt have."—"He who will not work, neither shall he eat."—"The world is his, who has patience and industry."

Shibuzawa Eiichi, *Autobiography*

I . . . felt that it was necessary to raise the social standing of those who engaged in commerce and industry. By way of setting an example, I began studying and practicing the teachings of the *Analects of Confucius*. It contains teachings first enunciated more than twenty-four hundred years ago. Yet it supplies the ultimate in practical ethics for all of us to follow in our daily living. It has many golden rules for businessmen. For example, there is a saying: "Wealth and respect are what men desire, but unless a right way is followed, they cannot be obtained; poverty and lowly position are what men despise, but unless a right way is found, one cannot leave that status once reaching it." It shows very clearly how a businessman must act in this world.

Shibuzawa Eiichi on Progress

One must beware of the tendency of some to argue that it is through individualism or egoism that the State and society can progress most rapidly. They claim that under individualism, each individual competes with the others, and progress results from this competition. But this is to see merely the advantages and ignore the disadvantages, and I cannot support such a theory. Society exists, and a State has been founded. Although people desire to rise to positions of wealth and honor, the social order and the tranquility of the State will be disrupted if this is done egoistically. Men should not do battle in competition with their fellow men. Therefore, I believe that in order to get along together in society and serve the State, we must by all means abandon this idea of independence and self-reliance and reject egoism completely.

ARTS AND IDEAS: Which of these works are Romantic and which are in the style of Realism? What inspired Romanticism? In what sense might Romanticism have been a reaction to the inhuman aspects of industrialization? How is that reflected in the Romantic work that you see here? Why did some nineteenth-century observers classify Realism as part of a cult of ugliness? What did they think was the proper function of art? How did industrialization help lead to realistic thinking?

Which style do you think has had the more lasting impact? What does that say about modern society?

Eugène Delacroix, Women of Algiers

EDGAR ALLAN POE, "THE FALL OF THE HOUSE OF USHER"

No sooner had these syllables passed my lips, than—as if a shield of brass had indeed, at the moment, fallen heavily upon a floor of silver—I became aware of a distinct, hollow, metallic, and clangorous, yet apparently muffled, reverberation. Completely unnerved, I leaped to my feet; but the measured rocking movement of Usher was undisturbed. I rushed to the chair in which he sat. His eyes were bent fixedly before him, and throughout his whole countenance there reigned a stony rigidity. But, as I placed my hand upon his shoulder, there came a strong shudder over his whole person; a sickly smile quivered about his lips; and I saw that he spoke in a low, hurried, and gibbering murmur, as if unconscious of my presence. Bending closely over him, I at length drank in the hideous import of his words.

"Not hear it?—yes, I hear it, and *have* heard it. Long—long—long—many minutes, many hours, many days, have I heard it—yet I dared not—oh, pity me, miserable wretch that I am!—I dared not—I *dared* not speak! *We have put her living in the tomb!* Said I not that my senses were acute? I *now* tell you that I heard her first feeble movements in the hollow coffin. I heard them—many, many days ago—yet I dared not—I *dared not speak!* And now—to-night— . . . the rending of her coffin, and the grating of the iron hinges of her prison, and her struggles within the coppered archway of the vault! Oh whither shall I fly? Will she not be here anon? Is she not hurrying to upbraid me for my haste? Have I not heard her footstep on the stair? Do I not distinguish that heavy and horrible beating of her heart? MADMAN!"—here he sprang furiously to his feet, and shrieked out his syllables, as if in the effort he were giving up his soul—"MADMAN! I TELL YOU THAT SHE NOW STANDS WITHOUT THE DOOR!"

Gustave Courbet, *The Stonebreakers*

19

THE EMERGENCE OF MASS SOCIETY
IN THE WESTERN WORLD

Swimmers gather in front of concession stands at Coney Island

$\mathcal{A}$FTER 1870, NEW WORK PATTERNS in the Western world established the "weekend" as a distinct time of recreation and fun, while new forms of mass transportation—railroads and streetcars—enabled even workers to make brief excursions to amusement parks. Coney Island was only 8 miles from central New York City; Blackpool in England was a short train ride from nearby industrial towns. With their Ferris wheels and other daring rides that threw young men and women together, amusement parks offered a whole new world of entertainment. Thanks to the railroad, seaside resorts, once the preserve of the wealthy, became accessible to more people for weekend visits, much to the disgust of one upper-class regular, who complained about the new "day trippers": "They swarm upon the beach, wandering listlessly about with apparently no other aim than to get a mouthful of fresh air." Enterprising entrepreneurs in resorts like Blackpool welcomed the masses of new visitors, however, and built piers laden with food, drink, and entertainment to serve them.

Mass leisure was but one aspect of the new mass society that emerged in the West during the fifty years leading up to 1914. Those fifty years marked a dynamic age of material prosperity. The new industries, new sources of energy, and new goods of the Second Industrial Revolution transformed the human environment and led people to believe that their material progress reflected human progress. Scientific and technological achievements, many naively believed, would improve the human condition and solve all problems. The doctrine of progress became an article of faith.

The rapid economic changes of the nineteenth century led to the emergence of mass society in the Western world. Mass society meant improvements for the lower classes, who benefited from the extension of voting rights, a better standard of living, and free education. The coming of mass society also created new roles for the governments of European nation-states, which now fostered national loyalty, built vast armies by conscription, and took more responsibility for public health and housing measures in their cities. The period after 1871 also witnessed the growth of political democracy as the right to vote was extended to all adult males; women would still have to fight for the same political rights. With political democracy came a new mass politics that would become a regular feature of the twentieth century.

The period between 1870 and 1914 was also a time of great tension. Europeans engaged in a race for colonies that intensified existing antagonisms among European states, while the creation of huge conscript armies and enormous military establishments served to heighten tensions among the major powers. At the same time, despite the appearance of progress, Western philosophers, writers, and artists were exploring modern cultural expressions that questioned traditional ideas and values and increasingly provoked a crisis of confidence. ◆

The Fotomas Index

An Age of Progress. Between 1871 and 1914, the Second Industrial Revolution led many Europeans to believe that they were living in an age of progress when most human problems would be solved by scientific achievements. This illustration is taken from a special issue of *The Illustrated London News* celebrating the Diamond Jubilee of Queen Victoria in 1897. On the left are scenes from 1837, when Victoria came to the British throne; on the right are scenes from 1897. The vivid contrast underscored the magazine's conclusion: "The most striking . . . evidence of progress during the reign is the ever increasing speed which the discoveries of physical science have forced into everyday life. Steam and electricity have conquered time and space to a greater extent during the last sixty years than all the preceding six hundred years witnessed."

The Growth of Industrial Prosperity

At the heart of Europe's belief in progress between 1870 and 1914 was the stunning material growth produced by what historians have called the Second Industrial Revolution.

New Products

The first major change in industrial development between 1870 and 1914 was the substitution of steel for iron. New methods for shaping steel made it useful in the construction of lighter, smaller, and faster machines and engines, as well as railways, ships, and armaments. In 1860, Great Britain, France, Germany, and Belgium produced 125,000 tons of steel; by 1913, the total was 32 million tons.

Electricity was a major new form of energy that could be easily converted into other forms of energy, such as heat, light, and motion, and moved relatively effortlessly through space by means of transmitting wires. In the 1870s, the first commercially practical generators of electrical current were developed, and by 1910, hydroelectric power stations and coal-fired steam-generating plants enabled homes and factories in whole neighborhoods to be tied into a single, common source of power.

Electricity spawned a number of inventions. The lightbulb, developed independently by the American Thomas Edison and the Briton Joseph Swan, permitted homes and cities to be illuminated by electric lights. By the 1880s, streetcars and subways powered by electricity had appeared in major European cities. Electricity also transformed the factory. Conveyor belts, cranes, machines, and machine tools could all be powered by electricity and located anywhere. Similarly, a revolution in communications began when Alexander Graham Bell invented the telephone in 1876 and Guglielmo Marconi sent the first radio waves across the Atlantic in 1901.

The development of the internal combustion engine, fired by oil and gasoline, provided a new source of power in transportation and gave rise to ocean liners as well as to the airplane and the automobile. In 1900, world production stood at 9,000 cars, but an American, Henry Ford, revolutionized the automotive industry with the mass production of the Model T. By 1916, Ford's factories were producing 735,000 cars a year. In 1903, at Kitty Hawk, North Carolina, brothers Orville and Wilbur Wright made the first flight in a fixed-wing airplane. In 1919, the first regular passenger air service was established.

New Patterns

Industrial production grew rapidly at this time because of the greatly increased sales of manufactured goods. An increase in real wages for workers after 1870, combined with lower prices for manufactured goods because of reduced transportation costs, made it easier for Europeans to buy consumer products. In the cities, the first department stores began to sell a whole new range of consumer goods made possible by the development of the steel and electrical industries. The desire to own sewing machines, clocks, bicycles, electric lights, and typewriters was rapidly generating a new consumer ethic that has been a crucial part of the modern economy.

Not all nations benefited from the Second Industrial Revolution. Between 1870 and 1914, Germany replaced Great Britain as the industrial leader of Europe. Moreover, by 1900, Europe was divided into two economic zones. Great Britain, Belgium, France, the Netherlands, Germany, the western part of the Austro-Hungarian Empire, and northern Italy constituted an advanced industrialized core that had a high standard of living, decent systems of transportation, and relatively healthy and educated peoples (see Map 19.1). Another part of Europe, the backward and little industrialized area to the south and east, consisting of southern Italy, most of Austria-Hungary, Spain, Portugal, the Balkan kingdoms, and Russia, was still largely agricultural and relegated by the industrial countries to the function of providing food and raw materials.

Toward a World Economy

The economic developments of the late nineteenth century, combined with the transportation revolution that saw the growth of marine transport and railroads, fostered a true world economy. By 1900, Europeans were receiving beef and wool from Argentina and Australia, coffee from Brazil, iron ore from Algeria, and sugar from Java. European capital was also invested abroad to develop railways, mines, electrical power plants, and banks. Of course, foreign countries also provided markets for the surplus manufactured goods of Europe. With its capital, industries, and military might, Europe dominated the world economy by the beginning of the twentieth century.

The Spread of Industrialization

After 1870, industrialization began to spread beyond western and central Europe and North America. Especially noticeable was its rapid development, fostered by governments, in Russia and Japan. A surge of industrialization began in Russia in the 1890s under the guiding hand of Sergei Witte, the minister of finance. Witte pushed the government toward a program of massive railroad construction. By 1900, 35,000 miles of track had been laid. Witte's program also made possible the rapid growth of a modern steel and coal industry, making Russia by 1900 the fourth-largest producer of steel, behind the United States, Germany, and Great Britain. At the same time, Russia was also turning out half of the world's oil production.

In Japan, the imperial government took the lead in promoting industry (see Chapter 21). The government financed industries, built railroads, brought foreign experts to train Japanese employees in new industrial techniques, and instituted a universal educational system based on applied science. By the end of the nineteenth century, Japan had developed key industries in tea, silk, armaments, and shipbuilding.

Women and Work: New Job Opportunities

During the course of the nineteenth century, working-class organizations upheld the belief that women should remain at home to bear and nurture children and not be allowed in the industrial workforce. Working-class men argued that keeping women out of industrial work would ensure the moral and physical well-being of families. In reality, however, when their husbands were unemployed, women had to do low-wage work at home or labor part time in sweatshops to support their families.

The Second Industrial Revolution opened the door to new jobs for women. The development of larger industrial plants and the expansion of government services created a wide number of service and white-collar jobs. The increased demand for white-collar workers at relatively low wages coupled with a shortage of male workers led employers to hire women. Big businesses and retail shops needed clerks, typists, secretaries, file clerks, and salesclerks. The expansion of government services opened opportunities for women to be secretaries and telephone operators and to take jobs in health care and social services. Compulsory education necessitated more teachers, and the development of modern hospital services opened the way for an increase in nurses.

Many of the new white-collar jobs were far from exciting. The work was routine and, except for teaching and nursing, required few skills beyond basic literacy. Nevertheless, these jobs had distinct advantages for many women. For some middle-class women, the new jobs offered freedom from the domestic patterns expected of them. Most of the new positions, however, were filled by working-class women who saw them as an opportunity to escape from the "dirty" work of the lower-class world.

MAP 19.1 **The Industrial Regions of Europe at the End of the Nineteenth Century.** By the end of the nineteenth century, the Second Industrial Revolution—in steelmaking, electricity, petroleum, and chemicals—had spurred substantial economic growth and prosperity in western and central Europe; it also sparked economic and political competition between Great Britain and Germany. **?** Look back at Map 18.1. What parts of Europe not industrialized in 1850 had become industrialized in the ensuing decades?

Organizing the Working Classes

The desire to improve their working and living conditions led many industrial workers to form socialist political parties and socialist trade unions. These emerged after 1870, but the theory that made them possible had been developed more than two decades earlier in the work of Karl Marx. **Marxism** made its first appearance on the eve of the revolutions of 1848 with the publication of a short treatise titled *The Communist Manifesto,* written by two Germans, Karl Marx (1818–1883) and Friedrich Engels (1820–1895).

Marxist Theory Marx and Engels began their treatise with the statement that "the history of all hitherto existing society is the history of class struggles." Throughout history, then, oppressor and oppressed have "stood in constant opposition to one another."[1] One group of people—the oppressors—owned the means of production and thus had the power to control government and society.

THE CLASSLESS SOCIETY

FAMILY & SOCIETY

In *The Communist Manifesto,* Karl Marx and Friedrich Engels projected as the end product of the struggle between the bourgeoisie and the proletariat the creation of a classless society. In this selection, they discuss the steps by which that classless society would be reached.

How did Marx and Engels define the proletariat? The bourgeoisie? Why did Marxists come to believe that this distinction was paramount for understanding history? For shaping the future?

Karl Marx and Friedrich Engels, *The Communist Manifesto*

We have seen . . ., that the first step in the revolution by the working class is to raise the proletariat to the position of ruling class. . . . The proletariat will use its political supremacy to wrest, by degrees, all capital from the bourgeoisie, to centralize all instruments of production in the hands of the State, i.e., of the proletariat organized as the ruling class; and to increase the total of productive forces as rapidly as possible.

Of course, in the beginning, this cannot be effected except by means of despotic inroads on the rights of property, and on the conditions of bourgeois production; by means of measures, therefore, which appear economically insufficient and untenable, but which, in the course of the movement, outstrip themselves, necessitate further inroads upon the old social order, and are unavoidable as a means of entirely revolutionizing the mode of production.

These measures will of course be different in different countries.

Nevertheless, in the most advanced countries, the following will be pretty generally applicable:

1. Abolition of property in land and application of all rents of land to public purposes.
2. A heavy progressive or graduated income tax.
3. Abolition of all right of inheritance. . . .

5. Centralization of credit in the hands of the State, by means of a national bank with State capital and an exclusive monopoly.
6. Centralization of the means of communication and transport in the hands of the State.
7. Extension of factories and instruments of production owned by the State. . . .
8. Equal liability of all to labor. Establishment of industrial armies, especially for agriculture.
9. Combination of agriculture with manufacturing industries; gradual abolition of the distinction between town and country, by a more equable distribution of the population over the country.
10. Free education for all children in public schools. Abolition of children's factory labor in its present form. . . .

When, in the course of development, class distinctions have disappeared, and all production has been concentrated in the whole nation, the public power will lose its political character. Political power, properly so called, is merely the organized power of one class for oppressing another. If the proletariat during its contest with the bourgeoisie is compelled, by the force of circumstances, to organize itself as a class, if, by means of a revolution, it makes itself the ruling class, and, as such, sweeps away by force the old conditions of production, then it will, along with these conditions, have swept away the conditions for the existence of class antagonisms and of classes generally, and will thereby have abolished its own supremacy as a class.

In place of the old bourgeois society, with its classes and class antagonisms, we shall have an association, in which the free development of each is the condition for the free development of all.

ThomsonNOW To read more of *The Communist Manifesto,* enter the *ThomsonNOW* documents area using the access card that is available for *The Essential World History.*

Indeed, government itself was but an instrument of the ruling class. The other group, which depended on the owners of the means of production, were the oppressed.

In the industrialized societies of Marx's day, the **class struggle** continued. According to Marx, "Society as a whole is more and more splitting up into two great hostile camps, into two great classes directly facing each other: Bourgeoisie and Proletariat." Marx predicted that the struggle between the bourgeoisie and the proletariat would finally break into open revolution, "where the violent overthrow of the bourgeoisie lays the foundation for the sway of the proletariat." Hence the fall of the bourgeoisie "and the victory of the proletariat are equally inevitable."[2] For a while, the proletariat would

form a dictatorship in order to organize the means of production, but the end result would be a classless society, since classes themselves arose from the economic differences that would have been abolished. The state—itself an instrument of the bourgeois interests—would wither away (see the box above).

Socialist Parties In time, Marx's ideas were picked up by working-class leaders who formed socialist parties. Most important was the German Social Democratic Party (SPD), which emerged in 1875 and espoused revolutionary Marxist rhetoric while organizing itself as a mass political party competing in elections for the Reichstag (the lower house of parliament). Once in the Reichstag,

SPD delegates worked to achieve legislation to improve the condition of the working class. When it received four million votes in the 1912 elections, the SPD became the largest single party in Germany.

Socialist parties also emerged in other European states. In 1889, leaders of the various socialist parties formed the Second International, an association of national socialist groups that would fight against capitalism worldwide. (The First International had failed in 1872.) The Second International took some coordinated actions—May Day (May 1), for example, was made an international labor holiday—but differences often wreaked havoc at the organization's congresses.

Marxist parties divided over the issue of **revisionism**. Pure Marxists believed in the imminent collapse of capitalism and the need for socialist ownership of the means of production. But others, called revisionists, rejected **revolutionary socialism** and argued that workers must organize mass political parties and work together with other progressive elements to gain reform. Evolution by democratic means, not revolution, would achieve the desired goal of socialism.

Another force working for evolutionary rather than revolutionary socialism was the development of trade unions. In Great Britain, unions won the right to strike in the 1870s. Soon after, the masses of workers in factories were organized into trade unions so that they could use the instrument of the strike. By 1900, there were two million workers in British trade unions; by 1914, there were almost four million union members. Trade unions in the rest of Europe had varying degrees of success, but by the outbreak of World War I, they had made considerable progress in bettering both the living and the working conditions of workers.

The Emergence of Mass Society

The rapid economic and social changes of the nineteenth century led to the emergence of **mass society** by the century's end. For the lower classes, mass society brought voting rights, an improved standard of living, and access to education. However, mass society also made possible the development of organizations that manipulated the populations of the nation-states. To understand this mass society, we need to examine some aspects of its structure.

The New Urban Environment

One of the most important consequences of industrialization and the population explosion of the nineteenth century was urbanization. In the course of the nineteenth century, more and more people came to live in cities. In 1800, city dwellers constituted 40 percent of the population in Britain, 25 percent in France and Germany, and only 10 percent in eastern Europe. By 1914, urban residents had increased to 80 percent of the population in Britain, 45 percent in France, 60 percent in Germany, and

30 percent in eastern Europe. The size of cities also expanded dramatically, especially in industrialized countries. Between 1800 and 1900, London's population grew from 960,000 to 6.5 million and Berlin's from 172,000 to 2.7 million.

Urban populations grew faster than the general population primarily because of the vast migration from rural areas to cities. But cities also grew faster in the second half of the nineteenth century because health and the conditions of life in them were improving as urban reformers and city officials used new technology to ameliorate the urban landscape. In the 1840s, a number of urban reformers had pointed to filthy living conditions as the primary cause of deadly epidemic diseases in the cities. Following the reformers' advice, city governments set up boards of health to improve the quality of housing and instituted regulations requiring all new buildings to have running water and internal drainage systems.

Essential to the public health of the modern European city was the ability to bring in clean water and to expel sewage. The problem of fresh water was solved by a system of dams and reservoirs that stored the water and aqueducts and tunnels that carried it from the countryside to the city and into individual dwellings. Gas heaters in the 1860s, and later electric heaters, made regular hot baths available to many people. The treatment of sewage was also improved by building mammoth underground pipes that carried raw sewage far from the city for disposal. The city of Frankfurt, Germany, for example, began its program for sewers with a lengthy public campaign featuring the slogan "From the toilet to the river in half an hour."

Middle-class reformers also focused on the housing needs of the working class. Overcrowded, disease-ridden slums were seen as dangerous not only to physical health but also to the political and moral health of the entire nation. V. A. Huber, a German housing reformer, wrote in 1861: "Certainly it would not be too much to say that the home is the communal embodiment of family life. Thus the purity of the dwelling is almost as important for the family as is the cleanliness of the body for the individual."[3] To Huber, good housing was a prerequisite for stable family life, and without stable family life, society would fall apart.

Early efforts to attack the housing problem emphasized the middle-class, liberal belief in the power of private enterprise. Reformers such as Huber believed that the building of model dwellings renting at a reasonable price would force other private landlords to elevate their housing standards. A fine example of this approach was the work of Octavia Hill (see the box on p. 431). By the 1880s, as the number and size of cities continued to mushroom, governments concluded that private enterprise could not solve the housing crisis. In 1890, a British law empowered local town councils to construct cheap housing for the working classes. More and more, governments were stepping into areas of activity that they would not have touched earlier.

THE HOUSING VENTURE OF OCTAVIA HILL

FAMILY & SOCIETY

Octavia Hill was a practical-minded British housing reformer who believed that workers and their families were entitled to happy homes. At the same time, she was convinced that the poor needed guidance and encouragement, not charity. In this selection, she describes her housing venture.

Did Octavia Hill's housing venture create financial returns for her initial investment? What benefits did her tenants receive in turn? What feelings and beliefs about the lower classes are evident in Hill's account?

Octavia Hill, *Homes of the London Poor*

About four years ago I was put in possession of three houses in one of the worst courts of Marylebone. Six other houses were bought subsequently. All were crowded with inmates.

The first thing to be done was to put them in decent tenantable order. The set last purchased was a row of cottages facing a bit of desolate ground, occupied with wretched, dilapidated cowsheds, manure heaps, old timber, and rubbish of every description. The houses were in a most deplorable condition—the plaster was dropping from the walls; on one staircase a pail was placed to catch the rain that fell through the roof. All the staircases were perfectly dark; the banisters were gone, having been burnt as firewood by tenants. The grates, with large holes in them, were falling forward into the rooms. The washhouse, full of lumber belonging to the landlord, was locked up; thus the inhabitants had to wash clothes, as well as to cook, eat and sleep in their small rooms. The dustbin, standing in the front part of the houses, was accessible to the whole neighbourhood, and boys often dragged from it quantities of unseemly objects and spread them over the court. The state of the drainage was in keeping with everything else. The pavement of the backyard was all broken up, and great puddles stood in it, so that the damp crept up the outer walls. . . .

As soon as I entered into possession, each family had an opportunity of doing better: those who would not pay, or who led clearly immoral lives, were ejected. The rooms they vacated were cleansed; the tenants who showed signs of improvement moved into them, and thus, in turn, an opportunity was obtained for having each room distempered and papered. The drains were put in order, a large slate cistern was fixed, the washhouse was cleared of its lumber, and thrown open on stated days to each tenant in turn. The roof, the plaster, the woodwork was repaired; the staircase walls were distempered; new grates were fixed; the layers of paper and rag (black with age) were torn from the windows, and glass was put in; out of 192 panes only eight were found unbroken. The yard and footpath were paved.

The rooms, as a rule, were re-let at the same prices at which they had been let before; but tenants with large families were counselled to take two rooms, and for these much less was charged than if let singly: this plan I continue to pursue. Incoming tenants are not allowed to take a decidedly insufficient quantity of room, and no subletting is permitted. . . .

The pecuniary result has been very satisfactory. Five per cent has been paid on all the capital invested. A fund for the repayment of capital is accumulating. A liberal allowance has been made for repairs. . . .

My tenants are mostly of a class far below that of mechanics. They are, indeed, of the very poor. And yet, although the gifts they have received have been next to nothing, none of the families who have passed under my care during the whole four years have continued in what is called "distress," except such as have been unwilling to exert themselves. Those who will not exert the necessary self-control cannot avail themselves of the means of livelihood held out to them. But, for those who are willing, some small assistance in the form of work has, from time to time, been provided—not much, but sufficient to keep them from want or despair.

ThomsonNOW To read a similar account of city existence by Charles Dickens, enter the *ThomsonNOW* documents area using the access card that is available for *The Essential World History.*

The Social Structure of Mass Society

At the top of European society stood a wealthy elite, constituting but 5 percent of the population while controlling between 30 and 40 percent of its wealth. In the course of the nineteenth century, landed aristocrats had joined with the most successful industrialists, bankers, and merchants (the wealthy upper middle class) to form a new elite. Members of this elite, whether aristocratic or middle class in background, assumed leadership roles in government bureaucracies and military hierarchies. Marriage also united the two groups. Daughters of business tycoons gained titles, while aristocratic heirs gained new sources of cash. When the American Consuelo Vanderbilt married the duke of Marlborough, the new duchess brought $10 million to her husband.

The middle classes consisted of a variety of groups. Below the upper middle class was a group that included lawyers, doctors, and members of the civil service, as well as business managers, engineers, architects, accountants, and chemists benefiting from industrial expansion. Beneath this solid and comfortable middle group was a lower middle class of small shopkeepers, traders, manufacturers, and prosperous peasants.

Standing between the lower middle class and the lower classes were new groups of white-collar workers who were the product of the Second Industrial Revolution. They were the salespeople, bookkeepers, bank tellers, telephone operators, and secretaries. Though often paid little more than skilled laborers, these white-collar workers were committed to middle-class ideals.

The middle classes shared a certain lifestyle, the values of which dominated much of nineteenth-century society. This was especially evident in Victorian Britain, often considered a model of middle-class society. The European middle classes believed in hard work, which was open to everyone and guaranteed to have positive results. They were also regular churchgoers who believed in the good conduct associated with traditional Christian morality. The middle class was concerned with propriety, the right way of doing things, which gave rise to an incessant stream of books aimed at the middle-class market with such titles as *The Habits of Good Society* or *Don't: A Manual of Mistakes and Improprieties More or Less Prevalent in Conduct and Speech*.

Below the middle classes on the social scale were the working classes, who constituted almost 80 percent of the European population. Many of them were landholding peasants, agricultural laborers, and sharecroppers, especially in eastern Europe. The urban working class consisted of many different groups, including skilled artisans in such traditional trades as cabinetmaking, printing, and the making of jewelry and semiskilled laborers, who included such people as carpenters, bricklayers, and many factory workers. At the bottom of the urban working class stood the largest group of workers, the unskilled laborers. They included day laborers, who worked irregularly for very low wages, and large numbers of domestic servants, most of whom were women.

The Experiences of Women

In 1800, women were largely defined by family and household roles. They remained legally inferior and economically dependent. Women struggled to change their status throughout the nineteenth century.

Marriage and the Family   Many women in the nineteenth century aspired to the ideal of femininity popularized by writers and poets. Alfred Lord Tennyson's poem *The Princess* expressed it well:

> *Man for the field and woman for the hearth:*
> *Man for the sword and for the needle she:*
> *Man with the head and woman with the heart:*
> *Man to command and woman to obey;*
> *All else confusion.*

This traditional characterization of the sexes, based on gender-defined social roles, was virtually elevated to the status of universal male and female attributes in the nineteenth century. As the chief family wage earners, men worked outside the home for pay, while women were left with the care of the family, for which they were paid nothing.

For most women throughout most of the nineteenth century, marriage was viewed as the only honorable and available career. Though the middle class glorified the ideal of domesticity, for most women, marriage was a matter of economic necessity. The lack of meaningful work and the lower wages paid to women for their work made it difficult for single women to earn a living. Most women chose to marry.

The most significant development in the modern family was the decline in the number of offspring born to the average woman. While some historians attribute increased birth control to more widespread use of coitus interruptus, or male withdrawal before ejaculation, others have emphasized female control of family size through abortion and even infanticide or abandonment. That a change in attitude occurred was apparent in the development of a movement to increase awareness of birth control methods. Europe's first birth control clinic opened in Amsterdam in 1882.

The family was the central institution of middle-class life. Men provided the family income while women focused on household and child care. The use of domestic servants in many middle-class homes, made possible by an abundant supply of cheap labor, reduced the amount of time middle-class women had to spend on household chores. At the same time, by reducing the number of children in the family, mothers could devote more time to child care and domestic leisure.

A Middle-Class Family.   Nineteenth-century middle-class moralists considered the family the fundamental pillar of a healthy society. The family was a crucial institution in middle-class life, and togetherness constituted one of the important ideals of the middle-class family. This painting by William P. Frith, titled *Many Happy Returns of the Day*, shows a family birthday celebration for a little girl in which grandparents, parents, and children are taking part. The servant at the left holds the presents for the little girl.

The middle-class family fostered an ideal of togetherness. The Victorians devised the family Christmas with its Yule log, Christmas tree, songs, and exchange of gifts. In the United States, Fourth of July celebrations changed from drunken revels to family picnics by the 1850s.

Women in working-class families were more accustomed to hard work. Daughters in working-class families were expected to work until they married; even after marriage, they often did piecework at home to help support the family. For the children of the working classes, childhood was over by the age of nine or ten, when they became apprentices or were employed at odd jobs.

Between 1890 and 1914, however, family patterns among the working class began to change. High-paying jobs in heavy industry and improvements in the standard of living made it possible for working-class families to depend on the income of husbands and the wages of grown children. By the early twentieth century, some working-class mothers could afford to stay at home, following the pattern of middle-class women. At the same time, working-class families also aspired to buy new consumer products, such as sewing machines, clocks, bicycles, and cast-iron stoves.

The Movement for Women's Rights   Modern European feminism, or the movement for women's rights, had its beginnings during the French Revolution, when some women advocated equality for women based on the doctrine of natural rights. In the 1830s, a number of women in the United States and Europe, who worked together in several reform movements, argued for the right of women to divorce and own property. These early efforts were not overly successful; women did not gain the right to their own property until 1870 in Britain, 1900 in Germany, and 1907 in France.

The fight for property rights was only a beginning for the women's movement, however. Some middle- and upper-middle-class women gained access to higher education, and others sought entry into occupations dominated by men. The first to fall was teaching. As medical training was largely closed to women, they sought alternatives in the development of nursing. Nursing pioneers included the British nurse Florence Nightingale, whose efforts during the Crimean War (1854–1856), along with those of Clara Barton in the American Civil War (1861–1865), transformed nursing into a profession of trained, middle-class "women in white."

By the 1840s and 1850s, the movement for women's rights had entered the political arena with the call for equal political rights. Many feminists believed that the right to vote was the key to all other reforms to improve the position of women. **Suffragists** had one basic aim, the right of women to full citizenship in the nation-state.

The British women's movement was the most vocal and active in Europe. Emmeline Pankhurst (1858–1928) and her daughters, Christabel and Sylvia, founded the Women's Social and Political Union in 1903, which enrolled mostly middle- and upper-class women. Pankhurst's organization realized the value of the media and used unusual publicity stunts to call attention to its demands. Derisively labeled "suffragettes" by male politicians, they pelted government officials with eggs, chained themselves to lampposts, smashed the windows of department stores on fashionable shopping streets, burned railroad cars, and went on hunger strikes in jail.

Before World War I, the demands for women's rights were being heard throughout Europe and the United States, although only in Norway and some American states did women receive the right to vote before 1914. It would take the dramatic upheaval of World War I before male-dominated governments capitulated on this basic issue.

Women reformers also took on issues besides suffrage. In many countries, women supported peace movements. Bertha von Suttner (1843–1914) became head of the Austrian Peace Society and protested against the growing arms race of the 1890s. Her novel, *Lay Down Your Arms*, became a best-seller and brought her the Nobel Peace Prize in 1905. Lower-class women also took up the cause of peace. A group of women workers marched in Vienna in 1911 and demanded: "We want an end to armaments, to the means of murder and we want these millions to be spent on the needs of the people."

Bertha von Suttner was but one example of the "new women" who were becoming more prominent at the turn of the twentieth century. These women rejected traditional feminine roles (see the box on p. 434) and sought new freedom outside the household and new roles other than those of wives and mothers.

Education in an Age of Mass Society

Education in the early nineteenth century was primarily for the elite or the wealthier middle class, but between 1870 and 1914, most Western governments began to offer at least primary education to both boys and girls between the ages of six and twelve. States also assumed responsibility for better training of teachers by establishing teacher-training schools. By the beginning of the twentieth century, many European states, especially in northern and western Europe, were providing state-financed primary schools, salaried and trained teachers, and free, compulsory elementary education.

Why did Western nations make this commitment to **mass education?** One reason was industrialization. The new firms of the Second Industrial Revolution demanded skilled labor. Both boys and girls with an elementary education had new possibilities of jobs beyond their villages or small towns, including white-collar jobs in railways and subways, post offices, banking and shipping firms, teaching, and nursing. Mass education furnished the trained workers industrialists needed. For most students, elementary education led to apprenticeship and a job.

The chief motive for mass education, however, was political. The increase in suffrage created the need for a more educated electorate. Even more important, however,

ADVICE TO WOMEN: BE INDEPENDENT

FAMILY & SOCIETY

Although a majority of women probably followed the nineteenth-century middle-class ideal of women as keepers of the household and nurturers of husband and children, an increasing number of women fought for the rights of women. This selection is taken from Act III of Henrik Ibsen's play *A Doll's House* (1879), in which the character Nora Helmer declares her independence from her husband's control over her life.

In Ibsen's play, what challenges does Nora Helmer make to the prevailing view of the proper role and behavior of wives? Why is her husband so shocked? Why did Ibsen title this play A Doll's House?

Henrik Ibsen, *A Doll's House*

Nora: (*Pause*) Does anything strike you as we sit here?

Helmer: What should strike me?

Nora: We've been married eight years; does it not strike you that this is the first time we two, you and I, man and wife, have talked together seriously?

Helmer: Seriously? What do you mean, *seriously?*

Nora: For eight whole years, and more—ever since the day we first met—we have never exchanged one serious word about serious things. . . .

Helmer: Why, my dearest Nora, what have you to do with serious things?

Nora: There we have it! You have never understood me. I've had great injustice done to me, Torvald; first by father, then by you.

Helmer: What! Your father and me? We, who have loved you more than all the world?

Nora (*Shaking her head*): You have never loved me. You just found it amusing to think you were in love with me.

Helmer: Nora! What a thing to say!

Nora: Yes, it's true, Torvald. When I was living at home with father, he told me his opinions and mine were the same. If I had different opinions, I said nothing about them, because he would not have liked it. He used to call me his doll-child and played with me as I played with my dolls. Then I came to live in your house.

Helmer: What a way to speak of our marriage!

Nora (*Undisturbed*): I mean that I passed from father's hands into yours. You arranged everything to your taste and I got the same tastes as you; or pretended to—I don't know which—both, perhaps; sometimes one, sometimes the other. When I look back on it now, I seem to have been living here like a beggar, on hand-outs. I lived by performing tricks for you, Torvald. But that was how you wanted it. You and father have done me a great wrong. It is your fault that my life has come to naught.

Helmer: Why, Nora, how unreasonable and ungrateful! Haven't you been happy here?

Nora: No, never. I thought I was, but I never was.

Helmer: Not—not happy! . . .

Nora: I must stand quite alone if I am ever to know myself and my surroundings; so I cannot stay with you.

Helmer: Nora! Nora!

Nora: I am going at once. I daresay [my friend] Christina will take me in for tonight.

Helmer: You are mad! I shall not allow it! I forbid it!

Nora: It's no use your forbidding me anything now. I shall take with me only what belongs to me; from you I will accept nothing, either now or later.

Helmer: This is madness!

Nora: Tomorrow I shall go home—I mean to what was my home. It will be easier for me to find a job there.

Helmer: Oh, in your blind inexperience—

Nora: I must try to gain experience, Torvald.

Helmer: Forsake your home, your husband, your children! And you don't consider what the world will say.

Nora: I can't pay attention to that. I only know that I must do it.

Helmer: This is monstrous! Can you forsake your holiest duties?

Nora: What do you consider my holiest duties?

Helmer: Need I tell you that? Your duties to your husband and children.

Nora: I have other duties equally sacred.

Helmer: Impossible! What do you mean?

Nora: My duties toward myself.

Helmer: Before all else you are a wife and a mother.

Nora: That I no longer believe. Before all else I believe I am a human being, just as much as you are—or at least that I should try to become one. I know that most people agree with you, Torvald, and that they say so in books. But I can no longer be satisfied with what most people say and what is in books. I must think things out for myself and try to get clear about them.

ThomsonNOW To read more of Ibsen's plays, enter the *ThomsonNOW* documents area using the access card that is available for *The Essential World History.*

---

mass compulsory education instilled patriotism and nationalized the masses, providing an opportunity for even greater national integration. As people lost their ties to local regions and even to religion, nationalism supplied a new faith (see the comparative essay "The Rise of Nationalism" on p. 435).

Compulsory elementary education created a demand for teachers, and most of them were women. Many men viewed the teaching of children as an extension of women's "natural role" as nurturers of children. Moreover, females were paid lower salaries, in itself a considerable incentive for governments to encourage the

COMPARATIVE ESSAY

THE RISE OF NATIONALISM

POLITICS & GOVERNMENT

Like the Industrial Revolution, the concept of nationalism originated in eighteenth-century Europe, where it was the product of a variety of factors, including the spread of printing and the replacement of Latin with vernacular languages, the secularization of the age, and the experience of the French revolutionary and Napoleonic eras. The French were the first to show what a nation in arms could accomplish, but peoples conquered by Napoleon soon created their own national armies. At the beginning of the nineteenth century, peoples who had previously focused their identity on a locality or a region, on loyalty to a monarch or to a particular religious faith, now shifted their political allegiance to the idea of a nation, based on ethnic, linguistic, or cultural factors. The idea of the nation had explosive consequences: by the end of the first two decades of the twentieth century, the world's three largest multiethnic states—Imperial Russia, Austria-Hungary, and the Ottoman Empire—had all given way to a number of individual nation-states.

The idea of establishing political boundaries on the basis of ethnicity, language, or culture had a broad appeal throughout Western civilization, but it had unintended consequences. Although the concept provided the basis for a new sense of community that was tied to liberal thought in the first half of the nineteenth century, it also gave birth to ethnic tensions and hatred in the second half of the century that resulted in bitter disputes and contributed to the competition between nation-states that eventually erupted into world war. Governments, following the lead of the radical government in Paris during the French Revolution, took full advantage of the rise of a strong national consciousness and transformed war from the sport of kings into a matter of national honor and commitment. Universal schooling enabled states to arouse patriotic enthusiasm and create national unity. Most soldiers who joyfully went to war in 1914 were convinced that their nation's cause was just.

But if the concept of nationalism was initially the product of conditions in modern Europe, it soon spread to other parts of the world. Although a few societies, such as Vietnam, had already developed a strong sense of national identity, most of the peoples in Asia and Africa lived in multiethnic and multireligious communities and were not yet ripe for the spirit of nationalism. As we shall see, the first attempts to resist European colonial rule were thus often based on religious or ethnic identity, rather than on the concept of denied nationhood. But the imperialist powers, which at first benefited from the lack of political cohesion among their colonial subjects, eventually reaped what they had sowed. As the colonial peoples became familiar with Western concepts of democracy and self-determination, they too began to manifest a sense of common purpose that helped knit together the different elements in their societies to oppose colonial regimes and create the conditions for the emergence of future nations. For good or ill, the concept of nationalism had now achieved global proportions. We shall explore such issues, and their consequences, in greater detail in the chapters that follow.

---

establishment of teacher-training institutes for women. The first female colleges were really teacher-training schools. It was not until the beginning of the twentieth century that women were permitted to enter the male-dominated universities.

The most immediate result of mass education was an increase in literacy. In Germany, Great Britain, France, and the Scandinavian countries, adult illiteracy was virtually eliminated by 1900. Where there was less schooling, the story was very different. Adult illiteracy rates were 79 percent in Serbia, 78 percent in Romania, and 79 percent in Russia.

Leisure in an Age of Mass Society

With the Industrial Revolution came new forms of leisure. Work and leisure became opposites as leisure was viewed as what people do for fun after work. The new leisure hours created by the industrial system—evening hours after work, weekends, and later a week or two in the summer—largely determined the contours of the new **mass leisure.**

New technology created novel experiences for leisure, such as the Ferris wheel at amusement parks, while the subways and streetcars of the 1880s meant that even the working classes were no longer dependent on neighborhood facilities but could make their way to athletic games, amusement parks, and dance halls. Railroads could take people to the beaches on weekends.

By the late nineteenth century, team sports had also developed into another important form of mass leisure. Unlike the old rural games, they were no longer chaotic and spontaneous activities but became strictly organized with sets of rules and officials to enforce them. These rules were the products of organized athletic groups, such as the English Football Association (1863) and the American Bowling Congress (1895). The development of urban transportation systems made possible the construction of stadiums where thousands could attend, making mass spectator sports into a big business.

The National State

Throughout much of the Western world by 1870, the national state had become the focus of people's loyalties. Only in Russia, eastern Europe, Austria-Hungary, and Ireland did national groups still struggle for independence.

Tradition and Change in Latin America

After 1870, Latin America began to experience an era of rapid economic growth based to a large extent on the export of a few basic items, such as wheat and beef from Argentina, coffee from Brazil, nitrates from Chile, coffee and bananas from Central America, and sugar and silver from Peru. These foodstuffs and raw materials were exchanged for finished goods—textiles, machines, and luxury goods—from Europe and the United States. Despite their economic growth, Latin American nations remained economic colonies of Western nations.

Old patterns also still largely prevailed in society. Rural elites dominated their estates and their workers. Although slavery was abolished by 1888, former slaves and their descendants were at the bottom of their society. The Indians remained poverty-stricken.

One result of the new prosperity that came from increased exports was growth in the middle sectors of Latin American society—lawyers, merchants, shopkeepers, businesspeople, schoolteachers, professors, bureaucrats, and military officers. These middle sectors, which made up only 5 to 10 percent of the population, depending on the country, were hardly large enough in numbers to constitute a true middle class. Nevertheless, after 1900, the middle sectors continued to expand. They lived in the cities, sought education and decent incomes, and increasingly saw the United States as the model to emulate, especially in regard to industrialization and education.

As Latin American export economies boomed, the working class expanded, which in turn led to the growth of labor unions, especially after 1914. Radical unions often advocated the use of the general strike as an instrument for change. By and large, the governing elites succeeded in stifling the political influence of the working class by restricting workers' right to vote.

Political Change in Latin America Latin America also experienced a political transformation after 1870. Large landowners began to take a more direct interest in national politics and even in governing. In Argentina and Chile, for example, landholding elites controlled the governments, and although they produced constitutions similar to those of the United States and European nations, they ensured their power by regulating voting rights.

In some countries, large landowners supported dictators to ensure the interests of the ruling elite. Porfirio Díaz, who ruled Mexico from 1876 to 1910, created a conservative, centralized government with the support of the army, foreign capitalists, large landowners, and

Emiliano Zapata. The inability of Francisco Madero to carry out far-reaching reforms led to a more radical upheaval in the Mexican countryside. Emiliano Zapata led a band of Indians in a revolt against the large landowners of southern Mexico and issued his own demands for land reform.

the Catholic church. Nevertheless, there were forces for change in Mexico that led to a revolution in 1910.

During Díaz's dictatorial reign, 95 percent of the rural population owned no land while about one thousand families owned almost all of Mexico. When a liberal landowner, Francisco Madero, forced Díaz from power, he opened the door to a wider revolution. Madero's ineffectiveness created a demand for agrarian reform led by Emiliano Zapata, who aroused the masses of landless peasants and began to seize the estates of the wealthy landholders. Between 1910 and 1920, the revolution caused untold destruction to the Mexican economy. Finally, a new constitution in 1917 established a strong presidency, implemented land reform policies, placed limits on foreign investors, and set an agenda for social welfare for workers.

By this time, a new power had begun to wield its influence over Latin America. By 1900, the United States, which had begun to emerge as a great world power, began to interfere in the affairs of its southern neighbors. As a result of the Spanish-American War (1898), Cuba became a U.S. protectorate, and Puerto Rico was annexed outright to the United States. American investments in Latin America soon followed; so did American resolve to protect these investments. Between 1898 and 1934, American military forces were sent to Cuba, Mexico, Guatemala, Honduras, Nicaragua, Panama, Colombia, Haiti, and the Dominican Republic to protect American interests. At the same time, the United States became the chief foreign investor in Latin America.

The Rise of the United States

Four years of bloody civil war had preserved American national unity, but the old South had been destroyed. Between 1860 and 1914, the United States made the shift from an agrarian to an industrial nation. American heavy industry stood unchallenged in 1900. In that year, the Carnegie Steel Company alone produced more steel than Great Britain's entire steel industry. Industrialization also led to urbanization. Whereas 20 percent of Americans lived in cities in 1860, over 40 percent did forty years later.

By 1900, the United States had become the world's richest nation and greatest industrial power. Yet serious questions remained about the quality of American life. In 1890, the richest 9 percent of Americans owned an incredible 71 percent of all the wealth. Labor unrest over unsafe working conditions, strict work discipline, and periodic cycles of high unemployment led workers to organize. By the turn of the twentieth century, the American Federation of Labor had emerged as labor's dominant voice, but it lacked real power; in 1900, only 8.4 percent of American workers were members.

During the Progressive Era after 1900, the reform of many features of American life became a primary issue. Under President Theodore Roosevelt (1901–1909), the federal government began to regulate corrupt industrial practices. President Woodrow Wilson (1913–1921) was responsible for the creation of a graduated federal income tax. Like European states, the United States was moving slowly into policies that extended the functions of the state.

The United States as a World Power   At the end of the nineteenth century, the United States began to expand abroad. The Samoan Islands in the Pacific became the first important U.S. colony; the Hawaiian Islands were the next to fall. By 1887, U.S. settlers had gained control of the sugar industry on the islands. As more Americans settled in Hawaii, they sought to gain political power. In 1893, American residents, aided by U.S. Marines from the U.S.S. *Boston,* overthrew the monarchy of Queen Liliuokalani. Five years later Hawaii was formally annexed by the United States.

Its defeat of Spain in the Spanish-American War in 1898 encouraged the United States to extend its empire by acquiring Cuba, Puerto Rico, Guam, and the Philippine Islands. Although the Filipinos hoped for independence,

the Americans refused to grant it. As President William McKinley said, the United States had the duty "to educate the Filipinos and uplift and Christianize them," a remarkable statement in view of the fact that most of them had been Roman Catholics for centuries. It took three years and sixty thousand troops to pacify the Philippines and establish U.S. control. By the beginning of the twentieth century, the United States had an empire.

The Growth of Canada

Canada, too, faced problems of national unity between 1870 and 1914. At the beginning of 1870, the Dominion of Canada had only four provinces: Quebec, Ontario, Nova Scotia, and New Brunswick. With the addition of two more provinces in 1871—Manitoba and British Columbia—the Dominion of Canada now extended from the Atlantic Ocean to the Pacific. As the first prime minister, John Macdonald (1815–1891) moved to strengthen Canadian unity. He pushed for the construction of a transcontinental railroad, which was finally completed in 1885 and opened the western lands to industrial and commercial development.

Canada, 1914

This also led to the incorporation of two more provinces—Alberta and Saskatchewan—into the Dominion of Canada in 1905.

Real unity was difficult to achieve, however, because of the distrust between the English-speaking majority and the French-speaking Canadians, living primarily in Quebec. Wilfred Laurier (1841–1919), who became the first French Canadian prime minister in 1896, was able to reconcile Canada's two major groups and resolve the issue of separate schools for French Canadians. During Laurier's administration, industrialization boomed, especially the production of textiles, furniture, and railway equipment. Hundreds of thousands of immigrants, primarily from central and eastern Europe, also flowed into Canada. Many settled on lands in the west, thus helping to populate Canada's vast territories.

Europe

Within the major European states, considerable progress was made in achieving such liberal practices as constitutions and parliaments, but it was largely in the western European states that **mass politics** became a reality. Reforms encouraged the expansion of political democracy through voting rights for men and the creation of mass political parties. At the same time, however, similar reforms were strongly resisted in parts of Europe where the old political forces remained strong.

Western Europe: The Growth of Political Democracy

By 1871, Great Britain had a functioning two-party parliamentary system. For the next fifty years, Liberals and Conservatives alternated in power at regular intervals. Both parties were dominated by a ruling class composed of aristocratic landowners and upper-middle-class businesspeople. And both competed with each other in passing laws that expanded the right to vote. By 1918, all males over twenty-one and women over thirty could vote. Political democracy was soon accompanied by social welfare measures for the working class.

The growth of trade unions, which advocated more radical change of the economic system, and the emergence in 1900 of the Labour Party, which dedicated itself to the interests of the workers, caused the Liberals, who held the government from 1906 to 1914, to realize that they would have to create a program of social welfare or lose the support of the workers. Therefore, they voted for a series of social reforms. The National Insurance Act of 1911 provided benefits for workers in case of sickness and unemployment. Additional legislation provided a small pension for those over seventy.

In France, the confusion that ensued after the collapse of Louis Napoleon's Second Empire finally ended when an improvised constitution in 1875 established a republican form of government—the Third Republic—that lasted sixty-five years. France's parliamentary system was weak, however, because the existence of a dozen political parties forced the premier (or prime minister) to depend on a coalition of parties to stay in power. The Third Republic was notorious for its changes of government. Nevertheless, by 1914, the French Third Republic commanded the loyalty of most French people.

Central and Eastern Europe: Persistence of the Old Order

The constitution of the new imperial Germany begun by Chancellor Otto von Bismarck in 1871 provided for a bicameral legislature. The lower house of the German parliament, the Reichstag, was elected by universal male suffrage, but it did not have ministerial responsibility. Ministers of government, among whom the most important was the chancellor, were responsible to the emperor, not the parliament. The emperor also commanded the armed forces and controlled foreign policy and the government.

During the reign of Emperor William II (1888–1918), the new imperial Germany begun by Bismarck continued as an "authoritarian, conservative, military-bureaucratic power state." By the end of William's reign, Germany had become the strongest military and industrial power on the Continent, but the rapid change had also helped produce a society torn between modernization and traditionalism. With the expansion of industry and cities came demands for true democracy. Conservative forces, especially the landowning nobility and industrialists, two of the powerful ruling groups in imperial Germany, tried to block the movement for democracy by supporting William II's activist foreign policy. Expansion abroad,

CHRONOLOGY	The National State, 1870–1914
Great Britain	
Formation of Labour Party	1900
National Insurance Act	1911
France	
Republican constitution (Third Republic)	1875
Germany	
Bismarck as chancellor	1871–1890
Emperor William II	1888–1918
Austria-Hungary	
Emperor Francis Joseph	1848–1916
Russia	
Tsar Alexander III	1881–1894
Tsar Nicholas II	1894–1917
Russo-Japanese War	1904–1905
Revolution	1905
Latin America	
Rule of Porfirio Díaz in Mexico	1876–1910
Mexican Revolution begins	1910
United States	
Spanish-American War	1898
Theodore Roosevelt	1901–1909
Woodrow Wilson	1913–1921
Canada	
Transcontinental railroad	1885
Wilfred Laurier as prime minister	1896

they believed, would divert people's attention from the yearning for democracy at home.

After the creation of the Dual Monarchy of Austria-Hungary in 1867, the Austrian part received a constitution that theoretically established a parliamentary system. However, Emperor Francis Joseph (1848–1916) largely ignored parliament, ruling by decree when parliament was not in session. The problem of the various nationalities also remained troublesome. The German minority that governed Austria felt increasingly threatened by the Czechs, Poles, and other Slavic groups within the empire. Their agitation in the parliament for autonomy led prime ministers after 1900 to ignore the parliament and rely increasingly on imperial decrees to govern.

In Russia, the assassination of Alexander II in 1881 convinced his son and successor, Alexander III (1881–1894), that reform had been a mistake, and he lost no time in persecuting both reformers and revolutionaries. When Alexander III died, his weak son and successor, Nicholas II (1894–1917), began his rule with his father's conviction that the absolute power of the tsars should be preserved: "I shall maintain the principle of autocracy just as firmly and unflinchingly as did my unforgettable father."[4] But conditions were changing.

Industrialization progressed rapidly in Russia after 1890, and with industrialization came factories, an industrial working class, and the development of socialist parties, including the Marxist Social Democratic Party and the Social Revolutionaries. Repression forced both parties to go underground. The growing opposition to the tsarist regime finally exploded into revolution in 1905.

The defeat of the Russians by the Japanese in 1904–1905 encouraged antigovernment groups to rebel against the tsarist regime. Nicholas II granted civil liberties and created a legislative assembly, the Duma, elected directly by a broad franchise. But real constitutional monarchy proved short-lived. By 1907, the tsar

had curtailed the power of the Duma and relied again on the army and bureaucracy to rule Russia.

International Rivalries and the Winds of War

Bismarck had realized in 1871 that the emergence of a unified Germany as the most powerful state on the Continent (see Map 19.2) had upset the balance of power established at Vienna in 1815. Fearful of a possible anti-German alliance between France, Russia, and possibly even Austria, Bismarck made a defensive alliance with Austria in 1879. Three years later, this German-Austrian alliance was enlarged with the entrance of Italy, angry with the French over conflicting colonial ambitions in North Africa. The Triple Alliance of 1882—Germany,

MAP 19.2 **Europe in 1871.** German unification in 1871 upset the balance of power established at Vienna in 1815 and eventually led to a realignment of European alliances. By 1907, Europe was divided into two opposing camps: the Triple Entente of Great Britain, Russia, and France and the Triple Alliance of Germany, Austria-Hungary, and Italy. ❓ How was Germany affected by the formation of the Triple Entente? 🐭 **View an animated version of this map or related maps at** http://worldrc.wadsworth.com/

Austria-Hungary, and Italy—committed the three powers to a defensive alliance against France. At the same time, Bismarck maintained a separate treaty with Russia.

When Emperor William II cashiered Bismarck in 1890 and took over direction of Germany's foreign policy, he embarked on an activist foreign policy dedicated to enhancing German power by finding, as he put it, Germany's rightful "place in the sun." One of his changes in Bismarck's foreign policy was to drop the treaty with Russia, which he viewed as being at odds with Germany's alliance with Austria. The ending of the alliance brought France and Russia together, and in 1894, the two powers concluded a military alliance. During the next ten years, German policies abroad caused the British to draw closer to France. By 1907, an alliance of Great Britain, France, and Russia—known as the Triple Entente—stood opposed to the Triple Alliance of Germany, Austria-Hungary, and Italy. Europe became divided into two opposing camps that became more and more inflexible and unwilling to compromise. A series of crises in the Balkans between 1908 and 1913 set the stage for World War I.

Crisis in the Balkans   Over the course of the nineteenth century, the Balkan provinces of the Ottoman Empire had gradually gained their freedom, although the rivalry in the region between Austria and Russia complicated the process. By 1878, Greece, Serbia, and Romania had become independent states. Although freed from Ottoman rule, Montenegro was placed under an Austrian protectorate, while Bulgaria achieved autonomous status under Russian protection. Bosnia and Herzegovina were placed under Austrian protection; Austria could occupy but not annex them.

Nevertheless, in 1908, Austria did annex the two Slavic-speaking territories. Serbia was outraged because the annexation dashed the Serbs' hopes of creating a large

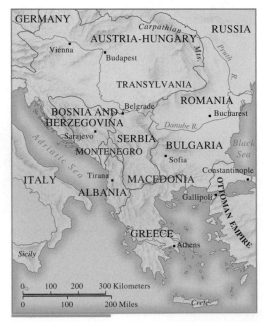

The Balkans in 1913

Serbian kingdom that would unite most of the southern Slavs. The Russians, as protectors of their fellow Slavs, supported the Serbs and opposed the Austrian action. Backed by the Russians, the Serbs prepared for war against Austria. At this point, William II intervened and demanded that the Russians accept Austria's annexation of Bosnia and Herzegovina or face war with Germany. Weakened from their defeat in the Russo-Japanese War in 1904–1905, the Russians backed down but vowed revenge. Two wars between the Balkan states in 1912–1913 further embittered the inhabitants of the region and generated more tensions among the great powers.

Serbia's desire to create a large Serbian kingdom remained unfulfilled. In their frustration, Serbian nationalists blamed the Austrians. Austria-Hungary was convinced that Serbia was a mortal threat to its empire and must at some point be crushed. As Serbia's chief supporters, the Russians were determined not to back down again in the event of a confrontation with Austria or Germany in the Balkans. The allies of Austria-Hungary and Russia were also determined to be more supportive of their respective allies in another crisis. By the beginning of 1914, two armed camps viewed each other with suspicion.

Toward the Modern Consciousness: Intellectual and Cultural Developments

Before 1914, many people in the Western world continued to believe in the values and ideals that had been generated by the Scientific Revolution and the Enlightenment. The idea that human beings could improve themselves and achieve a better society seemed to be proved by a rising standard of living, urban comforts, and mass education. It was easy to think that the human mind could make sense of the universe. Between 1870 and 1914, radically new ideas challenged these optimistic views and opened the way to a modern consciousness.

A New Physics

Science was one of the chief pillars underlying the optimistic and rationalistic view of the world that many Westerners shared in the nineteenth century. Supposedly based on hard facts and cold reason, science offered a certainty of belief in the orderliness of nature. The new physics dramatically altered that perspective.

Throughout much of the nineteenth century, Westerners adhered to the mechanical conception of the universe postulated by the classical physics of Isaac Newton. In this perspective, the universe was viewed as a giant machine in which time, space, and matter were objective realities that existed independently of the observers. Matter was thought to be composed of indivisible and solid material bodies called atoms.

FREUD AND THE CONCEPT OF REPRESSION

RELIGION & PHILOSOPHY

Freud's psychoanalytical theories resulted from his attempt to understand the world of the unconscious. This excerpt is taken from a lecture given in 1909 in which Freud describes how he arrived at his theory of the role of repression. Although Freud valued science and reason, his theories of the unconscious produced a new image of the human being as governed less by reason than by irrational forces.

According to Freud, how did he discover the existence of repression? What function does repression perform?

Sigmund Freud, *Five Lectures on Psychoanalysis*

I did not abandon [the technique of encouraging patients to reveal forgotten experiences], however, before the observations I made during my use of it afforded me decisive evidence. I found confirmation of the fact that the forgotten memories were not lost. They were in the patient's possession and were ready to emerge in association to what was still known by him; but there was some force that prevented them from becoming conscious and compelled them to remain unconscious. The existence of this force could be assumed with certainty, since one became aware of an effort corresponding to it if, in opposition to it, one tried to introduce the unconscious memories into the patient's consciousness. The force which was maintaining the pathological condition became apparent in the form of resistance on the part of the patient.

It was on this idea of resistance, then, that I based my view of the course of psychical events in hysteria. In order to effect a recovery, it had proved necessary to remove these resistances. Starting out from the mechanism of cure, it now became possible to construct quite definite ideas of the origin of the illness. The same forces which, in the form of

resistance, were now offering opposition to the forgotten material's being made conscious, must formerly have brought about the forgetting and must have pushed the pathogenic experiences in question out of consciousness. I gave the name of "repression" to this hypothetical process, and I considered that it was proved by the undeniable existence of resistance.

The further question could then be raised as to what these forces were and what the determinants were of the repression in which we now recognized the pathogenic mechanism of hysteria. A comparative study of the pathogenic situations which we had come to know through the cathartic procedure made it possible to answer this question. All these experiences had involved the emergence of a wishful impulse which was in sharp contrast to the subject's other wishes and which proved incompatible with the ethical and aesthetic standards of his personality. There had been a short conflict, and the end of this internal struggle was that the idea which had appeared before consciousness as the vehicle of this irreconcilable wish fell a victim to repression, was pushed out of consciousness with all its attached memories, and was forgotten. Thus the incompatibility of the wish in question with the patient's ego was the motive for the repression; the subject's ethical and other standards were the repressing forces. An acceptance of the incompatible wishful impulse or a prolongation of the conflict would have produced a high degree of unpleasure; this unpleasure was avoided by means of repression, which was thus revealed as one of the devices serving to protect the mental personality.

ThomsonNOW To read excerpts from Freud's *Interpretation of Dreams,* enter the *ThomsonNOW* documents area using the access card that is available for *The Essential World History.*

Albert Einstein (1879–1955), a German-born patent officer working in Switzerland, questioned this view of the universe. In 1905, Einstein published his special theory of relativity, which stated that space and time are not absolute but relative to the observer. Neither space nor time had an existence independent of human experience. As Einstein later explained simply to a journalist: "It was formerly believed that if all material things disappeared out of the universe, time and space would be left. According to the **relativity theory,** however, time and space disappear together with the things."[5] Einstein concluded that matter was nothing but another form of energy. His epochal formula $E = mc^2$—stating that each particle of matter is equivalent to its mass times the square of the velocity of light—was the key theory explaining the vast energies contained within the atom. It led to the atomic age and to uncertainty. To some, a relative universe—unlike Newton's universe—seemed a universe without certainty.

Sigmund Freud and the Emergence of Psychoanalysis

At the turn of the twentieth century, Viennese physician Sigmund Freud (1856–1939) advanced a series of theories that undermined optimism about the rational nature of the human mind. Freud's thought, like the new physics, added to the uncertainties of the age. His major ideas were published in 1900 in *The Interpretation of Dreams.*

According to Freud, human behavior was strongly determined by the unconscious, by past experiences and internal forces of which people were largely oblivious. For Freud, human behavior was no longer truly rational but rather instinctive or irrational. He argued that painful and unsettling experiences were blotted from conscious awareness but still continued to influence behavior since they had become part of the unconscious (see the box above). Repression began in childhood. Freud devised a method, known as **psychoanalysis,** by which a psychotherapist and patient could probe deeply into the memory in order to retrace the chain of repression all the way back to its childhood origins. By making the conscious mind aware of the unconscious and its repressed contents, the patient's psychic conflict was resolved.

The Impact of Darwin: Social Darwinism and Racism

In the second half of the nineteenth century, scientific theories were sometimes wrongly applied to meet other ends. For example, Charles Darwin's principle of organic evolution was applied to the social order as **social Darwinism,** the belief that societies were organisms that evolved through time from a struggle with their environment. Such ideas were used in a radical way by rabid nationalists and racists. In their pursuit of national greatness, extreme nationalists insisted that nations, too, were engaged in a "struggle for existence" in which only the fittest survived.

Perhaps nowhere was the combination of extreme nationalism and racism more evident or more dangerous than in Germany. One of the chief propagandists of German racism was Houston Stewart Chamberlain (1855–1927), a Briton who became a German citizen. According to Chamberlain, modern-day Germans were the only pure successors of the **Aryans,** who were portrayed as the true and original founders of Western culture. The Aryan race, under German leadership, must be prepared to fight for Western civilization and save it from the destructive assaults of such lower races as Jews, Negroes, and Orientals. Chamberlain singled out the Jews as the racial enemy who wanted to destroy the Aryan race.

Anti-Semitism   **Anti-Semitism** had a long history in European civilization, but in the nineteenth century, as a result of the ideals of the Enlightenment and the French Revolution, Jews were increasingly granted legal equality in many European countries. Many Jews now left the ghetto and became assimilated into the cultures around them. Many became successful as bankers, lawyers, scientists, scholars, journalists, and stage performers.

These achievements represent only one side of the picture, however. In Germany and Austria during the 1880s and 1890s, conservatives founded right-wing anti-Jewish parties that used anti-Semitism to win the votes of traditional lower-middle-class groups who felt threatened by the new economic forces of the times. The worst treatment of Jews at the turn of the century, however, occurred in eastern Europe, where 72 percent of the entire world Jewish population lived. Russian Jews were forced to live in certain regions of the country, and persecutions and pogroms were widespread. Hundreds of thousands of Jews decided to emigrate to escape the persecution.

Many Jews went to the United States, although some moved to Palestine, which soon became the focus of a Jewish nationalist movement called **Zionism.** For

Palestine

many Jews, Palestine, the land of ancient Israel, had long been the land of their dreams. Settlement in Palestine was difficult, however, because it was then part of the Ottoman Empire, which was opposed to Jewish immigration. Despite the problems, however, the First Zionist Congress, which met in Switzerland in 1897, proclaimed as its aim the creation of a "home in Palestine secured by public law" for the Jewish people. In 1900, around a thousand Jews migrated to Palestine, and the trickle rose to about three thousand a year between 1904 and 1914, keeping the Zionist dream alive.

The Culture of Modernity

The revolution in physics and psychology was paralleled by a revolution in literature and the arts. Before 1914, writers and artists were rebelling against the traditional literary and artistic styles that had dominated European cultural life since the Renaissance. The changes that they produced have since been called **Modernism.**

At the beginning of the twentieth century, a group of writers known as the Symbolists caused a literary revolution. Primarily interested in writing poetry and strongly influenced by the ideas of Freud, the Symbolists believed that an objective knowledge of the world was impossible. The external world was not real but only a collection of symbols that reflected the true reality of the individual human mind.

The period from 1870 to 1914 was one of the most fertile in the history of art. By the late nineteenth century, artists were seeking new forms of expression. The preamble to modern painting can be found in **Impressionism,** a movement that originated in France in the 1870s when a group of artists rejected the studios and museums and went out into the countryside to paint nature directly. Camille Pissarro (1830–1903), one of Impressionism's founders, expressed what they sought: "Don't proceed according to rules and principles, but paint what you observe and feel. Paint generously and unhesitatingly, for it is best not to lose the first impression."[6]

An important Impressionist painter was Berthe Morisot (1841–1895), who believed that women had a special vision, which was, as she said, "more delicate than that of men." She made use of lighter colors and flowing brushstrokes (see the comparative illustration on p. 443). Near the end of her life, she lamented the refusal of men to take her work seriously: "I don't think there has ever been a man who treated a woman as an equal, and that's all I would have asked, for I know I'm worth as much as they."[7]

COMPARATIVE ILLUSTRATION

Painting—West and East. Berthe Morisot, the first female painter to join the Impressionists, developed her own unique style. Her gentle colors and strong use of pastels are especially evident in *Young Girl by the Window,* seen at the left. The French Impressionist style also spread abroad. One of the most outstanding Japanese artists of the time was Kuroda Seiki (1866–1924), who returned from nine years in Paris to open a Western-style school of painting in Tokyo. Shown at the right is his *By the Lake,* painted in 1897, an excellent example of the fusion of contemporary French Impressionist painting with the Japanese tradition of courtesan prints.

Pablo Picasso, *Les Demoiselles d'Avignon.* Pablo Picasso, a major pioneer and activist of modern art, experimented with a remarkable variety of modern styles. *Les Demoiselles d'Avignon* was the first great example of Cubism, which one art historian called "the first style of this [twentieth] century to break radically with the past." Geometrical shapes replace traditional forms, forcing the viewer to re-create reality in his or her own mind. The head at the upper right of the painting reflects Picasso's attraction to aspects of African art, as is evident from the Congo mask included at the right.

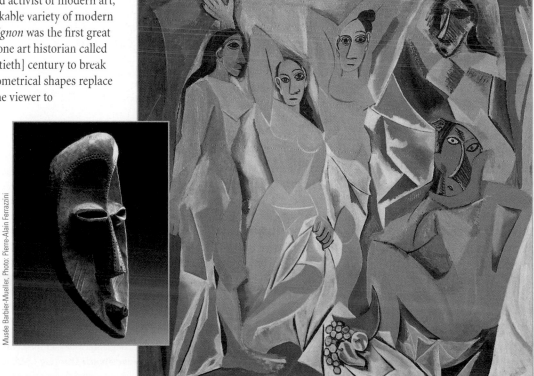

In the 1880s, a new movement known as **Post-Impressionism** arose in France and soon spread to other European countries. A famous Post-Impressionist was the tortured and tragic figure Vincent van Gogh (1853–1890). For van Gogh, art was a spiritual experience. He was especially interested in color and believed that it could act as its own form of language.

By the beginning of the twentieth century, the belief that the task of art was to represent "reality" had lost much of its meaning. The growth of photography gave artists one reason to reject Realism. Invented in the 1830s, photography became popular and widespread after George Eastman created the first Kodak camera in 1888 for the mass market. What was the point of an artist's doing what the camera did better? Unlike the camera, which could only mirror reality, artists could create reality.

By 1905, one of the most important figures in modern art was just beginning his career. Pablo Picasso (1881–1973) was from Spain but settled in Paris in 1904. Picasso was extremely flexible and painted in a remarkable variety of styles. He was instrumental in the development of a new style called **Cubism** that used geometrical designs as visual stimuli to re-create reality in the viewer's mind.

The modern artist's flight from "visual reality" reached a high point in 1910 with the beginning of **abstract painting.** A Russian who worked in Germany, Vasily Kandinsky (1866–1944) was one of its founders. Kandinsky sought to avoid representation altogether. He believed that art should speak directly to the soul. To do so, it must avoid any reference to visual reality and concentrate on line and color.

CONCLUSION

ETWEEN **1870** AND **1914,** the national state began to expand its functions beyond all previous limits. Fearful of the growth of socialism and trade unions, governments attempted to appease the working masses by adopting such **social insurance** measures as compensation for accidents, illness, and old age. These social welfare measures were limited in benefits before 1914, but they signaled a new direction for state action to benefit all citizens.

This extension of state functions took place in an atmosphere of increased national loyalty. After 1870, nation-states increasingly sought to solidify the social order and win the active loyalty and support of their citizens by deliberately cultivating national feelings. Yet this policy contained potentially great dangers. Nations had discovered once again that imperialistic adventures and military successes could arouse nationalistic passions and smother domestic political unrest. But they also found—belatedly in 1914—that nationalistic feelings could also lead to intense international rivalries that made war almost inevitable.

What many Europeans liked to call their "age of progress" between 1870 and 1914 was also an era of anxiety. Frenzied imperialist expansion had created vast European empires and **spheres of influence** around the globe. This feverish competition for colonies, however, had markedly increased the existing antagonisms among the European states. At the same time, the Western treatment of native peoples as racial inferiors caused educated, non-Western elites in these colonies to initiate movements for national independence. We turn now to the Western impact on the rest of the world.

CHAPTER NOTES

1. Karl Marx and Friedrich Engels, *The Communist Manifesto* (Harmondsworth, England, 1967), p. 80. Originally published in 1848.
2. Ibid., pp. 91, 94.
3. Quoted in Nicholas Bullock and James Read, *The Movement for Housing Reform in Germany and France, 1840–1914* (Cambridge, 1985), p. 42.
4. Quoted in Shmuel Galai, *The Liberation Movement in Russia, 1900–1905* (Cambridge, 1973), p. 26.
5. Quoted in Arthur E. E. McKenzie, *The Major Achievements of Science* (New York, 1960), vol. 1, p. 310.
6. Quoted in John Rewald, *History of Impressionism* (New York, 1961), pp. 456–458.
7. Quoted in Anne Higonnet, *Berthe Morisot's Images of Women* (Cambridge, Mass., 1992), p. 19.

SUGGESTED READING

The subject of the Second Industrial Revolution is well covered in **D. Landes, *The Unbound Prometheus,*** cited in Chapter 18. On Marx, there is the standard work by **D. McLellan, *Karl Marx: His Life and Thought*** (New York, 1974). For an introduction to international socialism, see **A. Lindemann, *A History of European Socialism*** (New Haven, Conn., 1983).

For a good introduction to housing reform on the Continent, see **N. Bullock** and **J. Read, *The Movement for Housing Reform in Germany and France, 1840–1914*** (Cambridge, 1985). An interesting work on aristocratic life is **D. Cannadine, *The Decline and Fall of the British Aristocracy*** (New Haven, Conn., 1990). On the middle classes, see **P. Pilbeam, *The Middle Classes in Europe, 1789–1914*** (Basingstoke, England, 1990). On the working classes, see **R. Magraw, *A History of the French Working Class*** (Cambridge, Mass., 1992). For a good overview of women's experiences in the nineteenth century, see

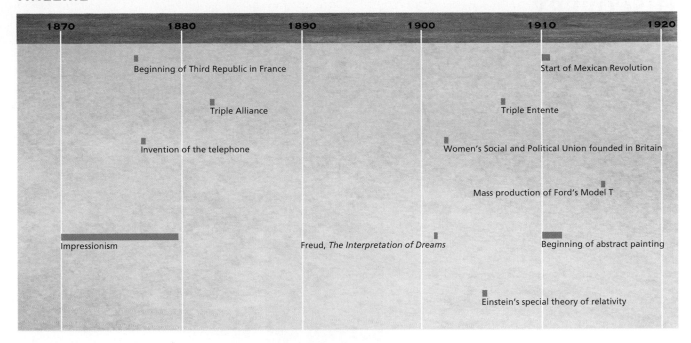

1870	1880	1890	1900	1910	1920

Beginning of Third Republic in France

Start of Mexican Revolution

Triple Alliance

Triple Entente

Invention of the telephone

Women's Social and Political Union founded in Britain

Mass production of Ford's Model T

Impressionism

Freud, *The Interpretation of Dreams*

Beginning of abstract painting

Einstein's special theory of relativity

B. Smith, *Changing Lives: Women in European History Since 1700* (Lexington, Mass., 1989). The rise of feminism is examined in **J. Rendall,** *The Origins of Modern Feminism: Women in Britain, France and the United States* (London, 1985). For a new perspective on domestic life, see **J. Flanders,** *Inside the Victorian Home: A Portrait of Domestic Life in Victorian England* (New York, 2004). On various aspects of education, see **M. J. Maynes,** *Schooling in Western Europe: A Social History* (Albany, N.Y., 1985). A concise and well-presented survey of leisure patterns is **G. Cross,** *A Social History of Leisure Since 1600* (State College, Pa., 1989).

The domestic politics of the period can be examined in the general works listed in the bibliography for Chapter 18. There are also specialized works on aspects of each country's history. On Britain, see **D. Read,** *The Age of Urban Democracy: England, 1868–1914* (New York, 1994). For a detailed examination of French history from 1871 to 1914, see **J.-M. Mayeur** and **M. Reberioux,** *The Third Republic from Its Origins to the Great War, 1871–1914* (Cambridge, 1984). On Germany, see **W. J. Mommsen,** *Imperial Germany, 1867–1918* (New York, 1995). On aspects of Russian history, see **H. Rogger,** *Russia in the Age of Modernization and Revolution, 1881–1917* (London, 1983), and **A. Ascher,** *The Revolution of 1905: Russia in Disarray* (New York, 1988). On the United States, see **D. Cashman,** *America in the Gilded Age: From the Death of Lincoln to the Rise of Theodore Roosevelt* (New York, 1984), and **J. W. Chambers,** *The Tyranny of Change: America in the Progressive Era, 1900–1917* (New York, 1980). On Latin American economic developments, see **B. Albert,** *South America and the World Economy from Independence to 1930* (London, 1983). For a comprehensive examination of the Mexican Revolution, see **A. Knight,** *The Mexican Revolution,* 2 vols. (Cambridge, 1986).

A well-regarded study of Freud is **P. Gay,** *Freud: A Life for Our Time* (New York, 1988). Modern anti-Semitism is covered in **A. S. Lindemann,** *Esau's Tears: Modern Anti-Semitism and the Rise of the Jews* (New York, 1997). European racism is analyzed in **G. L. Mosse,** *Toward the Final Solution* (New York, 1980). Very valuable on modern art are **M. Powell-Jones,** *Impressionism* (London, 1994); **G. Crepaldi,** *The Impressionists* (New York, 2002); and **B. Denvir,** *Post-Impressionism* (New York, 1992).

InfoTrac College Edition

Visit this chapter's InfoTrac College Edition/Research activities at the *Essential World History* Companion Website for activities related to the emergence of mass society.

ThomsonNOW for Duiker and Spielvogel's *The Essential World History, Third Edition*

Enter *ThomsonNOW* using the access card that is available with this text. *ThomsonNOW* will assist you in understanding the content in this chapter with lesson plans generated for your needs, as well as provide you with a connection to the *Wadsworth World History Resource Center* (see description below for details).

WORLD HISTORY
RESOURCE CENTER

Enter the Resource Center using either your *ThomsonNOW* access card or your standalone access card for the *Wadsworth World History Resource Center.* Organized by topic, this website includes quizzes; images; over 350 primary source documents; interactive simulations, maps, and timelines; movie explorations; and a wealth of other resources. You can read the following documents, and many more, at
http://worldrc.wadsworth.com/

Karl Marx and Friedrich Engels, *The Communist Manifesto*

Henrik Ibsen, *Ghosts; An Enemy of the People*; and *Pillars of Society*

Visit the *Essential World History* Companion Website for chapter quizzes and more:
http://www.thomsonedu.com/history/duiker

DISCOVERY

What was the relationship between economic, social, political, intellectual, and cultural developments between 1871 and 1914?

In thinking about this question, begin by breaking it down into the components shown below. A discussion of the significance of each component should appear in your answer.

ARTS AND IDEAS: As we moved from Romanticism to Realism in the previous chapter, how did Freud and Picasso both move away from using reality as a way to view and understand the world? Why would Freud and Picasso attempt to escape from the world that they saw around them? How would you relate their escape to the type of living conditions described in Octavia Hill's *Homes of the London Poor* (next page)? How would artists and thinkers use the concepts of repression or irrationality in attempting to deal with the economic pressures created by the industrialization and political developments of the nineteenth century? How would these lead to the further development of abstract art that completely avoids references to visual reality?

Musée Barbier-Mueller, Photo: Pierre-Alain Ferrazzini

© Museum of Modern Art/Licensed by SCALA/Art Resource, NY.
© 2006 Estate of Pablo Picasso/Artist's Rights Society (ARS), NY

Pablo Picasso, *Les Demoiselles d'Avignon*

SIGMUND FREUD, *FIVE LECTURES ON PSYCHOANALYSIS*

I did not abandon [the technique of encouraging patients to reveal forgotten experiences], however, before the observations I made during my use of it afforded me decisive evidence. I found confirmation of the fact that the forgotten memories were not lost. They were in the patient's possession and were ready to emerge in association to what was still known by him; but there was some force that prevented them from becoming conscious and compelled them to remain unconscious. The existence of this force could be assumed with certainty, since one became aware of an effort corresponding to it if, in opposition to it, one tried to introduce the unconscious memories into the patient's consciousness. The force which was maintaining the pathological condition became apparent in the form of resistance on the part of the patient.

It was on this idea of resistance, then, that I based my view of the course of psychical events in hysteria. In order to effect a recovery, it had proved necessary to remove these resistances. Starting out from the mechanism of cure, it now became possible to construct quite definite ideas of the origin of the illness. The same forces which, in the form of resistance, were now offering opposition to the forgotten material's being made conscious, must formerly have brought about the forgetting and must have pushed the pathogenic experiences in question out of consciousness. I gave the name

of "repression" to this hypothetical process, and I considered that it was proved by the undeniable existence of resistance.

The further question could then be raised as to what these forces were and what the determinants were of the repression in which we now recognized the pathogenic mechanism of hysteria. A comparative study of the pathogenic situations which we had come to know through the cathartic procedure made it possible to answer this question. All these experiences had involved the emergence of a wishful impulse which was in sharp contrast to the subject's other wishes and which proved incompatible with the ethical and aesthetic standards of his personality. There had been a short conflict, and the end of this internal struggle was that the idea which had appeared before consciousness as the vehicle of this irreconcilable wish fell a victim to repression, was pushed out of consciousness with all its attached memories, and was forgotten. Thus the incompatibility of the wish in question with the patient's ego was the motive for the repression; the subject's ethical and other standards were the repressing forces. An acceptance of the incompatible wishful impulse or a prolongation of the conflict would have produced a high degree of unpleasure; this unpleasure was avoided by means of repression, which was thus revealed as one of the devices serving to protect the mental personality.

FAMILY AND SOCIETY: Compare *The Communist Manifesto* and "An Age of Progress," on the next page. How did the artist view the nineteenth century? How did Marx view the nineteenth century? Why do they have such differing interpretations? What does the illustration suggest is the reason for human progress? How does this contrast with Marx's view? Based on this, would you say that Marx was a Realist or a Romantic?

In what ways do *Homes of the London Poor* and the painting on the next page reflect attitudes toward the lower working class and the middle class in Europe? What can you deduce about European values of the nineteenth century? How would Marx describe Octavia Hill's response to the problems that she believed existed in society?

Karl Marx and Friedrich Engels, *The Communist Manifesto*

We have seen . . ., that the first step in the revolution by the working class is to raise the proletariat to the position of ruling class. . . . The proletariat will use its political supremacy to wrest, by degrees, all capital from the bourgeoisie, to centralize all instruments of production in the hands of the State, i.e., of the proletariat organized as the ruling class; and to increase the total of productive forces as rapidly as possible.

Of course, in the beginning, this cannot be effected except by means of despotic inroads on the rights of property, and on the conditions of bourgeois production; by means of measures, therefore, which appear economically insufficient and untenable, but which, in the course of the movement, outstrip themselves, necessitate further inroads upon the old social order, and are unavoidable as a means of entirely revolutionizing the mode of production.

These measures will of course be different in different countries.

Nevertheless, in the most advanced countries, the following will be pretty generally applicable:

1. Abolition of property in land and application of all rents of land to public purposes.
2. A heavy progressive or graduated income tax.
3. Abolition of all right of inheritance. . . .
4. Centralization of credit in the hands of the State, by means of a national bank with State capital and an exclusive monopoly.
5. Centralization of the means of communication and transport in the hands of the State.
6. Extension of factories and instruments of production owned by the State. . . .
7. Equal liability of all to labor. Establishment of industrial armies, especially for agriculture.
8. Combination of agriculture with manufacturing industries; gradual abolition of the distinction between town and country, by a more equable distribution of the population over the country.
9. Free education for all children in public schools. Abolition of children's factory labor in its present form. . . .

When, in the course of development, class distinctions have disappeared, and all production has been concentrated in the whole nation, the public power will lose its political character. Political power, properly so called, is merely the organized power of one class for oppressing another. If the proletariat during its contest with the bourgeoisie is compelled, by the force of circumstances, to organize itself as a class, if, by means of a revolution, it makes itself the ruling class, and, as such, sweeps away by force the old conditions of production, then it will, along with these conditions, have swept away the conditions for the existence of class antagonisms and of classes generally, and will thereby have abolished its own supremacy as a class.

In place of the old bourgeois society, with its classes and class antagonisms, we shall have an association, in which the free development of each is the condition for the free development of all.

Octavia Hill, *Homes of the London Poor*

About four years ago I was put in possession of three houses in one of the worst courts of Marylebone. Six other houses were bought subsequently. All were crowded with inmates.

The first thing to be done was to put them in decent tenantable order. The set last purchased was a row of cottages facing a bit of desolate ground, occupied with wretched, dilapidated cowsheds, manure heaps, old timber, and rubbish of every description. The houses were in a most deplorable condition–the plaster was dropping from the walls; on one staircase a pail was placed to catch the rain that fell through the roof. All the staircases were perfectly dark; the banisters were gone, having been burnt as firewood by tenants. The grates, with large holes in them, were falling forward into the rooms. The washhouse, full of lumber belonging to the landlord, was locked up; thus the inhabitants had to wash clothes, as well as to cook, eat and sleep in their small rooms. The dustbin, standing in the front part of the houses, was accessible to the whole neighbourhood, and boys often dragged from it quantities of unseemly objects and spread them over the court. The state of the drainage was in keeping with everything else. The pavement of the backyard was all broken up, and great puddles stood in it, so that the damp crept up the outer walls. . . .

A Middle-Class Family

An Age of Progress

20

THE HIGH TIDE OF IMPERIALISM

Establishing British rule in Africa

© Mansell/Time Life Pictures/Getty Images

𝓘N 1877, THE YOUNG British empire builder Cecil Rhodes drew up his last will and testament. He bequeathed his fortune, achieved as a diamond magnate in South Africa, to two of his close friends and acquaintances. He also instructed them to use the inheritance to form a secret society with the aim of bringing about "the extension of British rule throughout the world, the perfecting of a system of emigration from the United Kingdom . . . especially the occupation by British settlers of the entire continent of Africa, the Holy Land, the valley of the Euphrates, the Islands of Cyprus and Candia [Crete], the whole of South America. . . . The ultimate recovery of the United States of America as an integral part of the British Empire . . . then finally the foundation of so great a power as to hereafter render wars impossible and promote the best interests of humanity."[1]

Preposterous as such ideas sound today, they serve as a graphic reminder of the hubris that characterized the worldview of Rhodes and many of his contemporaries during the age of imperialism, as well as the complex union of moral concern and vaulting ambition that motivated their actions on the world stage.

Through their efforts, Western colonialism spread throughout much of the non-Western world during the nineteenth and early twentieth centuries. Spurred by the demands of the Industrial Revolution, a few powerful Western states—notably, Great Britain, France, Germany, Russia, and the United States—competed avariciously for consumer markets and raw materials for their expanding economies. By the end of the nineteenth century, virtually all of the traditional societies in Asia and Africa were under direct or indirect colonial rule. As the new century began, the Western imprint on Asian and African societies, for better or for worse, appeared to be a permanent feature of the political and cultural landscape. ◇

The Spread of Colonial Rule

In the nineteenth century, a new phase of Western expansion into Asia and Africa began. Whereas European aims in the East before 1800 could be summed up in Vasco da Gama's famous phrase "Christians and spices," now a new relationship took shape as European nations began to view Asian and African societies as sources of industrial raw materials and as markets for Western manufactured goods. No longer were Western gold and silver exchanged for cloves, pepper, tea, silk, and porcelain. Now the prodigious output of European factories was sent to Africa and Asia in return for oil, tin, rubber, and the other resources needed to fuel the Western industrial machine.

The Motives

The reason for this change, of course, was the Industrial Revolution. Now industrializing countries in the West needed vital raw materials that were not available at home, as well as a reliable market for the goods produced in their factories. The latter factor became increasingly crucial as producers began to discover that their home markets could not always absorb domestic output and that they had to export their manufactures to make a profit.

As Western economic expansion into Asia and Africa gathered strength during the nineteenth century, it became fashionable to call the process **imperialism.** Although the term *imperialism* has many meanings, in this instance it referred to the efforts of capitalist states in the West to seize markets, cheap raw materials, and lucrative avenues for investment in the countries beyond Western civilization. In this interpretation, the primary motives behind the Western expansion were economic. Promoters of this view maintained that modern imperialism was a direct consequence of the modern industrial economy.

As in the earlier phase of Western expansion, however, the issue was not simply an economic one. Economic concerns were inevitably tinged with political overtones and with questions of national grandeur and moral purpose as well. In the minds of nineteenth-century Europeans, economic wealth, national status, and political power went hand in hand with the possession of a colonial empire. To

global strategists, colonies brought tangible benefits in the world of balance-of-power politics as well as economic profits, and many nations became involved in the pursuit of colonies as much to gain advantage over their rivals as to acquire territory for its own sake.

The relationship between colonialism and national survival was expressed directly in a speech by the French politician Jules Ferry in 1885. A policy of "containment or abstinence," he warned, would set France on "the broad road to decadence" and initiate its decline into a "third- or fourth-rate power." British imperialists, convinced by the theory of social Darwinism that in the struggle between nations, only the fit are victorious and survive, agreed. As the British professor of mathematics Karl Pearson argued in 1900, "The path of progress is strewn with the wrecks of nations; traces are everywhere to be seen of the [slaughtered remains] of inferior races. . . . Yet these dead people are, in very truth, the stepping stones on which mankind has arisen to the higher intellectual and deeper emotional life of today."[2]

For some, colonialism had a moral purpose, whether to promote Christianity or to build a better world. The British colonial official Henry Curzon declared that the British Empire "was under Providence, the greatest instrument for good that the world has seen." To Cecil Rhodes, the most famous empire builder of his day, the extraction of material wealth from the colonies was only a secondary matter. "My ruling purpose," he remarked, "is the extension of the British Empire."[3] That British Empire, on which, as the saying went, "the sun never set," was the envy of its rivals and was viewed as the primary source of British global dominance during the second half of the nineteenth century.

The Tactics

With the change in European motives for colonization came a corresponding shift in tactics. Earlier, when their economic interests were more limited, European states had generally been satisfied to deal with existing independent states rather than attempting to establish direct control over vast territories. There had been exceptions where state power at the local level was at the point of collapse (as in India), where European economic interests were especially intense (as in Latin America and the East Indies), or where there was no centralized authority (as in North America and the Philippines). But for the most part, the Western presence in Asia and Africa had been limited to controlling the regional trade network and establishing a few footholds where the foreigners could carry on trade and missionary activity.

After 1800, the demands of industrialization in Europe created a new set of dynamics. Maintaining access to industrial raw materials such as oil and rubber and setting up reliable markets for European manufactured products required more extensive control over colonial territories. As competition for colonies increased, the colonial powers sought to solidify their hold over their territories to protect them from attack by their rivals.

During the last two decades of the nineteenth century, the quest for colonies became a scramble as all the major European states, now joined by the United States and Japan, engaged in a global land grab. In many cases, economic interests were secondary to security concerns or the requirements of national prestige. In Africa, for example, the British engaged in a struggle with their rivals to protect their interests in the Suez Canal and the Red Sea.

By 1900, almost all the societies of Africa and Asia were either under full colonial rule or, as in the case of China and the Ottoman Empire, at a point of virtual collapse. Only a handful of states, such as Japan in East Asia, Thailand in Southeast Asia, Afghanistan and Iran in the Middle East, and mountainous Ethiopia in East Africa, managed to escape internal disintegration or subjection to colonial rule. For the most part, the exceptions were the result of good fortune rather than design. Thailand escaped subjugation primarily because officials in London and Paris found it more convenient to transform the country into a buffer state than to fight over it. Ethiopia and Afghanistan survived due to their remote location and mountainous terrain. Only Japan managed to avoid the common fate through a concerted strategy of political and economic reform.

The Colonial System

Now that they had control of most of the world, what did the colonial powers do with it? As we have seen, their primary objective was to exploit the natural resources of the subject areas and to open up markets for manufactured goods and capital investment from the mother country. In some cases, that goal could be realized in cooperation with local political elites, whose loyalty could be earned, or purchased, by economic rewards or by confirming them in their positions of authority and status in a new colonial setting. Sometimes, however, this policy of **indirect rule** was not feasible because local leaders refused to cooperate with their colonial masters or even actively resisted the foreign conquest. In such cases, the local elites were removed from power and replaced with a new set of officials recruited from the mother country.

In general, the societies most likely to actively resist colonial conquest were those with a long tradition of national cohesion and independence, such as Burma and Vietnam in Asia and the African Muslim states in northern Nigeria and Morocco. In those areas, the colonial powers tended to dispense with local collaborators and govern directly. In parts of Africa, the Indian subcontinent, and the Malayan peninsula, where the local authorities, for whatever reason, were willing to collaborate with the imperialist powers, indirect rule was more common.

Overall, colonialism in India, Southeast Asia, and Africa exhibited many similarities but also some differences. Some of these variations can be traced to political or social differences among the colonial powers themselves. The French, for example, often tried to impose a centralized administrative system on their colonies that mirrored the system in use in France, while the British sometimes attempted to transform local aristocrats into the equivalent of the landed gentry at home in Britain. Other differences stemmed from conditions in the colonies themselves.

The Philosophy of Colonialism

To justify their rule, the colonial powers appealed in part to the time-honored maxim of "might makes right." By the end of the nineteenth century, that attitude received pseudoscientific validity from the concept of social Darwinism, which maintained that only societies that moved aggressively to adapt to changing circumstances would survive and prosper in a world governed by the Darwinian law of "survival of the fittest."

Some people, however, were uncomfortable with such a brutal view of the law of nature and sought a moral justification that appeared to benefit the victim. Here again, the concept of social Darwinism pointed the way. By bringing the benefits of Western democracy, capitalism, and Christianity to the tradition-ridden societies of Africa and Asia, the colonial powers were enabling primitive peoples to adapt to the challenges of the modern world. Buttressed by such comforting theories, sensitive Western minds could ignore the brutal aspects of colonialism and persuade themselves that in the long run, the results would be beneficial for both sides (see the box on p. 449). Few were as adept at describing the "civilizing mission" of colonialism as the French administrator and twice governor-general of French Indochina Albert Sarraut. While admitting that colonialism was originally an "act of force" undertaken for commercial profit, he insisted that by redistributing the wealth of the earth, the colonial process would result in a better life for all: "Is it just, is it legitimate that such [an uneven distribution of resources] should be indefinitely prolonged? . . . No! . . . Humanity is distributed throughout the globe. No race, no people has the right or power to isolate itself egotistically from the movements and necessities of universal life."[4]

But what about the possibility that historically and culturally the societies of Asia and Africa were fundamentally different from those of the West and could not, or would not, be persuaded to transform themselves along Western lines? In that case, a policy of cultural transformation could not be expected to succeed and could even lead to disaster.

Assimilation or Association?   In fact, colonial theorists never decided this issue one way or the other. The French, who were most inclined to philosophize about the problem, adopted the terms **assimilation** (which implied an effort to transform colonial societies in the Western image) and **association** (implying collaboration with local elites while leaving local traditions alone) to describe the two alternatives and then proceeded to vacillate between them. French policy in

WHITE MAN'S BURDEN, BLACK MAN'S SORROW

POLITICS & GOVERNMENT

One of the justifications for modern imperialism was the notion that the allegedly "more advanced" white peoples had the moral responsibility to raise ignorant native peoples to a higher level of civilization. Few captured this notion better than the British poet Rudyard Kipling (1865–1936) in his famous poem *The White Man's Burden*. His appeal, directed to the United States, became one of the most famous set of verses in the English-speaking world.

That sense of moral responsibility, however, was often misplaced or, even worse, laced with hypocrisy. All too often, the consequences of imperial rule were detrimental to everyone living under colonial authority. Few observers described the destructive effects of Western imperialism on the African people as well as Edmund Morel, a British journalist whose book *The Black Man's Burden* pointed out some of the more harmful aspects of colonialism in the Belgian Congo.

According to Kipling, why should Western nations take up the "white man's burden," as indicated in this poem? What was the "black man's burden," as portrayed by Edmund Morel?

Rudyard Kipling, *The White Man's Burden*

Take up the White Man's burden—
Send forth the best ye breed—
Go bind your sons to exile
To serve your captives' need;
To wait in heavy harness,
On fluttered folk and wild—
Your new-caught sullen peoples,
Half-devil and half-child.

Take up the White Man's burden—
In patience to abide,
To veil the threat of terror
And check the show of pride;
By open speech and simple,
An hundred times made plain
To seek another's profit,
And work another's gain.

Take up the White Man's burden—
The savage wars of peace—
Fill full the mouth of Famine
And bid the sickness cease;
And when your goal is nearest
The end for others sought,
Watch Sloth and heathen Folly
Bring all your hopes to nought.

Edmund Morel, *The Black Man's Burden*

It is [the Africans] who carry the "Black man's burden." They have not withered away before the white man's occupation. Indeed . . . Africa has ultimately absorbed within itself every Caucasian and, for that matter, every Semitic invader, too. In hewing out for himself a fixed abode in Africa, the white man has massacred the African in heaps. The African has survived, and it is well for the white settlers that he has. . . .

What the partial occupation of his soil by the white man has failed to do; what the mapping out of European political "spheres of influence" has failed to do; what the Maxim and the rifle, the slave gang, labour in the bowels of the earth and the lash, have failed to do; what imported measles, smallpox and syphilis have failed to do; whatever the overseas slave trade failed to do; the power of modern capitalistic exploitation, assisted by modern engines of destruction, may yet succeed in accomplishing.

For from the evils of the latter, scientifically applied and enforced, there is no escape for the African. Its destructive effects are not spasmodic; they are permanent. In its permanence resides its fatal consequences. It kills not the body merely, but the soul. It breaks the spirit. It attacks the African at every turn, from every point of vantage. It wrecks his polity, uproots him from the land, invades his family life, destroys his natural pursuits and occupations, claims his whole time, enslaves him in his own home.

ThomsonNOW To read more of *The Black Man's Burden*, enter the *ThomsonNOW* documents area using the access card that is available for *The Essential World History*.

Indochina, for example, began as one of association but switched to assimilation under pressure from those who felt that colonial powers owed a debt to their subject peoples. But assimilation (which in any case was never accepted as feasible or desirable by many colonial officials) aroused resentment among the local population, many of whom opposed the destruction of their native traditions. In the end, the French abandoned the attempt to justify their presence and fell back on a policy of ruling by force of arms.

Other colonial powers had little interest in the issue. The British, whether out of a sense of pragmatism or of racial superiority, refused to entertain the possibility of assimilation and treated their subject peoples as culturally and racially distinct.

India Under the British Raj

By 1800, the once glorious empire of the Mughals had been reduced by British military power to a shadow of its former greatness. During the next few decades, the British sought to consolidate their control over the Indian subcontinent, expanding from their base areas along the

The Company Resident and His Puppet. The British East India Company gradually replaced the sovereigns of the once-independent Indian states with puppet rulers who carried out the company's policies. Here we see the company's resident dominating a procession in Tanjore in 1825, while the Indian ruler, Sarabhoji, follows like an obedient shadow. As a boy, Sarabhoji had been educated by European tutors and had filled his life and home with English books and furnishings.

coast into the interior. Some territories were taken over directly, first by the East India Company and later by the British crown; others were ruled indirectly through their local maharajas and rajas.

Colonial Reforms

Not all of the effects of British rule were bad. British governance over the subcontinent brought order and stability to a society that had been rent by civil war. By the early nineteenth century, British control had been consolidated and led to a relatively honest and efficient government that in many respects operated to the benefit of the average Indian. One of the benefits of the period was the heightened attention given to education. Through the efforts of the British administrator Thomas Babington Macaulay, a new school system was established to train the children of Indian elites, and the British civil service examination was introduced (see the box on p. 452). The instruction of young girls also expanded, with the primary purpose of making them better wives and mothers for the educated male population. In 1875, a Madras medical college accepted its first female student.

British rule also brought an end to some of the more inhumane aspects of Indian tradition. The practice of *sati* was outlawed, and widows were legally permitted to remarry. The British also attempted to put an end to the endemic brigandage (known as *thuggee*, which gave rise to the English word *thug*) that had plagued travelers in India since time immemorial. Railroads, the telegraph, and the postal service were introduced to India shortly after they appeared in Great Britain itself. Work began on the main highway from Calcutta to Delhi in 1839 (see Map 20.1), and the first rail network in northern India was opened in 1853.

The Costs of Colonialism

But the Indian people paid a high price for the peace and stability brought by the British **raj** (from the Indian *raja*, or prince). Perhaps the most flagrant cost was economic. While British entrepreneurs and a small percentage of the Indian population attached to the imperial system reaped financial benefits from British rule, it brought hardship to millions of others in both the cities and the rural areas. The introduction of British textiles put thousands of

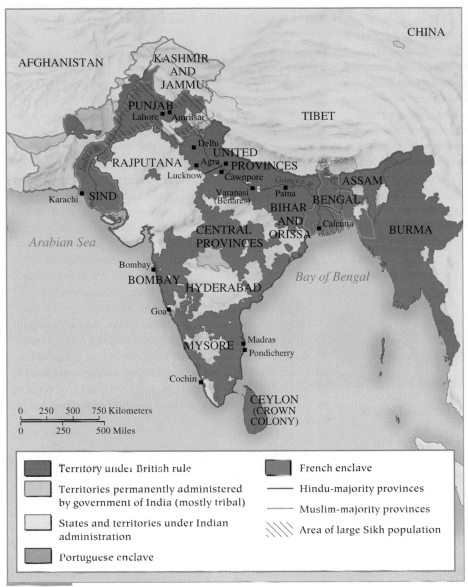

MAP 20.1 India Under British Rule, 1805–1931. This map shows the different forms of rule that the British applied in India under their control. **?** Where were the major cities of the subcontinent located, and under whose rule did they fall? **View an animated version of this map and related maps at** http://worldrc.wadsworth.com/

British colonialism was also remiss in bringing the benefits of modern science and technology to India. Some limited forms of industrialization took place, notably in the manufacturing of textiles and jute (used in making rope). The first textile mill opened in 1856. Seventy years later, there were eighty mills in the city of Bombay alone. Nevertheless, the lack of local capital and the advantages given to British imports prevented the emergence of other vital new commercial and manufacturing operations.

Foreign rule also had a psychological effect on the Indian people. Although many British colonial officials sincerely tried to improve the lot of the people under their charge, British arrogance and contempt for native tradition cut deeply into the pride of many Indians, especially those of high caste, who were accustomed to a position of superior status in India. Educated Indians trained in the Anglo-Indian school system for a career in the civil service, as well as Eurasians born to mixed marriages, often imitated the behavior and dress of their rulers, speaking English, eating Western food, and taking up European leisure activities, but many rightfully wondered where their true cultural loyalties lay (see the comparative illustration on p. 453).

Bengali women out of work and severely damaged the local textile industry.

In rural areas, the British introduced the *zamindar* system (see Chapter 15) in the misguided expectation that it would both facilitate the collection of agricultural taxes and create a new landed gentry, who could, as in Britain, become the conservative foundation of imperial rule. But the local gentry took advantage of this new authority to increase taxes and force the less fortunate peasants to become tenants or lose their land entirely. British officials also made few efforts during the nineteenth century to introduce democratic institutions or values to the Indian people. As one senior political figure remarked in Parliament in 1898, democratic institutions "can no more be carried to India by Englishmen . . . than they can carry ice in their luggage."[5]

Colonial Regimes in Southeast Asia

In 1800, only two societies in Southeast Asia were under effective colonial rule: the Spanish Philippines and the Dutch East Indies. During the nineteenth century, however, European interest in Southeast Asia increased rapidly, and by 1900, virtually the entire area was under colonial rule (see Map 20.2).

"Opportunity in the Orient": The Colonial Takeover in Southeast Asia

The process began after the Napoleonic wars, when the British, by agreement with the Dutch, abandoned their claims to territorial possessions in the East Indies in return for a free hand in the Malayan peninsula. In 1819, the colonial administrator Stamford Raffles founded a new British

The Esplanade. After occupying the island of Singapore early in the nineteenth century, the British turned what was once a pirate lair located at the entrance to the Strait of Malacca into one of the most important commercial seaports in Asia. By the end of the century, Singapore was home to a rich mixture of peoples, both European and Asian. This painting by a turn-of-the-century British artist graphically displays the multiracial character of the colony as strollers, rickshaw drivers, and lamplighters share space along the Esplanade, in Singapore Harbor. Almost all colonial port cities became a melting pot of peoples from various parts of the world. Many of the immigrants served as merchants, urban laborers, and craftsmen in the new colonial marketplace.

China's illimitable markets. We will not retreat from either. . . . We will not renounce our part in the mission of our race, trustee, under God, of the civilization of the world. And we will move forward to our work, not howling out regrets like slaves whipped to their burdens, but with gratitude for a task worthy of our strength, and thanksgiving to Almighty God that He has marked us as His chosen people, henceforth to lead in the regeneration of the world.[6]

Not all Filipinos agreed with Senator Beveridge's portrayal of the situation. Under the leadership of Emilio Aguinaldo, guerrilla forces fought bitterly against U.S. troops to establish their independence from both Spain and the United States. But America's first war against guerrilla forces in Asia was a success, and the bulk of the resistance collapsed in 1901. President McKinley had his stepping-stone to the rich markets of China.

The Nature of Colonial Rule

In Southeast Asia, economic profit was the immediate and primary aim of colonial enterprise. For that purpose, colonial powers tried wherever possible to work with local elites to facilitate the exploitation of natural resources. Indirect rule reduced the cost of training European administrators and had a less corrosive impact on the local culture. In the Dutch East Indies, for example, officials of the Dutch East India Company (VOC) entrusted local administration to the indigenous landed aristocracy, who maintained law and order and collected taxes in return for a payment from the VOC. The British followed a similar practice in Malaya. While establishing direct rule over the crucial commercial centers of Singapore and Malacca, the British allowed local Muslim rulers to maintain princely power in the interior of the peninsula.

Administration and Education Indirect rule, however convenient and inexpensive, was not always feasible. In some instances, local resistance to the colonial conquest made such a policy impossible. In Burma, the staunch opposition of the monarchy and other traditionalist forces caused the British to abolish the monarchy and administer the country directly through their colonial government in India. In Indochina, the French used both direct and indirect means. They imposed direct rule on the southern provinces in the Mekong delta but governed the north as a protectorate, with the emperor retaining titular authority from his palace in Huê. The French adopted a similar policy in Cambodia and Laos, where local rulers were left in charge with French advisers to counsel them.

Whatever method was used, colonial regimes in Southeast Asia, as elsewhere, were slow to create democratic institutions. The first legislative councils and assemblies were composed almost exclusively of European residents in the colony. The first representatives from the indigenous population were wealthy and conservative in their political views. When Southeast Asians complained, colonial officials gradually and reluctantly began to broaden the franchise. Albert Sarraut advised patience in awaiting the full benefits of colonial policy: "I will treat you like my younger brothers, but do not forget that I am the older brother. I will slowly give you the dignity of humanity."[7]

Colonial officials were also slow to adopt educational reforms. Although the introduction of Western education was one of the justifications of colonialism, colonial officials soon discovered that educating native elites could backfire. Often there were few jobs for highly trained lawyers, engineers, and architects in colonial societies, leading to the threat of an indigestible mass of unemployed intellectuals who would take out their frustrations on the colonial regime. As one French official noted in voicing his opposition to increasing the number of schools in Vietnam, educating the natives meant not "one coolie less, but one rebel more."

Stamford Raffles arrives in Singapore	1819
British attack lower Burma	1826
British rail network opened in northern India	1853
Sepoy Rebellion	1857
French attack Vietnam	1858
British and French agree to neutralize Thailand	1896
Commodore Dewey defeats Spanish fleet in Manila Bay	1898

Economic Development Colonial powers were equally reluctant to take up the "white man's burden" in the area of economic development. As we have seen, their primary goals were to secure a source of cheap raw materials and to maintain markets for manufactured goods. Such objectives would be undermined by the emergence of advanced industrial economies. So colonial policy concentrated on the export of raw materials—teakwood from Burma; rubber and tin from Malaya; spices, tea and coffee, and palm oil from the East Indies; and sugar and copra (the meat of a coconut) from the Philippines.

In some Southeast Asian colonial societies, a measure of industrial development did take place to meet the needs of the European population and local elites. Major manufacturing cities like Rangoon in lower Burma, Batavia on the island of Java, and Saigon in French Indochina grew rapidly. Although the local middle class benefited from the increased economic activity, most large industrial and commercial establishments were owned and managed by Europeans or, in some cases, by Indian or Chinese merchants.

Colonialism and the Countryside Despite the growth of an urban economy, the vast majority of people in the colonial societies continued to farm the land. Many continued to live by subsistence agriculture, but the colonial policy of emphasizing cash crops for export also led to the creation of a form of plantation agriculture in which peasants were recruited to work as wage laborers on rubber and tea plantations owned by Europeans. To maintain a competitive edge, the plantation owners kept the wages of their workers at poverty level. Many plantation workers were "shanghaied" (the English term originated from the practice of recruiting laborers, often from the docks and streets of Shanghai, by unscrupulous means such as the use of force, alcohol, or drugs) to work on plantations, where conditions were often so inhumane that thousands died. High taxes, enacted by colonial governments to pay for administrative costs or improvements in the local infrastructure, were a heavy burden for poor peasants.

The situation was made even more difficult by the steady growth of the population. Peasants in Asia had always had large families on the assumption that a high proportion of their children would die in infancy. But improved sanitation and medical treatment resulted in lower rates of infant mortality and a staggering increase

A Rubber Plantation. Natural rubber was one of the most impotant cash crops in European colonies in Asia. Rubber trees, native to the Amazon River basin in Brazil, were eventually transplanted to Southeast Asia, where they became a major source of profit. Workers on the plantations received few benefits, however. Once the sap of the tree (known as latex and shown on the left) was extracted, it was hardened and pressed into sheets (right photo) and then sent to Europe for refining.

© Bildarchiv Preussische Kulturbesitz, Berlin/Art Resource, NY

The Opening of the Suez Canal. The Suez Canal, which connected the Mediterranean and the Red seas, was constructed under the direction of the French promoter Ferdinand de Lesseps. Still in use today, the canal is Egypt's greatest revenue producer. This sketch shows the ceremonial passage of the first ships through the canal in 1869. Note the combination of sail and steam power, reflecting the transition to coal-powered ships in the mid-nineteenth century.

The Suez Canal

nineteenth century, and the sultan of Oman, who had reasserted Arab suzerainty over the region in the aftermath of the collapse of Portuguese authority, established his capital at Zanzibar in 1840.

The tenacity of the slave trade in East Africa—Zanzibar had now become the largest slave market in Africa—was undoubtedly a major reason for the rise of Western interest and Christian missionary activity in the region during the middle of the century. The most renowned missionary was the Scottish doctor David Livingstone, who arrived in Africa in 1841. Because Livingstone spent much of his time exploring the interior of the continent, discovering Victoria Falls in the process, he was occasionally criticized for being more explorer than missionary. But Livingstone was convinced that it was his divinely appointed task to bring Christianity to the far reaches of the continent, and his passionate opposition to slavery did far more to win public support for the abolitionist cause than did the efforts of any other figure of his generation. Public outcries provoked the British to redouble their efforts to bring the slave trade in East Africa to an end, and in 1873, the slave market at Zanzibar was finally closed as the result of

© Bojan Brecelj/CORBIS

Legacy of Shame. By the mid-nineteenth century, most European nations had prohibited the trade in African slaves, but slavery continued to exist in East Africa under the sponsorship of the sultan of Zanzibar. When the Scottish missionary David Livingstone witnessed a slave raid near Lake Tanganyika in 1871, he wrote, "It gave me the impression of being in Hell." Despite his efforts, the practice was not eradicated until well into the next century. Shown here are domestic slaves on the island of Zanzibar under the baton of a supervisor. The photograph was taken about 1890.

pressure from London. Shortly before, Livingstone had died of illness in Central Africa, but some of his followers brought his body to the coast for burial.

Bantus, Boers, and British in the South

Nowhere in Africa did the European presence grow more rapidly than in the south. During the eighteenth century, the Boers, Afrikaans-speaking farmers descended from the original Dutch settlers of the Cape Colony, began to migrate eastward. After the British seized control of the cape from the Dutch during the Napoleonic wars, the Boers' eastward migration intensified, culminating in the Great Trek of the mid-1830s. In part, the Boers' departure was provoked by the different attitude of the British to the native population. Slavery was abolished in the British Empire in 1834, and the British government was generally more sympathetic to the rights of the local African population than were the Afrikaners, many of whom believed that white superiority was ordained by God and fled from British rule to control their own destiny. Eventually, the Boers formed their own independent republics—the Orange Free State and the South African Republic (usually called the Transvaal; see Map 20.4).

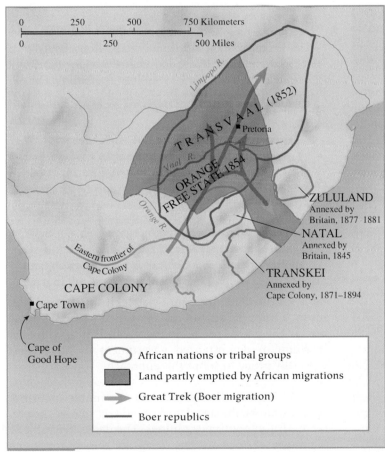

MAP 20.4 **The Struggle for Southern Africa.** Shown here is the expansion of European settlers from the Cape Colony into adjacent areas of southern Africa in the nineteenth century. The arrows indicate the routes taken by Afrikaans-speaking Boers. ❓ Who were the Boers, and why did they migrate eastward?

Although the Boer occupation of the eastern territory was initially facilitated by internecine warfare among the local inhabitants of the region, the new settlers met some resistance. In the early nineteenth century, the Zulus, a Bantu people led by a talented ruler named Shaka, engaged in a series of wars with the Europeans that ended only when Shaka was overthrown. Ultimately, most of the black Africans in the Boer republics were confined to reservations.

The Scramble for Africa

At the beginning of the 1880s, most of Africa was still independent. European rule was limited to the fringes of the continent, such as Algeria, the Gold Coast, and South Africa. Other areas like Egypt, lower Nigeria, Senegal, and Mozambique were under various forms of loose protectorate. But the pace of European penetration was accelerating, and the constraints that had limited European rapaciousness were fast disappearing.

The scramble began in the mid-1880s, when several European states, including Belgium, France, Germany, Great Britain, and Portugal, engaged in a feeding frenzy to seize a piece of African territory before the carcass had been picked clean. By 1900, virtually all of the continent had been placed under some form of European rule. The British had consolidated their authority over the Nile valley and seized additional territories in East Africa (see Map 20.3 on p. 457). The French retaliated by advancing eastward from Senegal into the central Sahara. They also occupied the island of Madagascar and other territories in West and Central Africa. In between, the Germans claimed the hinterland opposite Zanzibar, as well as coastal strips in West and Southwest Africa north of the cape, and King Leopold II of Belgium claimed the Congo. Eventually, Italy entered the contest and seized modern Libya and some of the Somali coast.

What had happened to spark the sudden imperialist hysteria that brought an end to African independence? Clearly, the level of trade between Europe and Africa was not sufficient to justify the risks and the expense of conquest. More important than economic interests were the intensified rivalries among the European states that led them to engage in imperialist takeovers out of fear that if they did not, another state might do so, leaving them at a disadvantage. In the most famous example, the British solidified their control over the entire Nile valley to protect the Suez Canal from seizure by the French.

Another consideration might be called the "missionary factor," as European missionary interests lobbied with their governments for colonial takeovers to facilitate their efforts to convert the African population to Christianity. The concept of social Darwinism and the "white man's burden" persuaded many that it was in the interests of the African people, as well as their conquerors, to be introduced more rapidly to the benefits of Western civilization. Even David Livingstone had become convinced that missionary work and economic development had to go hand in hand, pleading to his fellow Europeans to introduce the "three Cs" (Christianity, commerce, and civilization) to the continent. How much easier such a task would be if African peoples were under benevolent European rule!

There were more prosaic reasons as well. Advances in Western technology and European superiority in firearms made it easier than ever for a small European force to defeat superior numbers. Furthermore, life expectancy for Europeans living in Africa had improved. With the discovery that quinine (extracted from the bark of the cinchona tree) could provide partial immunity from the ravages of malaria, the mortality rate for Europeans living in Africa dropped dramatically in the 1840s. By the end of the century, European residents in tropical Africa faced only slightly higher risks of death by disease than individuals living in Europe.

Under these circumstances, King Leopold of Belgium used missionary activities as an excuse to claim vast territories in the Congo River basin (Belgium, he said, as "a small country, with a small people," needed a colony to enhance its image).[8] This set off a desperate race among European nations to stake claims throughout sub-Saharan Africa. Leopold ended up with the territories south of the Congo River, while France occupied areas to the north (Leopold bequeathed the Congo to Belgium on his death). Meanwhile, on the eastern side of the continent, Germany annexed the colony of Tanganyika. To avert the possibility of violent clashes among the great powers, the German chancellor, Otto von Bismarck, convened a conference in Berlin in 1884 to set ground rules for future annexations of African territory by European nations. Like the famous Open Door Notes fifteen years later (see Chapter 21), the conference combined high-minded resolutions with a hardheaded recognition of practical interests. The delegates called for free commerce in the Congo and along the Niger River as well as for further efforts to end the slave trade. At the same time, the participants recognized the inevitability of the imperialist dynamic, agreeing only that future annexations of African territory should not be given international recognition until effective occupation had been demonstrated. No African delegates were present.

The Berlin Conference had been convened to avert war and reduce tensions among European nations competing for the spoils of Africa. During the next few years, African territories were annexed without provoking a major confrontation between the Western powers, but in the late 1890s, Britain and France reached the brink of conflict at Fashoda, a small town on the Nile River in the Sudan. The French had been advancing eastward across the Sahara with the transparent objective of controlling

CHRONOLOGY Imperialism in Africa	
Dutch abolish slave trade in Africa	1795
Napoleonic invasion of Egypt	1798
Slave trade declared illegal in Great Britain	1808
Boers' Great Trek in southern Africa	1830s
French seize Algeria	1830
Sultan of Oman establishes capital at Zanzibar	1840
David Livingstone arrives in Africa	1841
Slavery abolished in the United States	1863
Completion of Suez Canal	1869
Zanzibar slave market closed	1873
British establish Gold Coast colony	1874
British establish informal protectorate over Egypt	1881
Berlin Conference on Africa	1884
Charles Gordon killed at Khartoum	1885
Confrontation at Fashoda	1898
Boer War	1899–1902
Union of South Africa established	1910

the regions around the upper Nile. In 1898, British and Egyptian troops seized the Sudan from successors of the Mahdi and then marched southward to head off the French. After a tense face-off at Fashoda, the French government backed down, and British authority over the area was secured.

Colonialism in Africa

Having seized Africa in what could almost be described as a fit of hysteria, the European powers had to decide what to do with it. With economic concerns relatively limited except for isolated areas like the gold mines in the Transvaal and copper deposits in the Belgian Congo, interest in Africa declined, and most European governments settled down to govern their new territories with the least effort and expense possible. In many cases, this meant a form of indirect rule similar to what the British used in the princely states in India. The British with their tradition of decentralized government at home were especially prone to adopt this approach.

Indirect Rule in West Africa In the minds of British administrators, the stated goal of indirect rule was to preserve African political traditions. The desire to limit cost and inconvenience was one reason for this approach, but it may also have been due to the conviction that Africans were inherently inferior to the white race and thus incapable of adopting European customs and institutions. In any event, indirect rule entailed relying to the greatest extent possible on existing political elites and institutions.

Initially, in some areas, the British simply asked a local ruler to formally accept British authority and to fly the Union Jack over official buildings. Sometimes it was the Africans who did the bidding, as in the case of the African leaders in Cameroons who wrote to Queen Victoria:

> We *wish* to have your laws in our towns. We want to have every *fashion* altered; also we will do according to your Consul's *word*. Plenty wars here in our country. Plenty murder and plenty idol worshippers. Perhaps these *lines* of our writing will look to you as an *idle* tale.
>
> We have *spoken* to the English consul plenty times about having an English *government* here. We never have answer from you, so we wish to write you *ourselves*.[9]

Nigeria offers a typical example of British indirect rule. British officials maintained the central administration, but local authority was assigned to native chiefs, with British district officers serving as intermediaries with the central administration. Where a local aristocracy did not exist, the British assigned administrative responsibility to clan heads from communities in the vicinity. The local authorities were expected to maintain law and order and to collect taxes from the native population. As a general rule, indigenous customs were left undisturbed, although the institution of slavery was abolished. A dual legal system was instituted that applied African laws to Africans and European laws to foreigners.

One advantage of such an administrative system was that it did not severely disrupt local customs and institutions. Nevertheless, it had several undesirable consequences. In the first place, it was essentially a fraud, since all major decisions were made by the British administrators while the native authorities served primarily as the means of enforcing decisions. Moreover, indirect rule served to perpetuate the autocratic system often in use prior to colonial takeover.

The British in East Africa The situation was somewhat different in East Africa, especially in Kenya, which had a relatively large European population attracted by the temperate climate in the central highlands. The local government had encouraged white settlers to migrate to the area as a means of promoting economic development and encouraging financial self-sufficiency. To attract Europeans, fertile farmlands in the central highlands were reserved for European settlement, while specified reserve lands were set aside for Africans. The presence of a substantial European minority (although, in fact, they represented only about 1 percent of the entire population) had an impact on Kenya's political development. The white settlers actively sought self-government and dominion status similar to that granted to such former British possessions as Canada and Australia. The British government, however, was not willing to run the risk of provoking racial tensions with the African majority and agreed only to establish separate government organs for the European and African populations.

British Rule in South Africa The British used a different system in southern Africa, where there was a high percentage of European settlers. The situation was further complicated by a growing division between English-speaking and Afrikaner elements within the European population. The discovery of gold and diamonds in the Boer republic of the Transvaal was the source of the problem. Clashes between the Afrikaner population and foreign (mainly British) miners and developers led to an attempt by Cecil Rhodes, prime minister of the Cape Colony and a prominent entrepreneur in the area, to subvert the Transvaal and bring it under British rule. In 1899, the so-called Boer War broke out between Britain and the Transvaal, which was backed by its fellow republic, the Orange Free State. Guerrilla resistance by the Boers was

Revere the Conquering Heroes.
European colonial officials were quick to place themselves at the top of the political and social hierarchy in their conquered territories. Here British officials accept the submission of the Ashanti king and queen, according to African custom, in 1896.

© Mansell/Time Life Pictures/Getty Images

fierce, but the vastly superior forces of the British were able to prevail by 1902. To compensate the defeated Afrikaner population for the loss of independence, the British government agreed that only whites would vote in the now essentially self-governing colony. The Boers were placated, but the brutalities committed during the war (the British introduced an institution later to be known as the concentration camp) created bitterness on both sides that continued to fester through future decades.

In 1910, the British agreed to the creation of the independent Union of South Africa, which combined the old Cape Colony and Natal with the Boer republics. The new union adopted a representative government, but only for the European population, while the African reserves of Basutoland (now Lesotho), Bechuanaland (now Botswana), and Swaziland were subordinated directly to the crown. The union was now free to manage its own domestic affairs and possessed considerable autonomy in foreign relations. Formal British rule was also extended to the remaining lands south of the Zambezi River, which were eventually divided into the territories of Northern and Southern Rhodesia. Southern Rhodesia attracted many British immigrants, and in 1922, after a popular referendum, it became a crown colony.

Direct Rule, French Style   Most other European nations governed their African possessions through a form of direct rule. The prototype was the French system, which reflected the centralized administrative system introduced in France itself by Napoleon. As in the British colonies, at the top of the pyramid was a French official, usually known as the governor-general, who was appointed from Paris and governed with the aid of a bureaucracy in the capital city. At the provincial level, French commissioners were assigned to deal with local administrators, but the latter were required to be conversant in French and could be transferred to a new position at the needs of the central government.

Moreover, the French ideal was to assimilate their African subjects into French culture rather than preserving their native traditions. Africans were eligible to run for office and to serve in the French National Assembly, and a few were appointed to high positions in the colonial administration. Such policies reflected the relative absence of racist attitudes in French society, as well as the conviction among the French of the superiority of Gallic culture and their revolutionary belief in the universality of human nature.

Women in Colonial Africa   The establishment of colonial rule had a mixed impact on the rights and status of women in Africa. Sexual relationships changed profoundly during the colonial era, sometimes in ways that could justly be described as beneficial. Colonial governments attempted to bring an end to forced marriage, bodily mutilation such as clitoridectomy, and polygamy. Missionaries introduced women to Western education and encouraged them to organize themselves to defend their interests.

But the colonial system had some unfavorable consequences as well. African women had traditionally benefited from the prestige of matrilineal systems and were empowered by their traditional role as the primary agricultural producers in their community. Under colonialism, European settlers not only took the best land for themselves but also, in introducing new agricultural techniques, tended to deal exclusively with males, encouraging them to develop lucrative cash crops, while women were restricted to traditional farming methods. Whereas African men applied chemical fertilizer to the fields, women used manure. While men began to use bicycles, and eventually trucks, to transport goods, women still carried their goods on their heads, a practice that continues today. In British colonies, Victorian attitudes of female subordination led to restrictions on women's freedom, and positions in government that they had formerly held were now closed to them.

The Emergence of Anticolonialism

Thus far we have looked at the colonial experience primarily from the point of view of the colonial powers. Equally important is the way the subject peoples reacted to the experience. From the perspective of nearly half a century, it seems clear that their primary response was to turn to nationalism.

Stirrings of Nationhood

As we have seen, nationalism refers to a state of mind rising out of an awareness of being part of a community that possesses common institutions, traditions, language, and customs (see the comparative essay "The Rise of Nationalism" on p. 435 in Chapter 19). Few nations in the world today meet such criteria. Most modern states contain a variety of ethnic, religious, and linguistic communities, each with its own sense of cultural and national identity. Should Canada, for example, which includes peoples of French, English, and Native American heritage, be considered a nation? Another question is how nationalism differs from other forms of tribal, religious, or linguistic affiliation. Should every group that resists assimilation into a larger cultural unity be called nationalist?

Such questions complicate the study of nationalism even in Europe and North America and make agreement on a definition elusive. They create even greater dilemmas in discussing Asia and Africa, where most societies are deeply divided by ethnic, linguistic, and religious differences and the very term *nationalism* is a foreign phenomenon imported from the West (see the box on p. 463). Prior to the colonial era, most traditional societies in Africa and Asia were formed on the basis of religious beliefs, tribal loyalties, or devotion to hereditary monarchies.

The advent of European colonialism brought the consciousness of modern nationhood to many of the societies of Asia and Africa. The creation of European

THE CIVILIZING MISSION IN EGYPT

FAMILY & SOCIETY

In many parts of the colonial world, European occupation served to sharpen class divisions in traditional societies. Such was the case in Egypt, where the British protectorate, established in the early 1880s, benefited many elites, who profited from the introduction of Western culture. Ordinary Egyptians, less inclined to adopt foreign ways, seldom profited from the European presence. In response, British administrators showed little patience for their subjects who failed to recognize the superiority of Western civilization. This view found expression in the words of the governor-general, Lord Cromer, who remarked in exasperation, "The mind of the Oriental, . . . like his picturesque streets, is eminently wanting in symmetry. His reasoning is of the most slipshod description." Cromer was especially irritated at the local treatment of women, arguing that the seclusion of women and the wearing of the veil were the chief causes of Islamic backwardness.

Such views were echoed by some Egyptian elites, who were utterly seduced by Western culture and embraced the colonialists' condemnation of native ways. The French-educated lawyer Qassim Amin was one example. His book *The Liberation of Women,* published in 1899 and excerpted here, precipitated a heated debate between those who considered Western nations the liberators of Islam and those who reviled them as oppressors.

Why does the author believe that Western culture would be beneficial to Egyptian society? How might a critic of colonialism respond?

Qassim Amin, *The Liberation of Women*

European civilization advances with the speed of steam and electricity, and has even overspilled to every part of the globe so that there is not an inch that he [European man] has not trodden underfoot. Any place he goes he takes control of its resources . . . and turns them into profit . . . and if he does harm to the original inhabitants, it is only that he pursues happiness in this world and seeks it wherever he may find it . . . . For the most part he uses his intellect, but when circumstances require it, he deploys force. He does not seek glory from his possessions and colonies, for he has enough of this through his intellectual achievements and scientific inventions. What drives the Englishman to dwell in India and the French in Algeria. . . . is profit and the desire to acquire resources in countries where the inhabitants do not know their value or how to profit from them.

When they encounter savages they eliminate them or drive them from the land, as happened in America . . . and is happening now in Africa. . . . When they encounter a nation like ours, with a degree of civilization, with a past, and a religion . . . and customs and . . . institutions . . . they deal with its inhabitants kindly. But they do soon acquire its most valuable resources, because they have greater wealth and intellect and knowledge and force. . . . [The veil constitued] a huge barrier between woman and her elevation, and consequently a barrier between the nation and its advance.

ThomsonNOW To read Cromer's "Why Britain Acquired Egypt in 1882," enter the *ThomsonNOW* documents area using the access card that is available for *The Essential World History*.

---

colonies with defined borders and a powerful central government led to the weakening of tribal and village ties and a significant reorientation in the individual's sense of political identity. The introduction of Western ideas of citizenship and representative government produced a new sense of participation in the affairs of government. At the same time, the appearance of a new elite class based not on hereditary privilege or religious sanction but on alleged racial or cultural superiority aroused a shared sense of resentment among the subject peoples who felt a common commitment to the creation of an independent society. By the first quarter of the twentieth century, political movements dedicated to the overthrow of colonial rule had arisen throughout much of the non-Western world.

Traditional Resistance: A Precursor to Nationalism

The beginnings of modern nationalism can be found in the initial resistance by the indigenous peoples to the colonial conquest. Although, strictly speaking, such resistance was not "nationalist" because it was essentially motivated by the desire to defend traditional institutions, it did reflect a primitive concept of nationhood in that it aimed at protecting the homeland from the invader; later patriotic groups have often hailed early resistance movements as the precursors of twentieth-century nationalist movements. Thus, traditional resistance to colonial conquest may logically be viewed as the first stage in the development of modern nationalism.

Such resistance took various forms. For the most part, it was led by the existing ruling class. In the Ashanti kingdom in Africa and in Burma and Vietnam in Southeast Asia, resistance to Western domination was initially directed by the imperial courts. In some cases, traditionalists continued to oppose foreign conquest even after resistance had collapsed at the center. After the decrepit monarchy in Vietnam had bowed to French pressure, a number of civilian and military officials set up an organization called Can Vuong (literally "save the king") and continued their resistance without imperial sanction (see the box on p. 464).

The first stirrings of nationalism in India took place in the early nineteenth century with the search for a

To Resist or Not to Resist

How to respond to the imposition of colonial rule was sometimes an excruciating problem for political elites in many Asian countries, since resistance often seemed futile while simply adding to the suffering of the indigenous population. Hoang Cao Khai and Phan Dinh Phung were members of the Confucian scholar-gentry from the same village in Vietnam. Yet they reacted in dramatically different ways to the French conquest of their country. Their exchange of letters, reproduced below, illustrates the dilemmas they faced.

Explain briefly the reasons advanced by each writer to justify his actions. Which argument do you believe would earn more support from contemporaries? Why?

Hoang Cao Khai's Letter to Phan Dinh Phung

Soon, it will be seventeen years since we ventured upon different paths of life. How sweet was our friendship when we both lived in our village. . . . At the time when the capital was lost and after the royal carriage had departed, you courageously answered the appeals of the King by raising the banner of righteousness. It was certainly the only thing to do in those circumstances. No one will question that.

But now the situation has changed and even those without intelligence or education have concluded that nothing remains to be saved. How is it that you, a man of vast understanding, do not realize this? . . . You are determined to do whatever you deem righteous. . . . But though you have no thoughts for your own person or for your own fate, you should at least attend to the sufferings of the population of a whole region. . . .

Until now your actions have undoubtedly accorded with your loyalty. May I ask however what sin our people have committed to deserve so much hardship? I would understand your resistance, did you involve but your family for the benefit of a large number. As of now, hundreds of families are subject to grief; how do you have the heart to fight on? I venture to predict that, should you pursue your struggle, not only will the population of our village be destroyed but our entire country will be transformed into a sea of blood and a mountain of bones. It is my hope that men of your superior morality and honesty will pause a while to appraise the situation.

Reply of Phan Dinh Phung to Hoang Cao Khai

In your letter, you revealed to me the causes of calamities and of happiness. You showed me clearly where advantages and disadvantages lie. All of which sufficed to indicate that your anxious concern was not only for my own security but also for the peace and order of our entire region. I understood plainly your sincere arguments.

I have concluded that if our country has survived these past thousand years when its territory was not large, its army not strong, its wealth not great, it was because the relationships between king and subjects, fathers and children, have always been regulated by the five moral obligations. In the past, the Han, the Sung, the Yuan, the Ming time and again dreamt of annexing our country and of dividing it up into prefectures and districts within the Chinese administrative system. But never were they able to realize their dream. Ah! if even China, which shares a common border with our territory, and is a thousand times more powerful than Vietnam, could not rely upon her strength to swallow us, it was surely because the destiny of our country had been willed by Heaven itself.

The French, separated from our country until the present day by I do not know how many thousand miles, have crossed the oceans to come to our country. Wherever they came, they acted like a storm, so much so that the Emperor had to flee. The whole country was cast into disorder. Our rivers and our mountains have been annexed by them at a stroke and turned into a foreign territory.

Moreover, if our region has suffered to such an extent, it was not only from the misfortunes of war. You must realize that wherever the French go, there flock around them groups of petty men who offer plans and tricks to gain the enemy's confidence. . . . They use every expedient to squeeze the people out of their possessions. That is how hundreds of misdeeds, thousands of offenses have been perpetrated. How can the French not be aware of all the suffering that the rural population has had to endure? Under these circumstances, is it surprising that families should be disrupted and the people scattered?

My friend, if you are troubled about our people, then I advise you to place yourself in my position and to think about the circumstances in which I live. You will understand naturally and see clearly that I do not need to add anything else.

---

renewed sense of cultural identity. In 1828, Ram Mohan Roy, a *brahmin* from Bengal, founded the Brahmo Samaj (Society of Brahma). Roy probably had no intention of promoting Indian national independence but created the new organization as a means of helping his fellow religionists defend the Hindu religion against verbal attacks by their British acquaintances.

Sometimes traditional resistance to Western penetration went beyond elite circles. Most commonly, it appeared in the form of peasant revolts. Rural rebellions were not uncommon in traditional Asian societies as a means of expressing peasant discontent with high taxes, official corruption, rising rural debt, and famine in the countryside. Under colonialism, rural conditions often deteriorated as population density increased and peasants were driven off the land to make way for plantation agriculture. Angry peasants then vented their frustration at the foreign invaders. For example, in Burma, the Buddhist monk Saya San led a peasant uprising against the British many years after they had completed their takeover.

The Sepoy Rebellion Sometimes the resentment had a religious basis, as in the Sudan, where the revolt led by the Mahdi had strong Islamic overtones, although it was initially provoked by Turkish misrule in Egypt. More significant than Roy's Brahmo Samaj in its impact on British policy was the famous Sepoy Rebellion of 1857 in India. The sepoys (derived from *sipahi*, a Turkish word meaning horseman or soldier) were native troops hired by the East India Company to protect British interests in the region. Unrest within Indian units of the colonial army had been common since early in the century, when it had been sparked by economic issues, religious sensitivities, or nascent anticolonial sentiment. In 1857, tension erupted when the British adopted the new Enfield rifle for use by sepoy infantrymen. The new weapon was a muzzle loader that used paper cartridges covered with animal fat and lard; because the cartridge had to be bitten off, it broke strictures against high-class Hindus' eating animal products and Muslim prohibitions against eating pork. Protests among sepoy units in northern India turned into a full-scale mutiny, supported by uprisings in rural districts in various parts of the country. But the revolt lacked clear goals, and rivalries between Hindus and Muslims and discord among the leaders within each community prevented coordination of operations. Although Indian troops often fought bravely and outnumbered the British six to one, they were poorly organized, and the British forces (supplemented in many cases by sepoy troops) suppressed the rebellion. Still, the revolt frightened the British, who introduced a number of reforms and suppressed the final remnants of the Mughal dynasty, which had supported the mutiny; responsibility for governing the subcontinent was then turned over to the crown.

Like the Sepoy Rebellion, traditional resistance movements usually met with little success. Peasants armed with pikes and spears were no match for Western armies possessing the most terrifying weapons then known to human society. In a few cases, such as the revolt of the Mahdi at Khartoum, the natives were able to defeat the invaders temporarily. But such successes were rare, and the late nineteenth century witnessed the seemingly inexorable march of the Western powers, armed with the Gatling gun (the first rapid-fire weapon and the precursor of the modern machine gun), to mastery of the globe.

CONCLUSION

*B*Y THE FIRST QUARTER of the twentieth century, virtually all of Africa and a good part of South and Southeast Asia were under some form of colonial rule. With the advent of the age of imperialism, a global economy was finally established, and the domination of Western civilization over those of Africa and Asia appeared to be complete.

Defenders of colonialism argue that the system was a necessary if painful stage in the evolution of human societies. Critics, however, charge that the Western colonial powers were driven by an insatiable lust for profits (see the comparative essay "Imperialism: The Balance Sheet" on p. 466). They dismiss the Western civilizing mission as a fig leaf to cover naked greed and reject the notion that imperialism played a salutary role in hastening the adjustment of traditional societies to the demands of industrial civilization. In the blunt words of two Western critics of imperialism: "Why is Africa (or for that matter Latin America and much of Asia) so poor? . . . The answer is very brief: we have made it poor."[10]

Between these two irreconcilable views, where does the truth lie? This chapter has contended that neither extreme position is justified. Although colonialism did introduce the peoples of Asia and Africa to new technology and the expanding economic marketplace, it was unnecessarily brutal in its application and all too often failed to realize the exalted claims and objectives of its promoters. Existing economic networks—often potentially valuable as a foundation for later economic development—were ruthlessly swept aside in the interests of providing markets for Western manufactured goods. Potential sources of native industrialization were nipped in the bud to avoid competition for factories in Amsterdam, London, Pittsburgh, or Manchester. Training in Western democratic ideals and practices was ignored out of fear that the recipients might use them as weapons against the ruling authorities.

The fundamental weakness of colonialism, then, was that it was ultimately based on the self-interests of the citizens of the colonial powers. Where those interests collided with the needs of the colonial peoples, those of the former always triumphed. The ultimate result was to deprive the colonial peoples of the right to make their own choices about their own destiny.

The continent of Africa and southern Asia were not the only areas of the world that were buffeted by the winds of Western expansionism in the late nineteenth century. The nations of eastern Asia, and those of Latin America and the Middle East as well, were also affected in significant ways. The consequences of Western political, economic, and military penetration varied substantially from one region to another, however, and therefore require separate treatment. The experience of East Asia will be dealt with in the next chapter. That of Latin America and the Middle East will be discussed in Chapter 23.

IMPERIALISM: THE BALANCE SHEET

INTERACTION & EXCHANGE

Few periods of history are as controversial among scholars and casual observers as the era of imperialism. To defenders of the colonial enterprise like the poet Rudyard Kipling, imperialism was the "white man's burden," a disagreeable but necessary phase in the evolution of human society, lifting up the toiling races from tradition to modernity and bringing an end to poverty, famine, and disease (see the box on p. 449).

Critics took exception to such views, portraying imperialism as a tragedy of major proportions. The insatiable drive of the advanced economic powers for access to raw materials and markets created an exploitative environment that transformed the vast majority of colonial peoples into a permanent underclass, while restricting the benefits of modern technology to a privileged few. Kipling's "white man's burden"

was dismissed as a hypocritical gesture to hoodwink the naive and salve the guilty feelings of those who recognized imperialism for what it was—a savage act of rape.

Defenders of the colonial experiment sometimes concede that there were gross inequities in the colonial system but point out that there was a positive side to the experience as well. The expansion of markets and the beginnings of a modern transportation and communications network, while bringing few immediate benefits to the colonial peoples, laid the groundwork for future economic growth. At the same time, the introduction of new ways of looking at human freedom, the relationship between the individual and society, and democratic principles set the stage for the adoption of such ideas after the restoration of independence following World War II. Finally, the colonial experience offered a new approach to the traditional relationship between men and women. Although colonial rule was by no means uniformly beneficial to the position of women in African and Asian societies, growing awareness of the struggle for equality by women in the West offered their counterparts in the colonial territories a weapon to fight against the long-standing barriers of custom and legal discrimination.

How, then, are we to draw up a final balance sheet on the era of Western imperialism? Both sides have good points to make, but perhaps the critics have the best of the argument. Although the colonial authorities sometimes did provide the beginnings of an infrastructure that could eventually serve as the foundation of an advanced industrial society, all too often they sought to prevent the rise of industrial and commercial sectors in their colonies that might provide competition to producers in the home country. Sophisticated, age-old societies that could have been left to respond to the technological revolution in their own way were thus squeezed dry of precious national resources under the false guise of a "civilizing mission." As the sociologist Clifford Geertz remarked in his book *Agricultural Involution: The Processes of Ecological Change in Indonesia,* the tragedy is not that the colonial peoples suffered through the colonial era but that they suffered for nothing.

Courtesy of William J. Duiker

Gateway to India? Built in the Roman imperial style by the British to commemorate the visit to India of King George V and Queen Mary in 1911, the Gateway of India was erected at the water's edge in the harbor of Bombay, India's greatest port city. For thousands of British citizens arriving in India, the Gateway of India was the first view of their new home and a symbol of the power and majesty of the British raj.

CHAPTER NOTES

1. Quoted in J. G. Lockhart and C. M. Wodehouse, *Rhodes* (London, 1963), pp. 69–70.
2. K. Pearson, *National Life from the Standpoint of Science* (London, 1905), p. 184.
3. Quoted in H. Braunschwig, *French Colonialism, 1871–1914* (London, 1961), p. 80.
4. Quoted in G. Garros, *Forceries Humaines* (Paris, 1926), p. 21.
5. Cited in B. Schwartz's review of D. Cannadine's *Ornamentalism: How the British Saw Their Empire, Atlantic,* November 2001, p. 135.

6. Quoted in R. Bartlett, ed., *The Record of American Diplomacy: Documents and Readings in the History of American Foreign Relations* (New York, 1952), p. 385.
7. Quoted in L. Roubaud, *Vietnam: La Tragédie Indochinoise* (Paris, 1926), p. 80.
8. Quoted in T. Pakenham, *The Scramble for Africa* (New York, 1991), p. 13.
9. Quoted in Pakenham, *Scramble for Africa,* p. 182, citing a letter to Queen Victoria dated August 7, 1879.
10. Quoted in P. C. W. Gutkind and I. Wallerstein, eds., *The Political Economy of Contemporary Africa* (Beverly Hills, Calif., 1976), p. 14.

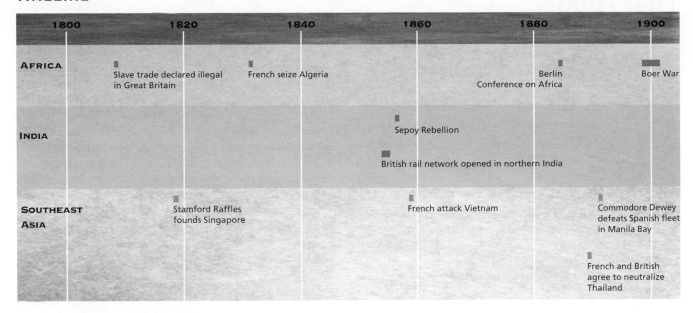

	1800	1820	1840	1860	1880	1900
AFRICA	Slave trade declared illegal in Great Britain	French seize Algeria			Berlin Conference on Africa	Boer War
INDIA				Sepoy Rebellion / British rail network opened in northern India		
SOUTHEAST ASIA		Stamford Raffles founds Singapore		French attack Vietnam	Commodore Dewey defeats Spanish fleet in Manila Bay / French and British agree to neutralize Thailand	

SUGGESTED READING

There are a number of good works on the subject of imperialism and colonialism. For a study that directly focuses on the question of whether colonialism was beneficial to subject peoples, see **D. K. Fieldhouse**, *The West and the Third World: Trade, Colonialism, Dependence, and Development* (Oxford, 1999). Also see **W. Baumgart**, *Imperialism: The Idea and Reality of British and French Colonial Expansion, 1880–1914* (Oxford, 1982), and **D. B. Abernathy**, *Global Dominance: European Overseas Empires, 1415–1980* (New Haven, Conn., 2000). On technology, see **D. R. Headrick**, *The Tentacles of Progress: Technology Transfer in the Age of Imperialism, 1850–1940* (Oxford, 1988). For a defense of the British imperial mission, see **N. Ferguson**, *Empire: The Rise and Demise of the British World Order* (New York, 2003).

On the imperialist age in Africa, above all see **R. Robinson** and **J. Gallagher**, *Africa and the Victorians: The Official Mind of Imperialism* (London, 1961). Also see **B. Vandervoort**, *Wars of Imperial Conquest in Africa, 1830–1914* (Bloomington, Ind., 1998), and two works by **T. Pakenham**, *The Scramble for Africa* (New York, 1991) and *The Boer War* (London, 1979). On southern Africa, see **J. Guy**, *The Destruction of the Zulu Kingdom* (London, 1979), and **D. Nenoon** and **B. Nyeko**, *Southern Africa Since 1800* (London, 1984). Also informative is **R. O. Collins**, ed., *Historical Problems of Imperial Africa* (Princeton, N.J., 1994).

For an overview of the British takeover and administration of India, see **S. Wolpert**, *A New History of India* (New York, 1989). **C. A. Bayly**, *Indian Society and the Making of the British Empire* (Cambridge, 1988), is a scholarly analysis of the impact of British conquest on the Indian economy. Also see **A. Wild's** elegant *East India Company: Trade and Conquest from 1600* (New York, 2000). For a comparative approach, see **R. Murphey**, *The Outsiders: The Western Experience in China and India* (Ann Arbor, Mich., 1977). In a provocative work, *Ornamentalism: How the British Saw Their Empire* (Oxford, 2000), **D. Cannadine** argues that it was class and not race that motivated British policy in the subcontinent.

General studies of the colonial period in Southeast Asia are rare because most authors focus on specific areas. For some stimulating essays on a variety of aspects of the topic, see *Continuity and Change in Southeast Asia: Collected Journal Articles of Harry J. Benda* (New

Haven, Conn., 1972). For an overview by several authors, see **N. Tarling**, ed., *The Cambridge History of Southeast Asia*, vol. 3 (Cambridge, 1992).

For an introduction to the effects of colonialism on women in Africa and Asia, see **S. Hughes** and **B. Hughes**, *Women in World History*, vol. 2 (Armonk, N.Y., 1997). Also consult the classic by **E. Boserup**, *Women's Role in Economic Development* (London, 1970); **J. Taylor**, *The Social World of Batavia* (Madison, Wis., 1983); and **L. Ahmed**, *Women and Gender in Islam* (New Haven, Conn., 1992).

InfoTrac College Edition

Visit this chapter's InfoTrac College Edition/Research activities at the *Essential World History* Companion Website for activities related to imperialism.

ThomsonNOW™ for Duiker and Spielvogel's *The Essential World History, Third Edition*

Enter *ThomsonNOW* using the access card that is available with this text. *ThomsonNOW* will assist you in understanding the content in this chapter with lesson plans generated for your needs, as well as provide you with a connection to the *Wadsworth World History Resource Center* (see description below for details).

WORLD HISTORY
RESOURCE CENTER

Enter the Resource Center using either your *ThomsonNOW* access card or your standalone access card for the *Wadsworth World History Resource Center*. Organized by topic, this website includes quizzes; images; over 350 primary source documents; interactive simulations, maps, and timelines; movie explorations; and a wealth of other resources. You can read the following documents, and many more, at http://worldrc.wadsworth.com/

J. A. Hobson, *Imperialism: A Study*

Henry Morton Stanley, *How I Found Livingstone*

Visit the *Essential World History* Companion Website for chapter quizzes and more:

http://www.thomsonedu.com/history/duiker

DISCOVERY

What were the consequences of the new imperialism of the nineteenth century for the colonies and the colonial powers? How do you feel the imperialist countries should be evaluated in terms of their motives and stated objectives?

In thinking about this question, begin by breaking it down into the components shown below. A discussion of the significance of each component should appear in your answer.

POLITICS AND GOVERNMENT: Why did European nations want more colonies? Looking at the map of Africa, think about why France would have benefited from its geographically concentrated colonies.

Look at Kipling's poem and Morel's excerpt. Why might nationalism have been a reason that European countries were again interested in acquiring colonies at the end of the nineteenth century? What is "the white man's burden"? Do you think the "civilizing missions" portrayed in the poem are examples of nationalism? According to Morel, why did colonialism "kill the soul in a people"? Do you agree with his statement that such harm "transcends physical murder"?

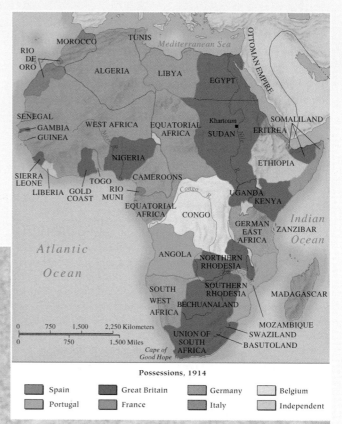

Possessions, 1914

Spain | Great Britain | Germany | Belgium
Portugal | France | Italy | Independent

Africa in 1914

WHITE MAN'S BURDEN, BLACK MAN'S SORROW

Rudyard Kipling, *The White Man's Burden*

Take up the White Man's burden—
Send forth the best ye breed—
Go bind your sons to exile
To serve your captives' need;
To wait in heavy harness,
On fluttered folk and wild—
Your new-caught sullen peoples,
Half-devil and half-child.

Take up the White Man's burden—
In patience to abide,
To veil the threat of terror
And check the show of pride;
By open speech and simple,
An hundred times made plain
To seek another's profit,
And work another's gain.

Take up the White Man's burden—
The savage wars of peace—
Fill full the mouth of Famine
And bid the sickness cease;
And when your goal is nearest
The end for others sought,
Watch Sloth and heathen Folly
Bring all your hopes to nought.

Edmund Morel, *The Black Man's Burden*

It is [the Africans] who carry the "Black man's burden." They have not withered away before the white man's occupation. Indeed . . . Africa has ultimately absorbed within itself every Caucasian and, for that matter, every Semitic invader, too. In hewing out for himself a fixed abode in Africa, the white man has massacred the African in heaps. The African has survived, and it is well for the white settlers that he has. . . .

What the partial occupation of his soil by the white man has failed to do; what the mapping out of European political "spheres of influence" has failed to do; what the Maxim and the rifle, the slave gang, labour in the bowels of the earth and the lash, have failed to do; what imported measles, smallpox and syphilis have failed to do; whatever the overseas slave trade failed to do; the power of modern capitalistic exploitation, assisted by modern engines of destruction, may yet succeed in accomplishing.

For from the evils of the latter, scientifically applied and enforced, there is no escape for the African. Its destructive effects are not spasmodic; they are permanent. In its permanence resides its fatal consequences. It kills not the body merely, but the soul. It breaks the spirit. It attacks the African at every turn, from every point of vantage. It wrecks his polity, uproots him from the land, invades his family life, destroys his natural pursuits and occupations, claims his whole time, enslaves him in his own home.

SCIENCE AND TECHNOLOGY: For what reason were plantations and transportation improvements made in the colonies? Who benefited? What role did colonists play in these economic endeavors? How did colonial economies impede the economic development of colonies? How has this colonial economic system continued to the present? How might the economic system create tensions between former colonies and Western nations?

A Rubber Plantation

The Opening of the Suez Canal

ARTS AND IDEAS: How do the images below convey cultural and political superiority? What does this underlying message reveal about European views of colonial peoples? How would these views affect the way they choose to rule colonies? To what degree do these ideas continue today?

The document reveals European views of Muslim society and ideas. How critical was the European view of Muslim society? Upon what was this assessment based? Compare the role of women in Europe in the nineteenth century with that of women in Muslim countries. Is it possible to measure whether one culture is "better" than another?

The Company Resident and His Puppet

Revere the Conquering Heroes

QASSIM AMIN, *THE LIBERATION OF WOMEN*

European civilization advances with the speed of steam and electricity, and has even overspilled to every part of the globe so that there is not an inch that he [European man] has not trodden underfoot. Any place he goes he takes control of its resources . . . and turns them into profit . . . and if he does harm to the original inhabitants, it is only that he pursues happiness in this world and seeks it wherever he may find it . . . . For the most part he uses his intellect, but when circumstances require it, he deploys force. He does not seek glory from his possessions and colonies, for he has enough of this through his intellectual achievements and scientific inventions. What drives the Englishman to dwell in India and the French in Algeria. . . . is profit and the desire to acquire resources in countries where the inhabitants do not know their value or how to profit from them.

When they encounter savages they eliminate them or drive them from the land, as happened in America . . . and is happening now in Africa. . . . When they encounter a nation like ours, with a degree of civilization, with a past, and a religion . . . and customs and . . . institutions . . . they deal with its inhabitants kindly. But they do soon acquire its most valuable resources, because they have greater wealth and intellect and knowledge and force. . . . [The veil constituted] a huge barrier between woman and her elevation, and consequently a barrier between the nation and its advance.

21

SHADOWS OVER THE PACIFIC: EAST ASIA UNDER CHALLENGE

CHAPTER OUTLINE AND FOCUS QUESTIONS

The Decline of the Manchus

▢ Why did the Qing dynasty decline and ultimately collapse, and what role did the Western powers play in this process?

Chinese Society in Transition

▢ What political, economic, and social reforms were instituted by the Qing dynasty during its final decades, and why were they not more successful in reversing the decline of Manchu rule?

A Rich Country and a Strong State: The Rise of Modern Japan

▢ To what degree was the Meiji Restoration a "revolution," and to what degree did it succeed in transforming Japan?

CRITICAL THINKING

▢ How did China and Japan each respond to Western pressures in the nineteenth century, and what implication did their different responses have for each nation's history?

The Opium War begins

National Maritime Museum, London

$\mathscr{T}$HE BRITISH EMISSARY Lord Macartney had arrived in Beijing in 1793 with a caravan loaded with six hundred cases of gifts for the emperor. Flags and banners provided by the Chinese proclaimed in Chinese characters that the visitor was an "ambassador bearing tribute from the country of England." But the tribute was in vain, for Macartney's request for an increase in trade between the two countries was flatly rejected, and he left Beijing in October with nothing to show for his efforts. Not until half a century later would the Qing dynasty—at the point of a gun—agree to the British demand for an expansion of commercial ties.

In fact, the Chinese emperor Qianlong had responded to the requests of his visitor with polite but poorly disguised condescension. To Macartney's proposal that a British ambassador be stationed in the capital of Beijing, the emperor replied that such a request was "not in harmony with the state system of our dynasty and will definitely not be permitted." As for the British envoy's suggestion that regular trade relations be established between the two countries, that proposal was also rejected. We receive all sorts of precious things, replied the Celestial Emperor, as gifts from the myriad nations. "Consequently," he added, "there is nothing we lack, as your principal envoy and others have themselves observed. We have never set much store on strange or ingenious objects, nor do we need more of your country's manufactures."

Historians have often viewed the failure of the Macartney mission as a reflection of the disdain of Chinese rulers toward their counterparts in other countries and their serene confidence in the superiority of Chinese civilization in a world inhabited by barbarians. If that was the case, Qianlong's confidence was misplaced, for as the eighteenth century came to an end, the country faced a growing challenge from the escalating power and ambitions of the West. When insistent British demands for the right to carry out trade and missionary activities in China were rejected, Britain resorted to force and in the Opium War, which broke out in 1839, gave Manchu troops a sound thrashing. A humiliated China was finally forced to open its doors. ◇

The Decline of the Manchus

In 1800, the Qing (Ch'ing) or Manchu dynasty was at the height of its power. China had experienced a long period of peace and prosperity under the rule of two great emperors, Kangxi and Qianlong. Its borders were secure, and its culture and intellectual achievements were the envy of the world. Its rulers, hidden behind the walls of the Forbidden City in Beijing, had every reason to describe their patrimony as the "Central Kingdom." But a little over a century later, humiliated and harassed by the black ships and big guns of the Western powers, the Qing dynasty, the last in a series that had endured for more than two thousand years, collapsed in the dust (see Map 21.1).

Historians once assumed that the primary reason for the rapid decline and fall of the Manchu dynasty was the intense pressure applied to a proud but somewhat complacent traditional society by the modern West. Now, however, most historians believe that internal changes played a major role in the dynasty's collapse and point out that at least some of the problems suffered by the Manchus during the nineteenth century were self-inflicted.

MAP 21.1 **The Qing Empire.** Shown here is the Qing Empire at the height of its power in the late eighteenth century, together with its shrunken boundaries at the moment of dissolution in 1911. ❓ How do China's tributary states on this map differ from those in Map 16.2? ◉ **View an animated version of this map or related maps at** http://worldrc.wadsworth.com/

Both explanations have some validity. Like so many of its predecessors, after an extended period of growth, the Qing dynasty began to suffer from the familiar dynastic ills of official corruption, peasant unrest, and incompetence at court. Such weaknesses were probably exacerbated by the rapid growth in population. The long era of peace and stability, the introduction of new crops from the Americas, and the cultivation of new, fast-ripening strains of rice enabled the Chinese population to double between 1550 and 1800. The population continued to grow, reaching the unprecedented level of 400 million by the end of the nineteenth century. Even without the irritating presence of the Western powers, the Manchus were probably destined to repeat the fate of their imperial predecessors. The ships, guns, and ideas of the foreigners simply highlighted the growing weakness of the Manchu dynasty and likely hastened its demise. In doing so, Western imperialism still exerted an indelible impact on the history of modern China—but as a contributing, not a causal, factor.

Opium and Rebellion

By 1800, Westerners had been in contact with China for more than two hundred years, but after an initial period of flourishing relations, Western traders had been limited to a small commercial outlet at Canton. This arrangement was not acceptable to the British, however. Not only did they chafe at being restricted to a tiny enclave, but the growing British appetite for Chinese tea created a severe balance-of-payments problem. After the failure of the Macartney mission in 1793, another mission, led by Lord Amherst, arrived in China in 1816. But it too achieved little except to worsen the already strained relations between the two countries. The British solution was opium. A product more addictive than tea, opium was grown in northeastern India and then shipped to China. Opium had been grown in southwestern China for

several hundred years but had been used primarily for medicinal purposes. Now, as imports increased, popular demand for the product in southern China became insatiable despite an official prohibition on its use. Soon bullion was flowing out of the Chinese imperial treasury into the pockets of British merchants.

The Chinese became concerned and tried to negotiate. In 1839, Lin Zexu (Lin Tse-hsu; 1785–1850), a Chinese official appointed by the court to curtail the opium trade, appealed to Queen Victoria on both moral and practical grounds and threatened to prohibit the sale of rhubarb (widely used as a laxative in nineteenth-century Europe) to Great Britain if she did not respond (see the box on p. 471). But moral principles, then as now, paled before the lure of commercial profits, and the British continued to promote the opium trade, arguing that if the Chinese did not want the opium, they did not have to buy it. Lin Zexu attacked on three fronts, imposing penalties on smokers, arresting dealers, and seizing supplies from importers as they attempted to smuggle the drug into China. The last tactic caused his downfall. When he blockaded the foreign factory area in Canton to force traders to hand over their remaining chests of opium, the British government, claiming that it could not permit British subjects "to be exposed to insult and injustice," launched a naval expedition to punish the Manchus and force the court to open China to foreign trade.[1]

The Opium War The Opium War (1839–1842) lasted three years and demonstrated the superiority of British firepower and military tactics (including the use of a shallow-draft steamboat that effectively harassed Chinese coastal defenses). British warships destroyed Chinese coastal and river forts and seized the offshore island of Chusan, not far from the mouth of the Yangtze River. When a British fleet sailed virtually unopposed up the

The Opium War. The Opium War, waged between China and Great Britain between 1839 and 1842, was China's first conflict with a European power. Lacking modern military technology, the Chinese suffered a humiliating defeat. In this painting, heavily armed British steamships destroy unwieldy Chinese junks along the Chinese coast. China's humiliation at sea was a legacy of its rulers' lack of interest in maritime matters since the middle of the fifteenth century, when Chinese junks were among the most advanced sailing ships in the world.

A LETTER OF ADVICE TO THE QUEEN

INTERACTION & EXCHANGE

Lin Zexu was the Chinese imperial commissioner in Canton at the time of the Opium War. Prior to the conflict, he attempted to use reason and the threat of retaliation to persuade the British to cease importing opium illegally into southern China. The following excerpt is from a letter that he wrote to Queen Victoria. In it, he appeals to her conscience while showing the condescension that the Chinese traditionally displayed to the rulers of other countries.

How does the imperial commissioner seek to persuade Queen Victoria to prohibit the sale of opium in China? To what degree are his arguments persuasive?

Lin Zexu, Letter to Queen Victoria

The kings of your honorable country by a tradition handed down from generation to generation have always been noted for their politeness and submissiveness. . . . Privately we are delighted with the way in which the honorable rulers of your country deeply understand the grand principles and are grateful for the Celestial grace. . . . The profit from trade has been enjoyed by them continuously for two hundred years. This is the source from which your country has become known for its wealth.

But after a long period of commercial intercourse, there appear among the crowd of barbarians both good persons and bad, unevenly. Consequently there are those who smuggle opium to seduce the Chinese people and so cause the spread of the poison to all provinces. . . .

The wealth of China is used to profit the barbarians. That is to say, the great profit made by barbarians is all taken from the rightful share of China. By what right do they then in return use the poisonous drug to injure the Chinese people? . . . Let us ask, where is your conscience? I have heard that the smoking of opium is very strictly forbidden by your country; that is because the harm caused by opium is clearly understood. Since it is not permitted to do harm to your own country, then even less should you let it be passed on to the harm of other countries—how much less to China! Of all that China exports to foreign countries, there is not a single thing which is not beneficial to people. . . . Is there a single article from China which has done any harm to foreign countries? Take tea and rhubarb, for example; the foreign countries cannot get along for a single day without them. . . . On the other hand, articles coming from the outside to China can only be used as toys. We can take them or get along without them. Nevertheless our Celestial Court lets tea, silk, and other goods be shipped without limit and circulated everywhere without begrudging it in the slightest. This is for no other reason but to share the benefit with the people of the whole world. . . .

May you, O King, check your wicked and sift your vicious people before they come to China, in order to guarantee the peace of your nation, to show further the sincerity of your politeness and submissiveness, and to let the two countries enjoy together the blessings of peace. . . . After receiving this dispatch will you immediately give us a prompt reply regarding the details and circumstances of your cutting off the opium traffic. Be sure not to put this off.

ThomsonNOW To read a full version of this document, enter the *ThomsonNOW* documents area using the access card that is available for *The Essential World History.*

Yangtze to Nanjing and cut off the supply of "tribute grain" from southern to northern China, the Qing finally agreed to British terms. In the Treaty of Nanjing in 1842, the Chinese agreed to open five coastal ports to British trade, limit tariffs on imported British goods, grant extraterritorial rights to British citizens in China, and pay a substantial indemnity to cover the costs of the war. China also agreed to cede the island of Hong Kong (dismissed by a senior British official as a "barren rock") to Great Britain. Nothing was said in the treaty about the opium trade, which continued unabated until it was brought under control through Chinese government efforts in the early twentieth century.

Although the Opium War has traditionally been considered the beginning of modern Chinese history, it is unlikely that many Chinese at the time would have seen it that way. This was not the first time that a ruling dynasty had been forced to make concessions to foreigners, and the opening of five coastal ports to the British hardly constituted a serious threat to the security of the empire. Although a few concerned Chinese argued that the court should learn more about European civilization, others contended that China had nothing to learn from the barbarians and that borrowing foreign ways would undercut the purity of Confucian civilization.

For the time being, the Manchus attempted to deal with the problem in the traditional way of playing the foreigners off against each other. Concessions granted to the British were offered to other Western nations, including the United States, and soon thriving foreign concession areas were operating in treaty ports along the southern Chinese coast from Canton to Shanghai.

The Taiping Rebellion In the meantime, the Qing court's failure to deal with pressing internal economic problems led to a major peasant revolt that shook the foundations of the empire. On the surface, the Taiping (T'ai p'ing) Rebellion owed something to the Western incursion; the leader of the uprising, Hong Xiuquan (Hung Hsiu-ch'uan), a failed examination candidate, was a Christian convert who viewed himself as a younger brother of Jesus and hoped to establish what

The Taiping Rebellion

he referred to as a "Heavenly Kingdom of Supreme Peace" in China. But there were many local causes as well. The rapid increase in population forced millions of peasants to eke out a living as sharecroppers or landless laborers. Official corruption and incompetence led to the whipsaw of increased taxes and a decline in government services; even the Grand Canal was allowed to silt up, hindering the shipment of grain. In 1853, the rebels seized the old Ming capital of Nanjing, but that proved to be the rebellion's high-water mark. Plagued by factionalism, the rebellion gradually lost momentum until it was finally suppressed in 1864.

One reason for the dynasty's failure to deal effectively with the internal unrest was its continuing difficulties with the Western imperialists. In 1856, the British and the French, still smarting from trade restrictions and limitations on their missionary activities, launched a new series of attacks against China and seized Beijing in 1860. As punishment, British troops destroyed the imperial summer palace just outside the city. In the ensuing Treaty of Tianjin (Tientsin), the Qing agreed to humiliating new concessions: the legalization of the opium trade, the opening of additional ports to foreign trade, and the cession of the peninsula of Kowloon (opposite the island of Hong Kong) to the British (see Map 21.2). Additional territories in the north were ceded to Russia.

Efforts at Reform

By the late 1870s, the old dynasty was well on the road to internal disintegration. In fending off the Taiping Rebellion, the Manchus had been compelled to rely for support on armed forces under regional command. After quelling the revolt, many of these regional

commanders refused to disband their units and, with the support of the local gentry, continued to collect local taxes for their own use. The dreaded pattern of imperial breakdown, so familiar in Chinese history, was beginning to appear once again.

In its weakened state, the court finally began to listen to the appeals of reform-minded officials, who called for a new policy of **"self-strengthening,"** in which Western technology would be adopted while Confucian principles and institutions were maintained intact. This policy, popularly known by its slogan "East for Essence, West for Practical Use," remained the guiding standard for Chinese foreign and domestic policy for nearly a quarter of a century. Some even called for reforms in education and in China's hallowed political institutions. Pointing to the power and prosperity of Great Britain, the journalist Wang Tao (Wang T'ao, 1828–1897) remarked, "The real strength of England . . . lies in the fact that there is a sympathetic understanding between the governing and the governed, a close relationship between the ruler and the people. . . . My observation is that the daily domestic political life of England actually embodies the traditional ideals of our ancient Golden Age."[2] Such democratic ideas were too radical for most reformers, however. One of the leading court officials of the day, Zhang Zhidong (Chang Chih-tung), countered:

> The doctrine of people's rights will bring us not a single benefit but a hundred evils. Are we going to establish a parliament? . . . Even supposing the confused and clamorous

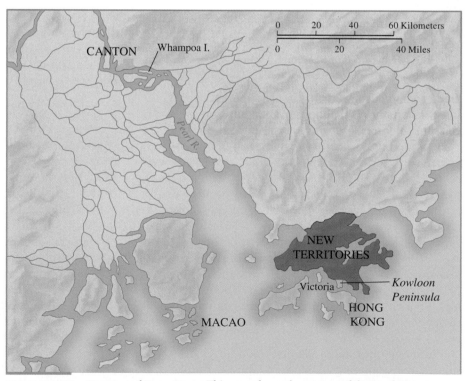

MAP 21.2 **Canton and Hong Kong.** This map shows the estuary of the Pearl River in southern China, an important area of early contact between China and Europe. ❓ What was the importance of Canton? What were the New Territories, and when were they annexed by the British?

people are assembled in one house, for every one of them who is clear-sighted, there will be a hundred others whose vision is beclouded; they will converse at random and talk as if in a dream—what use will it be?[3]

The Climax of Imperialism For the time being, Zhang Zhidong's arguments won the day. During the last quarter of the century, the Manchus attempted to modernize their military establishment and build up an industrial base without disturbing the essential elements of traditional Chinese civilization. Railroads, weapons arsenals, and shipyards were built, but the value system remained essentially unchanged.

In the end, the results spoke for themselves. During the last two decades of the nineteenth century, the European penetration of China, both political and military, intensified. Rapacious imperialists began to bite off the outer edges of the Qing Empire (see Map 21.1). The Gobi Desert north of the Great Wall, Central Asia, and Tibet, all inhabited by non-Chinese peoples and never fully assimilated into the Chinese Empire, were gradually lost. In the north and northwest, the main beneficiary was Russia, which took advantage of the dynasty's weakness to force the cession of territories north of the Amur River in Siberia. In Tibet, competition between Russia and Great Britain prevented either power from seizing the territory outright but at the same time enabled Tibetan authorities to revive local autonomy never recognized by the Chinese. In the south, British and French advances in mainland Southeast Asia removed Burma and Vietnam from their traditional vassal relationship to the Manchu court. Even more ominous were the foreign spheres of influence in the Chinese heartland, where local commanders were willing to sell exclusive commercial, railroad-building, or mining privileges.

The breakup of the Manchu dynasty accelerated at the end of the nineteenth century. In 1894, the Qing went to war with Japan over Japanese incursions into the Korean peninsula, which threatened China's long-held suzerainty over the area (see "Joining the Imperialist Club" later in this chapter). To the surprise of many observers, the Chinese were roundly defeated, confirming to some critics the devastating failure of the policy of self-strengthening by halfway measures. The disintegration of China accelerated in 1897, when Germany, a new entry in the race for spoils in East Asia, used the pretext of the murder of two German missionaries by Chinese rioters to demand the cession of territories in the Shandong (Shantung) peninsula. The approval of the demand by the imperial court set off a scramble for territory by other interested powers (see Map 21.3). Russia now demanded the Liaodong peninsula with its ice-free port at Port Arthur, and Great Britain weighed in with a request for a coaling station in northern China.

The government responded to the challenge with yet another effort at reform. In the spring of 1898, an outspoken advocate of change, the progressive Confucian scholar Kang Youwei (K'ang Yu-wei), won the support of the young Guangxu (Kuang Hsu) emperor for a comprehensive reform program patterned after recent measures in Japan. Without change, Kang argued, China would perish. During the next several weeks, the emperor issued edicts calling for major political, administrative, and educational reforms. Not surprisingly, Kang's proposals were opposed by many conservatives, who saw little advantage and much risk in copying the West. More important, the

MAP 21.3 **Foreign Possessions and Spheres of Influence About 1900.** At the end of the nineteenth century, China was being carved up like a melon by foreign imperialist powers. **?** Which of the areas marked on the map were removed from Chinese control during the nineteenth century?

🌐 **View an animated version of this map or related maps at** http://worldrc.wadsworth.com/

PROGRAM FOR A NEW CHINA

POLITICS & GOVERNMENT

In 1905, Sun Yat-sen united a number of anti-Manchu groups into a single patriotic organization called the Revolutionary Alliance (Tongmenghui). The new organization eventually formed the core of his *Guomindang*, or Nationalist Party. This excerpt is from the organization's manifesto, published in 1905 in Tokyo. Note that Sun believed that the Chinese people were not ready for democracy and required a period of tutelage to prepare them for the final era of constitutional political government. This was a formula that would be adopted by many other political leaders in Asia and Africa after World War II.

What are Sun Yat-sen's key proposals to transform China into a modern, technologically based society? How would you compare his program with the so-called Meiji reforms in Japan, discussed later in this chapter?

Sun Yat-sen, *Manifesto for the Tongmenghui*

By order of the Military Government, . . . the Commander-in-Chief of the Chinese National Army proclaims the purposes and platform of the Military Government to the people of the nation:

Therefore we proclaim to the world in utmost sincerity the outline of the present revolution and the fundamental plan for the future administration of the nation.

1. *Drive out the Tartars:* The Manchus of today were originally the eastern barbarians beyond the Great Wall. They frequently caused border troubles during the Ming dynasty; then when China was in a disturbed state they came inside Shanhaikuan, conquered China, and enslaved our Chinese people. . . . The extreme cruelties and tyrannies of the Manchu government have now reached their limit. With the righteous army poised against them, we will overthrow that government, and restore our sovereign rights.
2. *Restore China:* China is the China of the Chinese. The government of China should be in the hands of the Chinese. After driving out the Tartars we must restore our national state. . . .
3. *Establish the Republic:* Now our revolution is based on equality, in order to establish a republican

government. All our people are equal and all enjoy political rights. . . .
4. *Equalize land ownership:* The good fortune of civilization is to be shared equally by all the people of the nation. We should improve our social and economic organization, and assess the value of all the land in the country. Its present price shall be received by the owner, but all increases in value resulting from reform and social improvements after the revolution shall belong to the state, to be shared by all the people, in order to create a socialist state, where each family within the empire can be well supported, each person satisfied, and no one fail to secure employment. . . .

The above four points will be carried out in three steps in due order. The first period is government by military law. When the righteous army has arisen, various places will join the cause. . . . Evils like the oppression of the government, the greed and graft of officials, . . . the cruelty of tortures and penalties, the tyranny of tax collections, the humiliation of the queue [the requirement that all Chinese males braid their hair]—shall all be exterminated together with the Manchu rule. Evils in social customs, such as the keeping of slaves, the cruelty of foot binding, the spread of the poison of opium, should also all be prohibited. . . .

The second period is that of government by a provisional constitution. When military law is lifted in each *hsien* [district], the Military Government shall return the right of self-government to the local people. . . .

The third period will be government under the constitution. Six years after the provisional constitution has been enforced a constitution shall be made. The military and administrative powers of the Military Government shall be annulled; the people shall elect the president, and elect the members of parliament to organize the parliament.

ThomsonNOW To read Sun Yat-sen's *Principles of National Reconstruction,* enter the *ThomsonNOW* documents area using the access card that is available for *The Essential World History.*

The Revolution of 1911   In October 1911, Sun's followers launched an uprising in the industrial center of Wuhan, in central China. With Sun traveling in the United States, the insurrection lacked leadership, but the decrepit government's inability to react quickly encouraged political forces at the provincial level to take measures into their own hands. The dynasty was now in a state of virtual collapse: the empress dowager had died in 1908, one day after her nephew; the throne was now occupied by China's "last emperor," the infant Puyi (P'u Yi). Sun's party had neither the military strength nor the political base necessary to

seize the initiative, however, and was forced to turn to a representative of the old order, General Yuan Shikai (Yuan Shih-k'ai). A prominent figure in military circles since the beginning of the century, Yuan had been placed in charge of the imperial forces sent to suppress the rebellion, but now he abandoned the Manchus and acted on his own behalf. In negotiations with representatives of Sun Yat-sen's party (Sun himself had arrived in China in January 1912), he agreed to serve as president of a new Chinese republic. The old dynasty and the age-old system that it had attempted to preserve were no more.

Lord Macartney's mission to China	1793
Opium War	1839–1842
Taiping rebels seize Nanjing	1853
Taiping Rebellion suppressed	1864
Cixi becomes regent for nephew, the Guangxu emperor	1878
Sino-Japanese War	1894–1895
One Hundred Days reform	1898
Open Door policy	1899
Boxer Rebellion	1900
Commission to study constitution formed	1905
Deaths of Cixi and the Guangxu emperor	1908
Revolution in China	1911

Although the dynasty was gone, Sun and his followers were unable to consolidate their gains. The program of the Revolutionary Alliance was based on Western liberal democratic principles aimed at the urban middle class, but the middle class in China was still too small to form the basis for a new political order. The vast majority of the Chinese people still lived on the land. Sun had hoped to win their support with a land reform program, but few peasants had participated in the 1911 revolution. In failing to create new institutions and values to provide a framework for a changing society, the events of 1911 were less a revolution than a collapse of the old order. Weakened by imperialism and its own internal weaknesses, the old dynasty had come to an abrupt end before new political and social forces were ready to fill the vacuum.

What China had experienced was part of a historical process that was bringing down traditional empires across the globe, both in regions threatened by Western imperialism and in Europe itself, where tsarist Russia, the Austro-Hungarian Empire, and the Ottoman Empire all came to an end within a few years after the collapse of the Qing. The circumstances of their demise were not all the same. The Austro-Hungarian Empire, for example, was dismembered by the victorious allies after World War I, and the fate of tsarist Russia was directly linked to that conflict. Still, all four regimes shared the responsibility for their common fate in that they had failed to meet the challenges posed by the times. All had responded to the forces of industrialization and popular participation in the political process with hesitation and reluctance, and their attempts at reform were too little and too late. All paid the supreme price for their folly.

Chinese Society in Transition

The growing Western presence in China during the late nineteenth and early twentieth centuries obviously had a major impact on Chinese society; hence many historians have asserted that the arrival of the Europeans shook China out of centuries of slumber and launched it on the road to revolutionary change. In fact, when the European economic penetration began to accelerate in the mid-nineteenth century, Chinese society was already in a state of transition. The growth of industry and trade was particularly noticeable in the cities, where a national market for such commodities as oil, copper, salt, tea, and porcelain had developed. The foundation of an infrastructure more conducive to the rise of a money economy appeared to be in place. In the countryside, new crops introduced from abroad significantly increased food production and aided population growth. The Chinese economy had never been more productive or more complex.

Obstacles to Industrialization

Whether these changes by themselves would eventually have led to an industrial revolution and the rise of a capitalist society on the Western model in the absence of Western intervention is a question that historians cannot answer. Certainly, a number of obstacles would have made it difficult for China to embark on the Western path if it had wished to do so.

Although industrial production was on the rise, it was still based almost entirely on traditional methods. There was no uniform system of weights and measures, and the banking system was still primitive by European standards. The use of paper money, invented by the Chinese centuries earlier, had essentially been abandoned. The transportation system, which had been neglected since the end of the Yuan dynasty, was increasingly chaotic. There were few paved roads, and the Grand Canal, long the most efficient means of carrying goods from north to south, was silting up. As a result, merchants had to rely more and more on the coastal route, where they faced increasing competition from foreign shipping.

Although foreign concession areas in the coastal cities provided a conduit for the importation of Western technology and modern manufacturing methods, the Chinese borrowed less than they might have. Foreign manufacturing enterprises could not legally operate in China until the last decade of the nineteenth century, and their methods had little influence beyond the concession areas. Chinese efforts to imitate Western methods, notably in shipbuilding and weapons manufacture, were dominated by the government and often suffered from mismanagement.

Equally serious problems persisted in the countryside. The rapid increase in population had led to smaller plots and burgeoning numbers of tenant farmers. Whether per capita consumption of food was on the decline is not clear from the available evidence, but apparently rice as a staple of the diet was increasingly being replaced by less nutritious foods. Some farmers benefited from switching to commercial agriculture to supply the markets of the growing coastal cities, but the shift entailed a sizable investment. Many farmers went so deeply into debt that they eventually lost their land.

"IN THE BEGINNING, WE WERE THE SUN"

FAMILY & SOCIETY

One aspect of Western thought that the Meiji reformers did not seek to imitate was the idea of sexual equality. Although Japanese women sometimes tried to be "modern" like their male counterparts, Japanese society as a whole continued to treat women differently, as had been the case during the Tokugawa era. In 1911, a young woman named Hiratsuka Raicho founded a journal named *Seito (Blue Stockings)* to promote the liberation of women in Japan. The goal of the new movement was to encourage women to develop their own latent talents, rather than to demand legal changes in Japanese society. The following document is the proclamation that was issued at the creation of the Seito Society. Compare it to Mary Wollstonecraft's discussion of the rights of women in Chapter 17.

What, in the author's view, was necessary to bring about the liberation of women in Meiji Japan? Were her proposals similar to those set forth by her counterparts in the West?

Hiratsuka Raicho, Proclamation at the Founding of the Seito Society

Freedom and Liberation! Oftentimes we have heard the term "liberation of women." But what is it then? Are we not seriously misunderstanding the term freedom or liberation? Even if we call the problem the liberation of women, are there not many other issues involved? Assuming that women are freed from external oppression, liberated from constraint, given the so-called higher education, employed in various occupations, given the franchise, and provided an opportunity to be independent from the protection of their parents and husbands, and to be freed from the little confinement of their homes, can all of these be called liberation of women? They may provide proper surroundings and opportunities to let us fulfill the true goal of liberation. Yet they remain merely the means, and do not represent our goal or ideals.

However, I am unlike many intellectuals in Japan who suggest that higher education is not necessary for women. Men and women are endowed by nature to have equal faculties. Therefore, it is odd to assume that one of the sexes requires education while the other does not. This may be tolerated in a given country and in a given age, but it is fundamentally a very unsound proposition.

I bemoan the facts that there is only one private college for women in Japan, and that there is no tolerance on man's part to permit entrance of women into many universities maintained for men. However, what benefit is there when the intellectual level of women becomes similar to that of men? Men seek knowledge in order to escape from their lack of wisdom and lack of enlightenment. They want to free themselves. . . . Yet multifarious thought can darken true wisdom, and lead men away from nature. . . .

Now, what is the true liberation which I am seeking? It is none other than to provide an opportunity for women to develop fully their hidden talents and hidden abilities. We must remove all the hindrances that stand in the way of women's development, whether they be external oppression or lack of knowledge. And above and beyond these factors, we must realize that we are the masters in possession of great talents, for we are the bodies which enshrine the great talents.

ThomsonNOW To read a different view of women in Japan, enter the *ThomsonNOW* documents area using the access card that is available for *The Essential World History*.

---

arena. Their territory was small, lacking in resources, and densely populated, and they had no natural outlet for expansion. To observant Japanese, the lessons of history were clear. Western nations had amassed wealth and power not only because of their democratic systems and high level of education but also because of their colonies.

The Japanese began their program of territorial expansion close to home (see Map 21.4). In 1874, after a brief conflict with China, Japan was able to claim suzerainty over the Ryukyu Islands, long tributary to the Chinese Empire. Two years later, Japanese naval pressure forced Korea to open three ports to Japanese commerce.

During the early decades of the nineteenth century, Korea had followed Japan's example and attempted to isolate itself from outside contact except for periodic tribute missions to China. Christian missionaries, mostly Chinese or French, were vigorously persecuted. But Korea's problems were basically internal. In the early 1860s, a peasant revolt, inspired in part by the Taiping Rebellion in China, caused considerable devastation before being crushed in 1864. In succeeding years, the Yi dynasty sought to strengthen the country by returning to traditional values and fending off outside intrusion, but rural poverty and official corruption remained rampant. A U.S. fleet, following the example of Commodore Perry in Japan, sought to open the country in 1871 but was driven off with considerable loss of life.

Korea's most persistent suitor, however, was Japan, which was determined to bring an end to Korea's dependency status with China and modernize it along Japanese lines. In 1876, the two countries signed an agreement opening three treaty ports to Japanese commerce in

THE RULES OF GOOD CITIZENSHIP IN JAPAN

FAMILY & SOCIETY

After seizing power from the Tokugawa shogunate in 1868, the new Japanese leaders turned their attention to the creation of a new political system that would bring the country into the modern world. After exploring various systems in use in the West, a constitutional commission decided to adopt the system used in imperial Germany because of its paternalistic character. To promote civic virtue and obedience among the citizenry, the government then drafted an imperial rescript that was to be taught to every schoolchild in the country. The rescript instructed all children to obey their sovereign and place the interests of the community and the state above their own personal desires.

What, according to this document, was the primary purpose of education in Meiji Japan? How did these goals compare with those in China and the West?

Imperial Rescript on Education, 1890

Know ye, Our subjects:
Our Imperial Ancestors have founded Our Empire on a basis broad and everlasting, and have deeply and firmly implanted virtue. Our subjects ever united in loyalty and filial piety have from generation to generation illustrated the beauty thereof. This is the glory of the fundamental character of Our Empire, and herein also lies the source of Our education. Ye, Our subjects, be filial to your parents, affectionate to your brothers and sisters, as husbands and wives be harmonious, as friends true; bear yourselves in modesty and moderation; extend your benevolence to all; pursue learning and cultivate arts, and thereby develop intellectual faculties and perfect moral powers; furthermore, advance public good and promote common interests; always respect the Constitution and observe the laws; should emergency arise, offer yourselves to the State; and thus guard and maintain the prosperity of Our Imperial Throne coeval with heaven and earth. So shall ye not only be Our good and faithful subjects, but render illustrious the best traditions of your forefathers.

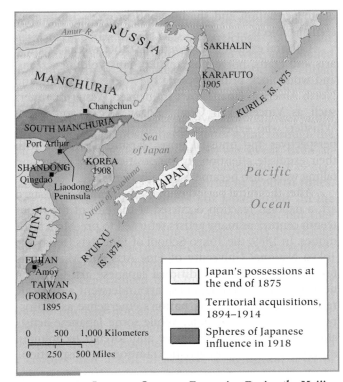

MAP 21.4 Japanese Overseas Expansion During the Meiji Era. Beginning in the late nineteenth century, Japan ventured beyond its home islands and became an imperialist power. The extent of Japanese colonial expansion through World War I is shown here. ❓ Which parts of imperial China were now under Japanese influence?

return for Japanese recognition of Korean independence. During the 1880s, Sino-Japanese rivalry over Korea intensified. When a new peasant rebellion broke out in Korea in 1894, China and Japan intervened on opposite sides. During the war, the Japanese navy destroyed the Chinese fleet and seized the Manchurian city of Port Arthur. In the Treaty of Shimonoseki, the Chinese were forced to recognize the independence of Korea and cede Taiwan and the Liaodong peninsula with its strategic naval base at Port Arthur to Japan.

Shortly thereafter, under pressure from the European powers, the Japanese returned the Liaodong peninsula to China, but in the early twentieth century, they went back on the offensive. Rivalry with Russia over influence in Korea led to increasingly strained relations between the two countries. In 1904, Japan launched a surprise attack on the Russian naval base at Port Arthur, which Russia had taken from China in 1898. The Japanese armed forces were weaker, but Russia faced difficult logistical problems along its new Trans-Siberian Railway and severe political instability at home. In 1905, after Japanese warships sank almost the entire Russian fleet off the coast of Korea, the Russians agreed to a humiliating peace, ceding the strategically located Liaodong peninsula back to Japan, as well as southern Sakhalin and the Kurile Islands. Russia also agreed to abandon its political and economic influence in Korea and southern Manchuria, which now came increasingly under Japanese control. The Japanese victory stunned

THE BEGINNING OF THE TWENTIETH-CENTURY CRISIS: WAR AND REVOLUTION

CHAPTER OUTLINE AND FOCUS QUESTIONS

The Road to World War I

▢ What were the long-range and immediate causes of World War I?

The Great War

▢ Why did the course of World War I turn out to be so different from what the belligerents had expected? How did World War I affect the belligerents' governmental and political institutions, economic affairs, and social life?

Crisis in Russia and the End of the War

▢ What were the causes of the Russian Revolution of 1917, and why did the Bolsheviks prevail in the civil war and gain control of Russia?

The Search for Stability

▢ What crises did Europe and the United States face in the interwar years?

In Pursuit of a New Reality: Cultural and Intellectual Trends

▢ How did the cultural and intellectual trends of the interwar years reflect the crises of the interwar years as well as the experience of World War I?

CRITICAL THINKING

▢ What was the relationship between World War I and the Russian Revolution?

British troops wait for the signal to attack

𝒪N JULY 1, 1916, BRITISH and French infantry forces attacked German defensive lines along a 25-mile front near the Somme River in France. Each soldier carried almost 70 pounds of equipment, making it "impossible to move much quicker than a slow walk." German machine guns soon opened fire: "We were able to see our comrades move forward in an attempt to cross No-Man's Land, only to be mown down like meadow grass," recalled one British soldier. "I felt sick at the sight of this carnage and remember weeping." In one day, more than 21,000 British soldiers died. After six months of fighting, the British had advanced 5 miles; one million British, French, and German soldiers had been killed or wounded.

Philip Gibbs, an English war correspondent, described what he saw in the German trenches that the British forces overran: "Victory! . . . Some of the German dead were young boys, too young to be killed for old men's crimes, and others might have been old or young. One could not tell because they had no faces, and were just masses of raw flesh in rags of uniforms. Legs and arms lay separate without any bodies thereabout."

World War I (1914–1918) was the defining event of the twentieth century. Overwhelmed by the size of its battles, the extent of its casualties, and its impact on all facets of life, contemporaries referred to it simply as the "Great War." The Great War was all the more disturbing to Europeans because it came after a period that many believed to have been an age of progress. Material prosperity and a fervid belief in scientific and technological advancement had convinced many people that the world stood on the verge of creating the utopia that humans had dreamed of for centuries. The historian Arnold Toynbee expressed what the pre–World War I era had meant to his generation:

> [We had expected] that life throughout the world would become more rational, more humane, and more democratic and that, slowly, but surely, political democracy would produce greater social justice. We had also expected that the progress of science and technology would make mankind richer, and that this increasing wealth would gradually spread from a minority to a majority. We had expected that all this would happen peacefully. In fact we thought that mankind's course was set for an earthly paradise.[1]

After 1918, it was no longer possible to maintain naive illusions about the progress of Western civilization. As World War I was followed by revolutionary upheavals, the mass murder machines of totalitarian regimes, and the destructiveness of World War II, it became all too apparent that instead of a utopia, Western civilization had become a nightmare. World War I and the revolutions it spawned can properly be seen as the first stage in the crisis of the twentieth century. ◆

The Road to World War I

On June 28, 1914, the heir to the Austrian throne, Archduke Francis Ferdinand, was assassinated in the Bosnian city of Sarajevo. Although this event precipitated the confrontation between Austria and Serbia that led to World War I, underlying forces had been propelling Europeans toward armed conflict for a long time.

Nationalism and Internal Dissent

The system of nation-states that had emerged in Europe in the second half of the nineteenth century (see Map 22.1) had led to severe competition. Rivalries over colonies and trade intensified during an era of frenzied imperialist expansion, while the division of Europe's great powers into two loose alliances (Germany, Austria, and Italy on one side and France, Great Britain, and Russia on the other) only added to the tensions. The series of crises that tested these alliances in the 1900s and early 1910s had left European states embittered, eager for revenge, and willing to go to war to preserve the power of their national states.

The growth of nationalism in the nineteenth century had yet another serious consequence. Not all ethnic groups had achieved the goal of nationhood. Slavic minorities in the Balkans and the multinational Habsburg Empire, for example, still dreamed of creating their own national states. So did the Irish in the British Empire and the Poles in the Russian Empire.

National aspirations, however, were not the only source of internal strife at the beginning of the twentieth century. Socialist labor movements had grown more powerful and were increasingly inclined to use strikes, even violent ones, to achieve their goals. Some conservative leaders, alarmed at the increase in labor strife and class division, even feared that European nations were on the verge of revolution. Did these statesmen opt for war in 1914 because they believed that "prosecuting an active foreign policy," as some Austrian leaders expressed it, would smother "internal troubles"? Some historians have argued that the desire to suppress internal disorder may have encouraged some leaders to take the plunge into war in 1914.

Militarism

The growth of large mass armies after 1900 not only heightened the existing tensions in Europe but also made it inevitable that if war did come, it would be highly destructive. **Conscription**—obligatory military service—had been established as a regular practice in most Western countries before 1914 (the United States and Britain were major exceptions). European military machines had doubled in size between 1890 and 1914. The Russian army was the largest, with 1.3 million men, and the French and Germans were not far behind, with 900,000 each. The British, Italian, and Austrian armies numbered between 250,000 and 500,000 soldiers.

Militarism, however, involved more than just large armies. As armies grew, so did the influence of military leaders, who drew up vast and complex plans for quickly mobilizing millions of men and enormous quantities of supplies in the event of war. Fearful that changes in these plans would cause chaos in the armed forces, military leaders insisted that their plans could not be altered. In the crises during the summer of 1914, the generals' lack of flexibility forced European political leaders to make decisions for military instead of political reasons.

The Outbreak of War: Summer 1914

Militarism, nationalism, and the desire to stifle internal dissent may all have played a role in the coming of World War I, but the decisions made by European leaders in the summer of 1914 directly precipitated the conflict. It was another crisis in the Balkans that forced this predicament on European statesmen.

As we have seen, states in southeastern Europe had struggled to free themselves of Ottoman rule in the course of the nineteenth and early twentieth centuries.

the use of unrestricted submarine warfare could starve the British into submission within five months, certainly before the Americans could act. The return to unrestricted submarine warfare brought the United States into the war on April 6, 1917. Although U.S. troops did not arrive in large numbers in Europe until the following year, the entry of the United States into the war gave the Allied Powers a psychological boost when they needed it.

The year 1917 had not been a good year for them. Allied offensives on the Western Front were disastrously defeated. The Italian armies were smashed in October, and in November, the Bolshevik Revolution in Russia (see "The Russian Revolution" later in this chapter) led to Russia's withdrawal from the war, leaving Germany free to concentrate entirely on the Western Front. The cause of the Central Powers looked favorable, although war weariness in the Ottoman Empire, Bulgaria, Austria-Hungary, and Germany was beginning to take its toll. The home front was rapidly becoming a cause for as much concern as the war front.

The Home Front: The Impact of Total War

The prolongation of World War I made it a **total war** that affected the lives of all citizens, however remote they might be from the battlefields. The need to organize masses of men and matériel for years of combat (Germany alone had 5.5 million men in active units in 1916) led to increased centralization of government powers, economic regimentation, and manipulation of public opinion to keep the war effort going.

Political Centralization and Economic Regimentation
Because the war was expected to be short, little thought had been given to long-term wartime needs. Governments had to respond quickly, however, when the war machines failed to achieve their knockout blows and made ever-greater demands for men and matériel. To meet these needs, governments expanded their powers. Countries drafted tens of millions of young men for that elusive breakthrough to victory.

Throughout Europe, wartime governments also expanded their powers over their economies. Free market capitalistic systems were temporarily shelved as governments experimented with price, wage, and rent controls; rationed food supplies and materials; and nationalized transportation systems and industries. Under total war mobilization, the distinction between soldiers at war and civilians at home was narrowed. In the view of political leaders, all citizens constituted a national army.

Control of Public Opinion
As the Great War dragged on and casualties grew worse, the patriotic enthusiasm that had marked the early days of the conflict waned. By 1916, there were numerous signs that civilian morale was beginning to crack under the pressure of total war. Governments took strenuous measures to fight the

growing opposition to the war. Even parliamentary regimes resorted to an expansion of police powers to stifle internal dissent. The British Parliament, for example, passed the Defence of the Realm Act (DORA), which allowed the public authorities to arrest dissenters and charge them as traitors. Newspapers were censored, and sometimes their publication was even suspended.

Wartime governments also made active use of propaganda to arouse enthusiasm for the war. At first, public officials needed to do little to achieve this goal. The British and French, for example, exaggerated German atrocities in Belgium and found that their citizens were only too willing to believe these accounts. But as the war dragged on and morale sagged, governments were forced to devise new techniques for stimulating declining enthusiasm.

Women in the War Effort
World War I opened up new roles for women. Because so many men went off to fight at the front, women were called on to take over jobs and responsibilities that had not been available to them

British Recruiting Poster. As the conflict persisted month after month, governments resorted to active propaganda campaigns to generate enthusiasm for the war. In this British recruiting poster, the government tried to pressure men into volunteering for military service. By 1916, the British were forced to adopt compulsory military service.

before, including jobs that had been considered beyond the "capacity of women." These included such occupations as chimney sweeps, truck drivers, farm laborers, and factory workers in heavy industry. Thirty-eight percent of the workers in the Krupp Armaments works in Germany in 1918 were women. Nevertheless, despite the noticeable increase in women's wages that resulted from government regulations, women's industrial wages never equaled men's wages at any time during the war.

Even worse, women's place in the workforce was far from secure. Both men and women seemed to expect that many of the new jobs for women were only temporary, an expectation quite evident in the British poem "War Girls," written in 1916:

> There's the girl who clips your ticket for the train,
> And the girl who speeds the lift from floor to floor,
> There's the girl who does a milk-round in the rain,
> And the girl who calls for orders at your door.
> Strong, sensible, and fit,
> They're out to show their grit,
> And tackle jobs with energy and knack.
> No longer caged and penned up,
> They're going to keep their end up
> Till the khaki soldier boys come marching back.[4]

At the end of the war, governments moved quickly to remove women from the jobs they had been encouraged to take earlier, and wages for women who remained employed were lowered.

Nevertheless, in some countries, the role played by women in the wartime economies did have a positive impact on the women's movement for political emancipation. The most obvious gain was the right to vote, granted to women in Britain in January 1918 and in Germany and Austria immediately after the war. Contemporary media, however, tended to focus on the more noticeable yet in some ways more superficial social emancipation of upper- and middle-class women. In ever-larger numbers, these young women took jobs, had their own apartments, and showed their new independence by smoking in public, wearing shorter dresses, and adopting radical new hairstyles.

Crisis in Russia and the End of the War

By 1917, total war was creating serious domestic turmoil in all of the European belligerent states. Only one, however, experienced the kind of complete collapse that others were predicting might happen throughout Europe. Out of Russia's collapse came the Russian Revolution.

The Russian Revolution

Tsar Nicholas II was an autocratic ruler who relied on the army and the bureaucracy to uphold his regime. But World War I magnified Russia's problems and severely challenged the tsarist government. Russian industry was unable to produce the weapons needed for the army. Many soldiers were sent to the front without rifles and told to pick one up from a dead comrade. Ill-led and ill-armed, Russian armies suffered incredible losses. Between 1914 and 1916, two million soldiers were killed, and another four to six million were wounded or captured.

In the meantime, Tsar Nicholas II was increasingly insulated from events by his German-born wife, Alexandra, a well-educated woman who had fallen under the sway of Rasputin, a Siberian peasant whom she regarded as a holy man because he alone seemed able to stop the bleeding of her hemophiliac son. Rasputin's influence with the tsarina made him a power behind the throne, and he did not hesitate to interfere in government affairs. As the leadership at the top experienced a series of military and economic disasters, the middle class, aristocrats, peasants, soldiers, and workers grew more and more disenchanted with the tsarist regime. Even aristocrats who supported the monarchy felt the need to do something to reverse the deteriorating situation. For a start, they assassinated Rasputin in December 1916. But by then, it was too late to save the monarchy.

The March Revolution   At the beginning of March 1917, a series of strikes led by working-class women broke out in the capital city of Petrograd (formerly Saint Petersburg). A few weeks earlier, the government had introduced bread rationing in the capital city after the price of bread had skyrocketed. Many of the women who stood in the lines waiting for bread were also factory workers who had put in twelve-hour days. The Russian government had become aware of the volatile situation in the capital from a police report: "Mothers of families, exhausted by endless standing in line at stores, distraught over their half-starving and sick children, are today perhaps closer to revolution than [the liberal opposition leaders] and of course they are a great deal more dangerous because they are the combustible material for which only a single spark is needed to burst into flame."[5] On March 8, a day celebrated since 1910 as International Women's Day, about ten thousand women marched through Petrograd demanding "peace and bread." Soon the women were joined by other workers, and together they called for a general strike that succeeded in shutting down all the factories in the city on March 10. Nicholas ordered his troops to disperse the crowds by shooting them if necessary, but large numbers of the soldiers soon joined the demonstrators. The Duma (legislature), which the tsar had tried to dissolve, met anyway and on March 12 declared that it was assuming governmental responsibility. It established a provisional government on March 15; the tsar abdicated the same day.

The Provisional Government, headed by Alexander Kerensky, decided to carry on the war to preserve Russia's honor—a major blunder because it satisfied neither the workers nor the peasants, who wanted more than anything an end to the war. The Provisional Government also faced another authority, the **soviets,** or councils of workers' and soldiers' deputies. The soviet of Petrograd had been formed in March 1917; at the same time, soviets sprang up spontaneously in army units, factory towns, and rural areas. The soviets represented the more radical interests of the lower classes and were largely composed of socialists of various kinds. One group—the Bolsheviks—came to play a crucial role.

Lenin and the Bolshevik Revolution The Bolsheviks were a small faction of Russian Social Democrats who had come under the leadership of Vladimir Ulianov, known to the world as V. I. Lenin (1870–1924). Under Lenin's direction, the Bolsheviks became a party dedicated to violent revolution. He believed that only a revolution could destroy the capitalist system and that a "vanguard" of activists must form a small party of well-disciplined professional revolutionaries to accomplish this task. Between 1900 and 1917, Lenin spent most of his time in exile in Switzerland. When the Provisional Government was set up in March 1917, he believed that an opportunity for the Bolsheviks to seize power had come. A month later, with the connivance of the German High Command, which hoped to create disorder in Russia, Lenin was shipped to Russia in a "sealed train" by way of Finland.

Lenin believed that the Bolsheviks must work toward gaining control of the soviets of soldiers, workers, and peasants and then use them to overthrow the Provisional Government. At the same time, the Bolsheviks sought mass support through promises geared to the needs of the people: an end to the war, redistribution of all land to the peasants, the transfer of factories and industries from capitalists to committees of workers, and the relegation of government power from the Provisional Government to the soviets. Three simple slogans summed up the Bolshevik program: "Peace, Land, Bread," "Worker Control of Production," and "All Power to the Soviets."

By the end of October, the Bolsheviks had achieved a slight majority in the Petrograd and Moscow soviets. The number of party members had also grown from 50,000 to 240,000. With Leon Trotsky (1877–1940), a fervid revolutionary, as chairman of the Petrograd soviet, Lenin and the Bolsheviks were in a position to seize power in the name of the soviets. During the night of November 6, pro-soviet and pro-Bolshevik forces took control of Petrograd. The Provisional Government quickly collapsed, with little bloodshed. The following night, the All-Russian Congress of Soviets, representing local soviets from all over the country, affirmed the transfer of power. At the second session, on the night of November 8, Lenin announced the new Soviet government, the Council of People's Commissars, with himself as its head (see the box on p. 501).

But the Bolsheviks, soon renamed the Communists, still faced enormous obstacles. For one thing, Lenin had

Lenin and Trotsky. Vladimir Lenin and Leon Trotsky were important figures in the Bolsheviks' successful seizure of power in Russia. On the left, Lenin is seen addressing a rally in Moscow in 1917. On the right, Trotsky, who became commissar of war in the new regime, is shown haranguing his troops.

© Brown Brothers

© Underwood & Underwood/CORBIS

SOLDIER AND PEASANT VOICES

POLITICS & GOVERNMENT

In 1917, Russia experienced a cataclysmic upheaval as two revolutions overthrew the tsarist regime and then the Provisional Government that replaced it. Peasants, workers, and soldiers poured out their thoughts and feelings on these events, some of them supporting the Bolsheviks and others denouncing the Bolsheviks for betraying their socialist revolution. These selections are taken from two letters, the first from a soldier and the second from a peasant. Both are addressed to Bolshevik leaders.

What arguments do both of the writers of these letters use against Lenin and the Bolsheviks? Why do they feel so betrayed by the Bolsheviks?

Letter from a Soldier in Leningrad to Lenin, January 6, 1918

Bastard! What the hell are you doing? How long are you going to keep on degrading the Russian people? After all, it's because of you they killed the former minister . . . and so many other innocent victims. Because of you, they might kill even other former ministers belonging to the [Socialist Revolutionary] party because you call them counterrevolutionaries and even monarchists. . . . And you, you Bolshevik gang leader hired either by Nicholas II or by Wilhelm II, are waging this pogrom propaganda against men who may have done time with you in exile.

Scoundrel! A curse on you from the politically conscious Russian proletariat, the conscious ones and not the kind who are following you—that is, the Red Guards, the tally clerks, who, when they are called to military service, all hide at the factories and now are killing . . . practically their own father, the way the soldiers did in 1905 when they killed their own, or the way the police and gendarmes did in [1917]. That's who they're more like. They're not pursuing the ideas of socialism because they don't understand them (if they did they wouldn't act this way) but because they get paid a good salary both at the factory and in the Red Guards. But not all the workers are like that—there are very politically aware ones and the soldiers—again not all of them—are like that but only former policemen, constables, gendarmes and the very very ignorant ones who under the old regime tramped with hay on one foot and straw on the other because they couldn't tell their right foot from their left and they are pursuing not the ideas of socialism that you advocate but to be able to lie on their cots in the barracks and do absolutely nothing not even to be asked to sweep the floor, which is already piled with several inches of filth. And so the entire proletariat of Russia is following you, but count fewer than are against you, but they are only physically or rather technically stronger than the majority, and that is what you're abusing when you disbanded the Constituent Assembly the way Nicholas II disbanded the Duma. You point out that counterrevolutionaries gathered there. You lie, scoundrel, there wasn't a single counterrevolutionary and if there was then it was you, the Bolsheviks, which you proved by your actions when you encroached on the gains of the revolution: you are shutting down newspapers, even socialist ones, arresting socialists, committing violence and deceiving the people; you promised loads but did none of it.

Letter from a Peasant to the Bolshevik Leaders, January 10, 1918

To you!

Rulers, plunderers, rapists, destroyers, usurpers, oppressors of Mother Russia, citizens Lenin, Trotsky, Uritsky, Zinoviev, Spiridonova, Antonov, Lunacharsky, Krylenko, and Co. [leaders of the Bolshevik party]:

Allow me to ask you how long you are going to go on degrading Russia's millions, its tormented and exhausted people. Instead of peace, you signed an armistice with the enemy, and this gave our opponent a painful advantage, and you declared war on Russia. You moved the troops you had tricked to the Russian-Russian front and started a fratricidal war. Your mercenary Red Guards are looting, murdering, and raping everywhere they go. A fire has consumed all our dear Mother Russia. Rail transport is idle, as are the plants and factories; the entire population has woken up to find itself in the most pathetic situation, without bread or kerosene or any of the other essentials, unclothed or unshod in unheated houses. In short: hungry and cold. . . . You have strangled the entire press, and freedom with it, you have wiped out the best freedom fighters, you have destroyed all Russia. Think it over, you butchers, you hirelings of the Kaiser [William II]. Isn't your turn about up, too? For all you are doing, we, politically aware Great Russians, are sending you butchers, you hirelings of the Kaiser, our curse. May you be damned, you accursed one, you bloodthirsty butchers, you hirelings of the Kaiser—don't think you're in the clear, because the Russian people will sober up and that will be the end of you. I'm writing in red ink to show that you are bloodthirsty. . . . I'm writing these curses, a great Russian native of Orel Province, peasant of Mtsensk Uezd.

ThomsonNOW To read Lenin's "Call to Power," enter the *ThomsonNOW* documents area using the access card that is available for *The Essential World History*.

promised peace, and that, he realized, was not an easy promise to fulfill because of the humiliating losses of Russian territory that it would entail. There was no real choice, however. On March 3, 1918, Lenin signed the Treaty of Brest-Litovsk with Germany and gave up eastern Poland, the Ukraine, Finland, and the Baltic provinces. He had promised peace to the Russian people; but real peace did not come, for the country soon sank into civil war.

Civil War   There was great opposition to the new Communist regime, not only from groups loyal to the tsar but also from bourgeois and aristocratic liberals and anti-Leninist socialists. In addition, thousands of Allied troops were eventually sent to different parts of Russia.

Between 1918 and 1921, the Communist (Red) Army was forced to fight on many fronts. The first serious threat to the Communists came from Siberia, where a White (anti-Communist) force attacked westward and advanced almost to the Volga River. Attacks also came from the Ukrainians in the southwest and from the Baltic regions. In mid-1919, White forces swept through the Ukraine and advanced almost to Moscow before being pushed back. By 1920, the major White forces had been defeated, and the Ukraine had been retaken. The next year, the Communist regime regained control over the independent nationalist governments in the Caucasus: Georgia, Russian Armenia, and Azerbaijan.

How had Lenin and the Bolsheviks triumphed over what seemed at one time to be overwhelming forces? For one thing, the Red Army became a well-disciplined fighting force, largely due to the organizational genius of Leon Trotsky. As commissar of war, Trotsky reinstated the draft and insisted on rigid discipline; soldiers who deserted or refused to obey orders were summarily executed.

In addition, the disunity of the anti-Communist forces seriously weakened the efforts of the Whites. Political differences created distrust among the Whites and prevented them from cooperating effectively. It was difficult enough to achieve military cooperation; political differences made it virtually impossible. The lack of a common goal on the part of the Whites was in sharp contrast to the single-minded sense of purpose of the Communists.

The Communists also succeeded in translating their revolutionary faith into practical instruments of power. A policy of **"war communism,"** for example, was used to ensure regular supplies for the Red Army. "War communism" included the nationalization of banks and most industries, the forcible requisition of grain from peasants, and the centralization of state power under Bolshevik control. Another Bolshevik instrument was "revolutionary terror." A new Red secret police—known as the Cheka—instituted the Red Terror, aimed at nothing less than the destruction of all who opposed the new regime.

Finally, the intervention of foreign armies enabled the Communists to appeal to the powerful force of Russian patriotism. Appalled by the takeover of power in Russia by the radical Communists, the Allied Powers

intervened. At one point, over 100,000 foreign troops—mostly Japanese, British, American, and French—were stationed on Russian soil. This intervention by the Allies enabled the Communist government to appeal to patriotic Russians to fight the attempts of foreigners to control their country.

By 1921, the Communists were in control of Russia. In the course of the civil war, the Communist regime had also transformed Russia into a bureaucratically centralized state dominated by a single party. It was also a state that was largely hostile to the Allied Powers that had sought to assist the Communists' enemies in the civil war.

The Last Year of the War

For Germany, the withdrawal of the Russians in March 1918 offered renewed hope for a favorable end to the war. The victory over Russia persuaded Erich von Ludendorff (1865–1937), who guided German military operations, and most German leaders to make one final military gamble—a grand offensive in the west to break the military stalemate. The German attack was launched in March and lasted into July, but an Allied counterattack, supported by the arrival of 140,000 fresh American troops, defeated the Germans at the Second Battle of the Marne on July 18. Ludendorff's gamble had failed.

On September 29, 1918, General Ludendorff informed German leaders that the war was lost and insisted that the government sue for peace at once. When German officials discovered, however, that the Allies were unwilling to make peace with the autocratic imperial government, reforms were instituted to create a liberal government. Meanwhile, popular demonstrations broke out throughout Germany. William II capitulated to public pressure and abdicated on November 9, and the Socialists under Friedrich Ebert (1871–1925) announced the establishment of a republic. Two days later, on November 11, 1918, the new German government agreed to an armistice. The war was over.

The Casualties of the War   World War I devastated European civilization. Between 8 and 9 million soldiers died on the battlefields; another 22 million were wounded. Many of the survivors died later from war injuries or lived on without arms or legs or with other forms of mutilation. The birthrate in many European countries declined noticeably as a result of the death or maiming of so many young men. World War I also created a lost generation of war veterans who had become accustomed to violence and who would later band together in support of Mussolini and Hitler in their bids for power.

Nor did the killing affect only soldiers. Untold numbers of civilians died from war injuries or starvation. In 1915, after an Armenian uprising against the Ottoman government, the government retaliated with fury by killing Armenian men and expelling women and children. Within seven months, 600,000 Armenians had been killed, and 500,000 had been deported. Of the latter, 400,000 died while marching through the deserts and swamps of Syria and Mesopotamia. By September 1915, an estimated one million Armenians were dead, the victims of genocide.

The Peace Settlement

In January 1919, the delegations of twenty-seven victorious Allied nations gathered in Paris to conclude a final settlement of the Great War. Over a period of years, the reasons for fighting World War I had been transformed from selfish national interests to idealistic principles. No one expressed the latter better than the U.S. president Woodrow Wilson (1856–1924). Wilson's proposals for a truly just and lasting peace included "open covenants of peace, openly arrived at" instead of secret diplomacy; the reduction of national armaments to a "point consistent with domestic safety"; and the self-determination of people so that "all well-defined national aspirations shall be accorded the utmost satisfaction." As the spokesman for a new world order based on democracy and international cooperation, Wilson was enthusiastically cheered by many Europeans when he arrived in Europe for the peace conference.

Wilson soon found, however, that more practical motives guided other states at the Paris Peace Conference. The secret treaties and agreements that had been made before the war could not be totally ignored, even if they did conflict with the principle of self-determination enunciated by Wilson. National interests also complicated the deliberations of the Paris Peace Conference. David Lloyd George (1863–1945), prime minister of Great Britain, had won a decisive electoral victory in December 1918 on a platform of making the Germans pay for this dreadful war.

France's approach to peace was primarily determined by considerations of national security. To Georges Clemenceau (1841–1929), the feisty premier of France who had led his country to victory, the French people had borne the brunt of German aggression. They deserved revenge and security against future German aggression.

The most important decisions at the Paris Peace Conference were made by Wilson, Clemenceau, and Lloyd George. In the end, only compromise made it possible to achieve a peace settlement. Wilson's wish that the creation of an international peacekeeping organization be the first order of business was granted, and already on January 25, 1919, the conference adopted the principle of the League of Nations. In return, Wilson agreed to make compromises on territorial arrangements to guarantee the establishment of the League, believing that a functioning League could later rectify bad arrangements.

The Treaty of Versailles   The final peace settlement consisted of five separate treaties with the defeated nations—Germany, Austria, Hungary, Bulgaria, and Turkey. The Treaty of Versailles with Germany, signed on June 28, 1919, was by far the most important. The Germans considered it a harsh peace and were particularly unhappy with Article 231, the so-called **War Guilt Clause,** which declared Germany (and Austria) responsible for starting the war and ordered Germany to pay **reparations** for all the damage to which the Allied governments and their people were subjected as a result of the war.

The military and territorial provisions of the treaty also rankled Germans. Germany had to lower its army to 100,000 men, reduce its navy, and eliminate its air force. German territorial losses included the return of Alsace and Lorraine to France and sections of Prussia to the new Polish state (see Map 22.3). German land west and as far as 30 miles east of the Rhine was established as a demilitarized zone and stripped of all armaments or fortifications to serve as a barrier to any future German military moves westward against France. Outraged by the "dictated peace," the new German government complained but accepted the treaty.

The Other Peace Treaties   The separate peace treaties made with the other Central Powers extensively redrew the map of eastern Europe. Many of these changes merely ratified what the war had already accomplished. Both the German and Russian Empires lost considerable territory in eastern Europe, and the Austro-Hungarian Empire disappeared altogether. New nation-states emerged from the lands of these three empires: Finland, Latvia, Estonia, Lithuania, Poland, Czechoslovakia, Austria, and Hungary.

MAP 22.3   Territorial Changes in Europe and the Middle East After World War I. The victorious Allies met in Paris to determine the shape and nature of postwar Europe. At the urging of U.S. President Woodrow Wilson, many nationalist aspirations of former imperial subjects were realized with the creation of several new countries from the prewar territory of Austria-Hungary, Germany, Russia, and the Ottoman Empire. ❓ What new countries emerged in Europe and the Middle East?

🔹 **View an animated version of this map or related maps at** http://worldrc.wadsworth.com/

Territorial rearrangements were also made in the Balkans. Serbia formed the nucleus of a new southern Slavic state, called Yugoslavia, which combined Serbs, Croats, and Slovenes.

Although the Paris Peace Conference was supposedly guided by the principle of self-determination, the mixtures of peoples in eastern Europe made it impossible to draw boundaries along neat ethnic lines. As a result of compromises, virtually every eastern European state was left with a minorities problem that could lead to future conflicts. Germans in Poland; Hungarians, Poles, and Germans in Czechoslovakia; Hungarians in Romania; and the combination of Serbs, Croats, Slovenes, Macedonians, and Albanians in Yugoslavia all became sources of later conflict.

Yet another centuries-old empire, the Ottoman Empire, was dismembered by the peace settlement after the war. To gain Arab support against the Ottoman Turks during the war, the Western Allies had promised to recognize the independence of Arab states in the Middle Eastern lands of the Ottoman Empire. But the imperialist habits of Western nations died hard. After the war, France was given control of Lebanon and Syria, while Britain received Iraq and Palestine. Officially, both acquisitions were called **mandates,** a system whereby a nation officially administered a territory on behalf of the League

The Middle East in 1919

of Nations. The system of mandates could not hide the fact that the principle of national self-determination at the Paris Peace Conference was largely for Europeans.

The Search for Stability

The peace settlement at the end of World War I had tried to fulfill the nineteenth-century dream of nationalism by creating new boundaries and new states. From its inception, however, this peace settlement had left nations unhappy and only too eager to revise it.

Uneasy Peace, Uncertain Security

President Woodrow Wilson had recognized that the peace treaties contained unwise provisions that could serve as new causes for conflicts, and he had placed many of his hopes for the future in the League of Nations. The League, however, was not particularly effective in maintaining the peace. The failure of the United States to join the League in a backlash of isolationist sentiment undermined its effectiveness from the beginning. Moreover, the League could use only economic sanctions to halt aggression.

France's search for security between 1919 and 1924 was founded primarily on a strict enforcement of the Treaty of Versailles. This tough policy toward Germany began with the issue of reparations, the payments that the Germans were supposed to make to compensate for war damage. In April 1921, the Allied Reparations Commission settled on a sum of 132 billion marks ($33 billion) for German reparations, payable in annual installments of 2.5 billion (gold) marks. The new German republic made its first payment in 1921, but by the following year, facing financial problems, the German government announced that it was unable to pay more. Outraged, the French government sent troops to occupy the Ruhr valley, Germany's chief industrial and mining center. Because the Germans would not pay reparations, the French would collect reparations in kind by operating and using the Ruhr mines and factories.

Both Germany and France suffered from the French occupation of the Ruhr. The German government adopted a policy of passive resistance to French occupation that was largely financed by printing more paper money. This only intensified the inflationary pressures that had already begun in Germany by the end of the war. The German mark became worthless, and economic disaster fueled political upheavals. All the nations, including France, were happy to cooperate with the American suggestion for a new conference of experts to reassess the reparations problem.

In August 1924, an international commission produced a new plan for reparations. The Dawes Plan, named after the American banker who chaired the commission, reduced the reparations and stabilized Germany's payments on the basis of its ability to pay. The Dawes Plan also granted an initial $200 million loan for German recovery, which opened the door to heavy American investments in Europe that helped create a new era of European prosperity between 1924 and 1929.

With prosperity came a new age of European diplomacy. A spirit of cooperation was fostered by the foreign ministers of Germany and France, Gustav Stresemann and Aristide Briand, who concluded the Treaty of Locarno in 1925. This guaranteed Germany's new western borders with France and Belgium. Although Germany's new eastern borders with Poland were conspicuously absent from the agreement, the Locarno pact was viewed by many as the beginning of a new era of European peace.

The spirit of Locarno was based on little real substance, however. Germany lacked the military power to alter its western borders even if it wanted to. And the issue of disarmament soon proved that even the spirit of Locarno could not bring nations to cut back on their weapons. Germany, of course, had been disarmed with the expectation that other states would do likewise. Numerous disarmament conferences, however, failed to achieve anything substantial as states were unwilling to trust their security to anyone but their own military forces.

The Great Depression

Almost as devastating as the two world wars in the first half of the twentieth century was the economic collapse that ravaged the world in the 1930s. Two events set the stage for the Great Depression: a downturn in domestic economic activities and an international financial crisis precipitated by the collapse of the American stock market in 1929.

Already in the mid-1920s, prices for agricultural goods were beginning to decline rapidly due to overproduction of basic commodities, such as wheat. In addition to domestic economic troubles, much of the European prosperity between 1924 and 1929 had been built on American bank loans to Germany. The crash of the U.S. stock market in October 1929 led panicky American investors to withdraw many of their funds from Germany and other European markets. The withdrawal of funds seriously weakened the banks of Germany and other central European states. By 1931, trade was slowing down, industrialists were cutting back production, and unemployment was increasing as the effects of international bank failures had a devastating impact on domestic economies.

Economic depression was by no means a new phenomenon in European history, but the depth of the economic downturn after 1929 fully justifies the label Great Depression. During 1932, the worst year of the depression, one British worker in four was unemployed; in Germany, six million people, 40 percent of the labor force, were out of work. The unemployed and homeless filled the streets of the cities of the advanced industrial countries (see the box on p. 507).

The Great Depression: Bread Lines in Paris.
The Great Depression devastated the European economy and had serious political repercussions. Because of its more balanced economy, France did not feel the effects of the depression as quickly as other European countries. By 1931, however, even France was experiencing lines of unemployed people at free-food centers.

Governments seemed powerless to deal with the crisis. The classical liberal remedy for depression, a deflationary policy of balanced budgets, which involved cutting costs by lowering wages and raising tariffs to exclude other countries' goods from home markets, only served to worsen the economic crisis and cause even greater mass discontent. This in turn led to serious political repercussions. Increased government activity in the economy was one reaction. Another effect was a renewed interest in Marxist doctrines. Hadn't Marx predicted that capitalism would destroy itself through overproduction? Communism took on new popularity, especially with workers and intellectuals. Finally, the Great Depression increased the attractiveness of facile dictatorial solutions, especially from a new movement known as fascism. Everywhere, democracy seemed on the defensive in the 1930s.

The Democratic States

After World War I, Great Britain went through a period of serious economic difficulties. During the war, Britain had lost many of the markets for its industrial products, especially to the United States and Japan. The postwar decline of such staple industries as coal, steel, and textiles led to a rise in unemployment, which reached the two million mark in 1921. But Britain soon rebounded and from 1925 to 1929 experienced an era of renewed prosperity.

By 1929, however, Britain faced the growing effects of the Great Depression. A national government (a coalition of Liberals and Conservatives) claimed credit for bringing Britain out of the worst stages of the depression, primarily by using the traditional policies of balanced budgets and protective tariffs. British politicians had largely ignored the new ideas of a Cambridge economist, John Maynard Keynes (1883–1946), who published his *General Theory of Employment, Interest, and Money* in 1936. He condemned the traditional view that in a free economy, depressions should be left to work themselves out. Keynes argued that unemployment stemmed not from overproduction but from a decline in demand and that demand could be increased by putting people back to work building highways and public structures, even if governments had to go into debt to pay for these works, a concept known as **deficit spending.**

After the defeat of Germany, France had become the strongest power on the European continent, but between 1921 and 1926, no French government seemed capable of solving the country's financial problems. Like other European countries, though, France did experience a period of relative prosperity between 1926 and 1929.

Because it had a more balanced economy than other nations, France did not begin to feel the full effects of the Great Depression until 1932. Economic instability soon had political repercussions. During a nineteen-month period in 1932 and 1933, six different cabinets were formed as France faced political chaos. Finally, in June 1936, a coalition of leftist parties—Communists, Socialists, and Radicals—formed a new government, the Popular Front, but its policies failed to solve the problems of the depression. By 1938, the French were experiencing a serious decline of confidence in their political system.

After the imperial Germany of William II had come to an end in 1918 with Germany's defeat in World War I, a German democratic state known as the Weimar Republic was established. From its beginnings, the Weimar Republic was plagued by a series of problems. The republic had no truly outstanding political leaders and faced serious economic difficulties. Germany experienced runaway inflation in 1922 and 1923; widows, orphans, the retired elderly, army officers, teachers, civil servants, and others who lived on fixed incomes all watched their monthly stipends become worthless and their lifetime savings disappear. Their economic losses increasingly pushed the middle class to the rightist parties that were hostile to the republic. To make matters worse, after a period of prosperity

THE GREAT DEPRESSION: UNEMPLOYED AND HOMELESS IN GERMANY

FAMILY & SOCIETY

In 1932, Germany had six million unemployed workers, many of them wandering aimlessly about the country, begging for food and seeking shelter in city lodging houses for the homeless. The Great Depression was an important factor in the rise to power of Adolf Hitler and the Nazis. This selection presents a description of the unemployed homeless in 1932.

Why did Hauser compare the scene he describes from 1932 with the years of 1917 and 1918? Why does he compare the hungry men with animals?

Heinrich Hauser, "With Germany's Unemployed"

An almost unbroken chain of homeless men extends the whole length of the great Hamburg-Berlin highway. . . . All the highways in Germany over which I have traveled this year presented the same aspect. . . .

Most of the hikers paid no attention to me. They walked separately or in small groups, with their eyes on the ground. And they had the queer, stumbling gait of barefooted people, for their shoes were slung over their shoulders. Some of them were guild members—carpenters . . . milkmen . . . and bricklayers . . . but they were in a minority. Far more numerous were those whom one could assign to no special profession or craft—unskilled young people, for the most part, who had been unable to find a place for themselves in any city or town in Germany, and who had never had a job and never expected to have one. There was something else that had never been seen before—whole families that had piled all their goods into baby carriages and wheelbarrows that they were pushing along as they plodded forward in dumb despair. It was a whole nation on the march.

I saw them—and this was the strongest impression that the year 1932 left with me—I saw them, gathered into groups of fifty or a hundred men, attacking fields of potatoes. I saw them digging up the potatoes and throwing them into sacks while the farmer who owned the field watched them in despair and the local policeman looked on gloomily from the distance. I saw them staggering toward the lights of the city as night fell, with their sacks on their backs. What did it remind me of? Of the War, of the worst periods of starvation in 1917 and 1918, but even then people paid for the potatoes. . . .

I saw that the individual can know what is happening only by personal experience. I know what it is to be a tramp. I know what cold and hunger are. . . . But there are two things that I have only recently experienced—begging and spending the night in a municipal lodging house.

I entered the huge Berlin municipal lodging house in a northern quarter of the city. . . .

Distribution of spoons, distribution of enameled-ware bowls with the words "Property of the City of Berlin" written on their sides. Then the meal itself. A big kettle is carried in. Men with yellow smocks have brought it in, and men with yellow smocks ladle out the food. These men, too, are homeless and they have been expressly picked by the establishment and given free food and lodging and a little pocket money in exchange for their work about the house.

Where have I seen this kind of food distribution before? In a prison that I once helped to guard in the winter of 1919 during the German civil war. There was the same hunger then, the same trembling, anxious expectation of rations. Now the men are standing in a long row, dressed in their plain nightshirts that reach to the ground, and the noise of their shuffling feet is like the noise of big wild animals walking up and down the stone floor of their cages before feeding time. The men lean far over the kettle so that the warm steam from the food envelops them, and they hold out their bowls as if begging and whisper to the attendant, "Give me a real helping. Give me a little more." A piece of bread is handed out with every bowl.

My next recollection is sitting at table in another room on a crowded bench that is like a seat in a fourth-class railway carriage. Hundreds of hungry mouths make an enormous noise eating their food. The men sit bent over their food like animals who feel that someone is going to take it away from them. They hold their bowl with their left arm partway around it, so that nobody can take it away, and they also protect it with their other elbow and with their head and mouth, while they move the spoon as fast as they can between their mouth and the bowl.

ThomsonNOW™ To read about World War I rationing in Germany, enter the *ThomsonNOW* documents area using the access card that is available for *The Essential World History*.

---

from 1924 to 1929, Germany faced the Great Depression. Unemployment increased to 3 million in March 1930 and 4.4 million by December of the same year. The depression paved the way for the rise of extremist parties.

After Germany, no Western nation was more affected by the Great Depression than the United States. By 1932, U.S. industrial production fell to 50 percent of what it had been in 1929. By 1933, there were fifteen million unemployed. Under these circumstances, the Democrat

Franklin Delano Roosevelt (1882–1945) was able to win a landslide electoral victory in 1932. He and his advisers pursued a policy of active government intervention in the economy that came to be known as the New Deal. Economic intervention included a stepped-up program of public works, such as the Works Progress Administration (WPA), which was established in 1935 and employed between two and three million people who worked at building bridges, roads, post offices, and airports. In 1935, the Social Security Act created a system of old-age pensions and unemployment insurance.

The New Deal provided some social reform measures, but it did not solve the unemployment problems of the Great Depression. In May 1937, during what was considered a period of full recovery, American unemployment still stood at seven million.

Socialism in Soviet Russia

The civil war in Russia had taken an enormous toll of life. Lenin had pursued a policy of war communism, but once the war was over, peasants began to sabotage the program by hoarding food. Added to this problem was drought, which caused a famine between 1920 and 1922 that claimed as many as five million lives. Industrial collapse paralleled the agricultural disaster. By 1921, industrial output was only 20 percent of its 1913 levels. Russia was exhausted. A peasant banner proclaimed, "Down with Lenin and horseflesh, Bring back the Tsar and pork." As Leon Trotsky said, "The country, and the government with it, were at the very edge of the abyss."[6]

In March 1921, Lenin pulled Russia back from the abyss by adopting his **New Economic Policy** (NEP), a modified version of the old capitalist system. Peasants were now allowed to sell their produce openly. Retail stores as well as small industries that employed fewer than twenty employees could now operate under private ownership, although heavy industry, banking, and mines remained in the hands of the government.

In 1922, Lenin and the Communists formally created a new state called the Union of Soviet Socialist Republics, known as the USSR by its initials or the Soviet Union by its shortened form. Already by that year, a revived market and a good harvest had brought the famine to an end; Soviet agricultural production climbed to 75 percent of its prewar level. Overall the NEP had saved the nation from complete economic disaster even though Lenin and other leading Communists intended it to be only a temporary, tactical retreat from the goals of communism.

Lenin's death in 1924 inaugurated a struggle for power among the seven members of the Politburo, the institution that had become the leading organ of the party. The Politburo was divided over the future direction of Soviet Russia. The Left, led by Leon Trotsky, wanted to end the NEP, launch Russia on the path of rapid industrialization, and spread the revolution abroad. Another group in the Politburo, called the Right, rejected the cause of world revolution and wanted instead to concentrate on constructing a socialist state in Russia. This group also favored a continuation of Lenin's NEP.

These ideological divisions were underscored by an intense personal rivalry between Leon Trotsky and Joseph Stalin. In 1924, Trotsky held the post of commissar of war and was the leading spokesman for the Left in the Politburo. Joseph Stalin (1879–1953) was content to hold the dull bureaucratic job of party general secretary while other Politburo members held party positions that enabled them to display their brilliant oratorical abilities. Stalin was skillful in avoiding allegiance to either the Left or Right factions in the Politburo. He was also a good organizer (his fellow Bolsheviks called him "Comrade Index-Card") and used his post as party general secretary to gain complete control of the Communist Party. Trotsky was expelled from the party in 1927. By 1929, Stalin had succeeded in eliminating the Bolsheviks of the revolutionary era from the Politburo and establishing a dictatorship.

In Pursuit of a New Reality: Cultural and Intellectual Trends

Four years of devastating war left many Europeans with a profound sense of despair and a conviction that something was dreadfully wrong with Western values. The Great Depression only added to the despair lingering from World War I.

Political and economic uncertainties were paralleled by social innovations. The Great War had served to break down many traditional middle-class attitudes, especially toward sexuality. In the 1920s, women's physical appearance changed dramatically. Short skirts, short hair, the use of cosmetics that were once thought to be the preserve of prostitutes, and the new practice of suntanning gave women a new image. This change in physical appearance, which stressed more exposure of a woman's body, was also accompanied by frank discussions of sexual matters. In 1926, the Dutch physician Theodor van de Velde published *Ideal Marriage: Its Physiology and Technique,* which became an international best-seller. Van de Velde described female and male anatomy and glorified sexual pleasure in marriage.

Nightmares and New Visions

Uncertainty also pervaded the cultural and intellectual achievements of the interwar years. Postwar artistic trends were largely a working out of the implications of prewar developments. Abstract painting, for example, became ever more popular (see the comparative essay "A Revolution in the Arts" on p. 509). In addition, prewar fascination with the absurd and the unconscious content of the mind seemed even more appropriate after the nightmare landscapes of World War I battlefronts. This gave rise to both the Dada movement and Surrealism.

Dadaism enshrined the purposelessness of life; revolted by the insanity of life, the Dadaists tried to give it expression by creating "anti-art." The 1918 Berlin Dada Manifesto maintained that "Dada is the international expression of our times, the great rebellion of artistic movements." Many Dadaists assembled pieces of junk (wire, string, rags, scraps of newspaper, nails, washers) into collages, believing that they were transforming the refuse of their culture into art. In the hands of Hannah Höch (1889–1978), Dada became an instrument to comment on women's roles in the new mass culture.

COMPARATIVE ESSAY

A REVOLUTION IN THE ARTS

The period between 1880 and 1930 witnessed a revolution in the arts throughout Western civilization. Fueled in part by developments in physics and psychology, artists and writers rebelled against the traditional belief that the task of art was to represent "reality" and experimented with innovative new techniques in order to approach reality from a totally fresh perspective.

From Impressionism and Expressionism to Cubism, abstract art, Dadaism, and Surrealism, painters seemed intoxicated with the belief that their canvases would help reveal the radically changing world. Especially after the cataclysm of World War I, which shattered the image of a rational society, artists sought an absolute freedom of expression, confident that art could redefine humanity in the midst of chaos. Other arts soon followed their lead: James Joyce turned prose on its head by focusing on his characters' innermost thoughts, and Arnold Schönberg created atonal music by using a scale composed of twelve notes independent of any tonal key.

This revolutionary spirit is exemplified by Pablo Picasso's canvas *Les Demoiselles d'Avignon,* painted in 1907 (see the illustration on p. 443). Picasso used geometrical designs to create a new reality and appropriated other cultural resources, including African masks, in his effort to revitalize Western art.

Another illustration of the revolutionary approach to art was the decision by the French artist Marcel Duchamp to enter a porcelain urinal in a 1917 art exhibit held in New York City. By signing it and giving it the title "Fountain," Duchamp proclaimed that he had transformed the urinal into a work of art. His "ready-mades" (as such art would henceforth be labeled) declared that art was whatever the artist proclaimed as art.

Such intentionally irreverent acts demystified the nearly sacred reverence that had traditionally been attached to works of art. Essentially, Duchamp and others claimed that anything under the sun could be selected as a work of art because the mental choice itself equaled the act of artistic creation. Therefore, art need not be a manual construct; it need only be a mental conceptualization. This liberating concept opened the floodgates of the art world, causing the new century to swim in this free-flowing, exploratory torrent.

Perhaps more important as an artistic movement was **Surrealism,** which sought a reality beyond the material, sensible world and found it in the world of the unconscious through the portrayal of fantasies, dreams, or nightmares. The Spaniard Salvador Dalí (1904–1989) became the high priest of Surrealism and in his mature phase became a master of representational Surrealism. Dalí portrayed recognizable objects entirely divorced from their normal context. By placing objects into unrecognizable relationships, Dalí created a disturbing world in which the irrational had become tangible.

Probing the Unconscious

Interest in the unconscious, evident in Surrealism, was also apparent in the development of new literary techniques that emerged in the 1920s. One of its most apparent

Hannah Höch, Cut with the Kitchen Knife Dada Through the Last Weimar Beer Belly Cultural Epoch of Germany. Hannah Höch, a prominent figure in the postwar Dada movement, used photomontage to create images that reflected on women's issues. In *Cut with the Kitchen Knife,* she combined pictures of German political leaders with sports stars, Dada artists, and scenes from urban life. One major theme emerged: the confrontation between the anti-Dada world of German political leaders and the Dada world of revolutionary ideals. Höch associated women with Dada and the new world.

manifestations was in a "stream of consciousness" technique in which the writer presented an interior monologue or a report of the innermost thoughts of each character. The most famous example of this genre was written by the Irish exile James Joyce (1882–1941). His *Ulysses,* published in 1922, told the story of one day in the life of ordinary people in Dublin by following the flow of their inner dialogue.

The German writer Hermann Hesse (1877–1962) dealt with the unconscious in a different fashion. His novels reflected the influence of new psychological theories and Eastern religions and focused on, among other things, the spiritual loneliness of modern human beings in a mechanized urban society. Hesse's novels made a large impact on German youth in the 1920s. He won the Nobel Prize for literature in 1946.

For much of the Western world, the best way to find (or escape) reality was through mass entertainment. The 1930s was the heyday of the Hollywood studio system, which in the single year of 1937 turned out nearly six hundred feature films. Supplementing the movies were cheap paperbacks and radio, which brought sports, soap operas, and popular music to the depression-weary masses.

The increased size of audiences and the ability of radio and cinema, unlike the printed word, to provide an immediate mass experience added new dimensions to mass culture. Favorite film actors and actresses became stars, whose lives then became subject to public adoration and scrutiny. Sensuous actresses such as Marlene Dietrich, whose appearance in the early sound film *The Blue Angel* catapulted her to fame, popularized new images of women's sexuality.

CONCLUSION

ORLD WAR I SHATTERED the society of late nineteenth- and early twentieth-century Europe. The incredible destruction and the deaths of almost ten million people undermined the whole idea of progress. New propaganda techniques had manipulated entire populations into sustaining their involvement in a meaningless slaughter.

World War I was a total war that involved a mobilization of resources and populations and increased government centralization of power over the lives of its citizens. Civil liberties, such as freedom of the press, speech, assembly, and movement, were circumscribed in the name of national security. The war made the practice of strong central authority a way of life.

The turmoil wrought by the Great War seemed to lead to even greater insecurity. Revolutions dismembered old empires and created new states that fostered unexpected problems. Expectations that Europe and the world would return to normalcy were soon dashed by the failure to achieve a lasting peace, economic collapse, and the rise of authoritarian governments that not only restricted individual freedoms but also sought even greater control over the lives of their subjects in order to guide them to achieve the goals of their totalitarian regimes.

Finally, World War I was the beginning of the end of European hegemony over world affairs. By weakening their own civilization on the battlegrounds of Europe, Europeans inadvertently encouraged the subject peoples of their vast colonial empires to initiate movements for national independence. In the next chapter, we examine some of those movements.

CHAPTER NOTES

1. Arnold Toynbee, *Surviving the Future* (New York, 1971), pp. 106–107.
2. Quoted in Joachim Remak, "1914—The Third Balkan War: Origins Reconsidered," *Journal of Modern History* 43 (1971): 364–365.
3. Quoted in J. M. Winter, *The Experience of World War I* (New York, 1989), p. 142.
4. Quoted in Catherine W. Reilly, ed., *Scars upon My Heart: Women's Poetry and Verse of the First World War* (London, 1981), p. 90.
5. Quoted in William M. Mandel, *Soviet Women* (Garden City, N.Y., 1975), p. 43.
6. Quoted in Irving Howe, ed., *The Basic Writings of Trotsky* (London, 1963), p. 162.

SUGGESTED READING

The historical literature on the causes of World War I is vast. A good starting point is the work by **J. Joll,** *The Origins of the First World War,* 2d ed. (London, 1992). On the events leading to war, see **D. Fromkin,** *Europe's Last Summer: Who Started the Great War in 1914?* (New York, 2004). On the role of militarism, see **D. Hermann,** *The Arming of Europe and the Making of the First World War* (New York, 1997).

The best account of World War I is now **H. Strachan,** *The First World War* (New York, 2004). See also **J. Keegan,** *An Illustrated History of the First World War* (New York, 2001). Two other worthy accounts are **M. Gilbert,** *The First World War* (New York, 1994), and the lavishly illustrated book by **J. M. Winter,** *The Experience of World War I* (New York, 1989). The nature of trench warfare is examined in **T. Ashworth,** *Trench Warfare, 1914–1918: The Live-and-Let-Live System* (London, 1980). For a new interpretation, see **D. Stevenson,** *Cataclysm: The First World War as Political Tragedy* (New York, 2004).

On the role of women in World War I, see **G. Braybon,** *Women Workers in the First World War: The British Experience* (London, 1981); **J. M. Winter** and **R. M. Wall,** eds., *The Upheaval of War: Family, Work and Welfare in Europe, 1914–1918* (Cambridge, 1988); and **G. Braybon** and **P. Summerfield,** *Women's Experiences in Two World Wars* (London, 1987).

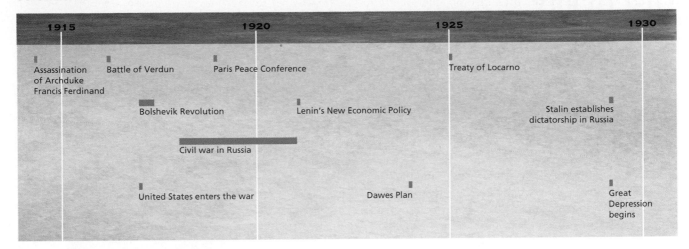

The role of war aims in shaping the peace settlement is examined in **V. H. Rothwell,** *British War Aims and Peace Diplomacy, 1914–1918* (Oxford, 1971), and **D. R. Stevenson,** *French War Aims Against Germany, 1914–1919* (New York, 1982).

A good introduction to the Russian Revolution can be found in **R. A. Wade,** *The Russian Revolution, 1917* (Cambridge, 2000), and **S. Fitzpatrick,** *The Russian Revolution, 1917–1932,* 2d ed. (New York, 1994). See also **R. Pipes,** *The Russian Revolution* (New York, 1990). For a study that puts the Russian Revolution into the context of World War I, see **P. Holquist,** *Making War, Forging Revolution* (Cambridge, Mass., 2002). There is a good analysis as well as a good collection of the thoughts and experiences of ordinary Russian people in 1917 in **M. D. Steinberg,** *Voices of Revolution, 1917* (New Haven, Conn., 2001). On Lenin, see **R. Service,** *Lenin: A Biography* (Cambridge, Mass., 2000). A comprehensive study of the Russian civil war is **W. B. Lincoln,** *Red Victory: A History of the Russian Civil War* (New York, 1989).

For a general introduction to the interwar period, see **M. Kitchen,** *Europe Between the Wars* (London, 1988). The best study on the problem of reparations is **M. Trachtenberg,** *Reparations in World Politics* (New York, 1980), which paints a more positive view of French policies. The "return to normalcy" after the war is analyzed in **C. S. Maier,** *Recasting Bourgeois Europe: Stabilization in France, Germany, and Italy in the Decade After World War I* (Princeton, N.J., 1975). Also valuable is **D. P. Silverman,** *Reconstructing Europe After the Great War* (Cambridge, Mass., 1982). On the Great Depression, see **C. P. Kindleberger,** *The World in Depression, 1929–39,* rev. ed. (Berkeley, Calif., 1986). On Weimar Germany, see **P. Bookbinder,** *Weimar Germany* (New York, 1996), and **R. Henig,** *The Weimar Republic, 1919–1933* (New York, 1998), a brief study.

InfoTrac College Edition

Visit this chapter's InfoTrac College Edition/Research activities at the *Essential World History* Companion Website for activities related to World War I.

ThomsonNOW™ for Duiker and Spielvogel's *The Essential World History,* Third Edition

Enter *ThomsonNOW* using the access card that is available with this text. *ThomsonNOW* will assist you in understanding the content in this chapter with lesson plans generated for your needs, as well as provide you with a connection to the *Wadsworth World History Resource Center* (see description below for details).

WORLD HISTORY
RESOURCE CENTER

Enter the Resource Center using either your *ThomsonNOW* access card or your standalone access card for the *Wadsworth World History Resource Center.* Organized by topic, this website includes quizzes; images; over 350 primary source documents; interactive simulations, maps, and timelines; movie explorations; and a wealth of other resources. You can read the following documents, and many more, at http://worldrc.wadsworth.com/

    Samuel Williamson, *The Origins of World War I*

    World War I poetry

Visit the *Essential World History* Companion Website for chapter quizzes and more:

    http://www.thomsonedu.com/history/duiker

DISCOVERY

What conclusions can you draw about the impact of World War I on the political and social structure of Europe?

In thinking about this question, begin by breaking it down into the components shown below. A discussion of the significance of each component should appear in your answer.

FAMILY AND SOCIETY: Why were young men willing and even eager to fight in World War I? What did the motivations of Zweig, Graves, and Limmer have in common? What impact would these motivations have on Europeans after the war? How long did Zweig and Graves expect the war to last? What does the poster tell you about the feeling for war by 1916? How do you account for the change?

British troops wait for the signal to attack

British Recruiting Poster

THE EXCITEMENT OF WAR

Stefan Zweig, *The World of Yesterday*

The next morning I was in Austria. In every station placards had been put up announcing general mobilization. The trains were filled with fresh recruits, banners were flying, music sounded, and in Vienna I found the entire city in a tumult. . . . There were parades in the street, flags, ribbons, and music burst forth everywhere, young recruits were marching triumphantly, their faces lighting up at the cheering. . . .

And to be truthful, I must acknowledge that there was a majestic, rapturous, and even seductive something in this first outbreak of the people from which one could escape only with difficulty. And in spite of all my hatred and aversion for war, I should not like to have missed the memory of those days. As never before, thousands and hundreds of thousands felt what they should have felt in peace time, that they belonged together. A city of two million, a country of nearly fifty million, in that hour felt that they were participating in world history, in a moment which would never recur, and that each one was called upon to cast his infinitesimal self into the glowing mass, there to be purified of all selfishness. All differences of class, rank, and language were flooded over at that moment by the rushing feeling of fraternity. . . .

What did the great mass know of war in 1914, after nearly half a century of peace? They did not know war, they had hardly given it a thought. It had become legendary, and distance had made it seem romantic and heroic. They still saw it in the perspective of their school readers and of paintings in museums; brilliant cavalry attacks in glittering uniforms, the fatal shot always straight through the heart, the entire campaign a resounding march of victory—"We'll be home at Christmas," the recruits shouted laughingly to their mothers in August of 1914. . . . A rapid excursion into the romantic, a wild, manly adventure—that is how the war of 1914 was painted in the imagination of the simple man, and the younger people were honestly afraid that they might miss this most wonderful and exciting experience of their lives; that is why they hurried and thronged to the colors, and that is why they shouted and sang in the trains that carried them to the slaughter; wildly and feverishly the red wave of blood coursed through the veins of the entire nation.

Robert Graves, *Goodbye to All That*

I had just finished with Charterhouse and gone up to Harlech, when England declared war on Germany. A day or two later I decided to enlist. In the first place, though the papers predicted only a very short war—over by Christmas at the outside—I hoped that it might last long enough to delay my going to Oxford in October, which I dreaded. Nor did I work out the possibilities of getting actively engaged in the fighting, expecting garrison service at home, while the regular forces were away. In the second place, I was outraged to read of the German's cynical violation of Belgian neutrality. Though I discounted perhaps twenty per cent of the atrocity details as wartime exaggeration, that was not, of course, sufficient.

Walter Limmer, Letter to His Parents

In any case I mean to go into this business. . . . That is the simple duty of every one of us. And this feeling is universal among the soldiers, especially since the night when England's declaration of war was announced in the barracks. We none of us got to sleep till three o'clock in the morning, we were so full of excitement, fury, and enthusiasm. It is a joy to go to the Front with such comrades. We are bound to be victorious! Nothing else is possible in the face of such determination to win.

POLITICS AND GOVERNMENT: What do the photos of Lenin and Trotsky suggest about why they were able to bring about a revolution in Russia? How do the authors of the letters suggest Lenin and Trotsky were able to seize and hold power? Why do the letters' authors feel so betrayed? What impact would such attitudes have on the political and social structure of the new Soviet Union?

© Brown Brothers

© Underwood & Underwood/CORBIS

Lenin and Trotsky

SOLDIER AND PEASANT VOICES

Letter from a Soldier in Leningrad to Lenin, January 6, 1918

Bastard! What the hell are you doing? How long are you going to keep on degrading the Russian people? After all, it's because of you they killed the former minister . . . and so many other innocent victims. Because of you, they might kill even other former ministers belonging to the [Socialist Revolutionary] party because you call them counterrevolutionaries and even monarchists. . . . And you, you Bolshevik gang leader hired either by Nicholas II or by Wilhelm II, are waging this pogrom propaganda against men who may have done time with you in exile.

Scoundrel! A curse on you from the politically conscious Russian proletariat, the conscious ones and not the kind who are following you—that is, the Red Guards, the tally clerks, who, when they are called to military service, all hide at the factories and now are killing . . . practically their own father, the way the soldiers did in 1905 when they killed their own, or the way the police and gendarmes did in [1917]. That's who they're more like. They're not pursuing the ideas of socialism because they don't understand them (if they did they wouldn't act this way) but because they get paid a good salary both at the factory and in the Red Guards. But not all the workers are like that—there are very politically aware ones and the soldiers—again not all of them—are like that but only former policemen, constables, gendarmes and the very very ignorant ones who under the old regime tramped with hay on one foot and straw on the other because they couldn't tell their right foot from their left and they are pursuing not the ideas of socialism that you advocate but to be able to lie on their cots in the barracks and do absolutely nothing not even to be asked to sweep the floor, which is already piled with several inches of filth. And so the entire proletariat of Russia is following you, but count fewer than are against you, but they are only physically or rather technically stronger than the majority, and that is what you're abusing when you disbanded the Constituent Assembly the way Nicholas II disbanded the Duma. You point out that counterrevolutionaries gathered there. You lie, scoundrel, there wasn't a single counterrevolutionary and if there was then it was you, the Bolsheviks, which you proved by your actions when you encroached on the gains of the revolution: you are shutting down newspapers, even socialist ones, arresting socialists, committing violence and deceiving the people; you promised loads but did none of it.

Letter from a Peasant to the Bolshevik Leaders, January 10, 1918

To you!

Rulers, plunderers, rapists, destroyers, usurpers, oppressors of Mother Russia, citizens Lenin, Trotsky, Uritsky, Zinoviev, Spiridonova, Antonov, Lunacharsky, Krylenko, and Co. [leaders of the Bolshevik party]:

Allow me to ask you how long you are going to go on degrading Russia's millions, its tormented and exhausted people. Instead of peace, you signed an armistice with the enemy, and this gave our opponent a painful advantage, and you declared war on Russia. You moved the troops you had tricked to the Russian-Russian front and started a fratricidal war. Your mercenary Red Guards are looting, murdering, and raping everywhere they go. A fire has consumed all our dear Mother Russia. Rail transport is idle, as are the plants and factories; the entire population has woken up to find itself in the most pathetic situation, without bread or kerosene or any of the other essentials, unclothed or unshod in unheated houses. In short: hungry and cold. . . . You have strangled the entire press, and freedom with it, you have wiped out the best freedom fighters, you have destroyed all Russia. Think it over, you butchers, you hirelings of the Kaiser [William II]. Isn't your turn about up, too? For all you are doing, we, politically aware Great Russians, are sending you butchers, you hirelings of the Kaiser, our curse. May you be damned, you accursed one, you bloodthirsty butchers, you hirelings of the Kaiser—don't think you're in the clear, because the Russian people will sober up and that will be the end of you. I'm writing in red ink to show that you are bloodthirsty. . . . I'm writing these curses, a great Russian native of Orel Province, peasant of Mtsensk Uezd.

ARTS AND IDEAS: Compare "Cut with the Kitchen Knife . . ." with the Mona Lisa or the Sistine Chapel or any "classical" artwork with which you are familiar. How would you relate Hannah Höch's artistic vision to all the events of this chapter: the excitement of war, its reality, changes that war made in the lives of women, events in Russia, and the economic collapse of Europe in the 1920s and 1930s?

© Erich Lessing/Art Resource, NY; © 2006 Artist's Rights Society (ARS), New York/VG Bild-Kunst, Bonn

Hannah Höch, Cut with the Kitchen Knife Dada through the Last Weimar Beer Belly Cultural Epoch of Germany

23

NATIONALISM, REVOLUTION, AND DICTATORSHIP: ASIA, LATIN AMERICA, AND THE MIDDLE EAST FROM 1919 TO 1939

CHAPTER OUTLINE AND FOCUS QUESTIONS

The Rise of Nationalism

▢ What were the various stages in the rise of nationalist movements in Asia and the Middle East, and what problems did they face?

Revolution in China

▢ What problems did China encounter between the two world wars, and what solutions did the Nationalists and the Communists propose to solve them?

Japan Between the Wars

▢ How did Japan address the problems of nation building in the first decades of the twentieth century, and why did democratic institutions not take hold more effectively?

Nationalism and Dictatorship in Latin America

▢ What problems did the nations of Latin America face in the interwar years? To what degree were they a consequence of foreign influence?

CRITICAL THINKING

▢ How did the societies discussed in this chapter deal with the political, economic, and social challenges that they faced after World War I, and how did these challenges differ from one region to another?

Nehru confers with Mahatma Gandhi, the "Soul of India"

AP Images/Max Desfor

IN 1930, MOHANDAS GANDHI, the sixty-one-year-old leader of the nonviolent movement for Indian independence from British rule, began a march to the sea with seventy-eight followers. Their destination was Dandi, a little coastal town some 240 miles away. The group covered about 12 miles a day. As they went, Gandhi preached his doctrine of nonviolent resistance to British rule in every village he passed through: "Civil disobedience is the inherent right of a citizen. He dare not give it up without ceasing to be a man." By the time he reached Dandi, twenty-four days later, his small group had become a nonviolent army of thousands. When they arrived at Dandi, Gandhi picked up a pinch of salt from the sand. All along the coast, thousands did likewise, openly breaking British laws that prohibited Indians from making their own salt. The British had long profited from their monopoly on the making and sale of salt, an item much in demand in a tropical country. By their simple acts of disobedience, Gandhi and the Indian people had taken a bold step on their long march to independence.

The salt march was but one of many nonviolent activities that Mohandas Gandhi undertook between World War I and World War II to win India's goal of national independence from British rule. World War I had not only deeply affected the lives of Europeans but had also undermined the prestige of Western civilization in the minds of many observers in the rest of the world. When Europeans devastated their own civilization on the battlefields of Europe, the subject peoples of their vast colonial empires were quick to understand what it meant. In Africa and Asia, where initial efforts to fend off Western encroachment in the late nineteenth century had failed, movements for national independence began to take shape. Some were inspired by the nationalist and liberal movements of the West, while others began to look toward the new Marxist model provided by the victory of the Communists in the Soviet Union, who soon worked to spread their revolutionary vision to African and Asian societies. In the Middle East, World War I ended the rule of the Ottoman Empire and led to the creation of new states, many of which soon fell under European domination. Latin American countries, although not fully subjected to colonial rule, watched with wary eyes the growing U.S. and European influence over their own national economies. ◆

The Rise of Nationalism

Although the West had emerged from World War I relatively intact, its political and social foundations and its self-confidence had been severely undermined. Within Europe, doubts about the future viability of Western civilization were widespread, especially among the intellectual elite. These doubts were quick to reach the attention of perceptive observers in Asia and Africa and contributed to a rising tide of unrest against Western political domination throughout the colonial and semicolonial world. That unrest took a variety of forms but was most notably displayed in increasing worker activism, rural protest, and a rising sense of national fervor among anticolonialist intellectuals. In areas of Asia, Africa, and Latin America where independent states had successfully resisted the Western onslaught, the discontent fostered by the war and later by the Great Depression led to a loss of confidence in democratic institutions and the rise of political dictatorships.

Modern Nationalism

The first stage of resistance to the West in Asia and Africa (see Chapters 20 and 21) had met with humiliation and failure and must have confirmed many Westerners' conviction that colonial peoples lacked both the strength and the know-how to create modern states and govern their own destinies. In fact, the process was just beginning. The next phase—the rise of modern nationalism—began to take shape at the beginning of the twentieth century and was the product of the convergence of several factors. The primary source of anticolonialist sentiment was a new urban middle class of Westernized intellectuals. In many cases, these merchants, petty functionaries, clerks, students, and professionals had been educated in Western-style schools. A few had spent time in the West. Many spoke Western languages, wore Western clothes, and worked in occupations connected with the colonial regime. Some even wrote in the languages of their colonial masters.

The results were paradoxical. On the one hand, this "new class" admired Western culture and sometimes harbored a deep sense of contempt for traditional ways. On the other hand, many strongly resented the foreigners and their arrogant contempt for colonial peoples. Though eager to introduce Western ideas and institutions into their own society, these intellectuals were dismayed at the gap between ideal and reality, theory and practice, in colonial policy. Although Western political thought exalted democracy, equality, and individual freedom, democratic institutions were primitive or nonexistent in the colonies.

Equality in economic opportunity and social life was also noticeably lacking. Normally, the middle classes did not suffer in the same manner as impoverished peasants or menial workers on sugar or rubber plantations, but they, too, had complaints. They were usually relegated to low-level jobs in the government or business and paid less than Europeans in similar positions. The superiority of the Europeans was expressed in a variety of ways, including "whites only" clubs and the use of the familiar form of the language (normally used by adults to children) when addressing the natives.

Under these conditions, many of the new urban educated class were very ambivalent toward their colonial masters and the civilization that they represented. Out of this mixture of hopes and resentments emerged the first stirrings of modern nationalism in Asia and Africa. During the first quarter of the century, in colonial and semicolonial societies from the Suez Canal to the shores of the Pacific Ocean, educated native peoples began to organize political parties and movements seeking reforms or the end of foreign rule and the restoration of independence.

Religion and Nationalism At first, many of the leaders of these movements did not focus clearly on the idea of nationhood but tried to defend native economic interests or religious beliefs. In Burma, for example, the first expression of modern nationalism came from students at the University of Rangoon, who protested against official persecution of the Buddhist religion and British lack of respect for local religious traditions. Adopting the name Thakin (a polite term in the Burmese language meaning "lord" or "master," thus emphasizing their demand for the right to rule themselves), they protested against British arrogance and failure to observe local customs in Buddhist temples (such as failing to remove their footwear). Only in the 1930s did the Thakins begin to focus specifically on national independence.

THE DILEMMA OF THE INTELLECTUAL

 Sutan Sjahrir (1909–1966) was a prominent leader of the Indonesian nationalist movement who briefly served as prime minister of the Republic of Indonesia in the 1950s. Like many Western-educated Asian intellectuals, he was tortured by the realization that by education and outlook he was closer to his colonial masters—in his case, the Dutch—than to his own people. He wrote the following passage in a letter to his wife in 1935 and later included it in his book *Out of Exile.*

Why does the author feel estranged from his native culture? What is his answer to the challenges faced by his country in coming to terms with the modern world?

Sutan Sjahrir, *Out of Exile*

Am I perhaps estranged from my people? . . . Why are the things that contain beauty for them and arouse their gentler emotions only senseless and displeasing for me? In reality, the spiritual gap between my people and me is certainly no greater than that between an intellectual in Holland . . . and the undeveloped people of Holland. . . . The difference is rather . . . that the intellectual in Holland does not feel this gap because there is a portion—even a fairly large portion—of his own people on approximately the same intellectual level as himself. . . .

This is what we lack here. Not only is the number of intellectuals in this country smaller in proportion to the total population—in fact, very much smaller—but in addition, the few who are here do not constitute any single entity in spiritual outlook, or in any spiritual life or single culture whatsoever. . . . It is for them so much more difficult than for the intellectuals in Holland. In Holland they build—both consciously and unconsciously—on what is already there. . . . Even if they oppose it, they do so as a method of application or as a starting point.

In our country this is not the case. Here there has been no spiritual or cultural life, and no intellectual progress for centuries. There are the much-praised Eastern art forms but what are these except bare rudiments from a feudal culture that cannot possibly provide a dynamic fulcrum for people of the twentieth century? . . . Our spiritual needs are needs of the twentieth century; our problems and our views are of the twentieth century. Our inclination is no longer toward the mystical, but toward reality, clarity, and objectivity. . . .

We intellectuals here are much closer to Europe or America than we are to the Borobudur or Mahabharata or to the primitive Islamic culture of Java and Sumatra. . . .

So, it seems, the problem stands in principle. It is seldom put forth by us in this light, and instead most of us search unconsciously for a synthesis that will leave us internally tranquil. We want to have both Western science and Eastern philosophy, the Eastern "spirit," in the culture. But what is this Eastern spirit? It is, they say, the sense of the higher, of spirituality, of the eternal and religious, as opposed to the materialism of the West. I have heard this countless times, but it has never convinced me.

In the Dutch East Indies, the Sarekat Islam (Islamic Association) began as a self-help society among Muslim merchants to fight against domination of the local economy by Chinese interests. Eventually, activist elements began to realize that the source of the problem was not the Chinese merchants but the colonial presence, and in the 1920s, Sarekat Islam was transformed into a new organization, the Nationalist Party of Indonesia (PNI), that focused on national independence. Like the Thakins in Burma, this party would eventually lead the country to independence after World War II.

Independence or Modernization? The Nationalist Quandary Building a new nation, however, requires more than a shared sense of grievances against the foreign invader. A host of other issues also had to be resolved. Soon patriots throughout the colonial world were engaged in a lively and sometimes acrimonious debate over such questions as whether independence or modernization should be their primary objective. The answer depended in part on how the colonial regime was perceived. If it was viewed as a source of needed reforms in a traditional society, a gradualist approach made sense. But if it was seen primarily as an impediment to change, the first priority was to bring it to an end. The vast majority of patriotic individuals were convinced that to survive, their societies must adopt much of the Western way of life; yet many were equally determined that the local culture would not, and should not, become a carbon copy of the West. What was the national identity, after all, if it did not incorporate some elements from the traditional way of life?

Another reason for using traditional values was to provide ideological symbols that the common people could understand and would rally around. Though aware that they needed to enlist the mass of the population in the common struggle, most urban intellectuals had difficulty communicating with the teeming population in the countryside who did not understand such complicated and unfamiliar concepts as democracy and nationhood. As the Indonesian intellectual Sutan Sjahrir lamented, many Westernized intellectuals had more in common with their colonial rulers than with the native population in the rural villages (see the box above). As one French colonial official remarked in some surprise to a Vietnamese reformist, "Why, Monsieur, you are more French than I am!"

Gandhi and the Indian National Congress

Nowhere in the colonial world were these issues debated more vigorously than in India. Before the Sepoy Rebellion (see Chapter 20), Indian consciousness had focused mainly on the question of religious identity. But in the latter half of the nineteenth century, a stronger sense of national consciousness began to arise, provoked by the conservative policies and racial arrogance of the British colonial authorities.

The first Indian nationalists were almost invariably upper class and educated. Many of them were from urban areas such as Bombay, Madras, and Calcutta. Some were trained in law and were members of the civil service. At first, many tended to prefer reform to revolution and believed that India needed modernization before it could handle the problems of independence. Such reformists did have some effect. In the 1880s, the government introduced a measure of self-government for the first time. All too often, however, such efforts were sabotaged by local British officials.

The slow pace of reform convinced many Indian nationalists that relying on British benevolence was futile. In 1885, a small group of Indians, with some British participation, met in Bombay to form the Indian National Congress (INC). They hoped to speak for all India, but most were high-class English-trained Hindus. Like their reformist predecessors, members of the INC did not demand immediate independence and accepted the need for reforms to end traditional abuses like child marriage and *sati*. At the same time, they called for an Indian share in the governing process and more spending on economic development and less on military campaigns along the frontier. The British responded with a few concessions, but change was glacially slow.

The INC also had difficulty reconciling religious differences within its ranks. The stated goal of the INC was to seek self-determination for all Indians regardless of class or religious affiliation, but many of its leaders were Hindu and inevitably reflected Hindu concerns. In the first decade of the twentieth century, the separate Muslim League was created to represent the interests of the millions of Muslims in Indian society.

Nonviolent Resistance In 1915, a young Hindu lawyer returned from South Africa to become active in the INC. He transformed the movement and galvanized India's struggle for independence and identity. Mohandas Gandhi was born in 1869 in Gujarat, in western India, the son of a government minister. In the late nineteenth century, he studied in London and became a lawyer. In 1893, he went to South Africa to work in a law firm serving Indian émigrés working as laborers there. He soon became aware of the racial prejudice and exploitation experienced by Indians living in the territory and tried to organize them to protect their interests.

On his return to India, Gandhi immediately became active in the independence movement, setting up a movement based on nonviolent resistance (the Hindi term was *satyagraha,* "hold fast to the truth") to try to force the British to improve the lot of the poor and grant independence to India. His goal was twofold: to convert the British to his views while simultaneously strengthening the unity and sense of self-respect of his compatriots. When the British attempted to suppress dissent, he called on his followers to refuse to obey British regulations. He began to manufacture his own clothes (Gandhi now dressed in a simple *dhoti* made of coarse homespun cotton) and adopted the spinning wheel as a symbol of Indian resistance to imports of British textiles.

British India Between the Wars

Gandhi, now increasingly known as India's "Great Soul" (*Mahatma*), organized mass protests to achieve his aims, but in 1919, they got out of hand and led to violence and British reprisals. British troops killed hundreds of unarmed protesters in the enclosed square in the city of Amritsar in northwestern India. When the protests spread, Gandhi was horrified at the violence and briefly retreated from active politics. Nevertheless, he was arrested for his role in the protests and spent several years in prison.

Gandhi combined his anticolonial activities with an appeal to the spiritual instincts of all Indians. Though he had been born and raised a Hindu, his universalist approach to the idea of God transcended individual religion, although it was shaped by the historical themes of Hindu belief. At a speech given in London in September 1931, he expressed his view of the nature of God as "an indefinable mysterious power that pervades everything . . . , an unseen power which makes itself felt and yet defies all proof."[1]

While Gandhi was in prison, the political situation continued to evolve. In 1921, the British passed the Government of India Act, transforming the heretofore advisory Legislative Council into a bicameral parliament, two-thirds of whose members would be elected. Similar bodies were created at the provincial level. In a stroke, five million Indians were enfranchised. But such reforms were no longer enough for many members of the INC, who wanted to push aggressively for full independence. The British exacerbated the situation by increasing the salt tax and prohibiting the Indian people from manufacturing or harvesting their own salt. Gandhi, now released from prison, returned to his earlier policy of **civil disobedience** by openly joining several dozen supporters in a 240-mile walk to the sea, where he picked up a lump of salt and

COMPARATIVE ILLUSTRATION

Masters and Disciples. When the founders of nationalist movements passed leadership over to their successors, the result was often a change in the strategy and tactics of the organizations. When Jawaharlal Nehru (left photo, on the left) replaced Mahatma Gandhi as leader of the Indian National Congress, the movement adopted a more secular posture. In China, Chiang Kai-shek (right photo, standing) took Sun Yat-sen's Nationalist Party in a more conservative direction after Sun's death in 1925.

urged Indians to ignore the law. Gandhi and many other members of the INC were arrested.

Organizations to promote women's rights in India had been established shortly after 1900, and Indian women now played an active role in the movement. Women accounted for about twenty thousand, or nearly 10 percent, of all those arrested and jailed for taking part in demonstrations during the interwar period. Women marched, picketed foreign shops, and promoted the spinning and wearing of homemade cloth. By the 1930s, women's associations were also actively involved in promoting social reforms, including women's education, the introduction of birth control devices, the abolition of child marriage, and universal suffrage. In 1929, the Sarda Act raised the minimum age of marriage to fourteen.

New Leaders and New Problems In the 1930s, a new figure entered the movement in the person of Jawaharlal Nehru (1889–1964), son of an earlier INC leader. Educated in the law in Great Britain and a *brahmin* by birth, Nehru personified the new Anglo-Indian politician: secular, rational, upper class, and intellectual. In fact, he appeared to be everything that Gandhi was not. With his emergence, the independence movement embarked on two paths, religious and secular, native and Western, traditional and modern. The dual character of the INC leadership may well have strengthened the movement by bringing together

the two primary impulses behind the desire for independence: elite nationalism and the primal force of Indian traditionalism. But it portended trouble for the nation's new leadership in defining India's future path in the contemporary world. In the meantime, Muslim discontent with Hindu dominance over the INC was increasing. In 1940, the Muslim League called for the creation of a separate Muslim state of Pakistan ("land of the pure") in the northwest. As communal strife between Hindus and Muslims increased, many Indians came to realize with sorrow (and some British colonialists with satisfaction) that British rule was all that stood between peace and civil war.

The Nationalist Revolt in the Middle East

In the Middle East, as in Europe, World War I hastened the collapse of old empires. The Ottoman Empire, which had dominated the eastern Mediterranean since the seizure of Constantinople in 1453, had been growing steadily weaker since the end of the eighteenth century, troubled by rising governmental corruption, a decline in the effectiveness of the sultans, and the loss of considerable territory in the Balkans and southwestern Russia. In North Africa, Ottoman authority, tenuous at best, had disintegrated in the nineteenth century, enabling the French to seize Algeria and Tunisia and the British to establish a protectorate over the Nile River valley.

Decline of the Ottoman Empire   Reformist elements in Istanbul, to be sure, had tried from time to time to resist the trend, but military defeats continued: Greece declared its independence, and Ottoman power declined steadily in the Middle East. A rising sense of nationality among Serbs, Armenians, and other minority peoples threatened the internal stability and cohesion of the empire. In the 1870s, a new generation of Ottoman reformers seized power in Istanbul and pushed through a constitution aimed at forming a legislative assembly that would represent all the peoples in the state. But the sultan they placed on the throne suspended the new charter and attempted to rule by traditional authoritarian means.

By the end of the nineteenth century, the defunct 1876 constitution had become a symbol of change for reformist elements, now grouped together under the common name **Young Turks.** They found support in the Ottoman army and administration and among Turks living in exile. In 1908, the Young Turks forced the sultan to restore the constitution, and he was removed from power the following year.

But the Young Turks had appeared at a moment of crisis for the empire. Internal rebellions, combined with Austrian annexations of Ottoman territories in the Balkans, undermined support for the new government and provoked the army to step in. With most minorities from the old empire now removed from Istanbul's authority, many ethnic Turks began to embrace a new concept of a Turkish state based on all those of Turkish nationality.

The final blow to the old empire came in World War I, when the Ottoman government allied with Germany in the hope of driving the British from Egypt and restoring Ottoman rule over the Nile valley. In response, the British declared an official protectorate over Egypt and, aided by the efforts of the dashing if eccentric British adventurer T. E. Lawrence (popularly known as Lawrence of Arabia), sought to undermine Ottoman rule in the Arabian peninsula by encouraging Arab nationalists there. In 1916, the local governor of Mecca declared Arabia independent from Ottoman rule, while British troops, advancing from Egypt, seized Palestine (see the spot map on p. 504 in Chapter 22). In October 1918, having suffered more than 300,000 casualties during the war, the Ottoman Empire negotiated an armistice with the Allied Powers.

Mustafa Kemal and the Modernization of Turkey   During the next few years, the tottering empire began to fall apart as the British and the French made plans to divide up Ottoman territories in the Middle East and the Greeks won Allied approval to seize the western parts of the Anatolian peninsula for their dream of re-creating the substance of the old Byzantine Empire. The impending collapse energized key elements in Turkey under the leadership of a war hero, Colonel Mustafa Kemal (1881–1938), who had commanded Turkish forces in their defense of the Dardanelles against a British invasion during World War I. Now he resigned from the army and convoked a national congress that called for the creation of an elected government and the preservation of the remaining territories of the old empire in a new republic of Turkey. Establishing his new capital at Ankara, Kemal's forces drove the Greeks from the Anatolian peninsula and persuaded the British to agree to a new treaty. In 1923, the last of the Ottoman sultans fled the country, which was now declared a Turkish republic. The Ottoman Empire had come to an end.

During the next few years, President Mustafa Kemal (now popularly known as Atatürk, or "Father Turk") attempted to transform Turkey into a modern secular republic. The trappings of a democratic system were put in place, centered on an elected Grand National Assembly, but the president was relatively intolerant of opposition and harshly suppressed critics of his rule. Turkish nationalism was emphasized, and the Turkish language, now written in the Roman alphabet, was shorn of many of its Arabic elements. Popular education was emphasized, old aristocratic titles like *pasha* and *bey* were abolished, and all Turkish citizens were given family names in the European style.

Atatürk also took steps to modernize the economy, overseeing the establishment of a light industrial sector producing textiles, glass, paper, and cement and instituting a five-year plan on the Soviet model to provide for state direction over the economy. Atatürk was no admirer of Soviet communism, however, and the Turkish economy can be better described as a form of state capitalism. He also encouraged the modernization of the agricultural sector through the establishment of training institutions and model farms, but such reforms had relatively little effect on the nation's predominantly conservative peasantry.

Perhaps the most significant aspect of Atatürk's reform program was his attempt to break the power of the Islamic clerics and transform Turkey into a secular state. The caliphate was formally abolished in 1924 (see the box on p. 518), and *Shari'a* (Islamic law) was replaced by a revised version of the Swiss law code. The fez (the brimless cap worn by Turkish Muslims) was abolished as a form of headdress, and women were discouraged from wearing the veil in the traditional Islamic custom. Women received the right to vote in 1934 and were legally guaranteed equal rights with men in all aspects of marriage and inheritance. Education and the professions were now open to citizens of both genders, and some women even began to participate in politics. All citizens were given the right to convert to another religion at will.

The legacy of Mustafa Kemal Atatürk was enormous. Although not all of his reforms were widely accepted in practice, especially by devout Muslims, most of the changes he introduced were retained after his death in 1938. In virtually every respect, the Turkish republic was the product of his determined efforts to create a modern Turkish nation.

Mustafa Kemal's Case Against the Caliphate

As part of his plan to transform Turkey into a modern society, Mustafa Kemal Atatürk proposed bringing an end to the caliphate, which had been in the hands of Ottoman sultans since the formation of the empire. In the following passage from a speech to the National Assembly, he gives his reasons.

When and why was the caliphate system first established? Why does Mustafa Kemal believe that it no longer meets the needs of the Turkish people?

Atatürk's Speech to the Assembly, October 1924

The monarch designated under the title of Caliph was to guide the affairs of [all] Muslim peoples and to secure the execution of the religious prescriptions which would best correspond to their worldly interests. He was to defend the rights of all Muslims and concentrate all the affairs of the Muslim world in his hands with effective authority.

The sovereign entitled Caliph was to maintain justice among the three hundred million Muslims on the terrestrial globe, to safeguard the rights of these peoples, to prevent any event that could encroach upon order and security, and confront every attack which the Muslims would be called upon to encounter from the side of other nations. It was to be part of his attributes to preserve by all means the welfare and spiritual development of Islam. . . .

If the Caliph and Caliphate, as they maintained, were to be invested with a dignity embracing the whole of Islam, ought they not to have realized in all justice that a crushing burden would be imposed on Turkey, on her existence; her entire resources and all her forces would be placed at the disposal of the Caliph? . . .

For centuries our nation was guided under the influence of these erroneous ideas. But what has been the result of it? Everywhere they have lost millions of men. "Do you know," I asked, "how many sons of Anatolia have perished in the scorching deserts of the Yemen? Do you know the losses we have suffered in holding Syria and Egypt and in maintaining our position in Africa? And do you see what has come out of it? Do you know?

"Those who favor the idea of placing the means at the disposal of the Caliph to brave the whole world and the power to administer the affairs of the whole of Islam must not appeal to the population of Anatolia alone but to the great Muslim agglomerations which are eight or ten times as rich in men.

"New Turkey, the people of New Turkey, have no reason to think of anything else but their own existence and their own welfare. She has nothing more to give away to others."

ThomsonNOW To read Atatürk's "Address to the Turkish Yash," enter the *ThomsonNOW* documents area using the access card that is available for *The Essential World History*.

Modernization in Iran In the meantime, a similar process was under way in Persia. Under the Qajar dynasty (1794–1925), the country had not been very successful in resisting Russian advances in the Caucasus or resolving its domestic problems. To secure themselves from foreign influence, the shahs moved the capital from Tabriz to Tehran, in a mountainous area just south of the Caspian Sea. During the mid-nineteenth century, one modernizing shah attempted to introduce political and economic reforms but was impeded by resistance from tribal and religious—predominantly Shi'ite—forces. To buttress its rule, the dynasty turned increasingly to Russia and Great Britain to protect itself from its own people.

Eventually, the growing foreign presence led to the rise of a native Persian nationalist movement. Supported actively by Shi'ite religious leaders, opposition to the regime rose steadily among both peasants and merchants in the cities, and in 1906, popular pressures forced the reigning shah to grant a constitution on the Western model.

As in the Ottoman Empire and Manchu China, however, the modernizers had moved too soon, before their power base was secure. With the support of the Russians and the British, the shah was able to regain control, while the two foreign powers began to divide the country into separate spheres of influence. One reason for the growing foreign presence in Persia was the discovery of oil reserves in the southern part of the country in 1908. Within a few years, oil exports increased rapidly, with the bulk of the profits going into the pockets of British investors.

In 1921, an officer in the Persian army by the name of Reza Khan (1878–1944) led a mutiny and seized power in Tehran. The new ruler's original intention had been to establish a republic; but resistance from traditional forces impeded his efforts, and in 1925, the new Pahlavi dynasty, with Reza Khan as shah, replaced the now defunct Qajar dynasty. During the next few years, Reza Khan attempted to follow the example of Atatürk in Turkey, introducing a number of reforms to strengthen the central government, modernize the civilian

Iran Under the Pahlavi Dynasty

and military bureaucracy, and establish a modern economic infrastructure. He also officially changed the name of the nation to Iran.

Unlike Atatürk, Reza Khan did not attempt to destroy the power of Islamic beliefs, but he did encourage the establishment of a Western-style educational system and forbade women to wear the veil in public. Women continued to be exploited, however; it was their intensive labor in the carpet industry that provided major export earnings—second only to oil—in the interwar period. To strengthen the sense of Persian nationalism and reduce the power of Islam, Reza Khan attempted to popularize the symbols and beliefs of pre-Islamic times. Like his Qajar predecessors, however, he was hindered by strong foreign influence. When the Soviet Union and Great Britain decided to send troops into the country during World War II, he resigned in protest and died three years later.

Nation Building in Iraq   One other consequence of the collapse of the Ottoman Empire was the emergence of a new political entity along the Tigris and Euphrates rivers, once the heartland of ancient empires. Lacking defensible borders and sharply divided along ethnic and religious lines—a Shi'ite majority in rural areas was balanced by a vocal Sunni minority in the cities and a largely Kurdish population in the northern mountains—the region had been under Ottoman rule since the seventeenth century. With the advent of World War I, British forces occupied the lowland area from Baghdad southward to the Persian Gulf in order to protect the oil-producing regions in neighboring Iran from a German takeover.

Although the British claimed to have arrived as liberators, in 1920 the League of Nations placed the country under British control as the mandate of Iraq. Civil unrest and growing anti-Western sentiment rapidly dispelled any plans for the possible emergence of an independent government, and in 1921, after the suppression of resistance forces, the country was placed under the titular authority of King Faisal of Syria, a descendant of Muhammad. Faisal relied for support primarily on the politically more sophisticated urban Sunni population, although they represented less than a quarter of the population. The discovery of oil near Kirkuk in 1927 increased the value of the area to the British, who granted formal independence to Iraq in 1932, although British advisers retained a strong influence over the fragile government.

The Rise of Arab Nationalism and the Issue of Palestine   Unrest against Ottoman rule had existed in the Arabian peninsula since the eighteenth century, when the Wahhabi revolt attempted to drive out the outside influences and cleanse Islam of corrupt practices that had developed in past centuries. The revolt was eventually suppressed, but Wahhabi influence persisted.

World War I offered an opportunity for the Arabs to throw off the shackles of Ottoman rule—but what would replace them? The Arabs were not a nation but an idea, and disagreement over what constitutes an Arab plagued generations of political leaders who sought unsuccessfully to knit together the disparate peoples of the region into a single Arab nation.

When the Arab leaders in Mecca declared their independence from Ottoman rule in 1916, they had hoped for British support, but they were to be sorely disappointed. As mentioned earlier, at the close of the war, the British and French agreed to create a number of mandates in the area under the general supervision of the League of Nations. Iraq and Trans-Jordan were assigned to the British; Syria and Lebanon (the two areas were separated so that Christian peoples in Lebanon could be placed under Christian administration) were given to the French.

The land of Palestine—once the home of the Jews but now inhabited primarily by Muslim Palestinians and a few thousand Christians—became a separate mandate. According to the Balfour Declaration, issued by the British foreign secretary, Lord Balfour, in November 1917, Palestine was to be a national home for the Jews.

© Illustrated London News

An Exercise in Nation Building.   When the Ottoman Empire collapsed after World War I, the victorious Allied Powers struggled to pick up the pieces and establish several fledgling new nations in the Middle East. It was a daunting task, given the ethnic diversity and the lack of any tradition of statehood in the area. Nowhere was the problem more acute than in Mesopotamia, where a British mandate—to be called Iraq—was created in 1921. Lacking a royal family with roots in the area, the British authorities selected Amir Faisal, a descendant of Muhammad, as constitutional monarch, although he had never visited the region. Shown here is the installation ceremony, held in August 1921. King Faisal, flanked by two British officials, is seated second from the left while a band plays the British anthem "God Save the King."

The declaration was ambiguous on the legal status of the territory and promised that the decision would not undermine the rights of the non-Jewish peoples currently living in the area. But Arab nationalists were incensed. How could a national home for the Jewish people be established in a territory where 90 percent of the population was Muslim?

In the early 1920s, a leader of the Wahhabi movement, Ibn Saud (1880–1953), united Arab tribes in the northern part of the Arabian peninsula and drove out the remnants of Ottoman rule. Ibn Saud was a descendant of the family that had led the Wahhabi revolt in the eighteenth century. Devout and gifted, he won broad support among Arab tribal peoples and established the kingdom of Saudi Arabia throughout much of the peninsula in 1932.

At first, his new kingdom, consisting essentially of the vast wastes of central Arabia, was desperately poor. But during the 1930s, American companies began to explore for oil, and in 1938, Standard Oil made a successful strike at Dhahran, on the Persian Gulf. Soon an Arabian-American oil conglomerate, popularly called Aramco, was established, and the isolated kingdom was suddenly inundated by Western oilmen and untold wealth.

In the meantime, Jewish settlers began to arrive in Palestine in response to the promises made in the Balfour Declaration. As tensions between the new arrivals and existing Muslim residents began to escalate, the British tried to restrict Jewish immigration into the territory and rejected the concept of a separate state. They also created a separate emirate of Trans-Jordan out of the eastern section of Palestine. After World War II, it would become the independent kingdom of Jordan. The stage was set for the conflicts that would take place in the region after World War II.

Nationalism and Revolution in Asia and Africa

Before the Russian Revolution, to most intellectuals in Asia and Africa, "Westernization" referred to the capitalist democratic civilization of western Europe and the United States, not the doctrine of social revolution developed by Karl Marx. Until 1917, Marxism was regarded as a utopian idea rather than a concrete system of government. Moreover, to many intellectuals, Marxism appeared to have little relevance to conditions in Asia and Africa. Marxist doctrine, after all, declared that a communist society would arise only from the ashes of an advanced capitalism that had already passed through an industrial revolution. From the perspective of Marxist historical analysis, most societies in Asia and Africa were still at the feudal stage of development; they lacked the economic conditions and political awareness to achieve a socialist revolution that would bring the working class to power. Finally, the Marxist view of nationalism and religion had little appeal to many patriotic intellectuals in the non-Western world. Marx believed that nationhood and religion were essentially false ideas that diverted the attention of the oppressed masses from the critical issues of class struggle. Instead, Marx stressed an "internationalist" outlook based on class consciousness and the eventual creation of a classless society with no artificial divisions based on culture, nation, or religion.

Lenin and the East   The situation began to change after the Russian Revolution in 1917. The rise to power of Lenin's Bolsheviks demonstrated that a revolutionary party espousing Marxist principles could overturn a corrupt, outdated system and launch a new experiment dedicated to ending human inequality and achieving a paradise on earth. In 1920, Lenin proposed a new revolutionary strategy designed to relate Marxist doctrine and practice to non-Western societies. His reasons were not entirely altruistic. Soviet Russia, surrounded by capitalist powers, desperately needed allies in its struggle to survive in a hostile world. To Lenin, the anticolonial movements emerging in North Africa, Asia, and the Middle East after World War I were natural allies of the beleaguered new regime in Moscow. Lenin was convinced that only the ability of the imperialist powers to find markets, raw materials, and sources of capital investment in the non-Western world kept capitalism alive. If the tentacles of capitalist influence in Asia and Africa could be severed, imperialism would weaken and collapse.

Establishing such an alliance was not easy, however. Most nationalist leaders in colonial countries belonged to the urban middle class, and many abhorred the idea of a comprehensive revolution to create a totally egalitarian society. In addition, many still adhered to traditional religious beliefs and were opposed to the atheistic principles of classical Marxism.

Since it was unrealistic to expect bourgeois nationalist support for social revolution, Lenin sought a compromise by which Communist parties could be organized among the working classes in the preindustrial societies of Asia and Africa. These parties would then forge informal alliances with existing middle-class parties to struggle against the traditional ruling class and Western imperialism. Such an alliance, of course, could not be permanent because many bourgeois nationalists in Asia and Africa would reject an egalitarian, classless society. Once the imperialists had been overthrown, therefore, the Communist parties would turn against their erstwhile nationalist partners to seize power on their own and carry out the socialist revolution.

Lenin's strategy became a major element in Soviet foreign policy in the 1920s. Soviet agents fanned out across the world to carry Marxism beyond the boundaries of industrial Europe. The primary instrument of this effort was the **Communist International,** or **Comintern** for short. Formed in 1919 at Lenin's prodding, the Comintern was a worldwide organization of Communist parties dedicated to the advancement of world revolution. At its headquarters in Moscow, agents from around the world were trained in the precepts of world communism and then sent back to their countries to form Marxist parties and promote the cause of social revolution. By the end of the 1920s, almost every colonial or semicolonial society in Asia had a party based on Marxist principles. The Soviets had less success in the Middle East, where Marxist ideology appealed mainly to minorities such as Jews and Armenians in the cities, and in black Africa, where Soviet strategists in any case felt that conditions were not sufficiently advanced for the creation of Communist organizations.

The Appeal of Communism According to Marxist doctrine, the rank and file of Communist parties should be urban factory workers alienated from capitalist society by inhuman working conditions. In practice, many of the leaders even in European Communist parties tended to be urban intellectuals or members of the lower middle class. That phenomenon was even more true in the non-Western world, where most early Marxists were rootless intellectuals. Some were probably drawn into the movement for patriotic reasons and saw Marxist doctrine as a new, more effective means of modernizing their societies and removing the colonial exploiters (see the box on p. 522). Others were attracted by the message of egalitarian communism and the utopian dream of a classless society. For those who had lost their faith in traditional religion, communism often served as a new secular ideology, dealing not with the hereafter but with the here and now or, indeed, with a remote future when the state would wither away and the "classless society" would replace the lost truth of traditional faiths.

Of course, the new doctrine's appeal was not the same in all non-Western societies. In Confucian societies such as China and Vietnam, where traditional belief systems had been badly discredited by their failure to counter the Western challenge, communism had an immediate impact and rapidly became a major factor in the anticolonial movement. In Buddhist and Muslim societies, where traditional religion remained strong and actually became a cohesive factor in the resistance movement, communism had less success. To maximize their appeal and minimize potential conflict with traditional ideas, Communist parties frequently attempted to adapt Marxist doctrine to indigenous values and institutions. In the Middle East, for example, the Ba'ath Party in Syria adopted a hybrid socialism combining Marxism with Arab nationalism. In Africa, radical intellectuals talked vaguely of a uniquely "African road to socialism."

The degree to which these parties were successful in establishing alliances with nationalist parties and building a solid base of support among the mass of the population also varied from place to place. In some instances, the Communists were briefly able to establish a cooperative relationship with the bourgeois parties. The most famous example was the alliance between the Chinese Communist Party and Sun Yat-sen's Nationalist Party (discussed in the next section). These efforts were abandoned in 1928 when the Comintern, reacting to Chiang Kai-shek's betrayal of the alliance with the Chinese Communist Party, declared that Communist parties should restrict their recruiting efforts to the most revolutionary elements in society—notably, the urban intellectuals and the working class. Harassed by colonial authorities and saddled with strategic directions from Moscow that often had little relevance to local conditions, Communist parties in most colonial societies had little success in the 1930s and failed to build a secure base of support among the mass of the population.

Revolution in China

Overall, revolutionary Marxism had its greatest impact in China, where a group of young radicals founded the Chinese Communist Party (CCP) in 1921. The rise of the CCP was a consequence of the failed revolution of 1911. When political forces are too weak or too divided to consolidate their power during a period of instability, the military usually steps in to fill the vacuum. In China, Sun Yat-sen and his colleagues had accepted General Yuan Shikai (Yuan Shih-k'ai) as president of the new Chinese republic in 1911 because they lacked the military force to compete with his control over the army. But some had misgivings about Yuan's intentions. As one remarked in a letter to a friend, "We don't know whether he will be a George Washington or a Napoleon."

As it turned out, he was neither. Understanding little of the new ideas sweeping into China from the West, Yuan ruled in a traditional manner, reviving Confucian rituals and institutions and eventually trying to found a new imperial dynasty. Yuan's dictatorial inclinations rapidly led to clashes with Sun's party, now renamed the *Guomindang* (*Kuomintang*), or Nationalist Party. When Yuan dissolved the new parliament, the Nationalists launched a rebellion. When it failed, Sun Yat-sen fled to Japan.

Yuan was strong enough to brush off the challenge from the revolutionary forces but not to turn back the clock of history. He died in 1916 and was succeeded by one of his military subordinates. For the next several

THE PATH OF LIBERATION

POLITICS & GOVERNMENT

In 1919, the Vietnamese revolutionary Ho Chi Minh (1890–1969) was living in exile in France, where he first became acquainted with the new revolutionary experiment in Bolshevik Russia. He became a leader of the Vietnamese Communist movement. In the following passage, written in 1960, he reminisces about his reasons for becoming a Communist. The Second International that he mentions was an organization created in 1889 by moderate socialists who pursued their goal by parliamentary means. Lenin created the Third International, or Comintern, in 1919 to promote violent revolution.

Why does Ho Chi Minh believe that the Third International was the key to the liberation of the colonial peoples? What were the essential elements of Lenin's strategy for bringing that about?

Ho Chi Minh, "The Path Which Led Me to Leninism"

After World War I, I made my living in Paris, now as a retoucher at a photographer's, now as a painter of "Chinese antiquities" (made in France!). I would distribute leaflets denouncing the crimes committed by the French colonialists in Vietnam.

At that time, I supported the October Revolution only instinctively, not yet grasping all its historic importance. I loved and admired Lenin because he was a great patriot who liberated his compatriots; until then, I had read none of his books.

The reason for my joining the French Socialist Party was that these "ladies and gentlemen"—as I called my comrades at that moment—had shown their sympathy toward me, toward the struggle of the oppressed peoples. But I understood neither what was a party, a trade union, nor what was Socialism nor Communism.

Heated discussions were then taking place in the branches of the Socialist Party, about the question whether the Socialist Party should remain in the Second International, should a Second-and-a-Half International be founded, or should the Socialist Party join Lenin's Third International? I attended the meetings regularly, twice or three times a week, and attentively listened to the discussion. First, I could not understand thoroughly. Why were the discussions so heated? Either with the Second, Second-and-a-Half, or Third International, the revolution could be waged. What was the use of arguing then? As for the First International, what had become of it?

What I wanted most to know—and this precisely was not debated in the meetings—was: which International sides with the peoples of colonial countries?

I raised this question—the most important in my opinion—in a meeting. Some comrades answered: It is the Third, not the Second International. And a comrade gave me Lenin's "Thesis on the national and colonial questions," published by *l'Humanité,* to read.

There were political terms difficult to understand in this thesis. But by dint of reading it again and again, finally I could grasp the main part of it. What emotion, enthusiasm, clear-sightedness, and confidence it instilled in me! I was overjoyed to tears. Though sitting alone in my room, I shouted aloud as if addressing large crowds: "Dear martyrs, compatriots! This is what we need, this is the path to our liberation!"

After that, I had entire confidence in Lenin, in the Third International.

ThomsonNOW To read more of Ho Chi Minh's writings, enter the *ThomsonNOW* documents area using the access card that is available for *The Essential World History.*

---

years, China slipped into semianarchy as the power of the central government disintegrated and military warlords seized power in the provinces.

Mr. Science and Mr. Democracy: The New Culture Movement

In the meantime, discontent with existing conditions continued to rise in various sectors of Chinese society. The most vocal protests came from radical intellectuals, who opposed Yuan Shikai's conservative rule but were now convinced that political change could not take place until the Chinese people were more familiar with trends in the outside world. Braving the displeasure of Yuan and his successors, progressive intellectuals at Peking University launched the **New Culture Movement,** aimed at abolishing the remnants of the old system and introducing Western values and institutions into China. Using the classrooms of China's most prestigious university as well as the pages of newly established progressive magazines and newspapers, the intellectuals introduced a bewildering mix of new ideas, from the philosophy of Friedrich Nietzsche to the feminist plays of Henrik Ibsen. As such ideas flooded into China, they stirred up a new generation of educated Chinese youth, who chanted "Down with Confucius and sons" and talked of a new era dominated by "Mr. Sai" (Mr. Science) and "Mr. De" (Mr. Democracy). No one was a greater defender of free thought and speech than the chancellor of Peking University, Cai Yuanpei (Ts'ai Yüan-p'ei): "Regardless of what school of thought a person may adhere to, so long as that person's ideas are justified and conform to reason and have not been passed by through the process of natural selection, although there may be controversy, such ideas have a right to be presented."[2] Not surprisingly, such views earned the distrust of conservative military officers, one of whom threatened to lob artillery shells into Peking University to destroy the poisonous new ideas and their advocates.

Discontent among intellectuals, however, was soon joined by the rising chorus of public protest against Japan's efforts to expand its influence on the mainland. During the first decade of the twentieth century, Japan had taken advantage of the Qing's decline to extend its domination over Manchuria and Korea (see Chapter 21). In 1915, the Japanese government insisted that Yuan Shikai accept a series of twenty-one demands that would have given Japan a virtual protectorate over the Chinese government and economy. Yuan was able to fend off the most far-reaching Japanese demands by arousing popular outrage in China, but at the Paris Peace Conference four years later, Japan received Germany's sphere of influence in Shandong Province as a reward for its support of the Allied cause in World War I. On hearing that the Chinese government had accepted the decision, on May 4, 1919, patriotic students, supported by other sectors of the urban population, demonstrated in Beijing and other major cities of the country. Although this May Fourth Movement did not lead to the restoration of Shandong, it did alert a substantial part of the politically literate population to the threat to national survival and the incompetence of the warlord government.

The Nationalist-Communist Alliance   By 1920, central authority had almost ceased to exist in China. Two competing political forces now began to emerge from the chaos. One was Sun Yat-sen's Nationalist Party. From Canton, Sun sought international assistance to carry out his national revolution. The other was the CCP. Following Lenin's strategy, Comintern agents soon advised the new party to link up with the more experienced Nationalists. Sun Yat-sen needed the expertise and the diplomatic support that the Soviet Union could provide because his anti-imperialist rhetoric had alienated many Western powers. In 1923, the two parties formed an alliance to oppose the warlords and drive the imperialist powers out of China.

For three years, with the assistance of a Comintern mission in Canton, the two parties submerged their mutual suspicions and mobilized and trained a revolutionary army to march north and seize control over China. The so-called Northern Expedition began in the summer of 1926 (see Map 23.1). By the following spring, revolutionary forces were in control of all Chinese territory south of the Yangtze River, including the major river ports of Wuhan and Shanghai. But tensions between the

Student Demonstrations in Beijing.   On May 4, 1919, students gathered at the Gate of Heavenly Peace in Beijing to protest against the Japanese takeover of the Shandong peninsula after World War I (left photo). The event triggered the famous May Fourth Movement, which highlighted the demands of progressive forces in China for political and social reforms. Eighty years to the day later, the event was repeated as students and their supporters gathered in the same spot to demand democracy and an end to official corruption in China. A portrait of the deceased Communist leader Mao Zedong looks down in seeming disdain (right photo).

MAP 23.1   **The Northern Expedition and the Long March.** This map shows the routes taken by the combined Nationalist-Communist forces during the Northern Expedition of 1926–1928. The thinner arrow indicates the route taken by Communist units during the Long March led by Mao Zedong. ❓ Where did Mao establish his new headquarters? 🌐 **View an animated version of this map or related maps at** http://worldrc.wadsworth.com/

two parties now surfaced. Sun Yat-sen had died of cancer in 1925 and was succeeded as head of the Nationalist Party by his military subordinate, Chiang Kai-shek (see the comparative illustration on p. 516). Chiang feigned support for the alliance with the Communists but actually planned to destroy them. In April 1927, he struck against the Communists and their supporters in Shanghai, killing thousands. After the massacre, most of the Communist leaders went into hiding in the city, where they attempted to revive the movement in its traditional base among the urban working class. Some party members, however, led by the young Communist organizer Mao Zedong (Mao Tse-tung), fled to the hilly areas south of the Yangtze River.

Unlike most CCP leaders, Mao was convinced that the Chinese revolution must be based on the impoverished peasants in the countryside. The son of a prosperous peasant, Mao served as an agitator in rural villages in his native province of Hunan during the Northern Expedition in the fall of 1926. At that time, he wrote a famous report to the party leadership suggesting that the CCP support peasant demands for a land revolution (see the box on p. 525). But his superiors refused, fearing that such radical policies would destroy the alliance with the Nationalists.

The Nanjing Republic

In 1928, Chiang Kai-shek founded a new Chinese republic at Nanjing, and over the next three years, he sought to reunify China by a combination of military operations and inducements to various northern warlords to join his movement. He also attempted to put an end to the Communists, rooting them out of their urban base in Shanghai and their rural redoubt in the rugged hills of Jiangxi (Kiangsi) Province. He succeeded in the latter task in 1931, when most party leaders were forced to flee Shanghai for Mao's base in southern China. Three years later, using their superior military strength, Chiang's troops surrounded the Communist base in Jiangxi, inducing Mao's young People's Liberation Army (PLA) to abandon its guerrilla lair and embark on the famous Long March, an arduous journey of thousands of miles on foot through mountains, marshes, and deserts to the small provincial town of Yan'an (Yenan) 200 miles north of the city of Xian in the dusty hills of northern China (see Map 23.1).

Meanwhile, Chiang was trying to build a new nation. When the Nanjing republic was established in 1928, Chiang publicly declared his commitment to Sun Yat-sen's Three People's Principles. In a program announced in 1918, Sun had written about the all-important second stage of "political tutelage":

> China . . . needs a republican government just as a boy needs school. As a schoolboy must have good teachers and helpful friends, so the Chinese people, being for the first time under republican rule, must have a farsighted revolutionary government for their training. This calls for the period of political tutelage, which is a necessary transitional stage from monarchy to republicanism. Without this, disorder will be unavoidable.[3]

In keeping with Sun's program, Chiang announced a period of political indoctrination to prepare the Chinese people for a final stage of constitutional government. In the meantime, the Nationalists would use their dictatorial power to carry out a land reform program and modernize the urban industrial sector.

But it would take more than paper plans to create a new China. Years of neglect and civil war had severely frayed the political, economic, and social fabric of the nation. There were faint signs of an impending industrial revolution in the major urban centers, but most of the people in the countryside, drained by warlord exactions and civil strife, were still grindingly poor and overwhelmingly illiterate. A Westernized middle class had begun to emerge in the cities and formed much of the natural constituency of the Nanjing government. But this new Westernized elite, preoccupied with bourgeois values of individual advancement and material accumulation, had

A CALL FOR REVOLT

POLITICS & GOVERNMENT

In the fall of 1926, Nationalist and Communist forces moved north from Canton on their Northern Expedition in an effort to defeat the warlords. The young Communist Mao Zedong accompanied revolutionary troops into his home province of Hunan, where he submitted a report to the CCP Central Committee calling for a massive peasant revolt against the ruling order. The report shows his confidence that peasants could play an active role in the Chinese revolution despite the skepticism of many of his colleagues.

Why does Mao Zedong believe that rural peasants could help bring about a social revolution in China? How does his vision compare with the reality of the Bolshevik Revolution in Russia?

Mao Zedong, "The Peasant Movement in Hunan"

During my recent visit to Hunan I made a firsthand investigation of conditions. . . . In a very short time, . . . several hundred million peasants will rise like a mighty storm, . . . a force so swift and violent that no power, however great, will be able to hold it back. They will smash all the trammels that bind them and rush forward along the road to liberation. They will sweep all the imperialists, warlords, corrupt officials, local tyrants, and evil gentry into their graves. Every revolutionary party and every revolutionary comrade will be put to the test, to be accepted or rejected as they decide. There are three alternatives. To march at their head and lead them? To trail behind them, gesticulating and criticizing? Or to stand in their way and oppose them? Every Chinese is free to choose, but events will force you to make the choice quickly.

The main targets of attack by the peasants are the local tyrants, the evil gentry and the lawless landlords, but in passing they also hit out against patriarchal ideas and institutions, against the corrupt officials in the cities and against bad practices and customs in the rural areas. . . . As a result, the privileges which the feudal landlords enjoyed for thousands of years are being shattered to pieces. . . . With the collapse of the power of the landlords, the peasant associations have now become the sole organs of authority, and the popular slogan "All power to the peasant associations" has become a reality.

The peasants' revolt disturbed the gentry's sweet dreams. When the news from the countryside reached the cities, it caused immediate uproar among the gentry. . . . From the middle social strata upwards to the Kuomintang right-wingers, there was not a single person who did not sum up the whole business in the phrase, "It's terrible!" . . . Even quite progressive people said, "Though terrible, it is inevitable in a revolution." In short, nobody could altogether deny the word "terrible." But . . . the fact is that the great peasant masses have risen to fulfill their historic mission. . . . What the peasants are doing is absolutely right; what they are doing is fine! "It's fine!" is the theory of the peasants and of all other revolutionaries. Every revolutionary comrade should know that the national revolution requires a great change in the countryside. The Revolution of 1911 did not bring about this change, hence its failure. This change is now taking place, and it is an important factor for the completion of the revolution. Every revolutionary comrade must support it, or he will be taking the stand of counterrevolution.

ThomsonNOW To read the quotations of Chairman Mao, enter the *ThomsonNOW* documents area using the access card that is available for *The Essential World History.*

---

few links with the peasants in the countryside or the rickshaw drivers "running in this world of suffering," in the poignant words of a Chinese poet. In an expressive phrase, some critics dismissed Chiang and his chief followers as "banana Chinese"—yellow on the outside, white on the inside.

The Best of East and West Chiang was aware of the difficulty of introducing exotic foreign ideas into a society still culturally conservative. While building a modern industrial sector, he attempted to synthesize modern Western ideas with traditional Confucian values of hard work, obedience, and moral integrity. In the officially promoted New Life Movement, sponsored by his Wellesley-educated wife, Mei-ling Soong, Chiang sought to propagate traditional Confucian social ethics such as integrity, propriety, and righteousness, while rejecting

what he considered the excessive individualism and material greed of Western capitalism.

Unfortunately for Chiang, Confucian ideas—at least in their institutional form—had been widely discredited by the failure of the traditional system to solve China's growing problems. With only a tenuous hold over the Chinese provinces, a growing Japanese threat in the north, and a world suffering from the Great Depression, Chiang made little progress with his program. Chiang repressed all opposition and censored free expression, thereby alienating many intellectuals and political moderates. A land reform program was enacted in 1930 but had little effect.

Chiang Kai-shek's government had little more success in promoting industrial development. During the decade of precarious peace following the Northern Expedition, industrial growth averaged only about 1 percent annually.

Mao Zadong *on the Long March.* In 1934, Mao Zedong led his bedraggled forces on the famous Long March from southern China to a new location at Yan'an, in the hills just south of the Gobi Desert. In the photo above, Mao Zedong poses with Zhou Enlai, one of his chief supporters. By this time, Mao had become the leader of the Communist movement, although the Communists did not take complete control of China until 1949.

Much of the national wealth was in the hands of senior officials and close subordinates of the ruling elite. Military expenses consumed half the budget, and distressingly little was devoted to social and economic development.

The new government, then, had little success in dealing with China's deep-seated economic and social problems. The deadly combination of internal disintegration and foreign pressure now began to coincide with the virtual collapse of the global economic order during the Great Depression and the rise of militant political forces in Japan determined to extend Japanese influence and power in an unstable Asia. These forces and the turmoil they unleashed will be examined in the next chapter.

"Down with Confucius and Sons": Economic, Social, and Cultural Change in Republican China

The transformation of the old order that had commenced at the end of the Qing era continued into the period of the early Chinese republic. The industrial sector continued to grow, albeit slowly. Although about 75 percent of all industrial production was still craft-produced in the early 1930s, mechanization was gradually beginning to replace manual labor in a number of traditional industries, notably in the manufacture of textile goods. Traditional Chinese exports, such as silk and tea, were hard-hit by the Great Depression, however, and manufacturing suffered a decline during the 1930s. It is difficult to gauge conditions in the countryside during the early republican era, but there is no doubt that farmers were often victimized by high taxes imposed by local warlords and the endemic political and social conflict.

Social Changes Social changes followed shifts in the economy and the political culture. By 1915, the assault on the old system and values by educated youth was intense. The main focus of the attack was the Confucian concept of the family—in particular, filial piety and the subordination of women. Young people demanded the right to choose their own mates and their own careers. Women demanded rights and opportunities equal to those enjoyed by men. More broadly, progressives called for an end to the concept of duty to the community and praised the Western individualist ethos. The popular short story writer Lu Xun (Lu Hsun) criticized the Confucian concept of family as a "man-eating" system that degraded humanity. In a famous short story titled "Diary of a Madman," the protagonist remarks:

> I remember when I was four or five years old, sitting in the cool of the hall, my brother told me that if a man's parents were ill, he should cut off a piece of his flesh and boil it for them if he wanted to be considered a good son. I have only just realized that I have been living all these years in a place where for four thousand years they have been eating human flesh.[4]

Such criticisms did have some beneficial results. During the early republic, the tyranny of the old family system began to decline, at least in urban areas, under the impact of economic changes and the urgings of the New Culture intellectuals. Women began to escape their cloistered existence and seek education and employment alongside their male contemporaries. Free choice in marriage and a more relaxed attitude toward sex became commonplace among affluent families in the cities, where the teenage children of Westernized elites aped the clothing, social habits, and even the musical tastes of their contemporaries in Europe and the United States.

But as a rule, the new individualism and women's rights did not penetrate to the textile factories, where more than a million women worked in conditions resembling slave labor, or to the villages, where traditional attitudes and customs still held sway (see the comparative essay "Out of the Doll's House" on p. 527). Arranged marriages continued to be the rule rather than the exception, and concubinage remained common. According to a survey taken in the 1930s, well over two-thirds of the

COMPARATIVE ESSAY

OUT OF THE DOLL'S HOUSE

FAMILY & SOCIETY

In Henrik Ibsen's play *A Doll's House*, published in 1879, Nora Helmer informs her husband, Torvald, that she will no longer accept his control over her life and announces her intention to leave home to start her life anew. When the outraged Torvald cites her sacred duties as wife and mother, Nora replies that she has other duties just as sacred, those to herself. "I can no longer content myself with what most people say," she declares. "I must think over things for myself and get to understand them."

To Ibsen's contemporaries, such remarks were revolutionary. In nineteenth-century Europe, the traditional characterization of the sexes, based on gender-defined social roles, had been elevated to the status of a universal law. As the family wage earners, men were expected to go off to work, while women were assigned the responsibility of caring for home and family. Women were advised to accept their lot and play their role as effectively and as gracefully as possible.

The ideal, however, did not always match reality. With the advent of the Industrial Revolution, many women, especially those from the lower classes, were driven by the need for supplemental income to seek employment outside the home, often in the form of menial labor. Some women, inspired by the ideals of human dignity and freedom expressed during the Enlightenment and the French Revolution, began to protest against a tradition of female inferiority that had long kept them in a "doll's house" of male domination and to claim equal rights before the law.

The movement to liberate women from the iron cage of legal and social inferiority first began to gain ground in English-speaking countries like Great Britain and the United States, but it gradually spread to the continent of Europe and then to colonial areas in Africa and Asia. By the first decades of the twentieth century, women's liberation movements were under way in parts of North Africa, the Middle East, and East Asia, voicing a growing demand for access to education, equal treatment before the law, and the right to vote.

Progress was often agonizingly slow, however, especially in societies where age-old traditional values had not yet been undermined by the corrosive force of the Industrial Revolution. In many colonial societies, the effort to improve the condition of women was subordinated to the goal of gaining national independence. In some instances, women's liberation movements were led by educated elites who failed to include the concerns of working-class women in their agendas. Colonialism, too, was a double-edged sword, as the sexist bias of European officials combined with indigenous traditions of male superiority to marginalize women even further. As men moved to the cities to exploit opportunities provided by the new colonial administration, women were left to cope with their traditional responsibilities in the villages, often without the safety net of male support that had sustained them during the precolonial era.

---

marriages even among urban couples had been arranged by their parents.

A New Culture Nowhere was the struggle between traditional and modern more visible than in the field of culture. Beginning with the New Culture era, radical reformists criticized traditional culture as the symbol and instrument of feudal oppression that must be entirely eradicated before a new China could stand with dignity in the modern world. During the 1920s and 1930s, Western literature and art became highly popular, especially among the urban middle class. Traditional culture continued to prevail among more conservative elements, and some intellectuals argued for a new art that would synthesize the best of Chinese and foreign culture. But the most creative artists were interested in imitating foreign trends, while traditionalists were more concerned with preservation.

Literature in particular was influenced by foreign ideas as Western genres like the novel and the short story attracted a growing audience. Although most Chinese novels written after World War I dealt with Chinese subjects, they reflected the Western tendency toward social realism and often dealt with the new Westernized middle class (Mao Dun's *Midnight*, for example, describes the changing mores of Shanghai's urban elites) or the disintegration of the traditional Confucian family (Ba Jin's famous novel *Family* is an example). Most of China's modern authors displayed a clear contempt for the past.

Japan Between the Wars

During the first two decades of the twentieth century, Japan made remarkable progress toward the creation of an advanced society on the Western model. The political system based on the Meiji Constitution of 1890 began to evolve along Western pluralistic lines, and a multiparty system took shape. The economic and social reforms launched during the Meiji era led to increasing prosperity and the development of a modern industrial and commercial sector.

Experiment in Democracy

During the first quarter of the twentieth century, Japanese political parties expanded their popular following and became increasingly competitive. Individual pressure groups began to appear in Japanese society, along with an independent press and a bill of rights. The influence of the old ruling oligarchy, the *genro*, had not yet been significantly challenged, however, nor had that of its ideological foundation the *kokutai*.

These fragile democratic institutions were able to survive throughout the 1920s. During that period, the military budget was reduced, and a suffrage bill enacted in 1925 granted the vote to all Japanese males, thus continuing the process of democratization begun earlier in the century. Women remained disenfranchised; but women's associations gained increasing visibility during the 1920s, and many women were active in the labor movement and in campaigning for various social reforms.

But the era was also marked by growing social turmoil, and two opposing forces within the system were gearing up to challenge the prevailing wisdom. On the left, a Marxist labor movement began to take shape in the early 1920s in response to growing economic difficulties. On the right, ultranationalist groups called for a rejection of Western models of development and a more militant approach to realizing national objectives.

This cultural conflict between old and new, native and foreign, was reflected in literature. Japanese self-confidence had been somewhat restored after the victories over China and Russia, and this resurgence sparked a great age of creativity in the early twentieth century. Now more adept at handling European literary forms, Japanese writers blended Western psychology with Japanese sensibility in exquisite novels reeking with nostalgia for the old Japan. A well-known example is Junichiro Tanizaki's *Some Prefer Nettles,* published in 1928, which delicately juxtaposes the positive aspects of both traditional and modern Japan. By the 1930s, however, military censorship increasingly inhibited free literary expression. Many authors continued to write privately, producing works that reflected the gloom of the era. This attitude is perhaps best exemplified by Shiga Naoya's novel *A Dark Night's Journey,* written during the early 1930s and capturing a sense of the approaching global catastrophe. It is regarded as the masterpiece of modern Japanese literature.

© Retrofile/Getty Images

East Meets West, Tokyo, 1930s. Whereas women of the old regime were swathed in colorful floor-length kimonos, elaborate coiffures, and traditional Japanese sandals, by the early 1930s many young Japanese had adopted Western dress and "modern" pursuits. Here we see young people in Western suits, overcoats, fedora hats, and high heels, strolling in the then-well-established Ginza business district of Tokyo. The young woman in the center seems to be sporting a combination of Eastern and Western styles. And overhead is evidence of the flourishing urban economy of the time—neon signs and art deco street lamps—all in the shadow of the Wako Department Store's famous clock tower.

A Zaibatsu Economy

Japan also continued to make impressive progress in economic development. Spurred by rising domestic demand as well as continued government investment in the economy, the production of raw materials tripled between 1900 and 1930, and industrial production increased more than twelvefold. Much of the increase went into exports, and Western manufacturers began to complain about increasing competition from the Japanese.

As often happens, rapid industrialization was accompanied by some hardship and rising social tensions. In the Meiji model, various manufacturing processes were concentrated in a single enterprise, the **zaibatsu,** or financial clique. Some of these firms were existing merchant companies that had the capital and the foresight to move into new areas of opportunity. Others were formed by enterprising samurai, who used their status and experience in management to good account in a new environment. Whatever their origins, these firms, often with official encouragement, gradually developed into large conglomerates that controlled a major segment of the Japanese economy. By 1937, the four largest *zaibatsu* (Mitsui, Mitsubishi, Sumitomo, and Yasuda) controlled

21 percent of the banking industry, 26 percent of mining, 35 percent of shipbuilding, 38 percent of commercial shipping, and more than 60 percent of paper manufacturing and insurance.

This concentration of power and wealth in a few major industrial combines created problems in Japanese society. In the first place, it resulted in the emergence of a dual economy: on the one hand, a modern industry characterized by up-to-date methods and massive government subsidies, and on the other, a traditional manufacturing sector characterized by conservative methods and small-scale production techniques.

Concentration of wealth also led to growing economic inequalities. As we have seen, economic growth had been achieved at the expense of the peasants, many of whom fled to the cities to escape rural poverty. That labor surplus benefited the industrial sector, but the urban proletariat was still poorly paid and ill-housed. A rapid increase in population (the total population of the Japanese islands increased from an estimated 43 million in 1900 to 73 million in 1940) led to food shortages and the threat of rising unemployment. In the meantime, those left on the farm continued to suffer. As late as the beginning of World War II, an estimated one-half of all Japanese farmers were tenants.

Shidehara Diplomacy

A final problem for Japanese leaders in the post-Meiji era was the familiar dilemma of finding sources of raw materials and foreign markets for the nation's manufactured goods. Until World War I, Japan had dealt with the problem by seizing territories such as Taiwan, Korea, and southern Manchuria and transforming them into colonies or protectorates of the growing Japanese empire. That policy had begun to arouse the concern, and in some cases the hostility, of the Western nations. China was also becoming apprehensive; as we have seen, Japanese demands for Shandong Province at the Paris Peace Conference in 1919 aroused massive protests in major Chinese cities.

The United States was especially concerned about Japanese aggressiveness. Although the United States had been less active than some European states in pursuing colonies in the Pacific, it had a strong interest in keeping the area open for U.S. commercial activities. In 1922, in Washington, D.C., the United States convened a major conference of nations with interests in the Pacific to discuss problems of regional security. The Washington Conference led to agreements on several issues, but the major accomplishment was a nine-power treaty recognizing the territorial integrity of China and the Open Door. The other participants induced Japan to accept these provisions by accepting its special position in Manchuria.

During the remainder of the 1920s, Japanese governments attempted to play by the rules laid down at the Washington Conference. Known as Shidehara diplomacy, after the foreign minister (and later prime minister) who attempted to carry it out, this policy sought to use diplomatic and economic means to realize Japanese interests in Asia. But this approach came under severe pressure as Japanese industrialists began to move into new areas, such as heavy industry, chemicals, mining, and the manufacturing of appliances and automobiles. Because such industries desperately needed resources not found in abundance locally, the Japanese government came under increasing pressure to find new sources abroad.

In the early 1930s, with the onset of the Great Depression and growing tensions in the international arena, nationalist forces rose to dominance in the government. While party leaders during the 1920s had attempted to realize Japanese aspirations within the existing global political and economic framework, the dominant elements in the government in the 1930s, a mixture of military officers and ultranationalist politicians, were convinced that the diplomacy of the 1920s had failed; they advocated a more aggressive approach to protecting national interests in a brutal and competitive world. (see Chapter 24).

Nationalism and Dictatorship in Latin America

Although the nations of Latin America played little role in World War I, that conflict nevertheless exerted an impact on the region, especially on its economy. By the end of the 1920s, the region was also strongly influenced by another event of global proportions—the Great Depression.

The Economy and the United States

At the beginning of the twentieth century, virtually all of Latin America, except for the three Guianas, British Honduras, and some of the Caribbean islands, had achieved independence (see Map 23.2). The economy of the region was based largely on the export of foodstuffs and raw materials. Some countries relied on exports of only one or two products. Argentina, for example, exported primarily beef and wheat; Chile, nitrates and copper; Brazil and the Caribbean nations, sugar; and the Central American states, bananas. A few reaped large profits from these exports, but for the majority of the population, the returns were meager.

World War I led to a decline in European investment in Latin America and a rise in the U.S. role in the local economies. By the late 1920s, the United States had replaced Great Britain as the foremost source of investment in Latin America. Unlike the British, however, U.S. investors put their funds directly into production enterprises, causing large segments of the area's export industries to fall into American hands. A number of Central American states, for example, were popularly labeled "banana republics" because of the power and influence of the U.S.-owned United Fruit Company. American firms

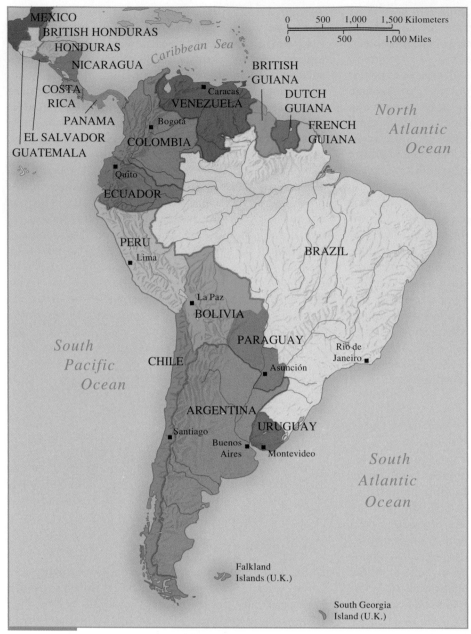

MAP 23.2 **Latin America in the First Half of the Twentieth Century.** Shown here are the boundaries dividing the countries of Latin America after the independence movements of the nineteenth century. ❓ Which areas remained under European rule?

U.S. economic influence; sometimes the United States even intervened militarily. In 1935, a bid to improve relations with Latin American countries, President Franklin D. Roosevelt promulgated the **Good Neighbor policy,** which rejected the use of U.S. military force in the region.

Because so many Latin American nations depended for their livelihood on the export of raw materials and food products, the Great Depression of the 1930s was a disaster for the region. Latin American exports in 1930 fell to barely half of their value in each of the previous five years. Spurred by the decline in foreign revenues, Latin American governments began to encourage the development of new industries. In some cases—the steel industry in Chile and Brazil, the oil industry in Argentina and Mexico—government investment made up for the absence of local sources of capital.

The Effects of Dependence

During the late nineteenth century, most governments in Latin America had been increasingly dominated by landed or military elites, who controlled the mass of the population—mostly impoverished peasants—by the blatant use of military force. This trend toward authoritarianism increased during the 1930s as domestic instability caused by the effects of the Great Depression led to the creation of dictatorships throughout the region. This trend was especially evident in Argentina and Brazil and to a lesser degree in Mexico—three countries that together possessed more than half of the land and wealth of Latin America.

Argentina The political domination of the country by an elite minority often had disastrous effects. The government of Argentina, controlled by landowners who had benefited from the export of beef and wheat, was slow to recognize the growing importance of establishing a local industrial base. In 1916, Hipólito Irigoyen (1852–1933), head of the Radical Party, was elected president on a program to improve conditions for the middle and lower

also dominated the copper mining industry in Chile and Peru and the oil industry in Mexico, Peru, and Bolivia.

Increasing economic power reinforced the traditionally high level of U.S. political influence in Latin America. This influence was especially evident in Central America and the Caribbean, regions that many Americans considered their backyard and thus vital to U.S. national security. The growing U.S. presence in the region provoked hostility among some Latin Americans, who viewed the United States as an aggressive imperialist power. Some charged that Washington worked to keep ruthless dictators, such as Juan Vicente Gómez of Venezuela and Fulgencio Batista of Cuba, in power in order to preserve

Hipólito Irigoyen becomes president of Argentina	1916
Argentinian military overthrows Irigoyen	1930
Rule of Getúlio Vargas in Brazil	1930–1945
Presidency of Lázaro Cárdenas in Mexico	1934–1940
Beginning of Good Neighbor policy	1935

classes. Little was achieved, however, as the party became increasingly corrupt and drew closer to the large landowners. In 1930, the army overthrew Irigoyen's government and reestablished the power of the landed class. But their efforts to return to the previous export economy and suppress the growing influence of labor unions failed.

Brazil   Brazil followed a similar path. In 1889, the army overthrew the Brazilian monarchy, installed by Portugal years before, and established a republic. But it was dominated by landed elites, many of whom had grown wealthy through their ownership of coffee plantations. By 1900, three-quarters of the world's coffee was grown in Brazil. As in Argentina, the ruling oligarchy ignored the importance of establishing an urban industrial base. When the Great Depression ravaged profits from coffee exports, a wealthy rancher, Getúlio Vargas (1883–1954), seized power and ruled the country as president from 1930 to 1945. At first, Vargas sought to appease workers by declaring an eight-hour workday and a minimum wage, but, influenced by the apparent success of fascist regimes in Europe, he ruled by increasingly autocratic means and relied on a police force that used torture to silence his opponents. His industrial policy was relatively enlightened, however, and by the end of World War II, Brazil had become Latin America's major industrial power. In 1945, the army, fearing that Vargas might prolong his power illegally after calling for new elections, forced him to resign.

Mexico   Mexico, in the years after World War I, was not an authoritarian state, but neither was it democratic. The Mexican Revolution at the beginning of the twentieth century had been the first significant effort in Latin American

Struggle for the Banner.   Like Diego Rivera, David Alfaro Siqueiros (1896–1974) painted on public buildings large murals that celebrated the Mexican Revolution and the workers' and peasants' struggle for freedom. Beginning in the 1930s, Siqueiros expressed sympathy for the exploited and downtrodden peoples of Mexico in dramatic frescoes such as this one. He painted similar murals in Uruguay, Argentina, and Brazil and was once expelled from the United States, where his political art and views were considered too radical.

history to overturn the system of large estates and improve the living standards of the masses. Out of the political revolution emerged a relatively stable political order based on the constitution of 1917, which established a strong presidency and introduced some social welfare reforms for workers (see Chapter 19). The revolution was democratic only in form, however, as the official political party, known as the Institutional Revolutionary Party (PRI), controlled the levers of power throughout society. Every six years, PRI bosses chose the party's presidential candidate, who was then dutifully elected by the people.

The situation began to change with the election of Lázaro Cárdenas (1895–1970) as president in 1934. Cárdenas won wide popularity with the peasants by ordering the redistribution of 44 million acres of land controlled by landed elites. He also won popular support by adopting a stronger stand against the United States, seizing control over the oil industry, which had hitherto been dominated by major U.S. oil companies. Alluding to the Good Neighbor policy, President Roosevelt refused to intervene, and eventually Mexico agreed to compensate U.S. oil companies for their lost property. It then set up PEMEX, a state-administered organization, to run the oil industry.

Latin American Culture

During the early twentieth century, modern European artistic and literary movements began to penetrate Latin America. In major cities, such as Buenos Aires and São Paulo, wealthy elites supported avant-garde trends, but other artists returned from abroad to adapt modern techniques to their native roots.

For many artists and writers, their work provided a means of promoting the emergence of a new national essence. An example was the Mexican muralist Diego Rivera (1886–1957). Rivera had studied in Europe, where he was influenced by fresco painting in Italy. After his return to Mexico, where the government provided financial support for the painting of murals on public buildings, he began to produce a monumental style of mural art that reflected indigenous styles and served two purposes: to illustrate the national past by portraying Aztec legends as well as Mexican festivals and folk customs and to promote a political message in favor of realizing the social goals of the Mexican Revolution. Rivera's murals can be found in such diverse locations as the Ministry of Education and the Social Security Hospital in Mexico City and the chapel of the Agricultural School at Chapingo.

CONCLUSION

THE TURMOIL BROUGHT about by World War I not only resulted in the destruction of several of the major Western empires and a redrawing of the map of Europe but also opened the door to political and social upheavals elsewhere in the world. In the Middle East, the decline and fall of the Ottoman Empire led to the creation of the secular republic of Turkey. The state of Saudi Arabia emerged in the Arabian peninsula, and Palestine became a source of tension between newly arrived Jewish settlers and longtime Muslim residents.

Other parts of Asia and Africa also witnessed the rise of movements for national independence. In Africa, these movements were spearheaded by native leaders educated in Europe or the United States. In India, Gandhi and his campaign of civil disobedience played a crucial role in his country's bid to be free of British rule. Communist movements also began to emerge in Asian societies as radical elements sought new methods of bringing about the overthrow of Western imperialism. Japan continued to follow its own path to modernization, which, although successful from an economic point of view, took a menacing turn during the 1930s.

Between 1919 and 1939, China experienced a dramatic struggle to establish a modern nation. Two dynamic political organizations—the Nationalists and the Communists—competed for legitimacy as the rightful heirs of the old order. At first, they formed an alliance in an effort to defeat their common adversaries, but cooperation ultimately turned to conflict. The Nationalists under Chiang Kai-shek emerged supreme, but Chiang found it difficult to control the remnants of the warlord regime in China, while the Great Depression undermined his efforts to build an industrial nation.

During the interwar years, the nations of Latin America faced severe economic problems because of their dependence on exports. Increasing U.S. investments in Latin America contributed to growing hostility against the powerful neighbor to the north. The Great Depression forced the region to begin developing new industries, but it also led to the rise of authoritarian governments, some of them modeled after the fascist regimes of Italy and Germany.

By demolishing the remnants of their old civilization on the battlefields of World War I, Europeans had inadvertently encouraged the subject peoples of their vast colonial empires to begin their own movements for national independence. The process was by no means completed in the two decades following the Treaty of Versailles, but the bonds of imperial rule had been severely strained. Once Europeans began to weaken themselves in the even more destructive conflict of World War II, the hopes of African and Asian peoples for national independence and freedom could at last be realized. It is to that devastating world conflict that we now turn.

TIMELINE

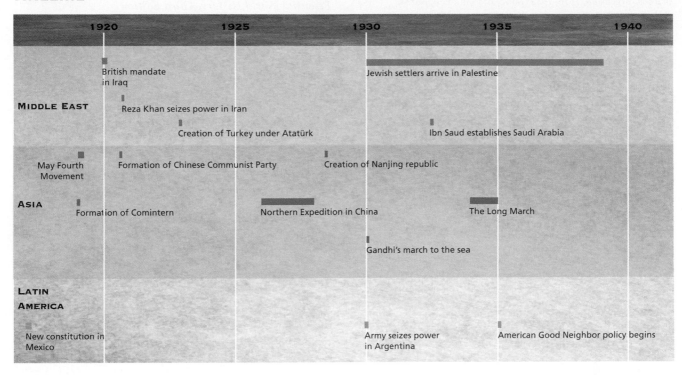

	1920	1925	1930	1935	1940

MIDDLE EAST

British mandate in Iraq

Jewish settlers arrive in Palestine

Reza Khan seizes power in Iran

Creation of Turkey under Atatürk

Ibn Saud establishes Saudi Arabia

ASIA

May Fourth Movement

Formation of Chinese Communist Party

Creation of Nanjing republic

Formation of Comintern

Northern Expedition in China

The Long March

Gandhi's march to the sea

LATIN AMERICA

New constitution in Mexico

Army seizes power in Argentina

American Good Neighbor policy begins

CHAPTER NOTES

1. Speech by Mahatma Gandhi, delivered in London in September 1931 during his visit for the first Roundtable Conference.
2. Ts'ai Yuan-p'ei, "Ta Lin Ch'in-nan Han," in *Ts'ai Yuan-p'ei Hsien-sheng Ch'uan-chi* [Collected Works of Mr. Ts'ai Yuan-p'ei] (Taipei, 1968), pp. 1057–1058.
3. Quoted in William Theodore de Bary et al., eds., *Sources of Chinese Tradition* (New York, 1963), p. 783.
4. Lu Xun, "Diary of a Madman," in *Selected Works of Lu Hsun* (Peking, 1957), vol. 1, p. 20.

SUGGESTED READING

The classic study of nationalism in the non-Western world is **R. Emerson**, *From Empire to Nation* (Boston, 1960). For a more recent approach, see **B. Anderson**, *Imagined Communities: Reflections on the Origin and Spread of Nationalism* (London, 1983). On nationalism in India, see **S. Wolpert**, *Congress and Indian Nationalism: The Pre-Independence Phase* (New York, 1988). Also see **P. Chatterjee**, *The Nation and Its Fragments: Colonial and Postcolonial Histories* (Princeton, N.J., 1993), and **E. Gellner**, *Nations and Nationalism* (Ithaca, N.Y., 1994).

There have been a number of studies of Mahatma Gandhi and his ideas. See, for example, **J. M. Brown**, *Gandhi: Prisoner of Hope* (New Haven, Conn., 1989), and **D. Dalton**, *Mahatma Gandhi: Nonviolent Power in Action* (New York, 1995). For a study of Nehru, see **J. M. Brown**, *Nehru* (New York, 2000).

For a general survey of events in the Middle East in the interwar era, see **H. M. Sachar**, *The Emergence of the Middle East, 1914–1924* (New York, 1969). For more specialized studies, see **I. Gershoni** et al.,

Egypt, Islam, and the Arabs: The Search for Egyptian Nationhood (Oxford, 1993), and **W. Laqueur**, *A History of Zionism: From the French Revolution to the Establishment of the State of Israel* (New York, 1996). The role of Atatürk is examined in **A. Mango**, *Atatürk: The Biography of the Founder of Modern Turkey* (New York, 2000). The Palestinian issue is dealt with in **B. Morris**, *Righteous Victims: The Palestinian Conflict, 1880–2000* (New York, 2001). On the founding of Iraq, see **S. Mackey**, *The Reckoning: Iraq and the Legacy of Saddam Hussein* (New York, 2002). Nascent nationalist movements in Africa are discussed in **R. Collins**, *Historical Problems of Imperial Africa* (Princeton, 1994).

On the early republic in China, see **L. Yu-sheng**, *The Crisis of Chinese Consciousness: Radical Antitraditionalism in the May Fourth Era* (Madison, Wis., 1979). The rise of the Chinese Communist Party is discussed in **A. Dirlik**, *The Origins of Chinese Communism* (Oxford, 1989). There are a number of biographies of Mao Zedong. A readable and informative one is **S. Schram**, *Mao Tse-tung: A Political Biography* (Baltimore, 1966). Also see **J. D. Spence**, *Mao Zedong: A Penguin Life* (New York, 1999). For an inside account of the Chinese Communist movement by a sympathetic Western journalist, see **E. Snow**, *Red Star over China* (New York, 1938). On Chiang Kai-shek, see **J. Fenby**, *Generalissimo: Chiang Kai-shek and the China He Lost* (New York, 2003). For a discussion of the role of ideology and nationalism in early-twentieth-century China, see **J. Fitzgerald**, *Awakening China: Politics, Culture, and Class in the Nationalist Revolution* (Stanford, Calif., 1997). On the interwar era in Japan, see **P. Duus**, ed., *The Cambridge History of Japan,* vol. 6 (Cambridge, 1989).

For an overview of Latin American history in the 1920s and 1930s, see **E. Williamson**, *The Penguin History of Latin America* (Harmondsworth, England, 1992). On U.S.-Latin American relations, see the classic study by **B. Wood**, *The Making of the Good Neighbor*

Policy (New York, 1960). On Argentina, Brazil, and Mexico, see
D. Rock, *Argentina, 1516–1982* (London, 1986); E. B. Burns,
A History of Brazil, 2d ed. (New York, 1980); and M. C. Meyer and
W. L. Sherman, *The Course of Mexican History,* 3d ed. (New York,
1987). On Getúlio Vargas, see R. Bourne, *Getúlio Vargas of Brazil,
1883–1954: Sphinx of the Pampas* (London, 1974). On culture, see
J. Franco, *The Modern Culture of Latin America: Society and the
Artist* (Harmondsworth, England, 1970).

For a general introduction to the women's movement during this
era, consult C. Johnson-Odim and M. Strobel, eds., *Restoring Women
to History* (Bloomington, Ind., 1999). For collections of essays concerning African women, see C. Robertson and I. Berger, *Women and
Class in Africa* (New York, 1986), and S. Stichter and J. I. Parparti,
eds., *Patriarchy and Class: African Women in the Home and
Workforce* (Boulder, Colo., 1988). To follow the women's movement
in India, see S. Tharu and K. Lalita, *Women Writing in India,* vol. 2
(New York, 1993). For Japan, see S. Sievers, *Flowers in Salt: The
Beginnings of Feminist Consciousness in Modern Japan* (Stanford,
Calif., 1983).

InfoTrac College Edition

Visit this chapter's InfoTrac College Edition/Research activities at
the *Essential World History* Companion Website for activities
related to Asia, Latin America, and the Middle East between the
world wars.

ThomsonNOW™ for Duiker and Spielvogel's *The
Essential World History, Third Edition*

Enter *ThomsonNOW* using the access card that is available with this
text. *ThomsonNOW* will assist you in understanding the content in
this chapter with lesson plans generated for your needs, as well as
provide you with a connection to the *Wadsworth World History
Resource Center* (see description below for details).

WORLD HISTORY
RESOURCE CENTER

Enter the Resource Center using either your *ThomsonNOW*
access card or your standalone access card for the *Wadsworth
World History Resource Center.* Organized by topic, this website
includes quizzes; images; over 350 primary source documents;
interactive simulations, maps, and timelines; movie explorations;
and a wealth of other resources. You can read the following
documents, and many more, at http://worldrc.wadsworth.com/

Mohandas Gandhi, "Indian Home Rule"

The Balfour Declaration

Visit the *Essential World History* Companion Website for chapter
quizzes and more:

http://www.thomsonedu.com/history/duiker

DISCOVERY

How did the societies discussed in this chapter deal with the political, economic, and social challenges that they faced after World War I, and how did these challenges differ from one region to another?

In thinking about this question, begin by breaking it down into the components shown below. A discussion of the significance of each component should appear in your answer.

POLITICS AND GOVERNMENT: Compare the different men who led their nations in the interwar years. How did each of them seek to gain more independence for his people? Who appears most likely to have taken up arms against the colonial rulers of his country?

Compare the ways in which you can still see continued Western influence in Iraq, Turkey, and India, even after the establishment of independence. Can you draw any conclusions about the way each country secured its indep

endence and its current political situation? What about the governments that ruled them? Compare the situation in Iraq with that of Turkey or India. Why would a postwar leader create future problems?

Nehru and Gandhi

Chiang Kai-shek and Sun Yat-sen

ATATÜRK'S SPEECH TO THE ASSEMBLY, OCTOBER 1924

The monarch designated under the title of Caliph was to guide the affairs of [all] Muslim peoples and to secure the execution of the religious prescriptions which would best correspond to their worldly interests. He was to defend the rights of all Muslims and concentrate all the affairs of the Muslim world in his hands with effective authority.

The sovereign entitled Caliph was to maintain justice among the three hundred million Muslims on the terrestrial globe, to safeguard the rights of these peoples, to prevent any event that could encroach upon order and security, and confront every attack which the Muslims would be called upon to encounter from the side of other nations. It was to be part of his attributes to preserve by all means the welfare and spiritual development of Islam. . . .

If the Caliph and Caliphate, as they maintained, were to be invested with a dignity embracing the whole of Islam, ought they not to have realized in all justice that a crushing burden would be imposed on Turkey, on her existence;

her entire resources and all her forces would be placed at the disposal of the Caliph? . . .

For centuries our nation was guided under the influence of these erroneous ideas. But what has been the result of it? Everywhere they have lost millions of men. "Do you know," I asked, "how many sons of Anatolia have perished in the scorching deserts of the Yemen? Do you know the losses we have suffered in holding Syria and Egypt and in maintaining our position in Africa? And do you see what has come out of it? Do you know?

"Those who favor the idea of placing the means at the disposal of the Caliph to brave the whole world and the power to administer the affairs of the whole of Islam must not appeal to the population of Anatolia alone but to the great Muslim agglomerations which are eight or ten times as rich in men.

"New Turkey, the people of New Turkey, have no reason to think of anything else but their own existence and their own welfare. She has nothing more to give away to others."

INTERACTION AND EXCHANGE: Compare the reasons given by Ho and Mao in the following documents for their people to rise up and revolt. Are their enemies the same? Although these are both communist revolutions,

how do they differ? Which leader was living in his country at the time, and which was not? Does anything about these documents reflect the different circumstances of their authors?

HO CHI MINH, "THE PATH WHICH LED ME TO LENINISM"

After World War I, I made my living in Paris, now as a retoucher at a photographer's, now as a painter of "Chinese antiquities" (made in France!). I would distribute leaflets denouncing the crimes committed by the French colonialists in Vietnam.

At that time, I supported the October Revolution only instinctively, not yet grasping all its historic importance. I loved and admired Lenin because he was a great patriot who liberated his compatriots; until then, I had read none of his books.

The reason for my joining the French Socialist Party was that these "ladies and gentlemen"—as I called my comrades at that moment—had shown their sympathy toward me, toward the struggle of the oppressed peoples. But I understood neither what was a party, a trade union, nor what was Socialism nor Communism.

Heated discussions were then taking place in the branches of the Socialist Party, about the question whether the Socialist Party should remain in the Second International, should a Second-and-a-Half International be founded, or should the Socialist Party join Lenin's Third International? I attended the meetings regularly, twice or three times

a week, and attentively listened to the discussion. First, I could not understand thoroughly. Why were the discussions so heated? Either with the Second, Second-and-a-Half, or Third International, the revolution could be waged. What was the use of arguing then? As for the First International, what had become of it?

What I wanted most to know—and this precisely was not debated in the meetings—was: which International sides with the peoples of colonial countries?

I raised this question—the most important in my opinion—in a meeting. Some comrades answered: It is the Third, not the Second International. And a comrade gave me Lenin's "Thesis on the national and colonial questions," published by *l'Humanité*, to read.

There were political terms difficult to understand in this thesis. But by dint of reading it again and again, finally I could grasp the main part of it. What emotion, enthusiasm, clear-sightedness, and confidence it instilled in me! I was overjoyed to tears. Though sitting alone in my room, I shouted aloud as if addressing large crowds: "Dear martyrs, compatriots! This is what we need, this is the path to our liberation!"

After that, I had entire confidence in Lenin, in the Third International.

MAO ZEDONG, "THE PEASANT MOVEMENT IN HUNAN"

During my recent visit to Hunan I made a firsthand investigation of conditions. . . . In a very short time, . . . several hundred million peasants will rise like a mighty storm, . . . a force so swift and violent that no power, however great, will be able to hold it back. They will smash all the trammels that bind them and rush forward along the road to liberation. They will sweep all the imperialists, warlords, corrupt officials, local tyrants, and evil gentry into their graves. Every revolutionary party and every revolutionary comrade will be put to the test, to be accepted or rejected as they decide. There are three alternatives. To march at their head and lead them? To trail behind them, gesticulating and criticizing? Or to stand in their way and oppose them? Every Chinese is free to choose, but events will force you to make the choice quickly.

The main targets of attack by the peasants are the local tyrants, the evil gentry and the lawless landlords, but in passing they also hit out against patriarchal ideas and institutions, against the corrupt officials in the cities and against bad practices and customs in the rural areas. . . . As a result, the privileges which the feudal landlords enjoyed for thousands of years are being shattered to pieces. . . . With the collapse of the power of the landlords, the

peasant associations have now become the sole organs of authority, and the popular slogan "All power to the peasant associations" has become a reality.

The peasants' revolt disturbed the gentry's sweet dreams. When the news from the countryside reached the cities, it caused immediate uproar among the gentry. . . . From the middle social strata upwards to the Kuomintang right-wingers, there was not a single person who did not sum up the whole business in the phrase, "It's terrible!" . . . Even quite progressive people said, "Though terrible, it is inevitable in a revolution." In short, nobody could altogether deny the word "terrible." But . . . the fact is that the great peasant masses have risen to fulfill their historic mission. . . . What the peasants are doing is absolutely right; what they are doing is fine! "It's fine!" is the theory of the peasants and of all other revolutionaries. Every revolutionary comrade should know that the national revolution requires a great change in the countryside. The Revolution of 1911 did not bring about this change, hence its failure. This change is now taking place, and it is an important factor for the completion of the revolution. Every revolutionary comrade must support it, or he will be taking the stand of counterrevolution.

FAMILY AND SOCIETY: After considering the excerpt from *Out of Exile*, what influence do you think colonial/Western culture seemed to have on the people, particularly the upper classes or intellectuals, of the non-Western world? How would this influence create internal divisions in those societies? Would this division and outside influence increase or decrease nationalism? How are these divisions still seen in many former colonies?

SUTAN SJAHRIR, *OUT OF EXILE*

Am I perhaps estranged from my people? . . . Why are the things that contain beauty for them and arouse their gentler emotions only senseless and displeasing for me? In reality, the spiritual gap between my people and me is certainly no greater than that between an intellectual in Holland . . . and the undeveloped people of Holland. . . . The difference is rather . . . that the intellectual in Holland does not feel this gap because there is a portion—even a fairly large portion—of his own people on approximately the same intellectual level as himself. . . .

This is what we lack here. Not only is the number of intellectuals in this country smaller in proportion to the total population—in fact, very much smaller—but in addition, the few who are here do not constitute any single entity in spiritual outlook, or in any spiritual life or single culture whatsoever. . . . It is for them so much more difficult than for the intellectuals in Holland. In Holland they build—both consciously and unconsciously—on what is already there. . . . Even if they oppose it, they do so as a method of application or as a starting point.

In our country this is not the case. Here there has been no spiritual or cultural life, and no intellectual progress for centuries. There are the

much-praised Eastern art forms but what are these except bare rudiments from a feudal culture that cannot possibly provide a dynamic fulcrum for people of the twentieth century? . . . Our spiritual needs are needs of the twentieth century; our problems and our views are of the twentieth century. Our inclination is no longer toward the mystical, but toward reality, clarity, and objectivity. . . .

We intellectuals here are much closer to Europe or America than we are to the Borobudur or Mahabharata or to the primitive Islamic culture of Java and Sumatra. . . .

So, it seems, the problem stands in principle. It is seldom put forth by us in this light, and instead most of us search unconsciously for a synthesis that will leave us internally tranquil. We want to have both Western science and Eastern philosophy, the Eastern "spirit," in the culture. But what is this Eastern spirit? It is, they say, the sense of the higher, of spirituality, of the eternal and religious, as opposed to the materialism of the West. I have heard this countless times, but it has never convinced me.

24

THE CRISIS DEEPENS: WORLD WAR II

CHAPTER OUTLINE
AND FOCUS QUESTIONS

Retreat from Democracy: Dictatorial Regimes

▫ What are the characteristics of totalitarian states, and to what degree were these characteristics present in Fascist Italy, Nazi Germany, and Stalinist Russia? To what extent, if any, was Japan a totalitarian state?

The Path to War

▫ What were the underlying causes of World War II, and what specific steps taken by Nazi Germany and Japan led to war?

World War II

▫ What were the main events of World War II in Europe and Asia?

The New Order

▫ What was the nature of the new orders that Germany and Japan attempted to establish in the territories they occupied?

The Home Front

▫ What were conditions like on the home front for the major belligerents in World War II?

Aftermath: Toward the Cold War

▫ How did the Allies' visions of the postwar differ, and how did these differences contribute to the emergence of the Cold War?

CRITICAL THINKING

▫ What was the relationship between World War I and World War II, and what were the differences in the ways the wars were fought?

Adolf Hitler salutes military leaders and soldiers during a military rally

© Bildarchiv Preussischer Kulturbesitz/Art Resource, NY

*O*N FEBRUARY 3, 1933, three days after he had been appointed chancellor of Germany, Adolf Hitler met secretly with Germany's leading generals. He revealed to them his desire to remove the "cancer of democracy," create a new authoritarian leadership, and forge a new domestic unity. All Germans would need to realize that "only a struggle [could save them] and that everything else must be subordinated to this idea." Since Germany's living space was too small for its people, Hitler said, Germany must rearm and prepare for "the conquest of new living space in the east and its ruthless Germanization." Even before he had consolidated his power, Adolf Hitler had a clear vision of his goals, and their implementation meant another war in Europe. World War II in Europe was Hitler's war. Other countries may have contributed by not resisting Hitler earlier, but Nazi Germany's actions alone made World War II inevitable.

It became far more than just Hitler's war, however. World War II was really two conflicts: one provoked by the ambitions of Germany in Europe, the other by the ambitions of Japan in Asia. When the United States and major European nations raised their tariff rates against Japanese imports in the early 1930s in a desperate effort to protect local businesses and jobs, militant groups in Tokyo began to argue that Japan must obtain by violent action what it could not secure by peaceful means. By 1941, with the United States embroiled in both wars, the two had merged into a single global conflict.

Although World War I had been described as a total war, World War II was even more so and was fought on a scale unique in history. Almost everyone in the warring countries was involved in one way or another—as soldiers; as workers in wartime industries; as ordinary citizens subject to invading armies, military occupation, or bombing raids; as refugees; or as victims of mass extermination. The world had never witnessed such widespread death and destruction at the hands of humans. ◇

Retreat from Democracy: Dictatorial Regimes

The rise of dictatorial regimes in the 1930s had a great deal to do with the coming of World War II. By 1939, only two major states in Europe, France and Great Britain, remained democratic. Italy and Germany had succumbed to the political movement called **fascism,** and Soviet Russia under Stalin moved toward repressive totalitarianism. A host of other European states and Latin American countries adopted authoritarian structures of different kinds, while a militarist regime in Japan moved that country down the path to war.

The dictatorial regimes between the wars assumed both old and new forms. Dictatorship was not new, but the modern **totalitarian state** was. The totalitarian regimes, best exemplified by Stalinist Russia and Nazi Germany, greatly extended the functions and power of the central state. The new "total states" expected the active loyalty and commitment of citizens to the regime's goals, whether they be war, a socialist society, or a thousand-year Reich. They used modern mass propaganda techniques and high-speed communications to conquer the minds and hearts of their subjects. The total state sought to control not only the economic, political, and social aspects of life but the intellectual and cultural aspects as well.

The modern totalitarian state was to be led by a single leader and a single party. It ruthlessly rejected the liberal ideal of limited government power and constitutional guarantees of individual freedoms. Indeed, individual freedom was to be subordinated to the collective will of the masses, organized and determined for them by the leader or leaders. Modern technology also gave total states unprecedented police controls to enforce their wishes on their subjects.

The Birth of Fascism

In the early 1920s, Benito Mussolini (1883–1945) burst on the Italian scene with the first fascist movement in Europe. In 1919, Mussolini, a veteran of World War I, had established a new political group, the *Fascio di Combattimento* (League of Combat), which won support from middle-class industrialists fearful of working-class agitation and large landowners who objected to agricultural strikes. The movement gained momentum as Mussolini's nationalist rhetoric and the middle-class fear of socialism, communist revolution, and disorder made the Fascists seem more and more attractive. On October 29, 1922, after Mussolini and the Fascists threatened to march on Rome if they were not given power, King Victor Emmanuel (1900–1946) capitulated and made Mussolini prime minister of Italy.

By 1926, Mussolini had established the institutional framework for a Fascist dictatorship. The prime minister was made "head of government" with the power to legislate by decree. The police were empowered to arrest and confine anybody for both nonpolitical and political crimes without due process of law. The government was given the power to dissolve political and cultural associations. In 1926, all anti-Fascist parties were outlawed, and a secret police force was established. By the end of the year, Mussolini ruled Italy as *Il Duce,* the leader.

Mussolini conceived of the Fascist state as totalitarian: "Fascism is totalitarian, and the Fascist State, the synthesis and unity of all values, interprets, develops and gives strength to the whole life of the people."[1] Mussolini did try to create a police state, but it was not very effective. Neither was the Italian Fascists' attempt to exercise control over all forms of mass media, including newspapers, radio, and cinema, in order to use propaganda as a means of integrating the masses into the state. Most commonly, Fascist propaganda was disseminated through simple slogans, such as "Mussolini is always right," plastered on walls all over Italy.

The Fascists portrayed the family as the pillar of the state and women as the basic foundation of the family. "Woman into the home" became the Fascist slogan. Women were to be homemakers and baby producers, "their natural and fundamental mission in life," according to Mussolini, for population growth was viewed as an indicator of national strength. Employment outside the home might distract women from conception: "It forms an independence and consequent physical and moral habits contrary to child bearing."[2]

Despite the instruments of repression, the use of propaganda, and the creation of numerous Fascist organizations, Mussolini never achieved the degree of totalitarian control attained in Hitler's Germany or Stalin's Soviet Union. Mussolini and the Fascist Party never completely destroyed the old power structure, and they were soon overshadowed by a much more powerful fascist movement to the north.

Hitler and Nazi Germany

In 1923, a small rightist party led by an obscure Austrian rabble-rouser named Adolf Hitler (1889–1945)

Mussolini, The Iron _Duce_.   One of Mussolini's favorite images of himself was that of the Iron _Duce_—the strong leader who is always right. Consequently, he was often seen in military-style uniforms and military poses. This photograph shows Mussolini in one of his numerous uniforms with his Black Shirt bodyguards giving the Fascist salute.

attempted to seize power in southern Germany in the notorious Beer Hall Putsch. Although the effort failed, the attempted putsch brought Hitler and the Nazis to national prominence.

Hitler's Rise to Power, 1919–1933   At the end of World War I, after four years of service on the Western Front, Hitler went to Munich and decided to enter politics. In 1919, he joined the obscure German Workers' Party, one of a number of right-wing extreme nationalist parties. By the summer of 1921, Hitler had assumed control of the party, which he renamed the National Socialist German Workers' Party, or Nazi Party for short. In two years, membership reached 55,000, including 15,000 in the party militia, the SA (for _Sturmabteilung_, or Storm Troops).

The overconfident Hitler staged an armed uprising against the government in Munich in November 1923, the Beer Hall Putsch. The putsch was quickly crushed, and Hitler was sentenced to prison. During his brief stay in jail, he wrote _Mein Kampf_ (_My Struggle_), an autobiographical account of his movement and its underlying ideology—extreme German nationalism, virulent anti-Semitism, and anticommunism linked together by a social Darwinian theory of struggle that stresses the right of superior nations to _Lebensraum_ (living space) through expansion and the right of superior individuals to secure authoritarian leadership over the masses.

During his imprisonment, Hitler also came to the realization that the Nazis would have to come to power by constitutional means, not by overthrowing the Weimar Republic. This implied the formation of a mass political party that would actively compete for votes with the other political parties. After his release from prison, Hitler reorganized the Nazi Party and expanded it to all parts of Germany. By 1929, the Nazis had a national party organization.

Three years later, the Nazi Party had 800,000 members and had become the largest party in the Reichstag. No doubt Germany's economic difficulties were a crucial factor in the Nazis' rise to power. Unemployment rose dramatically, from 4.35 million in 1931 to 6 million by the winter of 1932. Claiming to stand above all differences, Hitler promised that he would create a new Germany free of class differences and party infighting. His appeal to national pride, national honor, and traditional militarism struck receptive chords in his listeners. After attending one of Hitler's rallies, a schoolteacher in Hamburg said: "When the speech was over, there was roaring enthusiasm and applause. . . . Then he went—How many look up to him with touching faith as their savior, their deliverer from unbearable distress."[3]

Increasingly, the right-wing elites of Germany—the industrial magnates, landed aristocrats, military establishment, and higher bureaucrats—came to see Hitler as the man who had the mass support to establish a right-wing, authoritarian regime that would save Germany and

PROPAGANDA AND MASS MEETINGS IN NAZI GERMANY

POLITICS & GOVERNMENT

Propaganda and mass rallies were two of the chief instruments that Hitler used to prepare the German people for the tasks he set before them. In the first selection, taken from *Mein Kampf*, Hitler explains the psychological importance of mass meetings in creating support for a political movement. In the second excerpt, taken from his speech to a crowd at Nuremberg, he describes the kind of mystical bond he hoped to create through his mass rallies.

In Hitler's view, what do mass meetings accomplish for his movement? How do mass rallies further the development of nationalism?

Adolf Hitler, *Mein Kampf*

The mass meeting is also necessary for the reason that in it the individual, who at first, while becoming a supporter of a young movement, feels lonely and easily succumbs to the fear of being alone, for the first time gets the picture of a larger community, which in most people has a strengthening, encouraging effect. . . . When from his little workshop or big factory, in which he feels very small, he steps for the first time into a mass meeting and has thousands and thousands of people of the same opinions around him, when, as a seeker, he is swept away by three or four thousand others into the mighty effect of suggestive intoxication and enthusiasm, when the visible success and agreement of thousands confirm to him the rightness of the new doctrine and for the first time arouse doubt in the truth of his previous conviction—then he

himself has succumbed to the magic influence of what we designate as "mass suggestion." The will, the longing, and also the power of thousands are accumulated in every individual. The man who enters such a meeting doubting and wavering leaves it inwardly reinforced: he has become a link in the community.

Adolf Hitler, Speech at the Nuremberg Party Rally, 1936

Do we not feel once again in this hour the miracle that brought us together? Once you heard the voice of a man, and it struck deep into your hearts; it awakened you, and you followed this voice. Year after year you went after it, though him who had spoken you never even saw. You heard only a voice, and you followed it. When we meet each other here, the wonder of our coming together fills us all. Not every one of you sees me, and I do not see every one of you. But I feel you, and you feel me. It is the belief in our people that has made us small men great, that has made us poor men rich, that has made brave and courageous men out of us wavering, spiritless, timid folk; this belief made us see our road when we were astray; it joined us together into one whole! . . . You come, that . . . you may, once in a while, gain the feeling that now we are together; we are with him and he with us, and we are now Germany!

ThomsonNOW To read more works of Adolf Hitler, enter the *ThomsonNOW* documents area using the access card that is available for *The Essential World History*.

---

their privileged positions from a Communist takeover. Under pressure, President Paul von Hindenburg agreed to allow Hitler to become chancellor (on January 30, 1933) and form a new government.

Within two months, Hitler laid the foundations for the Nazis' complete takeover of Germany. The crowning step of Hitler's "legal seizure" of power came on March 23, when the Reichstag, by a two-thirds vote, passed the Enabling Act, which empowered the government to dispense with constitutional forms for four years while it issued laws to deal with the country's problems.

With their new source of power, the Nazis acted quickly to bring all institutions under their control. The civil service was purged of Jews and democratic elements, concentration camps were established for opponents of the new regime, trade unions were dissolved, and all political parties except the Nazis were abolished. By the end of the summer of 1933, Hitler and the Nazis had established the foundations for a totalitarian state. When Hindenburg died on August 2, 1934, the office of Reich president was abolished, and Hitler became *der Führer* (the leader)—sole ruler of Germany.

The Nazi State, 1933–1939 Having smashed the parliamentary state, Hitler now felt the real task was at hand: to develop the "total state." Hitler's goal was the development of an Aryan racial state that would dominate Europe and possibly the world for generations to come. Hitler stated:

> We must develop organizations in which an individual's entire life can take place. Then every activity and every need of every individual will be regulated by the collectivity represented by the party. There is no longer any arbitrary will, there are no longer any free realms in which the individual belongs to himself. . . . The time of personal happiness is over.[4]

The Nazis pursued the realization of this totalitarian ideal in a variety of ways.

Mass demonstrations and spectacles were orchestrated to draw the German nation into a collective fellowship and to mobilize it as an instrument for Hitler's policies (see the box above). These mass demonstrations, especially the party rallies that were held in Nuremberg every September, combined the symbolism

The Nazi Mass Spectacle. Hitler and the Nazis made clever use of mass spectacles to rally the German people behind the Nazi regime. These mass demonstrations evoked intense enthusiasm, as is evident in this photograph of Hitler arriving at the Bückeberg near Hamelin for the Harvest Festival in 1937. Almost one million people were present for the celebration.

of a religious service with the merriment of a popular amusement and usually evoked mass enthusiasm and excitement.

The state apparatus of Hitler's total state had some confusing features. One usually thinks of Nazi Germany as having an all-powerful government that maintained absolute control and order. In truth, Nazi Germany was the scene of almost constant personal and institutional conflict, which resulted in administrative chaos. Struggle characterized relationships within the party, within the state, and between party and state. Hitler, of course, remained the ultimate decision maker and absolute ruler.

In the economic sphere, Hitler and the Nazis also established control. Although the regime used public works projects and "pump-priming" grants to private construction firms to foster employment and end the depression, there is little doubt that rearmament did far more to solve the unemployment problem. Unemployment, which had stood at 6 million in 1932, dropped to 2.6 million in 1934 and less than 500,000 in 1937. This was an important factor in convincing many Germans to accept the new regime despite its excesses.

For those who needed coercion, the Nazi total state had its instruments of terror and repression. Especially important were the *Schutzstaffeln* (guard squadrons), known simply as the SS. The SS, under the direction of Heinrich Himmler (1900–1945), came to control all of the regular and secret police forces. Himmler and the SS functioned on the basis of two principles: terror and ideology. Terror included the instruments of repression and murder: secret police, criminal police, concentration camps, and later execution squads and death camps for the extermination of the Jews. For Himmler, the primary goal of the SS was to further the Aryan "master race."

The Nazi total state was intended to be an Aryan racial state. From its beginning, the Nazi Party reflected the strong anti-Semitic beliefs of Adolf Hitler. Women were to play a crucial role in the Aryan racial state as bearers of the children who would bring about the triumph of the Aryan race. To the Nazis, the differences between men and women were natural: men were destined to be warriors and political leaders; women were to be wives and mothers.

Once in power, the Nazis translated anti-Semitic ideas into anti-Semitic policies. In September 1935, at the annual party rally in Nuremberg, the Nazis announced new racial laws, which excluded German Jews from German citizenship and forbade marriages and extramarital relations between Jews and German citizens.

A more violent phase of anti-Jewish activity took place in 1938 and 1939, initiated on November 9–10, 1938, by the infamous *Kristallnacht,* the "night of shattered glass." The assassination of a third secretary in the German embassy in Paris became the excuse for a Nazi-led destructive rampage against the Jews in which synagogues were burned, seven thousand Jewish businesses were destroyed, and at least one hundred Jews were killed. Jews were barred from all public buildings and prohibited from owning or working in any retail store.

The Stalinist Era in the Soviet Union

Joseph Stalin made a significant shift in economic policy in 1928 when he launched his first five-year plan. Its real goal was nothing less than the transformation of the agrarian Soviet Union into an industrial country virtually overnight. Instead of producing consumer goods, the first five-year plan emphasized production of capital goods and armaments and succeeded in quadrupling the production of heavy machinery and doubling oil production. Between 1928 and 1937, during the first two five-year plans, steel production increased from 4 million to 18 million tons per year.

Rapid industrialization was accompanied by an equally rapid collectivization of agriculture. Its goal was to eliminate private farms and push people into collective farms. Strong resistance to Stalin's plans from peasants who hoarded crops and killed livestock only caused him to step up the program. By 1934, Russia's 26 million family farms had been collectivized into 250,000 units, though at a tremendous cost, since the hoarding of food and the slaughter of livestock produced widespread famine. Perhaps ten million peasants died in the artificially created famines of 1932 and 1933. The only concession Stalin made to the peasants was to allow each collective farm worker to have one tiny privately owned garden plot.

To achieve his goals, Stalin strengthened the party bureaucracy under his control. Those who resisted were sent into forced labor camps in Siberia. Stalin's desire for sole control of decision making also led to purges of the Old Bolsheviks. Between 1936 and 1938, the most prominent Old Bolsheviks were put on trial and condemned to death. During this same time, Stalin undertook a purge of army officers, diplomats, union officials, party members, intellectuals, and numerous ordinary citizens. Estimates are that eight million Russians were arrested; millions were sent to forced labor camps in Siberia from which they never returned.

The Stalinist era also reversed much of the permissive social legislation of the early 1920s. Advocating complete equality of rights for women, the Communists had made divorce and abortion easy to obtain while also encouraging women to work outside the home and to set their own moral standards. After Stalin came to power, the family was praised as a miniature collective in which parents were responsible for inculcating values of duty, discipline, and hard work. Abortion was outlawed, and divorced fathers who failed to support their children were fined heavily.

The Rise of Militarism in Japan

The rise of militant forces in Japan resulted not from a seizure of power by a new political party but from the growing influence of militant elements at the top of the political hierarchy. In the early 1930s, confrontations with China in Manchuria, combined with the onset of the Great Depression, brought an end to the fragile stability of the immediate postwar years.

The depression had a disastrous effect on Japan, as many European countries, along with the United States, raised stiff tariff walls against cheap Japanese imports in order to protect their struggling domestic industries. The ensuing economic slowdown imposed a heavy burden on the fragile democracy in Japan. Although civilian cabinets tried desperately to cope with the economic challenges

presented by the world depression, the political parties were no longer able to stem the growing influence of militant nationalist elements. Extremist patriotic organizations began to terrorize Japanese society by assassinating businessmen and public figures identified with the policy of conciliation toward the outside world. Some argued that Western-style political institutions should be replaced by a new system that would return to traditional Japanese values and imperial authority. Their message of "Asia for the Asians" became increasingly popular as the Great Depression convinced many Japanese that capitalism was unsuitable for Japan.

During the mid-1930s, the influence of the military and extreme nationalists over the government steadily increased. National elections continued to take place, but cabinets were dominated by the military or advocates of Japanese expansionism. In February 1936, junior army officers led a coup, briefly occupying the Diet building and other key government installations in Tokyo and assassinating several members of the cabinet. The ringleaders were quickly tried and convicted of treason, but under conditions that further strengthened the influence of the military.

The Path to War

Only twenty years after the "war to end war," the world plunged back into the nightmare. The efforts at collective security in the 1920s proved meaningless in view of the growth of Nazi Germany and the rise of Japan.

The Path to War in Europe

World War II in Europe had its beginnings in the ideas of Adolf Hitler, who believed that only the Aryans were capable of building a great civilization. To Hitler, Germany needed more land to support a larger population and be a great power. Already in the 1920s, in the second volume of *Mein Kampf,* Hitler had indicated that a National Socialist regime would find this land to the east—in Russia. Once it had been conquered, Russia could be resettled by German peasants while the Slavic population could be used as slave labor to build the Aryan racial state that would dominate Europe for a thousand years.

On March 9, 1935, in defiance of the Treaty of Versailles, Hitler announced the creation of an air force and one week later the introduction of a military draft that would expand Germany's army from 100,000 to 550,000 troops. Hitler's unilateral repudiation of the Versailles treaty brought a swift reaction as France, Great Britain, and Italy condemned Germany's action and warned against future aggressive steps. But nothing concrete was done.

On March 7, 1936, buoyed by his conviction that the Western democracies had no intention of using force to maintain the Treaty of Versailles, Hitler sent German troops into the demilitarized Rhineland. According to the Versailles treaty, the French had the right to use force against any violation of the demilitarized Rhineland. But France would not act without British support, and the British viewed the occupation of German territory by German troops as a reasonable action.

Meanwhile Hitler gained new allies. In October 1935, Benito Mussolini had committed Fascist Italy to imperial expansion by invading Ethiopia. Mussolini welcomed Hitler's support and began to draw closer to the German dictator. In October 1936, Hitler and Mussolini concluded an agreement that recognized their common interests, and one month later, Mussolini referred publicly to the new Rome-Berlin Axis. Also in November, Germany and Japan (the rising military power in the Far East) concluded the Anti-Comintern Pact and agreed to maintain a common front against communism.

By 1937, Germany was once more a "world power," as Hitler proclaimed. Hitler was convinced that neither the French nor the British would provide much opposition to his plans and decided in 1938 to move to achieve one of his longtime goals: *Anschluss* (union) with Austria. By threatening Austria with invasion, Hitler coerced the Austrian chancellor into putting Austrian Nazis in charge of the government. The new government promptly invited German troops to enter Austria and assist in maintaining law and order. One day later, on March 13, 1938, after his triumphal return to his native land, Hitler formally annexed Austria to Germany.

Hitler's next objective was the destruction of Czechoslovakia, and he believed that France and Britain would not use force to defend that nation. He was right again. On September 15, 1938, Hitler demanded the cession of the Sudetenland, in northern Czechoslovakia, to Germany and expressed his willingness to risk "world war" to achieve his objective. Instead of objecting, the British, French, Germans, and Italians—at a hastily arranged conference at Munich—reached an agreement that met all of Hitler's demands. German troops were allowed to occupy the Sudetenland. Increasingly, Hitler was convinced of his own infallibility, and he had by no means been satisfied at Munich. In March 1939, Hitler occupied all the Czech lands (Bohemia and Moravia), while the Slovaks, with Hitler's encouragement, declared their independence of the Czechs and became a puppet state (Slovakia) of Nazi Germany. On the evening of March 15, 1939, Hitler triumphantly declared in Prague that he would be known as the greatest German of them all.

At last, the Western states reacted to Hitler's threat. When Hitler began to demand the return of Danzig (which had been made a free city by the Treaty of Versailles to serve as a seaport for Poland) to Germany, Britain offered to protect Poland in the event of war. At the same time, both France and Britain realized that only the Soviet Union was powerful enough to help contain Nazi aggression and began political and military negotiations with Stalin and the Soviets.

Meanwhile, Hitler pressed on. To preclude an alliance between the West and the Soviet Union, which would open the danger of a two-front war, Hitler negotiated his own nonaggression pact with Stalin and shocked the world with its announcement on August 23, 1939. The treaty with the Soviet Union gave Hitler the freedom to attack Poland. He told his generals: "Now Poland is in the position in which I wanted her. . . . I am only afraid that at the last moment some swine or other will yet submit to me a plan for mediation."[5] He need not have worried. On September 1, German forces invaded Poland; two days later, Britain and France declared war on Germany. Europe was again at war.

The Path to War in Asia

During the mid-1920s, Japan had maintained a strong military and economic presence in Manchuria, an area in northeastern China controlled by the Chinese warlord Zhang Zuolin. But in 1928, the latter formed an alliance with Chiang Kai-shek, whose new Nanjing government was seeking to extend its sway northward from the Yangtze valley. Threatened with the loss of Manchuria's rich natural resources, in September 1931 Japanese military officers stationed in the area launched a coup to bring about a complete Japanese takeover of the region. Despite worldwide protests from the League of Nations, which eventually condemned the seizure, Japan steadily strengthened its control over Manchuria (now renamed Manchukuo) and began to expand its military presence south of the Great Wall in North China.

For the moment, Chiang Kai-shek attempted to avoid a direct confrontation with Japan so that he could deal with what he considered the greater threat from the Chinese Communists, still holed up in their mountain base at Yan'an. When clashes between Chinese and Japanese troops broke out, he sought to appease Tokyo by granting Japan the authority to administer areas in North China. But as Japan moved steadily southward, popular protests in Chinese cities against Japanese aggression intensified. In December 1936, Chiang ended his military efforts against the Communists in Yan'an and formed a new united front against the Japanese. When Chinese and Japanese forces clashed at the Marco Polo Bridge, south of Beijing, in July 1937, China refused to apologize, and hostilities spread.

A Monroe Doctrine for Asia To avoid provoking the United States, Japan did not declare war on China. Nevertheless, neither side would compromise, and the "China incident" of 1937 eventually turned into a major conflict. Japan advanced up the Yangtze River and seized the Chinese capital of Nanjing in December, but Chiang Kai-shek refused to capitulate and moved his government upriver to Hankou. When the Japanese seized that city, he retreated to Changqing, in remote Sichuan province, and kept his capital there for the remainder of the war.

A Japanese Victory in China.
After consolidating its authority over Manchuria, Japan began to expand into northern China. Direct hostilities between Japanese and Chinese forces began in 1937. This photograph shows victorious Japanese forces in January 1938 riding under the arched Chungshan Gate in Nanjing after they had conquered the Chinese capital city. By 1939, Japan had conquered most of eastern China.

Japanese strategists had hoped to force Chiang to agree to join a Japanese-dominated "New Order in East Asia," comprising Japan, Manchuria, and China, but when he refused to cooperate, Tokyo turned to the dissident politician Wang Jingwei, who agreed to form a pro-Japanese puppet government in Nanjing. The "New Order" was part of a larger Japanese plan to seize Soviet Siberia, with its rich resources, and create a new "Monroe Doctrine for Asia," with Japan guiding its Asian neighbors on the path to development and prosperity. After all, who better to instruct Asian societies on the path to modernization than the one Asian country that had already achieved it (see the box on p. 543)?

During the late 1930s, Japan had begun to cooperate with Nazi Germany on the assumption that the two countries would ultimately launch a joint attack on the Soviet Union and divide up its resources between them. But when Berlin suddenly surprised the world by signing a nonaggression pact with Moscow in August 1939, Japanese strategists were compelled to reevaluate their long-term objectives. Japan was not strong enough to defeat the Soviet Union alone and so began to shift its eyes southward, to the vast resources of Southeast Asia—the oil of the Dutch East Indies, the rubber and tin of Malaya, and the rice of Burma and Indochina.

A move southward, of course, would risk war with the European colonial powers and the United States. Japan's attack on China in the summer of 1937 had already aroused strong criticism abroad, particularly in the United States. When Japan demanded the right to occupy airfields and exploit economic resources in French Indochina in the summer of 1940, the United States warned the Japanese that it would cut off the sale of oil and scrap iron unless Japan withdrew from the area and returned to its borders of 1931.

In Tokyo, the American threat of retaliation was viewed as a threat to Japan's long-term objectives. It badly needed oil and scrap iron from the United States. Should they be cut off, Japan would have to find them elsewhere. Japan was thus caught in a dilemma. To obtain guaranteed access to natural resources that would be necessary to fuel the Japanese military machine, Japan must risk being cut off from its current source of raw materials that would be needed in the event of a conflict. After much debate, Japan decided to launch a surprise attack on American and European colonies in Southeast Asia in the hope of a quick victory that would evict the United States from the region.

World War II

Hitler stunned Europe with the speed and efficiency of the German *Blitzkrieg,* or "lightning war." Armored columns or panzer divisions (a panzer division was a strike force of about three hundred tanks and accompanying forces and supplies) supported by airplanes broke quickly through Polish lines and encircled the bewildered Polish troops. Conventional infantry units then moved in to hold the newly conquered territory. Within four weeks, Poland had surrendered. On September 28, 1939, Germany and the Soviet Union officially divided Poland between them.

Europe at War

After a winter of waiting, Hitler resumed the war on April 9, 1940, with another *Blitzkrieg* against Denmark and Norway (see Map 24.1). One month later, on May 10, the Germans launched their attack on the Netherlands, Belgium, and France. The main assault through Luxembourg and the Ardennes forest was completely

JAPAN'S JUSTIFICATION FOR EXPANSION

POLITICS & GOVERNMENT

Advocates of Japanese expansion justified their proposals by claiming both economic necessity and moral imperatives. Note the familiar combination of motives in this passage written by an extremist military leader in the late 1930s.

What arguments does Hashimoto Kingoro make in favor of territorial expansion? What is his reaction to the condemnation of western European nations?

Hashimoto Kingoro on the Need for Emigration and Expansion

We have already said that there are only three ways left to Japan to escape from the pressure of surplus population. We are like a great crowd of people packed into a small and narrow room, and there are only three doors through which we might escape, namely emigration, advance into world markets, and expansion of territory. The first door, emigration, has been barred to us by the anti-Japanese immigration policies of other countries. The second door, advance into world markets, is being pushed shut by tariff barriers and the abrogation of commercial treaties. What should Japan do when two of the three doors have been closed against her?

It is quite natural that Japan should rush upon the last remaining door.

It may sound dangerous when we speak of territorial expansion, but the territorial expansion of which we speak does not in any sense of the word involve the occupation of the possessions of other countries, the planting of the Japanese flag thereon, and the declaration of their annexation to Japan. It is just that since the Powers have suppressed the circulation of Japanese materials and merchandise abroad, we are looking for some place overseas where Japanese capital, Japanese skills and Japanese labor can have free play, free from the oppression of the white race.

We would be satisfied with just this much. What moral right do the world powers who have themselves closed to us the two doors of emigration and advance into world markets have to criticize Japan's attempt to rush out of the third and last door?

If they do not approve of this, they should open the doors which they have closed against us and permit the free movement overseas of Japanese emigrants and merchandise. . . .

At the time of the Manchurian incident, the entire world joined in criticism of Japan. They said that Japan was an untrustworthy nation. They said that she had recklessly brought cannon and machine guns into Manchuria, which was the territory of another country, flown airplanes over it, and finally occupied it. But the military action taken by Japan was not in the least a selfish one. Moreover, we do not recall ever having taken so much as an inch of territory belonging to another nation. The result of this incident was the establishment of the splendid new nation of Manchuria. The Powers are still discussing whether or not to recognize this new nation, but regardless of whether or not other nations recognize her, the Manchurian empire has already been established, and now, seven years after its creation, the empire is further consolidating its foundations with the aid of its friend, Japan.

And if it is still protested that our actions in Manchuria were excessively violent, we may wish to ask the white race just which country it was that sent warships and troops to India, South Africa, and Australia and slaughtered innocent natives, bound their hands and feet with iron chains, lashed their backs with iron whips, proclaimed these territories as their own, and still continues to hold them to this very day.

---

unexpected by the French and British forces. German panzer divisions were able to break through the weak French defensive positions there and race across northern France, splitting the Allied armies and trapping French troops and the entire British army on the beaches of Dunkirk. Only by heroic efforts did the British achieve a gigantic evacuation of 330,000 Allied troops. The French capitulated on June 22. German armies occupied about three-fifths of France while the French hero of World War I, Marshal Henri Pétain, established an authoritarian regime (known as Vichy France) over the remainder. Germany was now in control of western and central Europe, but Britain had still not been defeated.

As Hitler realized, an amphibious invasion of Britain would be possible only if Germany gained control of the air. At the beginning of August 1940, the *Luftwaffe* (the German air force) launched a major offensive against British air and naval bases, harbors, communication centers, and war industries. The British fought back doggedly, supported by an effective radar system that gave them early warning of German attacks. Nevertheless the British air force suffered critical losses by the end of August and was probably saved by Hitler's change of strategy. In September, in retaliation for a British attack on Berlin, Hitler ordered a shift from military targets to massive bombing of British cities to break British morale. The British rebuilt their air strength quickly and were soon inflicting major losses on *Luftwaffe* bombers. By the end of September, Germany had to postpone the invasion of Britain.

Although he had no desire for a two-front war, Hitler became convinced that Britain was remaining in the war only because it expected Soviet support. If the Soviet Union were smashed, Britain's last hope would be eliminated. Although the invasion of the Soviet Union was scheduled for spring 1941, the attack was delayed because

MAP 24.1 **World War II in Europe and North Africa.** With its fast and effective military, Germany quickly overwhelmed much of western Europe. However, Hitler overestimated his country's capabilities and underestimated those of his foes. By late 1942, his invasion of the Soviet Union was failing, and the United States had become a major factor in the war. The Allies successfully invaded Italy in 1943 and France in 1944. ❓ Which countries were neutral, and how did geography help make their neutrality an option? 🌐 **View an animated version of this map or related maps at** http://worldrc.wadsworth.com/

of problems in the Balkans. Hitler had already obtained the political cooperation of Hungary, Bulgaria, and Romania, but Mussolini's disastrous invasion of Greece in October 1940 exposed Hitler's southern flank to British air bases in Greece. To secure his Balkan flank, German troops seized both Yugoslavia and Greece in April. Now reassured, Hitler turned to the east and invaded the Soviet Union on June 22, 1941.

The massive attack stretched out along a 1,800-mile front. German troops advanced rapidly, capturing two million Soviet soldiers. By November, one German army group had swept through the Ukraine, while a second was besieging Leningrad; a third approached within 25 miles

of Moscow, the Soviet capital. An early winter and unexpected Soviet resistance, however, brought a halt to the German advance. For the first time in the war, German armies had been stopped. A Soviet counterattack in December 1941 came as an ominous ending to the year for the Germans. By that time, another of Hitler's decisions—the declaration of war on the United States—turned another European conflict into a global war.

Japan at War

On December 7, 1941, Japanese aircraft attacked the U.S. naval base at Pearl Harbor in the Hawaiian Islands. The

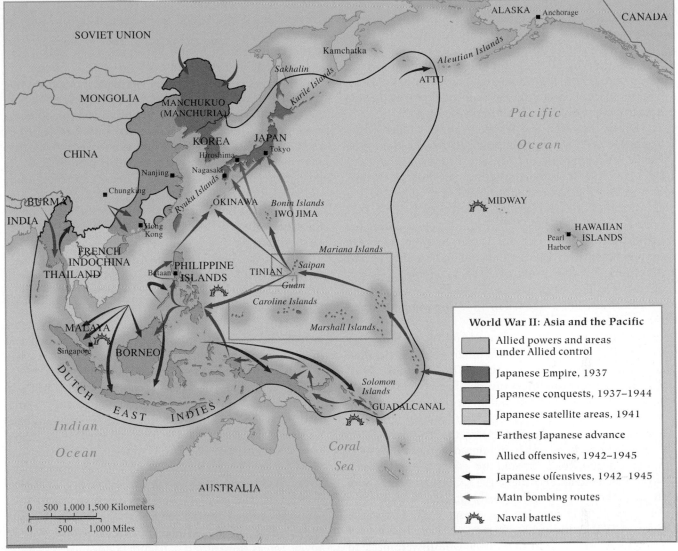

MAP 24.2 **World War II in Asia and the Pacific.** In 1937, Japan invaded northern China, beginning its effort to create a "Great East Asia Co-Prosperity Sphere." Further expansion induced the United States to end iron and oil sales to Japan. Deciding that war with the United States was inevitable, Japan engineered a surprise attack on Pearl Harbor. ❓ Why was control of the islands in the western Pacific of great importance both to the Japanese and to the Allies? ✇ **View an animated** version of this map or related maps at http://worldrc.wadsworth.com/

same day, other units launched additional assaults on the Philippines and began advancing toward the British colony of Malaya (see Map 24.2). Shortly after this, Japanese forces invaded the Dutch East Indies and occupied a number of islands in the Pacific Ocean. By the spring of 1942, almost all of Southeast Asia and much of the western Pacific had fallen to the Japanese. Japan declared the establishment of the Greater East Asia Co-Prosperity Sphere, encompassing the entire region under Japanese tutelage, and announced its intention to liberate the colonial areas of Southeast Asia from Western colonial rule. For the moment, however, Japan needed the resources of the region for its war machine and placed the countries under its own rule on a wartime basis.

Japanese leaders had hoped that their lightning strike at American bases would destroy the U.S. Pacific fleet

and persuade President Franklin D. Roosevelt to accept Japanese domination of the Pacific. But Japan had miscalculated. The attack on Pearl Harbor galvanized American opinion and won broad support for Roosevelt's war policy. The United States now joined with European nations and Nationalist China in a combined effort to defeat Japan and end its hegemony in the Pacific. Believing the American involvement in the Pacific would render the United States ineffective in the European theater of war, Hitler declared war on the United States four days after Pearl Harbor.

The Turning Point of the War, 1942–1943

The entry of the United States into the war created a coalition (the Grand Alliance) that ultimately defeated the Axis Powers (Germany, Italy, and Japan). To overcome mutual suspicions, the three major Allies, Britain, the United States, and the Soviet Union, agreed to stress military operations while ignoring political differences. At the beginning of 1943, the Allies also agreed to fight until the Axis Powers surrendered unconditionally, which had the effect of cementing the Grand Alliance by making it nearly impossible for Hitler to divide his foes.

Defeat, however, was far from Hitler's mind at the beginning of 1942. As Japanese forces advanced into the Pacific after crippling the American naval fleet at Pearl Harbor, Hitler continued the war in Europe against Britain and the Soviet Union. Until the fall of 1942, it appeared that the Germans might still prevail on the battlefield. Reinforcements in North Africa enabled the Afrika Korps under General Erwin Rommel to break through the British defenses in Egypt and advance toward Alexandria. In the spring of 1942, a renewed German offensive in the Soviet Union led to the capture of the entire Crimea. But by the fall of 1942, the war had turned against the Germans.

In North Africa, British forces had stopped Rommel's troops at El Alamein in the summer of 1942 and then forced them back across the desert. In November 1942, British and American forces invaded French North Africa and forced the German and Italian troops to surrender in May 1943. On the Eastern Front, the turning point of the war occurred at Stalingrad. After the capture of the Crimea, Hitler decided that Stalingrad, a major industrial center on the Volga, should be taken next. Between November 1942 and February 1943, German troops were stopped, then encircled, and finally forced to surrender on February 2, 1943 (see the box on p. 548). The entire German Sixth Army of 300,000 men was lost. By February 1943, German forces in the Soviet Union were back to their positions of June 1942.

The tide of battle in the Far East also turned dramatically in 1942. In the Battle of the Coral Sea on May 7–8, 1942, American naval forces stopped the Japanese advance. On June 4, at the Battle of Midway Island, American planes destroyed all four of the attacking Japanese aircraft carriers and established American naval superiority in the Pacific. By the fall of 1942, Allied forces were beginning to gather for offensive operations: into South China from Burma, through the East Indies by a process of "island hopping" by troops commanded by U.S. general Douglas MacArthur, and across the Pacific with a combination of U.S. Army, Marine, and Navy attacks on Japanese-held islands. After a series of bitter engagements in the waters of the Solomon Islands from August to November 1942, Japanese fortunes began to fade.

The Last Years of the War

By the beginning of 1943, the tide of battle had turned against Germany, Italy, and Japan. After the Axis forces had surrendered in Tunisia on May 13, 1943, the Allies crossed the Mediterranean and carried the war to Italy. After taking Sicily, Allied troops began the invasion of mainland Italy in September. In the meantime, after the ouster and arrest of Benito Mussolini, a new Italian government offered to surrender to Allied forces. But Mussolini was liberated by the Germans in a daring raid and then set up as the head of a puppet German state in northern Italy while German troops moved in and occupied much of Italy. The new defensive lines established by the Germans in the hills south of Rome were so effective that the Allied advance up the Italian peninsula was a painstaking affair accompanied by heavy casualties. Rome did not fall to the Allies until June 4, 1944. By that time, the Italian war had assumed a secondary role anyway as the Allies opened their long-awaited "second front" in western Europe.

Under the direction of the American general Dwight D. Eisenhower (1890–1969), the Allies landed five assault divisions on the beaches of Normandy on June 6 in history's greatest naval invasion. An initially indecisive German response enabled the Allied forces to establish a beachhead. Within three months, they had landed two million men and a half-million vehicles that pushed inland and broke through German defensive lines.

After the breakout, Allied troops moved south and east and liberated Paris by the end of August. By March 1945, they had crossed the Rhine River and advanced deep into Germany. At the end of April 1945, Allied armies in northern Germany moved toward the Elbe River, where they finally linked up with the Soviets. The Soviets had come a long way since the Battle of Stalingrad in 1943. In the summer of 1943, German forces were soundly defeated by the Soviets at the Battle of Kursk (July 5–12), the greatest tank battle of World War II. Soviet forces now began a relentless advance westward. The Soviets had reoccupied the Ukraine by the end of 1943 and lifted the siege of Leningrad and moved into the Baltic states by the beginning of 1944. Advancing along a northern front, Soviet troops occupied Warsaw in January 1945 and entered Berlin in April. Meanwhile, Soviet troops along a southern front swept through Hungary, Romania, and Bulgaria.

In January 1945, Hitler had moved into a bunker 55 feet under Berlin to direct the final stages of the war. In his final political testament, Hitler, consistent to the end in his rabid anti-Semitism, blamed the Jews for the war. Hitler committed suicide on April 30, two days after Mussolini had been shot by partisan Italian forces. On May 7, German commanders surrendered. The war in Europe was over.

Allied war plans for Asia had originally called for a massive military advance on the Japanese home islands through China, making full use of the latent strength of Chiang Kai-shek's armed forces. By 1943, however, President Roosevelt had lost confidence in the ability of Chiang Kai-shek's government to play a positive role in Allied operations and had turned to a "Pacific strategy" based on a gradual advance by U.S. military forces

CHRONOLOGY   The Course of World War II

Germany and the Soviet Union divide Poland	September 28, 1939
Blitzkrieg against Denmark and Norway	April 1940
Blitzkrieg against Belgium, Netherlands, and France	May 1940
France surrenders	June 22, 1940
Battle of Britain	Fall 1940
Nazi seizure of Yugoslavia and Greece	April 1941
Germany invades the Soviet Union	June 22, 1941
Japanese attack on Pearl Harbor	December 7, 1941
Battle of the Coral Sea	May 7–8, 1942
Battle of Midway Island	June 4, 1942
Allied invasion of North Africa	November 1942
German surrender at Stalingrad	February 2, 1943
Axis forces surrender in North Africa	May 1943
Battle of Kursk	July 5–12, 1943
Invasion of mainland Italy	September 1943
Allied invasion of France	June 6, 1944
Hitler commits suicide	April 30, 1945
Germany surrenders	May 7, 1945
Atomic bomb dropped on Hiroshima	August 6, 1945
Japan surrenders	August 14, 1945

across the Pacific Ocean. Beginning in 1943, American forces had gone on the offensive and proceeded, slowly at times, across the Pacific. The Americans took an increasing toll of enemy resources, especially at sea and in the air. As Allied military power drew inexorably closer to the main Japanese islands in the first months of 1945, President Harry Truman, who had succeeded to the presidency on the death of Franklin Roosevelt in April, decided to use atomic weapons to bring the war to an end without the necessity of an Allied invasion of the Japanese homeland. The first bomb was dropped on the city of Hiroshima on August 6. Three days later, a second bomb was dropped on Nagasaki. Japan surrendered unconditionally on August 14. World War II, in which seventeen million soldiers died in battle and perhaps eighteen million civilians perished as well, was finally over.

The New Order

The initial victories of the Germans and the Japanese had given them the opportunity to restructure society in Europe and Asia. Both followed policies of ruthless domination of their subject peoples.

The New Order in Europe

In 1942, the Nazi empire stretched across continental Europe from the English Channel in the west to the outskirts of Moscow in the east. Nazi-occupied Europe was largely organized in one of two ways. Some areas, such as western Poland, were directly annexed by Nazi Germany and made into German provinces. Most of occupied Europe was administered by German military or civilian officials, combined with different degrees of indirect control from collaborationist regimes.

Because the conquered lands in the east contained the living space for German expansion and were, in Nazi eyes, populated by racially inferior Slavic peoples, Nazi administration there was considerably more ruthless. Soon after the conquest of Poland, Heinrich Himmler, the leader of the SS, was put in charge of German resettlement plans in the east. Himmler's task was to evacuate the inferior Slavic peoples and replace them with Germans, a policy first applied to the new German provinces created from the lands of western Poland. One million Poles were uprooted and dumped in southern Poland. Hundreds of thousands of ethnic Germans (descendants of Germans who had migrated years earlier from Germany to different parts of southern and eastern Europe) were encouraged to colonize the designated areas in Poland. By 1942, two million ethnic Germans had been settled in Poland.

Labor shortages in Germany led to a policy of ruthless mobilization of foreign labor for Germany. In 1942, a special office was created to recruit labor for German farms and industries. By the summer of 1944, seven million foreign workers were laboring in Germany where they constituted 20 percent of the labor force. At the same time, another seven million workers were supplying forced labor in their own countries on farms, in industries, and even in military camps. The brutality of Germany's recruitment policies often led more and more people to resist the Nazi occupation forces.

The Holocaust

No aspect of the Nazi new order was more terrifying than the deliberate attempt to exterminate the Jews of Europe. Racial struggle was a key element in Hitler's ideology and meant to him a clearly defined conflict of opposites: the Aryans, creators of human cultural development, against the Jews, parasites who were trying to destroy the Aryans. Himmler and the SS organization closely shared Hitler's racial ideology. The SS was given responsibility for what the Nazis called their **Final Solution** to the "Jewish problem"—annihilation of the Jews. After the defeat of Poland, the SS ordered special strike forces (*Einsatzgruppen*) to round up all Polish Jews and concentrate them in ghettos established in a number of Polish cities.

In June 1941, the *Einsatzgruppen* were given new responsibilities as mobile killing units. These SS death squads followed the regular army's advance into Russia.

A GERMAN SOLDIER AT STALINGRAD

POLITICS & GOVERNMENT

The Soviet victory at Stalingrad was a major turning point in World War II. This excerpt comes from the diary of a German soldier who fought and died in the Battle of Stalingrad. His dreams of victory and a return home with medals are soon dashed by the realities of Soviet resistance.

What does this soldier believe about the Führer? Why? What has been the source of his information? Why is the battle for Stalingrad considered a major turning point in World War II?

Diary of a German Soldier

Today, after we'd had a bath, the company commander told us that if our future operations are as successful, we'll soon reach the Volga, take Stalingrad, and then the war will inevitably soon be over. Perhaps we'll be home by Christmas.

July 29. The company commander says the Russian troops are completely broken, and cannot hold out any longer. To reach the Volga and take Stalingrad is not so difficult for us. The Führer knows where the Russians' weak point is. Victory is not far away. . . .

August 10. The Führer's orders were read out to us. He expects victory of us. We are all convinced that they can't stop us.

August 12. This morning outstanding soldiers were presented with decorations. . . . Will I really go back to Elsa without a decoration? I believe that for Stalingrad the Führer will decorate even me. . . .

September 4. We are being sent northward along the front toward Stalingrad. We marched all night and by dawn had reached Voroponovo Station. We can already see the smoking town. It's a happy thought that the end of the war is getting nearer. That's what everyone is saying. . . .

September 8. Two days of nonstop fighting. The Russians are defending themselves with insane stubbornness. Our regiment has lost many men. . . .

September 16. Our battalion, plus tanks, is attacking the [grain storage] elevator, from which smoke is pouring—the grain in it is burning; the Russians seem to have set light to it themselves. Barbarism. The battalion is suffering heavy losses. . . .

October 10. The Russians are so close to us that our planes cannot bomb them. We are preparing for a decisive attack. The Führer has ordered the whole of Stalingrad to be taken as rapidly as possible. . . .

October 22. Our regiment has failed to break into the factory. We have lost many men; every time you move you have to jump over bodies. . . .

November 10. A letter from Elsa today. Everyone expects us home for Christmas. In Germany everyone believes we already hold Stalingrad. How wrong they are. If they could only see what Stalingrad has done to our army. . . .

November 21. The Russians have gone over to the offensive along the whole front. Fierce fighting is going on. So, there it is—the Volga, victory, and soon home to our families! We shall obviously be seeing them next in the other world.

November 29. We are encircled. It was announced this morning that the Führer has said: "The army can trust me to do everything necessary to ensure supplies and rapidly break the encirclement."

December 3. We are on hunger rations and waiting for the rescue that the Führer promised. . . .

December 14. Everybody is racked with hunger. Frozen potatoes are the best meal, but to get them out of the ice-covered ground under fire from Russian bullets is not so easy. . . .

December 26. The horses have already been eaten. I would eat a cat; they say its meat is also tasty. The soldiers look like corpses or lunatics, looking for something to put in their mouths. They no longer take cover from Russian shells; they haven't the strength to walk, run away, and hide. A curse on this war!

Their job was to round up Jews in their villages, execute them, and bury them in mass graves, often giant pits dug by the victims themselves before they were shot. But the constant killing led to morale problems among the SS executioners. During a visit to Minsk in the Soviet Union, Himmler tried to build morale by pointing out that he "would not like it if Germans did such a thing gladly. But their conscience was in no way impaired, for they were soldiers who had to carry out every order unconditionally. He alone had responsibility before God and Hitler for everything that was happening."[6]

Although it has been estimated that as many as one million Jews were killed by the *Einsatzgruppen,* this approach to solving the Jewish problem was soon perceived as inadequate. Instead, the Nazis opted for the systematic annihilation of the European Jewish population in specially built death camps. Jews from countries occupied by Germany (or sympathetic to Germany) were rounded up, packed like cattle into freight trains, and shipped to Poland, where six extermination centers were built to dispose of them. The largest and most famous was Auschwitz-Birkenau. Medical technicians chose Zyklon B (the commercial name for hydrogen cyanide) as the most effective gas for quickly killing large numbers of people in gas chambers designed to look like "shower rooms" to facilitate the cooperation of the victims. After gassing, the corpses were burned in specially built crematoria.

Library of Congress, Prints and Photographs Division

The Holocaust: Activities of the *Einsatzgruppen*. The mobile killing units known as the *Einsatzgruppen* were active during the first phase of mass killings of the Holocaust. This picture shows the execution of a Jew by a member of one of these SS killing squads. Onlookers include members of the German army, the German Labor Service, and even Hitler Youth. When it became apparent that this method of killing was inefficient, it was replaced by the death camps.

The death camps were in operation by the spring of 1942; by the summer, Jews were also being shipped from France, Belgium, and the Netherlands. Even as the Allies were making significant advances in 1944, Jews were being shipped from Greece and Hungary. A harrowing experience awaited the Jews when they arrived at one of the six death camps. Rudolf Höss, commandant at Auschwitz-Birkenau, described it:

> We had two SS doctors on duty at Auschwitz to examine the incoming transports of prisoners. The prisoners would be marched by one of the doctors who would make spot decisions as they walked by. Those who were fit for work were sent into the camp. Others were sent immediately to the extermination plants. Children of tender years were invariably exterminated since by reason of their youth they were unable to work. . . . At Auschwitz we endeavored to

fool the victims into thinking that they were to go through a delousing process. Of course, frequently they realized our true intentions and we sometimes had riots and difficulties due to that fact.[7]

About 30 percent of the arrivals at Auschwitz were sent to a labor camp; the remainder went to the gas chambers (see the box on p. 550). After they had been gassed, the bodies were burned in the crematoria. The victims' goods and even their bodies were used for economic gain. Female hair was cut off, collected, and turned into cloth or used to stuff mattresses. The Germans killed between five and six million Jews, more than three million of them in the death camps. Virtually 90 percent of the Jewish population of Poland, the Baltic countries, and Germany were exterminated.

The Nazis were also responsible for another **Holocaust,** the death by shooting, starvation, or overwork of at least another nine to ten million people. Because the Nazis considered the Gypsies of Europe a race containing alien blood (like the Jews), they were systematically rounded up for extermination. About 40 percent of Europe's one million Gypsies were killed in the death camps. The leading elements of the "subhuman" Slavic peoples—the clergy, intelligentsia, civil leaders, judges, and lawyers—were arrested and deliberately killed. Probably an additional four million Poles, Ukrainians, and Byelorussians lost their lives as slave laborers for Nazi Germany. Finally, at least three million Soviet prisoners of war, and probably more, were killed in captivity.

The New Order in Asia

Once Japan's takeover was completed, Japanese war policy in the occupied areas in Asia became essentially defensive, as Japan hoped to use its new possessions to meet its needs for raw materials, such as tin, oil, and rubber, as well as to serve as an outlet for Japanese manufactured goods. To provide a structure for the arrangement, Japanese leaders set up the Greater East Asia Co-Prosperity Sphere as a self-sufficient community designed to provide mutual benefits to the occupied areas and the home country.

The Japanese conquest of Southeast Asia had been accomplished under the slogan "Asia for the Asians." Japanese officials in occupied territories quickly promised that independent governments would be established under Japanese tutelage. Such governments were eventually established in Burma, the Dutch East Indies, Vietnam, and the Philippines.

In fact, however, real power rested with the Japanese military authorities in each territory, and the local Japanese military command was directly subordinated to the army general staff in Tokyo. The economic resources of the colonies were exploited for the benefit of the Japanese war machine, while natives were recruited to serve in local military units or conscripted to work on public works projects. In some cases, the people living in the occupied areas were subjected to severe hardships. In Indochina, for example, forced requisitions of rice by the

THE HOLOCAUST: THE CAMP COMMANDANT AND THE CAMP VICTIMS

FAMILY & SOCIETY

The systematic annihilation of millions of men, women, and children in extermination camps makes the Holocaust one of the most horrifying events in history. The first document is taken from an account by Rudolf Höss, commandant of the extermination camp at Auschwitz-Birkenau. In the second document, a French doctor explains what happened at one of the crematoria described by Höss.

What "equipment" does Höss describe? What process does the French doctor describe? Is there any sympathy for the victims in either account? Why or why not? How could such a horrifying process have been allowed to occur? Who was held responsible after the war? Was this sufficient?

Commandant Höss Describes the Equipment

The two large crematoria, Nos. I and II, were built during the winter of 1942–43. . . . Each . . . could cremate c. 2,000 corpses within twenty-four hours. . . . Crematoria I and II both had underground undressing and gassing rooms which could be completely ventilated. The corpses were brought up to the ovens on the floor above by lift. The gas chambers could hold c. 3,000 people.

The firm of Topf had calculated that the two smaller crematoria, III and IV, would each be able to cremate 1,500 corpses within twenty-four hours. However, owing to the wartime shortage of materials, the builders were obliged to economize, and so the undressing rooms and gassing rooms were built above ground and the ovens were of a less solid construction. But it soon became apparent that the flimsy construction of these two four-retort ovens was not up to the demands made on it. No. III ceased operating altogether after a short time and later was no longer used.

No. IV had to be repeatedly shut down since after a short period in operation of 4–6 weeks, the ovens and chimneys had burnt out. The victims of the gassing were mainly burnt in pits behind crematorium IV.

The largest number of people gassed and cremated within twenty-four hours was somewhat over 9,000.

A French Doctor Describes the Victims

It is mid-day, when a long line of women, children, and old people enter the yard. The senior official in charge . . . climbs on a bench to tell them that they are going to have a bath and that afterward they will get a drink of hot coffee. They all undress in the yard. . . . The doors are opened and an indescribable jostling begins. The first people to enter the gas chamber begin to draw back. They sense the death which awaits them. The SS men put an end to this pushing and shoving with blows from their rifle butts beating the heads of the horrified women who are desperately hugging their children. The massive oak double doors are shut. For two endless minutes one can hear banging on the walls and screams which are no longer human. And then—not a sound. Five minutes later the doors are opened. The corpses, squashed together and distorted, fall out like a waterfall. . . . The bodies, which are still warm, pass through the hands of the hairdresser, who cuts their hair, and the dentist, who pulls out their gold teeth. . . . One more transport has just been processed through No. IV crematorium.

ThomsonNOW To read more Nazi documents regarding concentration camps, enter the *ThomsonNOW* documents area using the access card that is available for *The Essential World History*.

---

local Japanese authorities for shipment abroad created a food shortage that caused the starvation of over a million Vietnamese in 1944 and 1945.

At first, many Southeast Asian nationalists took Japanese promises at face value and agreed to cooperate with their new masters. But as the exploitative nature of Japanese occupation policies became clear, sentiment turned against the new order. Japanese officials sometimes unwittingly provoked such attitudes by their arrogance and contempt for local customs.

Japanese military planners had little respect for their subject peoples and viewed the Geneva Convention on the laws of war as little more than a fabrication of Western countries to tie the hands of their adversaries. In conquering northern and central China, the Japanese freely used poison gas and biological weapons, which caused the deaths of millions of Chinese citizens. The Japanese occupation of the onetime Chinese capital of Nanjing was

especially brutal. In the notorious "Nanjing Incident," they spent several days killing, raping, and looting the local population.

Japanese soldiers also treated Koreans savagely. Almost 800,000 Koreans were sent overseas, most of them as forced laborers, to Japan. Tens of thousands of women from Korea and the Philippines were forced to be "comfort women" (prostitutes) for Japanese troops. In construction projects to help their war effort, the Japanese also made extensive use of labor forces composed of both prisoners of war and local peoples. In building the Burma-Thailand railway in 1943, for example, the Japanese used 61,000 Australian, British, and Dutch prisoners of war and almost 300,000 workers from Burma, Malaya, Thailand, and the Dutch East Indies. An inadequate diet and appalling work conditions in an unhealthy climate led to the deaths of 12,000 Allied prisoners of war and 90,000 native workers by the time the railway was completed.

The Home Front

World War II was even more of a total war than World War I. Fighting was much more widespread and covered most of the world. The number of civilians killed was far higher.

Mobilizing the People: Three Examples

The initial defeats of the Soviet Union led to drastic emergency mobilization measures that affected the civilian population. Leningrad, for example, experienced nine hundred days of siege, during which its inhabitants became so desperate for food that they ate dogs, cats, and mice. As the German army made its rapid advance into Soviet territory, the factories in the western part of the Soviet Union were dismantled and shipped to the interior—to the Urals, western Siberia, and the Volga region. Machines were set down on the bare earth, and walls went up around them as workers began their work.

Stalin called the widespread military and industrial mobilization of the nation a "battle of machines," and the Soviets won, producing 78,000 tanks and 98,000 artillery pieces. In 1943, fully 55 percent of Soviet national income went for war matériel, compared to 15 percent in 1940.

Soviet women played a major role in the war effort. Women and girls were enlisted for work in industries, mines, and railroads. Overall the number of women working in industry increased almost 60 percent. Soviet women were also expected to dig antitank ditches and work as air raid wardens. In addition, the Soviet Union was the only country in World War II to use women as combatants. Soviet women functioned as snipers and as crews in bomber squadrons.

In August 1914, Germans had enthusiastically cheered their soldiers marching off to war; in September 1939, the streets were quiet. Many Germans were apathetic or, even worse for the Nazi regime, had a foreboding of disaster. Hitler was very aware of the importance of the home front. He believed that the collapse of the home front in World War I had caused Germany's defeat. To avoid a repetition of that experience, he adopted economic policies that may indeed have cost Germany the war.

To maintain the morale of the home front during the first two years of the war, Hitler refused to cut production of consumer goods or increase the production of armaments. After German defeats on the Russian front and the American entry into the war, however, the situation changed. Early in 1942, Hitler finally ordered a massive increase in armaments production and the size of the army. Hitler's architect, Albert Speer, was made minister for armaments and munitions in 1942. By eliminating waste and rationalizing procedures, Speer was able to triple the production of armaments between 1942 and 1943, despite the intense Allied air raids. Speer's urgent plea for a total mobilization of resources for the war effort went unheeded, however. Hitler, fearful of civilian morale problems that would undermine the home front, refused any dramatic cuts in the production of consumer goods. A total mobilization of the economy was not implemented until 1944, but by that time, it was too late.

The war produced a reversal in Nazi attitudes toward women. Nazi resistance to female employment declined as the war progressed and more and more men were called up for military service. Nazi magazines now proclaimed, "We see the woman as the eternal mother of our people, but also as the working and fighting comrade of the man."[8] But the number of women working in industry, agriculture, commerce, and domestic service increased only slightly. The total number of employed women in September 1944 was 14.9 million, compared to 14.6 million in May 1939. Many women, especially those of the middle class, resisted regular employment, particularly in factories.

Wartime Japan was a highly mobilized society. To guarantee its control over all national resources, the government set up a planning board to control prices, wages, the utilization of labor, and the allocation of resources. Traditional habits of obedience and hierarchy, buttressed by the concept of imperial divinity, were emphasized to encourage citizens to sacrifice their resources, and sometimes their lives, for the national cause. The system culminated in the final years of the war, when young Japanese were encouraged to volunteer en masse to serve as pilots in the suicide missions (known as *kamikaze*, "divine wind") against U.S. battleships.

Women's rights too were to be sacrificed to the greater national cause. Already by 1937, Japanese women were being exhorted to fulfill their patriotic duty by bearing more children and by espousing the slogans of the Greater Japanese Women's Association. Japan was extremely reluctant to mobilize women on behalf of the war effort, however. General Hideki Tojo, prime minister from 1941 to 1944, opposed female employment, arguing that "the weakening of the family system would be the weakening of the nation. . . . We are able to do our duties only because we have wives and mothers at home."[9] Female employment increased during the war, but only in areas where women traditionally worked, such as the textile industry and farming. Instead of using women to meet labor shortages, the Japanese government brought in Korean and Chinese laborers.

The Frontline Civilians: The Bombing of Cities

Bombing was used in World War II against a variety of targets, including military targets, enemy troops, and civilian populations. The bombing of civilians made World War II as devastating for civilians as for frontline soldiers. A small number of bombing raids in the last year

COMPARATIVE ILLUSTRATION

The Bombing of Civilians—East and West. World War II was the most destructive war in world history, not only for frontline soldiers but for civilians at home as well. The most devastating bombing of civilians came near the end of World War II when the United States dropped atomic bombs on the Japanese cities of Hiroshima and Nagasaki. At the left is a view of Hiroshima after the bombing that shows the incredible devastation produced by the atomic bomb. The picture at the right shows a street in Clydebank, near Glasgow in Scotland, the day after the city was bombed by the Germans in March 1941. Only seven of the city's twelve thousand houses were left undamaged; 35,000 of the 47,000 inhabitants became homeless overnight.

of World War I had given rise to the argument that public outcry over the bombing of civilian populations would be an effective way to coerce governments into making peace. Consequently, European air forces began to develop long-range bombers in the 1930s.

The first sustained use of civilian bombing contradicted the theory. Beginning in early September 1940, the German *Luftwaffe* subjected London and many other British cities and towns to nightly air raids, making the Blitz (as the British called the German air raids) a national experience. Londoners took the first heavy blows, and it was their maintenance of morale that set the standard for the rest of the British population (see the comparative illustration above).

The British failed to learn from their own experience, however; Prime Minister Winston Churchill and his advisers believed that destroying German communities would break civilian morale and bring victory. Major bombing raids began in 1942. On May 31, 1942, Cologne became the first German city to be subjected to an attack by a thousand bombers. Bombing raids added an element of terror to circumstances already made difficult by

growing shortages of food, clothing, and fuel. Germans especially feared incendiary bombs, which ignited firestorms that swept destructive paths through the cities. The ferocious bombing of Dresden from February 13 to 15, 1945, set off a firestorm that may have killed as many as 100,000 inhabitants and refugees.

Germany suffered enormously from the Allied bombing raids. Millions of buildings were destroyed, and possibly half a million civilians died from the raids. Nevertheless, it is highly unlikely that Allied bombing sapped the morale of the German people. Instead Germans, whether pro-Nazi or anti-Nazi, fought on stubbornly, often driven simply by a desire to live. Nor did the bombing destroy Germany's industrial capacity. The Allied strategic bombing survey revealed that the production of war material actually increased between 1942 and 1944.

In Japan, the bombing of civilians reached a horrendous new level with the use of the first atomic bomb. Attacks on Japanese cities by the new American B-29 Superfortresses, the biggest bombers of the war, had begun on November 24, 1944. By the summer of 1945, many of Japan's industries had been destroyed, along with one-fourth of its dwellings. After the Japanese government decreed the mobilization of all people between the ages of thirteen and sixty into the so-called People's Volunteer Corps, President Truman and his advisers decided that Japanese fanaticism might mean a million American casualties, and Truman decided to drop the newly developed atomic bomb on Hiroshima and Nagasaki. The destruction was incredible. Of 76,000 buildings near the hypocenter of the explosion in Hiroshima, 70,000 were flattened, and 140,000 of the city's 400,000 inhabitants had died by the end of 1945. Over the next five years, another 50,000 perished from the effects of radiation. The dropping of the atomic bomb on Hiroshima on August 6, 1945, announced the dawn of the nuclear age.

Aftermath: Toward The Cold War

The total victory of the Allies in World War II was followed not by a real peace but by yet another period of conflict, known as the Cold War, that dominated world politics for the next fifty years.

The Conferences at Tehran, Yalta, and Potsdam

Stalin, Roosevelt, and Churchill, the leaders of the Big Three of the Grand Alliance, met at Tehran, the capital of Iran, in November 1943 to decide the future course of the war. Stalin and Roosevelt argued successfully for an American-British invasion of the Continent through France, which they scheduled for the spring of 1944. This meant that Soviet and British-American forces would meet in defeated Germany along a north-south dividing line and that Soviet forces would liberate eastern Europe. The Allies also agreed to a partition of postwar Germany.

By the time of the conference at Yalta in southern Russia in February 1945, the defeat of Germany was a foregone conclusion. The Western powers now faced the reality of eleven million Red Army soldiers taking possession of large portions of Europe. Stalin, deeply suspicious of the Western powers, desired a buffer to protect the Soviet Union from possible future Western aggression but at the same time was eager to obtain important resources and strategic military positions. Roosevelt by this time was moving toward the idea of self-determination for Europe. The Grand Alliance approved the "Declaration on Liberated Europe." This was a pledge to assist liberated European nations in the creation of "democratic institutions of their own choice." Liberated countries were to hold free elections to determine their political systems.

At Yalta, Roosevelt sought Russian military help against Japan. Development of the atomic bomb was not yet assured, and American military planners feared the possible loss of as many as one million men in invading the Japanese home islands. Roosevelt therefore agreed to Stalin's price for military assistance against Japan: possession of Sakhalin and the Kurile Islands, as well as railroad rights in Manchuria.

The creation of the United Nations was a major American concern at Yalta. Roosevelt hoped to ensure the participation of the Big Three in a postwar international organization before difficult issues divided them into hostile camps. After a number of compromises, both Churchill and Stalin accepted Roosevelt's plans for a United Nations organization and set the first meeting for San Francisco in April 1945.

The issues of Germany and eastern Europe were treated less decisively. The Big Three reaffirmed that Germany must surrender unconditionally and created four occupation zones (see Map 24.3). A compromise was also worked out in regard to Poland. Stalin agreed to free elections in the future to determine a new government. But the issue of free elections in eastern Europe caused a serious rift between the Soviets and the Americans. The principle was that eastern European governments would be freely elected, but they were also supposed to be pro-Russian. This attempt to reconcile two irreconcilable goals was doomed to failure, as soon became evident at the next conference of the Big Three.

The Potsdam conference of July 1945 began under a cloud of mistrust. Roosevelt had died on April 12 and had been succeeded as president by Harry Truman. At Potsdam, Truman demanded free elections throughout eastern Europe. Stalin responded, "A freely elected government in any of these East European countries would be anti-Soviet, and that we cannot allow."[10] After a bitterly fought and devastating war, Stalin sought absolute military security. To him, it could be gained only by the presence of Communist states in eastern Europe. Free elections might result in governments hostile to the Soviets. By the middle of 1945, only an invasion by Western forces could undo developments in eastern Europe, and few people favored such a policy.

As the war slowly receded into the past, the reality of conflicting ideologies reappeared (see the comparative essay "Paths to Modernization" on p. 555). Many in the West interpreted Soviet policy as part of a worldwide Communist conspiracy. The Soviets, for their part, viewed Western—especially American—policy as nothing less than global capitalist expansionism or, in Leninist terms, economic imperialism. In March 1946, in a speech to an American audience, former British prime minister Winston Churchill, declared that "an iron curtain" had "descended across the continent," dividing Germany and Europe into two hostile camps. Stalin branded Churchill's speech a "call to war with the Soviet Union." Only months after the world's most devastating conflict had ended, the world seemed once again bitterly divided.

MAP 24.3 **Territorial Changes in Europe After World War II.** In the last months of World War II, the Red Army occupied much of eastern Europe. Stalin sought pro-Soviet satellite states in the region as a buffer against future invasions from western Europe, whereas Britain and the United States wanted democratically elected governments. Soviet military control of the territory settled the question. ❓ Which country gained the greatest territory at the expense of Germany? 🌐 **View an animated version of this map or related maps at** http://worldrc.wadsworth.com/

CONCLUSION

𝒲ORLD WAR II was the most devastating total war in human history. Germany, Italy, and Japan had been utterly defeated. Perhaps as many as fifty million people—combatants and civilians—had been killed in only six years. In Asia and Europe, cities had been reduced to rubble, and millions of people faced starvation as once fertile lands stood neglected or wasted.

What were the underlying causes of the war? One direct cause was the effort by two rising powers, Germany and Japan, to make up for their relatively late arrival on the scene to carve out global empires. Key elements in both countries had resented the agreements reached after the end of World War I, which divided the world in a manner favorable to their rivals, and hoped to overturn them at the earliest opportunity. In Germany and Japan, the legacy of a past marked by a strong military tradition still wielded strong influence over the political system and the mindset of the entire population. It is no surprise that under the impact of the Great Depression, which had

PATHS TO MODERNIZATION

POLITICS &
GOVERNMENT

To the casual observer, the most important feature of the first half of the twentieth century was the rise of a virulent form of competitive nationalism that began in Europe and ultimately descended into the cauldron of two destructive world wars. Behind the scenes, however, the leading countries were also engaging in another form of competition over the most effective path to modernization.

The traditional approach, fostered by an independent urban merchant class, had been adopted by Great Britain, France, and the United States and led to the emergence of democratic societies on the capitalist model. A second approach, adopted in the late nineteenth century by imperial Germany and Meiji Japan, was carried out by traditional elites in the absence of a strong independent bourgeois class. They relied on strong government intervention to promote the growth of national wealth and power and led ultimately to the formation of fascist and militarist regimes during the depression years of the early 1930s.

The third approach, selected by Vladimir Lenin after the Bolshevik Revolution in 1917, was designed to carry out an industrial revolution without going through an intermediate capitalist stage. Guided by the Communist Party in the almost total absence of an urban middle class, this approach envisaged the creation of an advanced industrial society by destroying the concept of private property. Although Lenin's plans ultimately called for the "withering of the state," the party adopted totalitarian methods to eliminate enemies of the revolution and carry out the changes needed to create a future classless utopia.

How did these various approaches contribute to the series of crises that afflicted the world during the first half of the twentieth century? The democratic-capitalist approach proved to be a considerable success in an economic sense, leading to the creation of advanced economies that could produce manufactured goods at a rate never seen before. Societies just beginning to undergo their own industrial revolutions tried to imitate the success of the capitalist nations by carrying out their own "revolutions from above" in Germany and Japan. But the Great Depression and competition over resources and markets soon led to an intense rivalry between the established capitalist states and their ambitious late arrivals, a rivalry that ultimately erupted into global conflict.

In the first decade of the twentieth century, imperial Russia appeared ready to launch its own bid to join the ranks of the industrialized nations. But that effort was derailed by its entry into World War I, and before that conflict had come to an end, the Bolsheviks were in power. Isolated from the capitalist marketplace by mutual consent, the Soviet Union was able to avoid being dragged into the Great Depression but, despite Stalin's efforts, was unsuccessful in staying out of the "battle of imperialists" that followed at the end of the 1930s. As World War II came to an end, the stage was set for a battle of the victors—the United States and the Soviet Union—over political and ideological supremacy.

severe effects in both countries, militant forces determined to enhance national wealth and power soon overwhelmed fragile democratic institutions.

Whatever the causes of World War II, the consequences were soon evident. European hegemony over the world was at an end, and two new superpowers had emerged on the fringes of Western civilization to take its place. Even before the last battles had been fought, the United States and the Soviet Union had arrived at different visions of the postwar world, and their differences soon led to the new and potentially even more devastating conflict known as the Cold War. And even though Europeans seemed merely pawns in the struggle between the two superpowers, they managed to stage a remarkable recovery of their own civilization. In Asia, defeated Japan made a miraculous economic recovery, while the era of European domination finally came to an end.

CHAPTER NOTES

1. Benito Mussolini, "The Doctrine of Fascism," in Adrian Lyttleton, ed., *Italian Fascisms* (London, 1973), p. 42.
2. Quoted in Alexander De Grand, "Women Under Italian Fascism," *Historical Journal* 19 (1976), pp. 958–959.
3. Quoted in Jackson J. Spielvogel, *Hitler and Nazi Germany: A History*, 5th ed. (Upper Saddle River, N.J., 2005), p. 60.
4. Quoted in Joachim Fest, *Hitler*, trans. Richard Winston and Clara Winston (New York, 1974), p. 418.
5. *Documents on German Foreign Policy* (London, 1956), ser. D, vol. 7, p. 204.
6. Quoted in Raul Hilberg, *The Destruction of the European Jews*, rev. ed. (New York, 1985), vol. 1, pp. 332–333.
7. *Nazi Conspiracy and Aggression* (Washington, D.C., 1946), vol. 6, p. 789.
8. Quoted in Claudia Koonz, "Mothers in the Fatherland: Women in Nazi Germany," in Renate Bridenthal and Claudia Koonz, eds., *Becoming Visible: Women in European History* (Boston, 1977), p. 466.

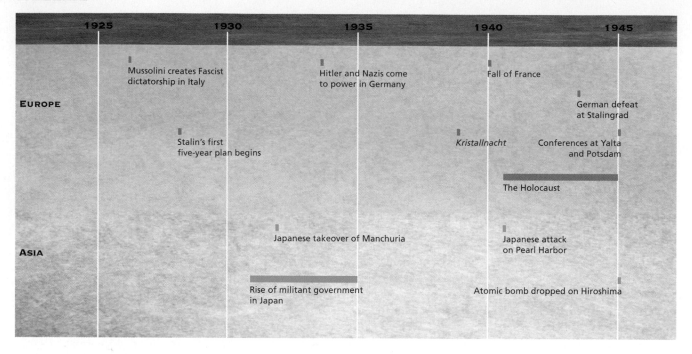

9. Quoted in John Campbell, *The Experience of World War II* (New York, 1989), p. 143.

10. Quoted in Norman Graebner, *Cold War Diplomacy, 1945–1960* (Princeton, N.J., 1962), p. 117.

SUGGESTED READING

For a general study of fascism, see **S. G. Payne, *A History of Fascism*** (Madison, Wis., 1996), and **R. O. Paxton, *The Anatomy of Fascism*** (New York, 2004). The best biography of Mussolini is **R. J. B. Bosworth, *Mussolini*** (London, 2002).

Two brief but sound surveys of Nazi Germany are **J. J. Spielvogel, *Hitler and Nazi Germany: A History,*** 5th ed. (Upper Saddle River, N.J., 2005), and **J. Dülffer, *Nazi Germany, 1933–1945*** (New York, 1996). A recent biography of Hitler is **I. Kershaw, *Hitler, 1889–1936: Hubris*** (New York, 1999), and ***Hitler: Nemesis*** (New York, 2000). Two works that examine the enormous literature on Hitler are **J. Lukacs, *The Hitler of History*** (New York, 1997), and **R. Rosenbaum, *Explaining Hitler*** (New York, 1998). On the rise of the Nazis to power, see **R. J. Evans *The Coming of the Third Reich*** (New York, 2004). On the Nazis in power, see **R. J. Evans, *The Third Reich in Power*** (New York, 2005). On women, see **C. Koonz, *Mothers in the Fatherland: Women, the Family, and Nazi Politics*** (New York, 1987). On Nazi anti-Jewish policies between 1933 and 1939, see **S. Friedländer, *Nazi Germany and the Jews,*** vol. 1, ***The Years of Persecution, 1933–1939*** (New York, 1997).

The collectivization of agriculture in the Soviet Union is examined in **S. Fitzpatrick, *Stalin's Peasants: Resistance and Survival in the Russian Village After Collectivization*** (New York, 1995). Industrialization is covered in **H. Kuromiya, *Stalin's Industrial Revolution: Politics and Workers, 1928–1932*** (New York, 1988). On Stalin himself, see **R. Service, *Stalin: A Biography*** (Cambridge, Mass., 2004).

A basic study of Germany's foreign policy from 1933 to 1939 can be found in **G. Weinberg, *The Foreign Policy of Hitler's Germany: Diplomatic Revolution in Europe, 1933–36*** (Chicago, 1970), and ***The Foreign Policy of Hitler's Germany: Starting World War II, 1937–1939*** (Chicago, 1980). Japan's march to war is examined in **A. Iriye, *The Origins of the Second World War in Asia and the Pacific*** (London, 1987).

A comprehensive study of World War II is provided in **G. Weinberg, *A World at Arms: A Global History of World War II,*** 2d ed. (New York, 2005). On Hitler as a military leader, see **R. Lewin, *Hitler's Mistakes*** (New York, 1986). On battles, see **J. Keegan, *The Second World War*** (New York, 1990).

Excellent studies of the Holocaust include **R. Hilberg, *The Destruction of the European Jews,*** rev. ed., 3 vols. (New York, 1985), and **L. Yahil, *The Holocaust*** (New York, 1990). For brief studies, see **J. Fischel, *The Holocaust*** (Westport, Conn., 1998), and **D. Dwork** and **R. J. van Pelt, *Holocaust: A History*** (New York, 2002). On the home front in Germany, see **M. Kitchen, *Nazi Germany at War*** (New York, 1995). The Soviet Union during the war is examined in **M. Harrison, *Soviet Planning in Peace and War, 1938–1945*** (Cambridge, 1985). The Japanese home front is examined in **T. R. H. Havens, *The Valley of Darkness: The Japanese People and World War Two*** (New York, 1978).

On the emergence of the Cold War, see **W. Loth, *The Division of the World, 1941–1955*** (New York, 1988), and **J. L. Gaddis, *The Cold War: A New History*** (New York, 2005).

InfoTrac College Edition

Visit this chapter's InfoTrac College Edition/Research activities at the *Essential World History* Companion Website for activities related to World War II.

ThomsonNOW™ for Duiker and Spielvogel's *The Essential World History, Third Edition*

Enter *ThomsonNOW* using the access card that is available with this text. *ThomsonNOW* will assist you in understanding the content in this chapter with lesson plans generated for your needs, as well as provide you with a connection to the *Wadsworth World History Resource Center* (see description at the right for details).

WORLD HISTORY
RESOURCE CENTER

Enter the Resource Center using either your *ThomsonNOW* access card or your standalone access card for the *Wadsworth World History Resource Center.* Organized by topic, this website includes quizzes; images; over 350 primary source documents; interactive simulations, maps, and timelines; movie explorations; and a wealth of other resources. You can read the following documents, and many more, at http://worldrc.wadsworth.com/

Franklin D. Roosevelt, "Four Freedoms" Speech

Wannsee Conference, Minutes of Discussion on the "Final Solution"

Visit the *Essential World History* Companion Website for chapter quizzes and more:

http://www.thomsonedu.com/history/duiker

DISCOVERY

What was the relationship between World War I and World War II, and what were the differences in the ways the wars were fought?

In thinking about this question, begin by breaking it down into the components shown below. A discussion of the significance of each component should appear in your answer.

POLITICS AND GOVERNMENT: Compare the maps showing the sides in both world wars. Which nations were neutrals in both conflicts? What geographical features made their neutrality possible? Which nations fought with the Triple Alliance, Triple Entente, Axis, and Allies? Which nations changed groups from war to war? What areas were conquered in World War II but not in World War I? Why or why not?

After reading the documents, what do you think were the objectives of each soldier? How did those objectives change over time? How did the way the war was fought affect their feelings about the war itself? Was the enemy clear in these readings? How are the comparisons of the war and fighting similar? At the end, what is the mind-set of each soldier? What does this say about modern warfare?

Europe in 1914

World War II in Europe and North Africa

DIARY OF A GERMAN SOLDIER

Today, after we'd had a bath, the company commander told us that if our future operations are as successful, we'll soon reach the Volga, take Stalingrad, and then the war will inevitably soon be over. Perhaps we'll be home by Christmas.

July 29. The company commander says the Russian troops are completely broken, and cannot hold out any longer. To reach the Volga and take Stalingrad is not so difficult for us. The Führer knows where the Russians' weak point is. Victory is not far away. . . .

August 10. The Führer's orders were read out to us. He expects victory of us. We are all convinced that they can't stop us.

August 12. This morning outstanding soldiers were presented with decorations. . . . Will I really go back to Elsa without a decoration? I believe that for Stalingrad the Führer will decorate even me. . . .

September 4. We are being sent northward along the front toward Stalingrad. We marched all night and by dawn had reached Voroponovo Station. We can already see the smoking town. It's a happy thought that the end of the war is getting nearer. That's what everyone is saying. . . .

September 8. Two days of nonstop fighting. The Russians are defending themselves with insane stubbornness. Our regiment has lost many men. . . .

September 16. Our battalion, plus tanks, is attacking the [grain storage] elevator, from which smoke is pouring—the grain in it is burning; the Russians seem to have set light to it themselves. Barbarism. The battalion is suffering heavy losses. . . .

October 10. The Russians are so close to us that our planes cannot bomb them. We are preparing for a decisive attack. The Führer has ordered the whole of Stalingrad to be taken as rapidly as possible. . . .

October 22. Our regiment has failed to break into the factory. We have lost many men; every time you move you have to jump over bodies. . . .

November 10. A letter from Elsa today. Everyone expects us home for Christmas. In Germany everyone believes we already hold Stalingrad. How wrong they are. If they could only see what Stalingrad has done to our army. . . .

November 21. The Russians have gone over to the offensive along the whole front. Fierce fighting is going on. So, there it is—the Volga, victory, and soon home to our families! We shall obviously be seeing them next in the other world.

November 29. We are encircled. It was announced this morning that the Führer has said: "The army can trust me to do everything necessary to ensure supplies and rapidly break the encirclement."

December 3. We are on hunger rations and waiting for the rescue that the Führer promised. . . .

December 14. Everybody is racked with hunger. Frozen potatoes are the best meal, but to get them out of the ice-covered ground under fire from Russian bullets is not so easy. . . .

December 26. The horses have already been eaten. I would eat a cat; they say its meat is also tasty. The soldiers look like corpses or lunatics, looking for something to put in their mouths. They no longer take cover from Russian shells; they haven't the strength to walk, run away, and hide. A curse on this war!

We wake up in the middle of the night. The earth booms. Heavy fire is falling on us. We crouch into corners. We distinguish shells of every calibre.

Each man lays hold of his things and looks again every minute to reassure himself that they are still there. The dugout heaves, the night roars and flashes. We look at each other in the momentary flashes of light, and with pale faces and pressed lips shake our heads.

Every man is aware of the heavy shells tearing down the parapet, rooting up the embankment and demolishing the upper layers of concrete. . . . Already by morning a few of the recruits are green and vomiting. They are too inexperienced. . . .

The bombardment does not diminish. It is falling in the rear too. As far as one can see it spouts fountains of mud and iron. A wide belt is being raked.

The attack does not come, but the bombardment continues. Slowly we become mute. Hardly a man speaks. We cannot make ourselves understood.

Our trench is almost gone. At many places it is only eighteen inches high; it is broken by holes, and craters, and mountains of earth. A shell lands square in front of our post. At once it is dark. We are buried and must dig ourselves out. . . .

Towards morning, while it is still dark, there is some excitement. Through the entrance rushes in a swarm of fleeing rats that try to storm the walls. Torches light up the confusion. Everyone yells and curses and slaughters. The madness and despair of many hours unloads itself in this outburst. Faces are distorted, arms strike out, the beasts scream; we just stop in time to avoid attacking one another. . . .

Suddenly it howls and flashes terrifically, the dugout cracks in all its joints under a direct hit, fortunately only a light one that the concrete blocks are able to withstand. It rings metallically; the walls reel; rifles, helmets, earth, mud, and dust fly everywhere. Sulfur fumes pour in. . . . The recruit starts to rave again and two others follow suit. One jumps up and rushes out, we have

trouble with the other two. I start after the one who escapes and wonder whether to shoot him in the leg—then it shrieks again; I fling myself down and when I stand up the wall of the trench is plastered with smoking splinters, lumps of flesh, and bits of uniform. I scramble back.

The first recruit seems actually to have gone insane. He butts his head against the wall like a goat. We must try tonight to take him to the rear. Meanwhile we bind him, but so that in case of attack he can be released.

Suddenly the nearer explosions cease. The shelling continues but it has lifted and falls behind us; our trench is free. We seize the hand grenades, pitch them out in front of the dugout, and jump after them. The bombardment has stopped and a heavy barrage now falls behind us. The attack has come.

No one would believe that in this howling waste there could still be men; but steel helmets now appear on all sides out of the trench, and fifty yards from us a machine gun is already in position and barking.

The wire entanglements are torn to pieces. Yet they offer some obstacle. We see the storm troops coming. Our artillery opens fire. Machine guns rattle, rifles crack. The charge works its way across. Haie and Kropp begin with the hand grenades. They throw as fast as they can; others pass them, the handles with the strings already pulled. Haie throws seventy-five yards, Kropp sixty; it has been measured; the distance is important. The enemy as they run cannot do much before they are within forty yards.

We recognize the distorted faces, the smooth helmets; they are French. They have already suffered heavily when they reach the remnants of the barbed-wire entanglements. A whole line has gone down before our machine guns; then we have a lot of stoppages and they come nearer.

I see one of them, his face upturned, fall into a wire cradle. His body collapses, his hands remain suspended as though he were praying. Then his body drops clean away and only his hands with the stumps of his arms, shot off, now hang in the wire.

SCIENCE AND TECHNOLOGY: Look at the differences in how the war was fought, comparing soldiers in the trenches during World War I with the streets of Glasgow in 1941 (below right). What made these different approaches possible?

Soldiers from around the World

FAMILY AND SOCIETY: How did World War II affect civilians? How was this different from the First World War? Why were civilians targets? How did the actions against civilians become a common tactic in modern warfare?

In what way is the Holocaust another example of attacks on civilians in war?

Based on the evidence in this chapter, which war was more deadly for civilians? World War I concluded with a large peace conference. World War II ended with the bombing of Hiroshima and Nagasaki. Do you see any relationship between the treatment of civilians in Europe and Japan and the end of the war without a formal treaty?

The Bombing of Civilians—
East and West

LOOKING BACK, LOOKING AHEAD

*H*OW ARE WE to draw up a final balance sheet on the era of Western imperialism? To its defenders, it was a necessary stage in the evolution of the human race, a flawed but essentially humanitarian effort to provide the backward peoples of Africa and Asia with a boost up the ladder of evolution. To its critics, it was a tragedy of major proportions. The insatiable drive of the advanced economic powers for access to raw materials and markets resulted in the widespread destruction of traditional cultures and created an exploitative environment that transformed the vast majority of colonial peoples into a permanent underclass while restricting the benefits of modern technology to a privileged few. Sophisticated, age-old societies that should have been left to respond to the technological revolution in their own way were subjected to foreign rule and squeezed

TIMELINE

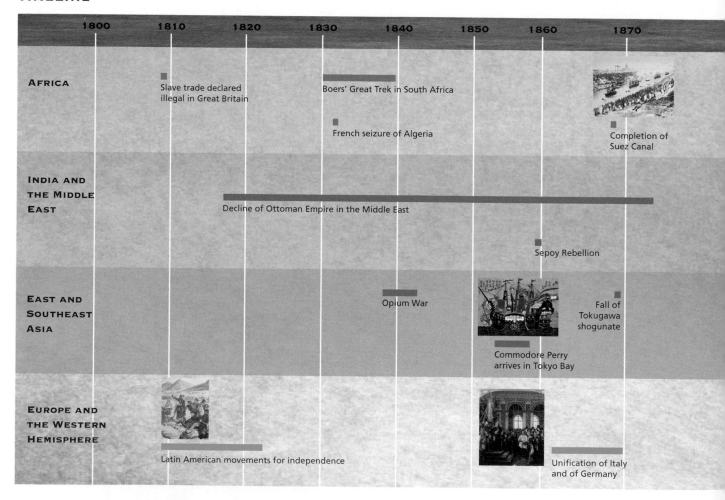

	1800	1810	1820	1830	1840	1850	1860	1870

AFRICA
- Slave trade declared illegal in Great Britain
- Boers' Great Trek in South Africa
- French seizure of Algeria
- Completion of Suez Canal

INDIA AND THE MIDDLE EAST
- Decline of Ottoman Empire in the Middle East
- Sepoy Rebellion

EAST AND SOUTHEAST ASIA
- Opium War
- Commodore Perry arrives in Tokyo Bay
- Fall of Tokugawa shogunate

EUROPE AND THE WESTERN HEMISPHERE
- Latin American movements for independence
- Unification of Italy and of Germany

dry of precious national resources under the guise of the "civilizing mission."

In this debate, the critics surely have the best argument. All in all, the colonial experience was brutal, and its benefits accrued almost entirely to citizens of the ruling power. The argument that the Western societies had a "white man's burden" to civilize the world was all too often a hypocritical gesture to salve the guilty feelings of

those who recognized imperialism for what it was—a savage act of rape.

But although the experience was a painful one, human societies were able to survive it and earn a second chance to make better use of the stunning promise of the industrial era. How they have fared in that effort will be the subject of the final section of this book.

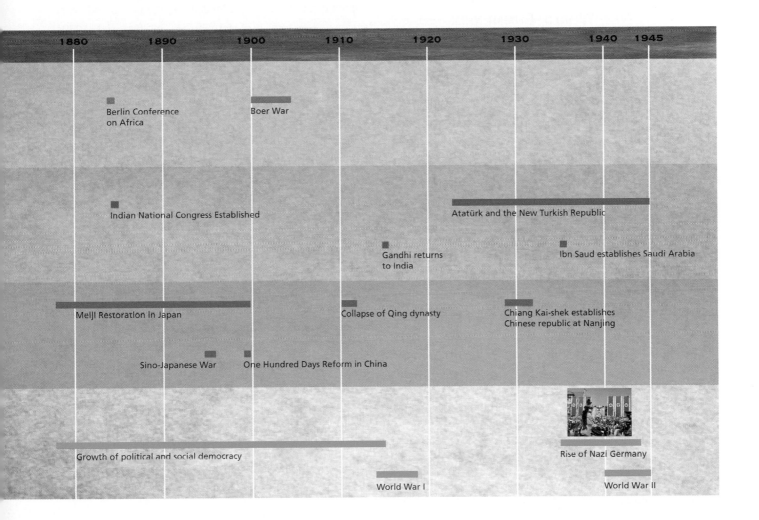

1880   1890   1900   1910   1920   1930   1940   1945

Berlin Conference on Africa

Boer War

Indian National Congress Established

Atatürk and the New Turkish Republic

Gandhi returns to India

Ibn Saud establishes Saudi Arabia

Meiji Restoration in Japan

Collapse of Qing dynasty

Chiang Kai-shek establishes Chinese republic at Nanjing

Sino-Japanese War

One Hundred Days Reform in China

Growth of political and social democracy

Rise of Nazi Germany

World War I

World War II

*A*s WORLD WAR II came to an end, the survivors of that bloody struggle could afford to face the future with a cautious optimism. Europeans might hope that the bitter rivalry that had marked relations among the Western powers would finally be put to an end and that the wartime alliance of the United States, Great Britain, and the Soviet Union could be maintained into the postwar era.

More than sixty years later, these hopes have been only partly realized. In the decades following the war, the Western capitalist nations managed to recover from the economic depression that had led into World War II and advanced to a level of economic prosperity never seen before. The bloody conflicts that had erupted among European nations during the first half of the twentieth century came to an end, and Germany and Japan were fully integrated into the world community.

At the same time, the prospects for a stable, peaceful world and an end to balance-of-power politics were hampered by the emergence of a grueling and sometimes tense ideological struggle between the socialist and capitalist camps, a competition headed by the only remaining great powers, the Soviet Union and the United States.

In the shadow of this rivalry, the Western European states made a remarkable economic recovery and reached untold levels of prosperity. In Eastern Europe, Soviet domination, both politically and economically, seemed so complete that many doubted it could ever be undone. But communism had never developed deep roots in Eastern Europe, and in the late 1980s, when Soviet leader Mikhail Gorbachev indicated that his government would no longer pursue military intervention, Eastern European states acted quickly to establish their freedom and adopt new economic structures based on Western models.

Outside the West, the peoples of Africa and Asia had their own reasons for optimism as World War II came to a close. In the Atlantic Charter, Franklin Roosevelt and Winston Churchill had set forth a joint declaration of their peace aims calling for the self-determination of all peoples and self-government and sovereign rights for all nations that had been deprived of them.

As it turned out, some colonial powers were reluctant to divest themselves of their colonies. Still, World War II had severely undermined the stability of the colonial order, and by the end of the 1940s, most colonies in Asia had received their independence. Africa followed a decade or two later.

Broadly speaking, the leaders of these newly liberated countries set forth three goals at the outset of independence. They wanted to throw off the shackles of Western economic domination and ensure material prosperity for all of their citizens. They wanted to introduce new political institutions that would enhance the right of self-determination of their peoples. And they wanted to develop a sense of common nationhood within the population and establish secure territorial boundaries. Most opted to follow a capitalist or a moderately socialist path toward economic development. In a few cases—most notably in China and Vietnam—revolutionary leaders opted for the communist mode of development.

Regardless of the path chosen, the results were often disappointing. Much of Africa and Asia remained economically dependent on the advanced industrial nations. Some societies faced severe problems of urban and rural poverty.

What had happened to tarnish the bright dream of economic affluence? During the late 1950s and early 1960s, one school of thought was dominant among scholars and government officials in the United States. Known as modernization theory, this school took the view that the problems faced by the newly independent countries were a consequence of the difficult transition from a traditional to a modern society. Modernization theorists were convinced that agrarian countries were destined to follow the path of the West toward the creation of modern industrial societies but would need time as well as substantial amounts of economic and technological assistance from the West to complete the journey.

Eventually, modernization theory began to come under attack from a new generation of younger scholars. In their view, the responsibility for continued economic underdevelopment in the developing world lay not with the countries themselves but with their continued domination by the ex-colonial powers. In this view, known as dependency theory, the countries of Asia, Africa, and Latin America were the victims of the international marketplace, which charged high prices for the manufactured goods of the West while dooming preindustrial countries to low prices for their own raw material exports. Efforts by such countries to build up their own industrial sectors and move into the stage of self-sustaining growth were hampered by foreign control—through European- and American-owned corporations—over many of their resources. To end this "neocolonial" relationship, the dependency theory advocates argued, developing societies should reduce their economic ties with the West and practice a policy of economic self-reliance, thereby taking control over their own destinies.

Leaders of African and Asian countries also encountered problems creating new political cultures responsive to the needs of their citizens. At first, most accepted the concept of democracy as the defining theme of that culture. Within a decade, however, democratic systems throughout the developing world were replaced by military dictatorships or one-party governments that redefined the concept of democracy to fit their own preferences. It was clear that the difficulties in building democratic political institutions in developing societies had been underestimated.

The problem of establishing a common national identity has in some ways been the most daunting of all the challenges facing the new nations of Asia and Africa. Many of these new states were a composite of a wide variety of ethnic, religious, and linguistic groups who found it difficult to agree on common symbols of nationalism. Problems of establishing an official language and delineating territorial boundaries left over from the colonial era created difficulties in many countries. Internal conflicts spawned by deep-rooted historical and ethnic hatreds have proliferated throughout the world, leading to a vast new movement of people across state boundaries equal to any that has occurred since the great population migrations of the thirteenth and fourteenth centuries.

The introduction of Western cultural values and customs has also had a destabilizing effect in many areas. Although such ideas are welcomed by some groups, they are firmly resisted by others. Where Western influence has the effect of undermining traditional customs and religious beliefs, it often provokes violent hostility and sparks tension and even conflict within individual societies. Much of the anger recently directed at the United States in Muslim countries has undoubtedly been generated by such feelings.

Nonetheless, social and political attitudes are changing rapidly in many Asian and African countries as new economic circumstances have led to a more secular worldview, a decline in traditional hierarchical relations, and a more open attitude toward sexual practices. In part, these changes have been a consequence of the influence of Western music, movies, and television. But they are also a product of the growth of an affluent middle class in many societies of Asia and Africa.

Today we live not only in a world economy but in a world society, where a revolution in the Middle East can cause a rise in the price of oil in the United States and a change in social behavior in Malaysia and Indonesia, where the collapse of an empire in Asia can send shock waves as far as Hanoi and Havana, and where a terrorist attack in New York City or London can disrupt financial markets around the world. ◆

25

EAST AND WEST IN THE GRIP
OF THE COLD WAR

CHAPTER OUTLINE
AND FOCUS QUESTIONS

The Collapse of the Grand Alliance

▢ Why were the United States and the Soviet Union suspicious of each other after World War II, and what events between 1945 and 1949 heightened the tensions between the two nations?

Cold War in Asia

▢ How and why did Mao Zedong and the Communists come to power in China, and what were the Cold War implications of their triumph?

From Confrontation to Coexistence

▢ What events led to the era of coexistence in the 1960s, and to what degree did each side contribute to the reduction in international tensions?

An Era of Equivalence

▢ Why did the Cold War briefly flare up again in the 1980s, and why did it come to a definitive end at the end of the decade?

CRITICAL THINKING

▢ How have historians answered the question of whether the United States or the Soviet Union bears the primary responsibility for the Cold War, and what evidence can be presented on each side of the issue?

Churchill, Roosevelt, and Stalin at Yalta

Art Archive, London

"*O*UR MEETING HERE in the Crimea has reaffirmed our common determination to maintain and strengthen in the peace to come that unity of purpose and of action which has made victory possible and certain for the United Nations in this war. We believe that this is a sacred obligation which our Governments owe to our peoples and to all the peoples of the world."[1]

With these ringing words, drafted at the Yalta Conference in February 1945, U.S. President Franklin D. Roosevelt, Soviet leader Joseph Stalin, and British Prime Minister Winston Churchill affirmed their common hope that the Grand Alliance that had been victorious in World War II could be sustained into the postwar era. Only through continuing and growing cooperation and understanding among the three Allies, the statement asserted, could a secure and lasting peace be realized that, in the words of the Atlantic Charter, would "afford assurance that all the men in all the lands may live out their lives in freedom from fear and want."

Roosevelt hoped that the decisions reached at Yalta would provide the basis for a stable peace in the postwar era. Allied occupation forces—American, British, and French in the west and Soviet in the east—were to bring about the end of Axis administration and to organize the free election of democratic governments throughout Europe. To foster mutual trust and an end to the suspicions that had marked relations between the capitalist world and the Soviet Union prior to the war, Roosevelt tried to reassure Stalin that Moscow's legitimate territorial aspirations and genuine security needs would be adequately met in a durable peace settlement.

This was not to be, however. Within months after the German surrender, the mutual trust among the Allies—if it had ever truly existed—rapidly disintegrated, and the dream of a stable peace was replaced by the specter of a potential nuclear holocaust. The United Nations, envisioned by its founders as a mechanism for adjudicating international disputes, became mired in partisan bickering. As the Cold War between Moscow and Washington intensified, Europe was divided into two armed camps, while the two superpowers, glaring at each other across a deep ideological divide, held the survival of the entire world in their hands. ◇

The Collapse of the Grand Alliance

When World War II finally ended, Soviet military forces occupied all of Eastern Europe and the Balkans (except Greece, Albania, and Yugoslavia), while U.S. and other Allied forces secured the western part of the Continent. Roosevelt had assumed that free elections, administered promptly by "democratic and peace-loving forces," would lead to democratic governments responsive to the local population. But it soon became clear that the Soviet Union interpreted the Yalta agreement differently. When Soviet occupation authorities began forming a new Polish government, Stalin refused to accept the Polish government-in-exile—headquartered in London during the war and composed primarily of landed aristocrats who harbored a deep distrust of the Soviet Union—and instead set up a government composed of Communists who had spent the war in Moscow. Roosevelt complained to Stalin but eventually agreed to a compromise whereby two members of the London government were included in the new Communist regime. A week later, Roosevelt was dead of a cerebral hemorrhage, emboldening Stalin to do pretty much as he pleased.

Soviet Domination of Eastern Europe

Similar developments took place in all of the states occupied by Soviet troops. Coalitions of all political parties (except fascist or right-wing parties) were formed to run the government, but within a year or two, the Communist Party in each coalition had assumed the lion's share of power. It was then a short step to the establishment of one-party Communist governments. Between 1945 and 1947, Communist governments became firmly entrenched in East Germany, Bulgaria, Romania, Poland, and Hungary. In Czechoslovakia, with its strong tradition of democratic

institutions, the Communists did not achieve their goals until 1948. After the Czech elections of 1946, the Communist Party shared control of the government with the non-Communist parties. When it appeared that the latter might win new elections early in 1948, the Communists seized control of the government on February 25. All other parties were dissolved, and the Communist leader Klement Gottwald became the new president of Czechoslovakia.

Yugoslavia was a notable exception to the pattern of Soviet dominance in Eastern Europe. The Communist Party there had led resistance to the Nazis during the war and easily assumed power when the war ended. Josip Broz, known as Tito (1892–1980), the leader of the Communist resistance movement, appeared to be a loyal Stalinist. After the war, however, he moved to establish an independent Communist state. Stalin hoped to take control of Yugoslavia, but Tito refused to capitulate to Stalin's demands and gained the support of the people (and some sympathy in the West) by portraying the struggle as one of Yugoslav national freedom. In 1958, the Yugoslav party congress asserted that Yugoslav Communists did not see themselves as deviating from communism, only from Stalinism. They considered their more decentralized system, in which workers managed themselves and local communes exercised some political power, closer to the Marxist-Leninist ideal.

To Stalin (who had once boasted, "I will shake my little finger, and there will be no more Tito"), the creation of pliant pro-Soviet regimes throughout Eastern Europe may simply have represented his interpretation of the Yalta peace agreement and a reward for sacrifices suffered during the war, satisfying Moscow's aspirations for a buffer zone against the capitalist West. If the Soviet leader had any intention of promoting future Communist revolutions in Western Europe—and there is some indication that he did—such developments would have to await the appearance of a new capitalist crisis a decade or more into the future. As Stalin undoubtedly recalled, Lenin had always maintained that revolutions come in waves.

Descent of the Iron Curtain

To the United States, however, the Soviet takeover of Eastern Europe represented an ominous development that threatened Roosevelt's vision of a durable peace. Public suspicion of Soviet intentions grew rapidly, especially among the millions of Americans who still had relatives living in Eastern Europe.

🌀 **Eastern Europe in 1948**

COMPARATIVE ILLUSTRATION

Across the Ideological Divide. Within five years of the end of World War II, the Grand Alliance that had brought victory over the Axis Powers was in tatters. In March 1946, former British Prime Minister Winston Churchill (top photo, with U.S. President Harry Truman looking on) declared that Soviet occupation of Eastern Europe had divided the Continent into two conflicting halves, separated by an iron curtain. In the lower photo, Soviet leader Nikita Khrushchev and North Vietnamese President Ho Chi Minh are hosted by CCP Chairman Mao at a banquet in Beijing in October 1959.

Winston Churchill was quick to put such fears into words. In a highly publicized speech at Westminster College in Fulton, Missouri, in March 1946, the former British prime minister declared that an "iron curtain" had "descended across the Continent," dividing Germany and Europe itself into two hostile camps (see the comparative illustration above). Stalin responded by branding Churchill's speech a "call to war with the Soviet Union." But he need not have worried. Although public opinion in the United States placed increasing pressure on Roosevelt's successor, Harry S. Truman (1884–1972), to devise an effective strategy to counter Soviet advances abroad, the American people were in no mood for another war.

The Truman Doctrine

A civil war in Greece created another potential arena for confrontation between the superpowers and an opportunity for the Truman administration to take a stand. Communist guerrilla forces supported by Tito's Yugoslavia had taken up arms against the pro-Western government in Athens. Great Britain had initially assumed primary responsibility for promoting postwar reconstruction in the eastern Mediterranean, but in 1947, continuing economic problems caused the British to withdraw from the active role they had been playing in both Greece and Turkey. President Truman, alarmed by British weakness and the possibility of Soviet expansion into the eastern Mediterranean, responded with the Truman Doctrine, which said in essence that the United States would provide money to countries that claimed they were threatened by Communist expansion. If the Soviets were not stopped in Greece, the Truman argument ran, then the United States would have to face the spread of communism throughout the free world. As Dean Acheson, the U.S. secretary of state, explained, "Like apples in a barrel infected by disease, the corruption of Greece would infect Iran and all the East . . . likewise Africa . . . Italy . . . France. . . . Not since Rome and Carthage has there been such a polarization of power on this earth."[2]

The U.S. suspicion that Moscow was actively supporting the insurgent movement in Greece turned out to be unfounded. Stalin was apparently unhappy with Tito's promoting the conflict, not only because he suspected that the latter was attempting to create his own sphere of influence in the Balkans but also because it risked provoking a direct confrontation between the United States and the Soviet Union.

The Marshall Plan

The proclamation of the Truman Doctrine was followed in June 1947 by the European Recovery Program, better known as the Marshall Plan, which provided $13 billion for the economic recovery of war-torn Europe. Underlying the program was the belief that Communist aggression fed off economic turmoil. General George C. Marshall noted in a speech at Harvard University, "Our policy is not directed against any country or doctrine but against hunger, poverty, desperation, and chaos."[3]

From the Soviet perspective, the Marshall Plan was capitalist imperialism, a thinly veiled attempt to buy the support of the smaller European countries "in return for the relinquishing . . . of their economic and later also their political independence."[4] A Soviet spokesperson described the United States as the "main force in the imperialist camp," whose ultimate goal was "the strengthening of imperialism, preparation for a new imperialist war, a struggle against socialism and democracy, and the support of reactionary and antidemocratic, pro-fascist regimes and movements." Although the Marshall Plan was open to the Soviet Union and its Eastern European satellite states, they refused to participate. The Soviets were in no position to compete financially with the United States, however, and could do little to counter the Marshall Plan except tighten their control in Eastern Europe.

Europe Divided

By 1947, the split in Europe between East and West had become a fact of life. At the end of World War II, the United States had favored a quick end to its commitments in Europe. But American fears of Soviet aims caused the United States to play an increasingly important role in European affairs. In an article in *Foreign Affairs* in July 1947, George Kennan, a well-known U.S. diplomat with much knowledge of Soviet affairs, advocated a policy of **containment** against further aggressive Soviet moves. Kennan favored the "adroit and vigilant application of counter-force at a series of constantly shifting geographical and political points, corresponding to the shifts and maneuvers of Soviet policy." When the Soviets blockaded Berlin in 1948, containment of the Soviet Union became formal U.S. policy.

The Berlin Airlift The fate of Germany had become a source of heated contention between East and West. Aside from **denazification** and the partitioning of Germany (and Berlin) into four occupied zones, the Allied powers had agreed on little with regard to the conquered nation. Even denazification proceeded differently in the various zones of occupation. The Americans and British proceeded methodically—the British had tried two million cases by 1948—while the Soviets (and French) went after major criminals and allowed lesser officials to go free. The Soviet Union, hardest hit by the war, took reparations from Germany by pillaging German industry. The technology-starved Soviets dismantled and removed to Russia 380 factories from the western zones of Berlin before transferring their control to the Western powers. By the summer of 1946, two hundred chemical, paper, and textile factories in the East German zone had likewise been shipped to the Soviet Union. At the same time, the German Communist Party was reestablished, under the control of Walter Ulbricht (1893–1973), and was soon in charge of the political reconstruction of the Soviet zone in eastern Germany.

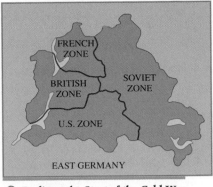

Berlin at the Start of the Cold War

Although the foreign ministers of the four occupying powers kept meeting in an attempt to arrive at a final peace treaty with Germany, they moved further and further apart. At the same time, the British, French, and Americans gradually began to merge their zones economically and by February 1948 were making plans for unification of these sectors and the formation of a national government. In an effort to secure all of Berlin and to halt the creation of a West German government, the Soviet Union imposed a blockade of West Berlin that prevented all traffic from entering the city's western zones through Soviet-controlled territory in East Germany.

The Western powers faced a dilemma. Direct military confrontation seemed dangerous, and no one wished to risk World War III. Therefore, an attempt to break through the blockade with tanks and trucks was ruled out. The solution was to deliver supplies for the city's inhabitants by plane. At its peak, the Berlin Airlift flew 13,000 tons of supplies daily into Berlin. The Soviets, also not wanting war, did not interfere and finally lifted the blockade in May 1949. The blockade of Berlin had severely increased tensions between the United States and the Soviet Union and brought the separation of Germany into two states. The Federal Republic of Germany was formally created from the three Western zones in September 1949, and a month later, the separate German Democratic Republic (GDR) was established in East Germany. Berlin remained a divided city and the source of much contention between East and West.

Cold War Alliances The search for security in the new world of the Cold War also led to the formation of military alliances. The North Atlantic Treaty Organization (NATO)

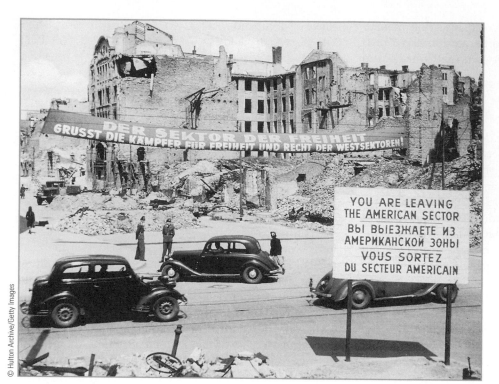

© Hulton Archive/Getty Images

A City Divided. In 1948, U.S. planes airlifted supplies into Berlin to break the blockade that Soviet troops had imposed to isolate the city. Shown here is "Checkpoint Charlie," located at the boundary between the U.S. and Soviet zones of Berlin, just as Soviet roadblocks are about to be removed. The banner at the entrance to the Soviet sector reads, ironically, "The sector of freedom greets the fighters for freedom and right of the Western sectors."

was formed in April 1949 when Belgium, Denmark, France, Great Britain, Iceland, Italy, Luxembourg, the Netherlands, Norway, and Portugal signed a treaty with the United States and Canada. All the powers agreed to provide mutual assistance if any one of them was attacked. A few years later, Greece, Turkey and West Germany joined NATO.

The Eastern European states soon followed suit. In 1949, they formed the Council for Mutual Economic Assistance (COMECON) for economic cooperation. Then, in 1955, Albania, Bulgaria, Czechoslovakia, East Germany, Hungary, Poland, Romania, and the Soviet Union organized a formal military alliance, the Warsaw Pact. Once again, Europe was tragically divided into hostile alliance systems (see Map 25.1).

Who Started the Cold War? There has been considerable historical debate over who bears responsibility for starting the Cold War. In the 1950s, most scholars in the West assumed that the bulk of the blame must fall on the shoulders of Stalin, whose determination to impose Soviet rule on Eastern Europe snuffed out hopes for freedom and self-determination there and aroused justifiable fears of Communist expansion in the West. During the next decade, however, revisionist historians—influenced in part by aggressive U.S. policies in Southeast Asia—began to argue that the fault lay primarily in Washington, where Truman and his anti-Communist advisers abandoned the precepts of Yalta and sought to encircle the Soviet Union with a tier of pliant U.S. client states.

In retrospect, both the United States and the Soviet Union took some unwise steps at the end of World War II.

Both nations, however, were working within a framework conditioned by the past. The rivalry between the two superpowers ultimately stemmed from their different historical perspectives and their irreconcilable political ambitions. Intense competition for political and military supremacy had long been a regular feature of Western civilization. The United States and the Soviet Union were the heirs of that European tradition of power politics, and it should not surprise us that two such different systems would seek to extend their way of life to the rest of the world. Because of its need to secure its western border, the Soviet Union was not prepared to give up the advantages it had gained in Eastern Europe from Germany's defeat. But neither were Western leaders prepared to accept without protest the establishment of a system of Soviet satellites that not only threatened the security of Western Europe but also deeply offended Western sensibilities because of its blatant disregard of the Western concept of human rights.

This does not necessarily mean that both sides bear equal responsibility for starting the Cold War. Some revisionist historians have claimed that the U.S. doctrine of containment was a provocative action that aroused Stalin's suspicions and drove Moscow into a position of hostility toward the West. This charge lacks credibility. As information from the Soviet archives and other sources has become available, it is increasingly clear that Stalin's suspicions of the West were rooted in his Marxist-Leninist worldview and long predated Washington's enunciation of the doctrine of containment. As his foreign minister, Vyacheslav Molotov, once remarked, Soviet policy was inherently aggressive and would be triggered

MAP 25.1 **The New European Alliance Systems During the Cold War.** This map shows postwar Europe as it was divided during the Cold War into two contending power blocs, the NATO alliance and the Warsaw Pact. Major military and naval bases are indicated by symbols on the map. ❓ Where on the map was the so-called Iron Curtain? 🐢 **View an animated version of this map or related maps at** http://worldrc.wadsworth.com/

whenever the opportunity offered. Although Stalin apparently had no master plan to advance Soviet power into Western Europe, he was probably prepared to make every effort to do so once the next revolutionary wave arrived. Western leaders were fully justified in reacting to this possibility by strengthening their own lines of defense. On the other hand, a case can be made that in deciding to respond to the Soviet challenge in a primarily military manner, Western leaders overreacted to the situation and virtually guaranteed that the Cold War would be transformed into an arms race that could conceivably result in a new and uniquely destructive war.

Cold War in Asia

The Cold War was somewhat slower to make its appearance in Asia. At Yalta, Stalin formally agreed to enter the Pacific War against Japan three months after the close of the conflict with Germany. As a reward for Soviet participation in the struggle against Japan, Roosevelt promised that Moscow would be granted "preeminent interests" in Manchuria (interests reminiscent of those possessed by imperial Russia prior to its defeat at the hands of Japan in 1904–1905) and the establishment of a Soviet naval base at Port Arthur. In return, Stalin promised to sign a treaty of alliance with the Republic of China, thus implicitly committing the Soviet Union not to provide the Chinese Communists with support in a possible future civil war. Although many observers would later question Stalin's sincerity in making such a commitment to the vocally anti-Communist Chiang Kai-shek, in Moscow the decision probably had a logic of its own. Stalin had no particular liking for the independent-minded Mao Zedong and indeed did not anticipate a Communist victory in any civil war in China. Only an agreement with Chiang could provide the Soviet Union with a strategically vital economic and political presence in northern China.

Despite these commitments, the Allied agreements soon broke down, and East Asia was sucked into the vortex of the Cold War by the end of the 1940s. The root of the problem lay in the underlying weakness of Chiang's regime, which threatened to create a political vacuum in East Asia that both Moscow and Washington would be tempted to fill.

The Chinese Civil War

As World War II came to an end in the Pacific, relations between the government of Chiang Kai-shek in China and its powerful U.S. ally had become frayed. Although Roosevelt had hoped that Republican China would be the keystone of his plan for peace and stability in Asia after the war, U.S. officials became disillusioned with the corruption of Chiang's government and his unwillingness to risk his forces against the Japanese (he hoped to save them for use against the Communists after the war in the Pacific ended), and China was no longer the focus of Washington's close attention as the war came to a close. Nevertheless, U.S. military and economic aid to China had been substantial, and at war's end, the new Truman administration still hoped that it could rely on Chiang to support U.S. postwar goals in the region.

While Chiang Kai-shek wrestled with Japanese aggression and problems of national development, the Communists were building up their strength in northern China. To enlarge their political base, they carried out a "mass line" policy (from the masses to the masses), reducing land rents and confiscating the lands of wealthy landlords. By the end of World War II, twenty to thirty million Chinese were living under the administration of the Communists, and their People's Liberation Army (PLA) included nearly one million troops.

As the war came to an end, world attention began to focus on the prospects for renewed civil strife in China. Members of a U.S. liaison team stationed in Yan'an were impressed by the performance of the Communists, and some recommended that the United States should support them or at least remain neutral in a possible conflict between Communists and Nationalists for control of China. The Truman administration, though skeptical of Chiang's ability to forge a strong and prosperous country, was increasingly concerned about the spread of communism in Europe and tried to find a peaceful solution through the formation of a coalition government of all parties in China.

The Communist Triumph   The effort failed. By 1946, full-scale war between the Nationalist government, now reinstalled in Nanjing, and the Communists resumed. Now Chiang Kai-shek's errors came home to roost. In the countryside, millions of peasants, attracted to the Communists by promises of land and social justice, flocked to serve in Mao Zedong's PLA. In the cities, middle-class Chinese, normally hostile to communism, were alienated by Chiang's brutal suppression of all dissent and his government's inability to slow the ruinous rate of inflation or solve the economic problems it caused. With morale dropping in the cities, Chiang's troops began to defect to the Communists. Sometimes whole divisions, officers as well as ordinary soldiers, changed sides. By 1948, the PLA was advancing south out of Manchuria and had encircled Beijing. Communist troops took the old imperial capital, crossed the Yangtze the following spring, and occupied the commercial hub of Shanghai (see Map 25.2). During the next few months, Chiang's government and two million of his followers

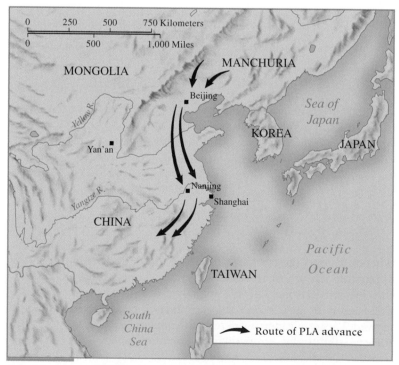

MAP 25.2   **The Chinese Civil War.** After the close of the Pacific War in 1945, the Nationalist government and the Chinese Communists fought a bitter civil war that ended with a victory by the latter in 1949. The path of Communist advance is displayed on the map. ❓ Where did Chang Kai-shek's government retreat to after its defeat?

WHO LOST CHINA?

**POLITICS &
GOVERNMENT**

In 1949, with China about to fall under the control of the Communists, President Truman instructed the State Department to prepare a White Paper explaining why the U.S. policy of seeking to avoid a Communist victory in China had failed. The authors of the paper concluded that responsibility lay at the door of Nationalist Chinese leader Chiang Kai-shek and that there was nothing the United States could have done to alter the result. Most China observers today would accept that assessment, but it did little at the time to deflect criticism of the administration for selling out the interests of our ally in China.

How do the authors of the White Paper explain the Communist victory in China? According to this argument, what actions might have prevented it?

U.S. State Department White Paper on China, 1949

When peace came the United States was confronted with three possible alternatives in China: (1) it could have pulled out lock, stock, and barrel; (2) it could have intervened militarily on a major scale to assist the Nationalists to destroy the Communists; (3) it could, while assisting the Nationalists to assert their authority over as much of China as possible, endeavor to avoid a civil war by working for a compromise between the two sides.

The first alternative would, and I believe American public opinion at the time so felt, have represented an abandonment of our international responsibilities and of our traditional policy of friendship for China before we had made a determined effort to be of assistance. The second alternative policy, while it may look attractive theoretically, in retrospect, was wholly impracticable. The Nationalists had been unable to destroy the Communists during the ten years before the war. Now after the war

the Nationalists were, . . . weakened, demoralized, and unpopular. They had quickly dissipated their popular support and prestige in the areas liberated from the Japanese by the conduct of their civil and military officials. The Communists on the other hand were much stronger than they had ever been and were in control of most of North China. Because of the ineffectiveness of the Nationalist forces, which was later to be tragically demonstrated, the Communists probably could have been dislodged only by American arms. It is obvious that the American people would not have sanctioned such a colossal commitment of our armies in 1945 or later. We therefore came to the third alternative policy whereunder we faced the facts of the situation and attempted to assist in working out a modus vivendi which would avert civil war but nevertheless preserve and even increase the influence of the National Government. . . .

The distrust of the leaders of both the Nationalist and Communist Parties for each other proved too deep-seated to permit final agreement, notwithstanding temporary truces and apparently promising negotiations. The Nationalists, furthermore, embarked in 1946 on an overambitious military campaign in the face of warnings by General Marshall that it not only would fail but would plunge China into economic chaos and eventually destroy the National Government. . . .

The unfortunate but inescapable fact is that the ominous result of the civil war in China was beyond the control of the government of the United States. Nothing that this country did or could have done within the reasonable limits of its capabilities could have changed that result; nothing that was left undone by this country has contributed to it. It was the product of internal Chinese forces, forces which this country tried to influence but could not. A decision was arrived at within China, if only a decision by default.

---

fled to Taiwan, which the Japanese had returned to Chinese control after World War II.

The Truman administration reacted to the spread of Communist power in China with acute discomfort. Washington had no desire to see a Communist government on the mainland, but it had little confidence in Chiang Kai-shek's ability to realize Roosevelt's dream of a strong, united, and prosperous China. In December 1945, President Truman sent General George C. Marshall to China in a last-ditch effort to bring about a peaceful settlement, but anti-Communist elements in the Republic of China resisted U.S. efforts to create a coalition government with the Chinese Communist Party (CCP). During the next two years, the United States gave limited military support to Chiang's regime but refused to commit U.S. power to guarantee its survival. The administration's hands-off policy deeply angered many members of Congress, who charged that the White House was "soft on

communism" and declared further that Roosevelt had betrayed Chiang Kai-shek at Yalta by granting privileges in Manchuria to the Soviet Union. In their view, Soviet troops had hindered the dispatch of Chiang's forces to the area and provided the PLA with weapons to use against its rivals.

In later years, sources in both Moscow and Beijing suggested that the Soviet Union gave little assistance to the CCP in its struggle against the Nanjing regime. In fact, Stalin periodically advised Mao against undertaking the effort. Although Communist forces undoubtedly received some assistance from Soviet occupation troops in Manchuria, their victory ultimately stemmed from conditions inside China, not from the intervention of outside powers. So indeed argued the Truman administration in 1949, when it issued a White Paper that placed most of the blame for the debacle at the feet of Chiang Kai-shek's regime (see the box above).

Many Americans, however, did not agree. With the Communist victory, Asia became a theater of the Cold War and an integral element of American politics. During the spring of 1950, under pressure from Congress and public opinion to define U.S. interests in Asia, the Truman administration adopted a new national security policy, known as NSC-68, that implied that the United States would take whatever steps were necessary to stem the further expansion of communism in the region.

The New China

Communist leaders in China, from their new capital of Beijing, hoped that their accession to power in 1949 would bring about an era of peace in the region and permit their new government to concentrate on domestic goals. But the desire for peace was tempered by their determination to erase a century of humiliation at the hands of imperialist powers and to restore the traditional outer frontiers of the empire. In addition to recovering territories that had been part of the Manchu Empire, such as Manchuria, Taiwan, and Tibet, the Chinese leaders also hoped to restore Chinese influence in former tributary areas such as Korea and Vietnam.

It soon became clear that these two goals were not always compatible. Negotiations with the Soviet Union led to Soviet recognition of Chinese sovereignty over Manchuria and Xinjiang (the desolate lands north of Tibet that were known as Chinese Turkestan because many of the peoples in the area were of Turkic origin), although the Soviets retained a measure of economic influence in both areas. Chinese troops occupied Tibet in 1950 and brought it under Chinese administration for the first time in more than a century. But in Korea and Taiwan, China's efforts to re-create the imperial buffer zone provoked new conflicts with foreign powers.

The problem of Taiwan was a consequence of the Cold War. As the civil war in China came to an end, the Truman administration appeared determined to avoid entanglement in China's internal affairs and indicated that it would not seek to prevent a Communist takeover of the island, now occupied by Chiang Kai-shek's Republic of China. But as tensions between the United States and the new Chinese government escalated during the winter of 1949–1950, influential figures in the United States began to argue that Taiwan was crucial to U.S. defense strategy in the Pacific.

The Korean War

The outbreak of war in Korea also helped bring the Cold War to East Asia. After the Sino-Japanese War in 1894–1895, Korea, long a Chinese tributary, had fallen increasingly under the rival influences of Japan and Russia. After the Japanese defeated the Russians in 1905, Korea became an integral part of the Japanese Empire and remained so until 1945. The removal of Korea from Japanese control had been one of the stated objectives of the Allies in World War II, and on the eve of Japanese surrender in August 1945, the Soviet Union and the United States agreed to divide the country into two separate occupation zones at the 38th parallel. They originally planned to hold national elections after the restoration of peace to reunify Korea under an independent government. But as U.S.-Soviet relations deteriorated, two separate governments emerged in Korea, a Communist one in the north and an anti-Communist one in the south.

Tensions between the two governments ran high along the dividing line, and on June 25, 1950, with the apparent approval of Stalin, North Korean troops invaded the south. The Truman administration immediately ordered U.S. naval and air forces to support South Korea, and the United Nations Security Council (with the Soviet delegate absent to protest the refusal of the UN to assign China's seat to the new government in Beijing) passed a resolution calling on member nations to jointly resist the invasion. By September, UN forces under the command of U.S. General Douglas MacArthur marched northward across the 38th parallel with the aim of unifying Korea under a single, non-Communist government.

President Truman worried that by approaching the Chinese border at the Yalu River, the UN troops could trigger Chinese intervention, but MacArthur assured him that China would not respond. In November, however, Chinese "volunteer" forces intervened in force on the side of North Korea and drove the UN troops southward in disarray. A static defense line was eventually established near the original dividing line at the 38th parallel (see Map 25.3), although the war continued.

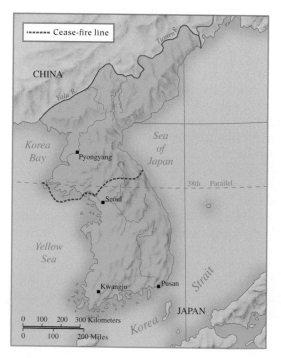

MAP 25.3 **The Korean Peninsula.** In January 1950, North Korean forces crossed the 38th parallel in a sudden invasion of the south. Shown here is the cease-fire line that brought an end to the war in 1953. ❓ What is the importance of the Yalu River?

To many Americans, the Chinese intervention in Korea was clear evidence that China intended to promote communism throughout Asia, and recent evidence suggests that Mao was convinced that a revolutionary wave was on the rise in Asia. In fact, however, China's decision to enter the war was probably motivated in large part by the fear that hostile U.S. forces might be stationed on the Chinese frontier and perhaps even launch an attack across the border. MacArthur intensified such fears by calling publicly for air attacks on Manchurian cities in preparation for an attack on Communist China.

In any case, the outbreak of the Korean War was particularly unfortunate for China. Immediately after the invasion, President Truman dispatched the U.S. Seventh Fleet to the Taiwan Strait to prevent a possible Chinese invasion of Taiwan. Even more unfortunate, the invasion hardened Western attitudes against the new Chinese government and led to China's isolation from the major capitalist powers for two decades. The United States continued to support the Nationalist government in Taiwan as the only legal representative of the Chinese people and supported its occupation of China's seat on the UN Security Council. As a result, China was cut off from all forms of economic and technological assistance and was forced to rely almost entirely on the Soviet Union, with which it had signed a pact of friendship and cooperation in early 1950.

Conflict in Indochina

During the mid-1950s, China sought to build contacts with the nonsocialist world. A cease-fire agreement brought the Korean War to an end in July 1953, and China signaled its desire to live in peaceful coexistence with other independent countries in the region. But a relatively minor conflict now began to intensify on China's southern flank, in French Indochina. The struggle had begun after World War II, when Ho Chi Minh's Indochinese Communist Party, at the head of a multiparty nationalist alliance called the Vietminh Front, seized power in northern and central Vietnam after the surrender of imperial Japan. After abortive negotiations between Ho's government and the returning French, war broke out in December 1946. French forces occupied the cities and the densely populated lowlands, while the Vietminh took refuge in the mountains.

For three years, the Vietminh gradually increased in size and effectiveness. What had begun as an anticolonial struggle by Ho's Vietminh Front against the French after World War II became entangled in the Cold War in the early 1950s, when both the United States and the new Communist government in China began to intervene in the conflict to promote their own national security objectives. China began to provide military assistance to the Vietminh to protect its own borders from hostile forces. The Americans supported the French but pressured the French government to prepare for an eventual transition to non-Communist governments in Vietnam, Laos, and Cambodia.

At the Geneva Conference in 1954, with the French public tired of fighting the "dirty war" in Indochina, the French agreed to a peace settlement with the Vietminh. Vietnam was temporarily divided into a northern Communist half (known as the Democratic Republic of Vietnam) and a non-Communist southern half based in Saigon (eventually to be known as the Republic of Vietnam). A demilitarized zone separated the two at the 17th parallel. Elections were to be held in two years to

Ho Chi Minh Plans an Attack on the French. Unlike many peoples in Southeast Asia, the Vietnamese had to fight for their independence after World War II. That fight was led by the talented Communist leader Ho Chi Minh. In this photograph, Ho (in the center), assisted by his chief strategist, Vo Nguyen Giap (at the far right), plans an attack on French positions in Vietnam.

Indochina After 1954

create a unified government. Cambodia and Laos were both declared independent under neutral governments.

China had played an active role in bringing about the settlement and clearly hoped that it would reduce tensions in the area, but subsequent efforts to improve relations between China and the United States foundered on the issue of Taiwan. In the fall of 1954, the United States signed a mutual security treaty with the Republic of China guaranteeing U.S. military support in case of an invasion of Taiwan. When Beijing demanded U.S. withdrawal from Taiwan as the price for improved relations, diplomatic talks between the two countries collapsed.

From Confrontation to Coexistence

The decade of the 1950s opened with the world teetering on the edge of a nuclear holocaust. The Soviet Union had detonated its first nuclear device in 1949, and the two blocs—capitalist and socialist—viewed each other across an ideological divide that grew increasingly bitter with each passing year. Yet as the decade drew to a close, a measure of sanity crept into the Cold War, and the leaders of the major world powers began to seek ways to coexist in a peaceful and stable world.

The first clear sign of change occurred after Stalin's death in early 1953. His successor, Georgy Malenkov (1902–1988), openly hoped to improve relations with the Western powers in order to reduce defense expenditures and shift government spending to growing consumer needs. Nikita Khrushchev (1894–1971), who replaced Malenkov in 1955, continued his predecessor's efforts to reduce tensions with the West and improve the living standards of the Soviet people.

In an adroit public relations touch, Khrushchev promoted an appeal for a policy of **peaceful coexistence** with the West. In 1955, he surprisingly agreed to negotiate an end to the postwar occupation of Austria by the victorious allies and allow the creation of a neutral country with strong cultural and economic ties with the West. He also called for a reduction in defense expenditures and reduced the size of the Soviet armed forces.

Ferment in Eastern Europe

At first, Western leaders were suspicious of Khrushchev's motives, especially in light of events that were taking place in Eastern Europe. The key to security along the western frontier of the Soviet Union was the string of Eastern European satellite states that had been assembled in the aftermath of World War II (see Map 25.1). Once Communist domination had been assured, a series of "little Stalins" put into power by Moscow instituted Soviet-type five-year plans that emphasized heavy industry rather than consumer goods, the collectivization of agriculture, and the nationalization of industry. They also appropriated the political tactics that Stalin had perfected in the Soviet Union, eliminating all non-Communist parties and establishing the classical institutions of repression—the secret police and military forces. Dissidents were tracked down and thrown into prison, and "national Communists" who resisted total subservience to the Soviet Union were charged with treason in mass show trials and executed.

Despite these repressive efforts, discontent became increasingly evident in several Eastern European countries. Hungary, Poland, and Romania harbored bitter memories of past Russian domination and suspected that Stalin, under the guise of proletarian internationalism, was seeking to revive the empire of the Romanovs. For the vast majority of peoples in Eastern Europe, the imposition of the so-called people's democracies (a term invented by Moscow to define a society in the early stage of socialist transition) resulted in economic hardship and severe threats to the most basic political liberties. The first indications of unrest appeared in East Berlin, where popular riots broke out against Communist rule in 1953. The riots eventually subsided, but the virus had spread to neighboring countries.

In Poland, public demonstrations against an increase in food prices in 1956 escalated into widespread protests against the regime's economic policies, restrictions on the freedom of Catholics to practice their religion, and the continued presence of Soviet troops (as called for by the Warsaw Pact) on Polish soil. In a desperate effort to defuse the unrest, the party leader stepped down and was replaced by Wladyslaw Gomulka (1905–1982), a popular figure who had previously been demoted for his "nationalist" tendencies. When Gomulka took steps to ease the crisis, Khrushchev flew to Warsaw to warn him against adopting policies that could undermine the political dominance of the party and weaken security links with the Soviet Union. Ultimately, Poland agreed to remain in the Warsaw Pact and to maintain the sanctity of party rule; in return, Gomulka was authorized to adopt domestic reforms, such as easing restrictions on religious practice and ending the policy of forced collectivization in rural areas.

The Hungarian Revolution The developments in Poland sent shock waves throughout the region. The impact

How the Mighty Have Fallen. In the fall of 1956, Hungarian freedom fighters rose up against Communist domination of their country in the short-lived Hungarian revolution. Their actions threatened Soviet hegemony in Eastern Europe, however, and in late October, Soviet leader Nikita Khrushchev dispatched troops to quell the uprising. In the meantime, the Hungarian people had demonstrated their discontent by toppling a gigantic statue of Joseph Stalin in the capital of Budapest. Statues of the Soviet dictator had been erected in all the Soviet satellites after World War II. ("W.C." identifies a public toilet in European countries.)

was strongest in neighboring Hungary, where the methods of the local "little Stalin," Matyas Rakosi, were so brutal that he had been summoned to Moscow for a lecture. In late October 1956, student-led popular riots broke out in the capital of Budapest and soon spread to other towns and villages throughout the country. Rakosi was forced to resign and was replaced by Imre Nagy (1896–1958), a national Communist who attempted to satisfy popular demands without arousing the anger of Moscow. Unlike Gomulka, however, Nagy was unable to contain the zeal of leading members of the protest movement, who sought major political reforms and the withdrawal of Hungary from the Warsaw Pact. On November 1, Nagy promised free elections, which, given the mood of the country, would probably have brought an end to Communist rule. After a brief moment of uncertainty, Moscow decided on firm action. Soviet troops, recently withdrawn at Nagy's request, returned to Budapest and installed a new government under the more pliant party leader János Kádár (1912–1989). While Kádár rescinded many of Nagy's measures, Nagy sought refuge in the Yugoslav embassy. A few weeks later, he left the embassy under the promise of safety but was quickly arrested, convicted of treason, and executed.

Different Roads to Socialism The dramatic events in Poland and Hungary graphically demonstrated the vulnerability of the Soviet satellite system in Eastern Europe, and many observers throughout the world anticipated that the United States would intervene on behalf of the

freedom fighters in Hungary. After all, the Eisenhower administration had promised that it would "roll back" communism, and radio broadcasts by the U.S.-sponsored Radio Liberty and Radio Free Europe had encouraged the peoples of Eastern Europe to rise up against Soviet domination. In reality, Washington was well aware that U.S. intervention could lead to nuclear war and limited itself to protests against Soviet brutality in crushing the uprising.

The year of discontent was not without consequences, however. Soviet leaders now recognized that Moscow could maintain control over its satellites in Eastern Europe only by granting them the leeway to adopt domestic policies appropriate to local conditions. Khrushchev had already embarked on this path in 1955 when he assured Tito that there were "different roads to socialism." Some Eastern European Communist leaders now took Khrushchev at his word and adopted reform programs to make socialism more palatable to their subject populations. Even Kádár, derisively labeled the "butcher of Budapest," managed to preserve many of Nagy's reforms to allow a measure of capitalist incentive and freedom of expression in Hungary.

The easing of Stalinist-style terror in some of Moscow's client states in Eastern Europe was accompanied by a new crisis over Berlin. The Soviet Union had launched its first intercontinental ballistic missile (ICBM) in August 1957, arousing U.S. fears of a missile gap between the United States and the Soviet Union. Khrushchev attempted to take advantage of the U.S. frenzy over missiles to solve the problem of West Berlin, which had remained a "Western island" of prosperity inside the relatively poverty-stricken state of East Germany. Many East Germans sought to escape to West Germany by fleeing through West Berlin, a serious blot on the credibility of the GDR and a potential source of instability in East-West relations. In November 1958, Khrushchev announced that unless the West removed its forces from West Berlin within six months, he would turn over control of the access routes to the East Germans. Unwilling to accept an ultimatum that would have abandoned West Berlin to the Communists, President Dwight D. Eisenhower and the West stood firm, and Khrushchev eventually backed down.

Despite such periodic crises in East-West relations, there were tantalizing signs that an era of true peaceful coexistence between the two power blocs could be achieved. In the late 1950s, the United States and the Soviet Union initiated a cultural exchange program. While the Leningrad Ballet appeared at theaters in the United States, Benny Goodman and the film *West Side Story* played in Moscow. In 1958, Khrushchev visited the United States and had a brief but friendly encounter with President Eisenhower at the presidential retreat in northern Maryland.

Rivalry in the Third World

Yet Khrushchev could rarely avoid the temptation to gain an advantage over the United States in the competition

The Kitchen Debate. During the late 1950s, the United States and the Soviet Union sought to defuse Cold War tensions by encouraging cultural exchanges between the two countries. On one occasion, U.S. Vice President Richard M. Nixon visited Moscow in conjunction with the arrival of an exhibit to introduce U.S. culture and society to the Soviet people. Here Nixon lectures Soviet Communist Party chief Nikita Khrushchev on the technology of the U.S. kitchen. On the other side of Nixon, at the far right, is future Soviet president Leonid Brezhnev.

for influence throughout the world, and this resulted in an unstable relationship between the two superpowers. Moscow also took every opportunity to promote its interests at the United Nations and in the Third World, as the unaligned countries of Asia, Africa, and Latin America were now popularly called. Unlike Stalin, Khrushchev viewed the dismantling of colonial regimes in the area as a potential advantage for the Soviet Union and sought especially to exploit the deep suspicions of the United States in Latin America. To improve Soviet influence in such areas, Khrushchev established alliances with key Third World leaders such as Sukarno in Indonesia, Gamel Abdul Nasser in Egypt, Jawaharlal Nehru in India, and Fidel Castro in Cuba (see Chapter 28). In January 1961, just as John F. Kennedy assumed the U.S. presidency, Khrushchev unnerved the new president at an informal summit meeting in Vienna by declaring that the Soviet Union would provide active support to national liberation movements throughout the world. There were rising fears in Washington of Soviet meddling in such sensitive trouble spots as Southeast Asia, Central Africa, and the Caribbean.

The Cuban Missile Crisis   The Cold War confrontation between the United States and the Soviet Union reached frightening levels during the Cuban Missile Crisis. In 1959, a left-wing revolutionary named Fidel Castro (b. 1927) overthrew the Cuban dictator Fulgencio Batista and established a Soviet-supported totalitarian regime. After the utter failure of a U.S.-supported attempt to overthrow Castro's regime in 1961 (known as the "Bay of Pigs" incident), the Soviet Union decided to place nuclear missiles in Cuba in 1962. The United States was not prepared to allow nuclear weapons within striking distance of the American mainland, even though it had placed some of its own nuclear weapons in Turkey, within range of the Soviet Union. Khrushchev was quick to point out that "your rockets are in Turkey. You are worried by

Cuba . . . because it is 90 miles from the American coast. But Turkey is next to us."[5] When U.S. intelligence discovered that a Soviet fleet carrying missiles was indeed heading to Cuba, President Kennedy decided to blockade Cuba and prevent the fleet from reaching its destination. This approach to the problem had the benefit of delaying confrontation and giving the two sides time to find a peaceful solution. Although hard-liners on both sides were reluctant to compromise, Khrushchev eventually agreed to turn back the fleet if Kennedy pledged not to invade Cuba (see the box on p. 575). In a conciliatory letter to Kennedy, Khrushchev wrote:

> We and you ought not to pull on the ends of the rope in which you have tied the knot of war, because the more the two of us pull, the tighter that knot will be tied. And a moment may come when that knot will be tied too tight that even he who tied it will not have the strength to untie it. . . . Let us not only relax the forces pulling on the ends of the rope; let us take measures to untie that knot. We are ready for this.[6]

The intense feeling that the world might have been annihilated in a few days had a profound influence on both sides. A hotline between Moscow and Washington was installed in 1963 to expedite communications between the two superpowers in time of crisis. In the same year, the two powers agreed to ban nuclear tests in the atmosphere, a step that served to lessen the tensions between the two nations.

The Sino-Soviet Dispute

Nikita Khrushchev had launched his slogan of peaceful coexistence as a means of improving relations with the capitalist powers; ironically, one result of the campaign was to undermine Moscow's ties with its close ally China. During Stalin's lifetime, Beijing had accepted the Soviet Union as the acknowledged leader of the socialist camp.

THE CUBAN MISSILE CRISIS FROM KHRUSHCHEV'S PERSPECTIVE

POLITICS & GOVERNMENT

The Cuban Missile Crisis was one of the sobering experiences of the Cold War. It led the two superpowers to seek new ways to lessen the tensions between them. This version of the events is taken from the memoirs of Nikita Khrushchev.

Why, according to his memoirs, did Nikita Khrushchev decide to place missiles in Cuba? Why did he agree to remove them later?

Khrushchev Remembers

I will explain what the Caribbean crisis of October 1962 was all about. . . . At the time that Fidel Castro led his revolution to victory and entered Havana with his troops, we had no idea what political course his regime would follow. . . . All the while the Americans had been watching Castro closely. At first they thought that the capitalist underpinnings of the Cuban economy would remain intact. So by the time Castro announced that he was going to put Cuba on the road toward Socialism, the Americans had already missed their chance to do anything about it by simply exerting their influence: there were no longer any forces left which could be organized to fight on America's behalf in Cuba. That left only one alternative—invasion! . . .

After Castro's crushing victory over the counterrevolutionaries we intensified our military aid to Cuba. . . . We were sure that the Americans would never reconcile themselves to the existence of Castro's Cuba. They feared, as much as we hoped, that a Socialist Cuba might become a magnet that would attract other Latin American countries to Socialism. . . . It was clear to me that we might very well lose Cuba if we didn't take some decisive steps in her defense. . . . We had to think up some way of confronting America with more than words. We had to establish a tangible and effective deterrent to American interference in the Caribbean. But what exactly? The logical answer was missiles. We knew that American missiles were aimed against us in Turkey and Italy, to say nothing of West Germany. . . . My thinking went like this: if we installed the missiles secretly and then if the United States discovered the missiles were there after they were already poised and ready to strike, the Americans would think twice before trying to liquidate our installations by military means. . . . I want to make one thing absolutely clear: when we put our ballistic missiles in Cuba we had no desire to start a war. On the contrary, our principal aim was only to deter America from starting a war. . . .

President Kennedy issued an ultimatum, demanding that we remove our missiles and bombers from Cuba. . . . We sent the Americans a note saying that we agreed to remove our missiles and bombers on the condition that the President give us his assurance that there would be no invasion of Cuba by the forces of the United States or anybody else. Finally Kennedy gave in and agreed to make a statement giving us such an assurance. . . . It had been, to say the least, an interesting and challenging situation. The two most powerful nations of the world had been squared off against each other, each with its finger on the button. You'd have thought that war was inevitable. But both sides showed that if the desire to avoid war is strong enough, even the most pressing dispute can be solved by compromise. And a compromise over Cuba was indeed found. The episode ended in a triumph of common sense. . . . It was a great victory for us, though, that we had been able to extract from Kennedy a promise that neither America nor any of her allies would invade Cuba. . . . The Caribbean crisis was a triumph of Soviet foreign policy and a personal triumph in my own career as a statesman and as a member of the collective leadership. We achieved, I would say, a spectacular success without having to fire a single shot!

ThomsonNOW To read several documents related to the Cuban Missile Crisis, enter the *ThomsonNOW* documents area using the access card that is available for *The Essential World History*.

After Stalin's death, however, relations began to deteriorate. Part of the reason may have been Mao Zedong's contention that he, as the most experienced Marxist leader, should now be acknowledged as the most authoritative voice within the socialist community. But another determining factor was that just as Soviet policies were moving toward moderation, China's were becoming more radical.

Several other issues were involved, including territorial disputes along the Sino-Soviet border and China's unhappiness with limited Soviet economic assistance. But the key sources of disagreement involved ideology and the Cold War. Chinese leaders were convinced that the successes of the Soviet space program confirmed that the socialists were now technologically superior to the capitalists (the East Wind, trumpeted the Chinese official press, had now triumphed over the West Wind), and they urged Khrushchev to go on the offensive to promote world revolution. Specifically, China wanted Soviet assistance in retaking Taiwan from Chiang Kai-shek. But Khrushchev was trying to improve relations with the West and rejected Chinese demands for support against Taiwan.

By the end of the 1950s, the Soviet Union had begun to remove its advisers from China, and in 1961, the dispute broke into the open. Increasingly isolated, China voiced its hostility to what Mao described as the "urban industrialized countries" (which included the

COMBATING THE AMERICANS

In December 1960, the National Front for the Liberation of South Vietnam, or NLF, was born. Composed of political and social leaders opposed to the anti-Communist government of Ngo Dinh Diem in South Vietnam, it operated under the direction of the Vietnam Workers' Party in North Vietnam and served as the formal representative of revolutionary forces in the south throughout the remainder of the Vietnam War. When, in the spring of 1965, President Lyndon Johnson began to dispatch U.S. combat troops to South Vietnam to prevent a Communist victory there, the NLF issued the following declaration.

How does the NLF justify its claim to represent the legitimate aspirations of the people of South Vietnam? How do you believe the Johnson administration would respond?

Statement of the National Liberation Front of South Vietnam

American imperialist aggression against South Vietnam and interference in its internal affairs have now continued for more than ten years. More American troops and supplies, including missile units, Marines, B-57 strategic bombers, and mercenaries from South Korea, Taiwan, the Philippines, Australia, Malaysia, etc., have been brought to South Vietnam. . . .

The Saigon puppet regime, paid servant of the United States, is guilty of the most heinous crimes. These despicable traitors, these boot-lickers of American imperialism, have brought the enemy into our country. They have brought to South Vietnam armed forces of the United States and its satellites to kill our compatriots, occupy and ravage our sacred soil and enslave our people.

The Vietnamese, the peoples of all Indo-China and Southeast Asia, supporters of peace and justice in every part of the world, have raised their voice in angry protest against this criminal unprovoked aggression of the United States imperialists.

In the present extremely grave situation, the South Vietnam National Liberation Front considers it necessary to proclaim anew its firm and unswerving determination to resist the U.S. imperialists and fight for the salvation of our country. . . . [It] will continue to rely chiefly on its own forces and potentialities, but it is prepared to accept any assistance, moral and material, including arms and other military equipment, from all the socialist countries, from nationalist countries, from international organizations, and from the peace-loving peoples of the world.

ThomsonNOW To read the U.S. State Department version of North Vietnamese aggression, enter the *ThomsonNOW* documents area using the access card that is available for *The Essential World History.*

Soviet Union) and portrayed itself as the leader of the "rural underdeveloped countries" of Asia, Africa, and Latin America in a global struggle against imperialist oppression. In effect, China had applied Mao Zedong's concept of people's war in an international framework.

The Second Indochina War

China's radicalism was intensified in the early 1960s by the outbreak of renewed war in Indochina. The Eisenhower administration had opposed the peace settlement at Geneva in 1954, which divided Vietnam temporarily into two separate regroupment zones, specifically because the provision for future national elections opened up the possibility that the entire country would come under Communist rule. But Eisenhower had been unwilling to introduce U.S. military forces to continue the conflict without the full support of the British and the French, who preferred to seek a negotiated settlement. In the end, Washington promised not to break the provisions of the agreement but refused to commit itself to the results.

During the next several months, the United States began to provide aid to a new government in South Vietnam. Under the leadership of the anti-Communist politician Ngo Dinh Diem, the South Vietnamese government began to root out dissidents. With the tacit approval of the United States, Diem refused to hold the national elections called for by the Geneva Accords. It was widely anticipated, even in Washington, that the Communists would win such elections. In 1959, Ho Chi Minh, despairing of the peaceful unification of the country under Communist rule, decided to promote revolutionary war in the south.

By 1963, South Vietnam was on the verge of collapse. Diem's autocratic methods and inattention to severe economic inequality had alienated much of the population, and revolutionary forces, popularly known as the Viet Cong (Vietnamese Communists) and supported by the Communist government in the North, expanded their influence throughout much of the country. In the fall of 1963, with the approval of the Kennedy administration, senior military officers overthrew the Diem regime. But factionalism kept the new military leadership from reinvigorating the struggle against the insurgent forces, and the situation in South Vietnam grew worse. By early 1965, the Viet Cong, whose ranks were now swelled by military units infiltrating from North Vietnam, were on the verge of seizing control of the entire country. In March, President Lyndon Johnson decided to send U.S. combat troops to South Vietnam to prevent a total defeat for the anti-Communist government in Saigon (see the box above).

The Role of China Chinese leaders observed the gradual escalation of the conflict in South Vietnam with mixed feelings. They were undoubtedly pleased to have a firm Communist ally—one that had in many ways followed the path of Mao Zedong—just beyond their southern frontier. Yet they were concerned that renewed bloodshed in South Vietnam might enmesh China in a new conflict with the United States. Nor did they welcome the specter of a powerful and ambitious united Vietnam, which might wish to extend its influence throughout mainland Southeast Asia, an area that Beijing considered its own backyard.

Chinese leaders therefore tiptoed delicately through the minefield of the Indochina conflict. As the war escalated in 1964 and 1965, Beijing publicly announced that the Chinese people fully supported their comrades seeking national liberation but privately assured Washington that China would not directly enter the conflict unless U.S. forces threatened its southern border. Beijing also refused to cooperate fully with Moscow in shipping Soviet goods to North Vietnam through Chinese territory.

Despite its dismay at the lack of full support from China, the Communist government in North Vietnam responded to U.S. escalation by infiltrating more of its own regular force troops into the south, and by 1968, the war had reached a stalemate. The Communists were not strong enough to overthrow the government in Saigon, whose weakness was shielded by the presence of half a million U.S. troops, but President Johnson was reluctant to engage in all-out war on North Vietnam for fear of provoking a global nuclear conflict. In the fall, after the Communist-led Tet offensive undermined claims of progress in Washington and aroused intense antiwar protests in the United States, peace negotiations began in Paris.

Richard Nixon (1913–1994) came into the White House in 1969 on a pledge to bring an honorable end to the Vietnam War. With U.S. public opinion sharply divided on the issue, he began to withdraw U.S. troops while continuing to hold peace talks in Paris. But the centerpiece of his strategy was to improve relations with China and thus undercut Chinese support for the North Vietnamese war effort. During the 1960s, relations between Moscow and Beijing had reached a point of extreme tension, and thousands of troops were stationed on both sides of their long common frontier. To intimidate their Communist rivals, Soviet sources hinted that they might launch a preemptive strike to destroy Chinese nuclear facilities in Xinjiang. Sensing an opportunity to split the two onetime allies, Nixon sent his emissary Henry Kissinger on a secret trip to China. Responding to assurances that the United States was determined to withdraw from Indochina and hoped to improve relations with the mainland regime, Chinese leaders invited President Nixon to visit China in early 1972. Nixon accepted, and the two sides agreed to set aside their differences over Taiwan to pursue a better mutual relationship.

The Fall of Saigon Incensed at the apparent betrayal by their close allies, North Vietnamese leaders decided to seek a peaceful settlement of the war in the south. In January 1973, a peace treaty was signed in Paris calling for the removal of all U.S. forces from South Vietnam. In return, the Communists agreed to halt military operations and to engage in negotiations to resolve their differences with the Saigon regime. But negotiations between

A Bridge Across the Cold War Divide. In January 1972, U.S. President Richard Nixon startled the world by visiting mainland China and beginning the long process of restoring normal relations between the two countries. Despite Nixon's reputation as a devout anti-Communist, the visit was a success as the two sides agreed to put aside their most bitter differences in an effort to reduce tensions in Asia. Here Nixon and Chinese leader Mao Zedong exchange a historic handshake in Beijing.

north and south over the political settlement soon broke down, and in early 1975, the Communists resumed the offensive. At the end of April, under a massive assault by North Vietnamese military forces, the South Vietnamese government surrendered. A year later, the country was unified under Communist rule.

The Communist victory in Vietnam was a severe humiliation for the United States, but its strategic impact was limited because of the new relationship with China. During the next decade, Sino-American relations continued to improve. In 1979, diplomatic ties were established between the two countries under an arrangement whereby the United States renounced its mutual security treaty with the Republic of China in return for a pledge from China to seek reunification with Taiwan by peaceful means. By the end of the 1970s, China and the United States had forged a "strategic relationship" in which they would cooperate against the common threat of Soviet hegemony in Asia.

Why had the United States failed to achieve its objective of preventing a Communist victory in Vietnam? One leading member of the Johnson administration later commented that Washington had underestimated the determination of its adversary in Hanoi and overestimated the patience of the American people. Deeper reflection suggests, however, that another factor was equally important: the United States had overestimated the ability of its client state in South Vietnam to defend itself against a disciplined adversary. In subsequent years, it became a crucial lesson to the Americans on the perils of nation building.

An Era of Equivalence

When the Johnson administration sent U.S. combat troops to South Vietnam in 1965, Washington's main concern was with Beijing, not Moscow. By the mid-1960s, U.S. officials viewed the Soviet Union as an essentially conservative power, more concerned with protecting its vast empire than with expanding its borders. In fact, U.S. policy makers periodically sought Soviet assistance in seeking a peaceful settlement of the Vietnam War. So long as Khrushchev was in power, they found a receptive ear in Moscow. Khrushchev was firmly dedicated to promoting peaceful coexistence (at least on his terms) and sternly advised the North Vietnamese against a resumption of revolutionary war in South Vietnam.

After October 1964, when Khrushchev was replaced by a new leadership headed by party chief Leonid Brezhnev (1906–1982) and Prime Minister Alexei Kosygin (1904–1980), Soviet attitudes about Vietnam became more ambivalent. On the one hand, the new Soviet leaders had no desire to see the Vietnam conflict poison relations between the great powers. On the other hand, Moscow was eager to demonstrate its support for the North Vietnamese to deflect Chinese charges that the Soviet Union had betrayed the interests of the oppressed peoples of the world. As a result, Soviet officials publicly voiced sympathy for the U.S. predicament in Vietnam but put no pressure on their allies to bring an end to the war. Indeed, the Soviet Union became Hanoi's main supplier of advanced military equipment in the final years of the war.

The Brezhnev Doctrine

In the meantime, new Cold War tensions were brewing in Eastern Europe, where discontent with Stalinist policies began to emerge in Czechoslovakia. The latter had not shared in the thaw of the mid-1950s and remained under the rule of the hard-liner Antonin Novotny (1904–1975), who had been placed in power by Stalin himself. By the late 1960s, however, Novotny's policies had led to widespread popular alienation, and in 1968, with the support of intellectuals and reformist party members, Alexander Dubček (1921–1992) was elected first secretary of the Communist Party. He immediately attempted to create what was popularly called "socialism with a human face," relaxing restrictions on freedom of speech and the press and the right to travel abroad. Economic reforms were announced, and party control over all aspects of society was reduced. A period of euphoria erupted that came to be known as the "Prague Spring."

It proved to be short-lived. Encouraged by Dubček's actions, some Czechs called for more far-reaching reforms, including neutrality and withdrawal from the Soviet bloc. To forestall the spread of this "spring fever," the Soviet Red Army, supported by troops from other Warsaw Pact states, invaded Czechoslovakia in August 1968 and crushed the reform movement. Gustav Husák (1913–1991), a committed Stalinist, replaced Dubček and restored the old order, while Moscow attempted to justify its action by issuing the so-called Brezhnev Doctrine (see the box on p. 579).

In East Germany, as well, Stalinist policies continued to hold sway. The ruling Communist government in East Germany, led by Walter Ulbricht, had consolidated its position in the early 1950s and became a faithful Soviet satellite. Industry was nationalized and agriculture collectivized. After the 1953 workers' revolt was crushed by Soviet tanks, a steady flight of East Germans to West Germany ensued, primarily through the city of Berlin. This exodus of mostly skilled laborers ("Soon only party chief Ulbricht will be left," remarked one Soviet observer sardonically) created economic problems and in 1961 led the East German government to erect a wall separating East Berlin from West Berlin, as well as even more fearsome barriers along the entire border with West Germany.

After building the Berlin Wall, East Germany succeeded in developing the strongest economy among the Soviet Union's Eastern European satellites. In 1971, Ulbricht was succeeded by Erich Honecker (1912–1994), a party hard-liner. Propaganda increased, and the use of the Stasi, the secret police, became a hallmark of

THE BREZHNEV DOCTRINE

In the summer of 1968, when the new Communist Party leaders in Czechoslovakia were seriously considering proposals for reforming the totalitarian system there, the Warsaw Pact nations met under the leadership of Soviet party chief Leonid Brezhnev to assess the threat to the socialist camp. Shortly after, military forces of several Soviet bloc nations entered Czechoslovakia and imposed a new government subservient to Moscow. The move was justified by the spirit of "proletarian internationalism" and was widely viewed as a warning to China and other socialist states not to stray too far from Marxist-Leninist orthodoxy, as interpreted by the Soviet Union. But Moscow's actions also raised tensions in the Cold War.

How does Leonid Brezhnev justify the Soviet decision to invade Czechoslovakia? To what degree do you find his arguments persuasive?

A Letter to the Central Committee of the Communist Party of Czechoslovakia

Dear comrades!

On behalf of the Central Committees of the Communist and Workers' Parties of Bulgaria, Hungary, the German Democratic Republic, Poland, and the Soviet Union, we address ourselves to you with this letter, prompted by a feeling of sincere friendship based on the principles of Marxism-Leninism and proletarian internationalism and by the concern of our common affairs for strengthening the positions of socialism and the security of the socialist community of nations.

The development of events in your country evokes in us deep anxiety. It is our firm conviction that the offensive of the reactionary forces, backed by imperialists, against your Party and the foundations of the social system in the Czechoslovak Socialist Republic, threatens to push your country off the road of socialism and that consequently it jeopardizes the interests of the entire socialist system. . .

We neither had nor have any intention of interfering in such affairs as are strictly the internal business of your Party and your state, nor of violating the principles of respect, independence, and equality in the relations among the Communist Parties and socialist countries. . . .

At the same time we cannot agree to have hostile forces push your country from the road of socialism and create a threat of severing Czechoslovakia from the socialist community. . . . This is the common cause of our countries, which have joined in the Warsaw Treaty to ensure independence, peace, and security in Europe, and to set up an insurmountable barrier against the intrigues of the imperialist forces, against aggression and revenge. . . . We shall never agree to have imperialism, using peaceful or nonpeaceful methods, making a gap from the inside or from the outside in the socialist system, and changing in imperialism's favor the correlation of forces in Europe. . . .

That is why we believe that a decisive rebuff of the anti-communist forces, and decisive efforts for the preservation of the socialist system in Czechoslovakia are not only your task but ours as well. . . .

We express the conviction that the Communist Party of Czechoslovakia, conscious of its responsibility, will take the necessary steps to block the path of reaction. In this struggle you can count on the solidarity and all-round assistance of the fraternal socialist countries.

Warsaw, July 15, 1968.

ThomsonNOW To read more of the Brezhnev Doctrine, enter the *ThomsonNOW* documents area using the access card that is available for *The Essential World History*.

Honecker's virtual dictatorship. Honecker ruled unchallenged for the next eighteen years.

An Era of Détente

Still, under Brezhnev and Kosygin, the Soviet Union continued to pursue peaceful coexistence with the West and adopted a generally cautious posture in foreign affairs. By the early 1970s, a new age in Soviet-American relations had emerged, often referred to by the French term *détente,* meaning a reduction of tensions between the two sides. One symbol of **détente** was the Antiballistic Missile (ABM) Treaty, often called SALT I (for Strategic Arms Limitation Talks), signed in 1972, in which the two nations agreed to limit the size of their ABM systems.

Washington's objective in pursuing the treaty was to make it unlikely that either superpower could win a nuclear exchange by launching a preemptive strike against the other. U.S. officials believed that a policy of "equivalence," in which the two sides had roughly equal power, was the best way to avoid a nuclear confrontation. Détente was pursued in other ways as well. When President Nixon took office in 1969, he sought to increase trade and cultural contacts with the Soviet Union. His purpose was to set up a series of "linkages" in U.S.-Soviet relations that would persuade Moscow of the economic and social benefits of maintaining good relations with the West.

A symbol of that new relationship was the Helsinki Agreement. Signed in 1975 by the United States, Canada, and all European nations on both sides of the Iron Curtain, these accords recognized all borders in Europe that had been established since the end of World War II, thereby formally acknowledging for the first time the

Soviet sphere of influence in Eastern Europe. The Helsinki Agreement also committed the signatories to recognize and protect the human rights of their citizens, a clear effort by the Western states to improve the performance of the Soviet Union and its allies in that arena.

Renewed Tensions in the Third World

Protection of human rights became one of the major foreign policy goals of the next U.S. president, Jimmy Carter (b. 1924). Ironically, just at the point when U.S. involvement in Vietnam came to an end and relations with China began to improve, U.S.-Soviet relations began to sour, for several reasons. Some Americans had become increasingly concerned about aggressive new tendencies in Soviet foreign policy. The first indication came in Africa. Soviet influence was on the rise in Somalia, across the Red Sea from South Yemen, and later in neighboring Ethiopia. In Angola, once a colony of Portugal, an insurgent movement supported by Cuban troops came to power. In 1979, Soviet troops were sent across the border into Afghanistan to protect a newly installed Marxist regime facing internal resistance from fundamentalist Muslims. Some observers suspected that the ultimate objective of the Soviet advance into hitherto neutral Afghanistan was to extend Soviet power into the oil fields of the Persian Gulf. To deter such a possibility, the White House promulgated the Carter Doctrine, which stated that the United States would use its military power, if necessary, to safeguard Western access to the oil reserves in the Middle East. In fact, sources in Moscow later disclosed that the Soviet advance had little to do with the oil of the Persian Gulf but was an effort to increase Soviet influence in a region increasingly beset by Islamic fervor. Soviet officials feared that Islamic activism could spread to the Muslim populations in the Soviet republics in Central Asia and were confident that the United States was too distracted by the **"Vietnam syndrome"** (the public fear of U.S. involvement in another Vietnam-type conflict) to respond.

Another reason for the growing suspicion of the Soviet Union in the United States was that some U.S. defense analysts began to charge that the Soviet Union had rejected the policy of equivalence and was seeking strategic superiority in nuclear weapons. Accordingly, they argued for a substantial increase in U.S. defense spending. Such charges, combined with evidence of Soviet efforts in Africa and the Middle East and reports of the persecution of Jews and dissidents in the Soviet Union, helped undermine public support for détente in the United States. These changing attitudes were reflected in the failure of the Carter administration to obtain congressional approval of a new arms limitation agreement (SALT II), signed with the Soviet Union in 1979.

Countering the Evil Empire

The early years of the administration of President Ronald Reagan (1911–2004) witnessed a return to the

harsh rhetoric, if not all of the harsh practices, of the Cold War. President Reagan's anti-Communist credentials were well known. In a speech given shortly after his election in 1980, he referred to the Soviet Union as an "evil empire" and frequently voiced his suspicion of its motives in foreign affairs. In an effort to eliminate perceived Soviet advantages in strategic weaponry, the White House began a military buildup that stimulated a renewed arms race. In 1982, the Reagan administration introduced the nuclear-tipped cruise missile, whose ability to fly at low altitudes made it difficult to detect by enemy radar. Reagan also became an ardent exponent of the Strategic Defense Initiative (SDI), nicknamed **"Star Wars."** The intent behind this proposed defense system was not only to create a space shield that could destroy incoming missiles but also to force Moscow into an arms race that it could not hope to win.

The Reagan administration also adopted a more activist, if not confrontational, stance in the Third World. That attitude was most directly demonstrated in Central America, where the revolutionary Sandinista regime had been established in Nicaragua after the overthrow of the Somoza dictatorship in 1979. Charging that the Sandinista regime was supporting a guerrilla insurgency movement in nearby El Salvador, the Reagan administration began to provide material aid to the government in El Salvador while

Northern Central America

COMPARATIVE ESSAY

GLOBAL VILLAGE OR CLASH OF CIVILIZATIONS?

As the Cold War came to an end in the early 1990s, statesmen, scholars, and political pundits began to forecast the emergence of a "new world order." One hypothesis was that the decline of communism signaled that the industrial capitalist democracies of the West had triumphed in the world of ideas and were now poised to remake the rest of the world in their own image.

Not all agreed with this optimistic view of the world situation. In *The Clash of Civilizations and the Remaking of the World Order*, the historian Samuel P. Huntington suggested that the post–Cold War era, far from marking the triumph of the Western idea, would be characterized by increased global fragmentation and a "clash of civilizations" based on ethnic, cultural, or religious differences. According to Huntington, the coming decades may see a world dominated by disputing cultural blocs in East Asia, Western Europe and the United States, Eurasia, and the Middle East. The dream of a universal order—a global village—dominated by Western values, he concludes, is a fantasy.

Events in recent years have lent some support to Huntington's hypothesis. The collapse of the Soviet Union led to the emergence of an atmosphere of conflict and tension all along the perimeter of the old Soviet Empire. More recently, the terrorist attack on the United States in September 2001 set the advanced nations of the West and much of the Muslim world on a collision course. As for the new economic order—now enshrined as official policy in Western capitals—public anger at the impact of globalization has reached disturbing levels in many countries, leading to a growing demand for self-protection and group identity in an impersonal and rapidly changing world.

Are we then headed toward Huntington's prediction of multiple power blocs divided by religion and culture? His thesis is indeed a useful corrective to the complacent tendency of many observers to view Western civilization as the zenith of human achievement. On the other hand, by dividing the world into competing cultural blocs, Huntington has underestimated the centrifugal forces at work in the various regions of the world. As the industrial and technological revolutions spread across the face of the earth, their impact is measurably stronger in some societies than in others, thus intensifying historical rivalries in a given region while establishing links between individual societies and counterparts in other parts of the world. In recent years, for example, Japan has had more in common with the United States than with its traditional neighbors, China and Korea.

The most likely scenario for the next few decades, then, is more complex than either the global village hypothesis or its rival, the clash of civilizations. The world of the twenty-first century will be characterized by simultaneous trends toward globalization and fragmentation as the thrust of technology and information transforms societies and gives rise to counterreactions among societies seeking to preserve a group identity and a sense of meaning and purpose in a confusing world.

---

simultaneously supporting an anti-Communist guerrilla movement (the **Contras**) in Nicaragua. Though the administration insisted that it was countering the spread of communism in the Western Hemisphere, its Central American policy aroused considerable controversy in Congress, where some members charged that growing U.S. involvement could lead to a repeat of the nation's bitter experience in Vietnam.

The Reagan administration also took the offensive in other areas. By providing military support to the anti-Soviet insurgents in Afghanistan, the White House helped maintain a Vietnam-like war in Afghanistan that entangled the Soviet Union in its own quagmire. Like the Vietnam War, the conflict in Afghanistan resulted in heavy casualties and demonstrated that the influence of a superpower was limited in the face of strong nationalist, guerrilla-type opposition.

The New World Order

In the early 1990s, the Soviet Union, which for so long had seemed to be a permanent fixture on the global scene, suddenly disintegrated. The Soviet satellites in Eastern Europe broke loose from Moscow's grip and declared their independence from Communist rule. Many are now being gradually integrated into an expanded Europe. In the meantime, massive protests shook the foundations of Communist power in China. Although the regime managed to survive, Mao Zedong's vision of a classless utopia has been replaced by a market-based economy every bit as focused on wealth and power as that of its capitalist rivals. These issues will be discussed in the next two chapters.

These cataclysmic events brought an end to the Cold War and lulled many observers into the seductive idea of a new world order that would be characterized by peaceful cooperation and increasing global prosperity (see the comparative essay "Global Village or Clash of Civilizations?" above). Unfortunately, such hopes were destined not to be realized. A bitter civil war in the Balkans in the mid-1990s graphically demonstrated that old fault lines of national and ethnic hostility were alive and well in the post Cold War world. In rapid succession, bloody ethnic and religious disputes broke out in Africa and the Middle East. Then, on September 11, 2001, the world entered a new era when terrorists attacked the nerve centers of U.S. power in New York

City and Washington, D.C., inaugurating a new round of tension between the West and the forces of militant Islam (see Chapters 28 and 29).

In the meantime, other issues beyond the headlines clamor for attention. Environmental problems and the threat of global warming, the growing gap between rich and poor nations, and tensions caused by the migrations of peoples all present a growing threat to political stability and the pursuit of happiness. As the new century progresses, the task of guaranteeing the survival of the human race appears to be equally as challenging, and even more complex, than it was during the Cold War.

CONCLUSION

*A*T THE END OF WORLD WAR II, a new conflict appeared in Europe as the two superpowers, the United States and the Soviet Union, began to compete for political domination. This ideological division soon spread to the rest of the world as the United States fought in Korea and Vietnam to prevent the spread of communism, promoted by the new Maoist government in China, while the Soviet Union used its influence to prop up pro-Soviet regimes in Asia, Africa, and Latin America.

What had begun, then, as a confrontation across the great divide of the Iron Curtain in Europe eventually took on global significance, much as the major European powers had jostled for position and advantage in Africa and eastern Asia prior to World War I. As a result, both Moscow and Washington became entangled in areas that in themselves had little importance in terms of real national security interests.

As the twentieth century entered its last two decades, however, there were tantalizing signs of a thaw in the Cold War. In 1979, China and the United States decided to establish mutual diplomatic relations, a consequence of Beijing's decision to focus on domestic reform and stop supporting wars of national liberation in Asia. Six years later, the ascent of Mikhail Gorbachev to leadership in the Soviet Union, culminating in the collapse of the Soviet Union in 1991, brought a final end to almost half a century of bitter rivalry between the world's two superpowers.

The Cold War thus ended without the horrifying vision of a mushroom cloud. Unlike the earlier rivalries that had resulted in two world wars, this time the antagonists had gradually come to realize that the struggle for supremacy could be carried out in the political and economic arena rather than on the battlefield. And in the final analysis, it was not military superiority, but political, economic, and cultural factors that brought about the triumph of Western civilization over the Marxist vision of a classless utopia. The world's statesmen could now shift their focus to other problems of mutual concern.

CHAPTER NOTES

1. Quoted in *Department of State Bulletin*, February 11, 1945, pp. 213–216.
2. Quoted in J. M. Jones, *The Fifteen Weeks (February 21–June 5, 1947)*, 2d ed. (New York, 1964), pp. 140–141.
3. Quoted in W. Laqueur, *Europe in Our Time* (New York, 1992), p. 111.
4. Quoted in W. Loth, *The Division of the World, 1941–1955* (New York, 1988), pp. 160–161.
5. Quoted in P. Lane, *Europe Since 1945: An Introduction* (Totowa, N.J., 1985), p. 248.
6. Quoted in R. F. Kennedy, *Thirteen Days: A Memoir of the Cuban Missile Crisis* (New York, 1969), pp. 89–90.

SUGGESTED READING

There is a detailed literature on the Cold War. Two general accounts are **R. B. Levering, *The Cold War, 1945–1972*** (Arlington Heights, Ill., 1982), and **B. A. Weisberger, *Cold War, Cold Peace: The United States and Russia Since 1945*** (New York, 1984). Two works that maintain that the Soviet Union was chiefly responsible for the Cold War are **H. Feis, *From Trust to Terror: The Onset of the Cold War, 1945–1950*** (New York, 1970), and **A. Ulam, *The Rivals: America and Russia Since World War II*** (New York, 1971). Revisionist studies on the Cold War have emphasized U.S. responsibility for the Cold War, especially its global aspects. These works include **J. Kolko** and **G. Kolko, *The Limits of Power: The World and United States Foreign Policy, 1945–1954*** (New York, 1972); **W. La Feber, *America, Russia, and the Cold War, 1945–1966*,** 2d ed. (New York, 1972); and **M. Sherwin, *A World Destroyed: The Atomic Bomb and the Grand Alliance*** (New York, 1975). For a critique of the revisionist studies, see **R. L. Maddox, *The New Left and the Origins of the Cold War*** (Princeton, N.J., 1973). **R. Garthoff, *Détente and Confrontation: American-Soviet Relations from Nixon to Reagan*** (Washington, D.C., 1985), provides a detailed analysis of U.S.-Soviet relations in the 1970s and 1980s. For a highly competent retrospective analysis of the Cold War era, see **J. L. Gaddis, *We Now Know: Rethinking Cold War History*** (Oxford, 1997). For the perspective of a veteran journalist, see **M. Frankel, *High Noon in the Cold War: Kennedy, Khrushchev, and the Cuban Missile Crisis*** (New York, 2004).

A number of studies of the early stages of the Cold War have been based on documents unavailable until the late 1980s or early

TIMELINE

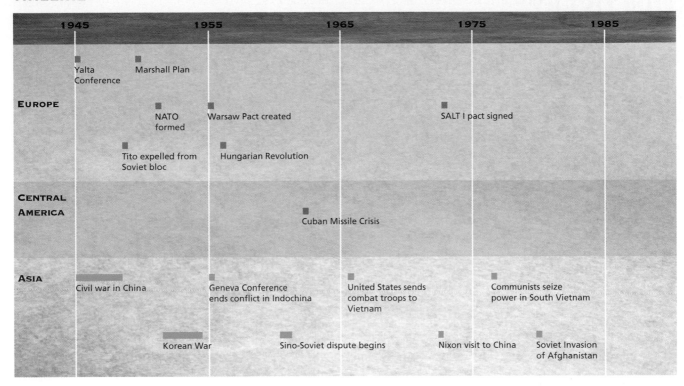

	1945	1955	1965	1975	1985
EUROPE	Yalta Conference · Marshall Plan · NATO formed · Tito expelled from Soviet bloc	Warsaw Pact created · Hungarian Revolution		SALT I pact signed	
CENTRAL AMERICA			Cuban Missile Crisis		
ASIA	Civil war in China · Korean War	Geneva Conference ends conflict in Indochina · Sino-Soviet dispute begins	United States sends combat troops to Vietnam	Communists seize power in South Vietnam · Nixon visit to China · Soviet Invasion of Afghanistan	

1990s. See, for example, **O. A. Westad,** *Cold War and Revolution: Soviet-American Rivalry and the Origins of the Chinese Civil War* (New York, 1993); **D. A. Mayers,** *Cracking the Monolith: U.S. Policy Against the Sino-Soviet Alliance, 1949–1955* (Baton Rouge, La., 1986); and **Chen Jian,** *China's Road to the Korean War: The Making of the Sino-American Confrontation* (New York, 1994). **S. Goncharov, J. W. Lewis,** and **Xue Litai,** *Uncertain Partners: Stalin, Mao, and the Korean War* (Stanford, Calif., 1993), provides a fascinating view of the war from several perspectives.

For important studies of Soviet foreign policy, see **A. B. Ulam,** *Expansion and Coexistence: Soviet Foreign Policy, 1917–1973,* 2d ed. (New York, 1974), and *Dangerous Relations: The Soviet Union in World Politics, 1970–1982* (New York, 1983). The effects of the Cold War on Germany are examined in **J. H. Backer,** *The Decision to Divide Germany: American Foreign Policy in Transition* (Durham, N.C., 1978). On atomic diplomacy in the Cold War, see **G. F. Herken,** *The Winning Weapon: The Atomic Bomb in the Cold War, 1945–1950* (New York, 1981). For a good introduction to the arms race, see **E. M. Bottome,** *The Balance of Terror: A Guide to the Arms Race,* rev. ed. (Boston, 1986).

There are several surveys of Chinese foreign policy since the Communist rise to power. For one important account, see **Chen Jian,** *Mao's China and the Cold War* (Chapel Hill, N.C., 2001). On Sino-U.S. relations, see **H. Harding,** *A Fragile Relationship: The United States and China Since 1972* (Washington, D.C., 1992), and **W. Burr,** ed., *The Kissinger Transcripts: The Top-Secret Talks with Beijing and Moscow* (New York, 1998). On Chinese policy in Korea, see **Shu Guang Zhang,** *Mao's Military Romanticism: China and the Korean War* (Lawrence, Kans., 2001), and **Xiaobing Li** et al., *Mao's Generals Remember Korea* (Lawrence, Kans., 2001). On Sino-Vietnamese relations, see **Ang Cheng Guan,** *Vietnamese Communists' Relations with China and the Second Indochina Conflict* (Jefferson, N.C., 1997).

InfoTrac College Edition

Visit this chapter's InfoTrac College Edition/Research activities at the *Essential World History* Companion Website for activities related to the Cold War.

ThomsonNOW™ for Duiker and Spielvogel's *The Essential World History, Third Edition*

Enter *ThomsonNOW* using the access card that is available with this text. *ThomsonNOW* will assist you in understanding the content in this chapter with lesson plans generated for your needs, as well as provide you with a connection to the *Wadsworth World History Resource Center* (see description below for details).

WORLD HISTORY RESOURCE CENTER

Enter the Resource Center using either your *ThomsonNOW* access card or your standalone access card for the *Wadsworth World History Resource Center.* Organized by topic, this website includes quizzes; images; over 350 primary source documents; interactive simulations, maps, and timelines; movie explorations; and a wealth of other resources. You can read the following documents, and many more, at http://worldrc.wadsworth.com/

  Charles Maier on the Cold War

  Winston Churchill's Iron Curtain speech

  John F. Kennedy, Address on the Cuban Missile Crisis

Visit the *Essential World History* Companion Website for chapter quizzes and more:

  http://www.thomsonedu.com/history/duiker

DISCOVERY

How have historians answered the question of whether the United States or the Soviet Union bears the primary responsibility for the Cold War, and what evidence can be presented on each side of the issue?

In thinking about this question, begin by breaking it down into the components shown below. A discussion of the significance of each component should appear in your answer.

INTERACTION AND EXCHANGE: Who coined the term *iron curtain* and why? What does such a phrase imply? How can you see this "iron curtain" on the accompanying maps? What were Soviet goals in Eastern Europe? How did the United States and the Soviet Union differ in their views of a postwar Germany? How did the use of language heighten tensions?

Were struggles in Third World nations really a part of the Cold War, or just regional conflicts or even civil wars? How did the United States view them, and how did this view determine American reactions? Was there such a thing as "monolithic communism," whereby all communist actions around the world were orchestrated by Moscow? In what ways did the policy of containment commit the United States to involvement around the world? How is the modern "war on terrorism" similar to the Cold War?

How do the first two documents reveal Soviet and Vietnamese views of the United States? What is the justification for their actions? How might the Vietnamese and Soviets view the Americans as the aggressors? Are they justified in their views? How are their justifications similar to the ones Truman uses in his doctrine?

Eastern Europe in 1948

Across the Ideological Divide

STATEMENT OF THE NATIONAL LIBERATION FRONT OF SOUTH VIETNAM

American imperialist aggression against South Vietnam and interference in its internal affairs have now continued for more than ten years. More American troops and supplies, including missile units, Marines, B-57 strategic bombers, and mercenaries from South Korea, Taiwan, the Philippines, Australia, Malaysia, etc., have been brought to South Vietnam. . . .

The Saigon puppet regime, paid servant of the United States, is guilty of the most heinous crimes. These despicable traitors, these bootlickers of American imperialism, have brought the enemy into our country. They have brought to South Vietnam armed forces of the United States and its satellites to kill our compatriots, occupy and ravage our sacred soil and enslave our people.

The Vietnamese, the peoples of all Indo-China and Southeast Asia, supporters of peace and justice in every part of the world, have raised their voice in angry protest against this criminal unprovoked aggression of the United States imperialists.

In the present extremely grave situation, the South Vietnam National Liberation Front considers it necessary to proclaim anew its firm and unswerving determination to resist the U.S. imperialists and fight for the salvation of our country. . . . [It] will continue to rely chiefly on its own forces and potentialities, but it is prepared to accept any assistance, moral and material, including arms and other military equipment, from all the socialist countries, from nationalist countries, from international organizations, and from the peace-loving peoples of the world.

Berlin at the Start of the Cold War

A Letter to the Central Committee of the Communist Party of Czechoslovakia

Dear comrades!

On behalf of the Central Committees of the Communist and Workers' Parties of Bulgaria, Hungary, the German Democratic Republic, Poland, and the Soviet Union, we address ourselves to you with this letter, prompted by a feeling of sincere friendship based on the principles of Marxism-Leninism and proletarian internationalism and by the concern of our common affairs for strengthening the positions of socialism and the security of the socialist community of nations.

The development of events in your country evokes in us deep anxiety. It is our firm conviction that the offensive of the reactionary forces, backed by imperialists, against your Party and the foundations of the social system in the Czechoslovak Socialist Republic, threatens to push your country off the road of socialism and that consequently it jeopardizes the interests of the entire socialist system. . . .

We neither had nor have any intention of interfering in such affairs as are strictly the internal business of your Party and your state, nor of violating the principles of respect, independence, and equality in the relations among the Communist Parties and socialist countries. . . .

At the same time we cannot agree to have hostile forces push your country from the road of socialism and create a threat of severing Czechoslovakia from the socialist community. . . . This is the common cause of our countries, which have joined in the Warsaw Treaty to ensure independence, peace, and security in Europe, and to set up an insurmountable barrier against the intrigues of the imperialist forces, against aggression and revenge. . . . We shall never agree to have imperialism, using peaceful or non-peaceful methods, making a gap from the inside or from the outside in the socialist system, and changing in imperialism's favor the correlation of forces in Europe. . . .

That is why we believe that a decisive rebuff of the anti-communist forces, and decisive efforts for the preservation of the socialist system in Czechoslovakia are not only your task but ours as well. . . .

We express the conviction that the Communist Party of Czechoslovakia, conscious of its responsibility, will take the necessary steps to block the path of reaction. In this struggle you can count on the solidarity and all-round assistance of the fraternal socialist countries.

Warsaw, July 15, 1968.

The Truman Doctrine

By 1947, the battle lines in the Cold War had been clearly drawn. This selection is taken from a speech by President Harry S Truman to the U.S. Congress in which he justified his request for aid to Greece and Turkey. Truman expressed the urgent need to contain the expansion of communism.

President Harry S Truman, Address to Congress, March 12, 1947

The peoples of a number of countries of the world have recently had totalitarian regimes forced upon them against their will. The Government of the United States has made frequent protests against coercion and intimidation, in violation of the Yalta agreement, in Poland, Romania, and Bulgaria. I must also state that in a number of other countries there have been similar developments.

At the present moment in world history nearly every nation must choose between alternative ways of life. The choice is too often not a free one.

One way of life is based upon the will of the majority, and is distinguished by free institutions, representative government, free elections, guarantees of individual liberty, freedom of speech and religion, and freedom from political oppression.

The second way of life is based upon the will of a minority forcibly imposed upon the majority. It relies upon terror and oppression, a controlled press and radio, fixed elections, and the suppression of personal freedoms.

I believe that it must be the policy of the United States to support free peoples who are resisting attempted subjugation by armed minorities or by outside pressures.

I believe that we must assist free people to work out their own destinies in their own way.

I believe that our help should be primarily through economic and financial aid which is essential to economic stability and orderly political processes. . . . I therefore ask the Congress for assistance to Greece and Turkey in the amount of $400,000,000.

POLITICS AND GOVERNMENT: How did Khrushchev and Kennedy view the events in Cuba in 1962? How were they similar and dissimilar in their views? If each nation believes it is right and justified in its actions, which is correct? Can any nation then justify taking hostile action? Why or why not?

Khrushchev Remembers

I will explain what the Caribbean crisis of October 1962 was all about. . . . At the time that Fidel Castro led his revolution to victory and entered Havana with his troops, we had no idea what political course his regime would follow. . . . All the while the Americans had been watching Castro closely. At first they thought that the capitalist underpinnings of the Cuban economy would remain intact. So by the time Castro announced that he was going to put Cuba on the road toward Socialism, the Americans had already missed their chance to do anything about it by simply exerting their influence: there were no longer any forces left which could be organized to fight on America's behalf in Cuba. That left only one alternative—invasion! . . .

After Castro's crushing victory over the counterrevolutionaries we intensified our military aid to Cuba. . . . We were sure that the Americans would never reconcile themselves to the existence of Castro's Cuba. They feared, as much as we hoped, that a Socialist Cuba might become a magnet that would attract other Latin American countries to Socialism. . . . It was clear to me that we might very well lose Cuba if we didn't take some decisive steps in her defense. . . . We had to think up some way of confronting America with more than words. We had to establish a tangible and effective deterrent to American interference in the Caribbean. But what exactly? The logical answer was missiles. We knew that American missiles were aimed against us in Turkey and Italy, to say nothing of West Germany. . . . My thinking went like this: if we installed the missiles secretly and then if the United States discovered the missiles were there after they were already poised and ready to strike, the Americans would think twice before trying to liquidate our installations by military means. . . . I want to make one thing absolutely clear: when we put our ballistic missiles in Cuba we had no desire to start a war. On the contrary, our principal aim was only to deter America from starting a war. . . .

President Kennedy issued an ultimatum, demanding that we remove our missiles and bombers from Cuba. . . . We sent the Americans a note saying that we agreed to remove our missiles and bombers on the condition that the President give us his assurance that there would be no invasion of Cuba by the forces of the United States or anybody else. Finally Kennedy gave in and agreed to make a statement giving us such an assurance. . . . It had been, to say the least, an interesting and challenging situation. The two most powerful nations of the world had been squared off against each other, each with its finger on the button. You'd have thought that war was inevitable. But both sides showed that if the desire to avoid war is strong enough, even the most pressing dispute can be solved by compromise. And a compromise over Cuba was indeed found. The episode ended in a triumph of common sense. . . . It was a great victory for us, though, that we had been able to extract from Kennedy a promise that neither America nor any of her allies would invade Cuba. . . . The Caribbean crisis was a triumph of Soviet foreign policy and a personal triumph in my own career as a statesman and as a member of the collective leadership. We achieved, I would say, a spectacular success without having to fire a single shot!

26

BRAVE NEW WORLD: COMMUNISM ON TRIAL

Shopping in Moscow

Courtesy of William J. Duiker

𝒜ccording to Karl Marx, capitalism is a system that involves the exploitation of man by man; under socialism, it is the other way around. That wry joke was typical of popular humor in post-World War II Moscow, where the dreams of a future utopia had faded in the grim reality of life in the Soviet Union.

For the average Soviet citizen after World War II, few images better symbolized the shortcomings of the Soviet system than a long line of people queuing up outside an official state store selling consumer goods. Because the command economy was so inefficient, items of daily use were chronically in such short supply that when a particular item became available, people often lined up immediately to buy several for themselves and their friends. Sometimes, if they saw a line forming, people would automatically join the queue without even knowing what item was available for purchase!

Despite the evident weaknesses of the centralized Soviet economy, the Communist monopoly on power seemed secure, as did Moscow's hold over its client states in Eastern Europe. In fact, for three decades after the end of World War II, the Soviet Empire appeared to be a permanent feature of the international landscape. But by the early

1980s, it was clear that there were cracks in the Kremlin wall. The Soviet economy was stagnant, the minority nationalities were restive, and Eastern European leaders were increasingly emboldened to test the waters of the global capitalist marketplace. In the United States, the newly elected president, Ronald Reagan, boldly predicted the imminent collapse of the "evil empire."

Within a period of less than three years (1989–1991), the Soviet Union ceased to exist as a nation. Russia and other former Soviet republics declared their separate independence, Communist regimes in Eastern Europe were toppled, and the long-standing division of postwar Europe came to an end. Although Communist parties survived the demise of the system and showed signs of renewed vigor in some countries in the region, their monopoly is gone, and they must now compete with other parties for power.

The fate of communism in China has been quite different. Despite some turbulence, communism has survived in China, even as that nation takes giant strides toward becoming an economic superpower. Yet, as China's leaders struggle to bring the nation into the twenty-first century, many of the essential principles of Marxist-Leninist dogma have been tacitly abandoned. ◇

The Postwar Soviet Union

World War II had left the Soviet Union as one of the world's two superpowers and its leader, Joseph Stalin, in a position of strength. He and his Soviet colleagues were now in control of a vast empire that included Eastern Europe, much of the Balkans, and new territory gained from Japan in East Asia.

From Stalin to Khrushchev

At the same time, World War II had devastated the Soviet Union. Twenty million citizens lost their lives, and cities such as Kiev, Kharkov, and Leningrad suffered enormous physical destruction. As the lands that had been occupied by the German forces were liberated, the Soviet government turned its attention to restoring their economic structures. Nevertheless, in 1945, agricultural production was only 60 percent and steel output only 50 percent of prewar levels. The Soviet people faced incredibly difficult conditions: ill-housed and poorly clothed, they worked longer hours and ate less they than before the war.

Stalinism in Action In the immediate postwar years, the Soviet Union removed goods and materials from occupied Germany and extorted valuable raw materials from its satellite states in Eastern Europe (see Map 26.1). More important, however, to create a new industrial base, Stalin returned to the method he had used in the 1930s— the extraction of development capital from Soviet labor. Working hard for little pay and for precious few consumer goods, Soviet laborers were expected to produce

goods for export with little in return for themselves. The incoming capital from abroad could then be used to purchase machinery and Western technology. The loss of millions of men in the war meant that much of this tremendous workload fell upon Soviet women, who performed almost 40 percent of the heavy manual labor.

The pace of economic recovery in the Soviet Union was impressive. By 1947, industrial production had attained 1939 levels. New power plants, canals, and giant factories were built, and industrial enterprises and oil fields were established in Siberia and Soviet Central Asia.

Although Stalin's economic recovery policy was successful in promoting growth in heavy industry, primarily for the benefit of the military, consumer goods remained scarce. Heavy industry grew at a rate three times that of personal consumption. Moreover, the housing shortage was acute, with living conditions especially difficult in the overcrowded cities.

When World War II ended in 1945, Stalin had been in power for more than fifteen years. Political terror enforced by several hundred thousand secret police ensured that he would remain in power. By the late 1940s, there were an estimated nine million Soviet citizens in Siberian concentration camps.

Increasingly distrustful of competitors, Stalin exercised sole authority and pitted his subordinates against each other. His morbid suspicions extended to even his closest colleagues, causing his associates to become completely cowed. As he remarked mockingly on one occasion, "When I die, the imperialists will strangle all of you like a litter of kittens."[1]

The Rise and Fall of Khrushchev Stalin died in 1953 and, after some bitter infighting within the party leadership, was succeeded by Georgy Malenkov, a veteran administrator and ambitious member of the Politburo (the party's governing body). But Malenkov's reform goals did not necessarily appeal to key groups, including the army, the Communist Party, the managerial elite, and the security services (now known as the Committee on Government Security, or KGB). In 1953, Malenkov was removed from his position, and power shifted to his rival, the new party general secretary, Nikita Khrushchev.

Once in power, Khrushchev moved vigorously to boost the performance of the Soviet economy and revitalize Soviet society. In an attempt to release the stranglehold of the central bureaucracy over the national economy, he abolished dozens of government ministries and split up the party and government apparatus. Khrushchev also attempted to rejuvenate the stagnant agricultural sector. He attempted to spur production by increasing profit incentives and opened "virgin lands" in Soviet Kazakhstan to bring thousands of acres of new land under cultivation.

An innovator by nature, Khrushchev had to overcome the inherently conservative instincts of the Soviet bureaucracy, as well as those of the mass of the Soviet population. His plan to remove the "dead hand" of the

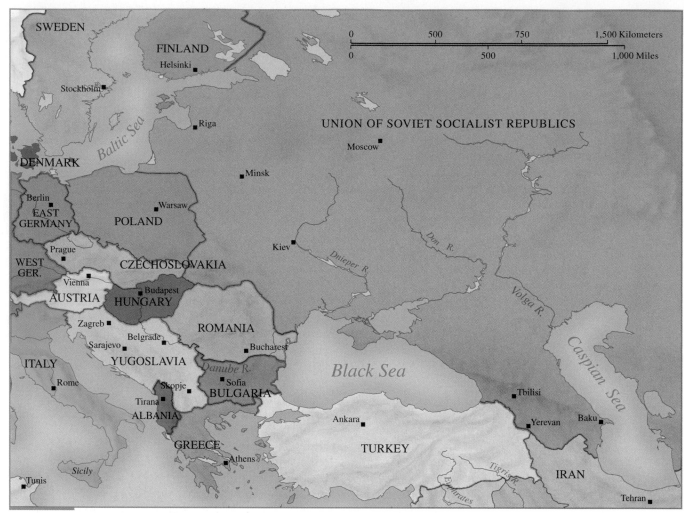

MAP 26.1 **Eastern Europe Under Soviet Rule.** After World War II, the boundaries of Eastern Europe were redrawn as a result of Allied agreements reached at the Tehran and Yalta conferences. This map shows the new boundaries that were established throughout the region, placing Soviet power at the center of Europe. ❓ How had the boundaries changed from the prewar era? 🌐 **View an animated version of this map or related maps at** http://worldrc.wadsworth.com/

state, however laudable in intent, alienated much of the Soviet official class, and his effort to split the party angered those who saw it as the central force in the Soviet system. Khrushchev's agricultural schemes inspired similar opposition. His effort to persuade Russians to eat more corn (an idea he had apparently picked up during a visit to the United States) earned him the mocking nickname "Cornman." The industrial growth rate, which had soared in the early 1950s, now declined dramatically, from 13 percent in 1953 to 7.5 percent in 1964.

Khrushchev was probably best known for his policy of **destalinization.** Khrushchev had risen in the party hierarchy as a Stalin protégé, but he had been deeply disturbed by his mentor's excesses and, once in a position of authority, moved to excise the Stalinist legacy from Soviet society. The campaign began at the Twentieth National Congress of the Communist Party in February 1956, when Khrushchev gave a long speech in private criticizing some of Stalin's major shortcomings. The speech had

apparently not been intended for public distribution, but it was quickly leaked to the Western press and created a sensation throughout the world (see the box on p. 588). Under Khrushchev's instructions, thousands of prisoners were released from concentration camps.

Khrushchev's personality, however, did not endear him to higher Soviet officials, who frowned at his tendency to crack jokes and play the clown. Foreign policy failures further damaged Khrushchev's reputation among his colleagues (see Chapter 25). While he was away on vacation in 1964, a special meeting of the Soviet Politburo voted him out of office (because of "deteriorating health") and forced him into retirement.

The Brezhnev Years (1964–1982)

The ouster of Nikita Khrushchev in October 1964 vividly demonstrated the challenges that would be encountered by any leader sufficiently bold to try to reform the Soviet

Courtesy of William J. Duiker

The Portals of Doom.   Perhaps the most feared location in the Soviet Union was Lyubyanka Prison, an ornate prerevolutionary building in the heart of Moscow. Taken over by the Bolsheviks after the 1917 Revolution, it became the headquarters of the Soviet secret police, the Cheka, later to be known as the KGB. It was here that many Soviet citizens accused of "counterrevolutionary acts" were imprisoned and executed. The figure on the pedestal is that of Felix Dzershinsky, first director of the Cheka. After the dissolution of the Soviet Union, the statue was removed.

system. Leonid Brezhnev (1906–1982), the new party chief, was undoubtedly aware of these realities of Soviet politics, and his long tenure in power was marked, above all, by the desire to avoid changes that might provoke instability, either at home or abroad. Brezhnev was himself a product of the Soviet system. He had entered the ranks of the party leadership under Stalin, and although he was not a particularly avid believer in party ideology, he was no partisan of reform.

Still, Brezhnev sought stability in the domestic arena. He and his prime minister, Alexei Kosygin, undertook what might be described as a program of "de-Khrushchevization," returning the responsibility for long-term planning to the central ministries and reuniting the Communist Party apparatus. Despite some cautious attempts to stimulate the stagnant farm sector, there was no effort to revise the basic collective system. In the industrial sector, the regime launched a series of reforms designed to give factory managers (themselves employees of the state) more responsibility for setting prices, wages, and production quotas. These **"Kosygin reforms"** had little effect, however, because they were stubbornly resisted by the bureaucracy.

A Controlled Society   Brezhnev also initiated a significant retreat from Khrushchev's policy of destalinization. Criticism of the "Great Leader" had angered conservatives both within the party hierarchy and among the public at large, many of whom still revered Stalin as a hero and a defender of Russia against Nazi Germany. Early in Brezhnev's reign, Stalin's reputation began to

revive. Although his alleged shortcomings were not totally ignored, he was now described in the official press as "an outstanding party leader" who had been primarily responsible for the successes achieved by the Soviet Union.

The regime also adopted a more restrictive policy toward dissidents in Soviet society. Critics of the Soviet system, such as the physicist Andrei Sakharov, were harassed and arrested or, like the famous writer Alexander Solzhenitsyn, forced to leave the country. Free expression was also restricted. The media were controlled by the state and presented only what the state wanted people to hear. The government made strenuous efforts to prevent the Soviet people from exposure to harmful foreign ideas, especially modern art, literature, and contemporary Western rock music. When the Summer Olympic Games were held in Moscow in 1980, Soviet newspapers advised citizens to keep their children indoors to keep them from being polluted with "bourgeois" ideas passed on by foreign visitors.

A Stagnant Economy   Soviet leaders also failed to achieve their objective of revitalizing the national economy. Whereas growth rates during the early Khrushchev era had been impressive (prompting Khrushchev during a reception at the Kremlin in the 1950s to chortle, "We will bury you," referring to the United States), under Brezhnev industrial growth declined to an annual rate of less than 4 percent in the early 1970s and less than 3 percent in the period from 1975 to 1980. Successes in the agricultural sector were equally meager.

Khrushchev Denounces Stalin

POLITICS & GOVERNMENT

Three years after Stalin's death, the new Soviet premier, Nikita Khrushchev, addressed the Twentieth Congress of the Communist Party and denounced the former Soviet dictator for his crimes. This denunciation was the beginning of a policy of destalinization.

What were the key charges that Khrushchev made against his predecessor? Can it be said that Khrushchev corrected these problems?

Khrushchev Addresses the Twentieth Party Congress, February 1956

Comrades, . . . quite a lot has been said about the cult of the individual and about its harmful consequences . . . . The cult of the person of Stalin . . . became at a certain specific stage the source of a whole series of exceedingly serious and grave perversions of Party principles, of Party democracy, of revolutionary legality.

Stalin absolutely did not tolerate collegiality in leadership and in work and . . . practiced brutal violence, not only toward everything which opposed him, but also toward that which seemed to his capricious and despotic character, contrary to his concepts.

Stalin abandoned the method of ideological struggle for that of administrative violence, mass repressions and terror . . . . Arbitrary behavior by one person encouraged and permitted arbitrariness in others. Mass arrests and deportations of many thousands of people, execution without trial and without normal investigation created conditions of insecurity, fear, and even desperation.

Stalin showed in a whole series of cases his intolerance, his brutality, and his abuse of power. . . . He often chose the path of repression and annihilation, not only against actual enemies, but also against individuals who had not committed any crimes against the Party and the Soviet government. . . .

Many Party, Soviet, and economic activists who were branded in 1937–8 as "enemies" were actually never enemies, spies, wreckers, and so on, but were always honest communists; they were only so stigmatized, and often, no longer able to bear barbaric tortures, they charged themselves (at the order of the investigative judges-falsifiers) with all kinds of grave and unlikely crimes.

This was the result of the abuse of power by Stalin, who began to use mass terror against the Party cadres. . . . Stalin put the Party and the NKVD [the Soviet police agency] up to the use of mass terror when the exploiting classes had been liquidated in our country and when there were no serious reasons for the use of extraordinary mass terror. The terror was directed . . . against the honest workers of the Party and the Soviet state. . . .

Stalin was a very distrustful man, sickly, suspicious. . . . Everywhere and in everything he saw "enemies," "two-facers," and "spies." Possessing unlimited power, he indulged in great willfulness and choked a person morally and physically. A situation was created where one could not express one's own will. When Stalin said that one or another would be arrested, it was necessary to accept on faith that he was an "enemy of the people." What proofs were offered? The confession of the arrested. . . . How is it possible that a person confesses to crimes that he had not committed? Only in one way—because of application of physical methods of pressuring him, tortures, bringing him to a state of unconsciousness, deprivation of his judgment, taking away of his human dignity.

ThomsonNOW™ To read more of Khrushchev's speech, enter the *ThomsonNOW* documents area using the access card that is available for *The Essential World History*.

One of the primary problems with the Soviet economy was the absence of incentives. Salary structures offered little reward for hard labor and extraordinary achievement. Pay differentials operated in a much narrower range than in most Western societies, and there was little danger of being dismissed. According to the Soviet constitution, every Soviet citizen was guaranteed an opportunity to work.

There were, of course, some exceptions to the general rule. Athletic achievement was highly prized, and a gymnast of Olympic stature would receive great rewards in the form of prestige and lifestyle. Senior officials did not receive high salaries but were provided with countless perquisites, such as access to foreign goods, official automobiles with a chauffeur, and entry into prestigious institutions of higher learning for their children.

An Aging Leadership Brezhnev died in November 1982 and was succeeded by Yuri Andropov (1914–1984), a party veteran and head of the Soviet secret services. During his brief tenure as party chief, Andropov was a vocal advocate of reform, but when he died after only a few months in office, little had been done to change the system. He was succeeded, in turn, by a mediocre party stalwart, the elderly Konstantin Chernenko (1911–1985). With the Soviet system in crisis, Moscow seemed stuck in a time warp.

Cultural Expression in the Soviet Bloc

In his occasional musings about the future communist utopia, Karl Marx had predicted that a new, classless society would replace the exploitative and hierarchical

Courtesy of William J. Duiker

How to Shop in Moscow.   Because of the policy of state control over the Soviet economy, the availability of goods was a consequence not of market factors but of decisions made by government bureaucrats. As a result, needed goods were often in short supply. When Soviet citizens heard that a shipment of a particular product had arrived at a state store, they queued up to buy it. Here shoppers line up in front of a store selling dinnerware in Moscow.

systems of feudalism and capitalism. In their free time, workers would produce a new, advanced culture, proletarian in character and egalitarian in content.

The reality in the post–World War II Soviet Union and Eastern Europe was somewhat different. Under Stalin, a series of government decrees made all forms of literary and scientific expression dependent on the state. All Soviet culture was expected to follow the party line. Historians, philosophers, and social scientists all grew accustomed to quoting Marx, Lenin, and, above all, Stalin as their chief authorities. Novels and plays, too, were supposed to portray Communist heroes and their efforts to create a better society. No criticism of existing social conditions was permitted. Some areas of intellectual activity were virtually abolished; the science of genetics disappeared, and few movies were made during Stalin's final years.

Stalin's death brought a modest respite from cultural repression. Writers and artists banned during the Stalin years were again allowed to publish. Still, Soviet authorities, including Khrushchev, were reluctant to allow cultural freedom to move far beyond official Soviet ideology.

These restrictions, however, did not prevent the emergence of some significant Soviet literature, although authors paid a heavy price if they alienated the Soviet authorities. Boris Pasternak (1890–1960), who began his literary career as a poet, won the Nobel Prize in 1958 for his celebrated novel *Doctor Zhivago*, written between 1945 and 1956 and published in Italy in 1957. But the Soviet government condemned Pasternak's anti-Soviet tendencies, banned the novel, and would not allow him to accept

the prize. The author had alienated the authorities by describing a society scarred by the excesses of Bolshevik revolutionary zeal.

Alexander Solzhenitsyn (b. 1918) created an even greater furor than Pasternak. Solzhenitsyn had spent eight years in forced labor camps for criticizing Stalin, and his *One Day in the Life of Ivan Denisovich*, which won him the Nobel Prize in 1970, was an account of life in those camps (see the box on p. 590). Khrushchev allowed the book's publication as part of his destalinization campaign. Solzhenitsyn then wrote *The Gulag Archipelago*, a detailed indictment of the whole system of Soviet oppression. Soviet authorities expelled Solzhenitsyn from the Soviet Union in 1973.

In the Eastern European satellites, cultural freedom varied considerably from country to country. In Poland, intellectuals had access to Western publications as well as greater freedom to travel to the West. Hungarian and Yugoslav Communists, too, tolerated a certain level of intellectual activity that was not liked but at least was not prohibited. Elsewhere

Courtesy of William J. Duiker

Stalinist Heroic: An Example of Socialist Realism.   Under Stalin and his successors, art was assigned the task of indoctrinating the Soviet population on the public virtues, such as hard work, loyalty to the state, and patriotism. Grandiose statuary erected to commemorate the heroic efforts of the Red Army during World War II appeared in every Soviet city. Here is an example in Minsk, today the capital of Belarus. The current president of Belarus, Alexander Lukashenko, still proclaims his allegiance to the principles of communism. Compare this example with the Chinese painting on p. 603.

ONE DAY IN THE LIFE OF IVAN DENISOVICH

ARTS & IDEAS

On November 20, 1962, a Soviet magazine published a work by Alexander Solzhenitsyn that created a literary and political furor. The short novel related one day in the life of its chief character, Ivan Denisovich, at a Siberian concentration camp, to which he had been sentenced at the end of World War II for supposedly spying for the Germans while a Soviet soldier. This excerpt narrates the daily journey from the prison camp to a work project through the 17 degrees-below-zero cold of Siberia. Many Soviet citizens who had suffered under Stalin identified with Ivan.

What was the author's purpose in writing this literary work? How did it contribute to Khrushchev's destalinization program?

Alexander Solzhenitsyn, *One Day in the Life of Ivan Denisovich*

There were escort guards all over the place. They flung a semicircle around the column on its way to the power station, their machine guns sticking out and pointing right at your face. And there were guards with gray dogs. One dog bared its fangs as if laughing at the prisoners. The escorts all wore short sheepskins, except for half a dozen whose coats trailed the ground. The long sheepskins were interchangeable: they were worn by anyone whose turn had come to man the watchtowers.

And once again as they brought the squads together the escort recounted the entire power-station column by fives. . . .

Out beyond the camp boundary the intense cold, accompanied by a headwind, stung even Shukhov's face, which was used to every kind of unpleasantness. Realizing that he would have the wind in his face all the way to the power station, he decided to make use of his bit of rag. To meet the contingency of a headwind he,

like many other prisoners, had got himself a cloth with a long tape on each end. The prisoners admitted that these helped a bit. Shukhov covered his face up to the eyes, brought the tapes around below his ears, and fastened the ends together at the back of his neck. Then he covered his nape with the flap of his hat and raised his coat collar. The next thing was to pull the front flap of the hat down into his brow. Thus in front only his eyes remained unprotected. He fixed his coat tightly at the waist with the rope. Now everything was in order except for his hands, which were already stiff with cold (his mittens were worthless). He rubbed them, he clapped them together, for he knew that in a moment he'd have to put them behind his back and keep them there for the entire march.

The chief of the escort guard recited the "morning prayer," which every prisoner was heartily sick of:

"Attention, prisoners. Marching orders must be strictly obeyed. Keep to your ranks. No hurrying, keep a steady pace. No talking. Keep your eyes fixed ahead and your hands behind your backs. A step to right or left is considered an attempt to escape and the escort has orders to shoot without warning. Leading guards, on the double."

The two guards in the lead of the escort must have set out along the road. The column heaved forward, shoulders swaying, and the escorts, some twenty paces to the right and left of the column, each man at a distance of ten paces from the next, machine guns held at the ready, set off too.

ThomsonNOW To read more of *One Day the Life of Ivan Denisovich*, enter the *ThomsonNOW* documents area using the access card that is available for *The Essential World History*.

---

intellectuals were forced to conform to the regime's demands. After the Soviet invasion of Czechoslovakia in 1968, Czech Communists pursued a policy of strict cultural control.

Social Changes According to Marxist doctrine, state control of industry and the elimination of private property were supposed to lead to a classless society. Although that ideal was never achieved, it did have important social consequences. The desire to create a classless society, for example, led to noticeable changes in education. In some countries, laws mandated quota systems based on class. As education became crucial for obtaining new jobs in the Communist system, enrollments rose in both secondary schools and universities.

The new managers of society, regardless of their class background, realized the importance of higher education and used their power to gain special privileges for their

children. By 1971, 60 percent of the children of white-collar workers attended university, but only 36 percent of the children of blue-collar families did so, although these families constituted 60 percent of the population.

Ideals of equality also did not include women. Men dominated the leadership positions of the Communist parties. Women did have greater opportunities in the workforce and even in the professions, however. In the Soviet Union, women comprised 51 percent of the labor force in 1980; by the mid-1980s, they constituted 50 percent of the engineers, 80 percent of the doctors, and 75 percent of the teachers and teachers' aides. But many of these were low-paying jobs; most female doctors, for example, worked in primary care and were paid less than skilled machinists. The chief administrators in hospitals and schools were still men.

Moreover, although women made up nearly half of the workforce, they were never freed from their traditional roles in the home. Most women had to work what came to be known as the "double shift." After working eight hours in their jobs, they came home to do the housework and care for the children. They might also spend two hours a day in long lines at a number of stores waiting to buy food and clothes. Because of the housing shortage, a number of families would share a kitchen, making even meal preparation a complicated task.

Nearly three-quarters of a century after the Bolshevik Revolution, then, the Marxist dream of an advanced, egalitarian society was as far away as ever. Although in some respects, conditions in the socialist camp were a distinct improvement over those before World War II, many problems and inequities were as intransigent as ever.

CHRONOLOGY The Soviet Bloc and Its Demise	
Death of Joseph Stalin	1953
Rise of Nikita Khrushchev	1955
Destalinization speech	1956
Removal of Khrushchev	1964
The Brezhnev era	1964–1982
Rule of Andropov and Chernenko	1982–1985
Gorbachev comes to power in Soviet Union	1985
Collapse of Communist governments in Eastern Europe	1989
Disintegration of Soviet Union	1991

The Disintegration of the Soviet Empire

On the death of Konstantin Chernenko in 1985, party leaders selected the talented and vigorous Soviet official Mikhail Gorbachev to succeed him. The new Soviet leader had shown early signs of promise. Born into a peasant family in 1931, Gorbachev combined farmwork with school and received the Order of the Red Banner for his agricultural efforts. This award and his good school record enabled him to study law at the University of Moscow. After receiving his law degree in 1955, he returned to his native southern Russia, where he eventually became first secretary of the Communist Party in the city of Stavropol. In 1978, he was made a member of the party's Central Committee in Moscow. Two years later, he became a full member of the ruling Politburo and secretary of the Central Committee.

During the early 1980s, Gorbachev began to realize the immensity of Soviet problems and the crucial need for massive reform to transform the system. During a visit to Canada in 1983, he discovered to his astonishment that Canadian farmers worked hard on their own initiative. "We'll never have this for fifty years," he reportedly remarked.[2] On his return to Moscow, he set in motion a series of committees to evaluate the situation and recommend measures to improve the system.

The Gorbachev Era

With his election as party general secretary in 1985, Gorbachev seemed intent on taking earlier reforms to their logical conclusions. The cornerstone of his program was **perestroika,** or "restructuring." At first, it meant only a reordering of economic policy, as Gorbachev called for the beginning of a market economy with limited free enterprise and some private property. But Gorbachev soon perceived that in the Soviet system, the economic sphere was intimately tied to the social and political spheres. Any efforts to reform the economy without political or social reform would be doomed to failure.

One of the most important instruments of *perestroika* was **glasnost,** or "openness." Soviet citizens and officials were encouraged to discuss openly the strengths and weaknesses of the Soviet Union. The arts also benefited from the new policy as previously banned works were now published and motion pictures were allowed to depict negative aspects of Soviet life. Music based on Western styles, such as jazz and rock, could now be performed openly. Religious activities, long banned by the authorities, were once again tolerated.

Political reforms were equally revolutionary. In June 1987, the principle of two-candidate elections was introduced; previously, voters had been presented with only one candidate. At the Communist Party conference in 1988, Gorbachev called for the creation of a new Soviet parliament, the Congress of People's Deputies, whose members were to be chosen in competitive elections. It convened in 1989, the first such meeting in the nation since 1918. Early in 1990, Gorbachev legalized the formation of other political parties and struck out Article 6 of the Soviet constitution, which guaranteed the "leading role" of the Communist Party. Hitherto, the position of first secretary of the party was the most important post in the Soviet Union, but as the Communist Party became less closely associated with the state, the powers of this office diminished. Gorbachev attempted to consolidate his power by creating a new state presidency, and in March 1990 he became the Soviet Union's first president.

The Beginning of the End One of Gorbachev's most serious problems stemmed from the character of the Soviet Union. The Union of Soviet Socialist Republics was a truly multiethnic country, containing 92 nationalities and 112 recognized languages. Previously, the iron hand of the Communist Party, centered in Moscow, had kept a lid on the centuries-old ethnic tensions that had periodically erupted throughout the history of this region. As Gorbachev released this iron grip, ethnic groups throughout the Soviet Union began to call for sovereignty of the republics and independence from Russian-based rule

MAP 26.2 **Eastern Europe and the Former Soviet Union.** After the disintegration of the Soviet Union in 1991, several onetime Soviet republics declared their independence. This map shows the new configuration of the states that emerged in the 1990s from the former Soviet Union. The breakaway region of Chechnya is indicated on the map. ❓ What new nations have appeared from the old Soviet Union since the end of the Cold War? 🔊 **View an animated version of this map or related maps at** http://worldrc.wadsworth.com/

centered in Moscow. Such movements sprang up first in Georgia in late 1988 and then in Latvia, Estonia, Moldavia, Uzbekistan, Azerbaijan, and Lithuania.

In December 1989, the Communist Party of Lithuania declared itself independent of the Communist Party of the Soviet Union. Despite pleas from Gorbachev, who supported self-determination but not secession, other Soviet republics eventually followed suit. Ukraine voted for independence on December 1, 1991. A week later, the leaders of Russia, Ukraine, and Belarus announced that the Soviet Union had "ceased to exist" and would be replaced by a "commonwealth of independent states." Gorbachev resigned on December 25, 1991, and turned over his responsibilities as commander in chief to Boris Yeltsin (b. 1931), the president of Russia. By the end of 1991, one of the largest empires in world history had come to an end, and a new era had begun in its lands (see Map 26.2 and Chapter 27).

Eastern Europe: From Satellites to Sovereign Nations

The disintegration of the Soviet Union had an immediate impact on its neighbors to the west. First to respond, as in 1956, was Poland, where popular protests at high food prices had erupted in the early 1980s, leading to the rise of an independent labor movement called Solidarity. Led by Lech Walesa (b. 1943), Solidarity rapidly became an influential force for change and a threat to the government's

monopoly of power. In 1988, the Communist government bowed to the inevitable and permitted free national elections to take place, resulting in the election of Walesa as president of Poland in December 1990. When Moscow took no action to reverse the verdict in Warsaw, Poland entered the post-Communist era.

In Hungary, as in Poland, the process of transition had begun many years previously. After crushing the Hungarian revolution of 1956, the Communist government of János Kádár had tried to assuage popular opinion by enacting a series of far-reaching economic reforms (labeled "communism with a capitalist face-lift"). But as the 1980s progressed, the economy sagged, and in 1989, the regime permitted the formation of opposition political parties, leading eventually to the formation of a non-Communist coalition government in elections held in March 1990.

The transition in Czechoslovakia was more abrupt. After Soviet troops crushed the Prague Spring in 1968, hard-line Communists under Gustav Husák followed a policy of massive repression to maintain their power. In 1977, dissident intellectuals formed an organization called Charter 77 as a vehicle for protest against violations of human rights. Dissident activities increased during the 1980s, and when massive demonstrations broke out in several major cities in 1989, President Husák's government, lacking any real popular support, collapsed. At the end of December, he was replaced by Václav Havel, a dissident playwright who had been a leading figure in Charter 77.

But the most dramatic events took place in East Germany, where a persistent economic slump and the ongoing oppressiveness of the regime of Erich Honecker led to a flight of refugees and mass demonstrations against the regime in the summer and fall of 1989. Capitulating to popular pressure, the Communist government opened its entire border with the West. The Berlin Wall, the most tangible symbol of the Cold War, became the site of a massive celebration, and most of it was dismantled by joyful Germans from both sides of the border. In March 1990, free elections led to the formation of a non-Communist government that rapidly carried out a program of political and economic reunification with West Germany (see Chapter 27).

The East Is Red: China Under Communism

In the fall of 1949, China was at peace for the first time in twelve years. The newly victorious Communist Party, under the leadership of its chairman, Mao Zedong, turned its attention to consolidating its power base and healing the wounds of war. Its long-term goal was to construct a socialist society, but its leaders realized that popular support for the revolution was based on the party's platform of honest government, land reform, social justice, and peace rather than on the utopian goal of a classless society. Accordingly, the new regime adopted a moderate program of political and economic recovery known as New Democracy.

New Democracy

With **New Democracy**—patterned roughly after Lenin's New Economic Policy in Soviet Russia in the 1920s (see Chapter 22)—the new Chinese leadership tacitly recognized that time and extensive indoctrination would be needed to convince the Chinese people of the superiority of socialism. In the meantime, the party would rely on capitalist profit incentives to spur productivity. Manufacturing and commercial firms were permitted to remain under private ownership, although with stringent government regulations. To win the support of the poorer peasants, who made up the majority of the population, a land redistribution program was adopted, but the collectivization of agriculture was postponed (see the box on p. 594).

In a number of key respects, New Democracy was a success. About two-thirds of the peasant households in the country received land and thus had reason to be grateful to the new regime. Spurred by official tolerance for capitalist activities and the end of internal conflict, the national economy began to rebound, although agricultural production still lagged behind both official targets and the growing population, which was increasing at an annual rate of more than 2 percent.

The Transition to Socialism

In 1953, party leaders launched the nation's first five-year plan (patterned after similar Soviet plans), which called for substantial increases in industrial output. Lenin had believed that mechanization would induce Russian peasants to join collective farms, which, because of their greater size and efficiency, could better afford to purchase expensive farm machinery. But the difficulty of providing tractors and reapers for millions of rural villages eventually convinced Mao that it would take years, if not decades, for China's infant industrial base to meet the needs of a modernizing agricultural sector. He therefore decided to begin collectivization immediately, in the hope that collective farms would increase food production and release land, labor, and capital for the industrial sector. Accordingly, beginning in 1955, virtually all private farmland was collectivized (although peasant families were allowed to retain small private plots), and most businesses and industries were nationalized.

Collectivization was achieved without provoking the massive peasant unrest that had taken place in the Soviet Union during the 1930s, but the hoped-for production increases did not materialize; in 1958, at Mao's insistent urging, party leaders approved a more radical program known as the **Great Leap Forward.** Existing rural collectives, normally the size of a traditional village, were combined into vast "people's communes," each containing more than thirty thousand people. These communes were to be responsible for all administrative and economic tasks at the local level. The party's official slogan promised "Hard work for a few years, happiness for a thousand."[3]

The communes were a disaster. Administrative bottlenecks, bad weather, and peasant resistance to the new system (which, among other things, attempted to eliminate work incentives and destroy the traditional family as the basic unit of Chinese society) combined to drive food production downward, and over the next few years, as many as fifteen million people may have died of starvation. In 1960, the experiment was essentially abandoned. Although the commune structure was retained, ownership and management were returned to the collective level. Mao was severely criticized by some of his more pragmatic colleagues.

The Great Proletarian Cultural Revolution

But Mao was not yet ready to abandon either his power or his dream of a totally egalitarian society. In 1966, he returned to the attack, mobilizing discontented youth and disgruntled party members into revolutionary units known as Red Guards, who were urged to take to the streets to cleanse Chinese society—from local schools and factories to government ministries in Beijing—of impure elements who (in Mao's mind, at least) were guilty of "taking the capitalist road." Supported by his wife, Jiang Qing, and other radical party figures, Mao launched China on a new forced march toward communism.

CONSOLIDATING POWER IN CHINA

POLITICS & GOVERNMENT

After the Communists came to power in China in 1949, Mao Zedong and his colleagues adopted a relatively moderate program designed to win the support of the Chinese people. Although major industries were to be placed under state ownership, the bulk of the manufacturing and commercial sector was to remain in private hands, while land would be confiscated from wealthy landlords and redistributed to the poor. In this excerpt from an article written in 1940, Mao predicted this policy.

Compare the New Democracy Program with the New Economic Policy of the Soviet Union, as described in Chapter 22.

Mao Zedong, "On New Democracy"

We must establish in China a republic that is politically new-democratic as well as economically new-democratic.

Big banks and big industrial and commercial enterprises shall be owned by this republic.

"Enterprises, whether Chinese-owned or foreign-owned, which are monopolistic in character or which are on too large a scale for private management, such as banks, railways and airlines shall be operated by the state so that private capital cannot dominate the livelihood of the people. This is the main principle of the control of capital."

This was also a solemn statement contained in the manifesto of the First National Congress of the Kuomintang during the period of the Kuomintang-Communist co-operation; this is the correct objective for the economic structure of the new-democratic republic. The state-operated enterprises of the new-democratic republic under the leadership of the proletariat are socialist in character and constitute the leading force in the national economy as a whole, but this republic does not take over other forms of capitalist private property, or forbid the development of capitalist production that "cannot dominate the livelihood of the people," for China's economy is still very backward.

This republic will adopt certain necessary measures to confiscate the land of landlords and distribute it to those peasants having no land or only a little land, carry out Din Sun Yat-sen's slogan of "land to the tillers," abolish the feudal relations in the rural areas, and turn the land into the private property of the peasants. In the rural areas, rich peasant economic activities will be tolerated. This is the line of "equalisation of land ownership." The correct slogan for this line is "land to the tillers." In this stage, socialist agriculture is in general not yet to be established though the various types of co-operative enterprises developed on the basis of "land to the tillers" will contain elements of socialism.

China's economy must develop along the path of "control of capital" and "equalisation of land ownership," and must never be "monopolist by a few"; we must never let the few capitalists and landlords "dominate the livelihood of the people"; we must never establish a capitalist society of the European-American type, nor allow the old semi-feudal society to remain. Whoever dares to run counter to this line will certainly fail to attain his aim, and will be knocked on the head.

Such are the internal economic relations which a revolutionary China, an anti-Japanese China, must and will necessarily establish.

Such an economy is new-democratic economy.

And new-democratic politics is the concentrated expression of such new-democratic economy.

ThomsonNOW™ To read more writings of Chairman Mao, enter the *ThomsonNOW* documents area using the access card that is available for *The Essential World History*.

The so-called **Great Proletarian Cultural Revolution** lasted for ten years, from 1966 to 1976. Some Western observers interpreted it as a simple power struggle between Mao Zedong and some of his key rivals such as Liu Shaoqi (Liu Shao-ch'i), Mao's designated successor, and Deng Xiaoping (Teng Hsiao-p'ing), the party's general secretary. Both were removed from their positions, and Liu later died, allegedly of torture, in a Chinese prison. But real policy disagreements were involved. Mao and his supporters feared that capitalist values and the remnants of "feudalist" Confucian ideas would undermine ideological fervor and betray the revolutionary cause. He was convinced that only an atmosphere of **"uninterrupted revolution"** could enable the Chinese to overcome the lethargy of the past and achieve the final stage of utopian communism.

Mao's opponents argued for a more pragmatic strategy that gave priority to nation building over the ultimate Communist goal of spiritual transformation. (Deng Xiaoping reportedly once remarked, "Black cat, white cat, what does it matter so long as it catches the mice?"). But with Mao's supporters now in power, the party carried out vast economic and educational reforms that virtually eliminated any remaining profit incentives, established a new school system that emphasized "Mao Zedong thought," and stressed practical education at the elementary level at the expense of specialized training in science and the humanities in the universities. School learning was discouraged as a legacy of capitalism, and Mao's famous *Little Red Book* (officially, *Quotations of Chairman Mao Zedong*, a slim volume of Maoist aphorisms to encourage good behavior and revolutionary zeal) was hailed as the most important source of knowledge in all areas (see the illustration on p. 603).

The radicals' efforts to destroy all vestiges of traditional society were reminiscent of the Reign of Terror in

Punishing Chinese Enemies During the Cultural Revolution. The Cultural Revolution, which began in 1966, was a massive effort by Mao Zedong and his radical supporters to eliminate rival elements within the Chinese Communist party and the government. Accused of being "capitalist roaders," such individuals were subjected to public criticism and removed from their positions. Some were imprisoned or executed. Here Red Guards have seized two members of an alleged "black gang" of traitors.

revolutionary France, when the Jacobins sought to destroy organized religion and even created a new revolutionary calendar. Red Guards rampaged through the country, attempting to eradicate the "four olds" (old thought, old culture, old customs, and old habits). They destroyed temples and religious sculptures; they tore down street signs and replaced them with new ones carrying revolutionary names. At one point, the city of Shanghai even ordered that the significance of colors in stoplights be changed so that red (the revolutionary color) would indicate that traffic could move.

But a mood of revolutionary ferment and enthusiasm is difficult to sustain. Key groups, including bureaucrats, urban professionals, and many military officers, did not share Mao's belief in the benefits of "uninterrupted revolution" and constant turmoil. Inevitably, the sense of anarchy and uncertainty caused popular support for the movement to erode, and when the end came in 1976, the vast majority of the population may well have welcomed its demise.

From Mao to Deng

Mao Zedong died in September 1976 at the age of eighty-three. After a short but bitter succession struggle, the pragmatists led by Deng Xiaoping (1904–1997) seized power from the radicals and formally brought the Cultural Revolution to an end. The egalitarian policies of the previous decade were reversed, and a new program emphasizing economic modernization was introduced.

Under the leadership of Deng Xiaoping, who placed his supporters in key positions throughout the party and the government, attention focused on what were called the **"Four Modernizations"**: industry, agriculture, technology, and national defense. Many of the restrictions against private activities and profit incentives were eliminated, and people were encouraged to work hard to benefit themselves and Chinese society. The familiar slogan "Serve the people" was replaced by a new one repugnant to the tenets of Mao Zedong thought: "Create wealth for the people."

By adopting this pragmatic approach in the years after 1976, China made great strides in ending its chronic problems of poverty and underdevelopment. Per capita income roughly doubled during the 1980s; housing, education, and sanitation improved; and both agricultural and industrial output skyrocketed.

But critics, both Chinese and foreign, complained that Deng Xiaoping's program had failed to achieve a "fifth modernization": democracy. In the late 1970s, ordinary citizens pasted "big character posters" criticizing the abuses of the past on the so-called Democracy Wall near Tiananmen Square in downtown Beijing. But it soon became clear that the new leaders would not tolerate any direct criticism of the Communist Party or of Marxist-Leninist ideology. Dissidents were suppressed, and some were sentenced to long prison terms.

Incident at Tiananmen Square

As long as economic conditions for the majority of Chinese were improving, the government was able to isolate dissidents from other elements in society. But in the late 1980s, an overheated economy led to rising inflation and growing discontent among salaried workers, especially in the cities. At the same time, corruption,

POLITICS & GOVERNMENT

COMPARATIVE ILLUSTRATION

Student Rebellions in France and China.   University students played an important role in revolutionary upheavals in the late 1960s in France and in the late 1980s in Eastern Europe and China. The discontent of university students in France exploded in the late 1960s in a series of student revolts. At the left is a scene from a student revolt in 1968. The photograph shows students hurling projectiles against riot police on a Parisian street. The demonstrations that erupted in Tiananmen Square in the spring of 1989 spread rapidly to other parts of China. Seen at the right is a group of students from a high school who are marching to the city of Guilin to display their determination to take part in the reform of Chinese society.

nepotism, and favored treatment for senior officials and party members were provoking increasing criticism. In May 1989, student protesters carried placards demanding "Science and Democracy," an end to official corruption, and the resignation of China's aging party leadership (see the comparative illustration on p. 523). These demands received widespread support from the urban population (although notably less in rural areas) and led to massive demonstrations in Tiananmen Square.

Deng Xiaoping and other aging party leaders turned to the army to protect their base of power and suppress what they described as "counterrevolutionary elements." Deng was undoubtedly counting on the fact that many Chinese, particularly in rural areas, feared a recurrence of the disorder of the Cultural Revolution and craved economic prosperity more than political reform. In the months after troops and tanks rolled into Tiananmen Square to crush the demonstrations, the government issued new regulations requiring courses on Marxist-Leninist ideology in the schools, suppressed dissidents within the intellectual community, and made it clear that while economic reforms would continue, the CCP's monopoly of power would not be allowed to decay. Harsh punishments were imposed on those accused of undermining the Communist system and supporting its enemies abroad.

From Marx to Confucius?

In the 1990s, the government began to nurture urban support by reducing the rate of inflation and guaranteeing the availability of consumer goods in great demand

among the rising middle class. Under Deng Xiaoping's successor, Jiang Zemin (b. 1926), who occupied the positions of both party chief and president of China, the government promoted rapid economic growth while cracking down harshly on political dissent. That policy paid dividends in bringing about a perceptible decline in alienation among the urban populations. Industrial production continued to increase rapidly, leading to predictions that China would become one of the economic superpowers of the twenty-first century. But discontent in rural areas began to increase, as lagging farm income, high taxes, and official corruption sparked resentment in the countryside.

Partly out of fear that such developments could undermine the socialist system and the rule of the CCP, conservative leaders attempted to curb Western influence and restore faith in Marxism-Leninism. In what may be a tacit recognition that Marxist exhortations were no longer an effective means of enforcing social discipline, the party turned to Confucianism as an antidote. Ceremonies celebrating the birth of Confucius now received official sanction, and the virtues promoted by the master, such as righteousness, propriety, and filial piety, were widely cited as an antidote to the tide of antisocial behavior. An article in the official newspaper *People's Daily* asserted that the spiritual crisis in contemporary Western culture stemmed from the incompatibility between science and the Christian religion. The solution, the author maintained, was Confucianism, "a nonreligious humanism that can provide the basis for morals and the value of life." Because a culture combining science and Confucianism was taking

MAP 26.3 **The People's Republic of China.** This map shows China's current boundaries. Major regions are indicated in capital letters. ❷ In which regions are there movements against Chinese rule?

shape in East Asia, he asserted, "it will thrive particularly well in the next century and will replace modern and contemporary Western culture."[4]

In the world arena, China now relies on the spirit of nationalism to achieve its goals, conducting an independent foreign policy and playing an increasingly active role in the region. To some of its neighbors, including Japan, India, and Russia, China's new posture is cause for disquiet and gives rise to suspicions that it is once again preparing to flex its muscle as in the imperial era. The first example of this new attitude took place as early as 1979, when Chinese forces briefly invaded Vietnam as punishment for the Vietnamese occupation of neighboring Cambodia. In the 1990s, China aroused concern in the region by claiming sole ownership over the Spratly Islands in the South China Sea and over Diaoyu Island (also claimed by Japan) near Taiwan (see Map 26.3).

To Chinese leaders, however, such actions simply represent legitimate efforts to resume China's rightful role in the affairs of the region. After a century of humiliation at the hands of the Western powers and neighboring Japan, the nation, in Mao's famous words of 1949, "has stood up" and no one will be permitted to humiliate it again. For the moment, at least, a fervent patriotism seems to be on the rise in China, actively promoted by the party as a means of holding the country together. Pride in the achievement of national sports teams is intense, and two young authors recently achieved wide acclaim with the publication of their book *The China That Can Say No,* a response to criticism of the country in the United States and Europe. The decision by the International Olympic Committee to award the 2008 Summer Games to Beijing led to widespread celebration throughout the country.

Pumping up the spirit of patriotism is not a solution to all problems, however. Unrest is growing among China's national minorities: in Xinjiang, where restless Muslim peoples are observing with curiosity the emergence of independent Islamic states in Central Asia, and in Tibet, where the official policy of quelling separation has led to the violent suppression of Tibetan culture and an influx of thousands of ethnic Chinese immigrants. In the meantime, the Falun Gong religious movement, which the government has attempted to suppress as a potentially serious threat to its authority, is an additional indication that with the disintegration of the old Maoist utopia, the Chinese people will need more than a pallid version of Marxism-Leninism or a revived Confucianism to fill the gap.

Whether the current leadership will be able to prevent further erosion of the party's power and prestige is unclear. In the short term, efforts to slow the process of change may succeed because many Chinese are understandably fearful of punishment and concerned for their careers. And high economic growth rates can sometimes obscure a multitude of problems as many individuals will opt to chase the fruits of materialism rather than the less tangible benefits of personal freedom. But in the long run, the party leadership must resolve the contradiction between political authoritarianism and economic prosperity. One is reminded of Chiang Kai-shek's failed attempt during the 1930s to revive Confucian ethics as a standard of behavior for modern China: dead ideologies cannot be revived by decree.

New leaders installed in 2002 and 2003 appear to recognize the challenge. Hu Jintao (b. 1943), who replaced Jiang Zemin as CCP general secretary and head of state, appears to recognize the need for further reforms to open up Chinese society and bridge the yawning gap between rich and poor. In recent years, the government has shown a growing tolerance for the public exchange of ideas, which has surfaced with the proliferation of bookstores, avant-garde theater, experimental art exhibits, and the Internet (although the government still attempts to limit access to certain websites). In 2005, an estimated 27 percent of all Chinese citizens possessed a cell phone.

"Serve the People": Chinese Society Under Communism

When the Communist Party came to power in 1949, Chinese leaders made it clear that their policies would differ from the Soviet model in one key respect. Whereas the Bolsheviks had distrusted nonrevolutionary elements in Russia and relied almost exclusively on the use of force to achieve their objectives, the CCP sought to win support from the mass of the population by carrying out reforms that could win popular support. This "mass line" policy, as it was known, worked fairly well until the late 1950s, when Mao and his radical allies adopted policies such as the Great Leap Forward that began to alienate much of the population. Ideological purity was valued over expertise in building an advanced and prosperous society.

Economics in Command

When he came to power in the late 1970s, Deng Xiaoping recognized the need to restore credibility to a system on the verge of breakdown and hoped that rapid economic growth would satisfy the Chinese people and prevent them from demanding political reforms. The post-Mao leaders clearly emphasized economic performance over ideological purity. To stimulate the stagnant industrial sector, which had been under state control since the end of the New Democracy era, they reduced bureaucratic controls over state industries and allowed local managers to have more say over prices, salaries, and quality control. Productivity was encouraged by permitting bonuses for extra effort, a policy that had been discouraged during the Cultural Revolution. The regime also tolerated the emergence of a small private sector. Unemployed youth were encouraged to set up restaurants, bicycle or radio repair shops, and handicraft shops on their own initiative.

Finally, the regime opened up the country to foreign investment and technology. Special economic zones were established in urban centers near the coast (ironically, many were located in the old nineteenth-century treaty ports), where lucrative concessions were offered to encourage foreign firms to build factories. The tourist industry was encouraged, and students were sent abroad to study.

The new leaders especially stressed educational reform. The system adopted during the Cultural Revolution, emphasizing practical education and ideology at the expense of higher education and modern science, was rapidly abandoned (the *Little Red Book* was even withdrawn from circulation and could no longer be found on bookshelves), and a new system based generally on the Western model was instituted. Admission to higher education was based on success in merit examinations, and courses on science and mathematics received high priority.

Agricultural Reform No economic reform program could succeed unless it included the countryside. Three decades of socialism had done little to increase food production or to lay the basis for a modern agricultural sector. China, with a population now numbering one billion, could still barely feed itself. Peasants had little incentive to work and few opportunities to increase production through mechanization, the use of fertilizer, or better irrigation.

Under Deng Xiaoping, agricultural policy made a rapid about-face. Under the new **rural responsibility system,** adopted shortly after Deng had consolidated his authority, collectives leased land to peasant families, who paid a quota in the form of rent to the collective. Anything produced on the land above that payment could be sold on the private market or consumed. To soak up excess labor in the villages, the government encouraged the formation of so-called sideline industries, a modern equivalent of the traditional cottage industries in premodern China. Peasants raised fish or shrimp, made consumer goods, and even assembled living room furniture and appliances for sale to their newly affluent compatriots.

The reform program had a striking effect on rural production. Grain production increased rapidly, and farm income doubled during the 1980s. Yet it also created problems. In the first place, income at the village level became more unequal as some enterprising farmers (known locally as "ten-thousand-dollar households") earned profits several times those realized by their less fortunate or less industrious neighbors. When some farmers discovered that they could earn more by growing cash crops or other specialized commodities, they devoted less land to rice and other grain crops, thus threatening to reduce the supply of China's most crucial staple. Finally, the agricultural policy threatened to undermine the government's population control program, which party leaders viewed as crucial to the success of the Four Modernizations.

Since a misguided period in the mid-1950s when Mao Zedong had argued that more labor would result in higher productivity, China had been attempting to limit its population growth. By 1970, the government had launched a stringent family planning program—including education, incentives, and penalties for noncompliance—to persuade the Chinese people to limit themselves to one child per family. The program has had some success, and population growth was reduced drastically in the early 1980s. The rural responsibility system, however, undermined the program because it encouraged farm families to pay the penalties for having additional children in the belief that their labor would increase family income and provide the parents with a form of social security for their old age. Today, China's population has surpassed 1.3 billion.

Evaluating the Four Modernizations Still, the overall effects of the modernization program were impressive. The standard of living improved for the majority of the population. Whereas a decade earlier, the average Chinese had struggled to earn enough to buy a bicycle, radio, watch, or washing machine, by the late 1980s, many were beginning to purchase videocassette recorders, refrigerators, and color television sets. Yet the rapid growth of the economy created its own problems: inflationary pressures, greed, envy, increased corruption, and—most dangerous of all for the regime—rising expectations. Young people in particular resented restrictions on employment (many young people in China are still required to accept the jobs that are offered to them by the government or school officials) and opportunities to study abroad. Disillusionment ran high, especially in the cities, where lavish living by officials and rising prices for goods aroused widespread alienation and cynicism.

During the 1990s, growth rates in the industrial sector continued to be high as domestic capital became increasingly available to compete with the growing presence of foreign enterprises. The government finally recognized the need to close down inefficient state enterprises, and by the end of the decade, the private sector, with official encouragement, accounted for over 10 percent of the gross domestic product. A stock market opened, and China's prowess in the international marketplace improved dramatically.

But as Chinese leaders now discovered, rapid economic change never comes without cost. The closing of state-run factories has led to the dismissal of millions of workers each year, and the private sector, although growing at over 20 percent annually, is unable to absorb them all. Discontent has been growing in the countryside as well, where a grain surplus has cut into farm incomes (the government tried to increase the official purchase price for grain but rescinded the order when it became too expensive). China's recent entrance into the

Nanjing Road: A Consumer's Paradise. Shanghai has become China's most affluent city, its forest of shimmering skyscrapers testifying to the phenomenal expansion of the Chinese economy in recent years. Nanjing Road, seen here, is one long avenue of towering banks, office buildings, hotels, and luxurious department stores. Along with these competing Chinese commercial signs, the ubiquitous American enterprises, such as KFC, Pepsi-Cola, and McDonald's, vie for the attention of the fashionably dressed Shanghainese as they shop for the latest styles.

World Trade Organization may help the national economy as a whole, but is less likely to benefit farmers, who now face the challenge of cheap foreign food imports. Millions of rural Chinese have left for the big cities, where many of them are unable to find steady employment and are forced to live in squalid conditions in crowded tenements or in the sprawling suburbs. Millions of others remain on the farm but attempt to maximize their income by producing for the market or by increasing the size of their families.

Another factor hindering China's economic advance is the impact on the environment. With the rising population, fertile land is in increasingly short supply (China, with twice the population, now has only two-thirds as much irrigable land as it had in 1950). Soil erosion is a major problem, especially in the north, where the desert is encroaching on farmlands. Water is also a problem. A massive dam project now under way in the Yangtze River valley has sparked protests from environmentalists, as well as from local peoples forced to migrate from the area. The rate of air pollution is ten times the level in the United States, contributing to growing health concerns. Chinese leaders now face the uncomfortable reality that the pains of industrialization are not exclusive to capitalist countries.

Social Problems

At the root of Marxist-Leninist ideology is the idea of building a new citizen free from the prejudices, ignorance, and superstition of the "feudal" era and the capitalist desire for self-gratification. This new citizen would be characterized not only by a sense of racial and sexual equality but also by the selfless desire to contribute his or her utmost for the good of all.

Women and the Family From the very start, the Chinese Communist government intended to bring an end to the Confucian legacy in modern China. Women were given the vote and encouraged to become active in the political process. At the local level, an increasing number of women became active in the CCP and in collective organizations. In 1950, a new marriage law guaranteed women equal rights with men (see the box on p. 601). Most important, perhaps, it permitted women for the first time to initiate divorce proceedings against their husbands. Within a year, nearly one million divorces had been granted.

The regime also undertook to destroy the influence of the traditional family system. To the Communists, loyalty to the family, a crucial element in the Confucian social order, undercut loyalty to the state and to the dictatorship of the proletariat.

At first, however, the new government moved carefully to avoid alienating its supporters in the countryside unnecessarily. When collective farms were established in the mid-1950s, payment for hours worked in the form of ration coupons was made not to the individual but to the family head, thus maintaining the traditionally dominant position of the patriarch. When people's communes were established in the late 1950s, payments went to the individual.

During the political radicalism of the Great Leap Forward, children were encouraged to report to the authorities any comments by their parents that criticized the system. Such practices continued during the Cultural Revolution, when children were expected to tell on their parents, students on their teachers, and employees on their superiors. Some have suggested that Mao deliberately encouraged such practices to bring an end to the traditional "politics of dependency." According to this theory, historically the famous "five relationships" forced individuals to swallow their anger and frustration and accept the hierarchical norms established by Confucian ethics (known in Chinese as "to eat bitterness"). By encouraging the oppressed elements in society—the young, the female, and the poor—to voice their bitterness, Mao was hoping to break the tradition of dependency. Such denunciations had been issued against landlords and other "local tyrants" in the land reform tribunals of the late 1940s and early 1950s. Later, during the Cultural Revolution, they were applied to other authority figures in Chinese society.

Lifestyle Changes The post-Mao era brought a decisive shift away from revolutionary utopianism and back toward the pragmatic approach to nation building. For most people, it meant improved living conditions and a qualified return to family traditions. For the first time, millions of Chinese saw the prospect of a house or an urban apartment with a washing machine, television set, and indoor plumbing. Young people whose parents had given them patriotic names such as Build the Country, Protect Mao Zedong, and Assist Korea began to choose more elegant and cosmopolitan names for their own children. Some names, such as Surplus Grain or Bring a Younger Brother, expressed hope for the future.

The new attitudes were also reflected in physical appearance. For a generation after the civil war, clothing had been restricted to the traditional baggy "Mao suit" in olive drab or dark blue, but by the 1980s, young people craved such fashionable Western items as designer jeans, trendy sneakers, and sweat suits (or reasonable facsimiles). Cosmetic surgery to create a more buxom figure or a more Western facial look became increasingly common among affluent young women in the cities. Many had the epicanthic fold over their eyelids removed or their noses enlarged—a curious decision in view of the tradition of referring derogatorily to foreigners as "big noses."

Religious practices and beliefs also changed. As the government became more tolerant, some Chinese began returning to the traditional Buddhist faith or to folk religions, and Buddhist and Taoist temples were once again crowded with worshipers. Despite official efforts to suppress its more evangelical forms, Christianity became increasingly popular; like the "rice Christians" (persons who supposedly converted for economic reasons)

VIEWS ON MARRIAGE

FAMILY & SOCIETY

One of the major goals of the Communist government in China was to reform the tradition of marriage and place it on a new egalitarian basis. In the following excerpt, a writer with the magazine China Youth Daily describes the ideal marriage and explains how socialist marriage differs from its capitalist counterpart.

How, according to this document, will socialist marriage differ from its capitalist counterpart? What changes will take place from traditional Chinese practices?

The Correct Viewpoint Toward Marriage

Now then, what is our viewpoint? Is it different from that of the exploiting bourgeois class?

For one thing, our basic concept on marriage is and must be that we build our happiness upon the premise that happiness should be shared by all. We advocate equal rights for man and woman, equal rights for husband and wife. We oppose the idea that man is superior to woman or that the husband has special prerogatives over his wife. We also oppose any discrimination against or ill treatment of the wife.

We believe that marriage should be based solely upon mutual consent. We oppose the so-called arranged marriage, or the use of any deceitful or compulsory method by one of the parties in this matter. We uphold the system of monogamy. Husband and wife ought to have true and exclusive love toward each other, and concubinage is not permitted.

We believe that the very basic foundations for love between man and woman are common political understanding, comradeship in work, mutual help, and mutual respect. Money, position, or the so-called prettiness should not be taken into consideration for a right marriage, because they are not reliable foundations for love.

We also believe that solemnity and fidelity are important elements for a correct relationship between husband and wife, and for a happy family life. To abandon one's partner by any improper means is to be opposed. In our society,

those who intend to pursue their happiness at the expense of others run contradictory to the moral principle of Communism and will never be happy.

For the exploiting class, the concept about marriage is just the opposite. The landlord class believes in pursuing happiness by making other people suffer. They subscribe to such biased viewpoints as "man is superior to woman," "man is more important than woman," "man should dominate woman," etc. Under this type of ideology, women are merely slaves and properties of men and marriage is nothing but a process of buying and selling with compulsion. In the bourgeois society the whole matrimonial relationship is built upon money, and becomes simply a "monetary relationship." In economic relationships women belong to men. Love is nothing but a merchandise; women trade their flesh for men's money. This concept about marriage is indeed reactionary and it shall meet with our firm opposition.

Among our young worker comrades there are still a few whose thinking is still under the influence of the exploiting class. They cannot do away with the thinking that man is superior to woman; they look down upon their own wives, especially those who have lower education and those who come from rural areas. When they look for lovers, what concerns the man most is whether the woman is pretty or not; what concerns the woman most is whether the man is earning high wages and has a high position. They disregard all the other elements for a good match.

Some of them even use deception to steal love or to force the other party to marry them. Their attitude toward love and marriage is most revolting. They love the new ones and forsake the old, get themselves involved in multi-angle romance, or even seek excuses as grounds for divorce. All this sort of thinking and behavior are certainly contradictory to the moral quality of the working class and Communism, and contradictory to the socialist concept and system of marriage. Therefore those who have formed such a wrong concept about marriage ought to adopt a correct one in accordance with the moral principle of Communism. Only then will there be possibility for true love and happy family life.

---

of the past, many viewed it as a symbol of success and cosmopolitanism.

As with all social changes, China's reintegration into the outside world has had a price. Arranged marriages, nepotism, and mistreatment of females (for example, under the one-child rule, parents reportedly killed female infants to regain the possibility of having a son) have come back, although such behavior likely survived under the cloak of revolutionary purity for a generation. Materialistic attitudes are prevalent among young people, along with a corresponding cynicism about politics and

the CCP (see the comparative essay "Family and Society in an Era of Change" on p. 602). Expensive weddings are now increasingly common, and bribery and favoritism are all too frequent. Crime of all types, including an apparently growing incidence of prostitution and sex crimes against women, appears to be on the rise. To discourage sexual abuse, the government now seeks to provide free legal services for women living in rural areas.

There is also a price to pay for the trend toward privatization. Under the Maoist system, the elderly and the sick were provided with retirement benefits and health

FAMILY AND SOCIETY IN AN ERA OF CHANGE

It is one of the paradoxes of the modern world that at a time of political stability and economic prosperity for many people in the advanced capitalist societies, public cynicism about the system is increasingly widespread. Alienation and drug use are at dangerously high levels, and the rate of criminal activities in most areas remains much higher than in the immediate postwar era.

Although the reasons advanced to explain this paradox vary widely, many observers place the responsibility for many contemporary social problems on the decline of the traditional family system. There has been a steady rise in the percentage of illegitimate births and single-parent families in countries throughout the Western world. In the United States, approximately half of all marriages end in divorce. Even in two-parent families, more and more parents work full time, leaving the children to fend for themselves on their return from school. In many countries in Europe, the birthrate has dropped to alarming levels, leading to a severe labor shortage that is attracting a rising number of immigrants from other parts of the world.

Observers point to several factors as an explanation for these conditions: the growing emphasis in advanced capitalist states on an individualistic lifestyle devoted to instant gratification, a phenomenon promoted vigorously by the advertising media; the rise of the feminist movement, which has freed women from the servitude imposed on their predecessors, but at the expense of removing them from full-time responsibility for the care of the next generation; and the increasing mobility of contemporary life, which disrupts traditional family ties and creates a sense of rootlessness and impersonality in the individual's relationship to the surrounding environment.

This phenomenon is not unique to Western civilization. The traditional nuclear family is also under attack in many societies around the world. Even in East Asia, where the Confucian tradition of family solidarity has been endlessly touted as a major factor in the region's economic success, the incidence of divorce and illegitimate births is on the rise, as is the percentage of women in the workforce. Older citizens frequently complain that the Asian youth of today

are too materialistic, faddish, and steeped in the individualistic values of the West. Such criticisms are now voiced in mainland China as well as in the capitalist societies around its perimeter (see Chapter 29).

In societies less exposed to the individualist lifestyle portrayed so prominently in Western culture, traditional attitudes about the family continue to hold sway. In the Middle East, governmental and religious figures seek to prevent the Western media from undermining accepted mores. Success is sometimes elusive, however, as the situation in Iran demonstrates. Despite the zealous guardians of Islamic morality, many young Iranians are clamoring for the individual freedoms that have been denied to them since the Islamic revolution took place over two decades ago (see Chapter 28).

Courtesy of William J. Duiker

China's "Little Emperors." Chinese leaders have launched a massive family planning program to curtail population growth. Urban families are restricted to a single child. In conformity with tradition, sons are especially prized, and some Chinese complain that many parents overindulge their children, turning them into spoiled "little emperors."

care by the state or by the collective organizations. Under current conditions, with the latter no longer playing such a social role and more workers operating in the private sector, the safety net has been removed. The government recently attempted to fill the gap by enacting a social security law, but because of lack of funds, eligibility is limited primarily to individuals in the urban sector of the economy. Those living in the countryside—who still represent 60 percent of the population—are essentially left to their own devices.

China's Changing Culture

The rise to power of the Communists in 1949 added a new dimension to the debate over the future of culture in China. The new leaders rejected the Western attitude of "art for art's sake" and, like their Soviet counterparts, viewed culture as an important instrument of indoctrination. The standard would no longer be aesthetic quality or the personal preference of the artist but "art for life's sake," whereby culture would serve the interests of socialism.

Hail the Great Helmsman! During the Great Proletarian Cultural Revolution, Chinese art was restricted to topics that promoted revolution and the thoughts of Chairman Mao Zedong. All the knowledge that the true revolutionary required was to be found in Mao's *Little Red Book,* a collection of his sayings on proper revolutionary behavior. In this painting, Chairman Mao stands among his admirers, who wave copies of the book as a symbol of their total devotion to him and his vision of a future China.

At first, the new emphasis on socialist realism did not entirely extinguish the influence of traditional culture. Mao and his colleagues tolerated—and even encouraged—efforts by artists to synthesize traditional ideas with socialist concepts and Western techniques. During the Cultural Revolution, however, all forms of traditional culture came to be viewed as reactionary. Socialist realism became the only acceptable standard in literature, art, and music. All forms of traditional expression were forbidden.

Nowhere were the dilemmas of the new order more challenging than in literature. In the heady afterglow of the Communist victory, many progressive writers supported the new regime and enthusiastically embraced Mao's exhortation to create a new Chinese literature for the edification of the masses. But in the harsher climate of the 1960s, many writers were criticized by the party for their excessive individualism and admiration for Western culture. Such writers either toed the new line and suppressed their doubts or were jailed and silenced, as was Ding Ling, the most prominent woman writer in China during the twentieth century. Born in 1904, she joined the Chinese Communist Party during the early 1930s and settled in Yan'an, where she authored her most famous novel, *The Sun Shines over the Sangan River,* which praised the land reform program. After the Communist victory in 1949, however, she was criticized for her individualism and outspoken views. During the Cultural Revolution, she was sentenced to hard labor. She died in 1981.

After Mao's death, Chinese culture was finally released from the shackles of socialist realism. In painting, where for a decade the only acceptable standard for excellence was praise for the party and its policies, the new permissiveness led to a revival of interest in both traditional and Western forms. Although some painters continued to blend Eastern and Western styles, others imitated trends from abroad, experimenting with a wide range of previously prohibited art styles, including Cubism and abstract painting.

In the late 1980s, two avant-garde art exhibits shocked the Chinese public and provoked the wrath of the party. An exhibition of nude paintings, the first ever held in China, attracted many viewers but reportedly offended the modesty of many Chinese. The second was an exhibit presenting the works of various schools of Modern and Postmodern art. The event resulted in considerable commentary and some expressions of public hostility. After a Communist critic lambasted the works as promiscuous and ideologically reactionary, the government declared that henceforth it would regulate all art exhibits.

The limits of freedom of expression were most apparent in literature. During the early 1980s, party leaders encouraged Chinese writers to express their views on the mistakes of the past, and a new "literature of the wounded" began to describe the brutal and arbitrary character of the Cultural Revolution. One of the most prominent writers was Bai Hua, whose script for the film *Bitter Love* described the life of a young Chinese painter who joined the revolutionary movement during the 1940s but was destroyed during the Cultural Revolution when his work was condemned as counterrevolutionary. The film depicts the condemnation through a view of a street in Beijing "full of people waving the *Quotations of Chairman Mao,* all those devout and artless faces fired by a feverish fanaticism." Driven from his home for posting a portrait of a third-century B.C.E. defender of human freedom on a Beijing wall, the artist flees the city. At the end of the film, he dies in a snowy field, where his corpse and a semicircle made by his footprints form a giant question mark.

In criticizing the excesses of the Cultural Revolution, Bai Hua was only responding to Deng Xiaoping's appeal for intellectuals to speak out, but he was soon criticized for failing to point out the essentially beneficial role of the CCP in recent Chinese history, and his film was withdrawn from circulation in 1981. Bai Hua was compelled to recant his errors and to state that the great ideas of Mao Zedong on art and literature were "still of universal guiding significance today."[5]

As the attack on Bai Hua illustrates, many party leaders remained suspicious of the impact that "decadent" bourgeois culture could have on the socialist foundations of Chinese society, and the official press periodically warned that China should adopt only the "positive" aspects of Western culture (notably, its technology and its work ethic) and not the "negative" elements such as drug use, pornography, and hedonism. Conservatives were especially incensed by the tendency of many writers to dwell on the shortcomings of the socialist system and to come uncomfortably close to direct criticism of the role of the CCP. One such example is the author Mo Yan (b. 1956), whose novels *The Garlic Ballads* (1988) and *The Republic of Wine* (2000) expose the rampant corruption of contemporary Chinese society, the roots of which he attributes to one-party rule.

Another author whose writings fell under the harsh glare of official disapproval is Zhang Xinxin (b. 1953). Her controversial novellas and short stories, which explored Chinese women's alienation and spiritual malaise, were viewed by many as a negative portrayal of contemporary society, provoking the government in 1984 to prohibit her from publishing for a year. Determined and resourceful, Zhang turned to reporting. With a colleague, she interviewed one hundred "ordinary" people to record their views on all aspects of everyday life.

One of the chief targets of China's recent "spiritual civilization" campaign is author Wang Shuo (b. 1958), whose writings have been banned for exhibiting a sense of "moral decay." In his novels *Playing for Thrills* (1989) and *Please Don't Call Me Human* (2000), Wang highlighted the seamier side of contemporary urban society, peopled with hustlers, ex-convicts, and other assorted hooligans. Spiritually depleted, hedonistic, and amoral in their approach to life, his characters represent the polar opposite of the socialist ideal.

CONCLUSION

𝐅OR FOUR DECADES after the end of World War II, the world's two superpowers competed for global hegemony. The Cold War became the dominant feature on the international scene and determined the internal politics of many countries around the world as well.

By the early 1980s, some of the tension had gone out of the conflict as it appeared that both Moscow and Washington had learned to tolerate the other's existence. Skeptical minds even suspected that both countries drew benefits from their mutual rivalry and saw it as an advantage in carrying on their relations with friends and allies. Few suspected that the Cold War, which had long seemed a permanent feature of world politics, was about to come to an end.

What brought about the collapse of the Soviet Empire? Some observers argue that the ambitious defense policies adopted by the Reagan administration forced Moscow into an arms race it could not afford, which ultimately led to a collapse of the Soviet economy. Others suggest that Soviet problems were more deep-rooted and would have ended in the disintegration of the Soviet Union even without outside stimulation. Both arguments have some validity, but the latter is surely closer to the mark. For years, if not decades, leaders in the Kremlin had disguised or ignored the massive inefficiencies of the Soviet system. In the 1980s, the perceptive Mikhail Gorbachev tried to save the system by instituting radical reforms. By then, however, it was too late.

Why has communism survived in China, albeit in a substantially altered form, when it failed in Eastern Europe and the Soviet Union? One of the primary factors is probably cultural. Although the doctrine of Marxism-Leninism originated in Europe, many of its main precepts, such as the primacy of the community over the individual and the denial of the concept of private property, run counter to trends in Western civilization. This inherent conflict is especially evident in the societies of central Europe, which were strongly influenced by Enlightenment philosophy and the Industrial Revolution. These forces were weaker in the countries farther to the east, but both had begun to penetrate tsarist Russia by the end of the nineteenth century.

By contrast, Marxism-Leninism found a more receptive climate in China and other countries in the region influenced by Confucian tradition. In its political culture, the Communist system exhibits many of the same characteristics as traditional Confucianism—a single truth, an elite governing class, and an emphasis on obedience to the community and its governing representatives—while feudal attitudes regarding female inferiority, loyalty to the family, and bureaucratic arrogance are hard to break. On the surface, China today bears a number of uncanny similarities to the China of the past.

Yet these similarities should not blind us to the real changes that are taking place in Chinese society today. Although the youthful protesters in Tiananmen Square were comparable in some respects to the reformist elements of the early republic, the China of today is fundamentally different from that of the early twentieth century. Literacy rates and the standard of living are far higher, the pressures of outside powers are less threatening, and China has entered its own industrial and technological revolution. For many Chinese, independent talk radio and the Internet are a greater source of news and views than are the official media. Where Sun Yat-sen, Chiang Kai-shek, and even Mao Zedong broke their lances on the rocks of centuries of tradition, poverty, and ignorance, China's present leaders rule a country much more aware of the world and its place in it.

TIMELINE

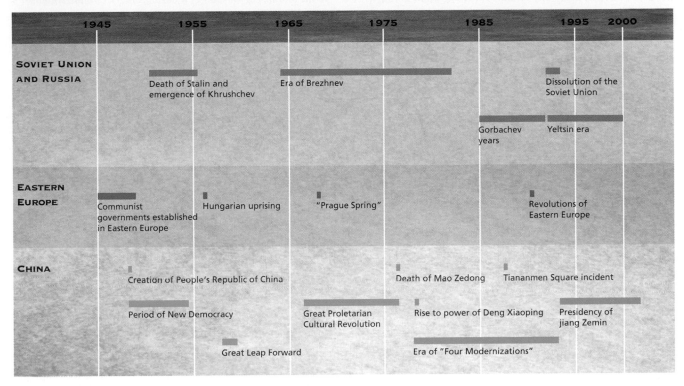

CHAPTER NOTES

1. Quoted in V. Zubok and C. Pleshakov, *Inside the Kremlin's Cold War: From Stalin to Khrushchev* (Cambridge, Mass., 1996), p. 166.
2. Quoted in H. Smith, *The New Russians* (New York, 1990), p. 74.
3. Quoted in S. Karnow, *Mao and China: Inside China's Cultural Revolution* (New York, 1972), p. 95.
4. Quoted in F. Ching, "Confucius, the New Saviour," *Far Eastern Economic Review*, November 10, 1994, p. 37.
5. Quoted in J. Spence, *Chinese Roundabout: Essays in History and Culture* (New York, 1992), p. 285.

SUGGESTED READING

For a general view of modern Russia, see **M. Malia,** *Russia Under Western Eyes* (Cambridge, Mass., 1999). On the Khrushchev years, see **E. Crankshaw,** *Khrushchev: A Career* (New York, 1966). For the final years of the Soviet era, see **S. F. Cohen,** *Rethinking the Soviet Experience* (New York, 1985); **R. J. Hill,** *The Soviet Union: Politics, Economics, and Society,* 2d ed. (London, 1989); **M. Lewin,** *The Gorbachev Phenomenon* (Berkeley, Calif., 1988); **G. Hosking,** *The Awakening of the Soviet Union* (London, 1990); and **S. White,** *Gorbachev and After* (Cambridge, 1991). For an inquiry into the reasons for the Soviet collapse, see **R. Conquest,** *Reflections on a Ravaged Century* (New York, 1999), and **R. Strayer,** *Why Did the Soviet Union Collapse? Understanding Historical Change* (New York, 1998).

For a general study of the Soviet satellites in Eastern Europe, see **S. Fischer-Galati,** *Eastern Europe in the 1980s* (London, 1981). The unique path of Yugoslavia is examined in **L. J. Cohen** and **P. Warwick,** *Political Cohesion in a Fragile Mosaic: The Yugoslav Experience* (Boulder, Colo., 1983). On East Germany, see **C. B. Scharf,** *Politics and Change in East Germany* (Boulder, Colo., 1984). Additional studies on the recent history of these countries include **T. G. Ash,** *The Polish Revolution: Solidarity* (New York, 1984); **B. Kovrig,** *Communism in Hungary from Kun to Kádár* (Stanford, Calif., 1979); **T. G. Ash,** *The Magic Lantern: The Revolution of '89 Witnessed in Warsaw, Budapest, Berlin, and Prague* (New York, 1990); **M. Shafir,** *Romania: Politics, Economics and Society* (London, 1985); **E. Biberaj,** *Albania: A Socialist Maverick* (Boulder, Colo., 1990); and **S. Ramet,** *Nationalism and Federalism in Yugoslavia* (Bloomington, Ind., 1992).

A number of useful surveys deal with China after World War II. The most comprehensive treatment of the Communist period is **M. Meisner,** *Mao's China and After: A History of the People's Republic* (New York, 1986). For documents, see **M. Selden, ed,** *The People's Republic of China: A Documentary History of Revolutionary Change* (New York, 1978). On Mao Zedong, see **Li Zhisui's** highly critical *The Private Life of Chairman Mao,* trans. Tai Hung-chao (New York, 1994). Also see **R. Evans,** *Deng Xiaoping and the Making of Modern China* (London, 1993).

There are countless specialized studies on various aspects of the Communist period in China. The Cultural Revolution is treated dramatically in **S. Karnow,** *Mao and China: Inside China's Cultural Revolution* (New York, 1972). For individual accounts of the impact of the revolution on people's lives, see the celebrated book by **Nien Cheng,** *Life and Death in Shanghai* (New York, 1986), and **Liang Heng** and **J. Shapiro,** *Son of the Revolution* (New York, 1984).

For the early post-Mao period, see **H. Harding,** *China's Second Revolution: Reform After Mao* (Washington, D.C., 1987), and **G. White,** *Riding the Tiger: The Politics of Economic Reform in Post-Mao China* (Stanford, Calif, 1993). Also see **O. Schell,** *Discos and Democracy: China in the Throes of Reform* (New York, 1988). Daily life is scrutinized in fascinating detail in **M. Dutton,** *Streetlife China* (Cambridge, 1998). Chinese politics is discussed in **R. MacFarquhar,** ed., *The Politics* of China: The Eras of Mao and Deng, 2d ed. (Cambridge, 1997), and **K. Lieberthal**, *Governing China: From Revolution Through Reform* (New York, 1995). The 1989 demonstrations and their aftermath are chronicled in **L. Feigon's** eyewitness account, *China Rising: The Meaning of Tiananmen* (Chicago, 1990), and **D. Morrison**, *Massacre in Beijing* (New York, 1989). For commentary by Chinese dissidents, see **Liu Binyan**, *China's Crisis, China's Hope* (Cambridge, 1990), and **Fang Lizhi**, *Bringing Down the Great Wall: Writings on Science, Culture, and Democracy in China* (New York, 1991). Documentary material relating to the events of 1989 are chronicled in **A. J. Nathan** and **P. Link**, eds., *The Tiananmen Papers* (New York, 2001). Subsequent events are analyzed in **J. Fewsmith**, *China Since Tiananmen: The Politics of Transition* (Cambridge, 2001).

For a comprehensive introduction to twentieth-century Chinese literature, consult **E. Widmer** and **D. Der-Wei Wang**, eds., *From May Fourth to June Fourth: Fiction and Film in Twentieth-Century China* (Cambridge, Mass., 1993), and **J. Lau** and **H. Goldblatt**, *The Columbia Anthology of Modern Chinese Literature* (New York, 1995). To witness daily life in the mid-1980s, see **Z. Xinxin** and **S. Ye**, *Chinese Lives: An Oral History of Contemporary China* (New York, 1987). An excellent survey of Chinese women writers is found in **M. S. Duke**, ed., *Modern Chinese Women Writers: Critical Appraisals* (Armonk, N.Y., 1989). See the interesting chapters on Ding Ling and her contemporaries in **J. Spence**, *The Gate of Heavenly Peace* (New York, 1981). For the most comprehensive analysis of twentieth-century Chinese art, consult **M. Sullivan**, *Arts and Artists of Twentieth-Century China* (Berkeley, Calif., 1996).

For a discussion of the women's movement in China during this period, see **J. Stacey**, *Patriarchy and Socialist Revolution in China* (Berkeley, Calif., 1983), and **M. Wolf**, *Revolution Postponed: Women in Contemporary China* (Stamford, Conn., 1985). Gender issues are treated in **B. Entwistle** and **G. E. Henderson**, eds., *Redrawing Boundaries: Work, Households, and Gender in China* (Berkeley, Calif., 2000). To follow the firsthand account of a

Chinese woman revolutionary, read **Y. Daiyun** and **C. Wakeman**, *To the Storm: The Odyssey of a Revolutionary Chinese Woman* (Berkeley, Calif., 1985).

InfoTrac College Edition

Visit this chapter's InfoTrac College Edition/Research activities at the *Essential World History* Companion Website for activities related to communism on trial.

ThomsonNOW™ for Duiker and Spielvogel's *The Essential World History, Third Edition*

Enter *ThomsonNOW* using the access card that is available with this text. *ThomsonNOW* will assist you in understanding the content in this chapter with lesson plans generated for your needs, as well as provide you with a connection to the *Wadsworth World History Resource Center* (see description below for details).

WORLD HISTORY
RESOURCE CENTER

Enter the Resource Center using either your *ThomsonNOW* access card or your standalone access card for the *Wadsworth World History Resource Center.* Organized by topic, this website includes quizzes; images; over 350 primary source documents; interactive simulations, maps, and timelines; movie explorations; and a wealth of other resources. You can read the following documents, and many more, at http://worldrc.wadsworth.com/

Mikhail Gorbachev, "On the End of the Cold War"

Lin Piao, "The Nature of People's War"

Visit the *Essential World History* Companion Website for chapter quizzes and more:

http://www.thomsonedu.com/history/duiker

DISCOVERY

Why has Communism survived in China when it failed in Eastern Europe and Russia? Compare conditions in China today with those in countries elsewhere in the world that have abandoned the Communist system. Are Chinese leaders justified in claiming that without party leadership, the country would fall into chaos?

In thinking about this question, begin by breaking it down into the components shown below. A discussion of the significance of each component should appear in your answer.

POLITICS AND GOVERNMENT: On the timeline, notice the key events in the Soviet Union and China. What are the key long-term events in Communist China? What are the key events in Soviet history? Which nation seemed to place more emphasis on the role of individual leaders in carrying out the revolutionary program? Why?

How does the timeline reveal a basic difference in the Chinese approach to dealing with problems that arise, as compared to the Soviets? Is this in part why Communism is still present in China? How have the Chinese differed from the Soviets in their approach to Communism?

TIMELINE

INTERACTION AND EXCHANGE: Compare these pictures of retail establishments in Communist Russia and China. Why would the Chinese allow such capitalistic establishments and advertisements? How is this a response to the problems of Communism as it developed in Russia? Is Chinese Communism more about political than about economic control?

Compare this evidence of capitalism to Lenin's economic policies in Chapter 22, page 500, and to Marx's original intention in the *Communist Manifesto*. How have the Chinese adapted to their conditions? Do most countries adapt their economic/political philosophies to fit their own culture? Has the United States done this?

Courtesy of William J. Duiker

How to Shop in Moscow

© Courtesy of William J. Duiker

Nanjing Road: A Consumer's Paradise

We have seen . . ., that the first step in the revolution by the working class is to raise the proletariat to the position of ruling class. . . . The proletariat will use its political supremacy to wrest, by degrees, all capital from the bourgeoisie, to centralize all instruments of production in the hands of the State, i.e., of the proletariat organized as the ruling class; and to increase the total of productive forces as rapidly as possible.

Of course, in the beginning, this cannot be effected except by means of despotic inroads on the rights of property, and on the conditions of bourgeois production; by means of measures, therefore, which appear economically insufficient and untenable, but which, in the course of the movement, outstrip themselves, necessitate further inroads upon the old social order, and are unavoidable as a means of entirely revolutionizing the mode of production.

These measures will of course be different in different countries.

Nevertheless, in the most advanced countries, the following will be pretty generally applicable:

1. Abolition of property in land and application of all rents of land to public purposes.
2. A heavy progressive or graduated income tax.
3. Abolition of all right of inheritance. . . .
4. Centralization of credit in the hands of the State, by means of a national bank with State capital and an exclusive monopoly.
5. Centralization of the means of communication and transport in the hands of the State.
6. Extension of factories and instruments of production owned by the State. . . .
7. Equal liability of all to labor. Establishment of industrial armies, especially for agriculture.
8. Combination of agriculture with manufacturing industries; gradual abolition of the distinction between town and country, by a more equable distribution of the population over the country.
9. Free education for all children in public schools. Abolition of children's factory labor in its present form. . . .

When, in the course of development, class distinctions have disappeared, and all production has been concentrated in the whole nation, the public power will lose its political character. Political power, properly so called, is merely the organized power of one class for oppressing another. If the proletariat during its contest with the bourgeoisie is compelled, by the force of circumstances, to organize itself as a class, if, by means of a revolution, it makes itself the ruling class, and, as such, sweeps away by force the old conditions of production, then it will, along with these conditions, have swept away the conditions for the existence of class antagonisms and of classes generally, and will thereby have abolished its own supremacy as a class.

In place of the old bourgeois society, with its classes and class antagonisms, we shall have an association, in which the free development of each is the condition for the free development of all.

ARTS AND IDEAS: Compare the two images. What are their similarities? What values do they attempt to glorify? Are they successful? How can art be used to instill a philosophy and its ideals among the people? Which of the two pictures do you find more appealing? Why?

What art in the United States is similar to these two images? What works of art symbolize American virtues?

Stalinist Heroic: An Example of Socialist Realism

Hail the Great Helmsman

Courtesy of William J. Duiker

© Private Collection/Bridgeman Art Library

27

EUROPE AND THE WESTERN HEMISPHERE SINCE 1945

CHAPTER OUTLINE AND FOCUS QUESTIONS

Recovery and Renewal in Europe

◻ What problems have the nations of Western Europe faced since 1945, and what steps have they taken to try to solve these problems?

Emergence of the Superpower: The United States

◻ What political, social, and economic changes has the United States experienced since 1945?

The Development of Canada

◻ What political, social, and economic developments has Canada experienced since 1945?

Latin America Since 1945

◻ What problems have the nations of Latin America faced since 1945, and what role has Marxist ideology played in their efforts to solve these problems?

Society and Culture in the Western World

◻ What major social, cultural, and intellectual developments have occurred in Western Europe and North America since 1945?

CRITICAL THINKING

◻ What are the similarities and differences between the major political, economic, and social developments in the first half of the twentieth century and those in the second half of the century?

Children play amid the ruins of Warsaw, Poland, at the end of World War II

THE END OF WORLD WAR II in Europe had been met with great joy. One visitor in Moscow reported, "I looked out of the window [at 2 A.M.], almost everywhere there were lights in the windows—people were staying awake. Everyone embraced everyone else, someone sobbed aloud." But after the victory parades and celebrations, Europeans awoke to a devastating realization: their civilization was in ruins. Almost forty million people (both soldiers and civilians) had been killed over the last six years. Massive air raids and artillery bombardments had reduced many of the great cities of Europe to heaps of rubble. The Polish capital of Warsaw had been almost completely obliterated. An American general described Berlin: "Wherever we looked, we saw desolation. It was like a city of the dead. Suffering and shock were visible in every face. Dead bodies still remained in canals and lakes and were being dug out from under bomb debris." Many Europeans were homeless.

Between 1945 and 1970, Europe not only recovered from the devastating effects of World War II but also experienced an economic resurgence that seemed nothing less than miraculous. Economic growth and virtually full employment continued so long that the first postwar recession, in 1973, came as a shock to Western Europe. It was short-lived, however, and economic growth returned. After the collapse of Communist governments in the revolutions of 1989, a number of Eastern European states sought to create market economies and join the military and economic unions first formed by Western European states.

The most significant factor after 1945 was the emergence of the United States as the world's richest and most powerful nation. American prosperity reached new heights in the two decades after World War II, but a series of economic and social problems—including racial division and staggering budget deficits—have given the nation plenty of internal matters to grapple with over the past half century.

To the south of the United States lay the vast world of Latin America, with its own unique heritage. Although some Latin Americans in the nineteenth century had looked to the United States as a model for their own development, in the twentieth century, many attacked the United States for its military and economic domination of Central and South America. At the same time, many Latin American countries struggled with economic and political instability.

In addition to the transformation from Cold War to post–Cold War realities, other changes were shaping the Western outlook. The demographic face of European countries changed as massive numbers of immigrants created more ethnically diverse populations. New artistic and intellectual currents, the continued advance of science and technology, the effort to come to grips with environmental problems, the surge of the women's liberation movement—all spoke of a vibrant, ever-changing world. At the same time, a devastating terrorist attack in the United States in 2001 made the Western world vividly aware of its vulnerability to international terrorism. ◆

Recovery and Renewal in Europe

The nations of Europe faced similar problems at the end of World War II. One was the need to let go of their colonial empires in Africa and Asia and allow the indigenous peoples to achieve national self-determination. **Decolonization** was a difficult and even bitter process (see Chapters 28 and 29), but it created a new world as the non-Western states ended the long era of Western domination.

Another problem for the European nations after World War II was the need to rebuild their shattered economies. Yet, within a few years after the defeat of Germany and Italy, an incredible economic revival brought renewed growth to Western Europe.

Western Europe: The Triumph of Democracy

With the economic aid of the Marshall Plan, the countries of Western Europe recovered relatively rapidly from the devastation of World War II. Between the early 1950s and late 1970s, industrial production surpassed all previous records, and Western Europe experienced virtually full employment.

France: From de Gaulle to New Uncertainties   The history of France for nearly a quarter century after the war was dominated by one man—Charles de Gaulle (1890–1970). Initially, he had withdrawn from politics, but in 1958, frightened by the bitter divisions within France caused by the Algerian crisis (see Chapter 28), the panic-stricken leaders of the Fourth Republic offered to let de Gaulle take over the government and revise the constitution.

In 1958, de Gaulle drafted a constitution for the Fifth Republic that greatly enhanced the power of the office of president, who now had the right to choose the prime minister, dissolve parliament, and supervise both defense and foreign policy. As the new president, de Gaulle sought to return France to a position of great power. With that goal in mind, de Gaulle invested heavily in the nuclear arms race. France exploded its first nuclear bomb in 1960. Despite his successes, de Gaulle did not really achieve his ambitious goals; in truth, France was too small for such global ambitions.

During de Gaulle's presidency, the French gross domestic product grew at an annual rate of 5.5 percent, faster than that of the United States. France became a major industrial producer and exporter, but problems remained. The expansion of traditional industries, such as coal, steel, and railroads, which had all been nationalized, led to large government deficits. The cost of living increased faster than in the rest of Europe. Increased dissatisfaction led in May 1968 to a series of student protests, followed by a general strike by the labor unions. After French voters rejected his suggested reforms of the constitution, de Gaulle resigned from office in April 1969 and died the next year.

The worsening of France's economic situation in the 1970s brought a shift to the left politically. By 1981, the Socialists had become the dominant party in the National Assembly, and the Socialist leader, François Mitterrand (1916–1995), was elected president. Mitterrand passed a number of measures to aid workers: an increased minimum wage, expanded social benefits, a mandatory fifth week of paid vacation for salaried workers, and a thirty-nine-hour workweek. The victory of the Socialists led them to enact some of their more radical reforms: the government nationalized the major banks, the space and electronics industries, and important insurance firms.

For the most part, however, the Socialist policies failed, and within three years, a decline in support caused the Mitterrand government to return some of the economy to private enterprise. But France's economic decline continued. In 1993, French unemployment stood at 10.6 percent, and in the elections in March of that year, the Socialists won only 28 percent of the vote; a coalition of conservative parties won 80 percent of the seats. The move to the right was strengthened when the conservative mayor of Paris, Jacques Chirac (b. 1932), was elected president in May 1995. Chirac pursued a plan of sending illegal immigrants back to their home countries and, after his reelection in 2002, strongly opposed the 2003 U.S. invasion of Iraq.

From West Germany to Germany   Under the pressures of the Cold War, the three western zones of Germany were unified as the Federal Republic of Germany in 1949. Konrad Adenauer (1876–1967), the leader of the Christian Democratic Union (CDU), served as chancellor from 1949 to 1963 and became the Federal Republic's "founding hero."

Adenauer's chancellorship is largely associated with the resurrection of the West German economy, often referred to as the "economic miracle." It was largely guided by the minister of finance, Ludwig Erhard. Although West Germany had only 52 percent of the territory of prewar Germany, by 1955 the West German gross domestic product exceeded that of prewar Germany. Real wages doubled between 1950 and 1965. Unemployment fell from 8 percent in 1950 to 0.4 percent in 1965.

After the Adenauer era, German voters moved politically from the center-right of the Christian Democrats to the center-left: in 1969, the Social Democrats became the leading party. The first Social Democratic chancellor was Willy Brandt (1913–1992), who was especially successful with his "opening toward the east" (known as *Ostpolitik*), for which he received the Nobel Peace Prize in 1972. On March 19, 1971, Brandt worked out the details of a treaty with East Germany (the former Russian zone) that led to greater cultural, personal, and economic contacts between West and East Germany.

In 1982, the Christian Democratic Union of Helmut Kohl (b. 1930) formed a new center-right government. Kohl was a clever politician who benefited greatly from an economic boom in the mid-1980s and the 1989 revolution in East Germany, which led to the reunification of the two Germanies, making the new Germany, with its 79 million people, the leading power in Europe. Reunification brought immediate political dividends to the Christian Democrats, but all too soon, the realization set in that the revitalization of eastern Germany would take far more money than was originally thought. Kohl's government soon faced the politically undesirable prospect of raising taxes substantially. Moreover, the virtual collapse of the economy in eastern Germany led to extremely high unemployment and severe discontent. One response was the return to power of the Social Democrats under the leadership of Gerhard Schroeder (b. 1944) in elections in 1998. But Schroeder failed to cure Germany's economic woes, and, as a result of elections in 2005, Angela Merkel (b. 1954), leader of the Christian Democrats, became the first female chancellor in German history.

The Decline of Great Britain   The end of World War II left Britain with massive economic problems. In elections held immediately after the war, the Labour Party overwhelmingly defeated Churchill's Conservatives. Labour had promised far-reaching reforms, particularly in the area of social welfare, and in a country with a tremendous shortage of consumer goods and housing, its platform was quite appealing. The new Labour government under Clement Attlee (1883–1967) proceeded to turn Britain into a modern **welfare state**.

The process began with the nationalization of the Bank of England, the coal and steel industries, public transportation, and public utilities, such as electricity and gas. In 1946, the new government established a comprehensive **social security** program and nationalized medical insurance, thereby enabling the state to subsidize the unemployed, the sick, and the aged. A health act established a system of socialized medicine that forced doctors and dentists to work with state hospitals, although private practice could be maintained. The British welfare state became the norm for most European nations after the war.

Continuing economic problems, however, brought the Conservatives back into power from 1951 to 1964. Although they favored private enterprise, the Conservatives accepted the welfare state. By now the British economy had recovered from the war, but the slow rate of its recovery reflected a long-term economic decline. As a result of World War II, Britain had lost much of its prewar revenues from abroad but was left with a burden of debt from its many international commitments. At the same time, as the influence of the United States and the Soviet Union continued to rise, Britain's ability to play the role of a world power declined substantially. Between 1964 and 1979, Conservatives and Labour alternated in power, but neither party was able to deal with Britain's ailing economy.

In 1979, the Conservatives returned to power under Margaret Thatcher (b. 1925), who became the first woman to serve as prime minister in British history (see the box on p. 610). Thatcher pledged to lower taxes, reduce government bureaucracy, limit social welfare, restrict union power, and end inflation. The "Iron Lady," as she was called, did break the power of the labor unions. Although she did not eliminate the basic components of the social welfare system, she did use austerity measures to control inflation. "Thatcherism," as her economic policy was termed, improved the British economic situation, but at a price. The south of England, for example, prospered, but the old industrial areas of the Midlands and north declined and were beset by high unemployment and poverty.

Margaret Thatcher dominated British politics in the 1980s. But in 1990, Labour's fortunes revived when Thatcher's government attempted to replace local property taxes with a flat-rate tax payable by every adult. Many British subjects argued that this was nothing more than a poll tax that would allow the rich to get away with paying the same rate as the poor. In 1990, Thatcher's popularity plummeted, and a revolt within her own party forced her to resign as prime minister. She was replaced by John Major (b. 1943), but his government failed to capture the imagination of most Britons. In new elections on May 1, 1997, the Labour

MARGARET THATCHER: ENTERING A MAN'S WORLD

FAMILY & SOCIETY

In 1979, Margaret Thatcher became the first woman to serve as Britain's prime minister. In this excerpt from her autobiography, Thatcher describes how she was interviewed by Conservative Party officials when they first considered her as a possible candidate for Parliament. Thatcher ran for Parliament for the first time in 1950; she lost but increased the Conservative vote total in the district by 50 percent over the previous election.

In this account, is Margaret Thatcher's being a woman more important to her or to others? Why would this disparity exist?

Margaret Thatcher, *The Path to Power*

And, as always with me, there was politics. I immediately joined the Conservative Association and threw myself into the usual round of Party activities. In particular, I thoroughly enjoyed what was called the "'39–'45" discussion group, where Conservatives of the war generation met to exchange views and argue about the political topics of the day. . . . It was as a representative of the Oxford University Graduate Conservative Association (OUGCA) that I went to the Llandudno Conservative Party Conference in October 1948.

It had originally been intended that I should speak at the Conference, seconding an OUGCA motion deploring the abolition of university seats. At that time universities had separate representation in Parliament, and graduates had the right to vote in their universities as well as in the constituency where they lived. (I supported separate university representation, but not the principle that graduates should have more than one vote. . . .) It would have been my first Conference speech, but in the end the seconder chosen was a City man, because the City seats were also to be abolished.

My disappointment at this was, however, very quickly overcome and in a most unexpected way. After one of the debates, I found myself engaged in one of those speculative conversations which young people have about their future prospects. An Oxford friend, John Grant, said he supposed that one day I would like to be a Member of Parliament. "Well, yes," I replied, "but there's not much hope of that. The chances of my being selected are just nil at the moment." I might have added that with no private income of my own there was no way I could have afforded to be an MP on the salary then available. I had not even tried to get on the Party's list of approved candidates.

Later in the day, John Grant happened to be sitting next to the Chairman of the Dartford Conservative Association, John Miller. The Association was in search of a candidate. I learned afterwards that the conversation went something like this: "I understand that you're still looking for a candidate at Dartford?" . . .

"That's right. Any suggestions?"

"Well, there's a young woman, Margaret Roberts, that you might look at. She's very good."

"Oh, but Dartford is a real industrial stronghold. I don't think a woman would do at all."

"Well, you know best of course. But why not just look at her?"

And they did. I was invited to have lunch with John Miller and his wife, Phee, and the Dartford Woman's Chairman, Mrs. Fletcher, on the Saturday on Llandudno Pier. Presumably, and in spite of any reservations about the suitability of a woman candidate for their seat, they liked what they saw. I certainly got on well with them. . . .

I did not hear from Dartford until December, when I was asked to attend an interview at Palace Chambers, Bridge Street. . . . Very few outside the political arena know just how nerve-racking such occasions are. The interviewee who is not nervous and tense is very likely to perform badly: for, as any chemist will tell you, the adrenaline needs to flow if one is to perform at one's best. . . .

I found myself short-listed, and was asked to go to Dartford itself for a further interview. . . . As one of five would-be candidates, I had to give a fifteen-minute speech and answer questions for a further ten minutes.

It was the questions which were more likely to cause me trouble. There was a good deal of suspicion of woman candidates, particularly in what was regarded as a tough industrial seat like Dartford. This was quite definitely a man's world into which not just angels feared to tread. . . .

The most reliable sign that a political occasion has gone well is that you have enjoyed it. I enjoyed that evening at Dartford, and the outcome justified my confidence. I was selected.

ThomsonNOW To read Margaret Thatcher on Christianity and wealth, enter the *ThomsonNOW* documents area using the access card that is available for *The Essential World History*.

Party won a landslide victory. The new prime minister, Tony Blair (b. 1953), was a moderate whose youthful energy immediately injected new vigor into British politics. Blair was one of the major leaders in forming an international coalition against terrorism after the terrorist attack on the United States in 2001. Four years later, his ongoing support for the U.S. war in Iraq when

a majority of Britons opposed it caused his popularity to decline.

Eastern Europe After Communism

The fall of Communist governments in Eastern Europe during the revolutions of 1989 brought a wave of euphoria

Margaret Thatcher. Great Britain's first female prime minister and also its longest-lasting, Margaret Thatcher was a strong leader who dominated British politics in the 1980s. This picture of Thatcher was taken at the Chelsea Flower Show in May 1990. Six months later, a revolt within her own party caused her to resign as prime minister.

to Europe. The new structures meant an end to a postwar European order that had been imposed on unwilling peoples by the victorious forces of the Soviet Union (see Chapter 25). In 1989 and 1990, new governments throughout Eastern Europe worked diligently to scrap the remnants of the old system and introduce the democratic procedures and market systems they believed would revitalize their scarred lands. But this process proved to be neither simple nor easy. Nevertheless, by the beginning of the twenty-first century, many of these states, especially Poland and the Czech Republic, were making a successful transition to both free markets and democracy.

The revival of the post-Cold War Eastern European states was evident in their desire to join both the North Atlantic Treaty Organization (NATO) and the European Union, the two major Cold War institutions of Western European unity. In 1997, Poland, the Czech Republic, and Hungary became full members of NATO. (On the European Union, see "The Unification of Europe" on p. 612.)

The Disintegration of Yugoslavia   From its beginning in 1919, Yugoslavia had been an artificial creation. After World War II, the dictatorial Marshal Tito had managed to hold together the six republics and two autonomous provinces that constituted Yugoslavia. After his death in

1980, no strong leader emerged, and at the end of the 1980s, Yugoslavia was caught up in the reform movements sweeping through Eastern Europe.

After negotiations among the six republics failed, Slovenia and Croatia declared their independence in June 1991. This action was opposed by Slobodan Milošević (1941–2006), the leader of the province of Serbia. He asserted that these republics could only be independent if new border arrangements were made to accommodate the Serb minorities in those republics who did not want to live outside the boundaries of Serbia. Serbian forces attacked both new states and although unsuccessful against Slovenia, captured one-third of Croatia's territory.

The international recognition of independent Slovenia and Croatia in 1992 and of Macedonia and Bosnia and Herzegovina soon thereafter did not deter the Serbs, who now turned their guns on Bosnia. By mid-1993, Serbian forces had acquired 70 percent of Bosnian territory. The Serbian policy of **ethnic cleansing**—killing or forcibly removing Bosnian Muslims from their lands—revived memories of Nazi atrocities in World War II. This account by one Muslim survivor from the town of Srebrenica is eerily reminiscent of the activities of the Nazi *Einsatzgruppen* (see Chapter 24):

> When the truck stopped, they told us to get off in groups of five. We immediately heard shooting next to the trucks. . . . About ten Serbs with automatic rifles told us to lie down on the ground face first. As we were getting down, they started to shoot, and I fell into a pile of corpses. I felt hot liquid running down my face. I realized that I was only grazed. As they continued to shoot more groups, I kept on squeezing myself in between dead bodies.[1]

As the fighting spread, European nations and the United States began to intervene to stop the bloodshed, and in the fall of 1995, a fragile cease-fire agreement was reached. An international peacekeeping force was stationed in the area to prevent further hostilities.

Peace in Bosnia, however, did not bring peace to Yugoslavia. A new war erupted in 1999 over Kosovo, an autonomous province within the Serbian republic. Kosovo's inhabitants were mainly ethnic Albanians, but the province was also home to a Serbian minority. In 1989, Yugoslav president Milosĕvić stripped Kosovo of its autonomous status. Four years later, some groups of ethnic Albanians founded the Kosovo Liberation Army (KLA) and began a campaign against Serbian rule in Kosovo. When Serb forces began to massacre ethnic Albanians in an effort to crush the KLA, the United States and its NATO allies mounted a bombing campaign that forced Milosĕvić to stop. In the fall elections of 2000, Milosĕvić himself was ousted from power, and he was later put on trial by an international tribunal for war crimes against humanity for his ethnic cleansing policies throughout Yugoslavia's disintegration. He died in 2006 during that trial.

The fate of Bosnia and Kosovo has not yet been finally determined. Thirty thousand NATO troops remain in Bosnia, trying to keep the peace, while other NATO military forces maintain an uneasy peace in Kosovo.

The last political vestige of Yugoslavia ceased to exist in 2004 when the new national government officially renamed the truncated country Serbia and Montenegro. Two years later, Montenegrins voted in favor of independence. Thus, by 2006, all six republics cobbled together to form Yugoslavia in 1918 were once again independent nations.

The New Russia: From Empire to Nation

Soon after the disintegration of the Soviet Union in 1991, a new era began in Russia with the presidency of Boris Yeltsin. A new constitution created a two-chamber parliament and established a strong presidency. During the mid-1990s, Yeltsin was able to maintain a precarious grip on power while seeking to implement reforms that would place Russia on a firm course toward a pluralistic political system and a market economy. But the new post-Communist Russia remained as fragile as ever. Burgeoning economic inequality and rampant corruption aroused widespread criticism and shook the confidence of the Russian people in the superiority of the capitalist system over the one that existed under Communist rule. A nagging war in the Caucasus—where the people of Chechnya have resolutely sought national independence from Russia—drained the government budget and exposed the decrepit state of the once vaunted Red Army. In presidential elections held in 1996, Yeltsin was reelected, but the rising popularity of a revived Communist Party and the growing strength of nationalist elements, combined with Yeltsin's precarious health, raised serious questions about the future of the country.

The Putin Era At the end of 1999, Yeltsin suddenly resigned his office and was replaced by Vladimir Putin (b. 1952), a former member of the KGB. Putin vowed to bring an end to the rampant corruption and inexperience that permeated Russian political culture and to strengthen the role of the central government in managing the affairs of state. During succeeding months, his proposal to centralize power in the hands of the federal government in Moscow was approved by the parliament; in early 2001, he presented a new plan to regulate political parties, which numbered more than fifty at the beginning of the decade.

Putin also vowed to bring the breakaway state of Chechnya back under Russian authority and to assume a more assertive role in international affairs. The new president took advantage of growing public anger at Western plans to expand the NATO alliance into Eastern Europe, as well as the aggressive actions by NATO countries against Serbia in the Balkans, to restore Russia's position as an influential force in the world.

Putin has attempted to deal with the chronic problems in Russian society by centralizing his control over the system, and by silencing critics—notably in the Russian media. Such moves have aroused unease among many observers in the West and provoked the United States to warn him against derailing the trend toward democratic institutions and practices in the old Soviet bloc. But there is a widespread sense of unease in Russia today about the decline of the social order—marked by a rising incidence of alcoholism, sexual promiscuity, and criminal activities and the disintegration of the traditional family system—and many of Putin's compatriots support his attempt to restore a sense of pride and discipline in Russian society. He was not alone in the spring of 2005 when he expressed the view that the breakup of the Soviet Union was a national tragedy.

The Unification of Europe

As we saw in Chapter 25, the divisions created by the Cold War led the nations of Western Europe to seek military security by forming NATO in 1949. The destructiveness of two world wars, however, caused many thoughtful Europeans to consider the need for some additional form of unity.

In 1957, France, West Germany, the Benelux countries (Belgium, the Netherlands, and Luxembourg), and Italy signed the Treaty of Rome, which created the European Economic Community (EEC). The EEC eliminated customs barriers for the six member nations and created a large free-trade area protected from the rest of the world by a common external tariff. All the member nations benefited economically. In 1973, Great Britain, Ireland, and Denmark gained membership in what now was called the European Community (EC). Greece joined in 1981, followed by Spain and Portugal in 1986. In 1995, Austria, Finland, and Sweden also became members of the EC.

The European Union The European Community was an economic union, not a political one. By 2000, the EC contained 370 million people and constituted the world's largest single trading entity, transacting one-fourth of the world's commerce. In the 1980s and 1990s, the EC moved toward even greater economic integration. The Treaty on European Union, which went into effect on January 1, 1994, turned the European Community into the European Union (EU), a true economic and monetary union. One of its first goals was achieved in 1999 with the introduction of a common currency, the euro. On January 1, 2002, the euro officially replaced twelve national currencies.

In addition to having a single internal market and a common currency for those twelve members, the EU has also established a common agricultural policy, which provides subsidies to farmers to enable them to sell their goods competitively on the world market. The end of national passports has given millions of Europeans greater flexibility in travel. The European Union has been less successful in setting common foreign policy goals, primarily because individual nations still see foreign policy as a national priority and are reluctant to give up this power to a single overriding institution.

Toward a United Europe At the beginning of the twenty-first century, the EU established a new goal: to incorporate into the union the states of eastern and southeastern Europe. Many of these states were considerably poorer than the current members, which raised the possibility that adding these nations might weaken the EU itself. To lessen that danger, EU members established a set of qualifications requiring applicants to demonstrate their commitment both to market capitalism and to democracy and to exhibit respect for minorities and human rights as well as for the rule of law. In May 2004, the European Union took the plunge and added ten new members: Cyprus, the Czech Republic, Estonia, Hungary, Latvia, Lithuania, Malta, Poland, Slovakia, and Slovenia, thereby enlarging the population of the EU to 455 million people (see Map 27.1).

MAP 27.1 **European Union, 2004.** Beginning in 1957 as the European Economic Community, also known as the Common Market, the union of European states seeking to integrate their economies has gradually grown from six members to twenty-five in 2004. The European Union has achieved two major goals—the creation of a single internal market and a common currency—although it has been less successful at working toward common political and foreign policy goals. ❓ What additional nations do you think will eventually join the European Union? Why?

Emergence of the Superpower: The United States

At the end of World War II, the United States emerged as one of the world's two superpowers. As its Cold War confrontation with the Soviet Union intensified, the United States directed much of its energy toward combating the spread of communism throughout the world. With the collapse of the Soviet Union at the beginning of the 1990s, the United States became the world's foremost military power.

American Politics and Society Through the Vietnam Era

Franklin Roosevelt's New Deal of the 1930s initiated a basic transformation of American society that continued between 1945 and 1970. It included a dramatic increase in the role and power of the federal government, the rise of organized labor as a significant force in the economy and politics, a commitment to the welfare state, and a grudging acceptance of minority problems. The New Deal in American politics was bolstered by the election of Democratic presidents—Harry Truman in 1948, John F. Kennedy in 1960, and Lyndon B. Johnson in 1964. Even the election of a Republican president, Dwight D. Eisenhower, in 1952 and 1956 did not significantly alter the fundamental direction of the New Deal.

The economic boom after World War II fueled confidence in the American way of life. A shortage of consumer goods during the war left Americans with both surplus income and the desire to purchase these goods after the war. Then, too, the growing influence of organized labor enabled more and more workers to get the wage increases that spurred the growth of the domestic market. Between 1945 and 1973, real wages grew an average of 3 percent a year, the most prolonged advance in U.S. history.

Starting in the 1960s, however, problems that had been glossed over earlier came to the fore. The decade began on a youthful and optimistic note when John F. Kennedy (1917–1963), at age forty-three, became the youngest elected president in the history of the United States and the first born in the twentieth century. His own administration, cut short by an assassin's bullet on November 22, 1963, focused primarily on foreign affairs. Kennedy's successor, Lyndon B. Johnson (1908–1973), who won a new term as president in a landslide in 1964, used his stunning mandate to pursue the growth of the welfare state, first begun in the New Deal. Johnson's programs included health care for the elderly and the War on Poverty, to be fought with food stamps and the Job Corps.

Johnson's other domestic passion was achieving equal rights for black Americans. In August 1963, the eloquent Reverend Martin Luther King Jr. (1929–1968) led the March on Washington for Jobs and Freedom to dramatize blacks' desire for freedom. This march and King's impassioned plea for racial equality had an electrifying effect on the American people. President Johnson pursued the cause of civil rights. As a result of his initiative, Congress enacted the Civil Rights Act of 1964, which created the machinery to end segregation and discrimination in the workplace and all public accommodations. The Voting Rights Act the following year eliminated obstacles to black participation in elections in southern states. But laws alone could not guarantee the Great Society that Johnson envisioned, and soon the administration faced bitter social unrest.

In the North and the West, blacks had had voting rights for many years, but local patterns of segregation resulted in considerably higher unemployment rates for blacks (and Hispanics) than for whites and left blacks segregated in huge urban ghettos. In the summer of 1965, race riots erupted in the Watts district of Los Angeles that led to thirty-four deaths and the destruction of over one thousand buildings. After King was assassinated in 1968, more than one hundred cities erupted in rioting, including Washington, D.C., the nation's capital. The riots led to a "white backlash" and a severe racial division of America.

Antiwar protests also divided the American people after President Johnson committed American troops to a costly war in Vietnam (see Chapter 25). The killing of four student protesters at Kent State University in 1970 by the Ohio National Guard shocked both activists and ordinary Americans, and thereafter the vehemence of the antiwar movement began to subside. But the combination of antiwar demonstrations and riots in the cities caused many people to call for "law and order," an appeal used by Richard Nixon (1913–1994), the Republican presidential candidate in 1968. With Nixon's election in 1968, a shift to the right in American politics had begun.

The Shift Rightward After 1973

Nixon eventually ended American involvement in Vietnam by gradually withdrawing American troops. Politically, he pursued a "southern strategy," carefully calculating that "law and order" issues would appeal to southern whites. The Republican strategy, however, also gained support among white Democrats in northern cities, where court-mandated busing to achieve racial integration had provoked a white backlash.

As president, Nixon was paranoid about conspiracies and resorted to subversive methods of gaining political intelligence on his political opponents. Nixon's zeal led to the Watergate scandal—a botched attempt to bug the Democratic National Headquarters and the ensuing coverup. Although Nixon repeatedly denied involvement in the affair, secret tapes he made of his own conversations in the White House revealed otherwise. On August 9, 1974, Nixon resigned in disgrace, an act that saved him from almost certain impeachment and conviction.

After Watergate, American domestic politics focused on economic issues. Gerald Ford (b. 1913) became president when Nixon resigned, only to lose in the 1976 election to the former governor of Georgia, Jimmy Carter (b. 1924), who campaigned as an outsider against the Washington establishment. By 1980, the Carter administration faced two devastating problems. High inflation and a decline in average weekly earnings were causing a perceptible drop in American living standards. At the same time, a crisis abroad had erupted when fifty-three Americans were taken hostage by the Iranian government of Ayatollah Khomeini and held for nearly fifteen months (see Chapter 28). Carter's inability to gain the release of the American hostages led to perceptions at home that he was a weak president. His overwhelming loss to Ronald Reagan (1911–2004) in the election of 1980 brought forward the chief exponent of right-wing Republican policies.

The Reagan Revolution, as it has been called, sent U.S. policy in a number of new directions. Reversing decades of changes, Reagan cut back on the welfare state by decreasing spending on food stamps, school lunch programs, and job programs. At the same time, his administration fostered the largest peacetime military buildup in American history. Total federal spending rose from $631 billion in 1981 to over $1 trillion by 1986. The administration's spending policies produced record government deficits, which loomed as an obstacle to long-term growth. In the 1970s, the total deficit was $420 billion; Reagan's budget deficits were three times that amount.

The inability of Reagan's successor, George H. W. Bush (b. 1924), to deal with the deficit problem, coupled with an economic downturn, led to the election of a Democrat, Bill Clinton (b. 1946), in November 1992. The new president was a southerner who claimed to be a new Democrat—one who favored a number of the Republican policies of the 1980s. This was a clear indication that the rightward drift in American politics was by no means ended by this Democratic victory.

President Clinton's political fortunes were aided considerably by a lengthy economic revival. A steady reduction in the annual government budget deficit strengthened confidence in the performance of the national economy. Much of Clinton's second term, however, was overshadowed by charges of misconduct stemming from the president's affair with Monica Lewinsky, a White House intern. After a bitter partisan struggle, the U.S. Senate acquitted the president on two articles of impeachment brought by the House of Representatives. But Clinton's problems helped the Republican candidate, George W. Bush (b. 1946), to win the presidential election in 2000. Although Bush lost the popular vote to Al Gore, he narrowly won the electoral vote after a highly controversial victory in the state of Florida.

The first four years of Bush's administration were largely occupied with the war on terrorism and the U.S.-led war on Iraq (see Chapter 28). The Department of Homeland Security was established after the 2001 terrorist assaults to help protect the country from future terrorist acts. At the same time, Bush pushed tax cuts through Congress that mainly favored the wealthy and helped produce record deficits reminiscent of the Reagan years. Environmentalists were especially disturbed by the Bush administration's efforts to weaken environmental laws and regulations to benefit American corporations. In November 2004, after a highly negative political campaign, Bush was narrowly elected to a second term. In 2005, his popularity plummeted as discontent grew over the war in Iraq and financial corruption in the Republican Party, as well as the administration's poor handling of relief efforts after Hurricane Katrina.

The Development of Canada

For twenty-five years after World War II, Canada realized extraordinary economic prosperity as it set out on a new path of industrial development, including electronic, aircraft, nuclear, and chemical engineering industries. Much of the Canadian growth, however, was financed by capital from the United States, which resulted in American ownership of Canadian businesses. While many Canadians welcomed the economic growth, others feared American economic domination of Canada.

After 1945, the Liberal Party continued to dominate Canadian politics. Under Lester Pearson (1897–1972), the Liberals created Canada's welfare state by enacting a national social security system (the Canada Pension Plan) and a national health insurance program. The most prominent Liberal government, however, was that of Pierre Trudeau (1919–2000), who came to power in 1968.

Trudeau's government pushed a vigorous program of industrialization, but inflation and Trudeau's efforts to impose the will of the federal government on the powerful provincial governments alienated voters and weakened his government. Economic recession in the early 1980s brought Brian Mulroney (b. 1939), leader of the Progressive Conservative Party, to power in 1984. Mulroney's government sought greater privatization of Canada's state-run corporations and negotiated a free-trade agreement with the United States. Bitterly resented by many Canadians, the agreement cost Mulroney's government much of its popularity. In 1993, the ruling Conservatives were overwhelmingly defeated, and the Liberal leader, Jean Chrétien (b. 1934), became prime minister. Chrétien's conservative fiscal policies, combined with strong economic growth, enabled his government to have a budgetary surplus by the late 1990s and led to another Liberal victory in the elections of 1997. Charges of widespread financial corruption in the government, however, led to a Conservative victory early in 2006, and Stephen Harper (b. 1959) became the new prime minister.

Latin America Since 1945

The Great Depression of the 1930s had led to political instability in many Latin American countries that resulted in military coups and militaristic regimes (see

Chapter 23). But the depression also provided the impetus for Latin America to move from a traditional to a modern economic structure. Since the nineteenth century, Latin Americans had exported raw materials, especially minerals and foodstuffs, while buying the manufactured goods of the industrialized countries in Europe and the United States. As a result of the depression, however, exports were cut in half, and the revenues available to buy manufactured goods declined. This encouraged many Latin American countries to develop industries to produce goods that were formerly imported. Due to a shortage of capital in the private sector, governments often invested in the new industries, thus leading, for example, to government-run steel industries in Chile and Brazil and oil industries in Argentina and Mexico.

By the 1960s, however, Latin American countries still found themselves dependent on the United States, Europe, and now Japan, especially for the advanced technology needed for modern industries. Because of the great poverty in many Latin American countries, domestic markets were limited in size, and many Latin American countries often failed to find markets abroad for their products. These failures led to instability and a new reliance on military regimes, especially to curb the power of the new industrial middle class and working classes, which had increased in size and power as a result of industrialization. In the 1960s, repressive military regimes in Chile, Brazil, and Argentina abolished political parties and often returned to export-import economies financed by foreigners.

In the 1970s, Latin American regimes grew even more dependent on borrowing from abroad, especially from banks in Europe and the United States, to maintain their failing economies. Between 1970 and 1982, debt to foreigners increased from $27 billion to $315.3 billion. By 1982, a number of governments announced that they could no longer pay interest on their debts to foreign banks, and their economies began to crumble.

In the 1980s, the debt crisis was paralleled by a movement toward democracy. Many people realized that military power without popular consent was incapable of providing a strong state. Then, too, there was a swelling of popular support for basic rights and free and fair elections. The movement toward democracy was the most noticeable trend of the 1980s and early 1990s in Latin America. In the mid-1980s, democratic regimes were established everywhere except Cuba, some of the Central American states, Chile, and Paraguay.

The United States has also played an important role in Latin America since 1945. Beginning in the 1920s, the United States replaced Britain as the foremost investor in Latin America. Unlike the British, however, American investors put funds directly into production enterprises, so that large segments of Latin America's export industries fell into American hands. The American-owned United Fruit Company turned a number of Central American nations into "banana republics," while American companies gained control of the copper-mining industry in Chile and Peru and the oil industry in Mexico, Peru, and Bolivia. The control of these industries by American investors reinforced a growing nationalist consciousness against America as a neo-imperialist power.

But the United States had also tried to pursue a new relationship with Latin America. In 1948, the nations of the Western Hemisphere formed the Organization of American States (OAS), which was intended to eliminate unilateral interference by one state in the internal or external affairs of any other state. But as the Cold War between the United States and the Soviet Union intensified, American policy makers grew anxious about the possibility of Communist regimes arising in Central America and the Caribbean and returned to a policy of unilateral action when they believed that Soviet agents were attempting to establish Communist governments. Especially after the success of Castro in Cuba (see the next section), the desire of the United States to prevent "another Cuba" largely determined American policy toward Latin America until the end of the Cold War in the 1990s. The United States provided massive military aid to anti-Communist regimes, regardless of their nature.

The Threat of Marxist Revolutions: The Example of Cuba

Since 1934, Cuba had been ruled by a dictatorship, headed by Fulgencio Batista (1901–1973) and closely tied economically to American investors. During the early 1950s, a strong opposition movement to Batista's government developed, led by Fidel Castro (b. 1926) assisted by Ernesto Ché Guevara (1928–1967), an Argentinean who believed in the need for revolutionary upheaval to change Latin America. Castro maintained that only armed force could overthrow Batista, but when their initial assaults on Batista's regime met with little success, Castro's forces, based in the Sierra Maestra, went over to guerrilla warfare (see the box on p. 617). As the rebels gained more support, Batista's regime responded with such brutality that he alienated his own supporters. The dictator fled in

Caribbean Sea
Caracas GUYANA
VENEZUELA   SURINAME
Bogotá   FRENCH GUIANA
COLOMBIA
Quito
ECUADOR
PERU   BRAZIL
Lima
BOLIVIA
La Paz
Pacific
Ocean   PARAGUAY   Rio de
           Asunción   Janeiro
                       Atlantic
CHILE Buenos URUGUAY Ocean
Santiago Aires Montevideo
ARGENTINA

0   750   1,500 Kilometers
0   500   1,000 Miles

Falkland
Islands (Br.)

South Georgia
Island (Br.)

South America

CASTRO'S REVOLUTIONARY IDEALS

POLITICS & GOVERNMENT

On July 26, 1953, Fidel Castro and a small group of supporters launched an ill-fated attack on the Moncada Barracks in Santiago de Cuba. Castro was arrested and put on trial. This excerpt is taken from the speech he presented in his defense, in which he discussed the goals of the revolutionaries.

What did Fidel Castro intend to accomplish by his revolution in Cuba? On whose behalf did he fight this revolution?

Fidel Castro, "History Will Absolve Me"

I stated that the second consideration on which we based our chances for success was one of social order because we were assured of the people's support. When we speak of the people we do not mean the comfortable ones, the conservative elements of the nation, who welcome any regime of oppression, any dictatorship, and despotism, prostrating themselves before the master of the moment until they grind their foreheads into the ground. When we speak of struggle, the people means the vast unredeemed masses, to whom all make promises and whom all deceive; we mean the people who yearn for a better, more dignified, and more just nation. . . .

In the brief of this cause there must be recorded the five revolutionary laws that would have been proclaimed immediately after the capture of the Moncada barracks and would have been broadcast to the nation by radio. . . .

The First Revolutionary Law would have returned power to the people and proclaimed the Constitution of 1940 the supreme Law of the land, until such time as the people should decide to modify or change it. . . .

The Second Revolutionary Law would have granted property, not mortgageable and not transferable, to all planters, subplanters, lessees, partners, and squatters who hold parcels of five or less *caballerias* [tracts of land, about 33 acres] of land, and the state would indemnify the former owners on the basis of the rental which they would have received for these parcels over a period of ten years.

The Third Revolutionary Law would have granted workers and employees the right to share 30 percent of the profits of all the large industrial, mercantile, and mining enterprises, including the sugar mills. . . .

The Fourth Revolutionary Law would have granted all planters the right to share 55 percent of the sugar production and a minimum quota of forty thousand *arrobas* [25 pounds] for all small planters who have been established for three or more years.

The Fifth Revolutionay Law would have ordered the confiscation of all holdings and ill-gotten gains of those who had committed frauds during previous regimes, as well as the holdings and ill-gotten gains of all their legatees and heirs.

ThomsonNOW To read more of Fidel Castro's writings on revolution, enter the *ThomsonNOW* documents area using the access card that is available for *The Essential World History*.

December 1958, and Castro's revolutionaries seized Havana on January 1, 1959.

Relations between Cuba and the United States quickly deteriorated early in 1960 when the Soviet Union agreed to buy Cuban sugar and provide $100 million in credits. In October 1960, the United States imposed a trade embargo on Cuba, thus driving Castro closer to the Soviet Union.

On January 3, 1961, the United States broke diplomatic relations with Cuba. The new American president, John F. Kennedy, supported a coup attempt against Castro's government, but the landing of fourteen hundred CIA-assisted Cuban exiles in Cuba at the Bay of Pigs on April 17, 1961, turned into a total military disaster. The Soviets were now encouraged to make an even greater commitment to Cuban independence by installing nuclear missiles in the country, an act that led to a showdown with the United States (see Chapter 25 on the Cuban Missile Crisis). As its part of the bargain to defuse the crisis, the United States agreed not to invade Cuba.

In Cuba, Castro's socialist revolution proceeded, with mixed results. The Cuban revolution did secure some social gains for its people, especially in health care and education. The regime provided free medical services for all citizens, and the population's health improved noticeably. Illiteracy was wiped out by developing new schools and establishing teacher-training institutes that tripled the number of teachers within ten years.

Eschewing rapid industrialization, Castro encouraged agricultural diversification. But the Cuban economy continued to rely on the production and sale of sugar. Economic problems forced Castro's regime to depend on Soviet subsidies and the purchase of Cuban sugar by Soviet bloc countries. After the collapse of these Communist regimes in 1989, Cuba lost their support. Although economic conditions in Cuba have steadily declined, Castro manages to remain in power.

Nationalism and the Military: The Example of Argentina

The military became the power brokers of many twentieth-century Latin American nations. Fearful of the forces unleashed by the development of industry, the military intervened in Argentinean politics in 1930 and propped up the cattle and wheat oligarchy that had controlled the reins of power since the beginning of the twentieth century. An organization of restless military officers overthrew the civilian oligarchy in June 1943. But the new military regime was unsure about how to deal with the working classes. One member, Juan Perón (1895–1974), used his position as labor secretary in the military government to curry favor with the workers. In 1944, Perón became vice president of the military government and made sure that people knew he was responsible for social welfare measures. But as Perón grew more popular, other army officers grew fearful of his power and arrested him. An uprising by workers forced the officers to back down, and in 1946, Perón was elected president.

Perón pursued a policy of increased industrialization in order to please his chief supporters—labor and the urban middle class. At the same time, he sought to free Argentina from foreign investors. The government bought the railways; took over the banking, insurance, shipping, and communications industries; and assumed regulation of imports and exports. But Perón's regime was also authoritarian. His wife, Eva Perón, founded women's organizations to support the government while Perón organized fascist gangs, modeled after Hitler's Brown Shirts, who used violence to intimidate his opponents. But growing corruption in Perón's government and the alienation of more and more people by the regime's excesses encouraged the military to overthrow him in September 1955. Perón went into exile in Spain.

Overwhelmed by problems, however, military leaders decided to allow Perón to come back from exile in Spain. Reelected as president in September 1973, Perón died one year later. In 1976, the military installed a new regime and used the occasion to kill more than six thousand leftists. But economic problems persisted, and the regime tried to divert people's attention by invading the Falkland Islands in April 1982. Great Britain, which had controlled the islands since the nineteenth century, decisively defeated the Argentinean forces. The loss discredited the military and opened the door to civilian rule. In 1983, Raúl Alfonsín (b. 1927) was elected president and sought to reestablish democratic practices. In elections in 1989, the Peronist Carlos Saúl Menem (b. 1930) won. This peaceful transfer of power gave hope that Argentina was moving on a democratic path. Despite problems of foreign debt and inflation, the government of President Néstor Kirchner (b. 1950) has witnessed economic growth since 2003.

The Mexican Way

During the 1950s and 1960s, Mexico's ruling party (known as the Institutional Revolutionary Party, or PRI) focused on a balanced program of industrial policy. Fifteen years of steady economic growth combined with low inflation and real gains in wages for more and more people made those years seem a golden age in Mexico's economic development. At the end of the 1960s, students began to protest Mexico's one-party system. On October 2, 1968, a demonstration of university students in Tlatelolco Square in Mexico City was met by police, who opened fire, killing hundreds of students. Leaders of the PRI became concerned about the need for change in the system.

The next two presidents, Luis Echeverría (1970–1976) and José López Portillo (1976–1982), introduced political reforms. Rules for the registration of political parties were eased, thus making their growth more likely, and greater freedom of debate in the press and at universities was allowed. But economic problems continued to trouble Mexico. In the late 1970s, vast new reserves of oil were discovered in Mexico, making the government even more dependent on oil revenues. When world oil prices dropped in the mid-1980s, Mexico was no longer able to make payments on its foreign debt, which had reached $80 billion in 1982.

The debt crisis and rising unemployment increased dissatisfaction with the government, which was especially evident in the 1988 election, when the PRI's choice for president, Carlos Salinas (b. 1948), who would be expected to win in a landslide, won by only a 50.3 percent majority. Increasing dissatisfaction with the government's economic policies finally led to the unthinkable: in 2000, Vicente Fox (b. 1942) defeated the PRI candidate

Juan and Eva Perón. Elected president of Argentina in 1946, Juan Perón soon established an authoritarian regime that nationalized some of Argentina's basic industries and organized fascist gangs to overwhelm its opponents. He is shown here with his wife, Eva, during the inauguration ceremonies initiating his second term as president in 1952.

© CORBIS

for the presidency. Despite high hopes, Fox's administration failed to deal with police corruption and bureaucratic inefficiency in the government.

Society and Culture in the Western World

Socially, culturally, and intellectually, the Western world during the second half of the twentieth century was marked by much diversity.

The Emergence of a New Society

During the postwar era, such products of new technologies as computers, television, jet planes, contraceptive devices, and new surgical techniques all dramatically altered the nature of human life. The rapid changes in postwar society were fueled by scientific advances and rapid economic growth. Called a technocratic society by some observers and the **consumer society** by others, postwar Western society was marked by a fluid social structure and new movements for change.

Especially noticeable in European society after 1945 were the changes in the middle class. Such traditional middle-class groups as businesspeople and professionals in law, medicine, and the universities were greatly augmented by a new group of managers and technicians as large companies and government agencies employed increasing numbers of white-collar supervisory and administrative personnel.

Changes also occurred among the traditional lower classes. Especially notable was the dramatic shift of people from rural to urban areas. The number of people in agriculture declined drastically. But the size of the industrial working class did not expand. In West Germany, industrial workers made up 48 percent of the labor force throughout the 1950s and 1960s. Thereafter the number of industrial workers began to dwindle as the number of white-collar service employees increased. At the same time, a substantial increase in real wages enabled the working classes to aspire to the consumption patterns of the middle class. Buying on the installment plan became widespread in the 1950s and gave workers a chance to imitate the middle class by buying such products as televisions, washing machines, refrigerators, vacuum cleaners, record players, and automobiles.

Rising incomes, combined with shorter working hours, created an even greater market for mass leisure activities. Between 1900 and 1980, the workweek was reduced from sixty hours to around forty hours, and the number of paid holidays increased. All aspects of popular culture—music, sports, media—became commercialized and opened opportunities for leisure activities.

Social change was also evident in both educational patterns and student attitudes. Before World War II, higher education had largely remained the preserve of Europe's wealthier classes. After the war, European states began to foster greater equality of opportunity in higher education by eliminating fees, and universities experienced an influx of students from the middle and lower classes. Enrollments grew dramatically; in France, 4.5 percent of young people went to a university in 1950. By 1965, the figure had increased to 14.5 percent.

But there were problems. Overcrowded classrooms, professors who paid little attention to students, administrators who acted in an authoritarian fashion, and an education that to many seemed irrelevant to the realities of the modern age led to an outburst of student revolts in the late 1960s. In part, these were an extension of the anti–Vietnam War protests in American universities in the mid-1960s. Perhaps the most famous student revolt occurred in France in 1968. It erupted at the University of Nanterre outside Paris but soon spread to the Sorbonne, the main campus of the University of Paris. French students demanded a greater voice in the administration of the university, took over buildings, and then expanded the scale of their protests by inviting workers to support them. Half of France's workforce went on strike in May 1968. After the Gaullist government instituted a hefty wage hike, the workers returned to work and the police repressed the remaining student protesters.

There were several reasons for the student radicalism. Some students were genuinely motivated by the desire to reform the university. Others were protesting the Vietnam War, which they viewed as a product of Western imperialism. They also attacked other aspects of Western society, such as its materialism, and expressed concern about becoming cogs in the large and impersonal bureaucratic mechanisms of the modern world.

The Permissive Society

Some critics referred to the new society of postwar Europe as the **permissive society.** Sweden took the lead in the propagation of the so-called sexual revolution of the 1960s, and the rest of Europe and the United States soon followed. Sex education in the schools and the decriminalization of homosexuality were but two aspects of Sweden's liberal approach. The introduction of the birth control pill, which became widely available by the mid-1960s, gave people more freedom in sexual behavior. Meanwhile, sexually explicit movies, plays, and books broke new ground in the treatment of once-hidden subjects. Cities like Amsterdam, which allowed open prostitution and the public sale of hard-core pornography, attracted thousands of curious tourists.

The new standards were evident in the breakdown of the traditional family. Divorce rates increased dramatically, especially in the 1960s, while premarital and extramarital sexual experiences also rose substantially. A survey in the Netherlands in 1968 revealed that 78 percent of men and 86 percent of women had participated in extramarital sex.

The 1960s also saw the emergence of the drug culture. Marijuana, though illegal, was widely used by college and

A "Love-In." In the 1960s, a number of outdoor public festivals for young people combined music, drugs, and sex. Flamboyant dress, facial painting, free-form dancing, and drugs were vital ingredients in creating an atmosphere dedicated to "love and peace." Shown here is a "love-in" that was held on the grounds of an English country estate in the "Summer of Love," 1967.

university students. For young people more interested in higher levels of consciousness, Timothy Leary, who had done research at Harvard on the psychedelic (perception-altering) effects of lysergic acid diethylamide (LSD), became the high priest of hallucinogenic experiences.

New attitudes toward sex and the use of drugs were only two manifestations of a growing youth movement in the 1960s that questioned authority and fostered rebellion against the older generation. Spurred on by opposition to the Vietnam War and a growing political consciousness, the youth rebellion became a youth protest movement by the second half of the 1960s (see the box on p. 621).

Women in the Postwar World

Despite their enormous contributions to the war effort, women at the end of World War II were removed from the workforce so that there would be jobs for the soldiers returning home. After the horrors of war, people seemed willing for a while to return to traditional family practices. Female participation in the workforce declined, and birthrates began to rise, creating a "baby boom." This increase in the birthrate, however, did not last, and the size of families began to decline by the mid-1960s. Largely responsible for this decline was the widespread practice of birth control. The condom, invented in the nineteenth century, was already in wide use, but the development in the 1960s of oral contraceptives, known as birth control pills or simply "the pill," provided a convenient and reliable means of birth control that quickly spread to all Western countries.

The trend toward smaller families contributed to changes in women's employment in both Europe and the United States, primarily because women now needed to devote far fewer years to rearing children. That led to a large increase in the number of married women in the workforce. At the beginning of the twentieth century, even working-class wives tended to stay at home if they could afford to do so. In the postwar period, this was no longer the case. In the United States, for example, in 1900, married women made up about 15 percent of the female labor force; by 1970, their number had increased to 62 percent.

But the increased number of women in the workforce did not change some old patterns. Working-class women in particular still earned salaries lower than those of men for equal work. In the 1960s, women earned only 60 percent of men's wages in Britain, 50 percent in France, and 63 percent in West Germany. In addition, women still tended to enter traditionally female jobs. Many European women also still faced the double burden of earning income on the one hand and raising a family and maintaining the household on the other. Such inequalities led increasing numbers of women to rebel.

The Feminist Movement: The Search for Liberation
Women's wartime participation helped them achieve one of the major aims of the nineteenth-century feminist movement—the right to vote. After World War I, many governments acknowledged the contributions of women to the war effort by granting them suffrage. Sweden, Great Britain, Germany, Poland, Hungary, Austria, and Czechoslovakia did so in 1918, followed by the United States in 1920. Women in France and Italy did not obtain the right to vote until 1945. After World War II, little was heard of feminist concerns, but by the 1960s, women began to assert their rights again and speak as feminists. Along with the student upheavals of the late 1960s came

"THE TIMES THEY ARE A-CHANGIN'": THE MUSIC OF YOUTHFUL PROTEST

In the 1960s, the lyrics of rock music reflected the rebellious mood of many young people. Bob Dylan (b. 1941), who became a vastly influential performer and recording artist, expressed the feelings of the younger generation. His song "The Times They Are a-Changin'," released in 1964, has been called an "anthem for the protest movement."

What caused the student campus revolts of the 1960s? What and whom does Dylan identify in this song as the problem?

Bob Dylan, "The Times They Are a-Changin'"

Come gather 'round people
Wherever you roam
And admit that the waters
Around you have grown
And accept it that soon
You'll be drenched to the bone
If your time to you
Is worth savin'
Then you better start swimmin'
Or you'll sink like a stone
For the times they are a-changin'

Come writers and critics
Who prophesize with your pen
And keep your eyes wide
The chance won't come again
And don't speak too soon
For the wheel's still in spin
And there's no tellin' who
That it's namin'
For the loser now
Will be later to win
For the times they are a-changin'

Come senators, congressmen
Please heed the call

Don't stand in the doorway
Don't block up the hall
For he that gets hurt
Will be he who has stalled
There's a battle outside
And it is ragin'
It'll soon shake your windows
And rattle your walls
For the times they are a-changin'

Come mothers and fathers
Throughout the land
And don't criticize
What you can't understand
Your sons and your daughters
Are beyond your command
Your old road
Is rapidly agin'
Please get out of the new one
If you can't lend your hand
For the times they are a-changin'

The line it is drawn
The curse it is cast
The slow one now
Will later be fast
As the present now
Will later be past
The order is
Rapidly fadin'
And the first one now
Will later be last
For the times they are a-changin'

ThomsonNOW™ To read more of Bob Dylan's song lyrics, enter the *ThomsonNOW* documents area using the access card that is available for *The Essential World History*.

---

renewed interest in **feminism,** or the **women's liberation movement,** as it was now called.

Of great importance to the emergence of the post-war women's liberation movement was the work of Simone de Beauvoir (1908–1986), who supported herself as a teacher and later as a novelist and writer. De Beauvoir believed that she lived a "liberated" life for a twentieth-century European woman, but for all her freedom, she still came to perceive that as a woman, she faced limits that men did not. In 1949, she published her highly influential work *The Second Sex,* in which she argued that as a result of male-dominated societies, women had been defined by their differences from men

and consequently received second-class status: "What particularly signalizes the situation of woman is that she—a free autonomous being like all human creatures—nevertheless finds herself in a world where men compel her to assume the status of the Other."[2] De Beauvoir took an active role in the French women's movement of the 1970s, and her book was a major influence on both sides of the Atlantic.

Transformation in Women's Lives To ensure natural replacement of a country's population, women need to produce an average of 2.1 children each. Many European countries fell far short of this mark; their populations stopped growing in the 1960s, and the trend has continued ever since. By the 1990s, among the nations of the European Union, the average number of children per mother was 1.4. Spain's rate, 1.15 in 2002, was among the lowest in the world.

At the same time, the number of women in the workforce has continued to rise. In Britain, for example, women accounted for 32 percent of the labor force in 1970 but 44 percent in 1990. Moreover, women have entered new employment areas. Greater access to universities and professional schools enabled women to take jobs in law, medicine, government, business, and education. In the Soviet Union, for example, about 70 percent of doctors and teachers were women. Nevertheless, economic inequality still often prevailed; women received lower wages than men for comparable work and received fewer promotions to management positions.

Feminists in the women's liberation movement came to believe that women themselves must transform the fundamental conditions of their lives. Women sought and gained a measure of control over their own bodies by seeking to legalize both contraception and abortion. In the 1960s and 1970s, hundreds of thousands of European women worked to repeal laws that outlawed contraception and abortion and began to meet with success. Even in Catholic countries, where the church remained opposed to abortion, legislation allowing contraception and abortion was passed in the 1970s and 1980s.

As more women became activists, they also became involved in new issues. Some women began to try to affect the political environment by allying with the antinuclear movement. In 1981, a group of women protested American nuclear missiles in Britain by chaining themselves to the fence of an American military base. Thousands more joined in creating a peace camp around the military compound. Enthusiasm ran high; one participant said, "I'll never forget that feeling; it'll live with me for ever. . . . As we walked round, and we clasped hands . . . It was for women; it was for peace; it was for the world."[3]

Some women joined the ecological movement. As one German writer who was concerned with environmental issues said, it is women "who must give birth to children, willingly or unwillingly, in this polluted world of ours." Especially prominent was the number of women members in the Green Party in Germany (see "The Environment and the Green Movements" later in this chapter).

Women in the West have also reached out to work with women from the rest of the world in international conferences to change the conditions of their lives. Between 1975 and 1995, the United Nations held conferences on women's issues in Mexico City, Copenhagen, Nairobi, and Beijing. These meetings made clear the differences between women from Western and non-Western countries. Whereas women from Western countries spoke about political, economic, cultural, and sexual rights, women from developing countries in Latin America, Africa, and Asia focused their attention on

bringing an end to the violence, hunger, and disease that haunt their lives.

The Growth of Terrorism

Acts of terror by individuals and groups opposed to governments became a frightening aspect of modern Western society. During the late 1970s and early 1980s, small bands of terrorists used assassination, indiscriminate killing of civilians, the taking of hostages, and the hijacking of airplanes to draw attention to their demands or to destabilize governments in the hope of achieving their political goals. Terrorist acts garnered considerable media attention. When Palestinian terrorists kidnapped and killed eleven Israeli athletes at the Munich Olympic Games in 1972, hundreds of millions of people watched the drama unfold on television.

Motivations for terrorist acts varied considerably. Left- and right-wing terrorist groups flourished in the late 1970s and early 1980s, but terrorist acts also stemmed from militant nationalists who wished to create separatist states. Most prominent was the Irish Republican Army (IRA), which resorted to vicious attacks against the ruling government and innocent civilians in Northern Ireland.

Although left- and right-wing terrorist activities declined in Europe in the 1980s, international terrorism remained rather commonplace. Angered over the loss of their territory to Israel, some militant Palestinians responded with a policy of terrorist attacks against Israel's supporters. Palestinian terrorists operated throughout European countries, attacking both Europeans and American tourists; Palestinian terrorists massacred vacationers at airports in Rome and Vienna in 1985. State-sponsored terrorism was often an integral part of international terrorism. Militant governments, especially in Iran, Libya, and Syria, assisted terrorist organizations that carried out attacks on Europeans and Americans. On December 21, 1988, Pan American flight 103 from Frankfurt to New York exploded over Lockerbie, Scotland, killing all 259 passengers and crew members. A massive investigation finally revealed that the bomb responsible for the explosion had been planted by two Libyan terrorists.

Terrorist Attack on the United States   One of the most destructive acts of terrorism occurred on September 11, 2001, in the United States. Four groups of terrorists hijacked four commercial jet airplanes after takeoff from Boston, Newark, and Washington, D.C. The hijackers flew two of the airplanes directly into the towers of the World Trade Center in New York City, causing these buildings, as well as a number of surrounding buildings, to collapse. A third hijacked plane slammed into the Pentagon near Washington, D.C. The fourth plane, apparently headed for Washington, crashed instead in an isolated area of Pennsylvania. In total, more than three thousand people were killed, including everyone aboard the four airliners.

POLITICS &
GOVERNMENT

COMPARATIVE ILLUSTRATION

International Terrorism. International terrorism had become commonplace by the start of the twenty-first century. At the left is a picture of a hijacked U.S. airliner about to hit one of the twin towers of the World Trade Center in New York City while smoke billows from the site of the first such attack on September 11, 2001. This devastating plot was carried out by an international terrorist group known as al-Qaeda. At the right is a scene from another al-Qaeda attack, the bombing of two nightclubs in Bali, a popular resort in Indonesia, on October 12, 2002. Almost two hundred people, including Indonesians, Australians, Canadians, French, and Britons were killed, and more than one hundred others were injured.

These coordinated acts of terror were carried out by hijackers connected to an international terrorist organization known as al-Qaeda (see the comparative illustration above), run by the mysterious Osama bin Laden. A native of Saudi Arabia of Yemeni extraction, bin Laden used an inherited fortune to set up terrorist training camps in Afghanistan, under the protection of that nation's militant fundamentalist Islamic rulers known as the Taliban.

U.S. president George W. Bush vowed to wage a lengthy and thorough war on terrorism and worked to create a coalition of nations to assist in ridding the world of al-Qaeda and other terrorist groups. Within weeks of the attack on America, U.S. and NATO air forces began bombing Taliban-controlled command centers, airfields, and al-Qaeda hiding places in Afghanistan. On the ground, Afghan forces, assisted by U.S. special forces, pushed the Taliban out and gained control of the country by the end of November. A democratic multiethnic government was installed but continues to face problems from revived Taliban activity (see Chapter 28).

The Environment and the Green Movements

Beginning in the 1970s, environmentalism became an important item on the European political agenda. By that time, serious ecological problems had become all too apparent. Air pollution, produced by nitrogen oxide and sulfur dioxide emissions from road vehicles, power plants, and industrial factories, was causing respiratory illnesses and having corrosive effects on buildings and monuments. Many rivers, lakes, and seas had become so polluted that they posed serious health risks. Dying forests and disappearing wildlife alarmed more and more people. The opening of Eastern Europe after the revolutions of 1989 brought to the world's attention the incredible environmental destruction of that region caused by unfettered industrial pollution.

Environmental concerns forced the major political parties in Europe to advocate new regulations for the protection of the environment. A disastrous accident at the Soviet nuclear power plant at Chernobyl, Ukraine, in 1986 made Europeans even more aware of potential environmental hazards, and 1987 was touted as the "year of the environment."

Growing ecological awareness also gave rise to Green movements and Green parties throughout Europe in the 1970s. Most visible was the Green Party in Germany, which was officially organized in 1979 and by 1987 had elected forty-two delegates to the West German parliament. Green parties also competed successfully in Sweden, Austria, and Switzerland.

Western Culture Since 1945

Intellectually and culturally, the Western world since World War II has been notable for its diversity and innovation. Especially since 1970, new directions have led some observers to speak of a postmodern cultural world.

Postwar Literature The most significant new trend in postwar literature was known as the Theater of the Absurd. Its most famous proponent was the Irishman Samuel Beckett (1906–1990), who lived in France. In Beckett's *Waiting for Godot* (1952), the action on the stage is transparently unrealistic. Two men wait around for the appearance of someone, with whom they may or may not have an appointment. During the course of the play, nothing seems to be happening. The audience is never told if the action in front of them is real or imagined. Suspense is maintained not by having the audience wonder "What is going to happen next?" but simply "What is happening now?"

The Theater of the Absurd reflected its time. The postwar period was one of disillusionment with fixed ideological beliefs in politics or religion. The same disillusionment that inspired the **existentialism** of writers Albert Camus (1913–1960) and Jean-Paul Sartre (1905–1980), with its sense of the world's meaninglessness, underscored the bleak worldview of absurdist drama and literature. The beginning point of the existentialism of Sartre and Camus was the absence of God in the universe. Although the death of God was tragic, it also meant that humans had no preordained destiny and were utterly alone in the universe with no future and no hope. As Camus expressed it:

> A world that can be explained even with bad reasons is a familiar world. But, on the other hand, in a universe suddenly divested of illusions and lights, man feels an alien, a stranger. His exile is without remedy since he is deprived of the memory of a lost home or the hope of a promised land. This divorce between man and his life, the actor and his setting, is properly the feeling of absurdity.[4]

According to Camus, then, the world was absurd and without meaning; humans, too, are without meaning and purpose. Reduced to despair and depression, humans have but one source of hope—themselves.

Postmodernism The term *Postmodern* covers a variety of intellectual and artistic styles and ways of thinking that have been prominent since the 1970s. In the broadest sense, **Postmodernism** rejects the modern Western belief in an objective truth and instead focuses on the relative nature of reality and knowledge.

While existentialism wrestled with notions of meaning and existence, a group of French philosophers in the 1960s attempted to understand how meaning and knowledge operate through the study of language and signs. **Poststructuralism** or **deconstruction,** formulated by Jacques Derrida (1930–2004), holds that culture is created and can therefore be analyzed in a variety of ways, according to the manner in which people create their own meaning. Hence there is no fixed truth or universal meaning.

Michel Foucault (1926–1984) drew on Derrida to explore relationships of power. Believing that "power is exercised, rather than possessed," Foucault argued that the diffusion of power and oppression marks all relationships. For example, any act of teaching entails components of assertion and submission, as the student adopts the ideas of the person in power. Therefore, all norms are culturally produced and entail some degree of power struggle.

Postmodernism was also evident in literature. One center of Postmodernism was in Central and Eastern Europe, especially in the work of Milan Kundera (b. 1929) of Czechoslovakia. Kundera blended fantasy with realism, using fantasy to examine moral issues while remaining optimistic about the human condition. Indeed, in his first novel, *The Unbearable Lightness of Being*, published in 1984, Kundera does not despair because of the political repression that he so aptly describes in his native Czechoslovakia but allows his characters to use love as a way to a better life. The human spirit can be lessened but not destroyed.

Trends in Art

Following the war, the United States dominated the art world, much as it did the world of popular culture. New York City replaced Paris as the artistic center of the West. The Guggenheim Museum, the Museum of Modern Art, and the Whitney Museum of Modern Art, together with New York's numerous art galleries, promoted modern art and helped determine artistic tastes throughout much of the world. One of the styles that became synonymous with the emergence of the New York art scene was **Abstract Expressionism.**

Dubbed "action painting" by one critic, Abstract Expressionism was energetic and spontaneous, qualities evident in the enormous canvases of Jackson Pollock (1912–1956). In such works as *Lavender Mist* (1950) paint seems to explode, enveloping the viewer with emotion and movement. Pollock's swirling forms and seemingly chaotic patterns broke all conventions of form and structure. His drip paintings, with their total abstraction, were extremely influential with other artists, and he eventually became a celebrity. Inspired by Native American sand painters, Pollock painted with the canvas on the floor. He explained, "On the floor I am more at ease. I feel nearer, more a part of the painting, since this way I can walk around it, work from four sides and be literally *in* the painting. When I am in the painting, I am not aware of what I am doing. There is pure harmony."

Postmodernism's eclectic commingling of past tradition with Modernist innovation became increasingly evident in architecture. Robert Venturi argued that architects should look as much to the commercial strips of Las Vegas as to the historical styles of the past for inspiration. One example is provided by Charles Moore. His *Piazza d'Italia* (1976–1980) in New Orleans is an outdoor plaza that combines classical Roman columns with stainless steel and neon lights. This blending of

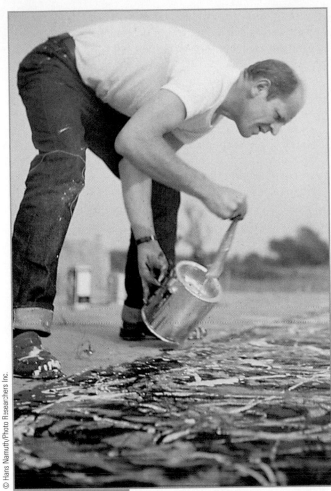

Jackson Pollock at Work. One of the best-known practitioners of Abstract Expressionism, which remained at the center of the artistic mainstream after World War II, was the American Jackson Pollock, who achieved his ideal of total abstraction in his drip paintings. He is shown here at work at his Long Island studio. Pollock found it easier to cover his large canvases with exploding patterns of color when he put them on the ground.

modern-day materials with historical references distinguished the Postmodern architecture of the late 1970s and 1980s from the Modernist glass box.

The World of Science and Technology

Many of the scientific and technological achievements since World War II have revolutionized people's lives. During World War II, university scientists were recruited to work for their governments and develop new weapons and practical instruments of war. British physicists played a crucial role in the development of an improved radar system that helped defeat the German air force in the Battle of Britain in 1940. German scientists created self-propelled rockets as well as jet airplanes to keep Hitler's hopes alive for a miraculous turnaround in the war. The computer, too, was a wartime creation. The British mathematician Alan Turing designed a primitive

computer to assist British intelligence in breaking the secret codes of German ciphering machines. The most famous product of wartime scientific research was the atomic bomb, created by a team of American and European scientists under the guidance of the physicist J. Robert Oppenheimer. Although most wartime devices were created for destructive purposes, they could easily be adapted for peacetime uses.

The postwar alliance of science and technology led to an accelerated rate of change that became a fact of life in Western society (see the comparative essay, "From the Industrial Age to the Technological Age" on p. 626). One product of this alliance—the computer—may yet prove to be the most revolutionary of all the technological inventions of the twentieth century. Early computers, which required thousands of vacuum tubes to function, were large and hot and took up considerable space. The development of the transistor and then the silicon chip produced a revolutionary new approach to computer design. With the invention in 1971 of the microprocessor, a machine that combines the equivalent of thousands of transistors on a single, tiny silicon chip, the road was open for the development of the personal computer. By the 1990s, the personal computer had become a regular fixture in businesses, schools, and homes. The Internet—the world's largest computer network—provides millions of people around the world with quick access to immense quantities of information, as well as rapid communication and commercial transactions. By 2000, an estimated 500 million people were using the Internet.

Despite the marvels produced by science and technology, some people came to question their underlying assumption—that scientific knowledge gave human beings the ability to manipulate the environment for their benefit. They maintained that some technological advances had far-reaching side effects that were damaging to the environment. Chemical fertilizers, for example, once touted for producing larger crops, wreaked havoc with the ecological balance of streams, rivers, and woodlands. *Small Is Beautiful*, written by the British economist E. F. Schumacher (1911–1977), was a fundamental critique of the dangers of the new science and technology (see the box on p. 627).

The Explosion of Popular Culture

Popular culture since 1900, and especially since World War II, has played an important role in helping Western people define themselves. It also reflects the economic system that supports it, for this system manufactures, distributes, and sells the images that people consume as popular culture. Modern popular culture is therefore inextricably tied to the mass consumer society in which it has emerged.

The United States has been the most influential force in shaping popular culture in the West and, to a lesser degree, the entire world. Through movies, music,

COMPARATIVE ESSAY

FROM THE INDUSTRIAL AGE TO THE TECHNOLOGICAL AGE

SCIENCE &
TECHNOLOGY

As many observers have noted, a key aspect of the world economy is that it is in the process of transition to what has been called a "postindustrial age," characterized by a system that is not only increasingly global in scope but also increasingly technology-intensive in character. Since World War II, a stunning array of technological changes—especially in transportation, communications, space exploration, medicine, and agriculture—have transformed the world in which we live. Technological changes have also raised new questions and concerns as well as producing some unexpected results. Some scientists have worried that genetic engineering might accidentally result in new strains of deadly bacteria that cannot be controlled outside the laboratory. Some doctors have recently warned that the overuse of antibiotics has created supergerms that are resistant to antibiotic treatment. The Technological Revolution has also led to the development of more advanced methods of destruction. Most frightening have been nuclear weapons.

The transition to a technology-intensive postindustrial world, which the futurologist Alvin Toffler has dubbed the Third Wave (the first two being the Agricultural and Industrial Revolutions), has produced difficulties for people in many walks of life—for blue-collar workers, whose high wages price them out of the market as firms begin to move their factories abroad; for the poor and uneducated, who lack the technical skills to handle complex tasks in the contemporary economy; and even for some members of the middle class, who have been fired or forced into retirement as their employers seek to reduce payrolls or outsource jobs to compete in the global marketplace.

It is now increasingly clear that the Technological Revolution, like the Industrial Revolution that preceded it, will entail enormous consequences and may ultimately give birth to a new era of social and political instability. The success of advanced capitalist states in the post–World War II era has been built on a broad consensus on the importance of two propositions: (1) the need for high levels of government investment in education, communications, and transportation as a means of meeting the challenges of continued economic growth and technological innovation and (2) the desirability of cooperative efforts in the international arena as a means of maintaining open markets for the free exchange of goods.

In the new century, these assumptions are increasingly under attack as citizens refuse to support education and oppose the formation of trading alliances to promote the free movement of goods and labor across national borders. The breakdown of the public consensus that brought modern capitalism to a pinnacle of achievement raises serious questions about the likelihood that the coming challenges of the Third Wave can be successfully met without a growing measure of political and social tension.

advertising, and television, the United States has spread its particular form of consumerism and the American dream to millions around the world. In 1923, the *New York Morning Post* noted that "the film is to America what the flag was once to Britain. By its means Uncle Sam may hope some day . . . to Americanize the world."[5] That day has already come.

Motion pictures were the primary vehicle for the diffusion of American popular culture in the years immediately following World War I and continued to find ever wider markets as the century rolled on. Television, developed in the 1930s, did not become readily available until the late 1940s, but by 1954, there were 32 million sets in the United States as television became the centerpiece of middle-class life. In the 1960s, as television spread around the world, American networks unloaded their products on Europe and the Third World at extraordinarily low prices.

The United States has also dominated popular music since the end of World War II. Jazz, blues, rhythm and blues, rap, and rock and roll have been by far the most popular music forms in the Western world—and much of the non-Western world—during this time. All of them originated in the United States, and all are rooted in African American musical innovations. These forms later spread to the rest of the world, inspiring local artists, who then transformed the music in their own ways.

The introduction of the video music channel MTV in the early 1980s radically changed the music scene by making image as important as sound in the selling of records. Artists like Michael Jackson and Madonna became superstars by treating the music video as an art form. Rather than merely a recorded performance, many videos were short films with elaborate staging and special effects set to music. The music of the 1980s was also affected by technological advances, especially the advent of the synthesizer, an electronic piano that produced computerized sounds.

In the postwar years, sports have become a major product of both popular culture and the leisure industry. The development of satellite television and various electronic breakthroughs have helped make sports a global phenomenon. Olympic Games can now be broadcast around the globe from anywhere in the world. Sports have become a cheap form of entertainment, as fans do not have to leave their homes to enjoy athletic competitions. As sports television revenues have escalated, many sports now receive the bulk of their yearly revenue from television contracts.

SMALL IS BEAUTIFUL: THE LIMITS OF MODERN TECHNOLOGY

Although science and technology have produced an amazing array of achievements in the postwar world, some voices have been raised in criticism of their sometimes destructive aspects. In 1975, in his book *Small is Beautiful,* the British economist E. F. Schumacher examined the effects modern industrial technology has had on the earth's resources.

According to Schumacher, under what illusion are modern humans living? What three irreplaceable things does he suggest people are consuming without noticing? What is "technology with a human face"? How does the author suggest this might transform modern life? Are Schumacher's ideas Postmodern? Why or why not?

E. F. Schumacher, *Small Is Beautiful*

Is it not evident that our current methods of production are already eating into the very substance of industrial man? To many people this is not at all evident. Now that we have solved the problem of production, they say, have we ever had it so good? Are we not better fed, better clothed, and better housed than ever before—and better educated? Of course we are: most, but by no means all, of us: in the rich countries. But this is not what I mean by "substance." The substance of [humankind] cannot be measured by Gross National Product. Perhaps it cannot be measured at all, except for certain symptoms of loss. However, this is not the place to go into the statistics of these symptoms, such as crime, drug addiction, vandalism, mental breakdown, rebellion, and so forth. Statistics never prove anything.

I started by saying that one of the most fateful errors of our age is the belief that the problem of production has been solved. This illusion, I suggested, is mainly due to our inability to recognize that the modern industrial system, with all its intellectual sophistication, consumes the very basis on which it has been erected. To use the language of the economist, it lives on irreplaceable capital which it cheerfully treats as income. I specified three categories of such capital: fossil fuels, the tolerance margins of nature, and the human substance. Even if some readers should refuse to accept all three parts of my argument, I suggest that any one of them suffices to make my case.

And what is my case? Simply that our most important task is to get off our present collision course. And who is there to tackle such a task? I think every one of us. . . . To talk about the future is useful only if it leads to action *now*. And what can we do *now*, while we are still in the position of "never having had it so good"? To say the least . . . we must thoroughly understand the problem and begin to see the possibility of evolving a new lifestyle, with new methods of production and new patterns of consumption: a lifestyle designed for permanence. To give only three preliminary examples: in agriculture and horticulture, we can interest ourselves in the perfection of production methods which are biologically sound, build up soil fertility, and produce health, beauty, and permanence. Productivity will then look after itself. In industry, we can interest ourselves in the evolution of small-scale technology, relatively nonviolent technology, "technology with a human face," so that people have a chance to enjoy themselves while they are working, instead of working solely for their pay packet and hoping, usually forlornly, for enjoyment solely during their leisure time.

CONCLUSION

ESTERN EUROPE BECAME a new community in the 1950s and 1960s as a remarkable economic recovery fostered a new optimism. Western European states became accustomed to political democracy, and with the development of the European Community, many of them began to move toward economic unity. But nagging economic problems, new ethnic divisions, environmental degradation, and the inability to work together to stop a civil war in their own backyard have all indicated that what had been seen as a glorious new path for Europe in the 1950s and 1960s had become laden with pitfalls in the 1990s and early 2000s.

In the Western Hemisphere, the two North American countries—the United States and Canada—built prosperous economies and relatively stable communities in the 1950s, but there too, new problems, including ethnic, racial, and linguistic differences as well as persistent

economic difficulties, dampened the optimism of the earlier decade. Though some Latin American nations shared in the economic growth of the 1950s and 1960s, it was not matched by any real political stability. Only in the 1980s did democratic governments begin to replace oppressive military regimes.

Western societies after 1945 were also participants in an era of rapidly changing international relationships. While Latin American countries struggled to find a new relationship with the colossus to the north, European states reluctantly let go of their colonial empires. Between 1947 and 1962, virtually every colony achieved independence and statehood. Decolonization was a difficult and even bitter process, but as we shall see in the next chapters, it created a new world as the non-Western states ended the long ascendancy of the Western nations.

TIMELINE

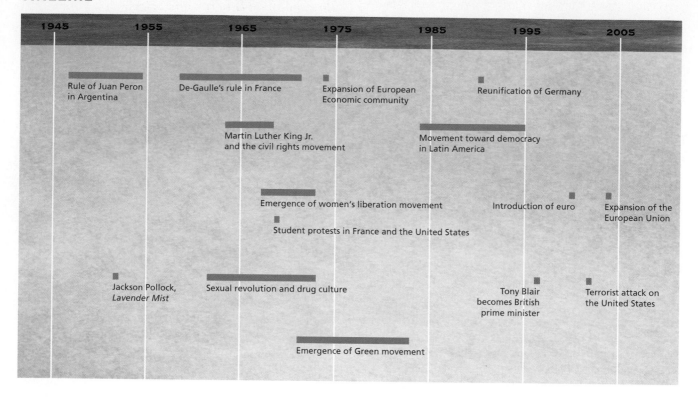

CHAPTER NOTES

1. Quoted in W. I. Hitchcock, *The Struggle for Europe: The Turbulent History of a Divided Continent, 1945–2002* (New York, 2003), pp. 399–400.

2. Simone de Beauvoir, *The Second Sex,* trans. H. M. Parshley (New York, 1961), p. xxviii.

3. Quoted in Renate Bridenthal, "Women in the New Europe," in Renate Bridenthal, Susan Mosher Stuard, and Merry E. Wiesner, eds., *Becoming Visible: Women in European History,* 3d ed. (Boston, 1998), pp. 564–565.

4. Quoted in Henry Grosshans, *The Search for Modern Europe* (Boston, 1970), p. 421.

5. Quoted in Richard Maltby, ed., *Passing Parade: A History of Popular Culture in the Twentieth Century* (New York, 1989), p. 11.

SUGGESTED READINGS

For a well-written survey on Europe since 1945, see **W. I. Hitchcock, *The Struggle for Europe: The Turbulent History of a Divided Continent, 1945–2002*** (New York, 2002), and **T. Judt, *Postwar: A History of Europe Since 1945*** (New York, 2005). The rebuilding of postwar Europe is examined in **D. W. Ellwood, *Rebuilding Europe: Western Europe, America, and Postwar Reconstruction*** (London, 1992). On the building of common institutions in Western Europe, see **S. Henig, *The Uniting of Europe: From Discord to Concord*** (London, 1997). For a survey of West Germany, see **H. A. Turner, *Germany from Partition to Reunification*** (New Haven, Conn., 1992). France under de Gaulle is examined in **A. Shennan, *De Gaulle***

(New York, 1993), and **D. J. Mahoney, *De Gaulle: Statesmanship, Grandeur, and Modern Democracy*** (Westport, Conn., 1996). On Britain, see **K. O. Morgan, *The People's Peace: British History, 1945–1990*** (Oxford, 1992). On the recent history of these countries, see **E. J. Evans, *Thatcher and Thatcherism*** (New York, 1997); **S. Baumann-Reynolds, *François Mitterrand*** (Westport, Conn., 1995); and **K. Jarausch, *The Rush to German Unity*** (New York, 1994).

For a general survey of American history, see **Stephan Thernstrom, *A History of the American People,*** 2d ed. (San Diego, Calif., 1989). **D. J. Garrow, *Martin Luther King Jr. and the Southern Christian Leadership Conference*** (New York, 1986), discusses the emergence of the civil rights movement. On the turbulent decade of the 1960s, see **W. O'Neill, *Coming Apart: An Informal History of America in the 1960s*** (Chicago, 1971). Works on more recent events include **B. Glad, *Jimmy Carter: From Plains to the White House*** (New York, 1980), and **G. Wills, *Reagan's America: Innocents at Home*** (New York, 1987). On Canadian history, see **R. Bothwell, I. Drummond,** and **J. English, *Canada Since 1945*** (Toronto, 1981).

For general surveys of Latin American history, see **E. B. Burns, *Latin America: A Concise Interpretive Survey,*** 4th ed. (Englewood Cliffs, N.J., 1986), and **E. Williamson, *The Penguin History of Latin America*** (London, 1992). The twentieth century is the focus of **T. E. Skidmore** and **P. H. Smith, *Modern Latin America,*** 3d ed. (New York, 1992). Works on other countries examined in this chapter include **L. A. Pérez, *Cuba: Between Reform and Revolution*** (New York, 1988); **J. A. Page, *Perón: A Biography*** (New York, 1983); **D. Rock, *Argentina, 1516–1987: From Spanish Colonization to Alfonsín,*** 2d ed. (Berkeley, Calif., 1987); and **M. C. Meyer** and **W. L. Sherman, *The Course of Mexican History,*** 4th ed. (New York, 1991).

The student revolts of the late 1960s are put into a broader context in **D. Caute,** *The Year of the Barricades: A Journey Through 1968* (New York, 1988). On the turbulent 1960s, see **A. Marwick,** *The Sixties: Social and Cultural Transformation in Britain, France, Italy, and the United States* (Oxford, 1999). On the women's liberation movement, see **D. Bouchier,** *The Feminist Challenge: The Movement for Women's Liberation in Britain and the United States* (New York, 1983); **T. Keefe,** *Simone de Beauvoir* (New York, 1998); and **C. Duchen,** *Women's Rights and Women's Lives in France, 1944–1968* (New York, 1994). On the sexual revolution, see **D. Allyn,** *Make Love, Not War—The Sexual Revolution: An Unfettered History* (New York, 2000). On terrorism, see **W. Laqueur,** *Terrorism,* 2d ed. (New York, 1988). On the development of the Green parties, see **M. O'Neill,** *Green Parties and Political Change in Contemporary Europe* (Aldershot, England, 1997).

For a general view of postwar thought, see **R. N. Stromberg,** *European Intellectual History Since 1789,* 5th ed. (Englewood Cliffs, N.J., 1990). On the arts, see **A. Marwick,** *Arts in the West Since 1945* (Oxford, 2002). There is an excellent survey of twentieth-century popular culture in **R. Maltby,** ed., *Passing Parade: A History of Popular Culture in the Twentieth Century* (New York, 1989)

InfoTrac College Edition

Visit this chapter's InfoTrac College Edition/Research activities at the *Essential World History* Companion Website for activities related to Europe and the Western Hemisphere since 1945.

ThomsonNOW™ for Duiker and Spielvogel's *The Essential World History, Third Edition*

Enter *ThomsonNOW* using the access card that is available with this text. *ThomsonNOW* will assist you in understanding the content in this chapter with lesson plans generated for your needs, as well as provide you with a connection to the *Wadsworth World History Resource Center* (see description below for details).

WORLD HISTORY
RESOURCE CENTER

Enter the Resource Center using either your *ThomsonNOW* access card or your standalone access card for the *Wadsworth World History Resource Center.* Organized by topic, this website includes quizzes; images; over 350 primary source documents; interactive simulations, maps, and timelines; movie explorations; and a wealth of other resources. You can read the following documents, and many more, at http://worldrc.wadsworth.com/

> Speeches by Ronald Reagan
>
> Joint speech on counterterrorism by George W. Bush and Vladimir Putin

Visit the *Essential World History* Companion Website for chapter quizzes and more:

> http://www.thomsonedu.com/history/duiker

DISCOVERY

What are the similarities and differences between the major political, economic, and social developments in the first half of the twentieth century and those in the second half of the century?

In thinking about this question, begin by breaking it down into the components shown below. A discussion of the significance of each component should appear in your answer.

POLITICS AND GOVERNMENT: Examine the map of the new Europe. Look also at the maps of Latin America, Africa, Asia, and the aftermath of World Wars I and II. What evidence can you find in this chapter that for the first time in many centuries, "Europe" exists entirely on the European continent? Why is this?

European Union, 2004

Latin America in the First Half of the Nineteenth Century

Africa in 1914

Territorial Changes in Europe and the Middle East after World War I

World War II in Europe and North Africa

World War II in Asia and the Pacific

FAMILY AND SOCIETY: What does the portion of Margaret Thatcher's autobiography about her political life reveal about the changing place of women in European society? Do you see the thread of a historical argument running through her interviewer's questions about her suitability for candidacy? Why couldn't Thatcher have won the office of prime minister at the beginning of the twentieth century? (Think not only about the political position of women but also about the social position of women.) Compare Thatcher's achievements with the fictional achievements of Nora in Ibsen's *A Doll's House.*

MARGARET THATCHER, *THE PATH TO POWER*

And, as always with me, there was politics. I immediately joined the Conservative Association and threw myself into the usual round of Party activities. In particular, I thoroughly enjoyed what was called the "'39–'45" discussion group, where Conservatives of the war generation met to exchange views and argue about the political topics of the day. . . . It was as a representative of the Oxford University Graduate Conservative Association (OUGCA) that I went to the Llandudno Conservative Party Conference in October 1948.

It had originally been intended that I should speak at the Conference, seconding an OUGCA motion deploring the abolition of university seats. At that time universities had separate representation in Parliament, and graduates had the right to vote in their universities as well as in the constituency where they lived. (I supported separate university representation, but not the principle that graduates should have more than one vote. . . .) It would have been my first Conference speech, but in the end the seconder chosen was a City man, because the City seats were also to be abolished.

My disappointment at this was, however, very quickly overcome and in a most unexpected way. After one of the debates, I found myself engaged in one of those speculative conversations which young people have about their future prospects. An Oxford friend, John Grant, said he supposed that one day I would like to be a Member of Parliament. "Well, yes," I replied, "but there's not much hope of that. The chances of my being selected are just nil at the moment." I might have added that with no private income of my own there was no way I could have afforded to be an MP on the salary then available. I had not even tried to get on the Party's list of approved candidates.

Later in the day, John Grant happened to be sitting next to the Chairman of the Dartford Conservative Association, John Miller. The Association was in search of a candidate. I learned afterwards that the conversation went something like this: "I understand that you're still looking for a candidate at Dartford?" . . .

"That's right. Any suggestions?"

"Well, there's a young woman, Margaret Roberts, that you might look at. She's very good."

"Oh, but Dartford is a real industrial stronghold. I don't think a woman would do at all."

"Well, you know best of course. But why not just look at her?"

And they did. I was invited to have lunch with John Miller and his wife, Phee, and the Dartford Woman's Chairman, Mrs. Fletcher, on the Saturday on Llandudno Pier. Presumably, and in spite of any reservations about the suitability of a woman candidate for their seat, they liked what they saw. I certainly got on well with them. . . .

HENRIK IBSEN, *A DOLL'S HOUSE*

Nora: (*Pause*) Does anything strike you as we sit here?

Helmer: What should strike me?

Nora: We've been married eight years; does it not strike you that this is the first time we two, you and I, man and wife, have talked together seriously?

Helmer: Seriously? What do you mean, *seriously?*

Nora: For eight whole years, and more—ever since the day we first met—we have never exchanged one serious word about serious things. . . .

Helmer: Why, my dearest Nora, what have you to do with serious things?

Nora: There we have it! You have never understood me. I've had great injustice done to me, Torvald; first by father, then by you.

Helmer: What! Your father and me? We, who have loved you more than all the world?

Nora (*Shaking her head*): You have never loved me. You just found it amusing to think you were in love with me.

Helmer: Nora! What a thing to say!

Nora: Yes, it's true, Torvald. When I was living at home with father, he told me his opinions and mine were the same. If I had different opinions, I said nothing about them, because he would not have liked it. He used to call me his doll-child and played with me as I played with my dolls. Then I came to live in your house.

Helmer: What a way to speak of our marriage!

Nora (*Undisturbed*): I mean that I passed from father's hands into yours. You arranged everything to your taste and I got the same tastes as you; or pretended to—I don't know which—both, perhaps; sometimes one, sometimes the other. When I look back on it now, I seem to have been living here like a beggar, on hand-outs. I lived by performing tricks for you, Torvald. But that was how you wanted it. You and father have done me a great wrong. It is your fault that my life has come to naught.

Helmer: Why, Nora, how unreasonable and ungrateful! Haven't you been happy here?

Nora: No, never. I thought I was, but I never was.

Helmer: Not—not happy! . . .

Nora: I must stand quite alone if I am ever to know myself and my surroundings; so I cannot stay with you.

Helmer: Nora! Nora!

Nora: I am going at once. I daresay [my friend] Christina will take me in for tonight.

Helmer: You are mad! I shall not allow it! I forbid it!

Nora: It's no use your forbidding me anything now. I shall take with me only what belongs to me; from you I will accept nothing, either now or later.

Helmer: This is madness!

Nora: Tomorrow I shall go home—I mean to what was my home. It will be easier for me to find a job there.

Helmer: Oh, in your blind inexperience—

Nora: I must try to gain experience, Torvald.

Helmer: Forsake your home, your husband, your children! And you don't consider what the world will say.

Nora: I can't pay attention to that. I only know that I must do it.

Helmer: This is monstrous! Can you forsake your holiest duties?

Nora: What do you consider my holiest duties?

Helmer: Need I tell you that? Your duties to your husband and children.

Nora: I have other duties equally sacred.

Helmer: Impossible! What do you mean?

Nora: My duties toward myself.

Helmer: Before all else you are a wife and a mother.

Nora: That I no longer believe. Before all else I believe I am a human being, just as much as you are—or at least that I should try to become one. I know that most people agree with you, Torvald, and that they say so in books. But I can no longer be satisfied with what most people say and what is in books. I must think things out for myself and try to get clear about them.

$\mathcal{28}$

CHALLENGES OF NATION BUILDING IN AFRICA AND THE MIDDLE EAST

CHAPTER OUTLINE AND FOCUS QUESTIONS

Uhuru: The Struggle for Independence in Africa

▢ What role did nationalist movements play in the transition to independence in Africa, and how did such movements differ from their counterparts elsewhere?

The Era of Independence

▢ How have dreams clashed with realities in the independent nations of Africa, and how have African governments sought to meet these challenges?

Continuity and Change in Modern African Societies

▢ How did the rise of independent states affect the lives and the role of women in African societies? How does that role compare with other parts of the contemporary world?

Crescent of Conflict

▢ What problems have the nations of the Middle East faced since the end of World War II, and to what degree have they managed to resolve those problems?

Society and Culture in the Contemporary Middle East

▢ How have religious issues affected economic, social, and cultural conditions in the Middle East in recent decades?

CRITICAL THINKING

▢ What factors can be advanced to explain the chronic instability and internal conflict that have characterized conditions in Africa and the Middle East since World War II?

The African community: soul of a continent

© Herbert M. Cole

$\mathcal{A}$T THE END OF WORLD WAR II, many societies in Asia and Africa had already been exposed to over half a century of colonial rule. Although Europeans complacently assumed that colonialism was a necessary evil in the process of introducing civilization to backward peoples around the globe, many Asians and Africans disagreed. Some even argued that the Western drive for political hegemony and economic profit, far from being a panacea for the world's ills, was a plague that threatened ultimately to destroy human civilization.

One aspect of Western civilization that many observers in Asia and Africa rejected was the concept of the nation-state as the natural unit of communal identity in the modern world. In their view, nationalism was at the root of many of the evils of the twentieth century and should be rejected as a model for development in the postwar period. In Africa, some intellectuals pointed to the traditional village community as a unique symbol of the humanistic and spiritual qualities of the African people and promoted the concept of "blackness" (**negritude**) as a common bond that could knit all the peoples of the continent into a cohesive community. A similar rejection of the nation-state was prevalent in the

Middle East, where many Muslims viewed Western materialist culture as a threat to the fundamental principles of Islam. To fend off the new threat from an old adversary, some dreamed of resurrecting the concept of a global caliphate (see Chapter 7) to unify all Muslim peoples in realizing their common destiny throughout the Islamic world.

Time has not been kind to such dreams of transnational solidarity and cooperation in the postwar world. Although the peoples of Africa and the Middle East were gradually liberated from the formal trappings of European authority, the legacy of colonialism in the form of political inexperience and continued European economic domination has frustrated the efforts of the leaders of the emerging new states to achieve political stability. At the same time, arbitrary boundaries imposed by the colonial powers, combined with ethnic and religious divisions, have led to bitter conflicts that have posed a severe obstacle to the dream of solidarity and cooperation in forging a common destiny. Today, these two regions, although blessed with enormous potential, are among the most volatile and conflict-ridden areas in the world. ◇

Uhuru: The Struggle for Independence in Africa

In the three decades following the end of World War II, the peoples of Africa were gradually liberated from the formal trappings of European colonialism.

The Colonial Legacy

As in Asia, colonial rule had a mixed impact on the societies and peoples of Africa (see Chapter 20). The Western presence brought a number of short-term and long-term benefits to Africa, such as improved transportation and communication facilities, and in a few areas laid the foundation for a modern industrial and commercial sector. Improved sanitation and medical care increased life expectancy. The introduction of selective elements of Western political systems after World War II laid the basis for the gradual creation of democratic societies.

Yet the benefits of Westernization were distributed very unequally, and the vast majority of Africans found their lives little improved, if at all. Only South Africa and French-held Algeria, for example, developed modern industrial sectors, extensive railroad networks, and modern communications systems. In both countries, European settlers were numerous, most investment capital for industrial ventures was European, and whites constituted almost the entire professional and managerial class. Members of the native population were generally restricted to unskilled or semiskilled jobs at wages less than one-fifth those enjoyed by Europeans.

Many colonies concentrated on export crops— peanuts in Senegal and Gambia, cotton in Egypt and Uganda, coffee in Kenya, palm oil and cocoa products in the Gold Coast. Here the benefits of development were somewhat more widespread. In some cases, the crops were grown on plantations, which were usually owned by Europeans. But plantation agriculture was not always suitable in Africa (sometimes the cultivation of cash crops eroded the fragile soil base and turned farmland into desert), and much farming was done by free or tenant farmers. In some areas, where landownership was traditionally vested in the community, the land was owned and leased by the corporate village. The vast majority of the profits from the exports, however, accrued to Europeans or to merchants from other foreign countries, such as India and the Arab emirates. The vast majority of Africans continued to be subsistence farmers growing food for their own consumption.

The Rise of Nationalism

Political organizations for African rights did not arise until after World War I, and then only in a few areas, such as British-ruled Kenya and the Gold Coast. After World War II, following the example of independence movements elsewhere, groups organized political parties with independence as their objective. In the Gold Coast, Kwame Nkrumah (1909–1972) led the Convention People's Party, the first formal political party in black Africa. In the late 1940s, Jomo Kenyatta (1894–1978) founded the Kenya African National Union (KANU), which focused on economic issues but had an implied political agenda as well.

For the most part, these political activities were basically nonviolent and were led by Western-educated African intellectuals. Their constituents were primarily urban professionals, merchants, and members of labor unions. But the demand for independence was not entirely restricted to the cities. In Kenya, for example, the widely publicized Mau Mau movement among the Kikuyu people used terrorism as an essential element of its program to achieve *uhuru* (Swahili for "freedom") from the British. Although most of the violence was directed against other Africans, the specter of Mau Mau terrorism alarmed the European population and convinced the British government in 1959 to promise eventual independence.

In areas such as South Africa and Algeria, where the political system was dominated by European settlers, the transition to independence was more complicated. In South Africa, political activity by local Africans began with the formation of the African National Congress (ANC) in 1912. Initially, the ANC was dominated by Western-oriented intellectuals and had little mass support. Its goal was to achieve economic and political reforms, including full equality for educated Africans, within the framework of the existing system. But the ANC's efforts met with little success, while conservative white parties managed to stiffen the segregation laws. In response, the ANC became increasingly radicalized, and by the 1950s, the prospects for a violent confrontation were growing.

In Algeria, resistance to French rule by Berbers and Arabs in rural areas had never ceased. After World War II, urban agitation intensified, leading to a widespread rebellion against colonial rule in the mid-1950s. At first, the French government tried to maintain its authority in Algeria. But when Charles de Gaulle became president in 1958, he reversed French policy, and Algeria became independent under President Ahmad Ben Bella (1918–2004) in 1962. The armed struggle in Algeria hastened the transition to statehood in its neighbors as well. Tunisia won its independence in 1956 after some urban agitation and rural unrest but retained close ties with Paris. The French attempted to suppress the nationalist movement in Morocco by sending Sultan Muhammad V into exile, but the effort failed; in 1956, he returned as the ruler of the independent state of Morocco.

Most black African nations achieved their independence in the late 1950s and 1960s, beginning with the Gold Coast, now renamed Ghana, in 1957 (see Map 28.1).

Nigeria, the Belgian Congo (renamed Zaire and then the Democratic Republic of the Congo), Kenya, Tanganyika (later, when joined with Zanzibar, renamed Tanzania), and several other countries soon followed. Most of the French colonies agreed to accept independence within the framework of de Gaulle's French Community. By the late 1960s, only parts of southern Africa and the Portuguese possessions of Mozambique and Angola remained under European rule.

Independence came later to Africa than to most of Asia. Several factors help explain the delay. For one thing, colonialism was established in Africa somewhat later than in most areas of Asia, and the inevitable reaction from the local population was consequently delayed. Furthermore, with the exception of a few areas in West Africa and along the Mediterranean, coherent states with a strong sense of cultural, ethnic, and linguistic unity did not exist in most of Africa. Most traditional states, such as Ashanti in West Africa, Songhai in the southern Sahara, and Bakongo in the Congo basin, were collections of heterogeneous peoples with little sense of national or cultural identity. It is hardly surprising that when opposition to colonial rule emerged, unity was difficult to achieve.

The Era of Independence

The newly independent African states faced intimidating challenges. Although Western political institutions, values, and technology had been introduced, at least in the cities, the exposure to European civilization had been superficial at best for most Africans and tragic for many. At the outset of independence, most African societies were still primarily agrarian and traditional, and their modern sectors depended mainly on imports from the West.

Pan-Africanism and Nationalism: The Destiny of Africa

Like the leaders of the new states in South and Southeast Asia, most African leaders came from the urban middle class. They had studied in either Europe or the United States and spoke and read European languages. Although most were profoundly critical of colonial policies, they appeared to accept the relevance of the

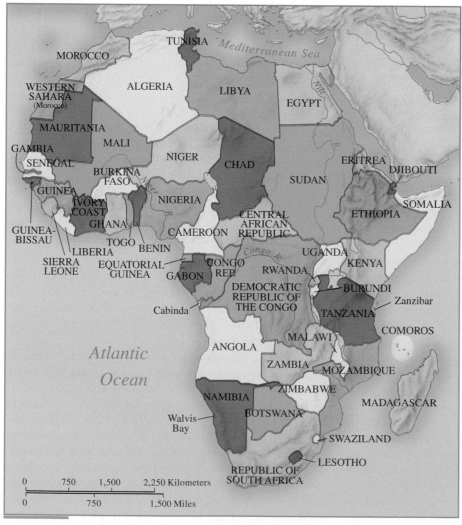

MAP 28.1 **Modern Africa.** This map shows the division of independent states in Africa today. ❓ Why was unity so difficult to achieve in African regions?

TOWARD AFRICAN UNITY

POLITICS & GOVERNMENT

In May 1963, the leaders of thirty-two African states met in Addis Ababa, the capital of Ethiopia, to discuss the creation of an organization that would represent the interests of all the newly independent countries of Africa. The result was the Organization of African Unity. An excerpt from its charter is presented here. Although the organization did not realize all of the aspirations of its founders, it provided a useful forum for the discussion and resolution of its members' common problems. In 2001, it was replaced by the new African Union, which was designed to bring about increased cooperation among the states on the continent.

What are the key objectives expressed in this charter? To what degree have they been achieved?

Charter of the Organization of African Unity

We, the Heads of African States and Governments assembled in the City of Addis Ababa, Ethiopia;

CONVINCED that it is the inalienable right of all people to control their own destiny;

CONSCIOUS of the fact that freedom, equality, justice, and dignity are essential objectives for the achievement of the legitimate aspirations of the African peoples;

CONSCIOUS of our responsibility to harness the natural and human resources of our continent for the total advancement of our peoples in spheres of human endeavor;

INSPIRED by a common determination to promote understanding among our peoples and cooperation among our States in response to the aspirations of our peoples for brotherhood and solidarity, in a larger unity transcending ethnic and national differences;

CONVINCED that, in order to translate this determination into a dynamic force in the cause of human progress, conditions for peace and security must be established and maintained;

DETERMINED to safeguard and consolidate the hard-won independence as well as the sovereignty and territorial integrity of our States, and to fight against neocolonialism in all its forms;

DEDICATED to the general progress of Africa; . . .

DESIROUS that all African States should henceforth unite so that the welfare and well-being of their peoples can be assured;

RESOLVED to reinforce the links between our states by establishing and strengthening common institutions;

HAVE agreed to the present Charter.

ThomsonNOW To read the full version of this document, enter the *ThomsonNOW* documents area using the access card that is available for *The Essential World History*.

Western model to Africa and gave at least lip service to Western democratic values.

Their views on economics were somewhat more diverse. Some, like Jomo Kenyatta of Kenya and General Mobutu Sese Seko (1930–1998) of Zaire, were advocates of Western-style capitalism. Others, like Julius Nyerere (1922–1999) of Tanzania, Kwame Nkrumah of Ghana, and Sékou Touré (1922–1984) of Guinea, preferred an "African form of socialism," which bore slight resemblance to the Marxist-Leninist socialism practiced in the Soviet Union. According to its advocates, it was descended from traditional communal practices in precolonial Africa.

Like the leaders of other developing countries, the new political leaders in Africa were highly nationalistic and generally accepted the colonial boundaries. But as we have seen, these boundaries were artificial creations of the colonial powers. Virtually all of the new states included widely diverse ethnic, linguistic, and territorial groups. Zaire, for example, was composed of more than two hundred territorial groups speaking seventy-five different languages.

A number of leaders—including Nkrumah of Ghana, Touré of Guinea, and Kenyatta of Kenya—were enticed by the dream of **pan-Africanism,** a concept of continental unity that transcended national boundaries. Nkrumah in particular hoped a pan-African union could be established that would unite all of the new countries of the continent in a broader community. His dream achieved concrete manifestation in the Organization of African Unity (OAU), which was founded in 1963 (see the box above).

Pan-Africanism originated among African intellectuals during the first half of the twentieth century. A basic element was the concept of **negritude,** which held that there was a distinctive "African personality" that owed nothing to Western materialism and provided a common sense of destiny for all black African peoples. Whereas Western civilization prized rational thought and material achievement, African culture emphasized emotional expression and a common sense of humanity.

Dream and Reality: Political and Economic Conditions in Independent Africa

The program of the OAU called for an Africa based on freedom, equality, justice, and dignity and on the unity, solidarity, prosperity, and territorial integrity of African states. It did not take long for reality to set in. Vast disparities in education and income made it hard to establish democracy in much of Africa. Expectations that independence would lead to stable political structures based on "one person, one vote" were soon disappointed as the initial phase of pluralistic governments gave way to a series of military regimes and one-party states. Between 1957 and 1982, more than seventy leaders of African countries were overthrown by violence, and the pace has not abated in recent years.

Hopes that independence would inaugurate an era of economic prosperity and equality were similarly dashed. Part of the problem could be (and was) ascribed to the lingering effects of colonialism. Most new countries in Africa were dependent on the export of a single crop or natural resource. When prices fluctuated or dropped, these countries were at the mercy of the vagaries of the international market. In several cases, the resources were still controlled by foreigners, leading to the charge that colonialism had been succeeded by **neocolonialism,** in which Western domination was maintained by economic rather than by political or military means. To make matters worse, most African states had to import technology and manufactured goods from the West, and the prices of those goods rose more rapidly than those of the export products.

World trade policies often exacerbated these problems. While advanced countries took aggressive action to reduce tariff barriers on the worldwide flow of industrial goods, at the same time they provided massive subsidies to protect domestic producers of agricultural goods, thus preventing poor countries in Africa and Asia from improving their economic conditions through agricultural exports.

The new states also contributed to their own problems. Scarce national resources were squandered on military equipment or expensive consumer goods rather than on building up their infrastructure to provide the foundation for an industrial economy. Corruption, a painful reality throughout the modern world, became almost a way of life in Africa as bribery became necessary to obtain even the most basic services.

Finally, population growth, which more than anything else has hindered economic growth in the new nations of Asia and Africa, became a serious problem and crippled efforts to create modern economies. By the mid-1980s, annual population growth averaged nearly 3 percent throughout Africa, the highest rate of any continent. Drought conditions and the inexorable spread of the Sahara (usually known as **desertification,** a condition caused partly by overcultivation of the land) have led to widespread hunger and starvation, first in West African countries such as Niger and Mali and then in Ethiopia, Somalia, and the Sudan. Over the next fifteen years, the population throughout the continent is predicted to increase by at least 300 million.

One factor that has begun to affect the rate of population growth is the spread of disease. In recent years, the prevalence of HIV and AIDS in Africa has reached epidemic proportions. According to one recent report, over 75 percent of all the AIDS cases reported around the world are on the continent of Africa. Some observers estimate that without measures to curtail the effects of the disease, it will have a significant impact on several African countries by reducing population growth.

Poverty is endemic in Africa, particularly among the three-quarters of the population still living off the land. Urban areas have grown tremendously, but as in much of Asia, most are surrounded by massive squatter settlements of rural peoples who had fled to the cities in search of a better life. The expansion of the cities has overwhelmed fragile transportation and sanitation systems and led to rising pollution and perpetual traffic jams, while millions are forced to live without running water and electricity. Meanwhile, the fortunate few (all too often government officials on the take) live the high life and emulate the consumerism of the West (in a particularly expressive phrase, the rich in many East African countries are known as *wabenzi,* or Mercedes-Benz people).

The Search for Solutions

While the problems of nation building mentioned so far have to one degree or another afflicted all of the emerging states of Africa throughout the continent, each has sought to deal with the challenge in its own way, and sometimes with strikingly different consequences. Despite all its shared difficulties, Africa today remains one of the most diverse regions on the globe.

Tanzania: An African Route to Socialism   Concern over the dangers of economic inequality inspired a number of African leaders to restrict foreign investment and nationalize the major industries and utilities while promoting democratic ideals and values. Julius Nyerere of Tanzania was the most consistent, promoting the ideals of socialism and self-reliance through his Arusha Declaration of 1967. Taking advantage of his powerful political influence, Nyerere placed limitations on income and established village collectives to avoid the corrosive effects of economic inequality and government corruption. Sympathetic foreign countries provided considerable economic aid to assist the experiment, and many observers noted that levels of corruption, political instability, and ethnic strife were lower in Tanzania than in many other African countries. Unfortunately, corruption has increased in recent years, while political elements on the island of Zanzibar, citing the stagnation brought by two decades of socialism, are agitating for autonomy or even total separation from the mainland. Tanzania also has poor soil, inadequate rainfall, and limited resources, all of which have contributed to its slow growth and continuing rural and urban poverty.

Kenya: The Perils of Capitalism   The countries that opted for capitalism faced their own dilemmas. Neighboring Kenya, blessed with better soil in the highlands, a local tradition of aggressive commerce, and a residue of European settlers, welcomed foreign investment and profit incentives. The results have been mixed. Kenya has a strong current of indigenous African capitalism and a substantial middle

Cape Town: A Tale of Two Cities.   First settled by the Dutch in the seventeenth century, Cape Town is the most modern city in Africa, as well as one of its most beautiful. Situated at the foot of scenic Table Mountain, its business and financial center has long been dominated by Europeans (see left photo). Despite the abolition of apartheid in the 1990s, much of Cape Town's black population still resides in the crowded "townships" located along the fringes of the city, as shown in the right photo.

class, mostly based in the capital, Nairobi. But landlessness, unemployment, and income inequities are high, even by African standards (almost one-fifth of the country's thirty million people are squatters, and unemployment is currently estimated at 45 percent). The rate of population growth—more than 3 percent annually—is one of the highest in the world. Eighty percent of the population remains rural, and 40 percent live below the poverty line. The result has been widespread unrest in a country formerly admired for its successful development.

Kenya's problems have been exacerbated by chronic disputes between disparate ethnic groups and a simmering tension in relations between farmers and pastoralists. For many years, the country maintained a fragile political stability under the dictatorial rule of President Daniel arap Moi, one of the most authoritarian of African leaders. Plagued by charges of corruption, Moi finally agreed to retire in 2002.

South Africa: An End to Apartheid   Perhaps Africa's greatest success story is South Africa, where the white government—which long maintained a policy of racial segregation (**apartheid**) and restricted black sovereignty to a series of small "Bantustans" in relatively infertile areas of the country—finally accepted the inevitability of African involvement in the political process and the national economy. In 1990, the government of President F. W. de Klerk (b. 1936) released African National Congress leader Nelson Mandela (b. 1918) from prison, where he had been held since 1964. In 1993, the two leaders agreed to hold democratic national elections the following spring. In the meantime, ANC representatives agreed to take part in a transitional coalition government with de Klerk's National Party. Those elections resulted in a substantial majority for the ANC, and Mandela became president. In May 1996, a new constitution was approved, calling for a multiracial state.

In 1999, a major step toward political stability was taken when Nelson Mandela stepped down from the presidency, to be replaced by his long-time disciple Thabo Mbeki. The new president faced a number of intimidating problems, including rising unemployment, widespread lawlessness, chronic corruption, and an ominous flight of capital and professional personnel from the country. Government promises to carry out an extensive land reform program—aimed at providing farmland to the nation's forty million black farmers—have not been fulfilled, provoking some squatters to seize unused private lands near Johannesburg.

Still, South Africa remains the wealthiest and most industrialized state in Africa and the best hope that a multiracial society can succeed on the continent. The country's black elite now number nearly one-quarter of its wealthiest households, compared with only 9 percent in 1991.

Nigeria: A Nation Divided   If the situation in South Africa provides grounds for modest optimism, the situation in Nigeria provides reason for serious concern. Africa's largest country in terms of population and one of its wealthiest because of substantial oil reserves, Nigeria had for many years been in the grip of military strongmen. During his rule, General Sani Abacha ruthlessly suppressed all opposition and in late 1995 ordered the execution of a writer despite widespread protests from human rights groups abroad. Abacha died in 1998, and national elections held the next year led to the creation of a civilian government under Olusegun Obasanjo (b. 1937). Civilian leadership has not been a panacea for Nigeria's problems, however. In early 2000, religious riots between Christians and Muslims broke out in several northern cities as a result of the decision by provincial officials to apply Islamic law throughout their jurisdictions.

© Herbert M. Cole

Performing a Ritual Dance. For many Africans, the focus of their historical identity lies not in the big cities but in the countless small communities that dot the landscape of their continent. Yet within that traditional concept lies the source of bitter conflict, as in the long-standing tension between cattle herders such as the Masai and the Fulani and the cultivators of the soil, many of them members of the Kikuyu language family. Shown here is a pastoral community in northern Kenya performing a traditional ritual dance. Desiccation of the savanna grasslands has forced many such communities to migrate southward, where they compete for precious lands with indigenous farmers. Conflicts over land—often exacerbated by religious differences—threaten the precarious stability of many African nations.

The dispute between Muslims and Christians in Nigeria is a contemporary variant of the traditional tensions that have existed between farmers and pastoralists throughout recorded history. Muslim cattle herders, migrating southward to escape the increasing desiccation of the grasslands south of the Sahara, compete for precious land with indigenous—primarily Christian—farmers. Often the confrontation leads to outbreaks of violence with strong religious and ethnic overtones. Although President Obasanjo has sought to defuse the crisis, the dispute threatens the fragile unity of Africa's most populous country.

A similar fault line between farmers and pastoralists has been at the root of the lengthy civil war that has been raging in the Sudan. Conflict between Muslim pastoralists—supported by the central government in Khartoum—and predominantly Christian black farmers in the southern part of the country was finally brought to an end in 2004, but new outbreaks of violence have erupted in western Darfur province, leading to reports of widespread starvation among the local villagers. At first, women singers, known as *hakamah,* chanted songs of bravery to inspire their Muslim brethren to victory. Later they were persuaded to change their lyrics and to entreat their compatriots to bring an end to the bloodshed, so far without success.

Central Africa: Cauldron of Conflict The most tragic situation is in the Central African states of Rwanda and Burundi, where a chronic conflict between the minority Tutsis and the Hutu majority has led to a bitter civil war, with thousands of refugees fleeing to the neighboring Congo. In another classic example of conflict between pastoral and farming peoples, the nomadic Tutsis, supported by the colonial Belgian government, had long dominated the sedentary Hutu population. It was the attempt of the Bantu-speaking Hutus to bring an end to Tutsi domination that initiated the most recent conflicts, marked by massacres on both sides. In the meantime, the presence of large numbers of foreign troops and refugees intensified centrifugal forces inside Zaire, where General Mobutu Sese Seko had long ruled with an iron hand. In 1997, military forces led by Mobutu's longtime opponent Lauren Kabila managed to topple the general's corrupt government. Once in power, Kabila renamed the country the Democratic Republic of the Congo and promised a return to democratic practices. The new government systematically suppressed political dissent, however, and in January 2001, Kabila was assassinated, to be succeeded by his son. Although peace talks to end the conflict began that fall and a United Nations peacekeeping force was stationed in the country, the situation remains unstable.

Sowing Seeds of Democracy Not all the news in Africa has been bad. Stagnant economies have led to the collapse of one-party regimes and the emergence of fragile democracies in several countries. Dictatorships were brought to an end in Ethiopia, Liberia, and Somalia, although in each case the fall of the regime was later followed by political instability or civil war. In Senegal, national elections held in the summer of 2000 brought an end to four decades of rule by the once-dominant Socialist Party. The new president, Abdoulaye Wade, is a staunch advocate of promoting development throughout Africa on the capitalist model. Perhaps the most notorious dictator was Idi Amin of Uganda, who led a military coup against Prime Minister Milton Obote in 1971. After ruling by terror and brutal repression of dissident elements, he was finally deposed in 1979. In recent years, stability has returned to the country, which in May 1996 held its first presidential election in more than fifteen years.

Statehood for Ghana	1957
Algeria gains independence from France	1962
Formation of the Organization of African Unity	1963
Release of ANC chairman Nelson Mandela from prison	1990
Nelson Mandela elected president of South Africa	1994
Civil War in Central Africa	1996–2000
Olusegun Obasanjo elected president of Nigeria	1999
Creation of African Union	2001

The African Union: A Glimmer of Hope It is clear that African societies have not yet begun to surmount the challenges they have faced since independence. Most African states are still poor and their populations illiterate. Moreover, African concerns continue to carry little weight in the international community. A recent agreement by the World Trade Organization on the need to reduce agricultural subsidies in the advanced nations has been widely ignored. In 2000, the United Nations General Assembly passed a Millennium Declaration calling for a dramatic reduction in the incidence of poverty, hunger, and illiteracy worldwide by the year 2015. So far, however, little has been done to realize these ambitious goals. At a conference held in September 2005, the participants squabbled over how best to fund the effort. Some delegations, including that of the United States, argued that external assistance cannot succeed unless African nations adopt measures to bring about good government and sound economic policies.

Certainly, part of the solution to the continent's multiple problems must come from within. Although there are gratifying signs of progress toward achieving political stability in some countries, including Senegal, Uganda, and South Africa, other nations like Sudan, Liberia, Somalia, and Zimbabwe are still racked by civil war or ruled by brutal dictatorships. Conflicts between Muslims and Christians in West Africa threaten to spread throughout the region. To alleviate such problems, UN peacekeeping forces have been sent to several African countries, including the Democratic Republic of the Congo, Eritrea, the Ivory Coast, and Sierra Leone.

A significant part of the problem is that the nation-state system is not particularly well suited to the African continent. Africans must find better ways to cooperate with each other and to protect and promote their own interests. A first step in that direction was taken in 1991, when the OAU agreed to establish the African Economic Community (AEC). In 2001, the OAU was replaced by the African Union, which is intended to provide greater political and economic integration throughout the continent on the pattern of the European Union (see Chapter 27). The new organization has already sought to mediate several of the conflicts in the region.

As Africa evolves, it is useful to remember that economic and political change is often an agonizingly slow and painful process. Introduced to industrialization and concepts of Western democracy only a century ago, African societies are still groping for ways to graft Western political institutions and economic practices onto a native structure still significantly influenced by traditional values and attitudes.

Continuity and Change in Modern African Societies

In general, the impact of the West has been greater on urban and educated Africans and more limited on their rural and illiterate compatriots. After all, the colonial presence was first and most firmly established in the cities. Many cities, including Dakar, Lagos, Johannesburg, Cape Town, Brazzaville, and Nairobi, are direct products of the colonial experience. Most African cities today look like their counterparts elsewhere in the world. They have high-rise buildings, blocks of residential apartments, wide boulevards, neon lights, movie theaters, and traffic jams.

Education

The educational system has been the primary means of introducing Western values and culture. In the precolonial era, formal schools did not really exist in Africa except for parochial schools in Christian Ethiopia and academies to train young males in Islamic doctrine and law in Muslim societies in North and West Africa. For the average African, education took place at the home or in the village courtyard and stressed socialization and vocational training. Traditional education in Africa was not necessarily inferior to that in Europe. Social values and customs were transmitted to the young by storytellers, often village elders, who could gain considerable prestige through their performance.

Europeans introduced modern Western education into Africa in the nineteenth century. At first, the schools concentrated on vocational training, with some instruction in European languages and Western civilization. Eventually, pressure from Africans led to the introduction of professional training, and the first institutes of higher learning were established in the early twentieth century.

With independence, African countries established their own state-run schools. The emphasis was on the primary level, but high schools and universities were established in major cities. The basic objectives have been to introduce vocational training and improve literacy rates. Unfortunately, both funding and trained teachers are scarce in most countries, and few rural areas have schools. As a result, illiteracy remains high, estimated at about 70 percent of the population across the continent. There has been a perceptible shift toward education in the vernacular languages. In West Africa, only about one in four adults is conversant in a Western language.

COMPARATIVE ILLUSTRATION

EARTH & ENVIRONMENT

Traditional Patterns in the Countryside. In various parts of the world, many people continue to follow patterns of living that are centuries old. In Africa, houses in the countryside are often constructed from a wooden frame woven from poles and branches, known as wattle, daubed with mud and then covered with a thatched roof. At the left is a scene from a Kenyan village not far from the Indian Ocean, where a young man is applying mud to the wall of his future house. The photo at the right shows a village in India, where housing styles and village customs have changed little since they were first described by Portuguese travelers in the sixteenth century. Note that the houses have thatched roofs and mud-and-straw walls plastered with dung reminiscent of those found in Africa.

Rural Life

Outside the major cities, where about three-quarters of the continent's inhabitants live, Western influence has had less of an impact. Millions of people throughout Africa (as in Asia) live much as their ancestors did, in thatched huts without modern plumbing and electricity (see the comparative illustration above); they farm or hunt by traditional methods, practice time-honored family rituals, and believe in the traditional deities. Even here, however, change is taking place. Slavery has been eliminated, for the most part, although there have been persistent reports of raids by slave traders on defenseless villages in the southern Sudan. Economic need, though, has brought about massive migrations as some leave to work on plantations, others move to the cities, and still others flee to refugee camps to escape starvation.

African Women

One of the consequences of colonialism and independence has been a change in the relationship between men and women. In precolonial Africa, as in traditional societies in Asia, men and women had distinctly different roles. Women in sub-Saharan Africa, however, generally did not live under the severe legal and social disabilities that we have seen in such societies as China and India (see Chapter 21). Their role, it has been said, was "complementary rather than subordinate to that of men."[1] As we

have seen, however, the role of women changed in a number of ways in colonial Africa, and not for the better (see Chapter 20).

The Impact of Independence   Independence has had a significant impact on gender roles in African society. Almost without exception, the new governments established the principle of sexual equality and permitted women to vote and run for political office. Yet as elsewhere, women continue to operate at a disability in a world dominated by males. Politics remains a male preserve, and although a few professions, such as teaching, child care, and clerical work, are dominated by women, most African women are employed in menial positions such as agricultural labor, factory work, and retail trade or as domestics. Education is open to all at the elementary level, but women comprise less than 20 percent of students at the upper levels in most African societies today.

Not surprisingly, women have made the greatest strides in the cities. Most urban women, like men, now marry on the basis of personal choice, although a significant minority are still willing to accept their parents' choice. After marriage, African women appear to occupy a more equal position than their counterparts in most Asian countries (see Chapters 27 and 29). Each marriage partner tends to maintain a separate income, and women often have the right to possess property separate from their husbands. While many wives still defer to their husbands in the traditional manner, others are like the woman in Abioseh Nicol's story "A Truly Married Woman," who, after years of living as a common law wife with her husband, is finally able to provide the price and finalize the marriage. After the wedding, she declares, "For twelve years I have got up every morning at five to make tea for you and breakfast. Now I am a truly married woman [and] you must treat me with a little more respect. You are now my husband and not a lover. Get up and make yourself a cup of tea."[2]

In rural areas, where traditional attitudes continue to exert a strong influence, individuals may still be subordinated to communalism. In some societies, female genital mutilation, the traditional rite of passage for a young girl's transit to womanhood, is still widely practiced. Polygamy is also not uncommon, and arranged marriages are still the rule rather than the exception. The dichotomy between rural and urban values can lead to acute tensions. Many African villagers regard the cities as the fount of evil, decadence, and corruption. Women in particular have suffered from the tension between the pull of the city and the village. As men are drawn to the cities in search of employment and excitement, their wives and girlfriends are left behind, both literally and figuratively, in the native village.

African Culture

Inevitably, the tension between traditional and modern, native and foreign, and individual and communal that has permeated contemporary African society has spilled over into culture. In general, in the visual arts and music, utility and ritual have given way to pleasure and decoration. In the process, Africans have been affected to a certain extent by foreign influences but have retained their distinctive characteristics. Wood carving, metalwork, painting, and sculpture, for example, have preserved their traditional forms but are now increasingly adapted to serve the tourist industry and the export market.

Literature No area of African culture has been so strongly affected by political and social events as literature. Except for Muslim areas in North and East Africa, precolonial Africans did not have a written literature, although their tradition of oral storytelling served as a rich repository of history, custom, and folk culture. The first written literature in the vernacular or in European languages emerged during the nineteenth century in the form of novels, poetry, and drama.

Angry at the negative portrayal of Africa in Western literature, African authors initially wrote primarily for a European audience as a means of establishing black dignity and purpose. Embracing the ideals of *négritude,* many glorified the emotional and communal aspects of the traditional African experience. The Nigerian Chinua Achebe is considered the first major African novelist to write in the English language. In his writings, he attempted to interpret African history from a native perspective and to forge a new sense of African identity.

In his trailblazing novel *Things Fall Apart* (1958), he recounted the story of a Nigerian who refused to submit to the new British order and eventually committed suicide. Criticizing his contemporaries who accepted foreign rule, the protagonist lamented that the white man "has put a knife on the things that held us together and we have fallen apart."

In recent decades, the African novel has taken a dramatic turn, shifting its focus from the brutality of the foreign oppressor to the shortcomings of the new native leadership. Having gained independence, African politicians were portrayed as mimicking and even outdoing the injustices committed by their colonial predecessors. A prominent example of this genre is the work of the Kenyan Ngugi Wa Thiong'o (b. 1938). His first novel, *A Grain of Wheat,* takes place on the eve of *uhuru,* or independence. Although it mocks the racism, snobbishness, and superficiality of local British society, its chief interest lies in its unsentimental and even unflattering portrayal of ordinary Kenyans in their daily struggle for survival.

Many of Ngugi's contemporaries have followed his lead and focused their frustration on the failure of the continent's new leadership to carry out the goals of independence (see the box on p. 640). One of the most outstanding is the Nigerian Wole Soyinka (b. 1934). His novel *The Interpreters* (1965) lambasted the corruption and hypocrisy of Nigerian politics. Succeeding novels and plays have continued that tradition, resulting in a Nobel Prize for literature in 1986. In 1994, however, Soyinka barely managed to escape arrest, and he now lives abroad.

A number of Africa's most prominent writers today are women. Traditionally, African women were valued for their talents as storytellers, but writing was strongly discouraged by both traditional and colonial authorities on the grounds that women should occupy themselves with their domestic obligations. In recent years, however, a number of women have emerged as prominent writers of African fiction. Two examples are Buchi Emecheta (b. 1940) of Nigeria and Ama Ata Aidoo (b. 1942) of Ghana. Beginning with *Second Class Citizen* (1975), which chronicled the breakdown of her own marriage, Emecheta has published numerous works exploring the role of women in contemporary African society and decrying the practice of polygamy. Ama Ata Aidoo has focused on the identity of today's African women and the changing relations between men and women in society. In her novel *Changes: A Love Story* (1991), she chronicles the lives of three women, none presented as a victim but all caught up in the struggle for survival and happiness.

The Destiny of Africa

Nowhere in the developing world is the dilemma of continuity and change more agonizing than in Africa. Mesmerized by the spectacle of Western affluence yet repulsed by the bloody trail from slavery to World War

STEALING THE NATION'S RICHES

ARTS & IDEAS

After 1965, African novelists transferred their anger from the foreign oppressor to their own national leaders, deploring their greed, corruption, and inhumanity. One of the most pessimistic expressions of this betrayal of newly independent Africa is found in *The Beautiful Ones Are Not Yet Born,* a novel published by the Ghanaian author Ayi Kwei Armah in 1968. The author decried the government of Kwame Nkrumah and was unimpressed with the rumors of a military coup, which, he predicted, would simply replace the present regime with a new despot and his entourage of "fat men."

According to the author of this passage, who is to blame for conditions in his country? Did the charter of the OAU (see the box on p. 633) make provision for dealing with this situation?

Ayi Kwei Armah, *The Beautiful Ones Are Not Yet Born*

The net had been made in the special Ghanaian way that allowed the really big corrupt people to pass through it. A net to catch only the small, dispensable fellows, trying in their anguished blindness to leap and to attain the gleam and the comfort the only way these things could be done. And the big ones floated free, like all the slogans. End bribery and corruption. Build Socialism. Equality. Shit. A man would just have to make up his mind that there was never going to be anything but despair, and there would be no way of escaping it. . . .

In the life of the nation itself, maybe nothing really new would happen. New men would take into their hands the power to steal the nation's riches and to use it for their own satisfaction. That, of course, was to be expected. New people would use the country's power to get rid of men and women who talked a language that did not flatter them. There would be nothing different in that. That would only be a continuation of the Ghanaian way of life. But here was the real change. The individual man of power now shivering, his head filled with the fear of the vengeance of those he had wronged. For him everything was going to change. And for those like him who had grown greasy and fat singing the praises of their chief, for those who had been getting themselves ready for the enjoyment of hoped-for favors, there would be long days of pain ahead. The flatterers with their new white Mercedes cars would have to find ways of burying old words. For those who had come directly against the old power, there would be much happiness. But for the nation itself there would only be a change of embezzlers and a change of the hunters and the hunted. A pitiful shrinking of the world from those days Teacher still looked back to, when the single mind was filled with the hopes of a whole people. A pitiful shrinking, to days when all the powerful could think of was to use the power of a whole people to fill their own paunches. Endless days, same days, stretching into the future with no end anywhere in sight.

ThomsonNOW To read Nkrumah's point of view, enter the *ThomsonNOW* documents area using the access card that is available for *The Essential World History.*

II and the atomic bombs over Hiroshima and Nagasaki, African intellectuals have been torn between the dual images of Western materialism and African negritude.

What is the destiny of Africa? Some Africans still yearn for the dreams embodied in the program of the OAU. Novelist Ngugi Wa Thiong'o calls for "an internationalization of all the democratic and social struggles for human equality, justice, peace, and progress."[3] Some African political leaders, however, have apparently discarded the democratic ideal and turned their attention to what is sometimes called the "East Asian model," based on the Confucian tenet of subordination of the individual to the community as the guiding principle of national development (see Chapter 29). Whether African political culture today is well placed to imitate the strategy adopted by the fast-growing nations of East Asia—which in any event are now encountering problems of their own—is questionable. Like all peoples, Africans must ultimately find their own solutions within the context of their own traditions, not by seeking to imitate the example of others.

Crescent of Conflict

"We Muslims are of one family even though we live under different governments and in various regions."[4] So said Ayatollah Ruholla Khomeini, the Islamic religious figure and leader of the 1979 revolution that overthrew the shah in Iran. The ayatollah's remark was not just a pious wish by a religious mystic but an accurate reflection of one crucial aspect of the political dynamics in the region.

If the concept of negritude represents an alternative to the system of nation-states in Africa, in the Middle East a similar role has been played by the forces of militant Islam. In both regions, a yearning for a sense of community beyond national borders tugs at the emotions and intellect of their inhabitants.

A dramatic example of the powerful force of pan-Islamic sentiment took place on September 11, 2001, when Muslim militants hijacked four U.S. airliners and turned them into missiles aimed at the center of world capitalism. The headquarters of the terrorist network that carried out the attack—known as al-Qaeda and led by Osama bin Laden (see Chapter 27)—was located in Afghanistan, but the militants themselves came from several different Muslim states. Although moderate Muslims throughout the world condemned the attack, it was clear that bin Laden and his cohorts had tapped into a wellspring of hostility and resentment directed at much of the Western world.

What were the sources of Muslim anger? In a speech released on videotape shortly after the attack, bin Laden declared that the attacks were a response to the "humiliation and disgrace" that have afflicted the Islamic world for over eighty years, a period dating back to the end of World War I. For the Middle East, the period between the two world wars was an era of transition. With the fall of the Ottoman and Persian Empires, new modernizing regimes emerged in Turkey and Iran, and a more traditionalist but fiercely independent government was established in Saudi Arabia. Elsewhere, European influence continued to be strong; the British and French had mandates in Syria, Lebanon, Jordan, and Palestine, and British influence persisted in Iraq, southern Arabia, and throughout the Nile valley.

During World War II, the region became the cockpit of European rivalries, as it had been during World War I. The region was more significant to the warring powers than previously because of the growing importance of oil and the Suez Canal's position as a vital sea route.

The Question of Palestine

As in other areas of Asia, the end of World War II led to the emergence of a number of independent states. Jordan, Lebanon, and Syria, all European mandates before the war, became independent. Egypt, Iran, and Iraq, though still under a degree of Western influence, became increasingly autonomous. Sympathy for the idea of Arab unity led to the formation of the Arab League in 1945, but different points of view among its members prevented it from achieving anything of substance.

The one issue on which all Arab states in the area could agree was the question of Palestine. As tensions between Jews and Arabs in that mandate intensified during the 1930s, the British attempted to limit Jewish immigration into the area and firmly rejected proposals for independence. After World War II, the Zionists turned for support to the United States, and in March 1948, the Truman administration approved the concept of an independent Jewish state, even though only about one-third of the local residents were Jews. In May, the new state of Israel was formally established.

To its Arab neighbors, the new state represented a betrayal of the interests of the Palestinian people, 90 percent of whom were Muslim. Outraged at the lack of Western support for Muslim interests in the area, several Arab countries invaded the new Jewish state. Because of internal divisions among the Arabs, the invasion did not succeed; but both sides remained bitter, and the Arab states refused to recognize Israel.

The war had other lasting consequences as well, because it led to the exodus of thousands of Palestinian refugees into neighboring Muslim states. Jordan was now flooded by the arrival of one million urban Palestinians in a country occupied by half a million Bedouins. To the north, the state of Lebanon had been created to provide the local Christian community with a country of their own, but the arrival of the Palestinian refugees upset the delicate balance between Christians and Muslims. In any event, the creation of Lebanon had angered the Syrians, who had lost it as a result of European decisions before and after the war.

Nasser and Pan-Arabism

The dispute over Palestine placed Egypt in an uncomfortable position. Technically, Egypt was not an Arab state. King Farouk, who had acceded to power in 1936, had frequently declared support for the Arab cause, but the Egyptian people were not Bedouins and shared little of the culture of the peoples across the Red Sea. In 1952, King Farouk, whose corrupt habits had severely eroded his early popularity, was overthrown by a military coup engineered by young military officers who abolished the monarchy and established a republic.

In 1954, one of those officers, Colonel Gamal Abdul Nasser (1918–1970), seized power in his own right and immediately instituted a land reform program. He also adopted a policy of neutrality in foreign affairs and expressed sympathy for the Arab cause. The British presence had rankled many Egyptians for years, for even after granting Egypt independence, Britain had retained control over the Suez Canal to protect its route to the Indian Ocean. In 1956, Nasser suddenly nationalized the Suez Canal Company, which had been under British and French administration. Seeing a threat to their route to the Indian Ocean, the British and the French launched a joint attack on Egypt to protect their investment. They were joined by Israel, whose leaders had grown exasperated at sporadic Arab commando raids on Israeli territory and now decided to strike back. But the Eisenhower administration in the United States, concerned that the attack smacked of a revival of colonialism, supported Nasser and brought about the withdrawal of foreign forces from Egypt and of Israeli troops from the Sinai peninsula.

The United Arab Republic   Nasser now turned to **pan-Arabism.** In 1958, Egypt united with Syria as the United Arab Republic (UAR). The union had been proposed by the Ba'ath Party, which advocated the unity of all Arab states in a new socialist society. In 1957, the Ba'ath Party assumed power in Syria and opened talks with Egypt on a union between the two countries, which took place in March 1958 following a plebiscite. Nasser was named president of the new state.

Egypt and Syria hoped that the union would eventually include all Arab states, but other Arab leaders, including young King Hussein of Jordan and the kings of Iraq and Saudi Arabia, were suspicious. The latter two in particular feared pan-Arabism on the reasonable assumption that they would be asked to share their vast oil revenues with the poorer states of the Middle East. Indeed, in Nasser's view, through Arab unity, this wealth could be used to improve the standard of living in the area.

In the end, Nasser's plans brought an end to the UAR. When the government announced the nationalization of a large number of industries and utilities in 1961, a military coup overthrew the Ba'ath leaders in Damascus, and the new authorities declared that Syria would end its relationship with Egypt.

The breakup of the UAR did not end the dream of pan-Arabism. During the mid-1960s, Egypt took the lead in promoting Arab unity against Israel. At a meeting of Arab leaders held in Jerusalem in 1964, the Palestine Liberation Organization (PLO) was set up under Egyptian sponsorship to represent the interests of the Palestinians. According to the charter of the PLO, only the Palestinian people (and thus not Jewish immigrants from abroad) had the right to form a state in the old British mandate. A guerrilla movement called al-Fatah, led by the dissident PLO figure Yasir Arafat (1929–2004), began to launch terrorist attacks on Israeli territory.

The Arab-Israeli Dispute

Growing Arab hostility was a constant threat to the security of Israel, whose leaders dedicated themselves to creating a Jewish homeland. The government attempted to build a democratic and modern state that would be a magnet for Jews throughout the world and a symbol of Jewish achievement.

Ensuring the survival of the tiny state surrounded by antagonistic Arab neighbors was a considerable challenge, made more difficult by divisions within the Israeli population. Some were immigrants from Europe, while others came from the Middle East. Some were secular and even socialist in their views, while others were politically and religiously conservative. The state was also home to Christians as well as Muslim Palestinians who had not fled to other countries. To balance these diverse interests, Israel established a parliament, called the Knesset, on the European model, with proportional representation based on the number of votes each party received in the general election. The parties were so numerous that none ever received a majority of votes, and all governments had to be formed from a coalition of several parties. As a result, moderate secular leaders such as longtime prime minister David Ben Gurion had to cater to more marginal parties composed of conservative religious groups.

The Six-Day War By the spring of 1967, relations between Israel and its Arab neighbors had deteriorated as Nasser attempted to improve his standing in the Arab world by imposing a blockade against Israeli commerce

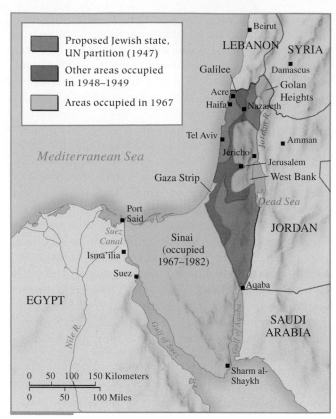

MAP 28.2 Israel and Its Neighbors. This map shows the evolution of the state of Israel since its founding in 1947. Areas occupied by Israel after the Six-Day War in 1967 are indicated in green. ❓ What is the significance of the West Bank?

through the Gulf of Aqaba. Concerned that it might be isolated, and lacking firm support from Western powers (which had originally guaranteed Israel the freedom to use the Gulf of Aqaba), in June 1967, Israel suddenly launched air strikes against Egypt and several of its Arab neighbors. Israeli armies then broke the blockade at the head of the Gulf of Aqaba and occupied the Sinai peninsula. Other Israeli forces attacked Jordanian territory on the West Bank of the Jordan River (Jordan's King Hussein had recently signed an alliance with Egypt and placed his army under Egyptian command), occupied the whole of Jerusalem, and seized Syrian military positions in the Golan Heights, along the Israeli-Syrian border (see Map 28.2). Israel's brief, six-day war had tripled the size of its territory but aroused even more bitter hostility among the Arabs; one million Palestinians were added inside its borders, most of them on the West Bank of the Jordan River.

During the next few years, the focus of the Arab-Israeli dispute shifted as Arab states demanded the return of the occupied territories. Nasser died in 1970 and was succeeded by his vice president, ex-general Anwar al-Sadat (1918–1981). Sadat attempted to renew Arab unity through a new confrontation with Israel. In 1973, on Yom Kippur (the Jewish Day of Atonement), an Israeli national holiday, Egyptian forces suddenly launched an air and artillery attack on Israeli positions in the Sinai just east of the Suez Canal. Syrian armies attacked Israeli positions in the Golan Heights. After early Arab successes, the Israelis managed to recoup some of their losses on both fronts. As a superpower confrontation between the United States and the Soviet Union loomed, a cease-fire was finally reached.

The Camp David Agreement   After his election as U.S. president in 1976, Jimmy Carter began to press for a compromise peace based on Israel's return of occupied Arab territories and Arab recognition of the state of Israel. By now, Sadat was anxious to reduce his military expenses and announced his willingness to seek peace. In September 1978, he and Israeli prime minister Menachem Begin met with Carter at Camp David, the presidential retreat in Maryland. Israel agreed to withdraw from the Sinai but not from other occupied territories unless other Arab countries recognized Israel.

The promise of the Camp David agreement was not fulfilled. One reason was the assassination of Sadat by Islamic militants in October 1981. But there were deeper causes, including the continued unwillingness of many Arab governments to recognize Israel and the Israeli government's encouragement of Jewish settlements on the occupied West Bank.

The PLO and the Intifada   During the early 1980s, the militancy of the Palestinians increased, leading to rising unrest, popularly labeled the *intifada* (uprising), among PLO supporters living inside Israel. As the 1990s began, U.S.-sponsored peace talks opened between Israel and a number of its neighbors, but progress was slow. Terrorist attacks by Palestinian militants resulted in heavy casualties and shook the confidence of many Jewish citizens that their security needs had been adequately protected. At the

CHRONOLOGY The Arab-Israeli Dispute	
Formation of the state of Israel	1948
Founding of the Palestine Liberation Organization	1964
Six-Day War between Arab states and Israel	1967
Yom Kippur War between Arab states and Israel	1973
Camp David accords	1978
Peace talks between Israel and Syria begin	1999
Election of Ariel Sharon as prime minister of Israel	2000
Death of Yasir Arafat	2004
Israeli forces occupy southern Lebanon	2006

same time, Jewish residents of the West Bank resisted the extension of Palestinian authority in the area.

A new Labour government under Prime Minister Ehud Barak sought to revitalize the peace process. Negotiations resumed with the PLO and also got under way with Syria over a peace settlement in Lebanon and the possible return of the Golan Heights. But in late 2000, peace talks broke down over the future of the city of Jerusalem, leading to massive riots by Palestinians and the election of a more hard-line Israeli prime minister, former defense minister Ariel Sharon. Sharon's ascent to leadership was accompanied by a rash of suicide attacks by Palestinians against Israeli targets, an intensive Israeli military crackdown on suspected terrorist sites inside Palestinian territory, and a dramatic increase in bloodshed on both sides. The death of Yasi Arafat in 2004 and his replacement by Palestinian moderate Mahmoud Abbas raised modest hopes for progress in peace talks, but key issues remain unresolved, including the future status of Jerusalem and Jewish settlements in the occupied territories. In 2006, radical Muslim forces operating in

The Temple Mount at Jerusalem.
The Temple Mount is one of the most sacred spots in the city of Jerusalem. Originally, it was the site of a temple built during the reign of Solomon, king of the Jews, about 1000 B.C.E. The western wall of the temple is shown in the foreground. Beyond the wall is the Dome of the Rock complex, built on the place from which Muslims believe that Muhammad ascended to heaven. Sacred to both religions, the Temple Mount is now a major bone of contention between Muslims and Jews and a prime obstacle to a final settlement of the Arab-Israeli dispute.

southern Lebanon launched massive attacks on Israeli cities. In response, Israeli troops crossed the border in an effort to wipe out the radical stronghold.

Revolution in Iran

In the late 1970s, another crisis arose in Iran, one of the key oil-exporting countries in the region. Under the leadership of Shah Mohammad Reza Pahlavi (1919–1980), who had taken over from his father in 1941, Iran had become one of the richest countries in the Middle East. During the 1950s and 1960s, Iran became a prime ally of the United States in the Middle East. With encouragement from the United States, which hoped that Iran could become a force for stability in the Persian Gulf, the shah attempted to carry through a series of social and economic reforms to transform the country into the most advanced in the region. Per capita income increased dramatically, literacy rates improved, a modern communications infrastructure took shape, and an affluent middle class emerged in the capital of Tehran.

Iran

Under the surface, however, trouble was brewing. Despite an ambitious land reform program, many peasants were still landless, unemployment among intellectuals was dangerously high, and the urban middle class was squeezed by high inflation. Some of the unrest took the form of religious discontent as millions of devout Muslims looked with distaste at a new Iranian civilization based on greed, sexual license, and material accumulation.

The Fall of the Shah Leading the opposition was Ayatollah Ruholla Khomeini (1900–1989), an austere Shi'ite cleric who had been exiled to Iraq and then to France because of his outspoken opposition to the shah's regime. From Paris, Khomeini continued his attacks in print, on television, and in radio broadcasts. By the late 1970s, large numbers of Iranians began to respond to Khomeini's diatribes against the "satanic regime," and demonstrations by his supporters were repressed with ferocity by the police. But workers' strikes grew in intensity. In 1979, the government collapsed and was replaced by a hastily formed Islamic republic. The new government, dominated by Shi'ite clergy under the guidance of Ayatollah Khomeini, immediately began to introduce traditional Islamic law. A new reign of terror ensued as supporters of the shah were rounded up and executed.

Though much of the outside world focused on the U.S. embassy in Tehran, where militants held a number of foreign hostages, the Iranian Revolution involved much

more. In the eyes of the ayatollah and his followers, the United States was "the great Satan," the powerful protector of Israel, and the enemy of Muslim peoples everywhere. Furthermore, it was responsible for the corruption of Iranian society under the shah. With economic conditions in Iran rapidly deteriorating, the Islamic revolutionary government finally agreed to free the hostages in return for the release of Iranian assets in the United States.

During the next few years, the intensity of the Iranian Revolution moderated slightly as the government displayed a modest tolerance for loosening clerical control over freedom of expression and social activities. But rising criticism of rampant official corruption and a high rate of inflation sparked a new wave of government repression in the mid-1990s; newspapers were censored, the universities were purged of disloyal or "un-Islamic" elements, and religious militants raided private homes in search of blasphemous activities.

In 1997, the moderate Muslim cleric Mohammad Khatemi was elected president of Iran. Khatemi, whose victory reflected a growing desire among many Iranians for a more pluralistic society open to the outside world, promoted a number of reforms, including an easing of press censorship, which led to the emergence of several reformist newspapers and magazines, as well as a relaxation of dress codes and restrictions on women's activities. After his reelection in August 2001, he immediately vowed to continue his reformist efforts. In the days following the terrorist attacks on the United States on September 11, he declared publicly that Muslims must

Iranian Woman Playing Soccer. Despite the restriction of having to cover their bodies in public, young Iranian women play soccer and other sports, attend schools and universities, and partake in other activities of the modern world. Here we see a female Iranian soccer player, fully covered compared to her Syrian opponent and wearing a traditional black hood. Although they rarely did so before the Islamic Revolution, today about two million Iranian women take part in sports.

reject terrorism as a tool in promoting Islam. But conservative clerics, anxious to contain the longing for personal freedom that is increasing among younger Iranians, have struck back by curtailing freedom of the press and defying parliamentary legislation that they consider destructive of the purity of the Islamic state. Although student protests erupted into the streets in 2003, hard-liners continued to reject proposals to expand civil rights and limit the power of the clerics. Two years later a militant Muslim fundamentalist, Mahmoud Ahmadinejad, was elected president, sparking new tensions with the West.

Crisis in the Gulf

Although much of the Iranians' anger was directed against the United States during the early phases of the revolution, Iran had equally hated enemies closer to home. To the north, the immense power of the Soviet Union, driven by atheistic communism, was viewed as a modern version of the Russian threat of previous centuries. To the west was a militant and hostile Iraq, now under the leadership of the ambitious Saddam Hussein (b. 1937). Iraq had just passed through a turbulent period. The monarchy had been overthrown by a military coup in 1958, but conflicts within the ruling military junta led to chronic instability, and in 1979 Colonel Saddam Hussein, a prominent member of the local Ba'athist Party, seized power on his own.

The Vision of Saddam Hussein   Saddam Hussein was a fervent believer in the creation of a single Arab state in the Middle East and soon began to persecute non-Arab elements in Iraq, including Persians and Kurds. He then turned his sights to territorial expansion to the east.

Iraq and Iran had long had an uneasy relationship, fueled by religious differences (Iranian Islam is predominantly Shi'ite, while the ruling caste in Iraq was Sunni) and a perennial dispute over borderlands adjacent to the Persian Gulf, the vital waterway for the export of oil from both countries. Like several of its neighbors, Iraq had long dreamed of unifying the Arabs but had been hindered by internal factions and suspicion among its neighbors.

During the mid-1970s, Iran gave some support to a Kurdish rebellion in the mountains of Iraq. In 1975, the government of the shah agreed to stop aiding the rebels in return for territorial concessions at the head of the Gulf. Five years later, however, the Kurdish revolt had been suppressed.

Saddam Hussein now saw his opportunity; accusing Iran of violating the territorial agreement, he launched an attack on his neighbor. The war was a bloody one and lasted for nearly ten years. Poison gas was used against civilians, and children were employed to clear minefields. Finally, with both sides virtually exhausted, a cease-fire was arranged in the fall of 1988.

The bitter conflict with Iran had not slaked Saddam Hussein's appetite for territorial expansion. In early August 1990, Iraqi military forces suddenly moved across the border and occupied the small neighboring country of Kuwait at the head of the Gulf. The immediate pretext was the claim that Kuwait was pumping oil from fields inside Iraqi territory. Baghdad was also angry over the Kuwaiti government's demand for repayment of loans it had made to Iraq during the war with Iran. But the underlying reason was Iraq's contention that Kuwait was legally a part of Iraq. Kuwait had been part of the Ottoman Empire until the beginning of the twentieth century, when the local prince had agreed to place his patrimony under British protection. When Iraq became independent in 1932, it claimed the area on the grounds that the state of Kuwait had been created by British imperialism, but opposition from major Western powers and other countries in the region, which feared the consequences of a "greater Iraq," prevented an Iraqi takeover.

Operation Desert Storm   The Iraqi invasion of Kuwait in 1990 sparked an international outcry, and the United States assembled a multinational coalition that under the name Operation Desert Storm liberated the country and destroyed a substantial part of Iraq's armed forces. President George H. W. Bush had promised the American people that U.S. troops would not fight with one hand tied behind their backs (a clear reference to the Vietnam War), but the allied forces did not occupy Baghdad at the end of the war out of fear that doing so would cause a breakup of the country, an eventuality that would operate to the benefit of Iran. The allies hoped instead that Saddam's regime would be ousted by an internal revolt. In the meantime, harsh economic sanctions were imposed on the Iraqi government as the condition for peace. The anticipated overthrow of Saddam Hussein did not materialize, however, and his tireless efforts to evade the conditions of the cease-fire continued to bedevil U.S. President Bill Clinton and his successor, George W. Bush.

Conflicts in Afghanistan and Iraq

The terrorist attacks launched against U.S. cities in September 2001 added a new dimension to the Middle Eastern equation. After the failure of the Soviet Union to quell the rebellion in Afghanistan during the 1980s, a fundamentalist Muslim group known as the Taliban, supported covertly by the United States, seized power in Kabul and ruled the country with a fanaticism reminiscent of the

Afghanistan

Cultural Revolution in China. Backed by conservative religious forces in Pakistan, the Taliban provided a base of operations for Osama bin Laden's al-Qaeda terrorist network. After the attacks of September 11, a coalition of forces led by the United States overthrew the Taliban and attempted to build a new and moderate government. But the country's history of bitter internecine warfare among various tribal groups represents a severe challenge to those efforts.

Iraq

In the meantime, the Bush administration, charging that Iraqi dictator Saddam Hussein not only had provided support to bin Laden's terrorist organization but also sought to develop weapons of mass destruction, threatened to invade Iraq and remove him from power. The plan, widely debated in the media and opposed by many of the United States' traditional allies, disquieted Arab leaders and fanned anti-American sentiment throughout the Muslim world. Nevertheless, in March 2003, American-led forces attacked Iraq and overthrew Saddam Hussein's regime. In the months that followed, occupation forces sought to restore stability to the country while setting forth plans to lay the foundations of a future democratic society. But although Saddam Hussein was later captured by U.S. troops, armed resistance by militant Muslim elements continues.

Efforts are under way to train an Iraqi military force capable of defeating the insurgents, and a provisional government has been formed, the embryo of a future pro-Western state that could serve as an emblem of democracy in the Middle East. Squabbling among Sunni, Shi'ite, and Kurdish elements within the country, however, is a vivid reminder that a similar effort by the British eighty years earlier ended without success.

Society and Culture in the Contemporary Middle East

To many seasoned observers, such plans seem unrealistic, since democratic values have laid down few roots in the region. In some cases—notably on the Arabian peninsula—feudal rulers remain in power. The kings of Saudi Arabia, for example, continue to rule by traditional precepts and, citing the distinctive character of Muslim political institutions, have been reluctant to establish representative political institutions. In general, these rulers maintain and even enforce the strict observance of traditional customs. Religious police in Saudi Arabia are responsible for enforcing the Muslim dress code, maintaining the prohibition against alcohol, and making sure businesses close during the time for prayer.

Varieties of Government

In other societies, traditional authority has been replaced by charismatic one-party rule or military dictatorships. Nasser's regime in Egypt is a good example of a single-party state where the leader won political power by the force of his presence or personality. Ayatollah Khomeini in Iran, Muammar Qadhafi in Libya, and Saddam Hussein in Iraq are other examples. Although their personal characteristics and images differed, they all owed much of their power to their personal appeal.

In other instances, charismatic rule has given way to modernizing bureaucratic regimes. Examples include the governments of Syria, Yemen, Turkey, and Egypt since Nasser, where Anwar al-Sadat and his successor, Hosni Mubarak, focused their regimes on performance (see Map 28.3). Sometimes the authoritarian character of the regimes has been modified by some democratic tendencies, especially in Turkey, where free elections and the sharing of power have become more prevalent in recent years. A few Arab nations, such as Bahrain, Kuwait, and Jordan, have also engaged in limited forms of democratic experimentation.

Only in Israel, however, are democratic institutions firmly established. The Israeli system suffers from the proliferation of minor parties, some of which are able to dictate policy because their support is essential to keeping a government in power. Nevertheless, the government generally reflects the popular will, and power is transferred by peaceful and constitutional means.

The Economics of Oil

Few areas exhibit a greater disparity of individual and national wealth than the Middle East. While millions live in abject poverty, a fortunate few rank among the wealthiest people in the world. The primary reason for this disparity is oil. Unfortunately for most of the peoples of the region, oil reserves are distributed unevenly and all too often are located in areas where the population density is low. Egypt and Turkey, with more than fifty million inhabitants apiece, have almost no oil reserves. The combined population of oil-rich Kuwait, the United Arab Emirates, and Saudi Arabia is well under ten million people.

Economics and Islam Not surprisingly, considering their different resources and political systems, the states of the Middle East have adopted diverse approaches to the problem of developing strong and stable economies. Some, like Nasser in Egypt and the leaders of the Ba'ath Party in Syria, attempted to create a form of Arab socialism, favoring a high level of government involvement in the economy to relieve the inequities of the free enterprise system. Others turned to the Western capitalist model to maximize growth while using taxes or development projects to build a modern infrastructure, redistribute wealth, and maintain political stability and economic opportunity for all.

Socialist theories of economic development such as Nasser's were often suggested as a way to promote economic growth while meeting the requirements of Islamic doctrine. Although the Qur'an has little to say about economics and can be variously interpreted as capitalist or socialist, it is clear in its opposition to charging interest and in its concern for the material welfare of the Muslim community, the *umma*. According to socialist theories, state intervention in the economic sector would bring about rapid development, while land redistribution and the nationalization or regulation of industry would minimize the harsh inequities of the marketplace. In general, however, the socialist approach has had little success, and most governments, including those of Egypt and Syria, have shifted to a more free enterprise approach while encouraging foreign investment to compensate for a lack of capital or technology.

Agricultural Policies Although the amount of arable land is relatively small, most countries in the Middle East rely on farming to supply food for their growing populations. Much of the fertile land was owned by wealthy absentee landlords, but land reform programs in several countries have attempted to alleviate this problem. The most comprehensive was instituted in Egypt, where Nasser and his successors managed to reassign nearly a quarter of all cultivable lands by limiting the amount a single individual could hold. Similar programs in Iran, Iraq, Libya, and Syria generally had less effect.

Agricultural productivity throughout the region has been plagued by the lack of water. With populations growing at more than 2 percent annually on average in the Middle East (more than 3 percent in some countries), several governments have tried to increase the amount of water available for irrigation. Many attempts have been sabotaged by government ineptitude, political disagreements,

CHRONOLOGY The Modern Middle East	
King Farouk overthrown in Egypt	1952
Egypt nationalizes the Suez Canal	1956
Formation of the United Arab Republic	1958
Iranian Revolution	1979
Iran-Iraq War begins	1980
Iraqi invasion of Kuwait	1990
Persian Gulf War	1991
Reformist wins presidency in Iran	2000
Al-Qaeda terrorist attack on the United States	2001
U.S.-led forces invade Iraq	2003
Formation of provisional government in Iraq	2005

See also the chronology of the Arab-Israeli conflict on p. 643.

MAP 28.3 **The Modern Middle East.** Shown here are the boundaries dividing the independent states in the contemporary Middle East. ❓ Which are the major oil-producing countries? How has the presence of oil affected political development in these countries? ✎ View an animated version of this map or related maps at http://worldrc.wadsworth.com/

ISLAM AND DEMOCRACY

RELIGION &
PHILOSOPHY

One of George W. Bush's key objectives in launching the invasion of Iraq in 2003 was to promote the emergence of democratic states throughout the Middle East. According to U.S. officials, one of the ultimate causes of the formation of terrorist movements in Muslim societies is the prevalence in such countries of dictatorial governments that do not serve the interests of their citizens. According to the Pakistani author of this editorial, the problem lies as much with the actions of Western countries as it does with political attitudes in the Muslim world.

How does the author answer the charge that democracy and Islam are incompatible? To what degree is the West responsible for problems in the Middle East?

M. J. Akbar, "Linking Islam to Dictatorship"

Let us examine a central canard, that Islam and democracy are incompatible. This is an absurdity. There is nothing Islamic or un-Islamic about democracy. Democracy is the outcome of a political process, not a religious process.

It is glibly suggested that "every" Muslim country is a dictatorship, but the four largest Muslim populations of the world—in Indonesia, India, Bangladesh, and Turkey—vote to change governments. Pakistan could easily have been on this list.

Voting does not make these Muslims less or more religious. There are dictators among Muslims just as there are dictators among Christians, Buddhists, and Hindus (check out Nepal). . . . Christian Latin America has seen ugly forms of dictatorship, as has Christian Africa.

What is unique to the Muslim world is not the absence of democracy but the fact that in 1918, after the defeat of the Ottoman Empire, every single Muslim in the world lived under foreign subjugation.

Every single one, from Indonesia to Morocco via Turkey. The Turks threw out their invaders within a few years under the great leadership of Kemal Atatürk, but the transition to self-rule in other Muslim countries was slow, uncertain, and full of traps planted by the world's preeminent powers.

The West, in the shape of Britain, France, or America, was never interested in democracy when a helpful dictator or king would serve. When people got a chance to express their wish, it was only logical that they would ask for popular rule. It was the street that brought Mossadegh to power in Iran and drove the shah of Iran to tearful exile in Rome. Who brought the shah of Iran and autocracy back to Iran? The CIA.

If Iranian democracy had been permitted a chance in 1953, there would have been no uprising led by Ayatollah Khomeini in 1979. In other countries, where the struggle for independence was long and brutal, as in Algeria and Indonesia, the militias who had fought the war institutionalized army authority. In other instances, civilian heroes confused their own well-being with national health. They became regressive dictators. Once again, there was nothing Islamic about it.

Muslim countries will become democracies, too, because it is the finest form of modern governance. But it will be a process interrupted by bloody experience as the street wrenches power from usurpers.

Democracy has happened in Turkey. It has happened in Bangladesh. It is happening in Indonesia. It almost happened in Pakistan, and the opportunity will return. Democracy takes time in the most encouraging environments.

Democracy has become the latest rationale for the occupation of Iraq. . . . Granted, democracy is always preferable to tyranny no matter how it comes. But Iraqis are not dupes. They will take democracy and place it at the service of nationalism. A decade ago, America was careless about the definition of victory. Today it is careless about the definition of democracy.

There is uncertainty and apprehension across the Muslim nations: uncertainty about where they stand, and apprehension about both American power and the repugnant use of terrorism that in turn invites the exercise of American power. There is also anger that a legitimate cause like that of Palestine can get buried in the debris of confusion. Muslims do not see Palestinians as terrorists.

---

and territorial conflicts, however. Today, the dearth of water in the region is reaching crisis proportions.

Migratory Workers Another way governments have attempted to deal with rapid population growth is to encourage emigration. Oil-producing states with small populations, such as Saudi Arabia and the United Arab Emirates, have imported labor from other countries in the region, mostly to work in the oil fields. By the mid-1980s, more than 40 percent of the population in those states was composed of foreign nationals, who often sent the bulk of their salaries back to their families in their home countries. When oil revenues declined in the late 1980s, and

1990s, however, several governments took measures to stabilize or reduce the migrant population.

Obstacles to Democracy What explains the failure of democratic institutions and values to take root in the contemporary Middle East? Some observers attribute the cause to the willingness of Western governments to coddle dictatorships as a means of preserving their access to the vast oil reserves located on the Arabian peninsula. Others ascribe it to deep-seated factors embedded in the history and culture of the region or in the religion of Islam itself. Whatever the cause, critics charge that the lack of personal freedom has aroused a level of popular discontent that local

COMPARATIVE ESSAY

RELIGION AND SOCIETY

The nineteenth and twentieth centuries witnessed a steady trend toward the secularization of society as people increasingly turned from religion to science for an explanation of natural phenomena and for answers to the challenges of everyday life.

In recent years, however, the trend has reversed, as religious faith in all its guises appears to be in a state of revival in much of the world. Although the percentage of people attending religious services on a regular basis or professing firm religious convictions has been dropping steadily in many countries, the intensity of religious belief appears to be growing among the faithful. This phenomenon has been widely publicized in the United States, where the evangelical movement has become a significant force in politics and an influential factor in defining many social issues. But it has also occurred in Latin America, where a drop in membership in the Roman Catholic church has been offset by significant increases in the popularity of evangelical Protestant sects. In the Muslim world, the influence of traditional Islam has been steadily on the rise, not only in the Middle East but also in non-Arab countries like Malaysia and Indonesia (see Chapter 29). Even in Russia and China, where half a century of Communist government sought to eradicate religion as the "opiate of the people," the popularity of religion is growing.

One major reason for the increasing popularity of religion in contemporary life is the desire to counter the widespread sense of malaise brought on by the absence of any sense of meaning and purpose in life—a purpose that religious faith provides. For many evangelical Christians in the United States, for example, the adoption of a Christian lifestyle is seen as a necessary prerequisite for resolving problems of crime, drugs, and social alienation. It is likely that a similar phenomenon is present with other religions and in other parts of the world.

Historical evidence suggests, however, that although religious fervor may serve to enhance the sense of community and commitment among believers, it can have a highly divisive impact on society as a whole, as the examples of Northern Ireland, Yugoslavia, and the Middle East vividly attest. Even if less dramatically, as in the United States, Latin America, and Africa, religion can divide as well as unite, and it will be a continuing task for religious leaders of all faiths to promote tolerance for peoples of other persuasions.

Another challenge for contemporary religion is to find ways to coexist with expanding scientific knowledge. Influential figures in the evangelical movement in the United States, for example, not only support a conservative social agenda but also express a growing suspicion of the role of technology and science in the contemporary world. Similar views are often expressed by significant factions in other world religions. Although fear over the impact of science on contemporary life is widespread, efforts to turn the clock back to a mythical golden age are not likely to succeed in the face of powerful forces for change set in motion by advances in scientific knowledge.

---

governments seek to deflect—often with great success—onto the West (see the box on p. 648). For their part, Middle Eastern political leaders undoubtedly fear that greater popular participation in the affairs of state could disrupt the precarious stability of many states in the region.

The Islamic Revival

In recent years, many developments in the Middle East have been described in terms of a resurgence of traditional values and customs in response to Western influence. Indeed, some conservative religious forces in the area have consciously attempted to replace foreign culture and values with allegedly "pure" Islamic forms of belief and behavior.

But the Islamic revival is not a simple dichotomy between traditional and modern, native and foreign, or irrational and rational. In the first place, many Muslims in the Middle East still believe that Islamic values and modern ways are not incompatible and may even be mutually reinforcing. Second, the resurgence of what are sometimes called "fundamentalist" Islamic groups may, in a Middle Eastern context, appear to be a rational and practical response to self-destructive practices, such as corruption and hedonism, drunkenness, prostitution, and the use of drugs. Finally, the reassertion of Islamic values is seen as a means of establishing a cultural identity and fighting off the overwhelming impact of Western ideas (see the comparative essay "Religion and Society" above).

Modernist Islam Initially, many Muslim intellectuals responded to Western influence by trying to create a "modernized" set of Islamic beliefs and practices that would not clash with the demands of the twentieth century. This process took place in most Islamic societies, but it was especially prevalent in Turkey, Egypt, and Iran, all of which attempted to make use of Islamic values while asserting the primacy of other issues such as political and economic development.

These secularizing trends were particularly noticeable among the political, intellectual, and economic elites in urban areas. They had less influence in the countryside, among the poor, and among devout elements within the clergy. Many of the clerics believed that Western influence in the cities had given birth to political and economic

Answering the Call of the *Muezzin*.
With the renewed fervor of Muslims in the world today, scenes such as this one in Kuwait exemplify the adherents' humble submission to God. Required to pray five times a day—at dawn, noon, mid-afternoon, sunset, and early evening—a Muslim, after ritual ablutions, prostrates himself facing Mecca to proclaim, "There is no god but Allah, and Muhammad is his prophet." Responding to the call of the *muezzin,* which today is often a recorded message from the minaret of a mosque, the faithful can perform their prayers in a few minutes, wherever they are, at home or in any public place. There are an estimated 1.3 billion Muslims in the world today, 175 million of whom are in Indonesia, 105 million in India, and 15 million in Europe.

corruption, sexual promiscuity, hedonism, individualism, and the prevalence of alcohol, pornography, and drugs. Although such practices had long existed in the Middle East, they were now far more visible and socially acceptable.

Return to Tradition   The movement to return to traditional practices strengthened after World War II and reached its zenith in Iran under Ayatollah Khomeini. It is not surprising that Iran took the lead, in light of its long tradition of ideological purity within the Shi'ite sect as well as the uncompromisingly secular character of the shah's reforms in the postwar era. In Iran today, traditional Islamic beliefs are all-pervasive and extend into education, clothing styles, social practices, and the legal system.

The cultural and social effects of the Iranian Revolution were profound as Iranian ideas spread throughout the area. In Algeria, the political influence of fundamentalist Islamic groups grew substantially and enabled them to win a stunning victory in the national elections in 1992. When the military stepped in to cancel the second round of elections and crack down on the militants, the latter responded with a campaign of terrorism against moderates that has claimed thousands of lives.

A similar trend emerged in Egypt, where militant groups such as the Muslim Brotherhood engaged in terrorism, including the assassination of Sadat and attacks on foreign tourists, who are considered carriers of corrupt Western influence.

Even in Turkey, generally considered the most secular of Islamic societies, a militant political group known as the Islamic Welfare Party took power in a coalition government formed in 1996. Worried moderates voiced their concern that the secular legacy of Kemal Atatürk was being eroded, and eventually the new prime minister

Necmettin Erbakan, agreed to resign under heavy pressure from the military. Frustrated with delays in its application for membership in the European Union and uncomfortable with the militancy of its Arab neighbors, Turkey has established a security relationship with Israel and seeks close ties with the United States. But religious and economic discontent lies just beneath the surface.

Women and Islam

Nowhere have the fault lines between tradition and modernity within Muslim societies in the Middle East been so sharp as in the ongoing debate over the role of women. At the beginning of the twentieth century, women's place in Middle Eastern society had changed little since the death of the prophet Muhammad. Women were secluded in their homes and had few legal, political, or social rights.

During the first decades of the twentieth century, advocates of modernist views began to contend that Islamic doctrine was not inherently opposed to women's rights. To modernists, Islamic traditions such as female seclusion, wearing the veil, and even polygamy were actually pre-Islamic folk traditions that had been tolerated in the early Islamic era and continued to be practiced in later centuries. Such views had considerable impact on a number of Middle Eastern societies, including Turkey and Iran. As we have seen, greater rights for women were a crucial element in the social revolution promoted by Kemal Atatürk in Turkey. In Iran, Shah Reza Khan and his son granted female suffrage and encouraged the education of women.

In recent years, a more traditional view of women's role has tended to prevail in many Middle Eastern countries. Attacks by religious conservatives on the growing role of women contributed to the emotions underlying

KEEPING THE CAMEL OUT OF THE TENT

FAMILY & SOCIETY

"Almighty God created sexual desire in ten parts; then he gave nine parts to women and one to men." So pronounced Ali, Muhammad's son-in-law, as he explained why women are held morally responsible as the instigators of sexual intercourse. Consequently, over the centuries, Islamic women have been secluded, veiled, and in many cases genitally mutilated in order to safeguard male virtue. Women are forbidden to look directly at, speak to, or touch a man prior to marriage. Even today, they are often sequestered at home or limited to strictly segregated areas away from all male contact. Women normally pray at home or in an enclosed antechamber of the mosque so that their physical presence will not disturb men's spiritual concentration.

Especially limiting today are the laws governing women's behavior in Saudi Arabia. Schooling for girls has never been compulsory because fathers believe that "educating women is like allowing the nose of the camel into the tent; eventually the beast will edge in and take up all the room inside." The country did not establish its first girls' school until 1956. The following description of Saudi women is from *Nine Parts Desire: The Hidden World of Islamic Women,* by the journalist Geraldine Brooks.

According to the author of this passage, do women in Saudi Arabia have an opportunity to receive an education? How do restrictions on women in Saudi Arabia compare with conditions elsewhere in the region?

Geraldine Brooks, *Nine Parts Desire*

Women were first admitted to university in Saudi Arabia in 1962, and all women's colleges remain strictly segregated. Lecture rooms come equipped with closed-circuit TVs and telephones, so women students can listen to a male professor and question him by phone, without having to contaminate themselves by being seen by him. When the first dozen women graduated from university in 1973, they were devastated to find that their names hadn't been printed on the commencement program. The old tradition, that it dishonors women to mention them, was depriving them of recognition they believed they'd earned. The women and their families protested, so a separate program was printed and a segregated graduation ceremony was held for the students' female relatives. . . .

But while the opening of women's universities widened access to higher learning for women, it also made the educational experience much shallower. Before 1962, many progressive Saudi families had sent their daughters abroad for education. They had returned to the kingdom not only with a degree but with experience of the outside world. . . . Now a whole generation of Saudi women have completed their education entirely within the country. . . .

Lack of opportunity for education abroad means that Saudi women are trapped in the confines of an education system that still lags men's. Subjects such as geology and petroleum engineering—tickets to influential jobs in Saudi Arabia's oil economy—remain closed to women. . . . Few women's colleges have their own libraries, and libraries shared with men's schools are either entirely off limits to women or open to them only one day per week. . . .

But women and men sit the same degree examinations. Professors quietly acknowledge the women's scores routinely outstrip the men's. "It's no surprise," said one woman professor. "Look at their lives. The boys have their cars, they can spend the evenings cruising the streets with their friends, sitting in cafés, buying black-market alcohol and drinking all night. What do the girls have? Four walls and their books. For them, education is everything."

---

the Iranian Revolution of 1979. Iranian women were instructed to wear the veil and to dress modestly in public. Films produced in postrevolutionary Iran rarely featured women, and when they did, physical contact between men and women was prohibited. The events in Iran had repercussions in secular Muslim societies such as Egypt, Turkey, and far-off Malaysia, where women began to dress more modestly in public, and criticism of open sexuality in the media became increasingly frequent.

The most conservative nation by far is still Saudi Arabia, where women are not only segregated and expected to wear the veil in public but are also restricted in education and forbidden to drive automobiles (see the box above). Still, women's rights have been extended in a few countries. In 1999, women obtained the right to vote in Kuwait, while they have been granted an equal right with their husbands to seek a divorce in Egypt. Even in Iran, women have many freedoms that they lacked before the twentieth century; for example, they can attend a university, receive military training, vote, practice birth control, and publish fiction.

Literature and Art

As in other areas of Asia and Africa, the encounter with the West in the nineteenth and twentieth centuries stimulated a cultural renaissance in the Middle East. Muslim authors translated Western works into Arabic and Persian and began to experiment with new literary forms.

Literature   Iran has produced one of the most prominent national literatures in the contemporary Middle East. Since World War II, Iranian literature has been hampered somewhat by political considerations, since it has been expected to serve first the Pahlavi monarchy and then the Islamic republic. Nevertheless, Iranian writers are among the most prolific in the region and often write in prose, which has finally been accepted as the equal of poetry.

Despite the male-oriented character of Iranian society, many of the new writers have been women. Since the revolution, the veil and the *chador,* an all-enveloping cloak, have become the central metaphor in Iranian women's writing. Those who favor the veil and *chador* praise them as the last bastion of defense against Western cultural imperialism. Behind the veil, the Islamic woman can breathe freely, unpolluted by foreign exploitation and moral corruption. Other Iranian women, however, consider the *chador* a "mobile prison" or an oppressive anachronism from the Dark Ages. As one writer, Sousan Azadi, expressed it, "As I pulled the *chador* over me, I felt a heaviness descending over me. I was hidden and in hiding. There was nothing visible left of Sousan Azadi."[5] Whether or not they accept the veil and *chador,* women writers are a vital part of contemporary Iranian literature and are addressing all aspects of social issues.

Like Iran, Egypt in the twentieth century has experienced a flowering of literature accelerated by the establishment of the Egyptian republic in the early 1950s. The most illustrious contemporary Egyptian writer was the late Naguib Mahfouz, who won the Nobel Prize for literature in 1988. His *Cairo Trilogy* (1952) chronicles three generations of a merchant family in Cairo during the tumultuous years between the world wars. Mahfouz was particularly adept at blending panoramic historical events with the intimate lives of ordinary human beings. Unlike many other modern writers, his message was essentially optimistic and reflected his hope that religion and science can work together for the overall betterment of humankind.

Art Like literature, the art of the modern Middle East has been profoundly influenced by its exposure to Western culture. At first, artists tended to imitate Western models, but later they began to experiment with national styles, returning to earlier forms for inspiration. Some emulated the writers in returning to the village to depict peasants and shepherds, but others followed international trends and attempted to express the alienation and disillusionment that characterize so much of modern life.

CONCLUSION

HE **MIDDLE EAST,** like the continent of Africa, is one of the most unstable regions in the the world today. In part, this turbulence is due to the continued interference of outsiders attracted by the massive oil reserves under the parched wastes of the Arabian peninsula and in the vicinity of the Persian Gulf. Oil is indeed both a blessing and a curse to the peoples of the region.

Another factor contributing to the volatility of the Middle East is the tug-of-war between the sense of ethnic identity in the form of nationalism and the intense longing to be part of a broader Islamic community, a dream that dates back to the time of the prophet Muhammad. The desire to create that community—a vision threatened by the presence of the alien state of Israel—inspired Gamal Abdul Nasser in the 1950s and Ayatollah Khomeini in the 1970s and 1980s and probably has motivated many of the actions of Saddam Hussein and Osama bin Laden.

A final reason for the turmoil currently affecting the Middle East is the intense debate over the role of religion in civil society. Although efforts in various Muslim countries to return to an allegedly purer form of Islam appear harsh and even repugnant to many observers, it is important to note that Muslim societies are not alone in deploring the sense of moral decline that is now allegedly taking place in societies throughout the world. Nor are they alone in advocating a restoration of traditional religious values as a means of reversing the trend. Not infrequently, members of such groups turn to violence as a means of making their point.

Whatever the reasons, it is clear that a deep-seated sense of anger is surging through much of the Islamic world today, an anger that transcends specific issues like the situation in Iraq or the Arab-Israeli dispute. Although economic privation and political oppression are undoubtedly important factors, the roots of Muslim resentment, as historian Bernard Lewis has pointed out, lie in a historical sense of humiliation at the hands of a Western colonialism that first emerged centuries ago, when the Arab hegemony in the Mediterranean region was replaced by European domination, and culminated early in the twentieth century, when much of the Middle East was occupied by Western colonial regimes. Today, the world is reaping the harvest of that long-cultivated bitterness, and the consequences cannot be foreseen.

CHAPTER NOTES

1. K. Little, *African Women in Towns: An Aspect of Africa's Social Revolution* (Cambridge, 1973), p. 6.

2. A. Nicol, *A Truly Married Woman and Other Stories* (London, 1965), p. 12.

3. Ngugi Wa Thiong'o, *Decolonizing the Mind: The Politics of Language in African Literature* (Portsmouth, N.H., 1986), p. 103.

4. Quoted in R. R. Andersen, R. F. Seibert, and J. G. Wagner, *Politics and Change in the Middle East: Sources of Conflict and Accommodation,* 4th ed. (Englewood Cliffs, N.J., 1982), p. 51.

5. S. Azadi, with A. Ferrante, *Out of Iran* (London, 1987), p. 223.

TIMELINE

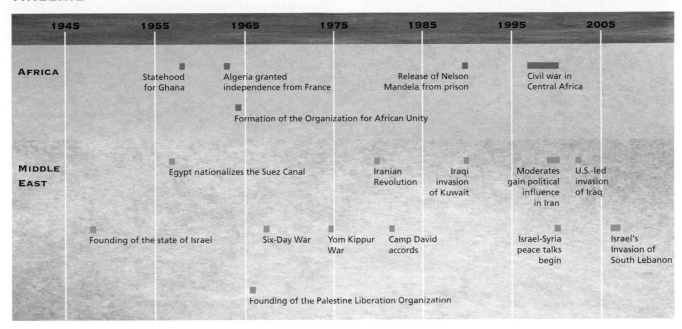

	1945	1955	1965	1975	1985	1995	2005

AFRICA

- Statehood for Ghana
- Algeria granted independence from France
- Formation of the Organization for African Unity
- Release of Nelson Mandela from prison
- Civil war in Central Africa

MIDDLE EAST

- Egypt nationalizes the Suez Canal
- Iranian Revolution
- Iraqi invasion of Kuwait
- Moderates gain political influence in Iran
- U.S.-led invasion of Iraq
- Founding of the state of Israel
- Six-Day War
- Yom Kippur War
- Camp David accords
- Israel-Syria peace talks begin
- Israel's Invasion of South Lebanon
- Founding of the Palestine Liberation Organization

SUGGESTED READING

For a general survey of contemporary African history, see **R. Oliver, *The African Experience*** (New York, 1992), which contains interesting essays on a variety of themes, and **K. Shillington, *History of Africa*** (New York, 1989), which takes a chronological and geographical approach and includes excellent maps and illustrations.

Two excellent treatments by preeminent historians of the African continent are **B. Davidson, *Africa in History: Themes and Outlines,*** rev. ed. (New York, 1991), and **P. Curtin** et al., ***African History*** (London, 1995). Also see **H. French, *A Continent for the Taking: The Tragedy and Hope of Africa*** (New York, 2004).

On nationalist movements, see **P. Gifford** and **W. R. Louis,** eds., ***The Transfer of Power in Africa*** (New Haven, Conn., 1982), and **J. D. Hargreaves, *Decolonisation in Africa*** (London, 1988). Also see **D. Birmingham, *Kwame Nkrumah: The Father of African Nationalism*** (Athens, Ohio, 1998). For a poignant analysis of the hidden costs of nation building, see **N. F. Mostert, *The Epic of South Africa's Creation and the Tragedy of the Xhosa People*** (London, 1992). Also see **A. Mazrui** and **M. Tidy, *Nationalism and New States in Africa*** (Portsmouth, N.H., 1984), and **S. Decalo, *Coups and Army Rule in Africa*** (New Haven, Conn., 1990).

For a survey of economic conditions in Africa, see ***Sub-Saharan Africa: From Crisis to Sustainable Growth*** (Washington, D.C., 1989), issued by the World Bank. Also see **A. O'Connor, *The African City*** (London, 1983), and **J. Illiffe, *The African Poor*** (Cambridge, 1983).

For a survey of African literature, see **O. Owomoyela,** ed., ***A History of Twentieth-Century African Literatures*** (Lincoln, Nebr., 1993); **M. J. Hay, *African Novels in the Classroom*** (Boulder, Colo., 2000); and **M. J. Daymond** et al., eds. ***Women Writing Africa: The Southern Region*** (New York, 2003). On art, see **S. L. Kasfir, *Contemporary African Art*** (London, 1999).

For interesting analyses of women's issues in the Africa of this time frame, see **S. B. Stichter** and **J. L. Parpart,** eds., ***Patriarchy and Class: African Women in the Home and the Workforce*** (Boulder,

Colo., 1988), and **M. Kevane, *Women and Development in Africa: How Gender Works*** (Boulder, Colo., 2004).

For contrasting views on the reasons for Africa's current difficulties, see **J. Marah, *The African People in the Global Village: An Introduction to Pan-African Studies*** (Lanham, Md., 1998), and **G. Ayittey, *Africa in Chaos*** (New York, 1998).

Good general surveys of the modern Middle East include **A. Goldschmidt Jr., *A Concise History of the Middle East*** (Boulder, Colo., 1991), and **G. E. Perry, *The Middle East: Fourteen Islamic Centuries*** (Elizabeth, N.J., 1992).

On Israel and the Palestinian question, see **D. Ross, *The Missing Peace: The Inside Story of the Fight for Middle East Peace*** (New York, 2004). On Jerusalem, see **B. Wasserstein, *Divided Jerusalem: The Struggle for the Holy City*** (New Haven, Conn., 2000).

The issue of oil is examined in **G. Luciani, *The Oil Companies and the Arab World*** (New York, 1984), and **P. Odell, *Oil and World Power*** (New York, 1986). Also see **M. H. Kerr** and **E. S. Yassin,** eds., ***Rich and Poor States in the Middle East: Egypt and the New Arab Order*** (Boulder, Colo., 1985).

On the Iranian Revolution, see **S. Bakash, *The Reign of the Ayatollahs*** (New York, 1984), and **B. Rubin, *Iran Since the Revolution*** (Boulder, Colo., 1985). On Ayatollah Khomeini's role and ideas, see **H. Algar, *Islam and Revolution: The Writings and Declarations of Imam Khomeini*** (Berkeley, Calif., 1981). The Iran-Iraq War is discussed in **C. Davies,** ed., ***After the War: Iran, Iraq and the Arab Gulf*** (Chichester, England, 1990), and **S. C. Pelletiere, *The Iran-Iraq War: Chaos in a Vacuum*** (New York, 1992).

For historical perspective on the invasion of Iraq, see **J. Kendell, *Iraq's Unruly Century*** (New York, 2003). **R. Khalidi's *Resurrecting Empire: Western Footprints and America's Perilous Path in the Middle East*** (Boston, 2003), is a critical look at U. S. policy in the region.

On the politics of the Middle East, see **J. A. Bill** and **R. Springborg, *Politics in the Middle East*** (London, 1990), and **R. R. Anderson, R. F. Seibert,** and **J. G. Wagner, *Politics and Change in the Middle***

East: Sources of Conflict and Accommodation (Englewood Cliffs, N.J., 1993). For expert analysis on the current situation in the region, see **B. Lewis**, *What Went Wrong? Western Impact and Middle Eastern Response* (Oxford, 2001), and **P. L. Bergen**, *Holy War, Inc.: Inside the Secret World of Osama bin Laden* (New York, 2001).

Two excellent surveys of women in Islam from pre-Islamic society to the present are **L. Ahmed**, *Women and Gender in Islam: Historical Roots of a Modern Debate* (New Haven, Conn., 1993), and **G. Nashat** and **J. E. Tucker**, *Women in the Middle East and North Africa* (Bloomington, Ind., 1999). Also consult **M. Afkhami** and **E. Friedl**, *In the Eye of the Storm: Women in Post-Revolutionary Iran* (Syracuse, N.Y., 1994), and **W. Wiebke**, *Women in Islam* (Princeton, N.J., 1995).

For a scholarly but accessible overview of Arabic literature, see **M. M. Badawi**, *A Short History of Modern Arab Literature* (Oxford, 1993). For Iranian literature, see **S. Sullivan** and **F. Milani**, *Stories by Iranian Women Since the Revolution* (Austin, Tex., 1991), and **M. M. Khorrami** and **S. Vatanabadi**, eds., *A Feast in the Mirror: Short Stories by Contemporary Iranian Women* (Boulder, Colo., 2000).

InfoTrac College Edition

Visit this chapter's InfoTrac College Edition/Research activities at the *Essential World History* Companion Website for activities related to nation building in Africa and the Middle East.

ThomsonNOW™ for Duiker and Spielvogel's *The Essential World History, Third Edition*

Enter *ThomsonNOW* using the access card that is available with this text. *ThomsonNOW* will assist you in understanding the content in this chapter with lesson plans generated for your needs, as well as provide you with a connection to the *Wadsworth World History Resource Center* (see description below for details).

WORLD HISTORY
RESOURCE CENTER

Enter the Resource Center using either your *ThomsonNOW* access card or your standalone access card for the *Wadsworth World History Resource Center*. Organized by topic, this website includes quizzes; images; over 350 primary source documents; interactive simulations, maps, and timelines; movie explorations; and a wealth of other resources. You can read the following documents, and many more, at http://worldrc.wadsworth.com/

> A. L. Geyer, "The Case for Apartheid"
>
> Speeches by Nelson Mandela

Visit the *Essential World History* Companion Website for chapter quizzes and more:

> http://www.thomsonedu.com/history/duiker

DISCOVERY

What factors can be advanced to explain the chronic instability and internal conflict that have characterized conditions in Africa and the Middle East since World War II?

In thinking about this question, begin by breaking it down into the components shown below. A discussion of the significance of each component should appear in your answer.

INTERACTION AND EXCHANGE: Look at the map of the Modern Middle East. Which of the nations in the Middle East are major oil producers? How have oil revenues affected political development in countries throughout the region? Which nations are democracies and which are dictatorships/monarchies?

Based on the document, what role has the West played in helping to support nondemocratic governments? What has been the reasoning for this? Is the lack of democracy a product of Islam or of economics? Within Islam, there are divisions, as seen in the map of Iraq. How do they contribute to political instability? To what degree is the West responsible for problems in the Middle East?

The Modern Middle East

Iraq

M. J. AKBAR, "LINKING ISLAM TO DICTATORSHIP"

Let us examine a central canard, that Islam and democracy are incompatible. This is an absurdity. There is nothing Islamic or un-Islamic about democracy. Democracy is the outcome of a political process, not a religious process.

It is glibly suggested that "every" Muslim country is a dictatorship, but the four largest Muslim populations of the world—in Indonesia, India, Bangladesh, and Turkey—vote to change governments. Pakistan could easily have been on this list.

Voting does not make these Muslims less or more religious. There are dictators among Muslims just as there are dictators among Christians, Buddhists, and Hindus (check out Nepal). . . . Christian Latin America has seen ugly forms of dictatorship, as has Christian Africa.

What is unique to the Muslim world is not the absence of democracy but the fact that in 1918, after the defeat of the Ottoman Empire, every single Muslim in the world lived under foreign subjugation.

Every single one, from Indonesia to Morocco via Turkey. The Turks threw out their invaders within a few years under the great leadership of Kemal Atatürk, but the transition to self-rule in other Muslim countries was slow, uncertain, and full of traps planted by the world's preeminent powers.

The West, in the shape of Britain, France, or America, was never interested in democracy when a helpful dictator or king would serve. When people got a chance to express their wish, it was only logical that they would ask for popular rule. It was the street that brought Mossadegh to power in Iran and drove the shah of Iran to tearful exile in Rome. Who brought the shah of Iran and autocracy back to Iran? The CIA.

If Iranian democracy had been permitted a chance in 1953, there would have been no uprising led by Ayatollah Khomeini in 1979. In other countries, where the struggle for independence was long and brutal, as in Algeria and Indonesia, the militias who had fought the war institutionalized army authority. In other instances, civilian heroes confused their own well-being with national health. They became regressive dictators. Once again, there was nothing Islamic about it.

Muslim countries will become democracies, too, because it is the finest form of modern governance. But it will be a process interrupted by bloody experience as the street wrenches power from usurpers.

Democracy has happened in Turkey. It has happened in Bangladesh. It is happening in Indonesia. It almost happened in Pakistan, and the opportunity will return. Democracy takes time in the most encouraging environments.

Democracy has become the latest rationale for the occupation of Iraq. . . . Granted, democracy is always preferable to tyranny no matter how it comes. But Iraqis are not dupes. They will take democracy and place it at the service of nationalism. A decade ago, America was careless about the definition of victory. Today it is careless about the definition of democracy.

There is uncertainty and apprehension across the Muslim nations: uncertainty about where they stand, and apprehension about both American power and the repugnant use of terrorism that in turn invites the exercise of American power. There is also anger that a legitimate cause like that of Palestine can get buried in the debris of confusion. Muslims do not see Palestinians as terrorists.

POLITICS AND GOVERNMENT: How has the Arab-Israeli dispute created lingering obstacles to peace and development in the Middle East? Is this a religious problem or a land problem? What role does religion play in the conflict, if any? How have both sides contributed to the ongoing inability to find a peaceful solution? What roles have the United States and Europe played in this ongoing conflict? How is that outside involvement viewed by the Arab states? How has it contributed to modern instability and conflict? What possible solutions do you see?

Israel and Its Neighbors

The Temple Mount at Jerusalem

INTERACTION AND EXCHANGE: How do these pictures and the reading illustrate economic factors that have blunted African development in the postcolonial period? How have the lingering effects of colonial rule contributed to these problems? How does tradition in Africa clash with modern development and economic progress? How have the Africans themselves contributed to these problems? What possible solutions do you see?

Cape Town: A Tale of Two Cities

AYI KWEI ARMAH, THE BEAUTIFUL ONES ARE NOT YET BORN

The net had been made in the special Ghanaian way that allowed the really big corrupt people to pass through it. A net to catch only the small, dispensable fellows, trying in their anguished blindness to leap and to attain the gleam and the comfort the only way these things could be done. And the big ones floated free, like all the slogans. End bribery and corruption. Build Socialism. Equality. Shit. A man would just have to make up his mind that there was never going to be anything but despair, and there would be no way of escaping it. . . .

In the life of the nation itself, maybe nothing really new would happen. New men would take into their hands the power to steal the nation's riches and to use it for their own satisfaction. That, of course, was to be expected. New people would use the country's power to get rid of men and women who talked a language that did not flatter them. There would be nothing different in that. That would only be a continuation of the Ghanaian way of life. But here was the real change. The individual man of power now shivering, his head filled with the fear of the vengeance of those he had wronged. For him everything was going to change. And for those like him who had grown greasy and fat singing the praises of their chief, for those who had been getting themselves ready for the enjoyment of hoped-for favors, there would be long days of pain ahead. The flatterers with their new white Mercedes cars would have to find ways of burying old words. For those who had come directly against the old power, there would be much happiness. But for the nation itself there would only be a change of embezzlers and a change of the hunters and the hunted. A pitiful shrinking of the world from those days Teacher still looked back to, when the single mind was filled with the hopes of a whole people. A pitiful shrinking, to days when all the powerful could think of was to use the power of a whole people to fill their own paunches. Endless days, same days, stretching into the future with no end anywhere in sight.

29

TOWARD THE PACIFIC CENTURY?

CHAPTER OUTLINE
AND FOCUS QUESTIONS

South Asia

▫ How did Mahatma Gandhi's and Jawaharlal Nehru's goals for India differ, and what role has each leader's views played in shaping modern India?

Southeast Asia

▫ What kinds of problems have the nations of Southeast Asia faced since 1945, and how have they attempted to solve these problems?

East Asia

▫ How did the Allied occupation after World War II change Japan's political and economic institutions, and what remained unchanged?

CRITICAL THINKING

▫ What factors have contributed to the economic successes achieved by Japan and the "Little Tigers"? Have the nations of South and Southeast Asia achieved the same results?

Hong Kong: symbol of the Pacific century

Courtesy of William J. Duiker

*F*IRST-TIME VISITORS to the Malaysian capital of Kuala Lumpur are astonished to observe a pair of twin towers thrusting up above the surrounding buildings into the clouds. The Petronas Towers rise 1,483 feet from ground level, leading to claims by Malaysian officials that they are the world's tallest buildings, at least for the time being.

More than an architectural achievement, the towers announced the emergence of Southeast Asia as a major player on the international scene. It is probably no accident that the foundations were laid on the site of the Selangor Cricket Club, symbol of colonial hegemony in Southeast Asia. "These towers," commented one local official, "will do wonders for Asia's self-esteem and confidence, which I think is very important, and which I think at this moment are at the point of takeoff."[1]

The Petronas Towers in Kuala Lumpur are only one symbol of the emergence of Asia as a major player in global politics in the century now unfolding. Several other cities in the region, including Hong Kong, Singapore, Tokyo, and Shanghai, have become major capitals of finance and monuments of economic prowess, rivaling traditional centers like New York, London, Berlin, and Paris. Together, they herald the opening of what has been called "the Pacific Century." ◇

South Asia

In 1947, nearly two centuries of British colonial rule came to an end when two new independent nations, India and Pakistan, came into being.

The End of the British Raj

During the 1930s, the nationalist movement in India was severely shaken by factional disagreements between Hindus and Muslims. The outbreak of World War II subdued these sectarian clashes, but they erupted again after the war ended in 1945. Battles between Hindus and Muslims broke out in several cities, and Mohammed Ali Jinnah (1876–1948), leader of the Muslim League, demanded the creation of a separate state for each. Meanwhile, the Labour Party, which had long been critical of the British colonial legacy on both moral and economic grounds, had come to power in Britain, and the new prime minister, Clement Attlee, announced that power would be transferred to "responsible Indian hands" by June 1948.

But the imminence of independence did not dampen communal strife. As riots escalated, the British reluctantly accepted the inevitability of partition and declared that on August 15, 1947, two independent nations—Hindu India and Muslim Pakistan—would be established. Pakistan would be divided between the main area of Muslim habitation in the Indus River valley in the west and a separate territory in east Bengal 2,000 miles to the east. Although Mahatma Gandhi warned that partition would provoke "an orgy of blood,"[2] he was increasingly regarded as a figure of the past, and his views were ignored.

The British instructed the rulers in the princely states to choose which state they would join by August 15, but problems arose in predominantly Hindu Hyderabad, where the nawab (viceroy) was a Muslim, and mountainous Kashmir, where a Hindu prince ruled over a Muslim population. After independence was declared, the flight of millions of Hindus and Muslims across the borders led to violence and the deaths of more than a million people. One of the casualties was Gandhi, who was assassinated on January 30, 1948, as he was going to morning prayer. The assassin, a Hindu militant, was apparently motivated by Gandhi's opposition to a Hindu India.

Independent India

With independence, the Indian National Congress, now renamed the Congress Party, moved from opposition to the responsibility of power under Jawaharlal Nehru, the new prime minister. The prospect must have been intimidating. The vast majority of India's 400 million people were poor and illiterate. The new nation encompassed a bewildering number of ethnic groups and fourteen major languages. Although Congress Party leaders spoke bravely of building a new nation, Indian society still bore the scars of past wars and divisions.

The government's first problem was to resolve disputes left over from the transition period. The rulers of Hyderabad and Kashmir had both followed their own preferences rather than the wishes of their subject populations. Nehru was determined to include both states within India. In 1948, Indian troops invaded Hyderabad and annexed the area. India was also able to seize most of Kashmir, but at the cost of creating an intractable problem that has poisoned relations with Pakistan down to the present day.

An Experiment in Democratic Socialism   Under Nehru's leadership, India adopted a political system on the British model, with a figurehead president and a parliamentary form of government. A number of political parties operated legally, but the Congress Party, with its enormous prestige and charismatic leadership, was dominant at both the central and the local levels.

Nehru had been influenced by British socialism and patterned his economic policy roughly after the program of the British Labour Party. The state took over ownership of the major industries and resources, transportation, and utilities, while private enterprise was permitted at the local and retail levels. Farmland remained in private hands, but rural cooperatives were officially encouraged.

In other respects, Nehru was a devotee of Western materialism. He was convinced that to succeed, India must industrialize. In advocating industrialization, Nehru departed sharply from Gandhi, who believed that materialism was morally corrupting and that only simplicity and nonviolence (as represented by the traditional Indian village and the symbolic spinning wheel) could save India, and the world itself, from self-destruction (see the box on p. 657).

The primary themes of Nehru's foreign policy were anticolonialism and antiracism. Under his guidance, India took a neutral stance in the Cold War and sought to provide leadership to all newly independent nations in Asia, Africa, and Latin America. India's neutrality put it at odds with the United States, which during the 1950s was trying to mobilize all nations against what it viewed as the menace of international communism.

Relations with Pakistan continued to be troubled. India refused to consider Pakistan's claim to Kashmir, even though the majority of the population there was Muslim. Tension between the two countries persisted, erupting into war in 1965. In 1971, when riots against the Pakistani government broke out in East Pakistan, India intervened on the side of East Pakistan, which declared its independence as the new nation of Bangladesh (see Map 29.1).

The Post-Nehru Era   Nehru's death in 1964 aroused concern that Indian democracy was dependent on the Nehru mystique. When his successor, a Congress Party veteran, died in 1966, party leaders selected Nehru's

TWO VISIONS FOR INDIA

POLITICS & GOVERNMENT

Although Jawaharlal Nehru and Mohandas Gandhi agreed on their desire for an independent India, their visions of the future of their homeland were dramatically different. Nehru favored industrialization to build material prosperity, whereas Gandhi praised the simple virtues of manual labor. The first excerpt is from a speech by Nehru; the second is from a letter written by Gandhi to Nehru.

What are the key differences between these two views on the future of India? Why do you think Nehru's proposals triumphed over those of Mahatma Gandhi?

Nehru's Socialist Creed

I am convinced that the only key to the solution of the world's problems and of India's problems lies in socialism, and when I use this word I do so not in a vague humanitarian way but in the scientific economic sense. . . . I see no way of ending the poverty, the vast unemployment, the degradation and the subjection of the Indian people except through socialism. That involves vast and revolutionary changes in our political and social structure, the ending of vested interests in land and industry, as well as the feudal and autocratic Indian states system. That means the ending of private property, except in a restricted sense, and the replacement of the present profit system by a higher ideal of cooperative service. . . . In short, it means a new civilization, radically different from the present capitalist order. Some glimpse we can have of this new civilization in the territories of the U.S.S.R. Much has happened there which has pained me greatly and with which I disagree, but I look upon that great and fascinating unfolding of a new order and a new civilization as the most promising feature of our dismal age.

A Letter to Jawaharlal Nehru

I believe that if India, and through India the world, is to achieve real freedom, then sooner or later we shall have to go and live in the villages—in huts, not in palaces. Millions of people can never live in cities and palaces in comfort and peace. Nor can they do so by killing one another, that is, by resorting to violence and untruth. . . . We can have the vision of . . . truth and nonviolence only in the simplicity of the villages. That simplicity resides in the spinning wheel and what is implied by the spinning wheel. . . .

You will not be able to understand me if you think that I am talking about the villages of today. My ideal village still exists only in my imagination. . . . In this village of my dreams the villager will not be dull—he will be all awareness. He will not live like an animal in filth and darkness. Men and women will live in freedom, prepared to face the whole world. There will be no plague, no cholera, and no smallpox. Nobody will be allowed to be idle or to wallow in luxury. Everyone will have to do body labor. Granting all this, I can still envisage a number of things that will have to be organized on a large scale. Perhaps there will even be railways and also post and telegraph offices. I do not know what things there will be or will not be. Nor am I bothered about it. If I can make sure of the essential thing, other things will follow in due course. But if I give up the essential thing, I give up everything.

ThomsonNOW To read more of Nehru's writings, enter the *ThomsonNOW* documents area using the access card that is available for *The Essential World History*.

---

daughter, Indira Gandhi (no relation to Mahatma Gandhi), as the new prime minister. Gandhi was inexperienced in politics, but she quickly showed the steely determination of her father.

Like Nehru, Gandhi embraced democratic socialism and a policy of neutrality in foreign affairs, but she was more activist than her father. To combat rural poverty, she nationalized banks, provided loans to peasants on easy terms, built low-cost housing, distributed land to the landless, and introduced electoral reforms to enfranchise the poor.

Gandhi was especially worried by India's growing population and in an effort to curb the growth rate, adopted a policy of enforced sterilization. This policy proved unpopular, however, and, along with growing official corruption and Gandhi's authoritarian tactics, led to her defeat in the general election of 1975, the first time the Congress Party had failed to win a majority at the national level.

A minority government of procapitalist parties was formed, but within two years, Gandhi was back in power. She now faced a new challenge, however, in the rise of religious strife. The most dangerous situation was in the Punjab, where militant Sikhs were demanding autonomy or even independence from India. Gandhi did not shrink from a confrontation and attacked Sikh rebels hiding in their Golden Temple in the city of Amritsar. The incident aroused widespread anger among the Sikh community, and in 1984, Sikh members of Gandhi's personal bodyguard assassinated her.

By now, Congress Party politicians were convinced that the party could not remain in power without a member of the Nehru family at the helm. Gandhi's son Rajiv, a commercial airline pilot with little interest in politics, was persuaded to replace his mother as prime minister. Rajiv lacked the strong ideological and political convictions of his mother and grandfather and allowed a greater role for private enterprise. But his

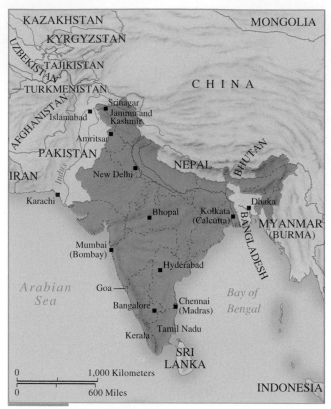

MAP 29.1 Modern South Asia. This map shows the boundaries of all the states in contemporary South Asia. India, the largest in area and population, is highlighted. ❓ Which of the countries in the region have primarily Muslim populations?

government was criticized for cronyism, inefficiency, and corruption.

Rajiv Gandhi also sought to play a role in regional affairs, mediating a dispute between the government in Sri Lanka and Tamil rebels (known as the "Elam tigers")

who were ethnically related to the majority population in southern India. The decision cost him his life: while campaigning for reelection in 1991, he was assassinated by a member of the Tiger organization. India faced the future without a member of the Nehru family as prime minister.

During the early 1990s, the Congress Party remained the leading party, but the powerful hold it once had on the Indian electorate was gone. New parties, such as the militantly Hindu Bharata Janata Party (BJP), actively vied with the Congress Party for control of the central and state governments. Growing political instability at the center was accompanied by rising tensions between Hindus and Muslims.

When a coalition government formed under Congress leadership collapsed, the BJP, under Prime Minister A. B. Vajpayee, ascended to power in 1998 and played on Hindu sensibilities to build its political base. The new government based its success on an aggressive program of privatization in the industrial and commercial sectors and made a major effort to support the nation's small but growing technological base. But BJP leaders had underestimated the discontent of India's less affluent citizens (an estimated 350 million Indians earn less than one U.S. dollar a day), and in the spring of 2004, a stunning defeat in national elections forced the Vajpayee government to resign. The Congress Party returned to power at the head of a coalition government based on a commitment to maintain economic growth while carrying out reforms in rural areas.

The Land of the Pure: Pakistan Since Independence

When Pakistan achieved independence in August 1947, it was, unlike its neighbor India, in all respects a new nation, based on religious conviction rather than historical or

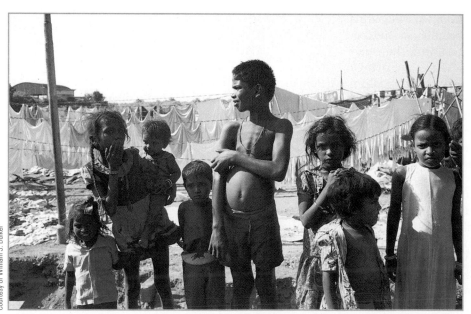

India's Hope, India's Sorrow. In India, as in many other societies in South Asia, overpopulation is a serious obstacle to economic development. The problem is particularly serious in large cities where thousands of poor children are forced into begging or prostitution. Shown here are a few of the thousands of street children in the commercial hub of Mumbai (Bombay). With the Indian economy experiencing rapid growth, the national government is aggressively addressing the issue of poverty.

ethnic tradition. The unique state consisted of two separate territories 2,000 miles apart. West Pakistan, including the Indus River basin and the West Punjab, was perennially short of water and was populated by dry crop farmers and peoples of the steppe. East Pakistan was made up of the marshy deltas of the Ganges and Brahmaputra rivers. Densely populated with rice farmers, it was the home of the artistic and intellectual Bengalis.

Even though the new state was an essentially Muslim society, its first years were marked by intense internal conflicts over religious, linguistic, and regional issues. Mohammed Ali Jinnah's vision of a democratic state that would assure freedom of religion and equal treatment for all was opposed by those who advocated a state based on Islamic principles.

Even more dangerous was the division between east and west. Many in East Pakistan felt that the government, based in the west, ignored their needs. In 1952, riots erupted in East Pakistan over the government's decision to adopt Urdu, a language derived from Hindi and used by Muslims in northern India, as the national language of the entire country. Most East Pakistanis spoke Bengali, an unrelated language. Tensions persisted, and in March 1971, East Pakistan declared its independence as the new nation of Bangladesh. Pakistani troops attempted to restore central government authority in the capital of Dhaka, but rebel forces supported by India went on the offensive, and the government bowed to the inevitable and recognized independent Bangladesh.

The breakup of the union between East and West Pakistan undermined the fragile authority of the military regime that had ruled Pakistan since 1958 and led to its replacement by a civilian government under Zulfikar Ali Bhutto. But now religious tensions came to the fore, despite a new constitution that made a number of key concessions to conservative Muslims. In 1977, a new military government under General Zia Ul Ha'q came to power with a commitment to make Pakistan a truly Islamic state. Islamic law became the basis for social behavior as well as for the legal system. Laws governing the consumption of alcohol and the role of women were tightened in accordance with strict Muslim beliefs. But after Zia was killed in a plane crash, Pakistanis elected Benazir Bhutto (b. 1953), the daughter of Zulfikar Ali Bhutto and a supporter of secularism who had been educated in the United States. She too was removed from power by a military regime, in 1990, on charges of incompetence and corruption. Reelected in 1993, she attempted to crack down on opposition forces but was removed once again amid renewed charges of official corruption. Her successor soon came under fire for the same reason and in 1999 was ousted by a military coup led by General Pervaiz Musharraf (b. 1943), who promised to restore political stability and honest government.

In September 2001, Pakistan became the focus of international attention when a coalition of forces arrived in Afghanistan to overthrow the Taliban regime and destroy the al-Qaeda terrorist network. Despite considerable support for the Taliban among the local population, President Musharraf pledged his help in bringing terrorists to justice. He also promised to return his country to the secular principles espoused by Mohammed Ali Jinnah. His situation was complicated by renewed tensions with India over Kashmir and a series of violent clashes between Muslims and Hindus in India. In 2003, however, relations began to improve as both sides promised to seek a peaceful solution to the Kashmir dispute.

Poverty and Pluralism in South Asia

The leaders of the new states that emerged in South Asia after World War II faced a number of problems. The peoples of South Asia were still overwhelmingly poor and illiterate, while the sectarian, ethnic, and cultural divisions that had plagued Indian society for centuries had not dissipated.

The Politics of Communalism   Perhaps the most sincere effort to create democratic institutions was in India, where the new constitution called for social justice, liberty, equality of status and opportunity, and fraternity. All citizens were guaranteed protection from discrimination based on religious belief, race, caste, gender, or place of birth.

In theory, then, India became a full-fledged democracy on the British parliamentary model. In actuality, a number of distinctive characteristics made the system less than fully democratic in the Western sense but may also have enabled it to survive. As we have seen, India became in essence a one-party state. By leading the independence movement, the Congress Party had amassed massive public support, which enabled it to retain its preeminent position in Indian politics for three decades. After Nehru's death in 1964, however, problems emerged that had been disguised by his adept maneuvering. Part of the problem was the familiar one of a party too long in power. Party officials became complacent and all too easily fell prey to the temptations of corruption and pork-barrel politics.

Another problem was **communalism.** Beneath the surface unity of the new republic lay age-old ethnic, linguistic, and religious divisions. Because of India's vast size and complex history, no national language had ever emerged. Hindi was the most prevalent, but it was the native language of less than one-third of the population. During the colonial period, English had served as the official language of government, but it was spoken only by the educated elite and represented an affront to national pride. Eventually, India recognized fourteen official tongues, making the parliament sometimes sound like the Tower of Babel.

Divisiveness increased after Nehru's death, and under his successors, official corruption grew. Only the lack of appeal of its rivals and the Nehru family charisma carried on by his daughter Indira Gandhi kept the Congress Party in power. But she was unable to prevent the progressive disintegration of the party's power base at the state level, where regional or ideological parties won the allegiance of voters by exploiting ethnic or social revolutionary themes.

During the 1980s, religious tensions began to intensify. As we have seen, Gandhi's uncompromising approach to Sikh separatism led to her assassination in 1984. In 1992, at Ayodhya, in northern India, Hindu militants destroyed a mosque allegedly built on the site of King Rama's birthplace, where a Hindu temple had once existed, and erected a temporary temple at the site. Their actions provoked clashes between Hindus and Muslims throughout India, and sparked protests in neighboring Pakistan where rioters destroyed a number of Hindu shrines.

In recent years, communal divisions have intensified, as militant Hindu groups agitate for a state that caters to the Hindu majority, now numbering more than 700 million people. In the spring of 2002, violence between Hindus and Muslims flared up again over plans by Hindu activists to build a permanent temple to Rama at the site of the destroyed mosque at Ayodhya. In the summer of 2006, unknown terrorists killed dozens of Indians in a series of bombings on commuter trains in Mumbai.

The Economy Nehru's answer to the social and economic inequality that had long afflicted the subcontinent was socialism. He instituted a series of five-year plans, which led to the creation of a relatively large and reasonably efficient industrial sector, centered on steel, vehicles, and textiles. Industrial production almost tripled between 1950 and 1965, and per capita income rose by 50 percent between 1950 and 1980, although it was still less than

$300 (in U.S. dollars). By the 1970s, however, industrial growth had slowed. The lack of modern infrastructure was a problem, as was the rising price of oil, most of which had to be imported.

India's major economic weakness, however, was in agriculture. At independence, mechanization was almost unknown, fertilizer was rarely used, and most farms were small and uneconomical because of the Hindu tradition of dividing the land equally among all male children. As a result, the vast majority of the Indian people lived in conditions of abject poverty. Landless laborers outnumbered landowners by almost two to one. The government attempted to relieve the problem by redistributing land to the poor, limiting the size of landholdings, and encouraging farmers to form voluntary cooperatives. But all three programs ran into widespread opposition.

Another problem was overpopulation. Even before independence, the country had had difficulty supporting its people. In the 1950s and 1960s, the population grew by more than 2 percent annually, twice the nineteenth-century rate. Beginning in the 1960s, the Indian government sought to curb population growth. Indira Gandhi instituted a program combining monetary rewards and compulsory sterilization. Males who had fathered too many children were sometimes forced to undergo a vasectomy. Popular resistance undermined the program, however, and the goals were scaled back in the 1970s. As a result, India has made little progress in holding down its burgeoning population, now estimated at more than one billion. Nevertheless, as a result of media popularization and better government programs, the trend today, even in poor rural villages, is toward smaller families. The average number of children a woman bears has declined from six in 1950 to three today.

After the death of Indira Gandhi in 1984, her son Rajiv proved more receptive to foreign investment and a greater role for the private sector in the economy. India began to export more manufactured goods, including computer software. The pace of change has accelerated under Rajiv Gandhi's successors, who have continued to transfer state-run industries to private hands. These policies have stimulated the growth of a prosperous new middle class, now estimated at more than 100 million. Consumerism has soared, and sales of television sets, automobiles, DVD players, and cell phones have increased dramatically. Equally important, Western imports are being replaced by new products manufactured in India with Indian brand names (see the box on p. 661).

One consequence of India's entrance into the industrial age is the emergence of a small but vibrant technological sector that provides many important services to the world's advanced nations. The city of Bangalore in South India has become an important technological center, benefiting from low wages and the presence of skilled labor with proficiency in the English language. It has also become a symbol of the "outsourcing" of jobs from the United States and Europe, a practice

SAY NO TO McDONALD'S AND KFC!

INTERACTION & EXCHANGE

One of the consequences of Rajiv Gandhi's decision to deregulate the Indian economy has been an increase in the presence of foreign corporations, including U.S. fast-food restaurant chains. Their arrival set off a storm of protest in India: from environmentalists concerned that raising grain for chickens is an inefficient use of land, from religious activists angry at the killing of animals for food, and from nationalists anxious to protect the domestic market from foreign competition. Fast-food restaurants now represent a growing niche in Indian society, but most cater to local tastes, avoiding beef products and offering many vegetarian dishes, such as the Veg Pizza McPuff. The author of this piece, which appeared in the *Hindustan Times,* was Maneka Gandhi, a daughter-in-law of Indira Gandhi and a onetime minister of the environment who has emerged as a prominent rival of Congress Party president Sonia Gandhi.

Why does the author of this article oppose the introduction of fast-food restaurants in India? Do you think her complaints apply in the United States as well?

Why India Doesn't Need Fast Food

India's decision to allow Pepsi Foods Ltd. to open 60 restaurants in India—30 each of Pizza Hut and Kentucky Fried Chicken—marks the first entry of multinational, meat-based junk-food chains into India. If this is allowed to happen, at least a dozen other similar chains will very quickly arrive, including the infamous McDonald's.

The implications of allowing junk-food chains into India are quite stark. As the name denotes, the foods served at Kentucky Fried Chicken (KFC) are chicken-based

and fried. This is the worst combination possible for the body and can create a host of health problems, including obesity, high cholesterol, heart ailments, and many kinds of cancer. Pizza Hut products are a combination of white flour, cheese, and meat—again, a combination likely to cause disease. . . .

Then there is the issue of the environmental impact of junk-food chains. Modern meat production involves misuse of crops, water, energy, and grazing areas. In addition, animal agriculture produces surprisingly large amounts of air and water pollution.

KFC and Pizza Hut insist that their chickens be fed corn and soybeans. Consider the diversion of grain for this purpose. As the outlets of KFC and Pizza Hut increase in number, the poultry industry will buy up more and more corn to feed the chickens, which means that the corn will quickly disappear from the villages, and its increased price will place it out of reach for the common man. Turning corn into junk chicken is like turning gold into mud. . . .

It is already shameful that, in a country plagued by famine and flood, we divert 37 percent of our arable land to growing animal fodder. Were all of that grain to be consumed directly by humans, it would nourish five times as many people as it does after being converted into meat, milk, and eggs. . . .

Of course, it is not just the KFC and Pizza Hut chains of Pepsi Foods Ltd. that will cause all of this damage. Once we open India up by allowing these chains, dozens more will be eagerly waiting to come in. Each city in America has an average of 5,000 junk-food restaurants. Is that what we want for India?

---

that has led to an increase in middle class, unemployment throughout the Western world (see the comparative illustration on p. 662).

As in the industrialized countries of the West, economic growth has been accompanied by environmental damage. Water and air pollution has led to illness and death for many people, and an environmental movement has emerged. Some critics, reflecting the traditional anti-imperialist attitude of Indian intellectuals, blame Western capitalist corporations for the problem, as in the highly publicized case of leakage from a foreign-owned chemical plant at Bhopal. Much of the problem, however, comes from state-owned factories erected with Soviet aid. And not all the environmental damage can be ascribed to industrialization. The Ganges River is so polluted by human overuse that it is risky for Hindu believers to bathe in it.

Moreover, many Indians have not benefited from the new prosperity. Nearly one-third of the population lives

below the national poverty line. Millions continue to live in urban slums, such as the famous "City of Joy" in Kolkata (Calcutta), and most farm families remain desperately poor. Despite the socialist rhetoric of India's leaders, the inequality of wealth in India is as pronounced as it is in capitalist nations in the West. Indeed, India has been described as two nations: an educated urban India of 100 million people surrounded by more than nine times that many impoverished peasants in the countryside.

Caste, Class, and Gender   Although the constitution of 1950 guaranteed equal treatment and opportunity for all, regardless of caste, and prohibited discrimination based on untouchability, prejudice is hard to eliminate. Untouchability persists, particularly in the villages, where *harijans,* now called **dalits,** still perform menial tasks and are often denied fundamental human rights.

After independence, India's leaders also sought to equalize treatment of the sexes. The constitution expressly

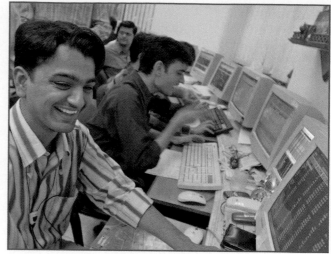

Courtesy of William J. Duiker

AP Images/Aijaz Rahi

COMPARATIVE ILLUSTRATION

Two Indias.   Contemporary India is a study in contrasts. In the right photo, middle class students learn to operate the computer, symbolizing their country's recent drive to join the global technological marketplace. Yet, India today remains above all, a nation of villages. On the left, women in colorful saris fill their pails of water at the village well. As in many developing countries, the scarcity of water is one of India's most crucial problems.

forbade discrimination based on gender and called for equal pay for equal work. Laws prohibited child marriage, *sati,* and the payment of a dowry by the bride's family. Women were encouraged to attend school and enter the labor market.

Such laws, along with the dynamics of economic and social change, have had a major impact on the lives of many Indian women. Middle-class women in urban areas are much more likely to seek employment outside the home, and many hold managerial and professional positions. Some Indian women, however, choose to play a dual role—a modern one in their work and in the marketplace and a more submissive, traditional one at home.

Like other aspects of life, the role of women has changed much less in rural areas. In the early 1960s, many villagers still practiced the institution of *purdah.* Female children are still much less likely to receive an education. The overall literacy rate in India today is less than 40 percent, but it is undoubtedly much lower among women. Laws relating to dowry, child marriage, and inheritance are routinely ignored in the countryside. There have been a few highly publicized cases of *sati,* although undoubtedly more women die of mistreatment at the hands of their husband or of other members of his family.

South Asian Art and Literature Since Independence

Recent decades have witnessed a prodigious outpouring of literature in India. Because of the vast quantity of

works published (India is currently the third-largest publisher of English-language books in the world), only a few of the most prominent fiction writers can be mentioned here. Anita Desai (b. 1937) was one of the first prominent female writers in contemporary India. Her writing focuses on the struggle of Indian women to achieve a degree of independence. In her first novel, *Cry, the Peacock,* the heroine finally seeks liberation by murdering her husband, preferring freedom at any cost to remaining a captive of traditional society.

The most controversial writer in India today is Salman Rushdie (b. 1947). In *Midnight's Children,* published in 1980, the author linked his protagonist, born on the night of independence, to the history of modern India, its achievements and its frustrations. Rushdie's later novels have tackled such problems as religious intolerance, political tyranny, social injustice, and greed and corruption. His attack on Islamic fundamentalism in *The Satanic Verses* (1988) won plaudits from literary critics but provoked widespread criticism among Muslims, including a death sentence by Ayatollah Khomeini in Iran.

Like Chinese and Japanese artists, Indian artists have agonized over how best to paint with a modern yet indigenous mode of expression. During the colonial period, Indian art went in several directions at once. One school of painters favored traditional themes; another experimented with a colorful primitivism founded on folk art. Many Indian artists painted representational social art extolling the suffering and silent dignity of India's impoverished millions. After 1960, however, most Indian artists adopted abstract art as their medium. Surrealism in particular, with its emphasis on spontaneity and the unconscious, appeared closer to the Hindu tradition of favoring intuition over reason. Yet Indian artists are still struggling to find the ideal way to be both modern and Indian.

Southeast Asia

As we have seen (see Chapter 24), Japanese wartime occupation had a great impact on attitudes among the peoples of Southeast Asia. It demonstrated the vulnerability of colonial rule in the region and showed that an Asian power could defeat Europeans. The Allied governments themselves also contributed—sometimes unwittingly—to rising aspirations for independence by promising self-determination for all peoples at the end of the war.

Some followed through on their promise. In July 1946, the United States granted total independence to the Philippines. The Americans maintained a military presence on the islands, however, and U.S. citizens retained economic and commercial interests in the new country.

The British, too, were willing to bring an end to a century of imperialism in the region. In 1948, the Union of Burma received its independence. Malaya's turn came in 1957, after a Communist guerrilla movement had been suppressed.

The French and the Dutch, however, both regarded their colonies in the region as economic necessities as well as symbols of national grandeur and refused to turn them over to nationalist movements at the end of the war. The Dutch attempted to suppress a rebellion in the East Indies led by Sukarno (1901–1970), leader of the Indonesian Nationalist Party. But the United States, which feared a Communist victory there, pressured the Dutch to grant independence to Sukarno and his non-Communist forces, and in 1950, the Dutch finally agreed to recognize the new Republic of Indonesia.

The situation was somewhat different in Vietnam, where the Communists seized power throughout most of the country. After the French refused to recognize the new government and reimposed their rule, war broke out in December 1946. At the time, it was only an anti-colonial war, but it would soon become much more (see Chapter 25).

The Era of Independent States

Many of the leaders of the newly independent states in Southeast Asia (see Map 29.2) admired Western political institutions and hoped to adapt them to their own countries. New constitutions were patterned on Western democratic models, and multiparty political systems quickly sprang into operation.

The Search for a New Political Culture By the 1960s, most of these budding experiments in pluralist democracy had been abandoned or were under serious threat.

Some had been replaced by military or one-party autocratic regimes. In Burma, a moderate government based on the British parliamentary system and dedicated to Buddhism and nonviolent Marxism had given way to a military government. In Thailand, too, the military now ruled. In the Philippines, President Ferdinand Marcos discarded democratic restraints and established his own centralized control. In South Vietnam, Ngo Dinh Diem and his successors paid lip service to the Western democratic model but ruled by authoritarian means.

One problem faced by most of these states was that independence had not brought material prosperity or ended economic inequality and the domination of the local economies by foreign interests. Most economies in the region were still characterized by tiny industrial sectors; they lacked technology, educational resources, and capital investment.

The presence of widespread ethnic, linguistic, cultural, and economic differences also made the transition to Western-style democracy difficult. In Malaya, for example, the majority Malays—most of whom were farmers—feared economic and political domination by the local Chinese minority, who were much more experienced in industry and commerce. In 1961, the Federation of Malaya, whose ruling party was dominated by Malays, integrated former British possessions on the island of Borneo into the new Union of Malaysia in a move to increase the non-Chinese proportion of the country's population.

The most publicized example of a failed experiment in democracy was in Indonesia. In 1950, the new leaders drew up a constitution creating a parliamentary system under a titular presidency. Sukarno was elected the first president. A spellbinding orator, Sukarno played a major role in creating a sense of national identity among the disparate peoples of the Indonesian archipelago.

In the late 1950s, Sukarno, exasperated at the incessant maneuvering among devout Muslims, Communists, and the army, dissolved the constitution and attempted to rule on his own through what he called **guided democracy.** As he described it, guided democracy was closer to Indonesian traditions and superior to the Western variety. Highly suspicious of the West, Sukarno nationalized foreign-owned enterprises and sought economic aid from China and the Soviet Union while relying for domestic support on the Indonesian Communist Party.

The army and conservative Muslims resented Sukarno's increasing reliance on the Communists, and the Muslims were further upset by his refusal to consider a state based on Islamic principles. In 1965, military officers launched a coup d'état that provoked a mass popular uprising, which resulted in the slaughter of several hundred thousand suspected Communists, many of whom were overseas Chinese, long distrusted by the Muslim majority. In 1967, a military government under General Suharto (b. 1921) was installed.

The new government made no pretensions of reverting to democratic rule, but it did restore good relations

MAP 29.2 Modern Southeast Asia. Shown here are the countries of contemporary Southeast Asia. The major islands that make up the Republic of Indonesia are indicated in italic type.
❓ Which of the countries in Southeast Asia now have functioning democratic governments? Which appear to be the most prosperous? 🔘 **View an animated version of this map or related maps at** http://worldrc.wadsworth.com/

with the West and sought foreign investment to repair the country's ravaged economy. But it also found it difficult to placate Muslim demands for an Islamic state.

The one country in Southeast Asia that explicitly rejected the Western model was North Vietnam. Its leaders opted for the Stalinist pattern of national development, based on Communist Party rule and socialist forms of ownership. In 1958, stimulated by the success of collectivization in neighboring China, the government launched a three-year plan to lay the foundation for a socialist society. Collective farms were established, and all industry and commerce above the family level were nationalized.

Recent Trends Toward Democracy In recent years, some Southeast Asian societies have shown signs of evolving toward more democratic forms. In the Philippines,

the dictatorial Marcos regime was overthrown by a massive public uprising in 1986 and replaced by a democratically elected government under President Corazon Aquino (b. 1933), the widow of a popular politician assassinated a few years earlier. Aquino was unable to resolve many of the country's chronic economic and social difficulties, however, and political stability remains elusive; one of her successors, ex-actor Joseph Estrada, was forced to resign on the charge of corruption. At the same time, Muslims in the southern island of Mindanao have mounted a terrorist campaign in their effort to obtain autonomy or independence.

In other nations, the results have also been mixed. Although Malaysia is a practicing democracy, tensions persist between Malays and Chinese as well as between secular and orthodox Muslims who seek to create an Islamic state. In neighboring Thailand, the military has found it expedient to hold national elections for civilian governments, but the danger of a military takeover is never far beneath the surface.

In Indonesia, difficult economic conditions caused by the financial crisis of 1997 (see the next section), combined with popular anger against the Suharto government (several members of his family had reportedly used their positions to amass considerable wealth), led to demands for his resignation and violent riots as Muslims and students took to the streets. Forced to step down in the spring of 1998, Suharto was replaced by his deputy, B. J. Habibie, who called for the establishment of a national assembly to select a new government based on popular aspirations. The assembly selected a moderate Muslim leader as president, but he was charged with corruption and incompetence and was replaced in 2001 by his vice president, Sukarno's daughter Megawati Sukarnoputri.

The new government faced a severe challenge, not only from the economic crisis but also from dissident elements seeking autonomy or even separation from the republic. Under pressure from the international community, Indonesia agreed to grant independence to the one-time Portuguese colony of East Timor, where the majority of the people are Roman Catholics. But violence provoked by pro-Indonesian militia units forced many refugees to flee the new country. Religious tensions have also erupted between Muslims and Christians elsewhere in the archipelago, and Muslim rebels in western Sumatra continue to agitate for a new state based on strict adherence to fundamentalist Islam.

In direct elections held in 2004, General Susilo Yudhyono defeated Megawati Sukarnoputri and ascended to the presidency. The new chief executive promised a new era of political stability, honest government, and economic reform but faces a number of severe challenges. Concerned about high wages and the risk of terrorism, a number of foreign firms have relocated their factories elsewhere in Asia, forcing thousands of workers to return to the countryside. Pressure from traditional Muslims to abandon the nation's secular tradition and move toward the creation of an Islamic state continues to grow. That the country was able to hold democratic elections in the midst of such tensions holds some promise for the future.

Elsewhere in the region, progress toward democracy has been mixed. In Vietnam, the trend has been toward a greater popular role in the governing process. Elections for the unicameral parliament are more open than in the past. The government remains suspicious of Western-style democracy, however, and represses any opposition to the Communist Party's guiding role over the state.

Only in Burma (now renamed Myanmar), where the military has been in complete control since the early 1960s, have the forces of greater popular participation been virtually silenced. Even there, however, the power of the ruling regime of General Ne Win (1911–2003) and his successors, known as SLORC, has been vocally challenged by Aung San Huu Kyi (b. 1952), the admired daughter of one of the heroes of the country's struggle for national liberation after World War II.

Increasing Prosperity and Financial Crisis The trend toward more representative systems of government has been due in part to increasing prosperity and the growth of an affluent and educated middle class. Although Indonesia, Burma, and the three Indochinese states are still overwhelmingly agrarian, Malaysia and

Soccer, a Global Obsession. Professional soccer has become the most popular sport in the world. It offers a diversion from daily drudgery and promotes intense patriotism as each nation supports its team. Moreover, children the world over enjoy playing soccer, even when there are no playing fields in the vicinity. Shown here is a match held in an ancestral Chinese temple in Hoi An, a town in central Vietnam that once served as a major entry point for European, Chinese, and Japanese merchants who took part in the regional trade network. Today, Vietnam is once again opening its doors to the outside world.

Thailand have been undergoing relatively rapid economic development.

In the late summer of 1997, however, these economic gains were threatened and popular faith in the ultimate benefits of globalization was shaken as a financial crisis swept through the region. The crisis was triggered by a number of problems, including growing budget deficits caused by excessive government expenditures on ambitious development projects, irresponsible lending and investment practices by financial institutions, and an overvaluation of local currencies relative to the U.S. dollar. An underlying cause of these problems was the prevalence of backroom deals between politicians and business leaders that temporarily enriched both groups at the cost of eventual economic dislocation.

As local currencies plummeted in value, the International Monetary Fund agreed to provide assistance, but only on the condition that the governments concerned permit greater transparency in their economic systems and allow market forces to operate more freely, even at the price of bankruptcies and the loss of jobs. By the early 2000s, there were signs that the economies in the region had weathered the crisis and were beginning to recover. But the massive tsunami that struck in December 2004 was another setback to economic growth, as well as a human tragedy of enormous proportions.

Regional Conflict and Cooperation: The Rise of ASEAN

In addition to their continuing internal challenges, Southeast Asian states have been hampered by serious tensions among themselves. Some of these tensions were a consequence of historical rivalries and territorial disputes that had been submerged during the long era of colonial rule. Cambodia, for example, has bickered with both of its neighbors, Thailand and Vietnam, over mutual frontiers drawn up originally by the French for their own convenience.

After the fall of Saigon and the reunification of Vietnam under Communist rule in 1975, the lingering border dispute between Cambodia and Vietnam erupted again. In April 1975, a brutal revolutionary regime under the leadership of the Khmer Rouge dictator Pol Pot came to power in Cambodia and proceeded to carry out the massacre of more than one million Cambodians. Then, claiming that vast territories in the Mekong delta had been seized from Cambodia by the Vietnamese in previous centuries, the Khmer Rouge regime launched attacks across the common border. In response, Vietnamese forces invaded Cambodia in December 1978 and installed a pro-Hanoi regime in Phnom Penh. Fearful of Vietnam's increasing power in the region, China launched a brief attack on Vietnam to demonstrate its displeasure.

The outbreak of war among the erstwhile Communist allies aroused the concern of other countries in the neighborhood. In 1967, several non-Communist countries

CHRONOLOGY Southeast Asia	
Philippines become independent	1946
Beginning of Franco-Vietminh War	1946
Burma becomes independent	1948
Recognition of the Republic of Indonesia	1950
Malaya becomes independent	1957
Beginning of Sukarno's "guided democracy" in Indonesia	1959
Military seizes power in Indonesia	1965
Foundation of ASEAN	1967
Fall of Saigon to North Vietnamese forces	1975
Vietnamese invade Cambodia	1978
Corazon Aquino elected president in the Philippines	1986
Vietnam becomes a member of ASEAN	1996
Islamic and student protests in Indonesia	1996–1997
Suharto steps down as president of Indonesia	1998
Tsunami causes widespread death and destruction throughout the region	2004

had established the Association of Southeast Asian Nations (ASEAN). Composed of Indonesia, Malaysia, Thailand, Singapore, and the Philippines, ASEAN at first concentrated on cooperative social and economic endeavors, but after the end of the Vietnam War, it cooperated with other states in an effort to force the Vietnamese to withdraw from Cambodia. In 1991, the Vietnamese finally withdrew, and a new government was formed in Phnom Penh.

The growth of ASEAN from a weak collection of diverse states into a stronger organization whose members cooperate militarily and politically has helped provide the nations of Southeast Asia with a more cohesive voice to represent their interests on the world stage. That Vietnam was admitted into ASEAN in 1996 should provide both Hanoi and its neighbors with greater leverage in dealing with China—their powerful neighbor to the north.

Daily Life: Town and Country in Contemporary Southeast Asia

The urban-rural dichotomy observed in India also is found in Southeast Asia, where the cities resemble those in the West while the countryside often appears little changed from precolonial days. In cities such as Bangkok, Manila, and Jakarta, broad boulevards lined with skyscrapers alternate with muddy lanes passing through neighborhoods packed with wooden shacks topped by thatch or rusty tin roofs. Nevertheless, in recent decades, millions of Southeast Asians have fled to these urban slums. Although most available jobs are menial, the pay is better than in the villages.

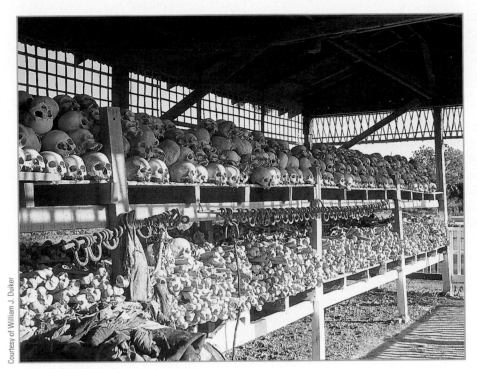

Courtesy of William J. Duiker

Holocaust in Cambodia. When the Khmer Rouge seized power in Cambodia in April 1975, they immediately emptied the capital of Phnom Penh and systematically began to eliminate opposition elements throughout the country. Thousands were tortured in the infamous Tuol Sleng prison and then marched out to the countryside, where they were massacred. Their bodies were thrown into massive pits. The succeeding government disinterred the remains, which are now displayed at an outdoor museum on the site. Today a measure of political and economic stability has begun to return to the country.

The Urban Impact   The urban migrants change not only their physical surroundings but their attitudes and values as well. Sometimes the move leads to a decline in traditional beliefs. Nevertheless, Buddhist, Muslim, and Confucian beliefs remain strong, even in cosmopolitan cities such as Bangkok, Jakarta, and Singapore. This preference for the traditional also shows up in lifestyle. Native dress—or an eclectic blend of Asian and Western dress—is still common. Traditional music, art, theater, and dance remain popular, although Western rock music has become fashionable among the young, and Indonesian filmmakers complain that Western films are beginning to dominate the market.

The Role of Women   One of the most significant changes that has taken place in Southeast Asia in recent decades is in the role of women in society. In general, women in the region have historically faced fewer restrictions on their activities and enjoyed a higher status than women elsewhere in Asia. Nevertheless, they were not the equal of men in every respect. With independence, Southeast Asian women gained new rights. Virtually all of the constitutions adopted by the newly independent states granted women full legal and political rights, including the right to work. Today, women have increased opportunities for education and have entered careers previously reserved for men. Women have become more active in politics, and as we have seen, some have served as heads of state.

Yet women are not truly equal to men in any country in Southeast Asia. In Vietnam, women are legally equal to men, yet until recently no women had served in the Communist Party's ruling Politburo. In Thailand, Malaysia, and Indonesia, women rarely hold senior positions in government service or in the boardrooms of major corporations.

A Region in Flux

Today, the Western image of a Southeast Asia mired in the Vietnam conflict and the tensions of the Cold War has become a memory. In ASEAN, the states in the region have created the framework for a regional organization that can serve their common political, economic, technological, and security interests. A few members of ASEAN are already on the road to advanced development.

To be sure, there are continuing signs of trouble. The financial crisis of the late 1990s aroused serious political unrest in Indonesia, and the region's economies, though recovering, still bear the scars of the crisis. There are disquieting signs that al-Qaeda has established a presence in the region. Myanmar remains isolated and appears mired in a state of chronic underdevelopment and brutal military rule. The three states of Indochina remain potentially unstable and have not yet been fully integrated into the region as a whole.

East Asia

In August 1945, Japan was in ruins, its cities destroyed, its vast Asian empire in ashes, its land occupied by a foreign army. Half a century later, Japan had emerged as the second-greatest industrial power in the world, democratic in form and content and a source of stability throughout the region. Japan's achievement spawned a number of Asian imitators.

The Japanese Miracle: The Transformation of Modern Japan

For five years after the end of the war in the Pacific, Japan was governed by an Allied administration under the command of U.S. general Douglas MacArthur. As commander of the occupation administration, MacArthur was responsible for demilitarizing Japanese society, destroying the Japanese war machine, trying Japanese civilian and military officials charged with war crimes, and laying the foundations of postwar Japanese society.

One of the sturdy pillars of Japanese militarism had been the giant business cartels, known as *zaibatsu*. Allied policy was designed to break up the *zaibatsu* into smaller units in the belief that corporate concentration not only hindered competition but was inherently undemocratic and conducive to political authoritarianism. Occupation planners also intended to promote the formation of independent labor unions in order to lessen the power of the state over the economy and provide a mouthpiece for downtrodden Japanese workers. Economic inequality in rural areas was to be reduced by a comprehensive land reform program that would turn the land over to those who farmed it. Finally, the educational system was to be remodeled along American lines so that it would turn out independent individuals rather than automatons subject to manipulation by the state.

The Allied program was an ambitious and even audacious plan to remake Japanese society and has been justly praised for its clear-sighted vision and altruistic motives. Parts of the program, such as the constitution, the land reforms, and the educational system, succeeded brilliantly. But as other concerns began to intervene, changes or compromises were made that were not always successful. In particular, with the rise of Cold War sentiment in the United States in the late 1940s, the goal of decentralizing the Japanese economy gave way to the desire to make Japan a key partner in the effort to defend East Asia against international communism. Convinced of the need to promote economic recovery in Japan, U.S. policy makers began to show more tolerance for the *zaibatsu*. Concerned at growing radicalism within the new labor movement, U.S. occupation authorities placed less emphasis on the independence of the labor unions.

The Cold War also affected U.S. foreign relations with Japan. On September 8, 1951, the United States and other former belligerent nations signed a peace treaty restoring Japanese independence. In turn, Japan renounced any claim to such former colonies or territories as Taiwan, Korea, and southern Sakhalin and the Kurile Islands (see Map 29.3). On the same day, Japan and the United States signed a defensive alliance and agreed that

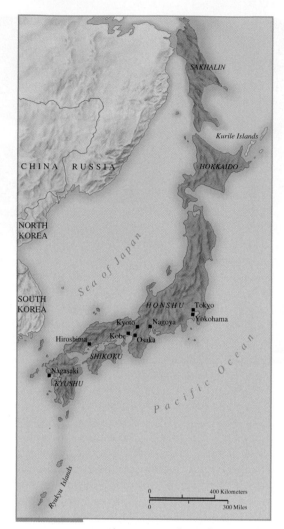

MAP 29.3 Modern Japan. Shown here are the four main islands that make up the contemporary state of Japan. ❓ Which is the largest?

the latter could maintain military bases on the Japanese islands. Japan was now formally independent but in a new dependency relationship with the United States. A provision in the new constitution renounced war as an instrument of national policy and prohibited the raising of an army.

Politics and Government The Allied occupation administrators started with the conviction that Japanese expansionism was directly linked to the institutional and ideological foundations of the Meiji constitution. Accordingly, they set out to change Japanese politics into something closer to the pluralistic model used in most Western nations. Yet a number of characteristics of the postwar Japanese political system reflected the tenacity of the traditional political culture. Although Japan had a multiparty system with two major parties, the Liberal Democrats and the Socialists, in practice there was a "government party" and a permanent opposition—the Liberal Democrats were not voted out of office for thirty years.

That tradition changed suddenly in 1993, when the ruling Liberal Democrats, shaken by persistent reports of corruption and cronyism between politicians and business interests, failed to win a majority of seats in parliamentary elections. The new coalition government, however, quickly split into feuding factions, and in 1995, the Liberal Democrats returned to power. Successive prime ministers proved unable to carry out promised reforms, and in 2001, Junichiro Koizumi, an ex-minister of health and welfare, was elected prime minister. He too promised far-reaching reforms to make the political system more responsive to the challenges facing the country—with mixed success.

These challenges include not only curbing persistent political corruption but also reducing the government's involvement in the economy. Since the Meiji period, the government has played an active role in mediating management-labor disputes, establishing price and wage policies, and subsidizing vital industries and enterprises producing goods for export. This government intervention in the economy was once cited as a key reason for the efficiency of Japanese industry and the emergence of the country as an industrial giant.

The issue of Japan's behavior during World War II has been especially sensitive. During the 1990s, critics at home and abroad charged that textbooks printed under the guidance of the Ministry of Education did not adequately discuss the atrocities committed by the Japanese government and armed forces during World War II. The government expressed remorse, but only in the context of the aggressive actions of all colonial powers during the imperialist era.

The Economy Nowhere are the changes in postwar Japan so visible as in the economic sector, where Japan developed into a major industrial and technological power in the space of a century, surpassing such advanced Western societies as Germany, France, and Great Britain.

Although this "Japanese miracle" has often been described as beginning after the war as a result of the Allied reforms, Japanese economic growth in fact began much earlier, with the Meiji reforms, which helped transform Japan from an autocratic society based on semifeudal institutions into an advanced capitalist democracy.

As noted, the officials of the Allied occupation identified the Meiji economic system with centralized power and the rise of Japanese militarism. But with the rise of Cold War tensions, the policy of breaking up the *zaibatsu* was scaled back. Looser ties between companies were still allowed, and a new type of informal relationship, sometimes called the **keiretsu,** or "interlocking arrangement," began to take shape. Through such arrangements among suppliers, wholesalers, retailers, and financial institutions, the *zaibatsu* system was reconstituted under a new name.

The occupation administration had more success with its program to reform the agricultural system. Half of the population still lived on farms, and half of all farmers were still tenants. Under the land reform program, all lands owned by absentee landlords and all cultivated landholdings over an established maximum were sold on easy credit terms to the tenants. The program created a strong class of yeoman farmers, and tenants declined to about 10 percent of the rural population.

During the next fifty years, Japan re-created the stunning results of the Meiji era. In 1950, the Japanese gross domestic product was about one-third that of Great Britain or France. Today, it is larger than both put together and well over half that of the United States. Japan is one of the greatest exporting nations in the world, and its per capita income equals or surpasses that of most advanced Western states.

In the last decades, however, the Japanese economy has run into serious difficulties, raising the question of whether the vaunted Japanese model is as appealing as many observers earlier declared. A rise in the value of the yen hurt exports and burst the bubble of investment by Japanese banks that had taken place under the umbrella of government protection. Lacking a domestic market equivalent in size to the United States, in the 1990s the Japanese economy slipped into a recession that persisted until recently.

These economic difficulties have placed heavy pressure on some of the vaunted features of the Japanese economy. The tradition of lifetime employment created a bloated white-collar workforce and has made downsizing difficult. Today, job security is on the decline as increasing numbers of workers are being laid off. A disproportionate burden has fallen on women, who lack seniority and continue to suffer from various forms of discrimination in the workplace.

A final change is that slowly but inexorably, the Japanese market is beginning to open up to international competition. Greater exposure to foreign competition may improve the performance of Japanese manufacturers. In recent years, Japanese consumers have become increasingly critical of the quality of some domestic products, provoking one cabinet minister to complain about "sloppiness and complacency" among Japanese firms. One apparent reason for the country's recent quality problems is the cost-cutting measures adopted by Japanese companies to meet the challenges from abroad.

A Society in Transition During the occupation, Allied planners set out to change social characteristics that they believed had contributed to Japanese aggressiveness before and during World War II. The new educational system removed all references to filial piety, patriotism, and loyalty to the emperor while emphasizing the

GROWING UP IN JAPAN

FAMILY & SOCIETY

Japanese schoolchildren are exposed to a much more regimented environment than U.S. children experience. Most Japanese schoolchildren, for example, wear black-and-white uniforms to school. These regulations are examples of rules adopted by middle school systems in various parts of Japan. The Ministry of Education in Tokyo concluded that these regulations were excessive, but they are probably typical.

What is the apparent purpose of these regulations? Why does Japan appear to place more restrictions on students' behavior than most Western countries do?

School Regulations, Japanese Style

1. Boys' hair should not touch the eyebrows, the ears, or the top of the collar.
2. No one should have a permanent wave, or dye his or her hair. Girls should not wear ribbons or accessories in their hair. Hair dryers should not be used.
3. School uniform skirts should be___ centimeters above the ground, no more and no less (differs by school and region).
4. Keep your uniform clean and pressed at all times. Girls' middy blouses should have two buttons on the back collar. Boys' pant cuffs should be of the prescribed width. No more than 12 eyelets should be on shoes. The number of buttons on a shirt and tucks in a shirt are also prescribed.
5. Wear your school badge at all times. It should be positioned exactly.
6. Going to school in the morning, wear your book bag strap on the right shoulder; in the afternoon on the way home, wear it on the left shoulder. Your book case thickness, filled and unfilled, is also prescribed.
7. Girls should wear only regulation white underpants of 100% cotton.
8. When you raise your hand to be called on, your arm should extend forward and up at the angle prescribed in your handbook.
9. Your own route to and from school is marked in your student rule handbook; carefully observe which side of each street you are to use on the way to and from school.
10. After school you are to go directly home, unless your parent has written a note permitting you to go to another location. Permission will not be granted by the school unless this other location is a suitable one. You must not go to coffee shops. You must be home by___ o'clock.
11. It is not permitted to drive or ride a motorcycle, or to have a license to drive one.
12. Before and after school, no matter where you are, you represent our school, so you should behave in ways we can all be proud of.

---

individualistic values of Western civilization. The new constitution and a revised civil code eliminated remaining legal restrictions on women's rights to obtain a divorce, hold a job, or change their domicile. Women were guaranteed the right to vote and were encouraged to enter politics.

Such efforts to remake Japanese behavior through legislation were only partially successful. During the past sixty years, Japan has unquestionably become a more individualistic and egalitarian society. At the same time, many of the distinctive characteristics of traditional Japanese society have persisted to the present day, although in somewhat altered form. The emphasis on loyalty to the group and community relationships, for example, is reflected in the strength of corporate loyalties in contemporary Japan.

Emphasis on the work ethic also remains strong. The tradition of hard work is taught at a young age. The Japanese school year runs for 240 days a year, compared to 180 days in the United States, and work assignments outside class tend to be more extensive. The results are impressive: Japanese schoolchildren consistently earn higher scores on achievement tests than children in other advanced countries. At the same time, this devotion to success has often been accompanied by bullying by teachers and what Americans might consider an oppressive sense of conformity (see the box above).

By all accounts, independent thinking is on the increase in Japan. In some cases, it leads to antisocial behavior, such as crime or membership in a teenage gang. Usually, it is expressed in more indirect ways, such as the recent fashion among young people of dyeing their hair brown (known in Japanese as "tea hair"). Because the practice is banned in many schools and generally frowned on by the older generation (one police chief dumped a pitcher of beer on a student with brown hair whom he noticed in a bar), many young Japanese dye their hair as a gesture of independence. When seeking employment or getting married, however, they often return their hair to its natural color.

One of the more tenacious legacies of the past in Japanese society is sexual inequality. Although women are now legally protected against discrimination in employment, very few have reached senior levels in business,

© Barry Cronin Newsmakers/Getty Images

Courtsey of William J. Duiker

From Conformity to Counterculture. Traditionally, schoolchildren in Japan have worn uniforms to promote conformity with the country's communitarian social mores. In the left photo, young students dressed in identical uniforms are on a field trip to Kyoto's Nijo Castle, built in 1603 by Tokugawa Ieyasu. Recently, however, a youth counterculture has emerged in Japan. On the right, fashion-conscious teenagers with "tea hair"—heirs of Japan's long era of affluence—revel in their expensive hip-hop outfits, platform shoes, and layered dresses. Such dress habits symbolize the growing revolt against conformity in contemporary Japan.

education, or politics. Women now constitute nearly 50 percent of the workforce; but most are in retail or service occupations, and their average salary is only about half that of men. There is a feminist movement in Japan, but it has none of the vigor and mass support of its counterpart in the United States.

Religion and Culture   When Japan was opened to the West in the nineteenth century, many Japanese became convinced of the superiority of foreign ideas and institutions and were especially interested in Western religion and culture. Although Christian converts were few, numbering less than 1 percent of the population, the influence of Christianity was out of proportion to the size of the community.

Today, Japan includes almost 1.5 million Christians, along with 93 million Buddhists. Many Japanese also follow Shinto, no longer identified with reverence for the emperor and the state. As in the West, increasing urbanization has led to a decline in the practice of organized religion, although evangelical sects have proliferated in recent years. The largest and best-known sect is Soka Gakkai, a lay Buddhist organization that has attracted millions of followers and formed its own political party, the Komeito. Zen Buddhism retains its popularity, and some businesspeople seek to use Zen techniques to learn how to focus on willpower as a means of outwitting a competitor.

Western literature, art, and music have also had a major impact on Japanese society. After World War II, many of the writers who had been active before the war resurfaced, but now their writing reflected demoralization. Many were attracted to existentialism, and some turned to hedonism and nihilism. For these disillusioned authors, defeat was compounded by fear of the Americanization of postwar Japan. One of the best examples of this attitude was the novelist Yukio Mishima, who led a crusade to stem the tide of what he described as America's "universal and uniform 'Coca-Colonization'" of the world in general and Japan in particular.[3] Mishima's ritual suicide in 1970 was the subject of widespread speculation and transformed him into a cult figure.

One of Japan's most serious-minded contemporary authors is Kenzaburo Oe (b. 1935). His work, rewarded with a Nobel Prize for literature in 1994, focuses on Japan's ongoing quest for modern identity and purpose. His characters reflect the spiritual anguish precipitated by the collapse of the imperial Japanese tradition and the subsequent adoption of Western culture—a trend that Oe contends has culminated in unabashed materialism, cultural decline, and a moral void. Yet unlike Mishima, Oe does not wish to reinstill the imperial traditions of the past but rather seeks to regain spiritual meaning by retrieving the sense of communality and innocence found in rural Japan.

Other aspects of Japanese culture have also been influenced by Western ideas. Western music is very popular in Japan, and scores of Japanese classical musicians have succeeded in the West. Even rap music has gained a foothold among Japanese youth, although without the association with sex, drugs, and violence that it has in the United States. As one singer remarked, "We've been very fortunate, and we don't want to bother our Moms and Dads. So we don't sing songs that would disturb parents."[4]

The Little Tigers

The success of postwar Japan in meeting the challenge from the capitalist West soon caught the eye of other Asian nations. By the 1980s, several smaller states in the region—known collectively as the "Little Tigers"—had successively followed the Japanese example.

South Korea: A Peninsula Divided   In 1953, the Korean peninsula was exhausted from three years of bitter fraternal war, a conflict that took the lives of an estimated four million Koreans on both sides of the 38th parallel. Although a cease-fire was signed in July 1953, it was a fragile peace that left two heavily armed and mutually hostile countries facing each other suspiciously.

North of the truce line was the People's Republic of Korea (PRK), a police state under the dictatorial rule of the Communist leader Kim Il Sung (1912–1994). To the south was the Republic of Korea, under the equally autocratic President Syngman Rhee (1875–1965), a fierce anti-Communist who had led the resistance to the northern invasion. After several years of harsh rule in the Republic of Korea, marked by government corruption, fraudulent elections, and police brutality, demonstrations broke out in the capital city of Seoul in the spring of 1960 and forced Rhee into retirement.

In 1961, a coup d'état in South Korea placed General Chung Hee Park (1917–1979) in power. The new regime promulgated a new constitution, and in 1963, Park was elected president of a civilian government. He set out to foster recovery of the economy from decades of foreign occupation and civil war. Because the private sector had been relatively weak under Japanese rule, the government played an active role in the process by instituting a series of five-year plans that targeted specific industries for development, promoted exports, and funded infrastructure development.

The program was a solid success. Benefiting from the Confucian principles of thrift, respect for education, and hard work, as well as from Japanese capital and technology, Korea gradually emerged as a major industrial power in East Asia. The largest corporations—including Samsung, Daewoo, and Hyundai—were transformed into massive conglomerates called **chaebol,** the Korean equivalent of the *zaibatsu* of prewar Japan. Korean businesses began to compete actively with the Japanese for export markets in Asia and throughout the world.

But like many other countries in the region, South Korea was slow to develop democratic principles. Although his government functioned with the trappings of democracy, Park continued to rule by autocratic means and suppressed all forms of dissidence. In 1979, Park was assassinated. But after a brief interregnum of democratic rule, in 1980 a new military government under General Chun Doo Hwan seized power. The new regime was as authoritarian as its predecessors; but opposition to autocratic rule had now spread from student riots in 1987 to much of the urban population, and national elections were finally held in 1989. A series of civilian rulers promised to make Korea "a freer and more mature democracy."

But the nation faced serious problems. A growing trade deficit, combined with a declining growth rate, led to increased unemployment and bankruptcy. After the Asian financial crisis developed in 1997, economic conditions worsened, leading to the election of a longtime opposition figure, Kim Dae Jung, to the presidency. The new leader promised drastic reforms, but his regime too was charged with corruption and incompetence. In the meantime, relations with North Korea, now on the verge of becoming a nuclear power, remain tense.

Taiwan: The Other China   After retreating to Taiwan following their defeat by the Communists, Chiang Kai-shek's government, which continued to refer to itself as the Republic of China (ROC), contended that it remained the legitimate representative of the Chinese people and would eventually return in triumph to the mainland.

The Nationalists had much more success on Taiwan than they had achieved on the mainland. In the relatively secure environment provided by a security treaty with the United States, signed in 1954, the ROC was able to concentrate on

The Korean Peninsula Since 1953

Modern Taiwan

The Chiang Kai-shek Memorial in Taipei. While the Chinese government on the mainland attempted to destroy all vestiges of traditional culture the Republic of China on Taiwan sought to preserve the cultural heritage as a line between past and present. This policy is graphically displayed in the mausoleum for Chiang Kai-shek in downtown Taipei, shown in this photograph. The mausoleum, with its massive entrance gate, not only glorifies the nations's leader but recalls the grandeur of old China.

economic growth without worrying about a Communist invasion.

The government moved rapidly to create a solid agricultural base. A land reform program led to the reduction of rents, and landholdings over 3 acres were purchased by the government and resold to the tenants at reasonable prices. At the same time, local manufacturing and commerce were strongly encouraged. By the 1970s, Taiwan had become one of the most dynamic industrial economies in East Asia.

In contrast to the Communist regime in the People's Republic of China (PRC), the ROC actively maintained Chinese tradition, promoting respect for Confucius and the ethical principles of the past, such as hard work, frugality, and filial piety. Although there was some corruption in both the government and the private sector, income differentials between the wealthy and the poor were generally less than elsewhere in the region, and the overall standard of living increased substantially. Health and sanitation improved, literacy rates were quite high, and an active family planning program reduced the rate of population growth.

After the death of Chiang Kai-shek in 1975, the ROC slowly began to move toward a more representative form of government, including elections and legal opposition parties. A national election in 1992 resulted in a bare majority for the Nationalists over strong opposition from the Democratic Progressive Party (DPP). But political liberalization had its dangers; some members of the DPP began to agitate for an independent Republic of Taiwan, a possibility that aroused concern within the Nationalist government in Taipei and frenzied hostility in the PRC. The election of DPP leader Chen Shuibian as ROC president in March 2000 angered Beijing, which threatened to invade Taiwan should the island continue to delay unification with the mainland.

The United States continues to provide defensive military assistance to the Taiwanese armed forces and has made it clear that it supports self-determination for the people of Taiwan and that it expects the final resolution of the Chinese civil war to be by peaceful means. In the meantime, economic and cultural contacts between Taiwan and the mainland are steadily increasing. Nevertheless, the Taiwanese have shown no inclination to accept the PRC's offer of "one country, two systems," under which the ROC would accept the PRC as the legitimate government of China in return for autonomous control over the affairs of Taiwan.

Singapore and Hong Kong: The Littlest Tigers The smallest but by no means the least successful of the Little Tigers are Singapore and Hong Kong. Both contain large

End of World War II in the Pacific	1945
Chiang Kai-shek retreats to Taiwan	1949
End of U.S. occupation of Japan	1950
Korean War	1950–1953
United States–Republic of China security treaty	1954
Syngman Rhee overthrown in South Korea	1960
Rise to power of Chung Hee Park in South Korea	1961
Independence of Republic of Singapore	1965
Death of Chiang Kai-shek	1975
Chung Hee Park assassinated	1979
First free general elections on Taiwan	1992
Return of Hong Kong to mainland control	1997
Financial crisis hits the region	1997
Chen Shuibian elected president of Taiwan	2000
Junichiro Koizumi elected prime minister of Japan	2001

The Republic of Singapore

Kuan-yew and his People's Action Party dominated Singapore politics, and opposition elements were intimidated into silence or arrested. The prime minister openly declared that the Western model of pluralist democracy was not appropriate for Singapore. Confucian values of thrift, hard work, and obedience to authority were promoted as the ideology of the state.

But economic success has begun to undermine the authoritarian foundations of the system as a more sophisticated citizenry voices aspirations for more political freedoms and an end to government paternalism. Lee Kuan-yew's successor, Goh Chok Tong, has promised a "kinder, gentler" Singapore, and political restrictions on individual behavior are gradually being relaxed.

The future of Hong Kong is not so clear-cut. As in Singapore, sensible government policies and the hard work of its people have enabled Hong Kong to thrive. At first, the prosperity of the colony depended on a plentiful supply of cheap labor. Inundated with refugees from the mainland during the 1950s and 1960s, the population of Hong Kong burgeoned to more than six million. More recently, Hong Kong has benefited from increased tourism, manufacturing, and the growing economic prosperity of neighboring Guangdong province, the most prosperous region of the PRC. Unlike the other societies discussed in this chapter, Hong Kong has relied on an unbridled free market system rather than active state intervention in the economy. At the same time, by allocating substantial funds for transportation, sanitation, education, and public housing, the government has created favorable conditions for economic development.

When Britain's ninety-nine-year lease on the New Territories, the foodbasket of the colony, expired on July 1, 1997, Hong Kong returned to mainland authority. Although the Chinese promised the British that for fifty years, the people of Hong Kong would live under a capitalist system and be essentially self-governing, recent

Hong Kong

statements by Chinese leaders have raised questions about the degree of autonomy Hong Kong will continue to receive under Chinese rule (see the box on p. 675).

populations densely packed into small territories. Singapore, once a British colony and briefly a part of the state of Malaysia, is now an independent nation. Hong Kong was a British colony until it was returned to PRC control in 1997. In recent years, both have emerged as industrial powerhouses, with standards of living well above those of their neighbors.

The success of Singapore must be ascribed in good measure to the will and energy of its political leaders. When it became independent in August 1965, Singapore's longtime position as an entrepôt for trade between the Indian Ocean and the South China Sea was on the wane.

Within a decade, Singapore's role and reputation had dramatically changed. Under the leadership of Prime Minister Lee Kuan-yew (b. 1923), the government cultivated an attractive business climate while engaging in public works projects to feed, house, and educate its two million citizens. The major components of success have been shipbuilding, oil refineries, tourism, electronics, and finance—the city-state has become the banking hub of the entire region.

As in the other Little Tigers, an authoritarian political system has guaranteed a stable environment for economic growth. Until his recent retirement, Lee

RETURN TO THE MOTHERLAND

POLITICS & GOVERNMENT

After lengthy negotiations, in December 1984, China and Great Britain agreed that on July 1, 1997, Hong Kong would return to Chinese sovereignty. Key sections of the agreement are included here. In succeeding years, authorities of the two countries held further negotiations. Some of the discussions raised questions in the minds of residents of Hong Kong as to whether their individual liberties would indeed be respected after the colony's return to China.

What restrictions does this document place on the autonomy of Hong Kong? How does the system in Hong Kong differ from that on the mainland of China?

The Joint Declaration on Hong Kong

The Hong Kong Special Administrative Region will be directly under the authority of the Central People's Government of the People's Republic of China. The Hong Kong Special Administrative Region will enjoy a high degree of autonomy, except in foreign and defense affairs, which are the responsibility of the Central People's Government.

The Hong Kong Special Administrative Region will be vested with executive, legislative, and independent judicial power, including that of final adjudication. The laws currently in force in Hong Kong will remain basically unchanged.

The Government of the Hong Kong Special Administrative Region will be composed of local inhabitants. The chief executive will be appointed by the Central People's Government on the basis of the results of elections or consultations to be held locally. Principal officials will be nominated by the chief executive of the Hong Kong Special Administrative Region for appointment by the Central People's Government. . . .

The current social and economic systems in Hong Kong will remain unchanged, and so will the lifestyle. Rights and freedoms, including those of the person, of speech, of the press, of assembly, of association, of travel, of movement, of correspondence, of strike, of choice of occupation, of academic research, and of religious belief will be ensured by law. . . . Private property, ownership of enterprises, legitimate right of inheritance, and foreign investment will be protected by law.

ThomsonNOW To read more of the declaration, enter the *ThomsonNOW* documents area using the access card that is available for *The Essential World History*.

The China Factor

One of the primary reasons for the growing preeminence of East Asia on the economic scene is the emergence of mainland China as a major player in the global marketplace. A quarter of a century ago, China was a predominantly rural nation with an archaic state-run industrial sector. Today, with a predominantly market-driven economy and an industrious low-wage workforce, it has become an economic powerhouse, taking over the role previously played by Japan in leading the resurgence of East Asia in world affairs (see Chapter 26).

What effect this will have on future developments in the region is still unclear. For the moment, the new China is both a blessing and a curse to its neighbors: a major importer of raw materials from other countries in Asia, but a dangerous competitor in the export market. A period of political instability in China, of course, would dramatically change the equation. Barring unforseen circumstances, however, the emergence of China represents a significant step in transforming the vision of the Pacific Century into a reality.

On the Margins of Asia: Postwar Australia and New Zealand

Technically, Australia and New Zealand are not part of Asia, and throughout their short history, both countries have identified culturally and politically with the West rather than with their Asian neighbors. Their political institutions and values are derived from Europe, and their economies resemble those of the advanced countries of the world rather than the preindustrial societies of much of Southeast Asia. Both are currently members of the British Commonwealth and of the U.S.-led ANZUS (Australia, New Zealand, and the United States) alliance.

Yet trends in recent years have been drawing both states, especially Australia, closer to Asia. In the first place, immigration from East and Southeast Asia has increased rapidly. More than one-half of current immigrants into Australia come from East Asia, and by early this century, about 7 percent of the population of about 18 million people will be of Asian descent. In New Zealand, residents of Asian descent represent only about 3 percent of the population of 3.5 million, but about 12 percent of the population are Maoris,

Polynesian peoples who settled on the islands about a thousand years ago. Second, trade relations with Asia are increasing rapidly. About 60 percent of Australia's export markets today are in East Asia, and the region is the source of about one-half of its imports. Asian trade with New Zealand is also on the increase.

Whether Australia and New Zealand will ever become an integral part of the Asia-Pacific region is uncertain. Cultural differences stemming from the European origins of the majority of the population in both countries hinder mutual understanding on both sides of the divide. But economic and geographic realities act as a powerful force, and should the Pacific region continue on its current course toward economic prosperity and political stability, the role of Australia and New Zealand will assume greater significance.

CONCLUSION

𝒯HE RISE OF ASIA as a crucial factor in the global economic order has sparked widespread debate, and sometimes concern, in major world capitals. Some observers see major Asian states like China, Japan, and even India as future competitors with advanced Western nations (see the comparative essay "Global Village or Clash of Civilizations?" in Chapter 25), an observation made more ominous in recent years by the outsourcing of jobs to the region.

To some observers, the economic achievements of the nations of the western Pacific have come at a high price, in the form of political authoritarianism and a lack of attention to human rights. Until recently, government repression of opposition has been common in many of these nations. In addition, the rights of national minorities and women are often still limited in comparison with the advanced nations of the West. Developments such as the financial crisis of 1997 and the long economic downturn in Japan have also somewhat tarnished the image of the "Asian miracle," raising concern that some of the factors that contributed to economic success in prior years are now making it difficult for governments to develop open and accountable financial systems.

Rapid economic development in eastern and southern Asia has also exacted an environmental price. Industrial pollution in China and India and the burning of forests in Indonesia and other Southeast Asian nations increasingly threaten the fragile ecosystem and create friction among nations within the region (see the comparative essay "One World, One Environment" on p. 677). Unless the region's nations learn to cooperate effectively to deal with the problem in future years, it will ultimately begin to undermine the dramatic economic and social progress that has taken place.

Still, it should be kept in mind that progress has not always been easy to achieve in the West and even now frequently fails to match expectations. A look at the historical record suggests that political pluralism is often a by-product of economic growth and that political values and institutions evolve in response to changing social conditions. A rising standard of living and increased social mobility should go far toward enhancing political freedom and promoting social justice in the countries bordering the western Pacific.

The efforts of these nations to find a way to accommodate traditional and modern, native and foreign, raise a final question. As we have seen, Mahatma Gandhi believed that materialism is ultimately a dead end. In light of contemporary concerns about the emptiness of life in the West and the self-destructiveness of material culture, can his message be ignored?

CHAPTER NOTES

1. *New York Times,* May 2, 1996.
2. Quoted in L. Collins and D. Lapierre, *Freedom at Midnight* (New York, 1975), p. 252.
3. Y. Mishima and G. Bownas, eds., *New Writing in Japan* (Harmondsworth, England, 1972), p. 16.
4. *New York Times,* January 29, 1996.

SUGGESTED READING

For a survey of postwar Indian history, see **S. Wolpert,** *A New History of India* (New York, 1989). Also see **P. Brass,** *The New Cambridge History of India: The Politics of Independence* (Cambridge, 1990), and **S. Tharoor,** *India: From Midnight to the Millennium* (New York, 1997). On India's founding father, see **J. Brown,** *Nehru: A Political Life* (New Haven, Conn., 2003). The life and career of Indira Gandhi have been well chronicled. Two fine biographies are **T. Ali,** *An Indian Dynasty: The Story of the Nehru-Gandhi Family* (New York, 1985), and **K. Frank,** *Indira: The Life of Indira Nehru Gandhi* (New York, 2000). On Pakistan, see **O. B. Jones,** *Pakistan: Eye of the Storm* (New Haven, Conn., 2002). Also of interest is **C. Baxter,** *Bangladesh: From a Nation to a State* (Boulder, Colo., 1997).

On Indian literature, see **D. Ray** and **A. Singh,** eds., *India: An Anthology of Contemporary Writing* (Athens, Ohio, 1983). See also **S. Tharu** and **K. Lalita,** eds., *Women Writing in India,* vol. 2 (New York, 1993).

There are a number of standard surveys of the history of modern Southeast Asia. Unfortunately, many of them are now out of date because of the changes that have taken place in the region since

COMPARATIVE ESSAY

ONE WORLD, ONE ENVIRONMENT

A crucial factor that is affecting the evolution of society and the global economy in the early twenty-first century is growing concern over the impact of industrialization on the earth's environment. Humans have always caused some harm to their natural surroundings, but never has the danger of significant ecological damage been as extensive as during the past century. The effects of chemicals introduced into the atmosphere or into rivers, lakes, and oceans have increasingly threatened the health and well-being of all living species.

For many years, the main focus of environmental concern was in the developed countries of the West, where industrial effluents, automobile exhaust, and the use of artificial fertilizers and insecticides led to urban smog, extensive damage to crops and wildlife, and a major reduction of the ozone layer in the upper atmosphere. In recent years, the problem has spread elsewhere. China's headlong rush to industrialization has resulted in major ecological damage in that country. Industrial smog has created almost unlivable conditions in many cities in Asia, while hillsides denuded of their forests have caused severe problems of erosion and destruction of farmlands. Destruction of the rain forest is a growing problem in many parts of the world, notably in Brazil and Indonesia. With the forest cover throughout the earth rapidly disappearing, there is less plant life to perform the crucial process of reducing carbon dioxide levels in the atmosphere.

Destruction of the Environment. This stunted tree has been killed by acid rain, a combination of sulfuric and nitric acids mixed with moisture in the air. Entire forests of trees killed by acid rain are becoming common sights in Canada, the United States, and northern Europe.

One of the few beneficial consequences of such incidents has been a growing international consensus that environmental concerns have taken on a truly global character. Although the danger of global warming—allegedly caused by the release, as a result of industrialization, of hothouse gases into the atmosphere—has not yet been definitively proved, it has become a source of sufficient concern to bring about an international conference on the subject in Kyoto, Japan, in December 1997. If, as many scientists predict, worldwide temperatures should continue to increase, the rise in sea levels could pose a significant threat to low-lying islands and coastal areas throughout the world, while climatic change could lead to severe droughts or excessive rainfall in cultivated areas.

It is one thing to recognize a problem, however, and another to solve it. So far, cooperative efforts among nations to alleviate environmental problems have all too often been hindered by economic forces or by political, ethnic, and religious disputes. The 1997 conference on global warming, for example, was marked by bitter disagreement over the degree to which developing countries should share the burden of cleaning up the environment. As a result, it achieved few concrete results. The fact is, few nations have been willing to take unilateral action that might pose an obstacle to economic development plans or lead to a rise in unemployment. In 2001, President George W. Bush refused to sign the Kyoto Agreement on the grounds that it discriminated against advanced Western countries.

the end of the Vietnam War. For an introduction with a strong emphasis on recent events, see **D. R. Sar Desai, Southeast Asia: Past and Present,** 2d ed. (Boulder, Colo., 1989). For a more scholarly approach, see **D. J. Steinberg,** ed., **In Search of Southeast Asia,** 2d ed. (New York, 1985).

For a broader perspective on Indonesian society and culture, see **T. Friend, Indonesian Destinies** (Cambridge, Mass., 2003). For a political perspective on the Suharto years, see **M. Vatiokis, Indonesian Politics Under Suharto** (London, 1993). The rise of terrorism in the region is discussed in **Z. Abuza, Militant Islam in Southeast Asia: Crucible of Terror** (Boulder, Colo., 2003). Also see **C. Christie, A Modern History of Southeast Asia: Decolonization, Nationalism and Separatism** (London, 1996).

For an overview of women's issues in contemporary South and Southeast Asia, consult **B. Ramusack** and **S. Sievers, Women in Asia** (Bloomington, Ind., 1999). Articles that focus on the socioeconomic problems of women in India in the 1980s are found in **M. Kishwar** and **R. Vanita,** eds., **In Search of Answers: Indian Women's Voices from Manushi** (London, 1991). **K. Bhasin, R. Menon,** and **N. S. Khan,** eds., **Against All Odds: Essays on Women, Religion and Development from India and Pakistan** (New Delhi, 1994), explores fundamentalist conservatism among both Hindu and Muslim women. Of interest on Southeast Asian women's issues are **W. Williams, Japanese Lives: Women and Men in Modern Indonesian Society** (New Brunswick, N.J., 1991), and **C. B. N. Chin, In Service and Servitude: Foreign Female Domestic Workers and the Malaysian "Modernity" Project** (New York, 1998).

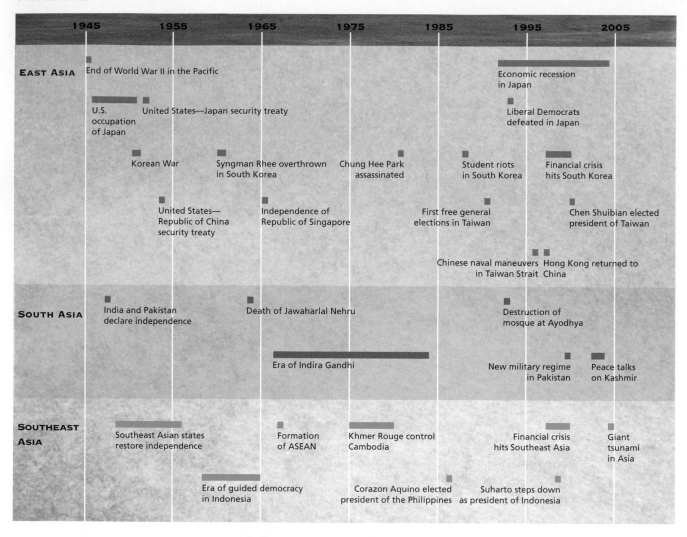

For a balanced treatment of all issues relating to postwar Japan, see **J. McLain, *Japan: A Modern History*** (New York, 2001). For a more journalistic approach that raises questions about the future of democracy in Japan, see **I. Buruma, *Inventing Japan*** (New York, 2002). For a topical approach with a strong emphasis on economic and social matters, **J. E. Hunter, *The Emergence of Modern Japan: An Introductory History Since 1853*** (London, 1989), is excellent. For an extensive analysis of Japan's adjustment to the Allied occupation, see **J. W. Dower, *Embracing Defeat: Japan in the Wake of World War II*** (New York, 1999). Political dissent and its consequences are dealt with in **N. Fields, *In the Realm of the Dying Emperor*** (New York, 1991).

Japanese social issues have often been examined from an economic perspective as foreign observers try to discover the reasons for the nation's economic success. **C. Nakane, *Japanese Society*** (Harmondsworth, England, 1979), provides a scholarly treatment, while **R. J. Hendry, *Understanding Japanese Society*** (Beckenham, England, 1987), is more accessible. For a more local treatment, see **R. P. Dore, *Shinohata: A Portrait of a Japanese Village*** (New York, 1978), and **T. C. Bestor, *Neighborhood Tokyo*** (Stanford, Calif., 1989). **T. Heymann, *On an Average Day in Japan*** (New York, 1992),

provides an interesting statistical comparison of Japanese and American society. On the role of women in modern Japan, see **D. Robins-Mowry, *The Hidden Sun: Women of Modern Japan*** (Boulder, Colo., 1983), and **N. Bornoff, *Pink Samurai: Love, Marriage, and Sex in Contemporary Japan*** (New York, 1991).

On the four Little Tigers and their economic development, see **E. F. Vogel, *The Four Little Dragons: The Spread of Industrialization in East Asia*** (Cambridge, Mass., 1991); **J. W. Morley**, ed., ***Driven by Growth: Political Change in the Asia-Pacific Region*** (Armonk, N.Y., 1992); and **J. Woronoff, *Asia's Miracle Economies*** (New York, 1986). For an interesting collection of articles on the role of Confucian ideology in promoting economic growth, see **Hung-chao Tai,** ed., ***Confucianism and Economic Development*** (Washington, D.C., 1989). For individual treatments of the Little Tigers, see **Hak-kyu Sohn, *Authoritarianism and Opposition in South Korea*** (London, 1989); **D. F. Simon, *Taiwan: Beyond the Economic Miracle*** (Armonk, N.Y., 1992); **Lee Kuan Yew, *From Third World to First: The Singapore Story, 1965-2000*** (New York, 2000); and **K. Rafferty, *City on the Rocks: Hong Kong's Uncertain Future*** (London, 1991). Also see **M. Rubinstein, *Taiwan: A New History*** (New York, 2001).

InfoTrac College Edition

Visit this chapter's InfoTrac College Edition/Research activities at the *Essential World History* Companion Website for activities related to South and East Asia in the late twentieth century.

ThomsonNOW™ for Duiker and Spielvogel's *The Essential World History, Third Edition*

Enter *ThomsonNOW* using the access card that is available with this text. *ThomsonNOW* will assist you in understanding the content in this chapter with lesson plans generated for your needs, as well as provide you with a connection to the *W adsworth World History Resource Center* (see description at the right for details).

WORLD HISTORY
RESOURCE CENTER

Enter the Resource Center using either your *ThomsonNOW* access card or your standalone access card for the *Wadsworth World History Resource Center*. Organized by topic, this website includes quizzes; images; over 350 primary source documents; interactive simulations, maps, and timelines; movie explorations; and a wealth of other resources. You can read the following documents, and many more, at http://worldrc.wadsworth.com/

> The Manila Accord
>
> Declaration of Pakistan and India on Jammu and Kashmir

Visit the *Essential World History* Companion Website for chapter quizzes and more:

> http://www.thomsonedu.com/history/duiker

DISCOVERY

What factors have contributed to the economic successes achieved by Japan and the "Little Tigers"? Have the other nations of South and Southeast Asia achieved the same results?

In thinking about this question, begin by breaking it down into the components shown below. A discussion of the significance of each component should appear in your answer.

POLITICS AND GOVERNMENT: What are the key differences in these two views on the future of India? Why do you think Nehru's proposals triumphed over those of Mahatma Gandhi? What has India gained by moving from a village to a modern urban culture? What might some people say it has lost? What role did Hinduism play in the development of modern India?

NEHRU'S SOCIALIST CREED

I am convinced that the only key to the solution of the world's problems and of India's problems lies in socialism, and when I use this word I do so not in a vague humanitarian way but in the scientific economic sense. . . . I see no way of ending the poverty, the vast unemployment, the degradation and the subjection of the Indian people except through socialism. That involves vast and revolutionary changes in our political and social structure, the ending of vested interests in land and industry, as well as the feudal and autocratic Indian states system. That means the ending of private property, except in a restricted sense, and the replacement of the present profit system by a higher ideal of cooperative service. . . . In short, it means a new civilization, radically different from the present capitalist order. Some glimpse we can have of this new civilization in the territories of the U.S.S.R. Much has happened there which has pained me greatly and with which I disagree, but I look upon that great and fascinating unfolding of a new order and a new civilization as the most promising feature of our dismal age.

A LETTER TO JAWAHARLAL NEHRU

I believe that if India, and through India the world, is to achieve real freedom, then sooner or later we shall have to go and live in the villages—in huts, not in palaces. Millions of people can never live in cities and palaces in comfort and peace. Nor can they do so by killing one another, that is, by resorting to violence and untruth. . . . We can have the vision of . . . truth and nonviolence only in the simplicity of the villages. That simplicity resides in the spinning wheel and what is implied by the spinning wheel. . . .

You will not be able to understand me if you think that I am talking about the villages of today. My ideal village still exists only in my imagination. . . . In this village of my dreams the villager will not be dull—he will be all awareness. He will not live like an animal in filth and darkness. Men and women will live in freedom, prepared to face the whole world. There will be no plague, no cholera, and no smallpox. Nobody will be allowed to be idle or to wallow in luxury. Everyone will have to do body labor. Granting all this, I can still envisage a number of things that will have to be organized on a large scale. Perhaps there will even be railways and also post and telegraph offices. I do not know what things there will be or will not be. Nor am I bothered about it. If I can make sure of the essential thing, other things will follow in due course. But if I give up the essential thing, I give up everything.

FAMILY AND SOCIETY: What is the apparent purpose of Japanese school regulations like those on the next page? Do you imagine Indian families and schools impose similar rules on school children? Why or why not? Why does Japan appear to place more restrictions on students' behavior than most Western countries do? Which of these regulations make the most sense to you? the least? What biases do you think inform your answers? What relationship do you think may exist between rules like these and a modern capitalist society?

From Conformity to Counterculture

Courtesy of William J. Duiker

1. Boys' hair should not touch the eyebrows, the ears, or the top of the collar.
2. No one should have a permanent wave, or dye his or her hair. Girls should not wear ribbons or accessories in their hair. Hair dryers should not be used.
3. School uniform skirts should be___ centimeters above the ground, no more and no less (differs by school and region).
4. Keep your uniform clean and pressed at all times. Girls' middy blouses should have two buttons on the back collar. Boys' pant cuffs should be of the prescribed width. No more than 12 eyelets should be on shoes. The number of buttons on a shirt and tucks in a shirt are also prescribed.
5. Wear your school badge at all times. It should be positioned exactly.
6. Going to school in the morning, wear your book bag strap on the right shoulder; in the afternoon on the way home, wear it on the left shoulder. Your book case thickness, filled and unfilled, is also prescribed.

7. Girls should wear only regulation white underpants of 100% cotton.
8. When you raise your hand to be called on, your arm should extend forward and up at the angle prescribed in your handbook.
9. Your own route to and from school is marked in your student rule handbook; carefully observe which side of each street you are to use on the way to and from school.
10. After school you are to go directly home, unless your parent has written a note permitting you to go to another location. Permission will not be granted by the school unless this other location is a suitable one. You must not go to coffee shops. You must be home by___o'clock.
11. It is not permitted to drive or ride a motorcycle, or to have a license to drive one.
12. Before and after school, no matter where you are, you represent our school, so you should behave in ways we can all be proud of.

INTERACTION AND EXCHANGE: Why does the author of the document think India should say no to fast food? Do you imagine the young men at their computers agree with her? Do you think fast food helps create a culture of modern economic prosperity, or does prosperity attract fast food? What are the apparent advantages of village life in contemporary India and urban life in contemporary Japan?

Two Indias

From Conformity to Counterculture

SAY NO TO McDONALD'S AND KFC!

Why India Doesn't Need Fast Food

India's decision to allow Pepsi Foods Ltd. to open 60 restaurants in India—30 each of Pizza Hut and Kentucky Fried Chicken—marks the first entry of multinational, meat-based junk-food chains into India. If this is allowed to happen, at least a dozen other similar chains will very quickly arrive, including the infamous McDonald's.

The implications of allowing junk-food chains into India are quite stark. As the name denotes, the foods served at Kentucky Fried Chicken (KFC) are chicken-based and fried. This is the worst combination possible for the body and can create a host of health problems, including obesity, high cholesterol, heart ailments, and many kinds of cancer. Pizza Hut products are a combination of white flour, cheese, and meat—again, a combination likely to cause disease. . . .

Then there is the issue of the environmental impact of junk-food chains. Modern meat production involves misuse of crops, water, energy, and grazing areas. In addition, animal agriculture produces surprisingly large amounts of air and water pollution.

KFC and Pizza Hut insist that their chickens be fed corn and soybeans. Consider the diversion of grain for this purpose. As the outlets of KFC and Pizza Hut increase in number, the poultry industry will buy up more and more corn to feed the chickens, which means that the corn will quickly disappear from the villages, and its increased price will place it out of reach for the common man. Turning corn into junk chicken is like turning gold into mud. . . .

It is already shameful that, in a country plagued by famine and flood, we divert 37 percent of our arable land to growing animal fodder. Were all of that grain to be consumed directly by humans, it would nourish five times as many people as it does after being converted into meat, milk, and eggs. . . .

Of course, it is not just the KFC and Pizza Hut chains of Pepsi Foods Ltd. that will cause all of this damage. Once we open India up by allowing these chains, dozens more will be eagerly waiting to come in. Each city in America has an average of 5,000 junk-food restaurants. Is that what we want for India?

LOOKING BACK, LOOKING AHEAD

*E*VEN AS THE WORLD becomes more global in culture and interdependent in its mutual relations, centrifugal forces are at work attempting to redefine the political, cultural, and ethnic ways in which it is divided. Such efforts are often disruptive and can sometimes work against measures to enhance our human destiny. But they also represent an integral part of human character and human history and cannot be suppressed in the relentless drive to create a world society. In his crusade against the "Coca-Colonization" of the world, the Japanese novelist Yukio Mishima was expressing a fear

that is shared today by millions throughout the world, as Walt Disney, rock music, and McDonald's relentlessly erode the boundaries that separate one culture and people from another. What will result from this concern is as yet unclear. The Technological Revolution is proceeding at a dizzying speed that can carry information, ideas, and images around the world in seconds.

What is already apparent is that technological advances will have an enormous impact on human society in coming generations. Although many of these consequences may be welcome, others represent a serious

TIMELINE

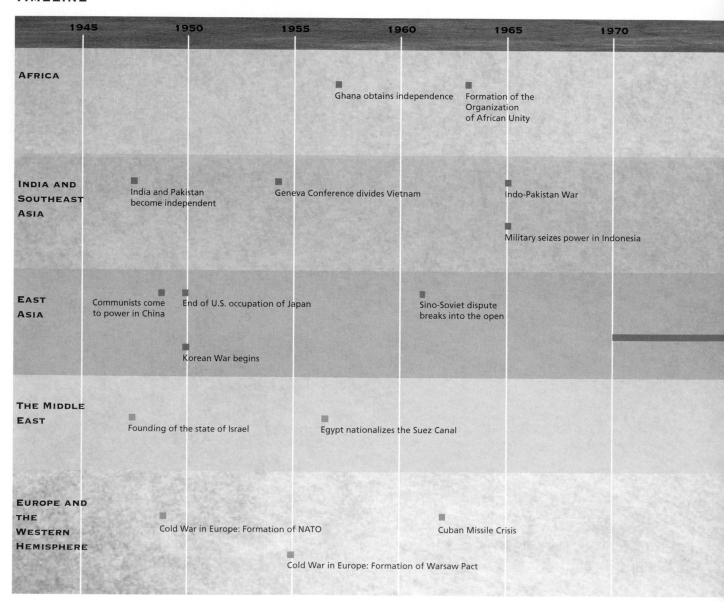

	1945	1950	1955	1960	1965	1970
AFRICA			Ghana obtains independence	Formation of the Organization of African Unity		
INDIA AND SOUTHEAST ASIA	India and Pakistan become independent		Geneva Conference divides Vietnam		Indo-Pakistan War / Military seizes power in Indonesia	
EAST ASIA	Communists come to power in China	End of U.S. occupation of Japan / Korean War begins		Sino-Soviet dispute breaks into the open		
THE MIDDLE EAST	Founding of the state of Israel		Egypt nationalizes the Suez Canal			
EUROPE AND THE WESTERN HEMISPHERE	Cold War in Europe: Formation of NATO / Cold War in Europe: Formation of Warsaw Pact			Cuban Missile Crisis		

challenge, as individuals raised on television, video games, and the computer find less and less time for human relationships or creative activities. To some, the only antidote to the sense of confusion and alienation afflicting contemporary life is to reject the scientific outlook, with its secularizing implications, and return to religious faith. Others hope that a combination of scientific knowledge and spiritual revival can spark a renewal that will enable people to deal constructively with contemporary alienation and confusion.

There are already initial signs that as the common dangers posed by environmental damage, overpopulation, and scarcity of resources become even more apparent, societies around the world will find ample reason to turn their attention from cultural differences to the demands of global interdependence. The greatest challenge of the twenty-first century may be to reconcile the drive for individual and group identity with the common needs of the human community.

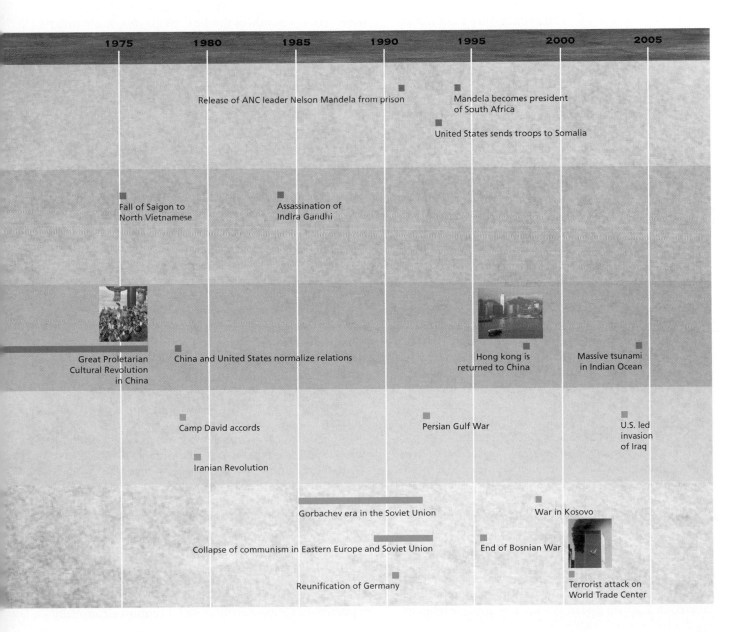

| 1975 | 1980 | 1985 | 1990 | 1995 | 2000 | 2005 |

Release of ANC leader Nelson Mandela from prison

Mandela becomes president of South Africa

United States sends troops to Somalia

Fall of Saigon to North Vietnamese

Assassination of Indira Gandhi

Great Proletarian Cultural Revolution in China

China and United States normalize relations

Hong kong is returned to China

Massive tsunami in Indian Ocean

Camp David accords

Persian Gulf War

U.S. led invasion of Iraq

Iranian Revolution

Gorbachev era in the Soviet Union

War in Kosovo

Collapse of communism in Eastern Europe and Soviet Union

End of Bosnian War

Reunification of Germany

Terrorist attack on World Trade Center

WORLD HISTORY

TO 1500

THE PEOPLES OF MESOPOTAMIA AND EGYPT, like the peoples of India and China, built the first civilizations. Blessed with an abundant environment in their fertile river valleys, beginning around 3000 B.C.E. they built technologically advanced societies, developed cities, and struggled with the problems of organized states. They developed writing to keep records and created literature. They constructed monumental architecture to please their gods, symbolize their power, and preserve their culture for all time. They developed new political, military, social, and religious structures to deal with the basic problems of human existence and organization. These first literate civilizations left detailed records that allow us to view how they grappled with three of the fundamental problems that humans have pondered: the nature of human relationships, the nature of the universe, and the role of divine forces in that cosmos. Although other peoples would provide different answers from those of the Mesopotamians and Egyptians, they posed the questions, gave answers, and wrote them down. Human memory begins with the creation of civilizations.

By the middle of the second millennium B.C.E., much of the creative impulse of the Mesopotamian and Egyptian civilizations was beginning to wane. Around 1200 B.C.E., the decline of the Hittites and Egyptians had created a power vacuum that allowed a number of small states to emerge and flourish temporarily. All of them were eventually overshadowed by the rise of the great empires of the Assyrians and Persians. The Assyrian Empire had been the first to unite almost all of the ancient Middle East. Even larger, however, was the empire of the Great Kings of Persia. The many years of peace that the Persian Empire brought to the Middle East facilitated trade and the general well-being of its peoples. It is no wonder that many peoples expressed their gratitude for being subjects of the Great Kings of Persia. Among these peoples were the Israelites, who created no empire but nevertheless left an important spiritual legacy. The evolution of monotheism created in Judaism one of the world's greatest religions;

moreover, Judaism influenced the development of both Christianity and Islam.

While the peoples of North Africa and the Middle East were actively building the first civilizations, a similar process was getting under way in India. The first civilization in India arose in the Indus River valley during the fourth millennium B.C.E. This Harappan civilization made significant political and social achievements for some two thousand years until the coming of the Aryans finally brought its end around 1500 B.C.E. The Aryans established political control throughout all of India and created a new Indian civilization. Two of the world's great religions, Hinduism and Buddhism, began in India. With its belief in reincarnation, Hinduism provided justification for the rigid class system of India. Buddhism was the product of one man, Siddhartha Gautama, whose simple message in the sixth century B.C.E. of achieving wisdom created a new spiritual philosophy that came to rival Hinduism.

With the rise of the Mauryan dynasty in the fourth century B.C.E., the distinctive features of a great civilization began to be clearly visible. It was extensive in its scope, embracing the entire Indian subcontinent and eventually, in the form of Buddhism and Hinduism, spreading to China and Southeast Asia. But the underlying ethnic, linguistic, and cultural diversity of the Indian people posed a constant challenge to the unity of the state. After the collapse of the Mauryas, the subcontinent would not come under a single authority again for several hundred years.

In the meantime, another great experiment was taking place far to the northeast, across the Himalaya Mountains. Like many other civilizations of antiquity, the first Chinese state was concentrated on a major river system. Beginning around 1600 B.C.E., the Shang dynasty created the first flourishing Chinese civilization. Under the Shang, China developed organized government, a system of writing, and advanced skills in the making of bronze vessels. During the Zhou dynasty, China began to adopt many of the features that characterized Chinese civilization for centuries. Especially important politically was the "mandate from Heaven," which, it was believed, gave kings a divine right to rule. The family, with its ideal of filial piety, also emerged as a powerful economic and social unit.

Once embarked on its own path toward the creation of a complex society, China achieved results that were in all respects the equal of its counterparts elsewhere. A new dynasty—the Han—then established a vast empire that lasted over four hundred years. During the glory years of the Han dynasty (202 B.C.E.–221 C.E.), China extended the boundaries of its empire far into the sands of central Asia and southward along the coast of the South China Sea into what is modern-day Vietnam. Chinese culture appeared to be unrivaled, and its scientific and technological achievements were unsurpassed.

Unlike the great centralized empires of the Persians and the Chinese, ancient Greece consisted of a larger number of small, independent city-states, most of which had populations of only a few thousand. Despite the small size of their city-states, these ancient Greeks created a civilization that was the fountainhead of Western culture. In classical Greece (c. 500–338 B.C.E.), Socrates, Plato, and Aristotle established the foundations of Western philosophy. Western literary forms are largely derived from Greek poetry and drama. Greek notions of harmony, proportion, and beauty have remained the touchstones for all subsequent Western art. A rational method of inquiry, so important to modern science, was conceived in ancient Greece. Many political terms are Greek in origin, and so too are concepts of the rights and duties of citizenship, especially as they were conceived in Athens, the first great democracy. The Greeks raised and debated the fundamental questions about the purpose of human existence, the structure of human society, and the nature of the universe that have concerned thinkers ever since.

For all of their brilliant accomplishments, however, the Greeks were unable to rise above the divisions and rivalries that caused them to fight each other and undermine their own civilization. Of course, their cultural contributions have outlived their political struggles. And the Hellenistic era, which emerged after the Greek city-states had lost their independence in 338 B.C.E. and Alexander the Great had defeated the Persian Empire and carved out a new kingdom in the Middle East, made possible the spread of Greek ideas to larger areas. New philosophical concepts captured the minds of many. Significant achievements were made in art, literature, and science. Greek culture spread throughout the Middle East and made an impact wherever it was carried. Although the Hellenistic world achieved a degree of political stability, by the late third century B.C.E. signs of decline were beginning to multiply, and the growing power of Rome would eventually endanger the Hellenistic world.

In the eighth and seventh centuries B.C.E., the Latin-speaking community of Rome emerged as an actual city.

Between 509 and 264 B.C.E., the expansion of this city brought about the union of almost all of Italy under Rome's control. Even more dramatically, between 264 and 133 B.C.E., Rome expanded to the west and east and became master of the Mediterranean Sea and its surrounding territories, creating one of the largest empires in antiquity. Rome's republican institutions proved inadequate for the task of ruling an empire, however, and after a series of bloody civil wars, Octavian created a new order that would rule the empire in an orderly fashion. His successors established a Roman imperial state.

The Roman Empire experienced a lengthy period of peace and prosperity between 14 and 180. During this era, trade flourished and the provinces were governed efficiently. In the course of the third century, however, the Roman Empire came near to collapse due to invasions, civil wars, and economic decline. Although the emperors Diocletian and Constantine brought new life to the so-called Late Empire, their efforts shored up the empire only temporarily. In its last two hundred years, as Christianity with its new ideals of spiritual equality and respect for human life grew, a slow transformation of the Roman world took place. The Germanic invasions greatly accelerated this process. Beginning in 395, the empire divided into western and eastern parts, and in 476, the Roman Empire in the west came to an end.

Although the Roman Empire in the west collapsed and lived on only as an idea, Roman achievements were bequeathed to the future. The Romance languages of today (French, Italian, Spanish, Portuguese, and Romanian) are based on Latin. Western practices of impartial justice and trial by jury owe much to Roman law. As great builders, the Romans left monuments to their skills throughout Europe, some of which, such as aqueducts and roads, are still in use today.

The fall of ancient empires did not mark the end of civilization. After 500 C.E., new societies eventually rose on the ashes of the ancient empires, while new civilizations were on the verge of creation across the oceans in the continents of North and South America. The Maya and Aztecs were especially successful in developing advanced and prosperous civilizations in central America. Both cultures built elaborate cities with pyramids, temples, and palaces. Both were polytheistic and practiced human sacrifice as a major part of their religions. Mayan civilization collapsed in the ninth century, whereas the Aztecs fell to Spanish invaders in the sixteenth century. In the fifteenth century, another remarkable civilization—that of the Inka—flourished in South America. The Inkan Empire was carefully planned and regulated, which is especially evident in the extensive network of roads that connected all parts of the empire. However, the Inka, possessing none of the new weapons of the Spaniards, eventually fell to the foreign conquerors.

All of these societies in the Americas developed in apparently total isolation from their counterparts elsewhere in the world. This lack of contact with other human beings deprived them of access to developments taking place in Africa, Asia, and Europe. They did not know of the wheel, for example, and their written languages were not as sophisticated as those in other parts of the world. In other respects, however, their cultural achievements were the equal of those realized elsewhere. One development that the peoples of the Americas lacked was the knowledge of firearms. In a few short years, tiny bands of Spanish explorers were able to conquer the magnificent civilizations of the Americas and turn them into ruins.

After the collapse of Roman power in the west, the eastern Roman Empire, centered in Constantinople, continued in the eastern Mediterranean and eventually emerged as the unique Christian civilization known as the Byzantine Empire, which flourished for hundreds of years. One of the greatest challenges to the Byzantine Empire, however, came from a new force—Islam—a new religion that arose in the Arabian peninsula at the beginning of the seventh century C.E. and spread rapidly throughout the Middle East. It was the work of a man named Muhammad. After Muhammad's death, his successors organized the Arabs and set in motion a great expansion. Arab armies moved westward across North Africa and into Spain, as well as eastward into the Persian Empire, conquering Syria and Mesopotamia. Internal struggles, however, soon weakened the empire, although the Abbasid dynasty established an Arab empire in 750 that flourished for almost five hundred years.

Like other empires in the region, however, the Arab Empire did not last. Nevertheless, Islam brought a code of law and a written language to societies that had previously not had them. By creating a flourishing trade network stretching from West Africa to East Asia, Islam also brought untold wealth to thousands and a better life to millions. By the end of the thirteenth century, the Arab Empire was no more than a memory. But it left a powerful legacy in Islam, which remains one of the great religions of the world. In succeeding centuries, Islam began to penetrate into Africa and across the Indian Ocean into the islands of Southeast Asia.

The mastery of agriculture gave rise to three early civilizations in northern Africa: Egypt, Kush, and Axum. Later, new states emerged in different parts of Africa, some of them strongly influenced by the spread of Islam. Ghana, Mali, and Songhai were three prosperous trading states that flourished in West Africa between the twelfth and fifteenth centuries. Zimbabwe, which emerged around 1300, played an important role in the southern half of Africa. Africa was also an active participant in emerging regional and global trade with the Mediterranean world and across the Indian Ocean. Although the state-building process in

sub-Saharan Africa was still in its early stages compared with the ancient civilizations of India, China, and Mesopotamia, in many respects the new African states were as impressive and sophisticated as their counterparts elsewhere in the world.

In the fifteenth century, a new factor came to affect Africa. Fleets from Portugal began to probe southward along the coast of West Africa. At first, their sponsors were in search of gold and slaves, but when Portuguese ships rounded the southern coast of Africa by 1500, they began to seek to dominate the trade of the Indian Ocean as well. The new situation posed a challenge to the peoples of Africa, whose states would be severely tested by the demands of the Europeans.

The peoples of Africa were not the only ones to confront a new threat from Europe at the beginning of the sixteenth century. When the Portuguese sailed across the Indian Ocean, they sought to reach India, where a new empire capable of rivaling the great kingdom of the Mauryas was in the throes of creation (see Chapter 15). Between 500 and 1500, Indian civilization had faced a number of severe challenges. One was an ongoing threat from beyond the mountains in the northwest. This challenge, which began in the eleventh century, led to the takeover of all of northern India in the eleventh century by Turkish warriors, who were Muslims. A second challenge came from the tradition of internal rivalry that had marked Indian civilization for hundreds of years and that continued almost without interruption down to the sixteenth century. The third challenge was the religious divisions between Hindus and Buddhists, and later between Hindus and Muslims, that existed throughout much of this period.

During the same period that Indian civilization faced these challenges at home, it was having a profound impact on the emerging states of Southeast Asia. Situated at the crossroads between two oceans and two great civilizations, Southeast Asia has long served as a bridge linking peoples and cultures. When complex societies began to appear in the region, they were strongly influenced by the older civilizations of neighboring China and India. All the young states throughout the region—Vietnam, Angkor, Thailand, the Burmese kingdom of Pagan, and several states on the Malay peninsula and Indonesian archipelago—were affected by foreign ideas and adopted them as a part of their own cultures. At the same time, the Southeast Asian peoples, like the Japanese, put their own unique stamp on the ideas that they adopted. The result was a region marked by cultural richness and diversity, yet rooted in the local culture.

One of the civilizations that spread its shadow over the emerging societies of Southeast Asia was China. Between the sixth and fifteenth centuries, China was ruled by a series of strong dynasties and had advanced in many ways. The industrial and commercial section had grown considerably in size, complexity, and technological capacity. In the countryside, a flourishing agriculture bolstered China's economic prosperity. The civil service provided for a stable government bureaucracy and an avenue of upward mobility that was virtually unknown elsewhere in the world. China's achievements were unsurpassed throughout the world and made it a civilization that was the envy of its neighbors.

And yet some things had not changed. By 1500, China was still a predominantly agricultural society, with wealth based primarily on the ownership of land. Commercial activities flourished but remained under a high level of government regulation. China also remained a relatively centralized empire based on an official ideology that stressed the virtue of hard work, social conformity, and hierarchy. In foreign affairs, the long frontier struggle with the nomadic peoples along the northern and western frontiers continued unabated.

Along the fringes of Chinese civilization were a number of other agricultural societies that were beginning to follow a pattern of development similar to that of China, although somewhat later in time. All of these early agricultural societies were eventually influenced to some degree by their great neighbor. Vietnam remained under Chinese rule for a thousand years. Korea retained its separate existence but was long a tributary state of China and in many ways followed China's cultural example. Cut off from the mainland by 120 miles of ocean, the Japanese had little contact with the outside world during most of their early development. However, once the Japanese became acquainted with Chinese culture, they were quick to take advantage of the opportunity. In the space of a few decades, the young state adopted many features of Chinese society and culture and thereby introduced major changes into the Japanese way of life. Nevertheless, Japan was a society that was able to make use of ideas imported from beyond its borders

without endangering its customs, beliefs, and institutions. Japan retained both its political independence and its cultural uniqueness.

After the collapse of the Roman Empire in the fifth century, a new European civilization slowly began to emerge in western Europe. The coronation of Charlemagne, the descendant of a Germanic tribe converted to Christianity, as Roman emperor in 800 symbolized the fusion of the three chief components of the new European civilization: the German tribes, the Roman legacy, and the Christian Church. Charlemagne's Carolingian Empire fostered the idea of a distinct European identity. With the disintegration of that empire, power fell into the hands of many different lords, who came to constitute a powerful group of nobles that dominated the political, economic, and social life of Europe. But quietly and surely, within this world of castles and private power, kings gradually began to extend their public power and laid the foundations for the European kingdoms that in one form or another have dominated European politics ever since.

European civilization began to flourish in the High Middle Ages (1000–1300). The revival of trade, the expansion of towns and cities, and the development of a money economy did not mean the end of a predominantly rural European society, but they did offer new opportunities for people to expand and enrich their lives. At the same time, the High Middle Ages also gave birth to an intellectual and spiritual revival that transformed European society. However, fourteenth-century Europe was challenged by an overwhelming number of disintegrative forces but proved remarkably resilient. Elements of recovery in the age of the Renaissance made the fifteenth century a period of significant artistic, intellectual, and political change in Europe. By the second half of the fifteenth century, the growth of strong, centralized monarchical states made possible the dramatic expansion of Europe into other parts of the world.

MAP CREDITS

The authors wish to acknowledge their use of the following books as reference in preparing the maps listed here:

SPOT MAP, PAGE 31 Geoffrey Barraclough, ed., *Times Atlas of World History*, (Maplewood, N.J.: Hammond Inc., 1978), p. 65.

MAP 3.1 Geoffrey Barraclough, ed., *Times Atlas of World History*, (Maplewood, N.J.: Hammond Inc., 1978), p. 63.

MAP 5.4 Hammond Past Worlds: *The Times Atlas of Archeology*, (Maplewood, N.J.: Hammond Inc. 1988), pp. 190–191.

MAP 5.5 Conrad Schirokauer, *A Brief History of Chinese and Japanese Civilizations*, 2d ed. (San Diego: Harcourt Brace Jovanovich, 1989), p. 52.

MAP 6.2 Michael Coe, Dean Snow and Elizabeth Benson, *Atlas of Ancient America* (New York: Facts on File, 1988), p. 144.

MAP 6.3 Geoffrey Barraclough, ed., *Times Atlas of World History*, (Maplewood, N.J.: Hammond Inc., 1978), p. 47.

MAP 6.4 Phillipa Fernandez-Arnesto, *Atlas of World Exploration*, (New York: Harper Collins, 1991), p. 35.

MAP 6.5 Geoffrey Barraclough, ed., *Times Atlas of World History*, (Maplewood, N.J.: Hammond Inc., 1978), p. 47.

MAP 7.3 Geoffrey Barraclough, ed., *Times Atlas of World History*, (Maplewood, N.J.: Hammond Inc., 1978), pp. 134–135.

MAP 7.4 Geoffrey Barraclough, ed., *Times Atlas of World History*, (Maplewood, N.J.: Hammond Inc., 1978), p. 135.

MAP 8.1 Geoffrey Barraclough, ed., *Times Atlas of World History*, (Maplewood, N.J.: Hammond Inc., 1978), pp. 44–45.

MAP 8.4 Geoffrey Barraclough, ed., *Times Atlas of World History*, (Maplewood, N.J.: Hammond Inc., 1978), pp. 136–137.

MAP 9.2 Michael Edwardes, *A History of India* (London: Thames and Hudson, 1961), p. 79.

MAP 10.1 John K. Fairbank, Edwin O. Reischauer, and Albert M. Craig, *East Asia: Tradition and Transformation* (Boston: Houghton Mifflin, 1973), p. 103.

SPOT MAP, PAGE 273 Albert Hermann, *An Historical Atlas of China* (Chicago: Aidine, 1966), p. 13.

MAP 11.1 John K. Fairbank, Edwin O. Reischauer, and Albert M. Craig, *East Asia: Tradition and Transformation* (Boston: Houghton Mifflin, 1973), p. 363.

MAP 13.2 Geoffrey Barraclough, ed., *Times Atlas of World History*, (Maplewood, N. J.:Hammond, Inc. 1978), p. 160.

MAP 15.3 Geoffrey Barraclough, ed., *Times Atlas of World History*, (Maplewood, N. J.: Hammond, Inc. 1978), p. 173.

MAP 16.1 Jonathan Spence, *The Search for Modern China*, (New York: W. W. Norton, 1990), p. 19.

MAP 16.2 Conrad Schirokauer, *A Brief History of Chinese and Japanese Civilizations*, 2d ed., (San Diego: Harcourt Brace Jovanovich, 1989), p. 330.

MAP 16.3 John K. Fairbank, Edwin O. Reischauer, and Albert M. Craig, *East Asia: Tradition and Tranformation*, (Boston: Houghton Mifflin, 1973), pp. 402–403.

GLOSSARY

absolutism   a form of government where the sovereign power or ultimate authority rested in the hands of a monarch who claimed to rule by divine right and was therefore responsible only to God.

Abstract Expressionism   a post–World War II artistic movement that broke with all conventions of form and structure in favor of total abstraction.

Agricultural (Neolithic) Revolution   the shift from hunting animals and gathering plants for sustenance to producing food by systematic agriculture that occurred gradually between 10,000 and 4000 B.C.E. (the Neolithic or "New Stone" Age).

agricultural revolution   the application of new agricultural techniques that allowed for a large increase in productivity in the eighteenth century.

Amerindian   earliest inhabitants of North and South America. Original theories suggested migration from Siberia across the Bering Land Bridge; more recent evidence suggests migration also occurred by sea from regions of the South Pacific to South America.

anarchism   a political theory that holds that all governments and existing social institutions are unnecessary and advocates a society based on voluntary cooperation.

ANC   the African National Congress. Founded in 1912, it was the beginning of political activity by South African blacks. Banned by politically dominant European whites in 1960, it was not officially "unbanned" until 1990. It is now the official majority party of the South African government.

Analects   the body of writing containing conversations between Confucius and his disciples that preserves his worldly wisdom and pragmatic philosophies.

anti-Semitism   hostility toward or discrimination against Jews.

apartheid   the system of racial segregation practiced in the Republic of South Africa until the 1990s, which involved political, legal, and economic discrimination against nonwhites.

appeasement   the policy, followed by the European nations in the 1930s, of accepting Hitler's annexation of Austria and Czechoslovakia in the belief that meeting his demands would assure peace and stability.

Aramaic   A Semitic language dominant in the Middle East in the first century B.C.E.; still in use in small regions of the Middle East and southern Asia.

Arianism   a Christian heresy that taught that Jesus was inferior to God. Though condemned by the Council of Nicaea in 325, Arianism was adopted by many of the Germanic peoples who entered the Roman Empire over the next centuries.

aristocracy   a class of hereditary nobility in medieval Europe; a warrior class who shared a distinctive lifestyle based on the institution of knighthood, although there were social divisions within the group based on extremes of wealth.

Arthasastra   an early Indian political treatise that sets forth many fundamental aspects of the relationship of rulers and their subjects. It has been compared to Machiavelli's well-known book, *The Prince,* and has provided principles upon which many aspects of social organization have developed in the region.

Aryans   Indo–European-speaking nomads who entered India from the Central Asian steppes between 1500 and 1000 B.C.E. and greatly affected Indian society, notably by establishing the caste system. The term was later adopted by German Nazis to describe their racial ideal.

asceticism   a lifestyle involving the denial of worldly pleasures. Predominantly associated with Hindu, Buddhist, or Christian religions, adherents perceive their practices as a path to greater spirituality.

ASEAN   the Association for the Southeast Asian Nations formed in 1967 to promote the prosperity and political stability of its member nations. Currently Brunei, Indonesia, Laos, Malaysia, Myanmar, the Philippines, Singapore, Thailand, and Vietnam are members. Other countries in the region participate as "observer" members.

Ausgleich   the "Compromise" of 1867 that created the dual monarchy of Austria-Hungary. Austria and Hungary each had its own capital, constitution, and legislative assembly, but were united under one monarch.

authoritarian state   a state that has a dictatorial government and some other trappings of a totalitarian state, but does not demand that the masses be actively involved in the regime's goals as totalitarian states do.

auxiliaries   troops enlisted from the subject peoples of the Roman Empire to supplement the regular legions composed of Roman citizens.

bakufu   the centralized government set up in Japan in the twelfth century. See shogunate system.

balance of power   a distribution of power among several states such that no single nation can dominate or interfere with the interests of another.

Banners   Originally established in 1639 by the Qing empire, the Eight Banners were administrative divisions into which all Manchu families were placed. Banners quickly evolved into the basis of Manchu military organization with each required to raise and support a prescribed number of troops.

Bao-jia system   the Chinese practice, reportedly originated by the Qin dynasty in the third century B.C.E., of organizing families into groups of five or ten to exercise mutual control and surveillance and reduce loyalty to the family.

Baroque   a style that dominated Western painting, sculpture, architecture and music from about 1580 to 1730, generally characterized by elaborate ornamentation and dramatic effects. Important practitioners included Bernini, Rubens, Handel, and Bach.

Bedouins   nomadic tribes originally from northern Arabia, who became important traders after the domestication of the camel during the first millennium B.C.E. Early converts to Islam, their values and practices deeply affected Muhammad.

benefice   in the Christian church, a position, such as a bishopric, that consisted of both a sacred office and the right of the holder to the annual revenues from the position.

Berbers   an ethnic group indigenous to western North Africa.

bey   a provincial governor in the Ottoman Empire.

bhakti   in Hinduism, devotion as a means of religious observance open to all persons regardless of class.

bodhi   Wisdom. Sometimes described as complete awareness of the true nature of the universe.

bicameral legislature   a legislature with two houses.

Black Death   the outbreak of plague (mostly bubonic) in the mid-fourteenth century that killed from 25 to 50 percent of Europe's population.

Blitzkrieg   "lightning war." A war conducted with great speed and force, as in Germany's advance at the beginning of World War II.

bodhisattvas   in some schools of Buddhism, individuals who have achieved enlightenment but, because of their great compassion, have chosen to renounce Nirvana and to remain on earth in spirit form to help all human beings achieve release from reincarnation.

Bolsheviks   a small faction of the Russian Social Democratic Party who were led by Lenin and dedicated to violent revolution; seized power in Russia in 1917 and were subsequently renamed the Communists.

bonsai   Originating in China in the first millenium B.C.E. and known there as *penzai,* it was imported to Japan between 700–900 C.E. Bonsai combines patience and artistry in the cultivation of stunted trees and shrubs to create exquisite nature scenes in miniature.

boyars   the Russian nobility.

Brahman   The Hindu word roughly equivalent to God; the Divine basis of all being; regarded as the source and sum of the cosmos.

brahmin   A member of the Hindu priestly caste or class; literally "one who has realized or attempts to realize Brahman." Traditionally, duties of a brahmin include studying Hindu religious scriptures and transmitting them to others orally. The priests of Hindu temples are brahmin.

Brezhnev Doctrine   the doctrine, enunciated by Leonid Brezhnev, that the Soviet Union had a right to intervene if socialism was threatened in another socialist state; used to justify the use of Soviet troops in Czechoslovakia in 1968.

Buddhism   A religion and philosophy based on the teachings of Siddhartha Gautama in about 500 B.C.E. Principally practiced in China, India, and other parts of Asia, Buddhism has 360 million followers and is considered a major world releigion.

Burakumin   A Japanese minority similar to dalits (or untouchables) in Indian culture. Past and current discrimination has resulted in lower educational attainment and socioeconomic status for members of this group. Movements with objectives ranging from "liberation" to integration have tried over the years to change this situation.

Bushido   The code of conduct observed by samurai warriors; comparable to the European concept of chilvalry.

caliph the secular leader of the Islamic community.

calpulli In Aztec society, a kinship group, often of a thousand or more, which served as an intermediary with the central government, providing taxes and conscript labor to the state.

capital material wealth used or available for use in the production of more wealth.

caste system a system of rigid social hierarchy in which all members of that society are assigned by birth to specific "ranks," and inherit specific roles and privileges.

cartel a combination of independent commercial enterprises that work together to control prices and limit competition.

Cartesian dualism Descartes's principle of the separation of mind and matter (and mind and body) that enabled scientists to view matter as something separate from themselves that could be investigated by reason.

caudillos strong leaders in nineteenth-century Latin America, who were usually supported by the landed elites and ruled chiefly by military force, though some were popular; they included both modernizers and destructive dictators.

censorate one of the three primary Chinese ministries, originally established in the Qin dynasty, whose inspectors surveyed the efficiency of officials throughout the system.

chaebol a South Korean business structure similar to the Japanese keiretsu.

Chan Buddhism a Chinese sect (Zen in Japanese) influenced by Daoist ideas, which called for mind training and a strict regimen as a means of seeking enlightenment.

chansons de geste a form of vernacular literature in the High Middle Ages that consisted of heroic epics focusing on the deeds of warriors.

chinampas in Mesoamerica, artifical islands crisscrossed by canals that provided water for crops and easy transportation to local markets.

chivalry the ideal of civilized behavior that emerged among the nobility in the eleventh and twelfth centuries under the influence of the church; a code of ethics knights were expected to uphold.

Christian (northern) humanism an intellectual movement in northern Europe in the late fifteenth and early sixteenth centuries that combined the interest in the classics of the Italian Renaissance with an interest in the sources of early Christianity, including the New Testament and the writings of the church fathers.

civic humanism an intellectual movement of the Italian Renaissance that saw Cicero, who was both an intellectual and a statesman, as the ideal and held that humanists should be involved in government and use their rhetorical training in the service of the state.

civil rights the basic rights of citizens including equality before the law, freedom of speech and press, and freedom from arbitrary arrest.

civil service examination an elaborate Chinese system of selecting bureaucrats on merit, first introduced in 165 C.E., developed by the Tang dynasty in the seventh century C.E. and refined under the Song dynasty; later adopted in Vietnam and with less success in Japan and Korea. It contributed to efficient government, upward mobility, and cultural uniformity.

class struggle the basis of the Marxist analysis of history, which says that the owners of the means of production have always oppressed the workers and predicts an inevitable revolution. See Marxism.

Cold War the ideological conflict between the Soviet Union and the United States after World War II.

collective farms large farms created in the Soviet Union by Stalin by combining many small holdings into one large farm worked by the peasants under government supervision.

collective security the use of an international army raised by an association of nations to deter aggression and keep the peace.

coloni free tenant farmers who worked as sharecroppers on the large estates of the Roman Empire (singular: *colonus*).

Comintern a worldwide organization of Communist parties, founded by Lenin in 1919, dedicated to the advancement of world revolution; also known as the Third International.

common law law common to the entire kingdom of England; imposed by the king's courts beginning in the twelfth century to replace the customary law used in county and feudal courts that varied from place to place.

commune in medieval Europe, an association of townspeople bound together by a sworn oath for the purpose of obtaining basic liberties from the lord of the territory in which the town was located; also, the self-governing town after receiving its liberties.

communalism in South Asia, the tendency of people to band together in mutually antagonistic social sub-groups; elsewhere used to describe unifying trends in the larger community.

conciliarism a movement in fourteenth- and fifteenth-century Europe that held that final authority in spiritual matters resided with a general church council, not the pope; emerged in response to the Avignon papacy and the Great Schism and used to justify the summoning of the Council of Constance (1414–1418).

condottieri leaders of bands of mercenary soldiers in Renaissance Italy who sold their services to the highest bidder.

Confucianism a system of thought based on the teachings of Confucius (551–479 B.C.E.) that developed into the ruling ideology of the Chinese state. See Neo-Confucianism.

conquistadors "conquerors." Leaders in the Spanish conquests in the Americas, especially Mexico and Peru, in the sixteenth century.

conscription a military draft.

conservatism an ideology based on tradition and social stability that favored the maintenance of established institutions, organized religion, and obedience to authority and resisted change, especially abrupt change.

consuls the chief executive officers of the Roman Republic. Two were chosen annually to administer the government and lead the army in battle.

consumer society a term applied to Western society after World War II as the working classes adopted the consumption patterns of the middle class and installment plans, credit cards, and easy credit made consumer goods such as appliances and automobiles widely available.

containment a policy adopted by the United States in the Cold War. Its goal was to use whatever means, short of all-out war, to limit Soviet expansion.

Continental System Napoleon's effort to bar British goods from the Continent in the hope of weakening Britain's economy and destroying its capacity to wage war.

Contras in Nicaragua in the 1980s, an anti-Sandinista guerrilla movement supported by the U.S. Reagan administration.

Coptic a form of Christianity, originally Egyptian, that has thrived in Ethiopia since the fourth century C.E.

cosmopolitanism the quality of being sophisticated and having wide international experience.

cottage industry a system of textile manufacturing in which spinners and weavers worked at home in their cottages using raw materials supplied to them by capitalist entrepreneurs.

Crusade in the Middle Ages, a military campaign in defense of Christendom.

cultural relativism the belief that no culture is superior to another because culture is a matter of custom, not reason, and derives its meaning from the group holding it.

cuneiform "wedge-shaped." A system of writing developed by the Sumerians that consisted of wedge-shaped impressions made by a reed stylus on clay tablets.

daimyo prominent Japanese families who provided allegiance to the local shogun in exchange for protection; similar to vassals in Europe.

dalits commonly referred to as untouchables; the lowest level of Indian society, technically outside the caste system and considered less than human; renamed harijans ("children of God") by Gandhi, they remain the object of discrimination despite affirmative action programs.

Dao a Chinese philosophical concept, literally "The Way," central to both Confucianism and Daoism, that describes the behavior proper to each member of society; somewhat similar to the Indian concept of dharma.

Daoism a Chinese philosophy traditionally ascribed to the perhaps legendary Lao Tzu, which holds that acceptance and spontaneity are the keys to harmonious interaction with the universal order; an alternative to Confucianism.

decolonization the process of becoming free of colonial status and achieving statehood; occurred in most of the world's colonies between 1947 and 1962.

deism belief in God as the creator of the universe who, after setting it in motion, ceased to have any direct involvement in it and allowed it to run according to its own natural laws.

deficit spending the concept, developed by John Maynard Keynes in the 1930s, that in times of economic depression governments should stimulate demand by hiring people to do public works, such as building highways, even if this increased public debt.

demesne the part of a manor retained under the direct control of the lord and worked by the serfs as part of their labor services.

denazification after World War II, the Allied policy of rooting out any traces of Nazism in German society by bringing prominent Nazis to trial for war crimes and purging any known Nazis from political office.

depression a very severe, protracted economic downturn with high levels of unemployment.

destalinization the policy of denouncing and undoing the most repressive aspects of Stalin's regime; begun by Nikita Khrushchev in 1956.

détente the relaxation of tension between the Soviet Union and the United States that occurred in the 1970s.

devshirme in the Ottoman Empire, a system (literally, "collection") of training talented children to be administrators or members of the sultan's harem; originally meritocratic, by the seventeenth century, it degenerated into a hereditary caste.

dharma in Hinduism and Buddhism, the law that governs the universe, and specifically human behavior.

dialectic logic, one of the seven liberal arts that made up the medieval curriculum. In Marxist thought, the process by which all change occurs through the clash of antagonistic elements.

Diaspora the scattering of Jews throughout the ancient world after the Babylonian captivity in the sixth century B.C.E.

dictator in the Roman Republic, an official granted unlimited power to run the state for a short period of time, usually six months, during an emergency.

diocese the area under the jurisdiction of a Christian bishop; based originally on Roman administrative districts.

direct representation a system of choosing delegates to a representative assembly in which citizens vote directly for the delegates who will represent them.

divination the practice of seeking to foretell future events by interpreting divine signs, which could appear in various forms, such as in entrails of animals, in patterns in smoke, or in dreams.

divine-right monarchy a monarchy based on the belief that monarchs receive their power directly from God and are responsible to no one except God.

domino theory the belief that if the Communists succeeded in Vietnam, other countries in Southeast and East Asia would also fall (like dominoes) to communism; a justification for the U.S. intervention in Vietnam.

dualism the belief that the universe is dominated by two opposing forces, one good and the other evil.

dyarchy during the Qing dynasty in China, a system in which all important national and provincial adminstrative positions were shared equally by Chinese and Manchus, which helped to consolidate both Manchu rule and their assimilation.

dynastic state a state where the maintenance and expansion of the interests of the ruling family is the primary consideration.

economic imperialism the process in which banks and corporations from developed nations invest in underdeveloped regions and establish a major presence there in the hope of making high profits; not necessarily the same as colonial expansion in that businesses invest where they can make a profit, which may not be in their own nation's colonies.

El Niño periodic changes in water temperature at the surface of the Pacific Ocean, which can lead to major environmental changes and may have led to the collapse of the Moche civilization in what is now Peru.

emir "commander" (Arabic), used by Muslim rulers in southern Spain and elsewhere.

empiricism the practice of relying on observation and experiment.

enclosure movement in the eighteenth century, the fencing in of the old open fields, combining many small holdings into larger units that could be farmed more efficiently.

encomienda a grant from the Spanish monarch to colonial conquistadors; see *encomienda system*.

encomienda system the system by which Spain first governed its American colonies. Holders of an encomienda were supposed to protect the Indians as well as using them as laborers and collecting tribute but in practice exploited them.

encyclical a letter from the pope to all the bishops of the Roman Catholic church.

enlightened absolutism an absolute monarchy where the ruler follows the principles of the Enlightenment by introducing reforms for the improvement of society, allowing freedom of speech and the press, permitting religious toleration, expanding education, and ruling in accordance with the laws.

Enlightenment an eighteenth-century intellectual movement, led by the philosophes, that stressed the application of reason and the scientific method to all aspects of life.

entrepreneur one who organizes, operates, and assumes the risk in a business venture in the expectation of making a profit.

Epicureanism a philosophy founded by Epicurus in the fourth century C.E. that taught that happiness (freedom from emotional turmoil) could be achieved through the pursuit of pleasure (intellectual rather than sensual pleasure).

equestrians a group of extremely wealthy men in the late Roman Republic who were effectively barred from high office, but sought political power commensurate with their wealth; called equestrians because many had gotten their start as cavalry officers (*equites*).

eta in feudal Japan, a class of hereditary slaves who were responsible for what were considered degrading occupations, such as curing leather and burying the dead.

ethnic cleansing the policy of killing or forcibly removing people of another ethnic group; used by the Serbs against Bosnian Muslims in the 1990s.

eucharist a Christian sacrament in which consecrated bread and wine are consumed in celebration of Jesus' Last Supper; also called the Lord's Supper or communion.

eunuch a man whose testicles have been removed; a standard feature of the Chinese imperial system, the Ottoman Empire, and the Mughal Dynasty, among others.

evolutionary socialism a socialist doctrine espoused by Eduard Bernstein who argued that socialists should stress cooperation and evolution to attain power by democratic means rather than by conflict and revolution.

fascism an ideology or movement that exalts the nation above the individual and calls for a centralized government with a dictatorial leader, economic and social regimentation, and forcible suppression of opposition; in particular, the ideology of Mussolini's Fascist regime in Italy.

feminism the belief in the social, political, and economic equality of the sexes; also, organized activity to advance women's rights.

fief a landed estate granted to a vassal in exchange for military services.

filial piety in traditional China, in particular, a hierarchical system in which every family member has his or her place, subordinate to a patriarch who has in turn reciprocal responsibilities.

Final Solution the physical extermination of the Jewish people by the Nazis during World War II.

five pillars of Islam the core requirements of the faith, observation of which would lead to paradise: belief in Allah and his Prophet Muhammad; prescribed prayers; observation of Ramadan; pilgrimage to Mecca; and giving alms to the poor.

five relationships in traditional China, the hierarchical interpersonal associations considered crucial to social order, within the family, between friends, and with the king.

folk culture the traditional arts and crafts, literature, music, and other customs of the people; something that people make, as opposed to modern popular culture, which is something people buy.

foot binding an extremely painful process, common in China throughout the second millenium C.E., that compressed girls' feet to half their natural size, representing submissiveness and self-discipline, which were considered necessary attributes for an ideal wife.

four modernizations the slogan for radical reforms of Chinese industry, agriculture, technology, and national defense, instituted by Deng Xiaoping after his accession to power in the late 1970s.

free trade the unrestricted international exchange of goods with low or no tariffs.

fundamentalism a movement that emphasizes rigid adherence to basic religious principles; often used to describe evangelical Christianity, it also characterizes the practices of Islamic conservatives.

general strike a strike by all or most workers in an economy; espoused by Georges Sorel as the heroic action that could be used to inspire the workers to destroy capitalist society.

genin landless laborers in feudal Japan, who were effectively slaves.

gentry well-to-do English landowners below the level of the nobility; played an important role in the English Civil War of the seventeenth century.

geocentric theory the idea that the earth is at the center of the universe and that the sun and other celestial objects revolve around the earth.

glasnost "openness." Mikhail Gorbachev's policy of encouraging Soviet citizens to openly discuss the strengths and weaknesses of the Soviet Union.

Gleichschaltung the coordination of all government institutions under Nazi control in Germany from 1933.

global civilization human society considered as a single world-wide entity, in which local differences are less important than overall similarities.

good emperors the five emperors who ruled from 96 to 180 (Nerva, Trajan, Hadrian, Antoninus Pius, and Marcus Aurelius), a period of peace and prosperity for the Roman Empire.

Grand Council the top of the government hierarchy in the Song dynasty in China.

grand vezir (*also*, vizier) the chief executive in the Ottoman Empire, under the sultan.

Great Leap Forward a short-lived, radical experiment in China, started in 1958, which created vast rural communes and attempted to replace the family as the fundamental social unit.

Great Proletarian Cultural Revolution an attempt to destroy all vestiges of tradition in China, in order to create a totally egalitarian society; launched by Mao Zedong in 1966, it became virtually anarchic and lasted only until Mao's death in 1976.

Great Schism the crisis in the late medieval church when there were first two and then three popes; ended by the Council of Constance (1414–1418).

green revolution the introduction of technological agriculture, especially in India in the 1960s, which increased food production substantially but also exacerbated rural inequality because only the wealthier farmers could afford fertilizer.

guest workers foreign workers working temporarily in European countries.

guided democracy the name given by President Sukarno of Indonesia in the late 1950s to his style of government, which theoretically operated by consensus.

guild an association of people with common interests and concerns, especially people working in the same craft. In medieval Europe, guilds came to control much of the production process and to restrict entry into various trades.

guru teacher, especially in the Hindu, Buddhist and Sikh religious traditions, where it is an important honorific.

gymnasium in classical Greece, a place for athletics; in the Hellenistic Age, a secondary school with a curriculum centered on music, physical exercise, and literature.

Hadith a collection of the sayings of the Prophet Muhammad, used to supplement the revelations contained in the Qur'an.

Hanseatic League a commercial and military alliance of north German coastal towns, increasingly powerful in the fifteenth century C.E.

harem the private domain of a ruler such as the sultan in the Ottoman Empire or the caliph of Baghdad, generally large and mostly inhabited by the extended family.

Hegira the flight of Muhammad from Mecca to Medina in 622, which marks the first date on the official calendar of Islam.

heliocentric theory the idea that the sun (not the earth) is at the center of the universe.

Hellenistic literally, "to imitate the Greeks"; the era after the death of Alexander the Great when Greek culture spread into the Near East and blended with the culture of that region.

helots serfs in ancient Sparta, who were permanently bound to the land that they worked for their Spartan masters.

heresy the holding of religious doctrines different from the official teachings of the church.

Hermeticism an intellectual movement beginning in the fifteenth century that taught that divinity is embodied in all aspects of nature; included works on alchemy and magic as well as theology and philosophy. The tradition continued into the seventeenth century and influenced many of the leading figures of the Scientific Revolution.

hetairai highly sophisticated courtesans in ancient Athens who offered intellectual and musical entertainment as well as sex.

hieroglyphics a highly pictorial system of writing most often associated with ancient Egypt. Also used (with different "pictographs") by other ancient peoples such as the Mayans.

high culture the literary and artistic culture of the educated and wealthy ruling classes.

Hinayana the scornful name for Theravada Buddhism ("lesser vehicle") used by devotees of Mahayana Buddhism.

Hinduism the main religion in India, it emphasizes reincarnation, based on the results of the previous life, and the desirability of escaping this cycle. Its various forms feature both asceticism and the pleasures of ordinary life, and encompass a multitude of gods as different manifestations of one ultimate reality.

Holocaust the mass slaughter of European Jews by the Nazis during World War II.

Hopewell culture a Native American society that flourished from about 200 B.C.E. to 400 C.E., noted for large burial mounds and extensive manufacture. Largely based in Ohio, its traders ranged as far as the Gulf of Mexico.

hoplites heavily armed infantry soldiers used in ancient Greece in a phalanx formation.

Huguenots French Calvinists.

humanism an intellectual movement in Renaissance Italy based upon the study of the Greek and Roman classics.

Hundred Schools (of philosophy) in China around the third century B.C.E., a wide-ranging debate over the nature of human beings, society, and the universe. The Schools included Legalism and Daoism, as well as Confucianism.

hydraulic society a society organized around a large irrigation system.

iconoclasm an eighth-century Byzantine movement against the use of icons (pictures of sacred figures), which was condemned as idolatry.

ideology a political philosophy such as conservatism or liberalism.

imam an Islamic religious leader; some traditions say there is only one per generation, others use the term more broadly.

imperialism the policy of extending one nation's power either by conquest or by establishing direct or indirect economic or cultural authority over another. Generally driven by economic self-interest, it can also be motivated by a sincere (if often misguided) sense of moral obligation.

imperium "the right to command." In the Roman Republic, the chief executive officers (consuls and praetors) possessed the *imperium*; a military commander was an *imperator*. In the Roman Empire, the title *imperator*, or emperor, came to be used for the ruler.

indirect representation a system of choosing delegates to a representative assembly in which citizens do not choose the delegates directly but instead vote for electors who choose the delegates.

indirect rule a colonial policy of foreign rule in cooperation with local political elites; implemented in much of India and Malaya, and parts of Africa, it was not feasible where resistance was greater.

individualism emphasis on and interest in the unique traits of each person.

indulgence the remission of part or all of the temporal punishment in purgatory due to sin; granted for charitable contributions and other good deeds. Indulgences became a regular practice of the Christian church in the High Middle Ages, and their abuse was instrumental in sparking Luther's reform movement in the sixteenth century.

infanticide the practice of killing infants.

inflation a sustained rise in the price level.

intifada the "uprising" of Palestinians living under Israeli control, especially in the 1980s and 1990s.

intendants royal officials in seventeenth-century France who were sent into the provinces to execute the orders of the central government.

intervention, principle of the idea, after the Congress of Vienna, that the great powers of Europe had the right to send armies into countries experiencing revolution to restore legitimate monarchs to their thrones.

Islam the religion derived from the revelations of Muhammad, the Prophet of Allah; literally, "submission" (to the will of Allah); also the culture and civilization based upon the faith.

isolationism a foreign policy in which a nation refrains from making alliances or engaging actively in international affairs.

Jainism an Indian religion, founded in the fifth century B.C.E., which stresses extreme simplicity.

Janissaries an elite core of eight thousand troops personally loyal to the sultan of the Ottoman Empire.

jati a kinship group, the basic social organization of traditional Indian society, to some extent specialized by occupation.

jihad In Islam, "striving in the way of the Lord." The term is ambiguous and has been subject to varying interpretations, from the practice of conducting raids against local neighbors to the conduct of "holy war" against unbelievers.

joint-stock company a company or association that raises capital by selling shares to individuals who receive dividends on their investment while a board of directors runs the company.

joint-stock investment bank a bank created by selling shares of stock to investors. Such banks potentially have access to much more capital than do private banks owned by one or a few individuals.

Jomon the earliest known Neolithic inhabitants of Japan, named for the cord pattern of their pottery.

justification by faith the primary doctrine of the Protestant Reformation; taught that humans are saved not through good works, but by the grace of God, bestowed freely through the sacrifice of Jesus.

Kabuki a form of Japanese theater which developed in the seventeenth century C.E.; originally disreputable, it became a highly stylized art form.

kami spirits who were worshiped in early Japan, and resided in trees, rivers and streams. See Shinto.

karma a fundamental concept in Hindu (and later Buddhist, Jain, and Sikh) philosophy, that rebirth in a future life is determined by actions in this or other lives; the word refers to the entire process, to the individual's actions, and also to the cumulative result of those actions, for instance a store of good or bad karma.

keiretsu a type of powerful industrial or financial conglomerate that emerged in post–World War II Japan following the abolition of zaibatsu.

khanates Mongol kingdoms, in particular the subdivisions of Genghis Khan's empire ruled by his heirs.

kokutai the core ideology of the Japanese state, particularly during the Meiji Restoration, stressing the uniqueness of the Japanese system and the supreme authority of the emperor.

kolkhoz a collective farm in the Soviet Union, in which the great bulk of the land was held and worked communally. Between 1928 and 1934, 250,000 kolkhozes replaced 26 million family farms.

kshatriya originally, the warrior class of Aryan society in India; ranked below (sometimes equal to) brahmins, in modern times often government workers or soldiers.

laissez-faire "to let alone." An economic doctrine that holds that an economy is best served when the government does not interfere but allows the economy to self-regulate according to the forces of supply and demand.

latifundia large landed estates in the Roman Empire (singular: *latifundium*).

lay investiture the practice in which a layperson chose a bishop and invested him with the symbols of both his temporal office and his spiritual office; led to the Investiture Controversy, which was ended by compromise in the Concordat of Worms in 1122.

Lebensraum "living space." The doctrine, adopted by Hitler, that a nation's power depends on the amount of land it occupies; thus, a nation must expand to be strong.

Legalism a Chinese philosophy that argued that human beings were by nature evil and would follow the correct path only if coerced by harsh laws and stiff punishments. Adopted as official ideology by the Qin dynasty, it was later rejected but remained influential.

legitimacy, principle of the idea that after the Napoleonic wars peace could best be reestablished in Europe by restoring legitimate monarchs who would preserve traditional institutions; guided Metternich at the Congress of Vienna.

Leninism Lenin's revision of Marxism that held that Russia need not experience a bourgeois revolution before it could move toward socialism.

liberal arts the seven areas of study that formed the basis of education in medieval and early modern Europe. Following Boethius and other late Roman authors, they consisted of grammar, rhetoric, and dialectic or logic (the *trivium*) and arithmetic, geometry, astronomy, and music (the *quadrivium*).

liberalism an ideology based on the belief that people should be as free from restraint as possible. Economic liberalism is the idea that the government should not interfere in the workings of the economy. Political liberalism is the idea that there should be restraints on the exercise of power so that people can enjoy basic civil rights in a constitutional state with a representative assembly.

limited liability the principle that shareholders in a joint-stock corporation can be held responsible for the corporation's debts only up to the amount they have invested.

limited (constitutional) monarchy a system of government in which the monarch is limited by a representative assembly and by the duty to rule in accordance with the laws of the land.

lineage group the descendants of a common ancestor; relatives, often as opposed to immediate family.

Longshan a Neolithic society from near the Yellow River in China, sometimes identified by its black pottery.

maharaja originally, a king in the Aryan society of early India (a great raja); later used more generally to denote an important ruler.

Mahayana a school of Buddhism that promotes the idea of universal salvation through the intercession of bodhisattvas; predominant in north Asia.

majlis a council of elders among the Bedouins of the Roman era.

mandate of Heaven the justification for the rule of the Zhou dynasty in China; the king was charged to maintain order as a representative of Heaven, which was viewed as an impersonal law of nature.

mandates a system established after World War I whereby a nation officially administered a territory (mandate) on behalf of the League of Nations. Thus, France administered Lebanon and Syria as mandates, and Britain administered Iraq and Palestine.

Manichaeanism an offshoot of the ancient Zorastrian religion, influenced by Christianity; became popular in central Asia in the eighth century C.E.

manor an agricultural estate operated by a lord and worked by peasants who performed labor services and paid various rents and fees to the lord in exchange for protection and sustenance.

Marshall Plan the European Recovery Program, under which the United States provided financial aid to European countries to help them rebuild after World War II.

Marxism the political, economic, and social theories of Karl Marx, which included the idea that history is the story of class struggle and that ultimately the proletariat will overthrow the bourgeoisie and establish a dictatorship en route to a classless society.

mass education a state-run educational system, usually free and compulsory, that aims to ensure that all children in society have at least a basic education.

mass leisure forms of leisure that appeal to large numbers of people in a society including the working classes; emerged at the end of the nineteenth century to provide workers with amusements after work and on weekends; used during the twentieth century by totalitarian states to control their populations.

mass politics a political order characterized by mass political parties and universal male and (eventually) female suffrage.

mass society a society in which the concerns of the majority—the lower classes—play a prominent role; characterized by extension of voting rights, an improved standard of living for the lower classes, and mass education.

materialism the belief that everything mental, spiritual, or ideal is an outgrowth of physical forces and that truth is found in concrete material existence, not through feeling or intuition.

matrilinear passing through the female line, for example from a father to his sister's son rather than his own, as practiced in some African societies; not necessarily, or even usually, combined with matriarchy, in which women rule.

megaliths large stones, widely used in Europe from around 4000 to 1500 B.C.E. to create monuments, including sophisticated astronomical observatories.

Meiji Restoration the period during the late 19th and early 20th century in which fundamental economic and cultural changes occured in Japan, tranforming it from a feudal and agrarian society to an industrial and technological society.

mercantilism an economic theory that held that a nation's prosperity depended on its supply of gold and silver and that the total volume of trade is unchangeable; therefore, advocated that the government play an active role in the economy by encouraging exports and discouraging imports, especially through the use of tariffs.

Mesoamerica the region stretching roughly from modern central Mexico to Honduras, in which the Olmec, Mayan, Aztec and other civilizations developed.

Mesolithic Age the period from 10,000 to 7000 C.E., characterized by a gradual transition from a food-gathering/hunting economy to a food-producing economy.

mestizos the offspring of intermarriage between Europeans, originally Spaniards, and native American Indians.

metics resident foreigners in ancient Athens; not permitted full rights of citizenship but did receive the protection of the laws.

Middle Passage the journey of slaves from Africa to the Americas as the middle leg of the triangular trade.

Middle Path a central concept of Buddhism, which advocates avoiding extremes of both materialism and asceticism; also known as the Eightfold Way.

mihrab the niche in a mosque's wall that indicates the direction of Mecca, usually containing an ornately decorated panel representing Allah.

militarism a policy of aggressive military preparedness; in particular, the large armies based on mass conscription and complex, inflexible plans for mobilization that most European nations had before World War I.

millet an administrative unit in the Ottoman empire used to organize religious groups.

ministerial responsibility a tenet of nineteenth-century liberalism that held that ministers of the monarch should be responsible to the legislative assembly rather than to the monarch.

Modernism the new artistic and literary styles that emerged in the decades before 1914 as artists rebelled against traditional efforts to portray reality as accurately as possible (leading to Impressionism and Cubism) and writers explored new forms.

monotheistic/monotheism having only one god; the doctrine or belief that there is only one god.

muezzin the man who calls Muslims to prayer at the appointed times; nowadays often a tape-recorded message played over loudspeakers.

mulattoes the offspring of Africans and Europeans, particularly in Latin America.

Munich syndrome a term used to criticize efforts to appease an aggressor, as in the Munich agreement of 1938, on the grounds that they only encourage his appetite for conquest.

mutual deterrence the belief that nuclear war could best be prevented if both the United States and the Soviet Union had sufficient nuclear weapons so that even if one nation launched a preemptive first strike, the other could respond and devastate the attacker.

mystery religions religions that involve initiation into secret rites that promise intense emotional involvement with spiritual forces and a greater chance of individual immortality.

nationalism a sense of national consciousness based on awareness of being part of a community—a "nation"—that has common institutions, traditions, language, and customs and that becomes the focus of the individual's primary political loyalty.

nationalities problem the dilemma faced by the Austro-Hungarian Empire in trying to unite a wide variety of ethnic groups including, among others, Austrians, Hungarians, Poles, Croats, Czechs, Serbs, Slovaks, and Slovenes in an era when nationalism and calls for self-determination were coming to the fore.

nationalization the process of converting a business or industry from private ownership to government control and ownership.

nation in arms the people's army raised by universal mobilization to repel the foreign enemies of the French Revolution.

nation-state a form of political organization in which a relatively homogeneous people inhabits a sovereign state, as opposed to a state containing people of several nationalities.

NATO the North Atlantic Treaty Organization; a military alliance formed in 1949 in which the signatories (Belgium, Canada, Denmark, France, Great Britain, Iceland, Italy, Luxembourg, the Netherlands, Norway, Portugal, and the United States) agreed to provide mutual assistance if any one of them was attacked; later expanded to include other nations, including former members of the Warsaw Pact—Poland, the Czech Republic, and Hungary.

natural laws a body of laws or specific principles held to be derived from nature and binding upon all human society even in the absence of positive laws.

natural rights certain inalienable rights to which all people are entitled; include the right to life, liberty, and property, freedom of speech and religion, and equality before the law.

natural selection Darwin's idea that organisms that are most adaptable to their environment survive and pass on the variations that enabled them to survive, while other, less adaptable organisms become extinct; "survival of the fittest."

Nazi New Order the Nazis' plan for their conquered territories; included the extermination of Jews and others considered inferior, ruthless exploitation of resources, German colonization in the east, and the use of Poles, Russians, and Ukrainians as slave labor.

negritude a philosophy shared among African blacks that there exists a distinctive "African personality" that owes nothing to Western values and provides a common sense of purpose and destiny for black Africans.

Neo-Confucianism the dominant ideology of China during the second millennium C.E., it combined the metaphysical speculations of Buddhism and Daoism with the pragmatic Confucian approach to society, maintaining that the world is real, not illusory, and that fulfillment comes from participation, not withdrawal. It encouraged an intellectual environment that valued continuity over change and tradition over innovation.

neocolonialism the use of economic rather than political or military means to maintain Western domination of developing nations.

Neolithic Revolution the development of agriculture, including the planting of food crops and the domestication of farm animals, around 10,000 B.C.E.

Neoplatonism a revival of Platonic philosophy; in the third century C.E., a revival associated with Plotinus; in the Italian Renaissance, a revival associated with Marsilio Ficino who attempted to synthesize Christianity and Platonism.

New Course a short-lived, liberalizing change in Soviet policy to its Eastern European allies instituted after the death of Stalin in 1953.

New Culture Movement a protest launched at Peking University after the failure of the 1911 revolution, aimed at abolishing the remnants of the old system and introducing Western values and institutions into China.

New Deal the reform program implemented by President Franklin Roosevelt in the 1930s, which included large public works projects and the introduction of Social Security.

New Democracy the initial program of the Chinese Communist government, from 1949 to 1955, focusing on honest government, land reform, social justice, and peace rather than on the utopian goal of a classless society.

New Economic Policy a modified version of the old capitalist system introduced in the Soviet Union by Lenin in 1921 to revive the economy after the ravages of the civil war and war communism.

new imperialism the revival of imperialism after 1880 in which European nations established colonies throughout much of Asia and Africa.

new monarchies the governments of France, England, and Spain at the end of the fifteenth century, where the rulers were successful in reestablishing or extending centralized royal authority, suppressing the nobility, controlling the church, and insisting upon the loyalty of all peoples living in their territories.

Nirvana in Buddhist thought, enlightenment, the ultimate transcendence from the illusion of the material world; release from the wheel of life.

nobiles "nobles." The small group of families from both patrician and plebeian origins who produced most of the men who were elected to office in the late Roman Republic.

Nok culture in northern Nigeria, one of the most active early ironworking societies in Africa, artifacts from which date back as far as 500 B.C.E.

nuclear family a family group consisting only of father, mother, and children.

nun female religious monk.

old regime/old order the political and social system of France in the eighteenth century before the Revolution.

oligarchy rule by a few.

Open Door notes a series of letters sent in 1899 by U.S. Secretary of State John Hay to Great Britain, France, Germany, Italy, Japan and Russia, calling for equal economic access to the China market for all states and for the maintenance of the territorial and administrative integrity of the Chinese Empire.

optimates "best men." Aristocratic leaders in the late Roman Republic who generally came from senatorial families and wished to retain their oligarchical privileges.

opium trade the sale of the addictive product of the poppy, specifically by British traders to China in the 1830s. Chinese attempts to prevent it led to the Opium War of 1839–1842, which resulted in British access to Chinese ports and has traditionally been considered the beginning of modern Chinese history.

orders/estates the traditional tripartite division of European society based on heredity and quality rather than wealth or economic standing, first established in the Middle Ages and continuing into the eighteenth century; traditionally consisted of those who pray (the clergy), those who fight (the nobility), and those who work (all the rest).

organic evolution Darwin's principle that all plants and animals have evolved over a long period of time from earlier and simpler forms of life.

Organization of African Unity founded in Addis Ababa in 1963, it was intended to represent the interests of all the newly independent countries of Africa and provided a forum for the discussion of common problems until 2001, when it was replaced by the African Union.

Paleolithic Age the period of human history when humans used simple stone tools (c. 2,500,000–10,000 B.C.E.).

pan-Africanism the concept of African continental unity and solidarity in which the common interests of African countries transcend regional boundaries.

pantheism a doctrine that equates God with the universe and all that is in it.

pariahs members of the lowest level of traditional Indian society, technically outside the class system itself; also known as untouchables.

pasha an administrative official of the Ottoman empire, responsible for collecting taxes and maintaining order in the provinces; later, some became hereditary rulers.

paterfamilias the dominant male in a Roman family whose powers over his wife and children were theoretically unlimited, though they were sometimes circumvented in practice.

patriarchal/patriarchy a society in which the father is supreme in the clan or family; more generally, a society dominated by men.

patriarchal family a family in which the husband/father dominates his wife and children.

patricians great landowners who became the ruling class in the Roman Republic.

patrilinear passing through the male line, from father to son; often combined with patriarchy.

patronage the practice of awarding titles and making appointments to government and other positions to gain political support.

Pax Romana "Roman peace." A term used to refer to the stability and prosperity that Roman rule brought to the Mediterranean world and much of western Europe during the first and second centuries C.E.

peaceful coexistence the policy adopted by the Soviet Union under Khrushchev in 1955, and continued by his successors, that called for economic and ideological rivalry with the West rather than nuclear war.

Pentateuch the first five books of the Hebrew Bible (Genesis, Exodus, Leviticus, Numbers, and Deuteronomy).

peoples' democracies a term invented by the Soviet Union to define a society in the early stage of socialist transition, applied to Eastern European countries in the 1950s.

perestroika "restructuring." A term applied to Mikhail Gorbachev's economic, political, and social reforms in the Soviet Union.

permissive society a term applied to Western society after World War II to reflect the new sexual freedom and the emergence of a drug culture.

Petrine supremacy the doctrine that the bishop of Rome—the pope—as the successor of Saint Peter (traditionally considered the first bishop of Rome) should hold a preeminent position in the church.

phalanx a rectangular formation of tightly massed infantry soldiers.

philosophes intellectuals of the eighteenth-century Enlightenment who believed in applying a spirit of rational criticism to all things, including religion and politics, and who focused on improving and enjoying this world, rather than on the afterlife.

plebeians the class of Roman citizens who included nonpatrician landowners, craftspeople, merchants, and small farmers in the Roman Republic. Their struggle for equal rights with the patricians dominated much of the Republic's history.

pluralism the practice in which one person holds several church offices simultaneously; a problem of the late medieval church.

pogroms organized massacres of Jews.

polis an ancient Greek city-state encompassing both an urban area and its surrounding countryside; a small but autonomous political unit where all major political and social activities were carried out in a central location.

political democracy a form of government characterized by universal suffrage and mass political parties.

politiques a group who emerged during the French Wars of Religion in the sixteenth century; placed politics above religion and believed that no religious truth was worth the ravages of civil war.

polygyny the practice of having more than one wife at a time.

polytheistic/polytheism having many gods; belief in or the worship of more than one god.

popular culture as opposed to high culture, the unofficial, written and unwritten culture of the masses, much of which was passed down orally; centers on public and group activities such as festivals. In the twentieth century, refers to the entertainment, recreation, and pleasures that people purchase as part of mass consumer society.

populares "favoring the people." Aristocratic leaders in the late Roman Republic who tended to use the people's assemblies in an effort to break the stranglehold of the *nobiles* on political offices.

popular sovereignty the doctrine that government is created by and subject to the will of the people, who are the source of all political power.

portolani charts of landmasses and coastlines made by navigators and mathematicians in the thirteenth and fourteenth centuries.

Poststructuralism a theory formulated by Jacques Derrida in the 1960s, holding that there is no fixed, universal truth since culture is created and can therefore be analyzed in various ways.

praetorian guard the military unit that served as the personal bodyguard of the Roman emperors.

praetors the two senior Roman judges, who had executive authority when the consuls were away from the city and could also lead armies.

Prakrit an ancient Indian language, a simplified form of Sanskrit.

predestination the belief, associated with Calvinism, that God, as a consequence of his foreknowledge of all events, has predetermined those who will be saved (the elect) and those who will be damned.

price revolution the dramatic rise in prices (inflation) that occurred throughout Europe in the sixteenth and early seventeenth centuries.

primogeniture an inheritance practice in which the eldest son receives all or the largest share of the parents' estate.

principate the form of government established by Augustus for the Roman Empire; continued the constitutional forms of the Republic and consisted of the *princeps* ("first citizen") and the senate, although the *princeps* was clearly the dominant partner.

proletariat the industrial working class. In Marxism, the class who will ultimately overthrow the bourgeoisie.

Protestant Reformation the western European religious reform movement in the sixteenth century C.E. that divided Christianity into Catholic and Protestant groups.

purdah the Indian term for the practice among Muslims and some Hindus of isolating women and preventing them from associating with men outside the home.

Pure Land a Buddhist sect, originally Chinese but later popular in Japan, which taught that devotion alone could lead to enlightenment and release.

Puritans English Protestants inspired by Calvinist theology who wished to remove all traces of Catholicism from the Church of England.

querelles des femmes "arguments about women." A centuries-old debate about the nature of women that continued during the Scientific Revolution as those who argued for the inferiority of women found additional support in the new anatomy and medicine.

quipu an Inka record-keeping system that used knotted strings rather than writing.

raj common name for the British colonial regime in India.

raja originally, a chieftain in the Aryan society of early India, a representative of the gods; later used more generally to denote a ruler.

Ramadan the holy month of Islam, during which believers fast from dawn to sunset; since the Islamic calendar is lunar, Ramadan migrates through the seasons.

rationalism a system of thought based on the belief that human reason and experience are the chief sources of knowledge.

realism in medieval Europe, the school of thought that, following Plato, held that the individual objects we perceive are not real but merely manifestations of universal ideas existing in the mind of God. In the nineteenth century, a school of painting that emphasized the everyday life of ordinary people, depicted with photographic realism.

Realpolitik "politics of reality." Politics based on practical concerns rather than theory or ethics.

real wages/income/prices wages/income/prices that have been adjusted for inflation.

reason of state the principle that a nation should act on the basis of its long-term interests and not merely to further the dynastic interests of its ruling family.

reincarnation the idea that the individual soul is reborn in a different form after death; in Hindu and Buddhist thought, release from this cycle is the objective of all living souls.

relativity theory Einstein's theory that holds, among other things, that (1) space and time are not absolute but are relative to the observer and interwoven into a four-dimensional space-time continuum and (2) matter is a form of energy ($E = mc^2$).

Renaissance the "rebirth" of classical culture that occurred in Italy between c. 1350 and c. 1550; also, the earlier revivals of classical culture that occurred under Charlemagne and in the twelfth century.

rentier a person who lives on income from property and is not personally involved in its operation.

reparations payments made by a defeated nation after a war to compensate another nation for damage sustained as a result of the war; required from Germany after World War I.

revisionism a socialist doctrine that rejected Marx's emphasis on class struggle and revolution and argued instead that workers should work through political parties to bring about gradual change.

revolution a fundamental change in the political and social organization of a state.

revolutionary socialism the socialist doctrine espoused by Georges Sorel who held that violent action was the only way to achieve the goals of socialism.

rhetoric the art of persuasive speaking; in the Middle Ages, one of the seven liberal arts.

Rococo a style, especially of decoration and architecture, that developed from the Baroque and spread throughout Europe by the 1730s. While still elaborate, it emphasized curves, lightness, and charm in the pursuit of pleasure, happiness, and love.

ronin Japanese warriors made unemployed by developments in the early modern era, since samurai were forbidden by tradition to engage in commerce.

rural responsibility system post-Maoist land reform in China, under which collectives leased land to peasant families, who could consume or sell their surplus production and keep the profits.

sacraments rites considered imperative for a Christian's salvation. By the thirteenth century consisted of the eucharist or Lord's Supper, baptism, marriage, penance, extreme unction, holy orders, and confirmation of children; Protestant reformers of the sixteenth century generally recognized only two—baptism and communion (the Lord's Supper).

samurai literally "retainer"; similar to European knights. Usually in service to a particular shogun, these Japanese warriors lived by a strict code of ethics and duty.

Sanskrit an early Indo-European language, in which the Vedas were composed, beginning in the second millenium B.C.E. It survived as the language of literature and the bureaucracy for centuries after its decline as a spoken tongue.

sans-culottes the common people who did not wear the fine clothes of the upper classes (sans-culottes means "without breeches") and played an important role in the radical phase of the French Revolution.

sati the Hindu ritual requiring a wife to throw herself upon her deceased husband's funeral pyre.

satori enlightenment, in the Japanese, especially Zen, Buddhist tradition.

satrap/satrapy a governor with both civil and military duties in the ancient Persian Empire, which was divided into satrapies, or provinces, each administered by a satrap.

satyagraha the Hindi term for the practice of nonviolent resistance, as advocated by Mohandas Gandhi; literally, "hold fast to the truth".

scholar-gentry in Song dynasty China, candidates who passed the civil service examinations and whose families were non-aristocratic landowners; eventually, a majority of the bureaucracy.

scholasticism the philosophical and theological system of the medieval schools, which emphasized rigorous analysis of contradictory authorities; often used to try to reconcile faith and reason.

School of Mind a philosophy espoused by Wang Yangming during the mid-Ming era of China, which argued that mind and the universe were a single unit and knowledge was therefore obtained through internal self-searching rather than through investigation of the outside world; for a while, a significant but unofficial rival to neo-Confucianism.

scientific method a method of seeking knowledge through inductive principles; uses experiments and observations to develop generalizations.

Scientific Revolution the transition from the medieval worldview to a largely secular, rational, and materialistic perspective; began in the seventeenth century and was popularized in the eighteenth.

secularization the process of becoming more concerned with material, worldly, temporal things and less with spiritual and religious things.

self-determination the doctrine that the people of a given territory or a particular nationality should have the right to determine their own government and political future.

self-strengthening a late-nineteenth-century Chinese policy, by which Western technology would be adopted while Confucian principles and institutions were maintained intact.

senate/senators the leading council of the Roman Republic; composed of about 300 men (senators) who served for life and dominated much of the political life of the Republic.

sepoys native troops hired by the East India Company to protect British interests in south Asia, who formed the basis of the British Indian Army.

serf a peasant who is bound to the land and obliged to provide labor services and pay various rents and fees to the lord; considered unfree but not a slave because serfs could not be bought and sold.

Shari'a a law code, originally drawn up by Muslim scholars shortly after the death of Muhammad, that provides believers with a set of prescriptions to regulate their daily lives.

sheikh originally, the ruler of a Bedouin tribe; later, also used as a more general honorific.

Shi'ite the second largest tradition of Islam, which split from the majority Sunni soon after the death of Muhammad, in a disagreement over the succession; especially significant in Iran and Iraq.

Shinto a kind of state religion in Japan, derived from beliefs in nature spirits and until recently linked with belief in the divinity of the emperor and the sacredness of the Japanese nation.

shogun a powerful Japanese leader, originally military, who ruled under the titular authority of the emperor.

shogunate system the system of government in Japan in which the emperor exercised only titular authority while the shogun (regional military dictators) exercised actual political power.

Sikhism a religion, founded in the early sixteenth century in the Punjab, which began as an attempt to reconcile the Hindu and Muslim traditions and developed into a significant alternative to both.

sipahis in the Ottoman empire, local cavalry elites, who held fiefdoms and collected taxes.

skepticism a doubtful or questioning attitude, especially about religion.

Social Darwinism the application of Darwin's principle of organic evolution to the social order; led to the belief that progress comes from the struggle for survival as the fittest advance and the weak decline.

socialism an ideology that calls for collective or government ownership of the means of production and the distribution of goods.

social security/social insurance government programs that provide social welfare measures such as old age pensions and sickness, accident, and disability insurance.

Socratic method a form of teaching that uses a question-and-answer format to enable students to reach conclusions by using their own reasoning.

Sophists wandering scholars and professional teachers in ancient Greece who stressed the importance of rhetoric and tended toward skepticism and relativism.

soviets councils of workers' and soldiers' deputies formed throughout Russia in 1917; played an important role in the Bolshevik Revolution.

sphere of influence a territory or region over which an outside nation exercises political or economic influence.

Star Wars nickname of the Strategic Defense Initiative, proposed by President Reagan, which was intended to provide a shield that would destroy any incoming missiles; named after a popular science-fiction movie series.

stateless societies the pre-Columbian communities in much of the Americas who developed substantial cultures without formal nation states.

State Confucianism the integration of Confucian doctrine with Legalist practice under the Han dynasty in China, which became the basis of Chinese political thought until the modern era.

Stoicism a philosophy founded by Zeno in the fourth century C.E. that taught that happiness could be obtained by accepting one's lot and living in harmony with the will of God, thereby achieving inner peace.

stupa originally a stone tower holding relics of the Buddha, more generally a place for devotion, often architecturally impressive and surmounted with a spire.

subinfeudation the practice in which a lord's greatest vassals subdivided their fiefs and had vassals of their own, and those vassals, in turn, subdivided their fiefs and so on down to simple knights whose fiefs were too small to subdivide.

Sublime Porte the office of the grand vezir in the Ottoman empire.

sudras the classes that represented the great bulk of the Indian population from ancient time, mostly peasants, artisans or manual laborers; ranked below brahmins, kshatriyas, and vaisyas, but above the pariahs.

suffrage the right to vote.

suffragists those who advocate the extension of the right to vote (suffrage), especially to women.

Sufism a mystical school of Islam, noted for its music, dance, and poetry, which became prominent in about the thirteenth century.

sultan "holder of power," a title commonly used by Muslim rulers in the Ottoman Empire, Egypt, and elsewhere; still in use in parts of Asia, sometimes for regional authorities.

Sunni the largest tradition of Islam, from which the Shi'ites split soon after the death of Muhammad, in a disagreement over the succession.

Supreme Ultimate according to Neo-Confucians, a transcendent world, distinct from the material world in which humans live, but to which humans may aspire; a set of abstract principles, roughly equivalent to the Dao.

surplus value in Marxism, the difference between a product's real value and the wages of the worker who produced the product.

Swahili a mixed African-Arabian culture that developed by the twelfth century along the east coast of Africa; also, the national language of Kenya and Tanzania.

syncretism the combining of different forms of belief or practice, as, for example, when two gods are regarded as different forms of the same underlying divine force and are fused together.

Taika reforms the seventh-century "great change" reforms that established the centralized Japanese state.

taille a French tax on land or property, developed by King Louis XI in the fifteenth century as the financial basis of the monarchy. It was largely paid by the peasantry; the nobility and the clergy were exempt.

Tantrism a mystical Buddhist sect, which emphasized the importance of magical symbols and ritual in seeking a path to enlightenment.

tariffs duties (taxes) imposed on imported goods; usually imposed both to raise revenue and to discourage imports and protect domestic industries.

tetrarchy rule by four; the system of government established by Diocletian (284–305) in which the Roman Empire was divided into two parts, each ruled by an "Augustus" assisted by a "Caesar."

theocracy a government based on a divine authority.

Theravada a school of Buddhism that stresses personal behavior and the quest for understanding as a means of release from the wheel of life, rather than the intercession of bodhisattvas; predominant in Sri Lanka and Southeast Asia.

three-field system in medieval agriculture, the practice of dividing the arable land into three fields so that one could lie fallow while the others were planted in winter grains and spring crops.

three kingdoms Koguryo, Paekche, and Silla, rivals but all under varying degrees of Chinese influence, which together controlled virtually all of Korea from the fourth to the seventh centuries.

three obediences the traditional duties of Japanese women, in permanent subservience: child to father, wife to husband, and widow to son.

tithe a tenth of one's harvest or income; paid by medieval peasants to the village church.

Tongmenghui the political organization—"Revolutionary Alliance"—formed by Sun Yat-sen in 1905, which united various revolutionary factions and ultimately toppled the Manchu dynasty.

Torah the body of law in Hebrew Scripture, contained in the Pentateuch (the first five books of the Hebrew Bible).

totalitarian state a state characterized by government control over all aspects of economic, social, political, cultural, and intellectual life, the subordination of the individual to the state, and insistence that the masses be actively involved in the regime's goals.

total war warfare in which all of a nation's resources, including civilians at home as well as soldiers in the field, are mobilized for the war effort.

trade union an association of workers in the same trade, formed to help members secure better wages, benefits, and working conditions.

transubstantiation a doctrine of the Roman Catholic church that teaches that during the eucharist the substance of the bread and wine is miraculously transformed into the body and blood of Jesus.

trench warfare warfare in which the opposing forces attack and counterattack from a relatively permanent system of trenches protected by barbed wire; characteristic of World War I.

tribunes of the plebs beginning in 494 B.C.E., Roman officials who were given the power to protect plebeians against arrest by patrician magistrates.

tribute system an important element of Chinese foreign policy, by which neighboring states paid for the privilege of access to Chinese markets, received legitimation and agreed not to harbor enemies of the Chinese Empire.

Truman Doctrine the doctrine, enunciated by Harry Truman in 1947, that the United States would provide economic aid to countries that said they were threatened by Communist expansion.

twice-born the males of the higher castes in traditional Indian society, who underwent an initiation ceremony at puberty.

tyrant/tyranny in an ancient Greek *polis* (or an Italian city-state during the Renaissance), a ruler who came to power in an unconstitutional way and ruled without being subject to the law.

uhuru "freedom" (Swahili), and so a key slogan in the African independence movements, especially in Kenya.

uji a clan in early Japanese tribal society.

ulama a convocation of leading Muslim scholars, the earliest of which shortly after the death of Muhammad drew up a law code, called the Shari'a, based largely on the Koran and the sayings of the Prophet, to provide believers with a set of prescriptions to regulate their daily lives.

umma the Muslim community, as a whole.

uncertainty principle a principle in quantum mechanics, posited by Heisenberg, that holds that one cannot determine the path of an electron because the very act of observing the electron would affect its location.

unconditional surrender complete, unqualified surrender of a nation.

uninterrupted revolution the goal of the Great Proletarian Cultural Revolution launched by Mao Zedong in 1966.

utopian socialists intellectuals and theorists in the early nineteenth century who favored equality in social and economic conditions and wished to replace private property and competition with collective ownership and cooperation; deemed impractical and "utopian" by later socialists.

vaisya the third-ranked class in traditional Indian society, usually merchants.

varna Indian classes, or castes. See caste system.

vassal a person granted a fief, or landed estate, in exchange for providing military services to the lord and fulfilling certain other obligations such as appearing at the lord's court when summoned and making a payment on the knighting of the lord's eldest son.

veneration of ancestors the extension of filial piety to include care for the deceased, for instance by burning replicas of useful objects to accompany them on their journey to the next world.

vernacular the everyday language of a region, as distinguished from a language used for special purposes. For example, in medieval Paris, French was the vernacular, but Latin was used for academic writing and for classes at the University of Paris.

Vietnam syndrome the presumption, from the 1970s on, that the U.S. public would object to a protracted military entanglement abroad, such as another Vietnam-type conflict.

vizier (*also*, vezir) the prime minister in the Abbasid caliphate and elsewhere, a chief executive.

volkish thought the belief that German culture is superior and that the German people have a universal mission to save Western civilization from inferior races.

war communism Lenin's policy of nationalizing industrial and other facilities and requisitioning the peasants' produce during the civil war in Russia.

War Guilt Clause the clause in the Treaty of Versailles that declared that Germany (and Austria) were responsible for starting World War I and ordered Germany to pay reparations for the damage the Allies had suffered as a result of the war.

Warsaw Pact a military alliance, formed in 1955, in which Albania, Bulgaria, Czechoslovakia, East Germany, Hungary, Poland, Romania, and the Soviet Union agreed to provide mutual assistance. Dissolved in 1991, most former members eventually joined NATO.

welfare state a social/political system in which the government assumes the primary responsibility for the social welfare of its citizens by providing such things as social security, unemployment benefits, and health care.

well field system the theoretical pattern of land ownership in early China, named for the appearance of the Chinese character for "well," in which farmland was divided into nine segments and a peasant family would cultivate one for their own use and cooperate with seven others to cultivate the ninth for the landlord.

wergeld "money for a man." In early Germanic law, a person's value in monetary terms, which was paid by a wrongdoer to the family of the person who had been injured or killed.

White Lotus a Chinese Buddhist sect, founded in 1133 C.E., that sought political reform; in 1796–1804, a Chinese peasant revolt.

women's liberation movement the struggle for equal rights for women, which has deep roots in history but achieved new prominence under this name in the 1960s, building on the work of, among others, Simone de Beauvoir and Betty Friedan.

world-machine Newton's conception of the universe as one huge, regulated, and uniform machine that operated according to natural laws in absolute time, space, and motion.

Yangshao a Neolithic society from near the Yellow River in China, sometimes identified by its painted pottery.

Young Turks a successful Turkish reformist group in the late nineteenth and early twentieth centuries.

zaibatsu powerful business cartels formed in Japan during the Meiji era and outlawed following World War II.

zamindars Indian tax collectors, who were assigned land, from which they kept part of the revenue; the British revived the system in a misguided attempt to create a landed gentry.

Zen Buddhism (in Chinese, Chan or Ch'an) a school of Buddhism particularly important in Japan, some of whose adherents stress that enlightenment (satori) can be achieved suddenly, though others emphasize lengthy meditation.

ziggurat a massive stepped tower upon which a temple dedicated to the chief god or goddess of a Sumerian city was built.

Zionism an international movement that called for the establishment of a Jewish state or a refuge for Jews in Palestine.

Zoroastrianism a religion founded by the Persian Zoroaster in the seventh century C.E.; characterized by worship of a supreme god Ahuramazda who represents the good against the evil spirit, identified as Ahriman.

PRONUNCIATION GUIDE

Abbasid   uh-BAH-sid *or* AB-uh-sid
Abd al-Rahman   ub-duh-rahkh-MAHN
Abu al-Abbas   uh-BOOL-uh-BUSS
Abu Bakr   uh-boo-BAHK-ur
Achebe, Chinua   ah-CHAY-bay, CHIN-wah
Achilles   uh-KIL-eez
Adenauer, Konrad   AD-uh-now-ur
aediles   EE-dylz
Aegospotami   ee-guh-SPOT-uh-mee
Aeolians   ee-OH-lee-unz
Aequi   EE-kwy
Aeschylus   ESS-kuh-luss
Aetius   ay-EE-shuss
Afrikaners   ah-fri-KAH-nurz
Agesilaus   uh-jess-uh-LAY-uss
Agincourt   AH-zhen-koor
Aguinaldo, Emilio   ah-gwee-NAHL-doh, ay-MEEL-yoh
Ahlwardt, Hermann   AHL-vart, hayr-MAHN
Ahuramazda   uh-hoor-uh-MAHZ-duh
Aix-la-Chapelle   ex-lah-shah-PELL
Ajanta   uh-JUHN-tuh
Akhenaten   ah-khuh-NAH-tun
Akhetaten   ah-khuh-TAH-tun
Akkadians   uh-KAY-dee-unz
Alaric   AL-uh-rik
Alberti, Leon Battista   al-BAYR-tee, LAY-un buh-TEESS-tuh
Albigensians   al-buh-JEN-see-unz
Albuquerque, Afonso de   AL-buh-kur-kee, ah-FAHN-soh day
Alcibiades   al-suh-BY-uh-deez
Alcuin   AL-kwin
Alemanni   al-uh-MAH-nee
al-Fatah   al-FAH-tuh
al-Hakim   al-hah-KEEM
Alia, Ramiz   AH-lee-uh, rah-MEEZ
al-Khwarizmi   al-KHWAR-iz-mee
Allah   AH-lah
al-Ma'mun   al-muh-MOON
Almeida, Francesco da   ahl-MAY-duh, frahn-CHAYSS-koh
al-Sadat, Anwar   ah-sah-DAHT, ahn-WAHR
Aidoo, Ama Ata   ah-EE-doo, AH-mah AH-tah
Amaterasu   ah-muh-teh-RAH-suh
Amenhotep   ah-mun-HOH-tep
Anasazi   ah-nuh-SAH-zee
Andreotti, Giulio   ahn-dray-AH-tee, JOOL-yoh
Andropov, Yuri   ahn-DRAHP-awf, YOOR-ee
Anjou   AHN-zhoo
Antigonid   an-TIG-uh-nid
Antigonus Gonatus   an-TIG-oh-nuss guh-NAH-tuss
Antiochus   an-TY-uh-kuss
Antonescu, Ion   an-tuh-NESS-koo, YON
Antoninus Pius   an-tuh-NY-nuss PY-uss
Anyang   ahn-YAHNG
apella   uh-PELL-uh
Apollonius   ap-uh-LOH-nee-uss
Aquinas, Thomas   uh-KWY-nuss

Arafat, Yasir   ah-ruh-FAHT, yah-SEER
aratrum   uh-RAH-trum
Arawak   AR-uh-wahk
Archimedes   ahr-kuh-MEE-deez
Argonautica   ahr-guh-NAWT-uh-kuh
Aristarchus   ar-iss-TAR-kus
Aristotle   AR-iss-tot-ul
Arjuna   ahr-JOO-nuh
Arsinoë   ahr-SIN-oh-ee
artium baccalarius   ar-TEE-um bak-uh-LAR-ee-uss
artium magister   ar-TEE-um muh-GISS-ter
Aryan   AR-ee-un
Ashikaga   ah-shee-KAH-guh
Ashkenazic   ash-kuh-NAH-zik
Ashoka   uh-SHOH-kuh
Ashurbanipal   ah-shur-BAH-nuh-pahl
Ashurnasirpal   ah-shur-NAH-zur-pahl
asiento   ah-SYEN-toh
assignat   ah-see-NYAH
Assyrians   uh-SEER-ee-unz
Astell, Mary   AST-ul
Atahualpa   ah-tuh-WAHL-puh
Attalid   AT-uh-lid
audiencias   ow-dee-en-SEE-uss
Auerstadt   OW-urr-shtaht
augur   AW-gurr
Augustine   AW-guh-steen
Aum Shinri Kyo   awm-shin-ree-KYO
Aung San Huu Kyi   AWNG-sawn-soo-chee
Aurelian   aw-REEL-yun
Auschwitz-Birkenau   OW-shvitz-BEER-kuh-now
Ausgleich   OWSS-glykh
auspices   AWSS-puh-sizz
Austerlitz   AWSS-tur-litz
Australopithecines   aw-stray-loh-PITH-uh-synz
Austrasia   awss-TRAY-zhuh
Autun   oh-TUNH
Avalokitesvara   uh-VAH-loh-kee-TESH-vuh-ruh
Avicenna   av-i-SENN-uh
Avignon   ah-veen-YOHNH
Ayacucho   ah-ya-KOO-choh
Ayodhya   ah-YOHD-hyah
Ayuthaya   ah-yoo-TY-yuh
Azerbaijan   az-ur-by-JAN
Ba'ath   BAHTH
Baader-Meinhof   BAH-durr-MYN-huff
Babeuf, Gracchus   bah-BUFF, GRAK-uss
Babur   BAH-burr
Bach, Johann Sebastian   BAKH, yoh-HAHN suh-BASS-chun
Baden-Powell, Robert   BAD-un-POW-ul
Bai Hua   by HWA
bakufu   buh-KOO-foo *or Japanese* bah-KOO-fuh
Bakunin, Michael   buh-KOON-yun
Balboa, Vasco Nuñez de   bal-BOH-uh, BAHS-koh
   NOON-yez day

Ballin, Albert   BAH-leen
Bandaranaike, Sirimavo   bahn-dur-uh-NY-uh-kuh, see-ree-MAH-voh
Banque de Belgique   BAHNK duh bel-ZHEEK
Ban Zhao   bahn ZHOW
Bao-jia   BOW-jah
Barbarossa   bar-buh-ROH-suh
Baroque   buh-ROHK
Barth, Karl   BAHRT
Basho   BAH-shoh
Bastille   bass-STEEL
Basutoland   buh-SOO-toh-land
Batista, Fulgencio   bah-TEES-tuh, full-JEN-see-oh
Bauhaus   BOW-howss
Bayazid   by-uh-ZEED
Bayle, Pierre   BELL, PYAYR
Beauharnais, Josephine de   boh-ar-NAY, zhoh-seff-FEEN duh
Beauvoir, Simone de   boh-VWAR, see-MUHN duh
Bebel, August   BAY-bul, ow-GOOST
Beccaria, Cesare   buh-KAH-ree-uh, CHAY-zuh-ray
Bechuanaland   bech-WAH-nuh-land
Bede   BEED
Begin, Menachem   BAY-gin, muh-NAH-khum
Beguines   bay-GEENZ
Beiderbecke, Bix   BY-der-bek, BIKS
Beijing   bay-ZHING
Belarus   bell-uh-ROOSS
Belgioioso, Cristina   bell-joh-YOH-soh
Belisarius   bell-uh-SAH-ree-uss
benefice   BEN-uh-fiss
Benin   bay-NEEN
Bergson, Henri   BAYRK-suhn, ahn-REE
Berlioz, Hector   BAYR-lee-ohz, hek-TOR
Berlusconi, Silvio   bayr-loo-SKOH-nee, SEEL-vee-oh
Bernhardi, Friedrich von   bayrn-HAR-dee, FREED-reekh fun
Bernini, Gian Lorenzo   bur-NEE-nee, JAHN loh-RENT-zoh
Bernstein, Eduard   BAYRN-shtyn, AY-doo-art
Bethman-Hollweg, Theobald von   BET-mun-HOHL-vek, TAY-oh-bahlt fun
Bhagavad Gita   bah-guh-vahd-GEE-tuh
Bharata Janata   BAR-ruh-tuh JAH-nuh-tuh
Bhutto, Zulfikar Ali   BOO-toh, ZOOL-fee-kahr ah-LEE
Bismarck, Otto von   BIZ-mark, OH-toh fun
Blanc, Louis   BLAHNH, LWEE
Blitzkrieg   BLITZ-kreeg
Blum, Léon   BLOOM, LAY-ohnh
Boccaccio, Giovanni   boh-KAH-choh, joe-VAH-nee
Bodichon, Barbara   boh-di-SHOHNH
Boer   BOOR *or* BOR
Boethius   boh-EE-thee-uss
Boleyn, Anne   BUH-lin *or* buh-LIN
Bolívar, Simón   boh-LEE-var, see-MOHN
Bologna   boh-LOHN-yuh
Bolsheviks   BOHL-shuh-viks
Bora, Katherina von   BOH-rah, kat-uh-REE-nuh fun
Borobudur   boh-roh-buh-DOOR
Bosnia   BAHZ-nee-uh
Bosporus   BAHSS-pruss
Bossuet, Jacques   baw-SWAY, ZHAHK
Botswana   baht-SWAH-nuh
Botta, Giuseppe   BOH-tah, joo-ZEP-pay
Botticelli, Sandro   bot-i-CHELL-ee, SAHN-droh
Boulanger, Georges   boo-lahnh-ZHAY, ZHORZH
boule   BOOL
Bracciolini, Poggio   braht-choh-LEE-nee, POH-djoh
Brahe, Tycho   BRAH, TY-koh

Brahmo Samaj   BRAH-moh suh-MAHJ
Bramante, Donato   brah-MAHN-tay, doh-NAH-toh
Brandt, Willy   BRAHNT, VIL-ee
Brasidas   BRASS-i-duss
Brest-Litovsk   BREST-li-TUFFSK
Brétigny   bray-tee-NYEE
Brezhnev, Leonid   BREZH-neff, lyee-oh-NYEET
Briand, Aristide   bree-AHNH, ah-ruh-STEED
Broz, Josip   BRAWZ, yaw-SEEP
Brunelleschi, Filippo   BROO-nuh-LESS-kee, fee-LEE-poh
Brüning, Heinrich   BRUR-ning, HYN-rikh
Bückeberg   BURK-uh-bayrk
Bulganin, Nicolai   bool-GAN-yin, nyik-uh-LY
Bund Deutscher Mädel   BOONT DOIT-chur MAY-dul
Bundesrat   BOON-duss-raht
Burckhardt, Jacob   BOORK-hart, YAK-ub
Burschenschaften   BOOR-shun-shahf-tun
Bushido   BOO-shee-doh
Cabral, Pedro   kuh-BRAL, PAY-droh
cahiers de doléances   ka-YAY duh doh-lay-AHNSS
Cai Yuanpei   TSY yoo-wan-PAY
Calais   ka-LAY
Calas, Jean   ka-LAH, ZHAHNH
Caligula   kuh LIG-yuh-luh
caliph   KAY-liff
caliphate   KAY-luh-fayt
Callicrates   kuh-LIK-ruh-teez
Calonne, Charles de   ka-LUNN, SHAHRL duh
Cambyses   kam-BY-seez
Camus, Albert   ka-MOO, ahl-BAYR
Can Vuong   kahn VWAHNG
Canaanites   KAY-nuh-nytss
Cannae   KAH-nee
Cao Cao   TSOW-tsow
Capet, Hugh   ka-PAY, YOO
Capetian   kuh-PEE-shun
Caracalla   kuh-RAK-uh-luh
Caraffa, Gian Pietro   kuh-RAH-fuh, JAHN PYAY-troh
carbonari   kar-buh-NAH-ree
Cárdenas, Lázaro   KAHR-day-nahss, LAH-zah-roh
Carolingian   kar-uh-LIN-jun
carruca   kuh-ROO-kuh
Carthage   KAHR-thij
Carthaginian   kahr-thuh-JIN-ee-un
Cartier, Jacques   kahr-TYAY, ZHAK
Casa de Contratación   KAH-sah day KOHN-trah-tahk-SYOHN
Cassiodorus   kass-ee-uh-DOR-uss
Castiglione, Baldassare   ka-steel-YOH-nay, bal-duh-SAH-ray
Castro, Fidel   KASS-troh, fee-DELL
Çatal Hüyük   chaht-ul-hoo-YOOK
Catharism   KATH-uh-riz-um
Catullus   kuh-TULL-uss
Cavendish, Margaret   KAV-un-dish
Cavour, Camillo di   kuh-VOOR, kuh-MEEL-oh dee
Ceauşescu, Nicolae   chow-SHES-koo, nee-koh-LY
celibacy   SELL-uh-buh-see
cenobitic   sen-oh-BIT-ik
Cereta, Laura   say-RAY-tuh, LOW-ruh
Cerularius, Michael   sayr-yuh-LAR-ee-uss
Cézanne, Paul   say-ZAHN, POHL
Chacabuco   chahk-ah-BOO-koh
Chaeronea   ker-uh-NEE-uh
Chaldean   kal-DEE-un
Chamorro, Violeta Barrios de   chah-MOH-roh, vee-oh-LET-uh bah-REE-ohss day

Champlain, Samuel de shonh-PLENH *or* sham-PLAYN, sahm-WEL duh

Chandragupta Maurya chun-druh-GOOP-tuh MOWR-yuh

Chang'an CHENG-AHN

chanson de geste shahn-SONH duh ZHEST

Chao Phraya chow-PRY-uh

Charlemagne SHAR-luh-mayn

Chateaubriand, François-René de shah-TOH-bree-AHNH, frahnh-SWAH-ruh-NAY duh

Châtelet, marquise du shat-LAY, mahr-KEEZ duh

Chauvet shoh-VAY

Chavín de Huántar chah-VEEN day HWAHN-tahr

Chechnya CHECH-nyuh

Cheka CHEK-uh

Chennai CHEN-ny

Chen Shuibian CHEN-shwee-BYAHN

Chiang Kai-shek CHANG ky-SHEK

Chichén Itzá chee-CHEN-eet-SAH

Chimor chee-MAWR

Chirac, Jacques shee-RAK, ZHAHK

Chongqing chung-CHING

Chrétien de Troyes kray-TYEN duh TRWAH

Chrétien, Jean kray-TYEN, ZHAHNH

Chrysoloras, Manuel kriss-uh-LAWR-uss, man-WEL

Cicero SIS-uh-roh

Cincinnatus sin-suh-NAT-uss

ciompi CHAHM-pee

Cistercians sis-TUR-shunz

Cixi TSEE-chee

Clairvaux klayr-VOH

Claudius KLAW-dee-uss

Cleisthenes KLYSS-thuh-neez

Clemenceau, Georges kluh-mahn-SOH, ZHORZH

Clovis KLOH-viss

Codreanu, Corneliu kaw-dree-AH-noo, kor-NELL-yoo

Colbert, Jean-Baptiste kohl-BAYR, ZHAHN-bap-TEEST

Colonia Agrippinensis kuh-LOH-nee-uh uh-grip-uh-NEN-suss

colonus kuh-LOH-nuss

Columbanus kah-lum-BAY-nuss

comitia centuriata kuh-MISH-ee-uh sen-choo-ree-AH-tuh

Commodus KAHM-uh-duss

Comnenus kahm-NEE-nuss

Comte, Auguste KOHNT, ow-GOOST

concilium plebis kahn-SILL-ee-um PLEE-biss

Concordat of Worms kun-KOR-dat uv WURMZ *or* VORMPS

Condorcet, Marie-Jean de konh-dor-SAY, muh-REE-ZHAHNH duh

condottieri kahn-duh-TYAY-ree

Confucius kun-FYOO-shuss

conquistador kahn-KEESS-tuh-dor

consul KAHN-sull

Contarini, Gasparo kahn-tuh-REE-nee, GAHS-puh-roh

conversos kohn-VAYR-sohz

Copán koh-PAHN

Copernicus, Nicolaus kuh-PURR-nuh-kuss, NEE-koh-lowss

Córdoba KOR-duh-buh

Corinth KOR-inth

Corpus Hermeticum KOR-pus hur-MET-i-koom

Corpus Iuris Civilis KOR-pus YOOR-iss SIV-i-liss

corregidores kuhr-reg-uh-DOR-ayss

Cortés, Hernán kor-TAYSS *or* kor-TEZ, hayr-NAHN

Corvinus, Matthias kor-VY-nuss, muh-THY-uss

Courbet, Gustave koor-BAY, goo-STAHV

Crassus KRASS-uss

Crécy kray-SEE

Credit Anstalt KRAY-deet AHN-shtahlt

Crédit Mobilier kray-DEE moh-bee-LYAY

Croatia kroh-AY-shuh

Croesus KREE-suss

cum manu koom MAH-noo

Curie, Marie kyoo-REE

Cypselus SIP-suh-luss

Cyrenaica seer-uh-NAY-uh-kuh

Dadaism DAH-duh-iz-um

Daimler, Gottlieb DYM-lur, GUHT-leeb

daimyo DYM-yoh

Dai Viet dy VYET

d'Albret, Jeanne dahl-BRAY, ZHAHN

Dalí, Salvador dah-LEE, sahl-vah-DOR

Dandin DUN-din

Danton, Georges dahn-TONH, ZHORZH

Dao de Jing DOW-deh-JING

Darius duh-RY-uss

Darmstadt DARM-shtaht

dauphin DAW-fin

David, Jacques-Louis dah-VEED, ZHAHK-LWEE

de Gaulle, Charles duh GOHL, SHAHRL

De Rerum Novarum day RAY-rum noh-VAR-um

Debelleyme, Louis-Maurice duh-buh-LAYM, LWEE-moh-REESS

Debussy, Claude duh-byoo-SEE, KLOHD

décades day-KAD

Decameron dee-KAM-uh-run

decarchies DEK-ar-keez

decemviri duh-SEM-vuh-ree

Deffand, marquise du duh-FAHNH, mar-KEEZ doo

Dei-Anang DAY-ah-NAHNG

Deir el Bahri dayr-ahl-BAH-ree

Delacroix, Eugène duh-lah-KRWAH, oo-ZHEN

Démar, Claire DAY-mar

Demosthenes duh-MAHSS-thuh-neez

Deng Xiaoping DENG-show-PING

Denikin, Anton dyin-YEE-kin, ahn-TOHN

Desai, Anita dess-SY

descamisados dayss-kah-mee-SAH-dohss

Descartes, René day-KART, ruh-NAY

Dessau DESS-ow

d'Este, Isabella DESS-tay, ee-suh-BELL-uh

détente day-TAHNT

devshirme dev-SHEER-may

dharma DAR-muh

d'Holbach, Paul dohl-BAHK, POHL

dhoti DOH-tee

Diaghilev, Sergei DYAHG-yuh-lif, syir-GAY

Dias, Bartholomeu DEE-ush, bar-toh-loh-MAY-oo

Diaspora dy-ASS-pur-uh

Diderot, Denis dee-DROH, duh-NEE

Ding Ling DING LING

Diocletian dy-uh-KLEE-shun

Disraeli, Benjamin diz-RAY-lee

Djibouti juh-BOO-tee

Djoser ZHOH-sur

Dollfuss, Engelbert DAWL-fooss, ENG-ul-bayrt

Domesday Book DOOMZ-day book

Domitian doh-MISH-un

Donatello, Donato di doh-nuh-TELL-oh, doh-NAH-toh dee

Donatist DOH-nuh-tist

Donatus duh-NAY-tus

Dopolavoro duh-puh-LAH-vuh-roh

Dorians DOR-ee-unz

Doryphoros   doh-RIF-uh-rohss
Dostoevsky, Fyodor   dus-tuh-YEF-skee, FYUD-ur
Douhet, Giulio   doo-AY, JOOL-yoh
Dreyfus, Alfred   DRY-fuss
Du Bois, W. E. B.   doo-BOISS
Dubček, Alexander   DOOB-chek
Dufay, Guillaume   doo-FAY, gee-YOHM
Duma   DOO-muh
Duong Thu Huong   ZHWAHNG too HWAHNG
Dupleix, Joseph-François   doo-PLEKS
Dürer, Albrecht   DOO-rur, AHL-brekht
Dzerzhinksy, Felix   djur-ZHIN-skee
Ebert, Friedrich   AY-bayrt, FREE-drikh
ecclesia   ek-KLEE-zee-uh
Eckhart, Meister   EK-hart, MY-stur
Einsatzgruppen   YN-zahtz-groop-un
Einstein, Albert   YN-styn
Ekaterinburg   i-kat-tuh-RIN-burk
Emecheta, Buchi   ay-muh-CHAY-tuh, BOO-chee
encomienda   en-koh-MYEN-duh
Engels, Friedrich   ENG-ulz, FREE-drikh
Enki   EN-kee
Enlil   EN-lil
Entente Cordiale   ahn-TAHNT kor-DYAHL
entrepôt   ahn-truh-POH
Epaminondas   i-PAM-uh-NAHN-duss
Ephesus   EFF-uh-suss
ephor   EFF-ur
Epicureanism   ep-i-kyoo-REE-uh-ni-zum
Epicurus   ep-i-KYOOR-uss
episcopos   i-PIS-kuh-puss
equestrians   i-KWES-tree-unz
equites   EK-wuh-teez
Erasistratus   er-uh-SIS-truh-tuss
Erasmus, Desiderius   i-RAZZ-mus, dez-i-DEER-ee-uss
Eratosthenes   er-uh-TAHSS-thuh-neez
eremitical   er-uh-MIT-i-kul
Erhard, Ludwig   AYR-hart, LOOD-vik
Estonia   ess-TOH-nee-uh
Etruscans   i-TRUSS-kunz
Euclid   YOO-klid
Euripides   yoo-RIP-uh-deez
exchequer   EKS-chek-ur
Execrabilis   ek-suh-KRAB-uh-liss
Eylau   Y-low
Falange   fuh-LANJ
Fang Lizhu   FAHNG lee-ZHOO
fasces   FASS-eez
Fascio di Combattimento   FASH-ee-oh dee com-bat-ee-MEN-toh
Fatimid   FAT-i-mid
Fedele, Cassandra   FAY-duh-lee
Feltre, Vittorino da   FELL-tray, vee-tor-EE-noh dah
Ficino, Marsilio   fee-CHEE-noh, mar-SIL-yoh
Fischer, Joschka   FISH-ur, YUSH-kah
Flaubert, Gustave   floh-BAYR, goo-STAHV
Fleury, Cardinal   floo-REE
fluyt   FLYT
Foch, Ferdinand   FUSH, fayr-di-NAWNH
Fontainebleau   FAWNH-ten-bloh
Fontenelle, Bernard de   fawnt-NELL, bayr-NAHR duh
Fouquet, Nicolas   foo-KAY, nee-koh-LAH
Fourier, Charles   foo-RYAY, SHAHRL
Francesca, Piero della   frahn-CHESS-kuh, PYAY-roh del-luh
Freud, Sigmund   FROID, SIG-mund *or* ZIG-munt
Friedan, Betty   free-DAN

Friedland   FREET-lahnt
Friedrich, Caspar David   FREED-rikh, kass-PAR dah-VEET
Froissart, Jean   frwah-SAR, ZHAHNH
Fronde   FROHND
Fu Xi   foo SHEE
Fu Xuan   foo SHWAHN
fueros   FWYA-rohss
Führerprinzip   FYOOR-ur-prin-TSEEP
Fujiwara   foo-jee-WAH-rah
gabelle   gah-BELL
Gaiseric   GY-zuh-rik
Galba   GAHL-buh
Galilei, Galileo   GAL-li-lay, gal-li-LAY-oh
Gama, Vasco da   GAHM-uh, VAHSH-koh dah
Gandhi, Mohandas (**Mahatma**)   GAHN-dee, moh-HAHN-dus
   (mah-HAHT-muh)
Garibaldi, Giuseppe   gar-uh-BAHL-dee, joo-ZEP-pay
Gasperi, Alcide de   GAHSS-puh-ree, ahl-SEE-day day
Gatti de Gamond, Zoé   gah-TEE duh gah-MOHNH, zoh-AY
Gaugamela   gaw-guh-MEE-luh
Gelasius   juh-LAY-shuss
Genghis Khan   JING-uss *or* GENG-uss KAHN
genin   gay-NIN
Gentileschi, Artemisia   jen-tuh-LESS-kee, ar-tuh-MEE-zhuh
Geoffrin, Marie-Thérèse de   zhoh-FRENH, ma-REE-tay-RAYZ duh
gerousia   juh-ROO-see-uh
Gesamtkunstwerk   guh-ZAHMT-koonst-vayrk
Gierek, Edward   GYER-ek, ED-vahrt
Gilgamesh   GILL-guh-mesh
Giolitti, Giovanni   joh-LEE-tee, joe-VAHN-nee
Giotto   JOH-toh
Girondins   juh-RAHN-dinz
glasnost   GLAHZ-nohst
Gleichschaltung   glykh-SHAHL-toonk
Goebbels, Joseph   GUR-bulz
Goethe, Johann Wolfgang von   GUR-tuh, yoh-HAHN VULF-gahnk fun
Gokhale, Gopal   GOH-ku-lay, goh-PAHL
Gömbös, Julius   GUM-buhsh
Gomulka, Wladyslaw   goh-MOOL-kuh, vlah-DIS-lahf
gonfaloniere   gun-fah-loh-NYAY-ray
Gonzaga, Gian Francesco   gun-DZAH-gah, JAHN frahn-CHES-koh
Gorbachev, Mikhail   GOR-buh-chof, meek-HAYL
Göring, Hermann   GUR-ing, hayr-MAHN
Gottwald, Clement   GAWT-valt, klay-MENT
Gouges, Olympe   GOOZH, oh-LAMP
Gracchus, Tiberius and Gaius   GRAK-us, ty-BEER-ee-uss *and* GY-uss
grandi   GRAHN-dee
Grieg, Edvard   GREEG, ED-vart
Groote, Gerard   GROH-tuh
Gropius, Walter   GROH-pee-uss, VAHL-tuh
Grossdeutsch   GROHS-doich
Groza, Petra   GRO-zhuh, PET-ruh
Guan Yin   gwahn-YIN
Guangdong   gwahng-DUNG
Guangxu   gwahng-SHOO
Guangzhou   gwahng-JOH
Guaraní   gwahr-uh-NEE
Guicciardini, Francesco   gwee-char-DEE-nee, frahn-CHESS-koh
Guindorf, Reine   GWIN-dorf, RY-nuh
Guise   GEEZ
Guizot, François   gee-ZOH, frahnh-SWAH

Gujarat goo-juh-RAHT
Guomindang gwoh-min-DAHNG
Gustavus Adolphus goo-STAY-vus uh-DAHL-fuss
Gutenberg, Johannes GOO-ten-bayrk, yoh-HAH-nuss
Guzman, Gaspar de goos-MAHN, gahs-PAR day
Habsburg HAPS-burg
Hadith huh-DEETH
Hadrian HAY-dree-un
Hagia Sophia HAG-ee-uh soh-FEE-uh
hajj HAJ
Hammurabi hahm-uh-RAH-bee
Han Gaozu HAHN gow-DZOO
Han Wudi HAHN woo-DEE
Handel, George Friedrich HAN-dul
Hankou HAHN-kow
Hannibal HAN-uh-bul
Hanukkah HAH-nuh-kuh
Harappa huh-RAP-uh
Hardenberg, Karl von HAR-den-bayrk, KARL fun
Harun al-Rashid huh-ROON ah-rah-SHEED
Hassan ben Sabbah khah-SAHN ben shah-BAH
Hatshepsut hat-SHEP-soot
Haushofer, Karl HOWSS-hoh-fuh
Haussmann, Baron HOWSS-mun
Havel, Vaclav HAH-vul, VAHT-slahf
Haydn, Franz Joseph HY-dun, FRAHNTS YO-zef
Hedayat, Sadeq hay-DY-yaht, sah-DEK
hegemon HEJ-uh-mun
Hegira hee-JY-ruh
Heian hay-AHN
Heisenberg, Werner HY-zun-bayrk, VAYR-nur
heliaea HEE-lee-ee
Hellenistic hel-uh-NIS-tik
helots HEL-uts
Heraclius he-ruh-KLY-uss *or* huh-RAK-lee-uss
Herculaneum hur-kyuh-LAY-nee-um
Herodotus huh-ROD-uh-tuss
Herophilus huh-ROF-uh-luss
Herzegovina HAYRT-suh-guh-VEE-nuh
Herzen, Alexander HAYRT-sun
Herzl, Theodor HAYRT-sul, TAY-oh-dor
Heshen HEH-shen
Hesiod HEE-see-ud
Hesse, Hermann HESS-uh, hayr-MAHN
hetairai huh-TY-ry
Heydrich, Reinhard HY-drikh, RYN-hart
Hideyoshi, Toyotomi hee-day-YOH-shee, toh-yoh-
    TOH-mee
hieroglyph HY-uh-roh-glif
Hildegard of Bingen HIL-duh-gard uv BING-un
Hindenburg, Paul von HIN-den-boork, POWL fun
Hiroshima hee-roh-SHEE-muh
Hisauchi, Michio hee-sah-OO-chee, mee-CHEE-OH
Hitler Jugend HIT-luh YOO-gunt
Ho Chi Minh HOH CHEE MIN
Höch, Hannah HURKH
Hohenstaufen hoh-en-SHTOW-fen
Hohenzollern hoh-en-TSULL-urn
Hohenzollern-Sigmaringen hoh-en-TSULL-urn-zig-mah-
    RING-un
Hokkaido hoh-KY-doh
Hokusai HOH-kuh-sy
Holtzendorf HOHLT-sen-dorf
Homo sapiens HOH-moh SAY-pee-unz
Honecker, Erich HOH-nek-uh, AY-reekh
Hong Xiuquan HOONG shee-oo-CHWAHN

Honorius hoh-NOR-ee-uss
hoplites HAHP-lyts
Horace HOR-uss
Horthy, Miklós HOR-tee, MIK-lohsh
Hosokawa, Mirohiro hoh-soh-KAH-wah, mee-roh-HEE-roh
Höss, Rudolf HURSS
Hoxha, Enver HAW-jah, EN-vayr
Huang Di hwahng-DEE
Huayna Inca WY-nuh INK-uh
Huê HWAY
Huguenots HYOO-guh-nots
Huitzilopochtli WEET-see-loh-POHCHT-lee
Humayun hoo-MY-yoon
Husák, Gustav HOO-sahk, goo-STAHV
Ibn Saud ib-un-sah-OOD
Ibn Sina ib-un SEE-nuh
iconoclasm y-KAHN-uh-claz-um
Ictinus ik-TY-nuss
Ife EE-fay
Ignatius of Loyola ig-NAY-shuss uv loi-OH-luh
Il Duce eel DOO-chay
Île-de-France EEL-duh-fronhss
illustrés ee-loo-STRAY
illustrissimi ee-loo-STREE-see-mee
imperator im-puh-RAH-tur
imperium im-PEER-ee-um
intendant anh-tahnh-DAHNH *or* in-TEN-dunt
Irigoyen, Hipólito ee-ree-GOH-yen, ee-POH-lee-toh
Isis Y-sis
Issus ISS-uss
Iturbide, Agustín de ee-tur-BEE-day, ah-goo-STEEN dat
Itzamna eet-SAHM-nuh
ius civile YOOSS see-VEE-lay
ius gentium YOOSS GEN-tee-um
ius naturale YOOSS nah-too-RAH-lay
Izanagi ee-zah-NAH-gee
Izanami ee-zah-NAH-mee
Izvestia iz-VESS-tee-uh
Jacobin JAK-uh-bin
Jacquerie zhak-REE
Jadwiga yahd-VEE-guh
Jagiello yahg-YEL-oh
Jahn, Friedrich Ludwig YAHN, FREED-rikh LOOD-vik
jati JAH-tee
Jaufré Rudel zhoh-FRAY roo-DEL
Jaurès, Jean zhaw-RESS, ZHAHNH
Jena YAY-nuh
Jiang Qing jahng-CHING
Jiang Zemin JAHNG zuh-MIN
Jiangxi JAHNG-shee
jihad jee-HAHD
Jinnah, Mohammed Ali JIN-uh, moh-HAM-ed ah-LEE
Joffre, Joseph ZHUFF-ruh, zhoh-ZEFF
Journal des Savants zhoor-NAHL day sah-VAHNH
Juana Inés de la Cruz, Sor HWAH-nuh ee-NAYSS day lah
    KROOZ, SAWR
Judaea joo-DEE-uh
Judas Maccabaeus JOO-dus mak-uh-BEE-uss
Jung, Carl YOONG
Junkers YOONG-kurz
Jupiter Optimus Maximus JOO-puh-tur AHP-tuh-muss
    MAK-suh-muss
Jurchen roor-ZHEN
Justinian juh-STIN-ee-un
Juvenal JOO-vuh-nul
Ka'aba KAH-buh
Kádár, János KAH-dahr, YAH-nush

Kalidasa   kah-lee-DAH-suh
kamikaze   kah-mi-KAH-zee
Kanagawa   kah-nah-GAH-wah
Kanchipuram   kahn-CHEE-poo-rum
Kandinsky, Wassily   kan-DIN-skee, vus-YEEL-yee
Kang Youwei   KAHNG yow-WAY
Kangxi   GANG-zhee
Kanishka   kuh-NISH-kuh
Kant, Immanuel   KAHNT, i-MAHN-yoo-el
Karisma Kapoor   kuh-RIZ-muh kuh-POOR
Karlowitz   KARL-oh-vits
Karlsbad   KARLSS-baht
Kaunitz, Wenzel von   KOW-nits, VENT-sul fun
Kautilya   kow-TIL-yuh
Kazakhstan   ka-zak-STAN *or* kuh-zahk-STAHN
Kemal Atatürk, Mustafa   kuh-MAHL ah-tah-TIRK, moos-tah-FAH
Kenyatta, Jomo   ken-YAHT-uh, JOH-moh
Kerensky, Alexander   kuh-REN-skee
Keynes, John Maynard   KAYNZ
Khadija   kaha-DEE-jah
Khajuraho   khah-joo-RAH-hoh
Khanbaliq   khahn-bah-LEEK
Khomeini, Ayatollah Ruholla   khoh-MAY-nee, ah-yah-TUL-uh roo-HUL-uh
Khrushchev, Nikita   KHROOSH-chawf, nuh-KEE-tuh
Khubilai Khan   KOO-bluh KAHN
Kikuya   ki-KOO-yuh
Kilwa   KIL-wuh
Kim Dae Jung   kim day JOONG
Kim Il Sung   kim il SOONG
Kirghiz   keer-GEEZ
Kleindeutsch   KLYN-doich
Knesset   kuh-NESS-it
Koguryo   koh-GOOR-yoh
Kohl, Helmut   KOHL, HEL-moot
koiné   koi-NAY
Koizumi, Junichero   koh-ee-ZOO-mee, joo-nee-CHAY-roh
kokutai   koh-kuh-TY
Kolchak, Alexander   kul-CHAHK
Kollantai, Alexandra   kul-lun-TY
Kongxi   koong-SHEE
Königgrätz   kur-nig-GRETS
Kornilov, Lavr   kor-NYEE-luff, LAH-vur
Koryo   KAWR-yoh
Kosciuszko, Thaddeus   kaw-SHOOS-koh, tah-DAY-oosh
Kosovo   KAWSS-suh-voh
Kossuth, Louis   KAWSS-uth *or* KAW-shoot
Kostunica, Vojislav   kuh-STOO-nit-suh, VOH-yee-slav
Kosygin, Alexei   kuh-SEE-gun, uh-LEK-say
kouros   KOO-rohss
Koyaanisqatsi   koh-YAH-niss-kaht-see
Kraft durch Freude   KRAHFT doorkh FROI-duh
Kreditanstalt   kray-deet-AHN-shtalt
Krishna   KRISH-nuh
Kristallnacht   kri-STAHL-nahkht
Krupp, Alfred   KROOP
Kuchuk-Kainarji   koo-CHOOK-ky-NAR-jee
Kukulcan   koo-kul-KAHN
kulaks   KOO-lahks
Kulturkampf   kool-TOOR-kahmpf
Kun, Béla   KOON, BAY-luh
Kundera, Milan   koon-DAYR-uh, MEE-lahn
Kursk   KOORSK
Kushanas   koo-SHAH-nuz
Kwasniewski, Aleksander   kwahsh-NYEF-skee

Kyangyi   kyang-YEE
Kyoto   KYOH-toh
Kyushu   KYOO-shoo
la belle époque   lah BEL ay-PUK
Lafayette, marquis de   lah-fay-ET, mar-KEE duh
laissez-faire   less-ay-FAYR
Lamarck, Jean-Baptiste   lah-MARK, ZHAHNH-bah-TEEST
Lancaster   LAN-kas-tur
Lao Tzu   LOW-dzuh
La Rochefoucauld-Liancourt, duc de   lah-RUSH-foo-koh-lee-ahnh-KOOR, dook duh
Las Navas de Tolosa   lahss nah-vahss day toh-LOH-suh
latifundia   lat-i-FOON-dee-uh
Latium   LAY-shum
Latvia   LAT-vee-uh
Launay, marquis de   loh-NAY, mar-KEE duh
Laurier, Wilfred   LOR-ee-ay
Lavoisier, Antoine   lah-vwah-ZYAY, an-TWAHN
Lazar   lah-ZAR
Le Tellier, François Michel   luh tel-YAY, frahnh-SWAH mee-SHEL
Lebensraum   LAY-benz-rowm
Lee Kuan-yew   LEE-kwahn-YOO
Les Demoiselles d'Avignon   lay dem-wah ZEL dah-vee-NYOHNH
Lespinasse, Julie de   less-pee-NAHSS, zhoo-LEE duh
Lévesque, René   lay-VEK, ruh-NAY
Leviathan   luh-VY-uh-thun
Leyster, Judith   LESS-tur
Liège   lee-EZH
Li Su   lee SOO
Li Yuan   lee YWAHN
Li Zicheng   lee zee-CHENG
Liaodong   LYOW-doong
Licinius   ly-SIN-ee-uss
Liebenfels, Lanz von   LEE-bun-felss, LAHNTS fun
Liebknecht, Karl   LEEP-knekht
Liebknecht, Wilhelm   LEEP-knekht, VIL-helm
Liliuokalani   LIL-ee-uh-woh-kuh-LAH-nee
Lin Zexu   LIN dzeh-SHOO
Lindisfarne   LIN-dis-farn
Lionne, Hugues de   LYUN, OOG duh
List, Friedrich   LIST, FREED-rikh
Liszt, Franz   LIST, FRAHNTS
Lithuania   lith-WAY-nee-uh
Liu Bang   lyoo BAHNG
Liu Ling   lyoo LING
Liu Shaoqi   lyoo show-CHEE
Livy   LIV-ee
Longshan   loong-SHAHN
L'Ouverture, Toussaint   loo-vayr-TOOR, too-SANH
Louvois   loo-VWAH
Lu Xun   loo SHUN
Lucretius   loo-KREE-shus
Luddites   LUD-yts
Ludendorff, Erich   LOO-dun-dorf
Lueger, Karl   LOO-gur
Luftwaffe   LOOFT-vahf-uh
l'uomo universale   LWOH-moh OO-nee-vayr-SAH-lay
Luoyang   LWOH-yahng
Lützen   LURT-sun
Luxemburg, Rosa   LOOK-sum-boork
Lyons   LYOHNH
Maastricht   MAHSS-trikht
Ma'at   MAH-ut
Macao   muh-KOW

Machiavelli, Niccolò mahk-ee-uh-VEL-ee, nee-koh-LOH
Maginot Line MA-zhi-noh lyn
Magna Graecia MAG-nuh GREE-shuh
Magyars MAG-yarz
Mahabharata muh-hahb-huh-RAH-tuh
maharaja mah-huh-RAH-juh
Mahavira mah-hah-VEE-ruh
Mahayana mah-huh-YAH-nuh
Mahfouz, Naguib mahkh-FOOZ, nah-GEEB
Mahmud of Ghazni MAHKH-mood uv GAHZ-nee
Maimonides my-MAH-nuh-deez
Maistre, Joseph de MESS-truh, zhoh-ZEF duh
maius imperium MY-yoos im-PEE-ree-um
Malaysia muh-LAY-zhuh
Malaya muh-LAY-uh
Malenkov, Georgy muh-LEN-kuf, gyee-OR-gyee
Mallarmé, Stéphane mah-lahr-MAY, stay-FAHN
Malleus Maleficarum mal-EE-uss mal-uh-FIK-uh-rum
Malthus, Thomas MAWL-thuss
Mamallapuram muh-MAH-luh-poor-um
Manchukuo man-CHOO-kwoh
Manetho MAN-uh-thoh
Mao Dun mow DOON
Mao Zedong mow zee-DOONG
Marconi, Guglielmo mahr-KOH-nee, gool-YEL-moh
Marcus Aurelius MAR-kuss aw-REE-lee-uss
Marcuse, Herbert mar-KOO-zuh
Marie Antoinette muh-REE an-twuh-NET
Marius MAR-ee-uss
Marquez, Gabriel Garcia mar-KEZ
Marseilles mar-SAY
Marsiglio of Padua mar-SIL-yoh uv PAD-juh-wuh
Masaccio muh-ZAH-choh
Masaryk, Thomas MAS-uh-rik
Mästlin, Michael MEST-lin
Matteotti, Giacomo mat-tay-AHT-tee, JAHK-uh-moh
Maxentius mak-SEN-shuss
Maximian mak-SIM-ee-un
Maya MY-uh
Mazarin maz-uh-RANH
Mazzini, Giuseppe maht-SEE-nee, joo-ZEP-pay
Megasthenes muh-GAS-thuh-neez
Mehmet meh-MET
Meiji MAY-jee
Mein Kampf myn KAHMPF
Meir, Golda may-EER
Melanchthon, Philip muh-LANK-tun
Menander muh-NAN-dur
Mencius MEN-shuss
Mendeleyev, Dmitri men-duh-LAY-ef, di-MEE-tree
Mensheviks MENS-shuh-viks
Mercator, Gerardus mur-KAY-tur, juh-RAHR-dus
Merian, Maria Sibylla MAY-ree-un
Merovingian meh-ruh-VIN-jee-un
Mesopotamia mess-uh-puh-TAY-mee-uh
Messiaen, Olivier meh-SYANH, oh-lee-VYAY
mestizos mess-TEE-zohz
Metaxas, John muh-tahk-SAHSS
Metternich, Klemens von MET-ayr-nikh, KLAY-menss fun
Mexica meh-SHEE-kuh
Michel, Louise mee-SHEL
Michelangelo my-kuh-LAN-juh-loh
Mieszko MYESH-koh
millet mi-LET
Millet, Jean-François mi-YEH, ZHAHNH-frahnh-SWAH
Milošević, Slobodan mi-LOH-suh-vich, sluh-BOH-dahn

Miltiades mil-TY-uh-deez
Minamoto Yoritomo mee-nah-MOH-toh, yoh-ree-TOH-moh
Minseito MEEN-say-toh
Mirandola, Pico della mee-RAN-doh-lah, PEE-koh DELL-uh
Mishima, Yukio mi-SHEE-muh, yoo-KEE-oh
missi dominici MISS-ee doh-MIN-i-chee
Mitterrand, François MEE-tayr-rahnh, frahnh-SWAH
Moche moh-CHAY
Moctezuma mahk-tuh-ZOO-muh
Mogadishu moh-guh-DEE-shoo
Mohács MOH-hach
Mohenjo-Daro mo-HEN-jo-DAH-roh
Moldavia mohl-DAY-vee-uh
Moldova mohl-DOH-vuh
Molière, Jean-Baptiste mohl-YAYR, ZHAHNH-bah-TEEST
Molotov, Vyacheslav MAHL-uh-tawf, vyich-chiss-SLAHF
Mombasa mahm-BAH-suh
Monet, Claude moh-NEH, KLOHD
Mongkut MAWNG-koot
Montaigne, Michel de mahn-TAYN, mee-SHEL duh
Montefeltro, Federigo da mahn-tuh-FELL-troh, fay-day-REE-goh dah
Montesquieu MOHN-tess-kyoo
Montessori, Maria mahn-tuh-SOR-ee
Morisot, Berthe mor-ee-ZOH, BAYRT
Mozambique moh-zam-BEEK
Mozart, Wolfgang Amadeus MOH-tsart, VULF-gahng ah-muh-DAY-uss
Muawiya moo-AH-wee-yah
Mudejares moo-theh-KHAH-rayss
Mughal MOO-gul
Muhammad moh-HAM-ud *or* moh-HAHM-ud
Mühlberg MURL-bayrk
Mukden MOOK-dun
mulattoes muh-LAH-tohz
Mumbai MUM-by
Müntzer, Thomas MURN-tsur
Murad moo-RAHD
Musharraf, Pervaiz moo-SHAHR-uf, pur-VEZ
Muslim MUZ-lum
Mutsuhito moo-tsoo-HEE-toh
Myanmar MYAN-mahr
Mycenaean my-suh-NEE-un
Nabonidas nab-uh-NY-duss
Nabopolassar nab-uh-puh-LASS-ur
Nagasaki nah-gah-SAH-kee
Nagy, Imry NAHJ, IM-ray
Nanjing nan-JING
Nantes NAHNT
Nara NAH-rah
Nasrin, Taslima naz-REEN, tah-SLEE-muh
Nasser, Gamal Abdul NAH-sur, juh-MAHL ahb-DOOL
Navarre nuh-VAHR
Nebuchadnezzar neb-uh-kud-NEZZ-ur
Nehru, Jawaharlal NAY-roo, juh-WAH-hur-lahl
Nero NEE-roh
Nerva NUR-vuh
Netanyahu, Benjamin net-ahn-YAH-hoo
Neumann, Balthasar NOI-mahn, BAHL-tuh-zahr
Neumann, Solomon NOI-mahn
Neustria NOO-stree-uh
Nevsky, Alexander NYEF-skee
Newcomen, Thomas NYOO-kuh-mun *or* nyoo-KUM-mun
Ngo Dinh Diem GOH din DYEM
Nguyen NGWEN
Nicias NISS-ee-uss

Nietzsche, Friedrich   NEE-chuh, FREED-rikh
Nimwegen   NIM-vay-gun
Ninhursaga   nin-HUR-sah-guh
Nkrumah, Kwame   en-KROO-muh, KWAH-may
nobiles   no-BEE-layz
Nobunaga, Oda   noh-buh-NAH-guh, OH-dah
Nogarola, Isotta   noh-guh-ROH-luh, ee-ZAHT-uh
Novalis, Friedrich   noh-VAH-lis, FREED-rikh
Novotny, Antonin   noh-VAHT-nee, AHN-toh-nyeen
novus homo   NOH-vuss HOH-moh
nuoc mam   NWAHK MAHM
Nyame   NYAH-may
Nystadt   NEE-shtaht
Oaxaca   wah-HAH-kuh
Octavian   ahk-TAY-vee-un
Odoacer   oh-doh-AY-sur
Odysseus   oh-DISS-ee-uss
Oe, Kenzaburo   OH-ay, ken-zuh-BOO-roh
Olivares   oh-lee-BAH-rayss
Olmec   AHL-mek *or* OHL-mek
Omar Khayyam   OH-mar ky-YAHM
Ometeotl   oh-met-tee-AH-tul
optimates   ahp-tuh-MAH-tayz
Oresteia   uh-res-TY-uh
Orkhan   or-KHAHN
Osaka   oh-SAH-kuh
Osama bin Laden   oh-SAH-muh bin LAH-dun
Osiris   oh-SY-russ
Ostara   oh-STAH-ruh
Ostpolitik   OHST-poh-lee-teek
ostrakon   AHSS-truh-kahn
Ostrogoths   AHSS-truh-gahthss
Ovid   OH-vid
Oxenstierna, Axel   OOK-sen-shur-nah, AHK-sul
Pacal   pa-KAL
Pachakuti   pah-chah-KOO-tee
Paekche   bayk-JEE
Pagan   puh-GAHN
Paleologus   pay-lee-AWL-uh-guss
Panaetius   puh-NEE-shuss
Pankhurst, Emmeline   PANK-hurst
papal curia   PAY-pul KYOOR-ee-uh
Papen, Franz von   PAH-pun, FRAHNTS fun
Paracelsus   par-uh-SELL-suss
Parlement   par-luh-MAHNH
Parti Québécois   par-TEE kay-bek-KWAH
Pascal, Blaise   pass-KAHL, BLEZ
Pasternak, Boris   PASS-tur-nak, buh-REESS
Pasteur, Louis   pass-TOOR, LWEE
Pataliputra   pah-tah-lee-POO-truh
paterfamilias   pay-tur-fuh-MEEL-yus
Pensées   pahnh-SAY
Pentateuch   PEN-tuh-took
Pepin   PEP-in *or* pay-PANH
perestroika   per-uh-STROI-kuh
Pergamum   PUR-guh-mum
Pericles   PER-i-kleez
perioeci   per-ee-EE-see
Perpetua   pur-PET-choo-uh
Pétain, Henri   pay-TANH, AHN-ree
Petite Roquette   puh-TEET raw-KET
Petrarch   PEE-trark *or* PET-trark
Petronius   pi-TROH-nee-uss
phalansteries   fuh-LAN-stuh-reez
philosophe   fee-loh-ZAWF
Phintys   FIN-tiss

Phoenicians   fuh-NEE-shunz
Photius   FOH-shuss
Picasso, Pablo   pi-KAH-soh
Pietism   PY-uh-tiz-um
Pilsudski, Joseph   peel-SOOT-skee
Piscator, Erwin   PIS-kuh-tor, AYR-vin
Pisistratus   puh-SIS-truh-tuss
Pissarro, Camille   pee-SAH-roh, kah-MEEL
Pizan, Christine de   pee-ZAHN, kris-TEEN duh
Pizarro, Francesco   puh-ZAHR-oh, frahn-CHESS-koh
Planck, Max   PLAHNK
Plantagenet   plan-TAJ-uh-net
Plassey   PLASS-ee
Plato   PLAY-toh
Plautus   PLAW-tuss
plebiscita   pleb-i-SEE-tuh
Poincaré, Raymond   pwanh-kah-RAY, ray-MOHNH
polis   POH-liss
politiques   puh-lee-TEEKS
Pollaiuolo, Antonio   pohl-ly-WOH-loh
Poltava   pul-TAH-vuh
Polybius   puh-LIB-ee-uss
Pombal, marquis de   pum-BAHL, mar-KEE duh
Pompadour, madame de   POM-puh-door, mah-DAHM duh
Pompeii   pahm-PAY
Pompey   PAHM-pee
pontifex maximus   PAHN-ti-feks MAK-si-muss
Popul Vuh   puh-PUL VOO
populares   PAWP-oo-lahr-ayss
populo grasso   PAWP-oo-loh GRAH-soh
Postumus   PAHS-choo-muss
Potosí   poh-toh-SEE
Potsdam   PAHTS-dam
Poussin, Nicholas   poo-SANH, NEE-koh-lah
Praecepter Germaniae   PREE-sep-tur gayr-MAHN-ee-ee
practor   PREE-tur
Prakrit   PRAH-krit
Pravda   PRAHV-duh
Primo de Rivera   PREE-moh day ri-VAY-ruh
primogeniture   pree-moh-JEN-i-chur
princeps   PRIN-seps
Principia   prin-SIP-ee-uh
Procopius   pruh-KOH-pee-uss
procurator   PROK-yuh-ray-tur
Ptolemaic   tahl-uh-MAY-ik
Ptolemy   TAHL-uh-mee
Pugachev, Emelyan   poo-guh-CHAWF, yim-yil-YAHN
Punic   PYOO-nik
Putin, Vladimir   POO-tin
Pyongyang   pyawng-YANG
Pyrrhic   PEER-ik
Pyrrhus   PEER-uss
Pythagoras   puh-THAG-uh-russ
Qajar   kuh-JAHR
Qianlong   CHAN-loong
Qin   CHIN
Qin Shi Huangdi   chin shee hwang-DEE
Qing   CHING
Qiu Jin   chee-oo-JIN
Qu   CHOO
quadrivium   kwah-DRIV-ee-um
quaestors   KWES-turs
querelle des femmes   keh-REL day FAHM
Quesnay, François   keh-NAY, frahnn-SWAH
Quetzelcoatl   KWET-sul-koh-AHT-ul
Quraishi   koo-RY-shee

Qur'an   kuh-RAN *or* kuh-RAHN
Rabe'a of Qozdar   rah-BAY-uh uv kuz-DAHR
Racine, Jean-Baptiste   ra-SEEN, ZHAHNH-buh-TEEST
Rahner, Karl   RAH-nur
Rajput   RAHJ-poot
Rama   RAH-mah
Ramayana   rah-mah-YAH-nah
Ramcaritmanas   RAM-kah-rit-MAH-nuz
Rameses   RAM-uh-seez
Raphael   RAFF-ee-ul
Rasputin   rass-PYOO-tin
Rathenau, Walter   RAH-tuh-now, VAHL-tuh
Realpolitik   ray-AHL-poh-lee-teek
Realschule   ray-AHL-shoo-luh
Reichsrat   RYKHSS-raht
Reichstag   RYKHSS-tahk
Rembrandt van Rijn   REM-brant vahn RYN
Rémy, Nicholas   ray-MEE, nee-koh-LAH
Renan, Ernst   re-NAHNH
Rhee, Syngman   REE, SING-mun
Ricci, Matteo   REE-chee, ma-TAY-oh
Richelieu   REESH-uh-lyuh
Ricimer   RISS-uh-mur
Rig Veda   RIK-vee-duh
Rikstag   RIKS-tahk
Rilke, Rainer Maria   RILL-kuh, RY-nuh mah-REE-uh
Rimbaud, Arthur   ram-BOH, ar-TOOR
risorgimento   ree-SOR-jee-men-toh
Riza-i-Abassi   ree-ZAH-yah-BAH-see
Robespierre, Maximilien   ROHBZ-pyayr,
   mak-see-meel-YENH
Rococo   ruh-KOH-koh
Rocroi   roh-KRWAH
Röhm, Ernst   RURM
Rommel, Erwin   RAHM-ul
Romulus Augustulus   RAHM-yuh-luss ow-GOOS-chuh-luss
Rossbach   RAWSS-bahkh
Rousseau, Jean-Jacques   roo-SOH, ZHAHNH-ZHAHK
Rurik   ROO-rik
Ryswick   RYZ-wik
Sacrosancta   sak-roh-SANK-tuh
Saikaku   sy-KAH-koo
Saint-Just   sanh-ZHOOST
Saint-Simon, Henri de   sanh-see-MOHNH, ahnh-REE duh
Sakharov, Andrei   SAH-kuh-rawf, ahn-DRAY
Saladin   SAL-uh-din
Salazar, Antonio   SAL-uh-zahr
Sallust   SAL-ust
Samnite   SAM-nyt
Samudragupta   suh-mood-ruh-GOOP-tuh
samurai   SAM-uh-ry
San Martín, José de   san mar-TEEN, hoh-SAY day
Sandinista   san-duh-NEES-tuh
sans-culottes   sahnh-koo-LUT *or* sanz-koo-LAHTSS
Sarraut, Albert   sah-ROH, ahl-BAYR
Sartre, Jean-Paul   SAR-truh, ZHAHNH-POHL
Sassanid   suh-SAN-id
sati   suh-TEE
satrap   SAY-trap
satrapy   SAY-truh-pee
Satyricon   sa-TEER-uh-kahn
Schaumburg-Lippe   SHOWM-boorkh-LEE-puh
Schleswig-Holstein   SHLESS-vik-HOHL-shtyn
Schlieffen, Alfred von   SHLEE-fun, AHL-fret fun
Schliemann, Heinrich   SHLEE-mahn, HYN-rikh
Schmidt, Helmut   SHMIT, HEL-moot

Schönberg, Arnold   SHURN-bayrk, AR-nawlt
Schönborn   SHURN-bawn
Schönerer, Georg von   SHURN-uh-ruh, GAY-ork fun
Schröder, Gerhard   SHRUR-duh, GAYR-hahrt
Schuschnigg, Karl von   SHOOSH-nik, KAHRL fun
Schutzmannschaft   SHOOTS-mahn-shahft
Scipio Aemilianus   SEE-pee-oh ee-mil-YAY-nuss
Scipio Africanus   SEE-pee-oh af-ree-KAY-nuss
scriptoria   skrip-TOR-ee-uh
Ségur   say-GOO-uh
Sejm   SAYM
Seleucid   suh-LOO-sid
Seleucus   suh-LOO-kuss
Seljuk   SEL-jook
Seneca   SEN-uh-kuh
Sephardic   suh-FAHR-dik
Septimius Severus   sep-TIM-ee-uss se-VEER-uss
serjents   sayr-ZHAHNH
Sforza, Ludovico   SFORT-sah, loo-doh-VEE-koh
Shakuntala   shah-koon-TAH-lah
Shalmaneser   shal-muh-NEE-zur
Shandong   SHAHN-doong
Shang   SHAHNG
Shari'a   shah-REE-uh
Shen Nong   shun-NOONG
Shi'ite   SHEE-YT
Shidehara   shee-de-HAH-rah
Shiga Naoya   SHEE-gah NOW-yah
Shikoku   shee-KOH-koo
Shimonoseki   shee-moh-noh-SEK-ee
Shiva   SHIV-uh
Shotoku Taishi   shoh-TOH-koo ty-EE-shee
Sichuan   SEECH-wahn
Siddhartha Gautama   si-DAR-tuh GAW-tuh-muh
Sieveking, Amalie   SEE-vuh-king, uh-MAHL-yuh
Sieyès, Abbé   syay-YESS, ab-BAY
Sigiriya   see-gee-REE-uh
signoria   seen-YOR-ee-uh
Silla   SIL-uh
Silva, Luis Inácio Lula de   LWEES ee-NAH-syoh LOO-luh
   duh-SEEL-vuh
Sima Qian   SEE-mah chee-AHN
sine manu   sy-nee-MAY-noo
sipahis   suh-PAH-heez
Sita   SEE-tuh
Slovenia   sloh-VEE-nee-uh
Société Générale   soh-see-ay-TAY zhay-nay-RAHL
Socrates   SAHK-ruh-teez
Solon   SOH-lun
Solzhenitsyn, Alexander   sohl-zhuh-NEET-sin
Somme   SUM
Song Taizu   SOONG ty-DZOO
Soong, Mei-ling   SOONG, may-LING
Sophocles   SAHF-uh-kleez
Sorel, Georges   soh-RELL, ZHORZH
Spartacus   SPAR-tuh-kuss
Spartiates   spar-tee-AH-teez
Speer, Albert   SHPAYR
Speransky, Michael   spyuh-RAHN-skee
Spinoza, Benedict de   spi-NOH-zuh
squadristi   skwah-DREES-tee
Srebrenica   sreb-bruh-NEET-suh
stadholder   STAD-hohl-dur
Staël, Germaine de   STAHL, zhayr-MEN duh
Stakhanov, Alexei   stuh-KHAH-nuf, uh-LEK-say
Stasi   SHTAH-see

Stauffenberg, Claus von   SHTOW-fen-berk, KLOWSS fun
Stein, Heinrich von   SHTYN, HYN-rikh fun
Stilicho   STIL-i-koh
Stoicism   STOH-i-siz-um
Stolypin, Peter   stuh-LIP-yin
strategoi   strah-tay-GOH-ee
Stravinsky, Igor   struh-VIN-skee, EE-gor
Stresemann, Gustav   SHTRAY-zuh-mahn, GOOS-tahf
Strozzi, Alessandra   STRAWT-see
Struensee, John Frederick   SHTROO-un-zay
Sturmabteilung   SHTOORM-ap-ty-loonk
Sudetenland   soo-DAY-tun-land
sudra   SOO-druh *or* SHOO-druh
Suger   soo-ZHAYR
Suharto   soo-HAHR-toh
Sui Wendi   SWEE wen-DEE
Sui Yangdi   SWEE yahng-DEE
Sukarno   soo-KAHR-noh
Sukarnoputri, Megawati   soo-kahr-noh-POO-tree,
   meg-uh-WAH-tee
Suleiman   SOO-lay-mahn
Suleymaniye   soo-lay-MAHN-ee-eh
Sulla   SUL-uh
Sumerians   soo-MER-ee-unz *or* soo-MEER-ee-unz
Summa Theologica   SOO-muh tay-oh-LAH-jee-kuh
Sun Yat-sen   SOON yaht-SEN
Suppiluliumas   suh-PIL-oo-LEE-uh-muss
Suttner, Bertha von   ZOOT-nuh, BAYR-tuh fun
Swaziland   SWAH-zee-land
Symphonie Fantastique   SANH-foh-nee fahn-tas-TEEK
Taaffe, Edward von   TAH-fuh, ED-vahrt fun
Taban lo Liyong   tuh-BAN loh-lee-YAWNG
Tacitus   TASS-i-tuss
Tahuantinsuyu   tuh-HWAHN-tin-SOO-yoo
Taika   TY-kuh
taille   TY
Taiping   ty-PING
Talleyrand, Prince   tah-lay-RAHNH
Tanganyika   tang-an-YEE-kuh
Tanizaki, Junichiro   tan-i-ZAH-kee, jun-i-CHEE-roh
Tanzania   tan-zuh-NEE-uh
Temuchin   TEM-yuh-jin
Tenochtitlán   tay-nawch-teet-LAHN
Teotihuacán   tay-noh-tee-hwa-KAHN
Tertullian   tur-TUL-yun
Texcoco   tess-KOH-koh
Thales   THAY-leez
Theocritus   thee-AHK-ruh-tuss
Theodora   thee-uh-DOR-uh
Theodoric   thee-AHD-uh-rik
Theodosius   thee-uh-DOH-shuss
Theognis   thee-AHG-nuss
Theravada   thay-ruh-VAH-duh
Thermopylae   thur-MAHP-uh-lee
Thiers, Adolphe   TYAYR, a-DAWLF
Thucydides   thoo-SID-uh-deez
Thutmosis   thoot-MOH-suss
Tiananmen   TYAHN-ahn-men
Tianjin   TYAHN-jin
Tiberius   ty-BEER-ee-uss
Tiglath-pileser   TIG-lath-py-LEE-zur
Tikal   tee-KAHL
Tirpitz, Admiral von   TEER-pits
Tisza, István   TISS-ah, ISHT-vun
Tito   TEE-toh
Titus   TY-tuss

Tlaloc   tuh-lah-LOHK
Tlaltelolco   tuh-lahl-teh-LOH-koh
Tlaxcala   tuh-lah-SKAH-lah
Toer, Pramoedya   TOOR, pra-MOO-dyah
Tojo, Hideki   TOH-joh, hee-DEK-ee
Tokugawa Ieyasu   toh-koo-GAH-wah ee-yeh-YAH-soo
Tolstoy, Leo   TOHL-stoy
Tongmenghui   toong-meng-HWEE
Topa Inca   TOH-puh INK-uh
Topkapi   tawp-KAH-pee
Torah   TOR-uh
Tordesillas   tor-day-SEE-yass
Touré, Sékou   too-RAY, say-KOO
Trajan   TRAY-jun
Trevithick, Richard   TREV-uh-thik
Tristan, Flora   TRISS-tun
trivium   TRIV-ee-um
Trotsky, Leon   TRAHT-skee
Troyes   TRWAH
Trudeau, Pierre   troo-DOH, PYAYR
Trufaut, François   troo-FOH, frahnh-SWAH
Tsara, Tristan   TSAHR-rah, TRISS-tun
Tübingen   TUR-bing-un
Tughluq   tug-LUK
Tulsidas   tool-see-DAHSS
Tutankhamun   too-tang-KAH-mun
Tyche   TY-kee
Uccello, Paolo   oo-CHEL-oh, POW-loh
uhuru   oo-HOO-roo
uji   OO-jee
Ulbricht, Walter   OOL-brikht, VAHL-tuh
Ulianov, Vladimir   ool-YA-nuf
Umayyads   oo-MY-adz
Unam Sanctam   OO-nahm **SAHNK-tahm**
universitas   yoo-nee-VAYR-see-tahss
Utamaro   OO-tah-mah-roh
Uzbekistan   ooz-BEK-i-stan
vaisya   VISH-yuh
Vajpayee, Atal Behari   VAHJ-py-ee, AH-tahl bi-HAH-ree
Valens   VAY-linz
Valentinian   val-en-TIN-ee-un
Valéry, Paul   vah-lay-REE, POHL
Valois   val-WAH
Van de Velde, Theodore   vahn duh VEL-duh, TAY-oh-dor
van Eyck, Jan   vahn YK *or* van AYK, YAHN
van Gogh, Vincent   van GOH
Vasa, Gustavus   VAH-suh, GUSS-tuh-vuss
Vega, Lope de   VAY-guh, LOH-pay day
Velde, Theodor van de   VEL-duh, tay-oh-DOR vahn duh
Vendée   vahnh-DAY
Venetia   vuh-NEE-shuh
Verdun   vur-DUN
Vergerio, Pietro Paolo   vur-JEER-ee-oh, PYAY-troh POW-loh
Versailles   vayr-SY
Vesalius, Andreas   vuh-SAY-lee-uss, ahn-DRAY-uss
Vespasian   vess-PAY-zhun
Vespucci, Amerigo   vess-POO-chee, ahm-ay-REE-goh
Vesuvius   vuh-SOO-vee-uss
Vichy   VISH-ee
Vierzehnheiligen   feer-tsayn-HY-li-gen
Virchow, Rudolf   FEER-khoh, ROO-dulf
Virgil   VUR-jul
Visconti, Giangaleazzo   vees-KOHN-tee,
   jahn-gah-lay-AH-tsoh
Vishnu   VISH-noo
Visigoths   VIZ-uh-gathz

Voilquin, Suzanne vwahl-KANH, soo-ZAHN
Volk FULK
Volkschulen FULK-shoo-lun
Voltaire vohl-TAYR
Wafd WAHFT
Wagner, Richard VAG-nur, RIKH-art
Walesa, Lech vah-WENT-sah, LEK
Wallachia wah-LAY-kee-uh
Wallenstein, Albrecht von VAHL-en-shtyn, AWL-brekht
Wang Anshi WAHNG ahn-SHEE
Wang Shuo wahng-SHWOH
Wang Tao wahng-TOW
Wannsee VAHN-zay
Watteau, Antoine wah-TOH, AHN-twahn
Weill, Kurt VYL
Weizsäcker, Richard von VYTS-zek-ur, RIKH-art
wergeld WUR-geld
Windischgrätz, Alfred VIN-dish-grets
Winkelmann, Maria VINK-ul-mahn
Witte, Sergei VIT-uh, syir-GYAY
Wittenberg VIT-ten-bayrk
Wojtyla, Karol voy-TEE-wah, KAH-rul
Wollstonecraft, Mary WULL-stun-kraft
Wu Zhao woo-ZHOW
Würzburg VURTS-boork
Wyclif, John WIK-lif
Xavier, Francis ZAY-vee-ur
Xerxes ZURK-seez
Xhosa KHOH-suh
Xia SHEE-ah
Xian SHEE-ahn
Xiangyang SHYAHNG-yahng
Ximenes khee-MAY-ness
Xinjiang SHIN-jyahng
Xiongnu SHYAHNG-noo
Xui Tong shwee-TOONG
Yahweh YAH-way
Yan'an yuh-NAHN

Yang Guifei yahng gwee-FAY
Yangshao yahng-SHOW
Yangtze YANG-tsee
Yayoi yah-YO-ee
Yeats, William Butler YAYTS
Yeltsin, Boris YELT-sun
Yi Jing yee-JING
Yi Song-gye YEE song-YEE
yishuv YISH-uv
Yuan Shikai yoo-AHN shee-KY
Yudhoyono, Susilo yood-hoh-YOH-noh, soo-SEE-loh
Yue yoo-EH
zaibatsu zy-BAHT-soo *or Japanese* DZY-bahtss
Zanj ZANJ
Zanzibar ZAN-zi-bar
Zasulich, Vera tsah-SOO-likh
Zemsky Sobor ZEM-skee suh-BOR
zemstvos ZEMPST-vohz
Zeno ZEE-noh
Zenobia zuh-NOH-bee-uh
zeppelin ZEP-puh-lin
Zeus ZOOSS
Zhang Zhidong JANG jee-DOONG
Zhao Ziyang JOW dzee-YAHNG
Zhenotdel zhen-ut-DEL
Zhivkov, Todor ZHIV-kuff, toh-DOR
Zia ul-Haq, Mohammad ZEE-uh ool-HAHK
ziggurat ZIG-uh-rat
Zimmermann, Dominikus TSIM-ur-mahn, doh-MEE-nee-kooss
Zinzendorf, Nikolaus von TSIN-sin-dorf, NEE-koh-LOWSS fun
Zola, Émile ZOH-lah, ay-MEEL
zollverein TSOHL-fuh-ryn
Zoroaster ZOR-oh-ass-tur
Zuanzong zwahn-ZOONG
Zuni ZOO-nee
Zwingli, Ulrich TSFING-lee, OOL-rikh

DOCUMENTS

This page constitutes an extension of the copyright page. We have made every effort to trace the ownership of all copyrighted material and to secure permission from copyright holders. In the event of any question arising as to the use of any material, we will be pleased to make the necessary corrections in future printings. Thanks are due to the following authors, publishers, and agents for permission to use the material indicated.

INDEX

impact of migratory workers on, 648
industrialization and, 405, 408–09
territorial expansion and, **543b**
See also Birth control
Pornography, 365, 604, 619, 650
Portillo, José López (Mexican president), 618
Portugal
African slave trade by, 299–300
arrival in China, 356
early exploration voyages, **294m**, 296–97
in India, 288–89, 344, **348b**
maritime empire of, 293–94
membership in the EC, 612–13
post-WWII, 566
Post-Impressionism, 444
Postmodernism, 624
Potsdam Conference (1945), 555
Prester John (king of Ethiopia), **292p**
The Prince (Machiavelli), 312
The Princess (Tennyson), 432
Principia (Newton), 379
Printing
in the Age of Enlightenment, 382–83
calligraphy in the absence of, 352
development in China, **357p**
movable type and, 313
Protestant Reformation and, 313
Property rights
French Civil Code on, 395
U.S. Constitution on, 387
women and, 433
Prostitution, 347, 372, 508, 550, 601, 619,
658p
Protestant Reformation
background and prelude to, 312–14
Luther's Ninety-five Theses, **315b**
Martin Luther and, 314
politics and religion of the, 314–15
Roman Catholic Church and, 317–18
social impact of, 316–17
spread of, 315–16
Protestantism
Calvin and, 315–16
Catholicism and the wars of religion, 318–22
Church of England and the Puritans, 327
Church of England break from Rome, 316
Peace of Augsburg (1555) and, 314–15
Peace of Westphalia (1648) and, 322
Prussia. *See* Germany
Ptolemy (astronomer), 378
Puerto Rico, 437
Putin, Vladimir (Russian president), 612
Puyi ("last emperor" of China), 476

al-Qaeda, 581–82, 623, 640–41, 646, 659, 667
Qianlong (Qing emperor), 358–59, **363b**, 468–69
Qin Jin (female revolutionary in China), 478
Quotations of Chairman Mao Zedong (Mao Zedong),
594, 598, 603
Qur'an. See Islam

Race/racism
apartheid and, 635
British attitude toward, 449, 461, 515
colonialism and, 385, 463
homogeneity and national identity, 487
intermarriage and, 385
Marxist-Leninist ideology on, 600
Nazi Holocaust, 547–**50b**
Nazi ideology on, 538–40, 547
Social Darwinism and, 442
South African apartheid, 635
United States and, 608, 614
Raffles, Stamford (British official), 451
Railroads/railroad industry, 405–07, 427, 437, 450,
473m, 550
Rakosi, Matyas (Hungarian leader), 573
Ramayana (Hindu), 352
Ramcaritmanas (Tulsidas), 352
Rasputin (Grigory Novykh, Russian mystic), 499
Reagan, Ronald (U.S. president), 580–81, 615
Realism in the Age of Enlightenment, 420–22
Realpolitik "politics of reality," 416
Red Guards, 593
Religion/religious beliefs
Age of Exploration and, 292
anticolonial nationalism and, 513–14
in China, 600
in China's Cultural Revolution, 595–96
humanist movement and, 313
in Japan, 367–68, **370b**, 671–72
in the "new world order," **581b**

secularization and, 421, **649b**
Sepoy Rebellion (1857) and, 465, 515
Shinto as, **370b**
in Southeast Asia, 305
in the Soviet Union, 591
Sufism, 289, 338, 341
Western materialism and, **514b**
See also Buddhism; Christianity; Hinduism; Islam;
Jewish people/Judaism; Missionary activities;
Sacred/moral writings
Religious conversions
assimilation by, 351
Christianity and, **306b**, 318, 357, 671
colonialism and, 386, 456
Hinduism and, 347, 351
Islam and, 290, **343b**, 517
Protestantism and, 315
Remarque, Erich Maria (French writer), **496b**
Reminiscences of Carl Schurz (Schurz), **413b**
Rémy, Nicholas (witchcraft judge), 320
Renaissance, 312–14
Republic of China (ROC). *See* China, Republic of;
Chinese Nationalist Party (*Guomindang*)
Republic of Indonesia. *See* Indonesia
Republic of Korea (ROK, South Korea). *See* Korea
Republic of Taiwan. *See* Taiwan
Republic of Vietnam (South Vietnam). *See* Vietnam
The Republic of Wine (Mo Yan), 604
Resistance movements/rebellions
anticolonial resistance in, 464–65, 632
in Canada, 420
in China, 356–59, **391p**, 471–72, 475–**76b**, 521,
596p
communism as, **525b**
in Europe, 319, 322, 391, **596p**
in India, 465
in Korea, 484–85
land reform and, 370–71
in Russia, 388
in Southeast Asia, 663
in Southwest Asia, 645
Tiananmen Square demonstrations, 595–96
in the U.S., **419b**, 620
See also Independence movements
Revolutionary socialism, 430
On the Revolutions of the Heavenly Spheres
(Copernicus), **379b**
Reza Kahn (shah of Iran), 518–19, 644, 650
Rhee, Syngman (S. Korean president), 672
Rhodes, Cecil (British empire builder), 446, 461
Rhodesia, 462
Ricci, Matteo (Jesuit missionary), 318, **357p**, 363
Rigaud, Hyacinth (French painter), **325p**
Right to vote
in Africa, 634, 638
in China, 600
colonialism and, 462
democracy and, 426, 436–38
feminist movement and, 433, 620
Hitler's rise to power from, 537
in India, 515–16
Islam and, **648b**, 650
in Japan, 528, 670
liberalism and, 411–12
mass society and, 430
in Turkey, 517
U.S. electoral process, 615
U.S. Voting Rights Act (1965), 614
women and, 499, 517, **527b**, 600, 620–21, 670
Rights of man
American Bill of Rights, 411
American Declaration of Independence, 387
French Civil Code and, 395
French Declaration of the Rights of Man, **392b**
Helsinki Agreement (1975), 579–80
"*natural laws*" philosophy as, 381
U.S. Civil Rights Act (1964), 614
See also Equality/equal rights;Feminist movement
Riots/rioting
American Revolution, 386–87
Christian vs. Muslim, 635
colonialism and, 656
Nazi death camps, 549
from politics, 572–73, 643, 659, 672
U.S. race, 614
Rivera, Diego (Mexican painter), 532
Riza-i-Abassi (Safavid artist), 344
Robespierre, Maximilien (French revolutionist),
393–94
Roman Catholic Church
abortion and, 622
Americas missionary activities, 296

colonialism and, 386
Council of Trent, 318
French Revolution and, 392
French Wars of Religion (1562–1598), 318–19
in Poland, 572
pre-Reformation failures of, 313–14
Protestant Reformation and, 314–16
Reformation within the, 317–18
religious orders and ideals, 317–18
women and, 386
Romania, 563, 566, 572
Romanov, Michael (Russian tsar), 326
Romanticism in the Age of Enlightenment, 420–22
Roosevelt, Franklin Delano (U.S. president), 507, 530,
545–47, 553–55, 562, 563, 567, 614
Roosevelt, Theodore (U.S. president), 437
Rousseau, Jean-Jacques (philosopher), 382
Rubens, Peter Paul (Flemish painter), 328, **330p**
Rushdie, Salman (Indian writer), 662
Russia (as post-Soviet republic), 591–93, 612
Russia, WW I
alliances for war, 440, **492m**, 493
Battle of Masurian Lakes, 493
Battle of Tannenberg, 493
Bolshevik Revolution (1917), 498–502
home front support for, **501b**
the road to war in, 492
See also Soviet Union (USSR)
Russian Empire
Catherine the Great and, 388
Chinese territory cessions to, 473
creation of the tsarist dynasty, 326–27
Crimean War (1853–1856), 415–16
defeat of Napoleon in 1812, 396–97
political democracy in, 438–39
relations with China, 360
revolutionary movements of 1848 and, 418
Russo-Japanese War (1904–1905), 439–40, 485
Rwanda, 636

Sacred/moral writings
Christian Bible, 313
Hindu, 352, 514
Qur'an, 647
See also Laws and justice system; Religion/religious
beliefs
Sadat, Anwar al- (president of Egypt), 642–43
Safavid dynasty of Persia (1501–1723 C.E.), 334,
341–44
Safi al-Din (sheikh), 341
Saikaku (Japanese writer), 372
Sakharov, Andrei (Russian physicist), 587
Salinas, Carlos (Mexican president), 618
Samoan Islands, 437
San Martín, José de (Latin American leader), 414
Sanai peninsula, **642m**
Sanskrit. *See* Language
Sarabhoji (Indian ruler), **450p**
Sartre, Jean-Paul (French writer), 624
The Satanic Verses (Rushdie), 662
Saudi Arabia, 517, 520, 623, **651b**
Saya San (Buddhist monk), 465
Schlieffen, Alfred von (German general), 492
Schönberg, Arnold (American composer), **509b**
Schroeder, Gerhard (German leader), 609
Schumacher, E. F. (British economist), 625, **627b**
Schurz, Carl (U.S. senator), **413b**
Science. *See* Philosophy and science
Scientific Revolution, 296, 378–83, 420–21, 440–44
Scotland, 327, 386
Scott, Walter (British writer), 420
Second Class Citizen (Aidoo), 639
Second Industrial Revolution. *See* Age of Progress
(Second Industrial Revolution)
Second International, 430, **522b**
The Second Sex (de Beauvoir), 621
Secondat, Charles de (baron of Montesquieu), 381
Seiki, Kuroda (Japanese painter), **443p**
Seito (Blue Stockings), **484b**
Self-Help (Smiles), **410b**
Selim I (Ottoman emperor), 335, 341
Seljuk Turks, 334
See also Ottoman Empire
Senegal, **301p**, 459, 631, 636–37
September 11, 581–82, 622–23, 640, 644–46
Serbia
annexation by Austria, 440
assassination of Francis Ferdinand, 491–92
independence movements and ethnic cleansing,
611–12
Ottoman Empire and, 334, 517
WW I realignments of, 504